INTERACTIVE COMPUTER GRAPHICS IN X

THE PWS SERIES IN COMPUTER SCIENCE

Abernethy/Allen, *Experiments in Computing: Laboratories for Introductory Computer Science in Think Pascal*
Abernethy/Allen, *Experiments in Computing: Laboratories for Introductory Computer Science in Turbo Pascal*
Abernethy/Allen, *Exploring the Science of Computing*
Ageloff/Mojena, *Essentials of Structured BASIC*
Bent/Sethares, *QBASIC*
Bent/Sethares, *QuickBASIC: An Introduction to Computer Science Programming with the IBM PC*
Coburn, *Visual BASIC Made Easy*
Cosnard/Trystram, *Parallel Algorithms and Architecture*
Decker/Hirshfield, *The Analytical Engine: An Introduction to Computer Science Using HyperCard 2.1, Second Edition*
Decker/Hirshfield, *The Analytical Engine: An Introduction to Computer Science Using ToolBook*
Decker/Hirshfield, *The Object Concept: An Introduction to Computer Programming Using C++*
Decker/Hirshfield, *Working Classes: Data Structures and Algorithms Using C++*
Dershem/Jipping, *Programming Languages: Structures and Models, Second Edition*
Drozdek, *Data Structures and Algorithms in C++*
Drozdek/Simon, *Data Structures in C*
Eggen/Eggen, *An Introduction to Computer Science Using C*
Firebaugh/Michie, *Artificial Intelligence: A Knowledge-Based Approach, Second Edition*
Flynn/McHoes, *Understanding Operating Systems*
Giarratano/Riley, *Expert Systems: Principles and Programming, Second Edition*
Hennefeld, *Using Turbo Pascal 6.0-7.0, Third Edition*
Hochbaum, *Approximation Algorithms for NP-Hard Problems*
House, *Beginning with C*
Jamison/Russell /Snover, *Laboratories for a Second Course in Computer Science: ANSI Pascal*
Jamison/Russell /Snover, *Laboratories for a Second Course in Computer Science: Turbo Pascal*
Lieberherr, *Adaptive Object-Oriented Programming: The Demeter Metiod with Propagation Patterns*
Louden, *Programming Languages: Principles and Practice*
Pavlidis, *Interactive Computer Graphics in X*
Runnion, *Structured Programming in Assembly Language for the IBM PC and PS/2, Second Edition*
Saad, *Iterative Methods for Sparse Linear Systems*
Shay, *Understanding Data Communications and Networks*
Sipser, *Introduction to the Theory of Computation*
Sowa, *Knowledge Representation*
Suhy, *CICS using COBOL: A Structured Approach*
Wang, *An Introduction to ANSI C on UNIX*
Wang, *An Introduction to Berkeley UNIX*
Wang, *C++ with Object-Oriented Programming*
Whale, *Data Structures and Abstraction Using C*

INTERACTIVE COMPUTER GRAPHICS IN X

Theo Pavlidis
State University of New York
Stony Brook

PWS Publishing Company
ITP An International Thomson Publishing Company

Boston • Albany • Bonn • Cincinnati • Detroit • London • Melbourne • Mexico City
New York • Paris • San Francisco • Singapore • Tokyo • Toronto

PWS PUBLISHING COMPANY
20 Park Plaza, Boston, Massachusetts 02116-4324

I(T)P™
International Thomson Publishing
The trademark ITP is used under license

This book is printed on recycled, acid-free paper

For more information, contact:
PWS Publishing Co.
20 Park Plaza
Boston, MA 02116

International Thomson Publishing Europe
Berkshire House I68-I73
High Holborn
London WC1V 7AA
England

Thomas Nelson Australia
102 Dodds Street
South Melbourne, 3205
Victoria, Australia

Nelson Canada
1120 Birchmont Road
Scarborough, Ontario
Canada M1K 5G4

International Thomson Editores
Campos Eliseos 385, Piso 7
Col. Polanco
11560 Mexico D.F., Mexico

International Thomson Publishing GmbH
Konigswinterer Strasse 418
53227 Bonn, Germany

International Thomson Publishing Asia
221 Henderson Road
#05-10 Henderson Building
Singapore 0315

International Thomson Publishing Japan
Hirakawacho Kyowa Building, 31
2-2-1 Hirakawacho
Chiyoda-ku, Tokyo 102
Japan

Library of Congress Cataloging-in-Publication Data
Pavlidis, Theodosios.
Interactive computer graphics in X / Theodosios Pavlidis.
p. cm.
Includes index.
ISBN 0-534-94986-X (hc)
1. Computer graphics. 2. X Window System (Computer system)
I. Title
T385.P382 1995 95-20040
006.6'6—dc20 CIP

***Motif** is a registered trademark of Open Software Foundation*
***SUN** is a registered trademark of Sun Microsystems*
***UNIX** and **OPEN LOOK** are registered trademarks of UNIX System Laboratories*
***X Window System** is a registered trademark of the Massachusetts Institute of Technology*

Managing Editor: *Michael J. Sugarman*
Production Editor: *Monique A. Calello*
Editorial Assistant: *Tanja Brull*
Marketing Manager: *Nathan Wilbur*
Manufacturing Coordinator: *Wendy Kilborn*
Insert Design: *Monique Calello/ Tanja Brull*
Interior Design/Compositor: *Theo Pavlidis*
Electronic Prepress: *Pure Imaging*
Cover Design: *John Sills*
Cover Image: *"SIMCITY 2000 ," Courtesy of Maxis*
Cover/Insert Printer: *New England Book Components*
Text Printer: *Quebecor Printing/ Martinsburg*

Printed and bound in the United States of America
95 96 97 98 99---10 9 8 7 6 5 4 3 2 1

Preface

This text provides an introduction to computer graphics in an X Window System environment. Window systems first appeared in research laboratories nearly 20 years ago, but they now are pervasive in both PCs and workstations. When window systems are run on bitmap displays, they offer wonderful opportunities for producing graphics, as well as for image processing. However, they impose quite a few restrictions on the applications programmers because the display device must be shared with other programs.

Besides displaying graphics, window systems offer opportunities for extensive user-machine interaction through programs that are user-action or event driven. Event-driven programs require a much different programming style than do batch programs, which must be taught together with graphics. A video game is a typical (and probably the best-known) example of a program in which graphic displays and event-driven programming are heavily used.

The idea of giving up control of the flow of execution is a novel one for people who have been writing batch programs; to ease the transition I have included many examples. Besides video games, a number of painting programs are also described.

This book could be characterized in a nutshell as a text that teaches people how to write interactive graphics programs in a window environment. Although most of the material touches on a wide range of graphics applications, a video game is incorporated as an ongoing project. Readers can create animated figures and elaborate backgrounds. The only limitation is their imagination. Virtually every aspect of computer graphics, image processing, image analysis, visualization, and even computational geometry can be used in a video game. Of course, only a small fraction of these subjects can be covered in an introductory book.

While using a fun, computer game project for motivation, I also demonstrate good programming techniques (emphasizing an object-oriented programming style), the fundamentals of graphics algorithms, and how to use the window environment.

Because computer graphics have gone beyond technical areas, such as CAD, and entered the worlds of business and art, use of mathematics is minimal and only as needed. Fewer than one-third of the chapters (and none of the first nine) have any equations; of those that do, only a few use any mathematics beyond the level of a college preparatory high school algebra course. However, because programming is emphasized so much in the book, students are expected to be familiar with the C programming language.

Today the X Window System has become the standard for UNIX workstations, the environment used in this book. Since the X Window System was developed as a standard for all graphics applications, it is necessarily large and complex, which often discourages the beginner. To overcome this problem I developed a Starter Toolkit, which contains a library of functions commonly used in graphics; these function are no more complex than the function of old graphics libraries such as the UNIX PLOT. Using the Starter Toolkit, a reader can write a fairly complex video game program with only a few hundred lines of code. (A painting program is even shorter.)

The Starter Toolkit has been designed so that it can be used in combination with the the X Toolkit and any widget set that is based on the X Toolkit. Thus transition can be gradual in a pragmatic as well as an educational sense. For this reason the book includes a discussion of the X Window System itself to enable students to write programs beyond those using only the Starter Toolkit. That discussion follows a *cookbook* style; that is describing how certain things can be done in the system, as opposed to describing what the system can do. Chapters that deal with the X Window System itself are clearly marked and may be omitted without losing continuity.

Organization

Chapters 1, 2, 3, and 7 provide the fundamental interactive graphics material and should always be covered in a course. Chapters 4, 5, 6, 8, and 9 discuss the X Window System and may be covered to a lesser extent or skipped entirely in a course that focuses exclusively on graphics. The material of the X related chapters requires more programming experience than the other chapters. Chapters 10, 11, 12, 13, 15, and 16 cover traditional two-dimensional graphics material. Chapter 14 emphasizes the type of interactive graphics needed for drawing. Chapter 17 deals with splines, and Chapter 19 is an introduction to three-dimensional graphics. Both require a somewhat more advanced mathematical background than does the rest of the book. Chapters 20 and 21 deal with picture display (either scanned or synthetic). Chapters 18 and 22 cover those aspects of the X Window System that are related to the later chapters of the book.

A course that limits the involvement with X to the use of the Starter Toolkit should be able to cover the 15 graphics chapters in one semester, about one chapter per week. Chapter 20 does not depend on Chapters 10-19 and can be covered earlier in the course because it describes methods for including multicolor characters in a video game.

Software

The text contains listings of many programs. Most of them are available in the diskette that comes with the book or can be obtained from an `ftp` site (see Appendix C). The name of the source file is given with each listing. If that name does not refer to any directory — for example `spiral.c` (Listing 1.3), the file is in the directory `examples`.

If the name contains a directory name, the file is part of the Starter Toolkit and can be found in the directory `starter`. For example, the contents of Listing 2.1 can be found in `starter/include/Starter.h`. Usually, the source code of the Starter Toolkit is not identical to the listings. However, the code in the `examples` directory is; and each file contains comment lines that refer to the sections of the text in which the program is discussed. You should read those sections before attempting to compile a program.

Acknowledgments

The book is based on material that I developed while teaching an introductory graphics course at the State University of New York at Stony Brook. The University helped with a sabbatical leave, and my colleagues and students have been very helpful with comments throughout the period of development for both the course and the supporting software.

First I want to thank Bill Sakoda who introduced me to X and provided the initial guidance. Besides keeping my laboratory in running order, he provided constant feedback and contributed directly with the *Motif* interface of the Starter Toolkit. Chi Hung Chan, Tae Joon Chung, Sandip Sanghvi, and Peter Zenzerovich helped with the porting of the Starter Toolkit to various platforms. Bruno Costa helped with testing of the program listings. Professor Amitabh Varshney provided extensive comments on a draft of the text for which I am grateful. Comments were also provided by Professors Prateek Mishra and Arie Kaufman. I want to thank Professor Kaufman for the image used in Plates 6 and 7, and Pat Tonra and Lichen Hong from his laboratory for help at various times. Professor Masayuki Nakajima of the Tokyo Institute of Technology provided the image used in Plates 8 and 9. My secretary, Stella Mannino, was helpful throughout the process.

The origins of the book go back to my involvement in interactive graphics when I was with AT&T Bell Labs. My former colleagues have continued to be helpful and I want to single out Howard Trickey for significant suggestions and feedback during the Starter Toolkit development.

The following people have been helpful with comments on various drafts of the text: George Wolberg, City University of New York; Steve Tanimoto, University of Washington, Seattle; Sung Yoo, Middle Tennessee State University; Deborah Wilbert, Loral; Colin Godfrey, University of Massachusetts, Boston; Charles Williams, Georgia State University; Isaac Victor Kerlow, Pratt Institute; Lanny Mullens, Northern Arizona University; Doug Robertson, Bentley College; and Shirley Hermitage, Augusta College. Extensive comments were received from Paul Nagin, Hofstra University; and Mitchel Soltys, University of North Carolina, Chapel Hill. Tim Love, Cambridge University, provided comments on the Starter Toolkit over the Internet.

I very much appreciate the collaboration of the PWS staff, in particular, managing editor, Mike Sugarman, editorial assistant, Tanja Brull, and production editor, Monique Calello.

Writing a book requires a good environment both at home and at work. My wife Marion provided it at home. The long-term support of my research by two organizations has been essential for sustaining my laboratory. They are the National Science Foundation (Program directors Drs. Y. T. Chien and Howard Moraff) and Symbol Technologies (Dr. Jerome Swartz, CEO, and Dr. Joseph Katz, Vice President for Research and Development).

The text was produced using the tools of the *Documenter's Work Bench* from AT&T. The line drawings were produced by an X program written using only the Starter Toolkit. The files produced by that program were converted into *troff* commands and then integrated with the rest of the text. The drawing and the conversion programs are descendents of the *ped* and *tped* programs that I wrote while at Bell Labs.

Theo Pavlidis

Contents

1 Windows and Graphics **1**

1.1 What Windows Look Like **1**

1.1.1 A Typical Window Screen 1 • 1.1.2 Types of Pictures Displayed on Windows 3

1.2 Graphics Hardware **5**

1.2.1 Hardware for Picture Display 5 • 1.2.2 Vector and Raster Graphics 6 • 1.2.3 A Closer Look at Raster Graphics 6 • 1.2.4 What Is in the Refresh Memory: Pixels 8 • 1.2.5 Bitmaps, Pixmaps, and Planes 8 • 1.2.6 Input Devices 10

1.3 The X Window System **11**

1.3.1 Historical Context 11 • 1.3.2 What Is the X Window System? 12 • 1.3.3 Toolkits 13

1.4 The Starter Toolkit **14**

1.4.1 Overview 14 • 1.4.2 Primitive Drawing Functions 15 • 1.4.3 Graphics Context 16 • 1.4.4 Fonts 18

1.5 Simple Examples **20**

1.5.1 A Visualization Window 20 • 1.5.2 Visualizing a Computation 22 • 1.5.3 Visualization of Data 24 • 1.5.4 Using Font Information 26

1.6 Conclusions **27**

1.7 Assignments **28**

2 Event Driven Computing 31

2.1 Basic Concepts 31

2.1.1 Introduction 31 • 2.1.2 Events 32 • 2.1.3 Two programming styles for event handling 34 • 2.1.4 Using Function Pointers 36

2.2 Event Handling 37

2.2.1 Types of Events and Event Handling 37 • 2.2.2 Event Interpretation by the Starter Toolkit 38 • 2.2.3 An Event Handler of the Starter Toolkit 40

2.3 Painting with Pixels 41

2.3.1 Using a Pointer to Paint the Display Screen 41 • 2.3.2 Changing the Size of Pixels 42 • 2.3.3 Creating a Backup 44

2.4 Drawing Polylines 46

2.4.1 An Event Handler for Drawing Polylines 46 • 2.4.2 Using Two Event Handlers 48

2.5 Handling of Text 50

2.5.1 A High-Level Event Handler for Typed Input — Preliminaries 50 • 2.5.2 A High-Level Event Handler for Typed Input — The Main Part 52 • 2.5.3 Using Typed Text 54

2.6 Painting with Color 56

2.6.1 Subdividing a Window 56 • 2.6.2 Making a Palette of Colors 58 • 2.6.3 Using the Palette of Colors 60

2.7 Conclusions 61

2.8 Assignments 62

3 Icons and Games 65

3.1 Introduction 65

3.1.1 Some Definitions 65 • 3.1.2 Icon Editors 66

3.2 Using Icons 67

3.2.1 File Format 67 • 3.2.2 An Example of Icon Processing - Cursor Masks 68 • 3.2.3 Making Icons Useful 71

3.3 Some New Functions of the Starter Toolkit 73

3.3.1 Definitions of the New Functions 73 • 3.3.2 Changing the Cursor Icon 74

3.4 Using Icons for Games 75

3.4.1 Creation of Game Objects 76 • 3.4.2 Animating a Graphin 77 • 3.4.3 Animating a Population of Graphins 79 • 3.4.4 Objects with Erratic Motion 80

3.5 Sea World 81

3.5.1 Preparing the Graphins 81 • 3.5.2 Creating the Graphins 83

3.6 Interaction Among Objects 86

3.7 **A Simple Video Game** 90
3.8 **Conclusions** 92
3.9 **Assignments** 92

4 Fundamentals of the X Window System 95

4.1 **Introduction** 95
4.1.1 Clients and Servers 95 • 4.1.2 X Protocol and Xlib 96 • 4.1.3 An Example of an X Protocol Message 97
4.2 **Windows** 99
4.2.1 What Is a Window? 99 • 4.2.2 Windows and Multitasking 100 • 4.2.3 Window Managers 101 • 4.2.4 Backing Up Windows 103 • 4.2.5 Server Resources 104
4.3 **A Simple Window Program** 104
4.3.1 The Simplest Possible Window Program 104 • 4.3.2 Connecting to the Server (Display) 105 • 4.3.3 Creating and Mapping a Window 106 • 4.3.4 X Identity Numbers (XID) 107 • 4.3.5 Dealing with Asynchrony 108 • 4.3.6 Reparenting and the Obligations It Imposes 108
4.4 **Features of Windows** 109
4.4.1 Overview 109 • 4.4.2 Attributes 109 • 4.4.3 Properties and Atoms 110 • 4.4.4 Convenience Functions 111
4.5 **Conclusions** 112
4.6 **Assignments** 113

5 Drawing with the X Window System 114

5.1 **The Basics of Drawing** 114
5.1.1 Drawables and Pixmaps 114 • 5.1.2 Pixmap Manipulation Functions 115 • 5.1.3 Graphics Context 116
5.2 **Functions for Plots** 117
5.2.1 Drawing Primitives 118 • 5.2.2 Graphics Context Functions 119
5.3 **Color** 120
5.3.1 Colormaps and Color Cells 120 • 5.3.2 Using Colors by Name 122
5.4 **Icons** 124
5.4.1 Creating Icons 124 • 5.4.2 Creating Cursors from Icons 126
5.5 **Fonts** 128
5.6 **Conclusions** 130
5.7 **Assignments** 130

6 **Event Handling in the X Window System** 131

6.1 **Introduction** 131

6.1.1 Checking for Events 131 • 6.1.2 The XEvent Data Structure 133 • 6.1.3 Analyzing Mouse Events 134 • 6.1.4 Input Selection 135 • 6.1.5 Dealing with Window Manager Events 136

6.2 **Categories of Events** 138

6.2.1 Overview 138 • 6.2.2 Events Generated by Immediate User Action 138 • 6.2.3 Events That Always Are Selected 138 • 6.2.4 Events Selected Through the Graphics Context 139 • 6.2.5 Events Generated by the Server or the Window Manager and Selected by `Select_Input()` 139

6.3 **Implementation of the draw_window() Procedure** 140

6.3.1 Structure of the Function 140 • 6.3.2 The Function `create_canvas()` 142 • 6.3.3 The Function `create_gc()` 143 • 6.3.4 The Function `process_event()` 144

6.4 **Event Translation by the Starter Toolkit** 145

6.5 **Conclusions** 148

6.6 **Assignments** 149

7 **Graphical Computing** 151

7.1 **Introduction** 151

7.2 **Computing with Menus** 152

7.2.1 What Is a Menu? 152 • 7.2.2 Pointing to an Item on a Computer Screen 154 • 7.2.3 Types of Graphical Menus 154 • 7.2.4 Sliders and Scrollbars 157

7.3 **Graphical Menu Programs** 158

7.3.1 Overview 158 • 7.3.2 A Starter Toolkit Function for Action Panels 159 • 7.3.3 A Starter Toolkit Function for Value Panels 161

7.4 **Creating and Using Panels** 164

7.4.1 A Simple Program Using Panels 164 • 7.4.2 Constructing a Value Panel from an Integer Array 166 • 7.4.3 Computing a Value Panel from a String Array 167

7.5 **Pixel Painting Revisited** 168

7.5.1 Panels for Color 168 • 7.5.2 Panels with Icons 170 • 7.5.3 Varying the Cursor to Match a Panel Selection. 172 • 7.5.4 A Dialogue Panel 174 • 7.5.5 Saving a File 175

7.6 **Video Games Revisited** 178

7.7 **Pipes** 180

7.7.1 One-Way Pipes 181 • 7.7.2 Two-Way Pipes 183

7.8 **Conclusions** 186

7.9 **Assignments** 186

8 The X Window System Toolkit 188

8.1 **Introduction** 188
8.1.1 Window Objects 188 • 8.1.2 Creating Window Objects 190 • 8.1.3 Creating Windows 191 • 8.1.4 Processing Events 193

8.2 **Components of the X Window System Toolkit** 194
8.2.1 Introduction 194 • 8.2.2 Relationship between Xlib, Toolkit, Widget Sets, and the Starter Toolkit 196 • 8.2.3 Widget Classes 198 • 8.2.4 Widget Class Hierarchy, Widget Tree, and Instances 201 • 8.2.5 Resources 203

8.3 **Callbacks and Event Handlers** 204
8.3.1 Introduction 204 • 8.3.2 Callbacks 205 • 8.3.3 Event Handlers 206 • 8.3.4 While Waiting Between Events 209

8.4 **Conclusions** 210

8.5 **Assignments** 210

9 Using Toolkits 212

9.1 **Introduction** 212
9.1.1 Toolkits 212 • 9.1.2 Simple Examples 213

9.2 **Advanced Use of the Starter Toolkit** 216
9.2.1 Using the Starter Toolkit and the X Toolkit Together — 1 216 • 9.2.2 Using the Starter Toolkit and the X Toolkit Together — 2 217 • 9.2.3 The Dialogue Window of the Starter Toolkit. 220 • 9.2.4 A Prototype for a Slider Widget 223

9.3 **Direct Use of the X Toolkit** 226
9.3.1 Creating Widgets 226 • 9.3.2 Starting an Application 228 • 9.3.3 Creating a Drawing Widget 230

9.4 **Creating Motif and OLIT Widgets** 231
9.4.1 Implementation of `begin_display()` and `complete_display()` 231 • 9.4.2 Implementation of the Panel Functions of the Starter Toolkit 234 • 9.4.3 Implementation of the Button Functions of the Starter Toolkit 236

9.5 **The Tk Toolkit** 238

9.6 **Conclusions** 239

9.7 **Assignments** 240

10 Plotting Lines and Circles 241

10.1 **Introduction** 241

10.2 **Plotting Straight Lines** 242
10.2.1 The Basics 242 • 10.2.2 Mathematical Foundations 243 • 10.2.3 The Line Plotting Program 245

10.3 **Difficulties of Geometry on Bitmaps** 247

10.4 **Plotting Circular Arcs** 250

10.5 **Plotting Arcs with Straight Lines** 252
10.5.1 The Basic Idea 252 • 10.5.2 A Dangerous Solution 253 • 10.5.3 A Remedy 254

10.6 **Plotting Functions for Arcs and Polylines** 255

10.7 **Accelerating Pixel Painting** 256
10.7.1 Another Case of Planning 256 • 10.7.2 Straight Lines and Rectangles 258 • 10.7.3 Curves 259 • 10.7.4 Resetting the Event Handler 260

10.8 **Writing Useful Event Driven Programs** 261

10.9 **Conclusions** 261

10.10 **Assignments** 263

11 Filling Areas 264

11.1 **Introduction** 264

11.2 **Connectivity Filling with Line Segments** 266

11.3 **Implementation of Connectivity Filling** 267
11.3.1 The Basics 267 • 11.3.2 Calling the Filling Module 268 • 11.3.3 Filling a Line Segment 269 • 11.3.4 Defensive Programming 271

11.4 **Testing Connectivity Filling** 272
11.4.1 Stand Alone Testing 272 • 11.4.2 Integrating Connectivity Filling in the Pixel Editor 274

11.5 **Conclusions** 274

11.6 **Assignments** 275

12 Filling Polygons 277

12.1 **Introduction** 277

12.2 **Parity Filling** 278
12.2.1 The Basic Method 278 • 12.2.2 Singularities 280

12.3 **The Line Sweep Method** 282
12.3.1 Finding the Intersection of Many Parallel Lines with a Polygon 282 • 12.3.2 Preparing the Segment List 283 • 12.3.3 Sorting the Segment List 284 • 12.3.4 Traversal of the Segment List 286 • 12.3.5 Implementation of the Traversal of the Segment List 286 • 12.3.6 The Drawing Function 288 • 12.3.7 Calling the Procedures 290 • 12.3.8 Directional Parity Fill 291

12.4 **Conclusions** 293

12.5 **Assignments** 294

13 **Geometric Objects and Transformations** 296

13.1 **Introduction** 296

13.1.1 The Limitations of Pixel Arrays 296 • 13.1.2 Why Do We Care About the Limitations? 298

13.2 **Object Types** 299

13.2.1 Pixels and Points 299 • 13.2.2 Lines, Polylines, and Circles 300

13.3 **Scaling** 301

13.3.1 Changing the Size of a Circle or a Polyline 301 • 13.3.2 Center of an Object 302 • 13.3.3 A Simple Generalization 303

13.4 **Generic Geometric Objects** 305

13.5 **Translation and Rotation** 306

13.5.1 Translation 306 • 13.5.2 The Rotation Equations 307 • 13.5.3 The Rotation Program 308

13.6 **Finding Objects** 309

13.6.1 The Easy (but User-Unfriendly) Way 309 • 13.6.2 The Hard (but User-Friendly) Way 310

13.7 **Lines and Points** 311

13.7.1 Equation of a Line Joining Two Points 311 • 13.7.2 Distance to a Point from a Line Joining Two Other Points 312 • 13.7.3 Distance to a Point from a Line 313 • 13.7.4 Distance of a Point from a Line Segment Joining Two Other Points 313

13.8 **Finding Objects Revisited** 315

13.8.1 Implementation of the User-Friendly Distance Computation 315 • 13.8.2 The Moral of the Story 318 • 13.8.3 Issues of Efficiency 318

13.9 **Conclusions** 319

13.10 **Assignments** 320

14 **Programs for Drawing** 321

14.1 **Introduction** 321

14.1.1 Why Use a Computer to Create Pictures 322 • 14.1.2 Drawing Editors 323 • 14.1.3 A Potential Danger 324

14.2 **Polygon Drawing** 324

14.2.1 Drawing Arbitrary Polylines 324 • 14.2.2 Drawing Right Rectangles (Boxes) 327

14.3 **Grabbing and Dragging** 329

14.3.1 Grabbing and Dragging a Single Object 329 • 14.3.2 Grabbing and Dragging Many Objects: First Approach 331 • 14.3.3 Object Selection 333 • 14.3.4 Grabbing and Dragging Many Objects: Second Approach 335 • 14.3.5 The Many Meaning of the Word Selection 336

14.4 **Structure of the Callbacks** **336**

14.5 **Conclusions** **338**

14.6 **Assignments** **338**

15 **Operations on Lines** **341**

15.1 **Introduction** **341**

15.2 **Homogeneous Coordinates** **344**

15.2.1 Duality 344 • 15.2.2 Implementation 345 • 15.2.3 Metrics: Finding the Midpoint of a Line Segment 347 • 15.2.4 Metrics: Finding the Distance of a Point from a Line 349

15.3 **Applications** **351**

15.3.1 Composing Triplets 351 • 15.3.2 Fun and Games 352

15.4 **Relative Position of Points and/or Line Segments** **355**

15.4.1 Some Rules 355 • 15.4.2 Position of a Point with Respect to a Line 356 • 15.4.3 Intersection of Line Segments 359 • 15.4.4 Murphy's Law in Computer Graphics 360

15.5 **Conclusions** **361**

15.6 **Assignments** **362**

15.7 NOTE 362

16 **Operations on Polygons** **363**

16.1 **Introduction** **363**

16.2 **Window Clipping** **365**

16.2.1 Point Clipping 365 • 16.2.2 Line Clipping — Preliminaries 365 • 16.2.3 Line Clipping — The Complete Solution 368 • 16.2.4 Polyline Clipping by a Window 371

16.3 **Position of a Point with Respect to a Polygon** **373**

16.3.1 The General Problem 373 • 16.3.2 A Method for Convex Polygons 374 • 16.3.3 An Application of the Point in Polygon Routine 378

16.4 **Clipping a Line Segment with a Convex Polygon** **378**

16.5 **Clipping of Polygons** **381**

16.6 **Conclusions** **381**

16.7 **Assignments** **382**

17 Splines 384
17.1 Introduction 384
17.1.1 The Need 384 • 17.1.2 Some Solutions 385
17.2 Drawing with Splines 387
17.2.1 Splines and Splines 387 • 17.2.2 Functions for Drawing and Editing Splines 389
17.3 Controlled Curves 391
17.3.1 Parabolic Arcs 391 • 17.3.2 More Properties of Parabolic Arcs 393 • 17.3.3 Reintroducing Splines 394
17.4 Parabolic Splines 397
17.4.1 The Basics 397 • 17.4.2 Efficient Computation of the Points of a Spline 398 • 17.4.3 A Program for Computing Parabolic Splines 400 • 17.4.4 A Geometric Method for Computing Parabolic Splines 401 • 17.4.5 Corners in Splines 404 • 17.4.6 Estimating the Placement of Spline Arcs 406
17.5 Cubic Splines 407
17.6 Conclusions 409
17.7 Assignments 410

18 Advanced Plotting with Xlib 411
18.1 Introduction 411
18.2 Circular and Elliptical Arcs 412
18.2.1 Plain Arcs 412 • 18.2.2 Filled Arcs 414
18.3 Polygon Plotting 415
18.3.1 The Basics 415 • 18.3.2 More on Plots with Pixmaps 417
18.4 Polygon Filling 419
18.4.1 The Basics 419 • 18.4.2 Fill Patterns 420 • 18.4.3 Drawing on Tiles and Stipples 422
18.5 Regions 424
18.5.1 The Basics 424 • 18.5.2 Region Algebra 427
18.6 Conclusions 428
18.7 Assignments 428

19 Projections and Visibility 430
19.1 Introduction 430
19.1.1 What Is a Projection? 430 • 19.1.2 What Is Visibility? 433
19.2 Homogeneous Coordinates in Space 435
19.2.1 Points and Planes 435 • 19.2.2 Straight Lines 437

19.3 **Analytic Expressions for Projections** 439
19.3.1 The Basic Expressions 439 • 19.3.2 The Perspective Projection Matrix 440 • 19.3.3 Why Project in Three Dimensions? Visibility Issues 442 • 19.3.4 Some Examples 445

19.4 **Ray Tracing** 448

19.5 **Conclusions** 449

19.6 **Assignments** 451

20 **Full Pictures** 452

20.1 **Introduction** 452
20.1.1 Requirements for Displaying Full Pictures 452 • 20.1.2 Pictures and Their Descriptions 453

20.2 **Creating Full Pictures** 454
20.2.1 Scanning 454 • 20.2.2 Synthesis 456 • 20.2.3 The Theory of Displaying 457 • 20.2.4 Reconstruction Filters 458 • 20.2.5 Choosing the Right Sampling Rate 460 • 20.2.6 Creating Smooth Displays 461

20.3 **Color and Colormaps** 461
20.3.1 The Basics of Colormaps 461 • 20.3.2 Colormaps for Real Color 463 • 20.3.3 Facilities for Colormaps of the Starter Toolkit 465

20.4 **Display of Full Pictures** 466
20.4.1 Image Structure and Image Files 466 • 20.4.2 Windows for Full Pictures 467 • 20.4.3 Colormaps for Grayscale Pictures 469 • 20.4.4 Creating an Application That Displays Full Pictures 470

20.5 **Conclusions** 472

20.6 **Assignments** 472

21 **Halftoning** 474

21.1 **Introduction** 474
21.1.1 Statement of the Problem 474 • 21.1.2 Outline of Solutions 475

21.2 **Dither Halftoning** 476
21.2.1 Analysis of Dither Halftoning 476 • 21.2.2 A Program to Generate Dither Matrices. 478 • 21.2.3 Implementation of Dither Halftoning 480 • 21.2.4 Properties of Dither Halftoning 482

21.3 **Error Diffusion Halftoning** 483
21.3.1 Analysis of Error Diffusion Halftoning 483 • 21.3.2 Implementation of Error Diffusion Halftoning 485 • 21.3.3 Improved Implementation of Error Diffusion Halftoning 486

21.4 **Multilevel and Color Halftoning** 488

21.4.1 Multilevel Dithering 488 • 21.4.2 Multilevel Error Diffusion 489

21.5 Conclusions **491**

21.6 Assignments **493**

22 Image Display in the X Window System 494

22.1 Colormaps and Visuals **494**

22.1.1 The Basics of Colormaps 494 • 22.1.2 Overview of Visuals 495 • 22.1.3 Checking Visuals 496

22.2 Creating and Using Colormaps **498**

22.2.1 Color Cells and Their Allocation 498 • 22.2.2 Initializing Colormaps 499

22.3 Image Structures **502**

22.3.1 The XImage Structure 502 • 22.3.2 Where to Store Image Data 503 • 22.3.3 Creating XImages with Full Depth 503 • 22.3.4 Creating XImages with Halftoning 505 • 22.3.5 Images from Bitmaps and Icons 507 • 22.3.6 Image Display with the Starter Toolkit 509

22.4 An Image Display Prototype Widget **510**

22.5 Conclusions **512**

22.6 Assignments **513**

A Object-Oriented Programming 514

B The Starter Toolkit 522

C Installation of the Software 539

Index 544

1

Windows and Graphics

Scope of the Chapter

Overview of window systems from a user's viewpoint • Hardware for such systems • What is the X Window System? • The Starter Toolkit as a way to develop simple graphics programs within the X Window System • Primitive graphics functions of the Starter Toolkit • Simple visualization programs

1.1 WHAT WINDOWS LOOK LIKE

1.1.1 A Typical Window Screen

Most people using computers today are familiar with the appearance of a *window screen* and such terms as *icons* (small pictures), *cursor* or *sprite* (a small picture that can be moved around the screen), and *mouse* (a device that is used to move the cursor). An example of such a screen is shown in Figure 1.1, with seven windows. In this display each window corresponds to a combination of a running program and part of the resources needed to create a display. Later we define such resources, but that is not necessary for a quick overview of screen appearance.

Near the upper right corner a window displays a clock. It identifies a program that loops indefinitely and changes the displayed image every minute to show the correct time of day.

Figure 1.1 Appearance of a typical screen of a machine running an X Window System.

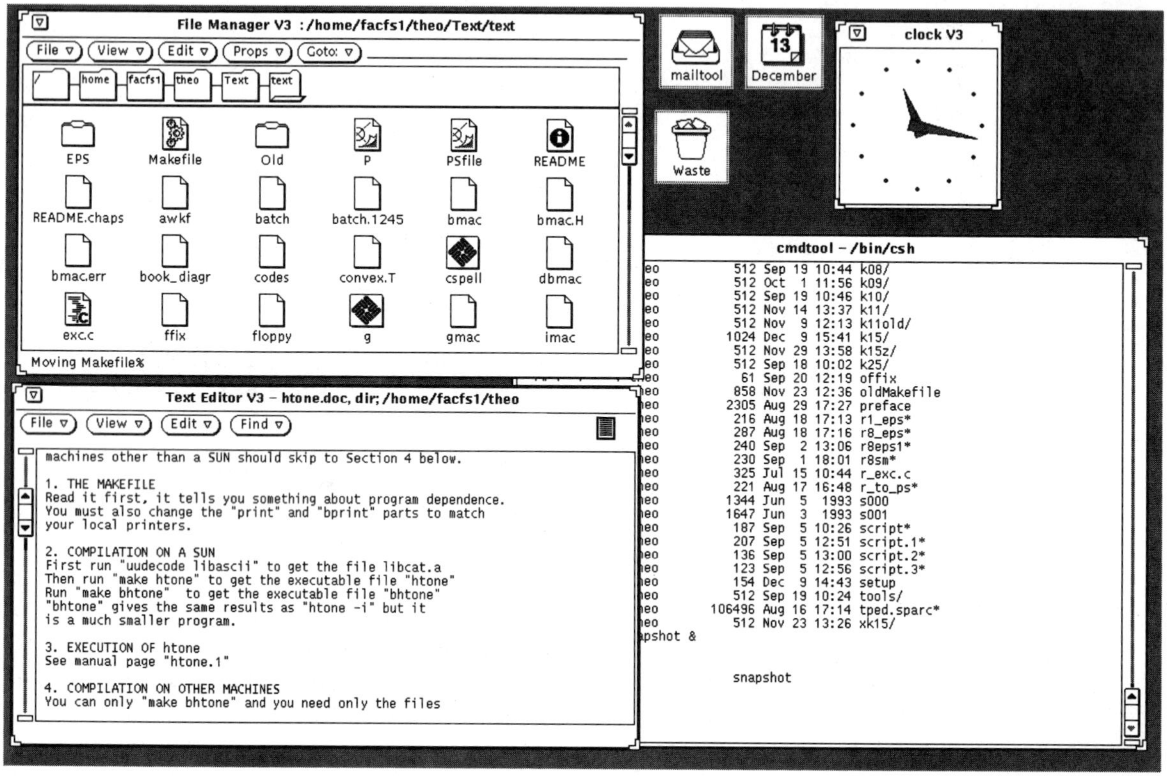

In the upper left part of the screen is a window entitled *file manager*. Its display resources are devoted to a program that displays the file names in a directory together with an icon that describes the type of the file. For example, a piece of paper with a folded corner is an ordinary text file. A square with the manufacturer's logo (SUN in this case) is an executable file, and so on. The user can access a file by using the mouse to move a cursor over the icon of the file and clicking on it.

The window at the lower left is running a *text editor*. That part of the screen behaves pretty much like "electronic paper." The user can select a point of the window with the mouse and then use the keyboard to type in text that will appear at that point. Depending on the setting of the parameters of the text editing program, such typed text will either replace or displace to the right any text that might have existed there.

A small window near the top of the screen is a *mailtool*, a program that deals with electronic mail. That window is *closed*. Its program has just enough access to the display resources to show an *icon*, which provides a hint about the function of the program running in the window. The user may *open* the window by pointing to it with the mouse and clicking. The program then takes control of a larger part of the display resources and shows a screen with detailed information. For example, it would list all electronic mail in the user's mailbox.

Next to the mailtool is a *calendar* window. It also is closed, but it performs a useful function by exhibiting the current date. When open it shows a full monthly or weekly calendar that can be used for scheduling purposes.

Note that one of the remaining windows is partially obscured by two of the others. Indeed windows can overlap, even when they are open. (It is probably a good practice not to have many windows open at the same time; some could be completely obscured and, possibly, forgotten.) The arrangement of the windows on the screen is under the control of a program called a *window manager*. That program also interprets user requests such as opening or closing a window, changing its size, and making it visible.

The creation and use of windows is tied closely to *computer graphics*. Many operating system and networking functions tend to be hidden not only from the user of such a system but also from most application programmers. In this book we focus on graphics and in particular on the type of graphics most relevant to writing window application programs.

1.1.2 Types of Pictures Displayed on Windows

We can characterize the screen of Figure 1.1 as a working person's screen. It displays file directories and a text editor, showing that the user was producing a document at that time. (Actually, it is a snapshot of a writing session for this book.)

Figure 1.2 shows part of another window screen whose appearance may be less familiar to you. It contains two windows that display pictures (an island and the head of a swan) and a window with an array of labels, some corresponding to the labels of the displayed pictures. It is an example of a *multimedia* screen. In this particular case a set of photographs taken on a trip have been scanned into electronic copies stored in a directory. A program that is a display tool shows the names of the files in the directory, and the user may select which of them are going to be displayed. This method is the latest way to go over the pictures taken on a trip. It also is the only way to review the pictures taken with a digital camera.

There are two significant differences between this example and the example of Section 1.1.1. The first has to do with the correspondence between programs and windows. In Figure 1.1 each window corresponded to a single program; in Figure 1.2 only one program is running, but it is controlling many windows.

Figure 1.2 Example of a multimedia display on a machine running an X window system

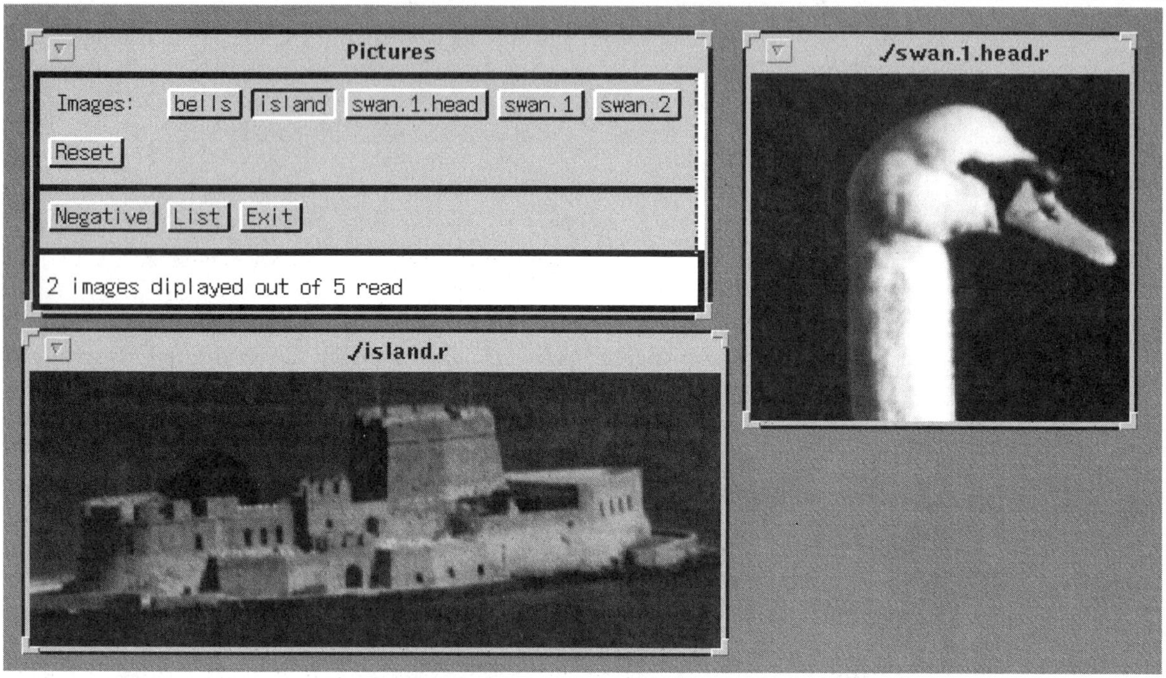

The second difference has to do with the types of pictures displayed. If you look closely at the two screens you will notice some differences in the nature of the displayed images. The images that are copies of black and white photographs have many levels of intensities. They are *grayscale* pictures. The windows of Figure 1.1 contain pictures that are *monochrome*. Note also that there are two types of monochrome pictures. Some, such as the icons of the mailtool and the text files, are *line drawings* but others, such as the clock, include *filled areas*.

Definition In this text we use the term *full picture* to refer either to a grayscale or a color picture with a wide range of intensities. We use the term *flat picture* for monochromes with filled areas. We use the term *line drawing* not only for drawings made with straight lines but also with curves.

These distinctions are important because each of the three types has different hardware requirements.

1.2 GRAPHICS HARDWARE

Any window system functions by displaying pictures and by receiving input from users not only through a keyboard but also through a *pointing device* such as a mouse. We describe only some of the fundamental aspects of such devices, without going into detail. Hardware technology changes constantly, and any detailed description is likely to be dated by the time it appears in print.

An even more important reason for providing only a limited description of hardware is that in modern systems, users and applications programmers are quite removed from the graphics hardware because of the intervening operating system and user interface programs. This separation is particularly true for the X Window System where a major effort has been made to allow programs written for one hardware platform to run on many others as well.

1.2.1 Hardware for Picture Display

Most graphics devices today are based on cathode ray tubes (CRTs), the same electronic device that is used in television sets. Such devices have a beam that strikes the material on the face of the screen and causes a spot to appear bright. The higher the intensity of the beam, the brighter is the spot. The position of the beam is controlled by a pair of plates that cause it to deflect vertically or horizontally.

Color displays are achieved by covering the face of the screen with three types of material and using three beams, each one striking only points that are covered with the material corresponding to a particular color. The impression of a full-color picture is the result of mixing the three *primary colors*: red, green, and blue. We use the terms red, green, or blue beam even though the beams themselves have no color; only the material they strike provides the color.

Television images are produced by having each beam move in a *raster* pattern — repeating horizontal motions while the vertical position changes. Such a pattern is repeated up to 60 times a second or even more. The intensity of each beam is determined by the received signal.

When a CRT device is used in a computer for picture display, the program must specify the location (both vertically and horizontally) and intensity of each of the three beams. (Or the single beam in monochrome displays.) The same basic relationship holds for other devices, such as *liquid crystal* displays, that are becoming increasingly common. The program must still specify a location and the intensity of the three primary colors to be displayed at that location.

1.2.2 Vector and Raster Graphics

There are two fundamental ways of creating an image from computer instructions. One is to execute a sequence of instructions, each positioning one of the color beams at a particular location with a specified intensity. Because screens tend to fade out, the display needs to be *refreshed*. Therefore a set of instructions is placed in a loop that is repeated while the image is being shown. Most of the display is generated not only by illuminating particular points but also by leaving the beam on while moving it from one point to another. Usually such a motion is along a straight line so that the displayed scene consists of a collection of straight line segments, or vectors. For this reason the name of this technology is *vector graphics*. The physics of beam motion can be used to generate more complex shapes as well.

In essence a vector graphics display consists of a *refresh buffer* containing the sequence of instructions and a processor that executes them in a loop. Through appropriate hardware, each instruction generates a signal for the actual electronic display.

Another way of creating an image with a program is to store position, color, and intensity information in a special part of the memory and then use a much simpler processor to examine this memory sequentially and, depending on the contents of its locations, to modulate the appropriate beam. Normally, the location is specified implicitly: The address of the memory where information about color and intensity is stored corresponds to a particular screen point. Special purpose hardware reads the memory continuously in synchrony with the raster pattern of the CRT device (left to right, top to bottom). The contents of each memory location determine the intensity of each of the three beams. Not surprisingly the name of this technology is *raster graphics*.

Most computer graphics systems today use raster graphics because they allow the generation of a much richer variety of pictures than do vector graphics.

1.2.3 A Closer Look at Raster Graphics

Raster graphics rely on a large memory that holds a copy of the picture to be displayed. This memory is used to refresh the display on the screen, so it is often called the *refresh memory*. Because this memory acts as a buffer between computation and display it is also called a *frame buffer*.

Raster graphics technology is quite old, but until the late 1970s had limited use because of the expense of the large high-speed memory required. The drop in computer memory prices in about 1975 made raster graphics widely available, and by the early 1980s they had displaced vector graphics in most applications.

As each location of a computer memory can hold only a string of bits set to 0s and 1s, some rules are needed to convert that information into color and brightness. One possibility is to have a fixed relationship between the bit pattern in each memory location and the colors. However, much greater flexibility is achieved if that relationship is under program control. The rules connecting the bit patterns and the actual color constitute the *colormap*, a table that assigns a combination of colors to a list of binary numbers. The colormap is loaded in a particular piece of hardware called the *video lookup table*.

Figure 1.3 shows the basic arrangement of a raster graphics system. The video lookup table converts the contents of each memory location to intensities for each one of the three primary colors. These intensities are expressed in digital form, so they must be passed through digital-to-analog (D/A) converters whose output is a voltage that controls the intensity of the tube's electronic beams. In this way the bit pattern in a memory location is converted to a particular color and brightness on the screen.

Figure 1.3 Basic hardware of a raster graphics display.

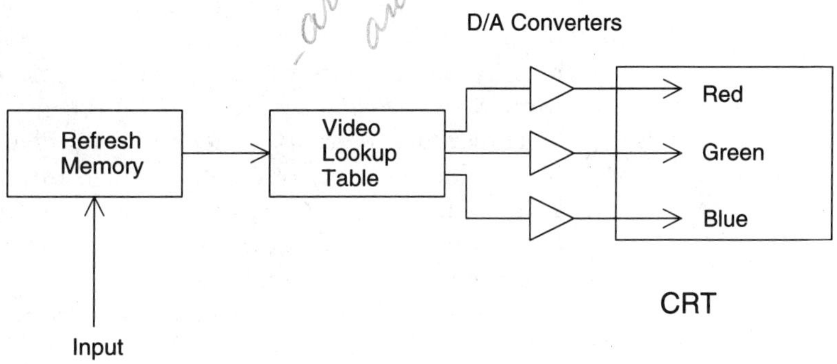

The major impact of this architecture on graphics programs is that they interact not with the actual display but only with the refresh memory and the lookup table. They *never access the real screen directly*. Because of the close correspondence between screen and refresh memory, the word *screen* is now used to refer to the combination of the lookup table and the refresh memory. This usage leads to paradoxical distinctions between *physical* and *logical* screens. Imagining a logical CRT or television monitor is difficult but thinking of logical memory is quite easy. Because this terminology is used extensively in X Window System data structures, we use it in this book and occasionally remind you of its exact meaning.

1.2.4 What Is in the Refresh Memory: Pixels

Like any other piece of computer memory, the refresh memory is organized in bits, bytes, and words. Because of the one-to-one correspondence between display screen locations and refresh memory locations, the following definition makes sense.

Definition A single addressable element of the display screen (refresh memory) is called a *pixel* (for picture element). The abbreviated term *pel* also is used.

The term pixel (but not the term pel) is now firmly established in the English language. *Webster's New World Dictionary, Third College Edition,* (1988) defines pixel as "the basic unit or picture element that makes up the image displayed on a video screen."

To produce a high-quality display, the pixels need to be packed at a high density so that each pixel corresponds to an extremely small area of the screen. Otherwise the jagged look associated in many people's minds with computer pictures will appear. The use of television technology makes convenient the use of a 480-by-640-pixel grid, with a diagonal of 800 pixels. For a 13-inch screen this amounts to about 60 pixels per inch. The same density for a 19-inch screen requires a grid of about 700 by 935 pixels. The higher density of 75 pixels per inch needs a grid of about 875 by 1170 pixels, or more than *one million pixels*!

How much memory is needed for a pixel? For a full picture (see Section 1.1.2) a large variety of intensity levels must be produced so a pixel must be bigger than a bit. Actually, people have trouble distinguishing intensities that differ from each other by less than 1 percent. Thus 100 different values might be enough to create the impression of a high-quality black and white photograph. An 8-bit byte can have 256 possible values, so *a byte per pixel* is a reasonable choice.

A full picture with color requires three times that amount of memory, one byte for each of the red, green, and blue images. Therefore *three bytes (24 bits) per pixel* are needed.

Flat pictures (see Section 1.1.2) and line drawings have only two intensities (usually black and white) so that *a bit per pixel* is enough. A similar picture with color requires *three bits per pixel,* one for each primary color.

1.2.5 Bitmaps, Pixmaps, and Planes

In computer graphics the term *bitmap* is used to describe the kind of memory needed to store pictures containing only 1 bit per pixel. Since computer memories tend to be organized in units no smaller than 8-bit bytes, addressing each pixel individually in such a memory is difficult. Instead pixels are packed 8 in a byte and appropriate bit masks are used to check individual pixel values.

Definition

The X Window System has popularized the term *pixmap* for a memory that is appropriate for storing multibit pixels. The word *depth* means the number of bits per pixel.

You might think of a pixmap as a volume where the x and y directions correspond to the screen coordinates and the z direction to the size of the pixels. You might also think of a pixmap as a stack of *planes*, each corresponding to one bit, as illustrated in Figure 1.4. The stack of planes is intersected by a line that is dashed for the portion between the top and bottom planes. Each plane separately then is a bitmap, the (dashed part of the) line is a pixel, and the whole set is a pixmap.

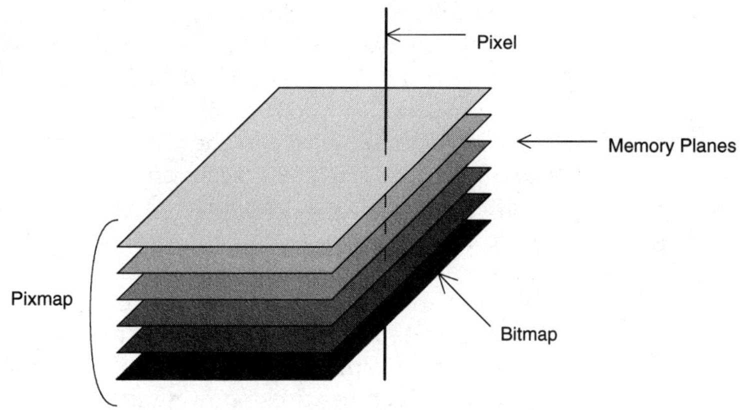

Figure 1.4 Pixmaps, planes, and bitmaps.

This conceptual memory organization does not necessarily correspond to an actual physical organization. Programming in a window environment allows us to rely on the operating system to do the appropriate translation.

Clearly, the refresh memory is either a pixmap or a bitmap. However, other parts of the computer memory also can be viewed in this way. The cursor icon is stored as a bitmap outside the refresh memory and then is copied to different locations in response to the mouse motion.

1.2.6 Input Devices

Besides the display, an interactive graphics system generally has input devices other than a keyboard. We need them for pointing to various parts of the screen, drawing shapes, and copying real pictures into computer memory. The following are some common input devices.

Digitizing tablets sense electronically the position of a pointing device (usually a stylus) on a surface. If we place a line drawing on such a surface, we can trace the drawing with a stylus and create a copy in computer memory.

Because the position of the stylus is not monitored continuously, but only at times determined by the computer clock, the data entry has a limited ability to follow small "wiggles" of the lines drawn. Additional errors are introduced because the position is described only by a fixed number of bits. Although accuracy is limited, it is still greater than that of other methods.

Touch sensitive screens offer a very convenient way for entering line pictures because we have immediate feedback of what is drawn. With digitizing tablets we must look at a screen for such feedback.

Motion sensing devices do not transmit their position to the computer, only their relative motion. The *mouse* and the *trackball* are two of the most common such devices. Details differ from device to device, but moving the mouse supplies to the controlling program two displacement values: `dx` in the horizontal and `dy` in the vertical directions. This information is used to move a *cursor* on the screen, and its position is then used by the program collecting the data. Similarly, the rolling motion of a trackball is translated into `dx` and `dy` displacements of the cursor.

Because of the indirect way in which location information is collected from a mouse or a trackball, accuracy is low and these devices are not appropriate for entering artwork or complex drawings. However they are adequate for simple line drawings and very convenient for interactive computing, which requires pointing to certain areas of the screen. In addition, a mouse may have one or more buttons that send a separate signal to the computer.

For example, if we are drawing a shape, we may move the cursor around until it is at a particular point that should be added to the shape. Then clicking on a mouse button informs the program that it should accept the current cursor position as input.

Scanners are devices that act like copying machines but store the result electronically rather than chemically. Simple scanners produce bitmaps, whereas high-quality scanners produce pixmaps, possibly with color. They are appropriate for entering full pictures into computer memory.

1.3 THE X WINDOW SYSTEM

1.3.1 Historical Context

In vector graphics a sequence of instructions had to be stored in the refresh buffer, which controlled the intensity and position of the beam. These were the *graphics primitives* that were interpreted by the hardware of the device. In raster graphics there is no such limitation. Any value can be stored at any location within that memory (provided there are enough bits to hold the value). However, such a programming style is quite laborious, and all graphics devices come with a library of graphics primitives that are interpreted, not as instructions for controlling the beam, but as values to be stored in the refresh memory.

Any program that is supposed to create a graphics display must produce a sequence of calls to such primitives: drawing a line segment, placing a character at a particular spot on the screen, and the like. An important distinction is the difference between the "low-level" library functions and the graphics primitives that they generate.

The sections of the Unix manual dealing with the *PLOT* libraries illustrate this point. *PLOT(3)* (accessed by the command `man 3 plot`) describes a set of low-level C language functions such as `line(x1, y1, x2, y2)`. This particular function causes a line segment to be drawn between the points with coordinates `x1, y1`, and `x2, y2`. However, when a program executes this function no line is drawn; instead a set of nine bytes is written to the standard output. The first byte contains the ASCII value of the character *l* (154 octal) and each of the four pairs of the following bytes contains the values of the four function arguments shown in Table 1.1. This

Table 1.1. The *PLOT* Graphics Primitive for Drawing a Line Segment

Bytes	Value	Description
First	0154	Operation Code
2 & 3	(short integer)	Value of x1
4 & 5	(short integer)	Value of y1
6 & 7	(short integer)	Value of x2
8 & 9	(short integer)	Value of y2

graphics primitive must be interpreted by a device to produce the actual plot of a line. Specifications for all such primitives can be found by running the command `man 5 plot`.

A set of such primitive instructions is called a *graphics file*, but the names *display list*, or *graphics metafile* also are used. (This terminology is general, not just for the Unix *PLOT*.)

The programs that convert the graphics file into an actual graphics display are listed in the first section of the manual and can be obtained by the command `man plot`. For example, *aed* is the program that converts the graphics file into a display on the AED 512 color graphics terminal, and *bgplot* does the same for the BBN bitgraph graphics terminal. (You can find more examples by running the command `man plot`.)

The Unix family of *PLOT* routines is obsolete today and reflects the technology of the 1970s and early 1980s. However, it illustrates one of the principles used in the X Window System: the distinction between the device and program that synthesize an image versus the device and program that do the actual display. In the X Window System the two parts communicate with messages of the type shown in Table 1.1.

1.3.2 What Is the X Window System?

A computer that has a window display needs a set of programs that manage the display and the interaction between the user and the machine. In addition, facilities must be available for writing new programs for that environment. There are various ways to build a window system and structure the interface between the system and the user or between the system and the applications programmer.

The X Window System (or simply X) was developed in the late 1980s and placed a great emphasis on networking. Some window systems require use of the same machine for running a program and for controlling the screen that displays the program results. The X Window System makes possible running the program on a machine that is quite remote, even on another continent, from the machine controlling the display. The system uses a somewhat counter-intuitive terminology for the two parts.

Definition The machine in which the display takes place and the program controlling the display are called the *server*. The machine in which the display is generated is called the *client*.

We provide a detailed discussion of this terminology and the other topics of this overview section in Chapter 4.

The heart of the X Window System is the X Protocol that both machines must understand and be able to generate. The messages exchanged between the two machines are similar (although more complex) to the kind shown in Table 1.1. Even when the program runs on the same machine that controls the display, the program communicates with the controller of the display through the X Protocol. This feature makes possible running the same program on a variety of display devices.

The communication between the two parts is *asynchronous*: When the program generating the display produces a message, it usually is buffered rather than sent immediately. This delay normally is not a problem (it might be only a fraction of a second) except in two situations. The first is debugging.

Important Point: *Because of the asynchronous communication between client and server, when the server part of the program crashes, the problem cannot be attributed to the last message sent. It may well be the result of an earlier one.*

The second situation occurs when a program displays messages at various stages of a long computation. We must flush the buffer explicitly if we want the message to appear at the time a particular computation is completed.

A library of C functions, called *Xlib,* generates protocol messages, so applications programmers do not have to deal directly with the protocol. Because X was developed as, and has become, a standard, it must provide facilities for every conceivable application. Therefore it is by necessity quite large and complex. *Xlib* contains more than 600 functions. In addition, most functions have a rather large list of arguments. For example, the line segment drawing function has seven arguments, as opposed to four of the corresponding function of the old Unix PLOT.

From an end user's viewpoint, the main feature of X is the ability to run programs on a remote machine. From an applications programmer's viewpoint, the system contains many other substantial features (see Chapters 4 to 6).

1.3.3 Toolkits

Programming in *Xlib* can be quite laborious. For this reason the X Window System provides a "toolkit," known as the X Window System Toolkit (often called simply the X Toolkit), consisting of a set of structures supporting windows, called *Widgets,* and a library of functions called *Intrinsics.* We discuss the X Toolkit (and its parts) systematically in Chapters 8 and 9 because it relies on concepts of computer graphics that we introduce in the intervening chapters. For now, think of a widget as a window with some functions associated with it.

For most of this text we use a *Starter Toolkit,* which hides the size and complexity of the X Window System from people who want to write relatively simple programs while at the same time preserving the key concepts of the X Toolkit and *Xlib*. This feature make possible a gradual transition from programming through the Starter Toolkit to programming with the X Toolkit or *Xlib*.

The Starter Toolkit has been designed in such a way that you need to learn only the parts needed for the simplest tasks before proceeding with more demanding applications. We introduce some of them in the next section and the rest throughout the rest of this text.

For those of you who want to write programs that go beyond the facilities of the Starter Toolkit, we included chapters describing additional facilities of the X Window System. In many cases the implementations of the Starter Toolkit functions are used as case studies for introducing more general concepts. The chapters (4, 5, 6, 8, 9, 18, and 22) that feature them are marked with a star (and a mountain icon) and may be skipped by those whose main focus is basic graphics. The Starter Toolkit is quite adequate for writing programs that illustrate all the basic concepts of computer graphics.

1.4 THE STARTER TOOLKIT

1.4.1 Overview

For the purpose of this chapter you should think of the Starter Toolkit as a library of functions that call some of the functions of *Xlib* with default arguments plus a few arguments supplied by the application. We avoided using macros in order to perform some error checking and avoid the inclusion of X definition files in application programs. All necessary information about the system can be limited to a *makefile* that, in a classroom environment, is provided by the instructor. Examples of such a makefile and instructions about the installation of the Starter Toolkit are given in Appendix C.

The Starter Toolkit may be used in conjunction with other toolkits and with direct calls to *Xlib* functions so that complex programs can be written while it is being used. We discuss how to do so in Chapters 9 and 18. When used alone, the Starter Toolkit limits application programs to one drawing window and a set of panels with buttons that can be used to select various operations or set parameters. (It also limits programs to one display, although they can be run on a remote machine by setting appropriate parameters in the Unix environment.) These restrictions allow the use of graphics primitive functions with a form as simple as the older Unix *PLOT*.

The Starter Toolkit preserves the important concepts of the X Window System, so you can use the toolkit and learn the "X style" of programming at the same time.

1.4.2 Primitive Drawing Functions

The following is a list of functions that are useful for drawing. The color of the drawing is left unspecified, so when one of these functions is called a default color is used. We explain in the next section how that color is set.

Important Point: *All these functions (as well as the **Xlib** functions) use a coordinate system that has its origin in the upper left corner of the window. Thus* `x` *increases from left to right (as in analytic geometry), but* `y` *increases from top to bottom, the opposite of the convention used in analytic geometry.*

A complete documentation of the function of the Starter Toolkit is given in Appendix B.

- **`void put_line(int x1, int y1, int x2, int y2)`**
  Display a straight line segment joining a pair of points with coordinates `x1, y1`, and `x2, y2`, respectively. ☜

- **`void put_rectangle(int x, int y, int w, int h)`**
  Display an unfilled rectangle with upper left corner at `x, y`, width `w` and height `h`. ☜

- **`void fill_rectangle(int x, int y, int w, int h)`**
  Display a filled rectangle with upper left corner coordinates `x, y` and dimensions `w` and `h`. ☜

Important Point: `fill_rectangle()` *is calling an **Xlib** function, which in most systems is built directly on top of a basic machine graphics primitive. Therefore it is the most efficient function to use to implement other graphics operations. In particular*

```
fill_rectangle(x, y, 1, 1)
```

is the best way to display a single pixel.

- **`int put_text(char *text, int x, int y)`**
  Display the string `text` so that it starts at `x` and its base line is at `y`. It returns the width of the displayed text in pixels. ☜

- **`void clear_screen(int x, int y, int w, int h)`**
  Erase whatever has been drawn in a rectangle with upper left corner coordinates `x, y` and dimensions `w` and `h`. However, if any argument is negative, the contents of the whole drawing window are erased. In such a case one argument is enough — for example, `clear_screen(-1)`. ☜

- **`void xflush()`**
  Flush the buffer and synchronize client and server. This function can be used after any of the drawing functions (such as those just described) to make sure that the server displays the drawing as soon as the client creates it. Section 1.3.2 explains why such a function is needed.

1.4.3 Graphics Context

The primitive functions described in Section 1.4.2 have no argument for color. These functions look at static variables that determine the color of what is drawn. Besides color, other parameters determined in this way are line thickness and text character size.

The static variables used by the various display functions are kept in a data structure called the *graphics context*. One of them is the *foreground* color, which is used for drawing lines and displaying text. Another is the *background* color, which is given to the empty areas. If the refresh memory has only one bit per pixel, only two colors are possible and the choice usually is between displaying dark on light or light on dark. For devices with more bits per pixel there are more choices. The Starter Toolkit has the following four functions that set colors.

- **`int fore_color(char *cname)`**
  Set the foreground color to the given name ("red," for example). It returns zero if the color has been set successfully, otherwise it returns – 1.

- **`int back_color(char *cname)`**
  Set the background color to the given name ("red," for example). It returns zero if the color has been set successfully, otherwise it returns – 1.

- **`void set_foregr(int c)`**
  Set the foreground color to the value `c`.

- **`void set_backgr(int c)`**
  Set the background color to the value `c`.

Although the first two functions are easier to use, the last two are more efficient. Of course, they place on the applications programmer the task of figuring out which value corresponds to a desired color.

A common error is to attempt to set the window background color by using one of the preceding functions. This approach does not work because the window color is selected when the window is created. (The Starter Toolkit always creates white windows.) To give the empty area of a window (of size, say, 200 by 300 pixels) a particular color (say, yellow), and then draw on it with another color (say, blue), the following sequence of instructions is needed.

```
fore_color("yellow");
fill_rectangle(0, 0, 200, 300);
back_color("yellow");
fore_color("blue");
```

Another important member of the graphics context is the *drawing mode*, which determines how the information drawn is combined with existing data in the refresh memory. Indeed drawing something on a raster display does not necessarily mean *replacing* what is there, but rather *changing* the values of certain locations in the refresh memory. For example, assume that the foreground color is `z` and that the old value in the refresh memory location corresponding to a pixel with coordinates `x, y` is `u`. Then executing `fill_rectangle(x, y, 1, 1)` may result in a new value `u+z` rather than `z`. Many other logical and arithmetic operations also are allowed.

One frequently used composition operation is *exclusive OR* between the bits of the two values (old and new). If both values are the same, the result is 0. This operation is useful because it removes the need to have separate functions for drawing and erasing. If a region of the screen (and refresh memory) is empty, that is, all pixels have 0 value, drawing with color `z` causes all pixels in the specified locations to have value `z`. Repeating the drawing operation with the same color addresses the same set of pixels, but they will already have value `z`. The result of the XOR operation will be 0, so the display will be erased.

The use of XOR becomes complicated when the background is not zero. For example, if the background is yellow and the foreground is blue, and you draw with the XOR mode, the result will not be blue but the color corresponding to the bit pattern produced by XORing the bit patterns that correspond to yellow and blue. To get the correct color under such circumstances requires changing the foreground to a bit pattern that is the result of applying XOR to bit patterns of the intended foreground color and the existing background color.

The Starter Toolkit contains two mode setting functions and a function to adjust the foreground color when the background is not zero.

☛ **`void use_xor_mode()`**
Set the drawing mode to exclusive OR. (The value in the refresh memory is formed by the bitwise exclusive OR of the old and the new value.) A warning is printed (once per application) if the background is nonzero. ☜

☛ **`void use_replace_mode()`**
Set the drawing mode to replacement. (The old value is replaced by the new.) ☜

☛ **`void xor_fore()`**
If the drawing mode is XOR and the background is nonzero, adjust the foreground value so that the correct color is displayed. ☜

Worrying about nonzero background for simple programs may seem unnecessary but, unfortunately, in some systems white corresponds to 1 and black corresponds to 0. Then you must call `xor_fore()` after calling `use_xor_mode()`.

Finally, the following three functions affect the appearance of the lines drawn by changing the value of elements of the graphics context.

☛ **`void make_dash()`**
All lines will be drawn dashed. ☜

☛ **`void make_solid()`**
All lines will be drawn solid. ☜

☛ **`void set_line_width(int n)`**
All lines (dashed or solid) will be drawn with thickness `n` pixels. If `n` is 0 it is treated as 1. ☜

1.4.4 Fonts

When you create a display that contains text, you must have some information about the size of the characters so that you can arrange text labels with the proper background space around them. In most graphics devices characters are stored as small matrices of 0s and 1s as illustrated in Figure 1.5 and are copied into the refresh memory when text has to be displayed. Actually, "copy" is not the right word. If a matrix element is 1, the bit pattern corresponding to the foreground color is placed in refresh memory. If the matrix element is 0, either the background color is stored or the memory contents are left undisturbed. The Starter Toolkit uses the option that leaves the contents undisturbed.

Figure 1.5 Examples of character images stored as 9 by 8 matrices.

```
11111111    11100000
01110001    01100000
01110000    01100000
01110001    01101110
01111111    01110001
01110001    01100001
01110000    01100001
01110001    01110001
11111111    11101110
```

Definition The collection of such matrices for all letters of the alphabet (lower- and uppercase), numerals, punctuation marks, and any special symbols such as the dollar sign are stored in a file together with a header that summarizes the properties of the characters. Such a file is called a *font*.

When a font file is copied into the memory of the display device we say that the font is loaded. The Starter Toolkit has three functions that deal with fonts.

- **`int select_font(char *font_name)`**
  Select the named font to be used for displaying text. The function returns 1 upon success and 0 otherwise. Note that a font corresponds to both a specific style and a specific size. ☜

- **`int get_font_height()`**
  If a font has been selected, the function returns the maximum vertical span (measured in pixels) of characters in the font used in the display. If there is no selected font, it returns 20 (a reasonable guess for most displays). ☜

- **`int fontlength(char *text_string)`**
  If a font has been selected, the function returns the length in pixels of the text string given as argument. If there is no selected font, it returns the number of characters in the string multiplied by 12 (a reasonable guess for most displays). ☜

The following three sets of fonts are listed in order of increasing size. (The printed version approximates the appearance of the font on the screen.)

Ordinary: "helvR08" "helvR10" "helvR12"
"helvR14" "helvR18" "helvR24"

Bold: "helvB08" "helvB10" "helvB12"
"helvB14" "helvB18" "helvB24"

Oblique: "helvO08" "helvO10" "helvO12"
"helvO14" "helvO18" "helvO24"

The server always has a font loaded, so text is always displayed. However, the information about it may not be available in the client, so from that side it appears that no font is loaded. (Recall the two-part nature of X discussed in Section 1.3.2.) The Starter Toolkit makes an effort to extract that information but does not guarantee success. In such cases the function `get_font_height()` returns the value 20 and `fontlength()` returns 12 times the string length of the text.

1.5 SIMPLE EXAMPLES

1.5.1 A Visualization Window

You may have noticed that none of the functions described in Sections 1.4.2 and 1.4.3 deal with window manipulation. For simple programs that need only one window to display some graphic information, that is not an issue. The Starter Toolkit has a function, `vis_window()`, that creates a single window that can be used to display graphs or plots that are useful for visualizing data. If the function is called with a 0 argument, it does nothing but create a window as shown in Listing 1.1.

Listing 1.1: Empty Window

```
main()
{
    vis_window(0);
}
```

This program asks the window manager to create a window in which nothing is displayed. The "nothing" is implied by the 0 argument. After compiling and running that program (see Assignment 1 at the end of the chapter) you get a display similar to that shown in Figure 1.6. The decorations of the frame depend on the particular system in which the program is running, although the message "Press any ..." should be the same.

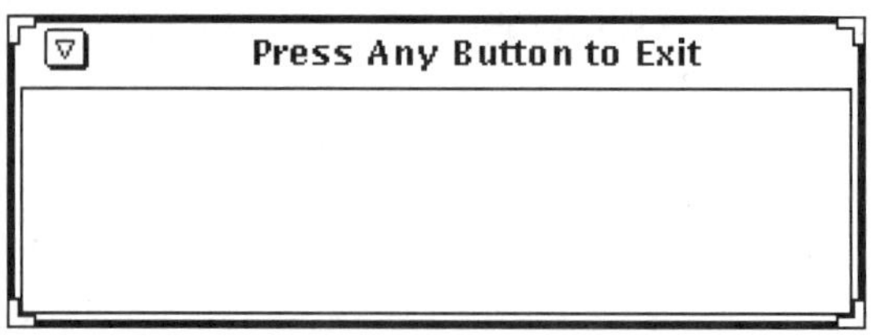

Figure 1.6 Display generated by the program of Listing 1.1.

This display is not particularly interesting, so let's try to give `vis_window()` an argument. The function `vis_window()` accepts as arguments a pointer to a function and, optionally, two integers with the values of the desired width and height. Listing 1.2 shows another program.

Listing 1.2: Window with Message — `File world.c`

```
void hello()
{
     put_text("The end of the world is near", 20, 20);
}

main()
{
     vis_window(hello);
}
```

The function `put_text()` places the string defined by its first argument so that it will start at a horizontal position given by its second argument and its baseline will be at a distance from the top of the window equal to its third argument. Figure 1.7 shows the output of the program.

Figure 1.7 Display generated by the program of Listing 1.2.

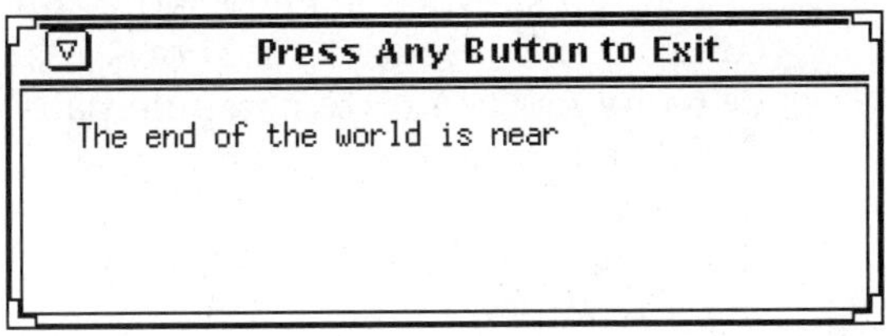

This program is slightly more complex than the famous "hello world" program that is considered the simplest C program. The main intricacy is the nature of the first argument to the `vis_window()` function. Here is the formal specification of this function.

☛ **`void vis_window(void (*f)(), int width, int height)`**
Create a window with width `width` and height `height` or use default values for the dimensions if the arguments are out of range. Once the window is ready, call `f()` to create the contents of the display. Depending on the system, `f()` might also be called any time the window has to be redrawn in response to changes in the window display. For example, one

window obscured by another may become visible again. ☜

C language aside The declaration

```
int (*fun)()
```

states that the variable `fun` is a pointer to functions that return an integer value. The declaration

```
void (*fun)()
```

states that the variable `fun` is a pointer to functions that have no return value. The variable `fun` can be used as an argument to functions or assigned to specific functions with statements of the form

```
fun = read_mail;
```

A subsequent call to `fun()` is equivalent to `read_mail()`.

The X Toolkit makes extensive use of function pointers, so you need to understand well both the example of Listing 1.2 and the C Language concept. The function `vis_window()` also provides a special example of a *Widget*. The function `vis_window()` creates a window of given dimensions and associates with it a function that produces the display on it. Think of the result as a *visualization* widget.

1.5.2 Visualizing a Computation

Listing 1.3 shows a slightly more complex program than the two just discussed, and Figure 1.8 shows its output. The main function calls `create_spiral()` to compute pairs of x-y coordinates of the points of a spiral and stores their values in the two arrays `X[]` and `Y[]`. Then it calls `vis_window()` to create the display window. It passes as argument to it the name of the function, `show_spiral()`, which creates the display from the precomputed coordinates.

Listing 1.3: Spiral Plot — `File spiral.c`

```
/*   Spiral Display      */
#define SIZE  150
#define MXP   4000

static int X[MXP], Y[MXP], npts=0;

void create_spiral()    /* Compute the x and y coordinates    */
{
     double x0 = 10, y0 = 10, x, y;
     do {
          x   = x0 - 0.05 * y0;
```

```
            y  = y0 + 0.05 * x0;
            x0 = x;
            y0 = y;
            X[npts]    = SIZE + x + 0.5;
            Y[npts++] = SIZE + y + 0.5;
        } while(npts<MXP && -SIZE < x && x < SIZE && -SIZE <y && y < SIZE);
}

void show_spiral()
{
        register i;
        for(i=1; i<npts; i++) put_line( X[i-1], Y[i-1], X[i], Y[i]);
}

main()
{
        create_spiral();
        vis_window(show_spiral, 2*SIZE, 2*SIZE);
}
```

Figure 1.8 Display generated by the program of Listing 1.3.

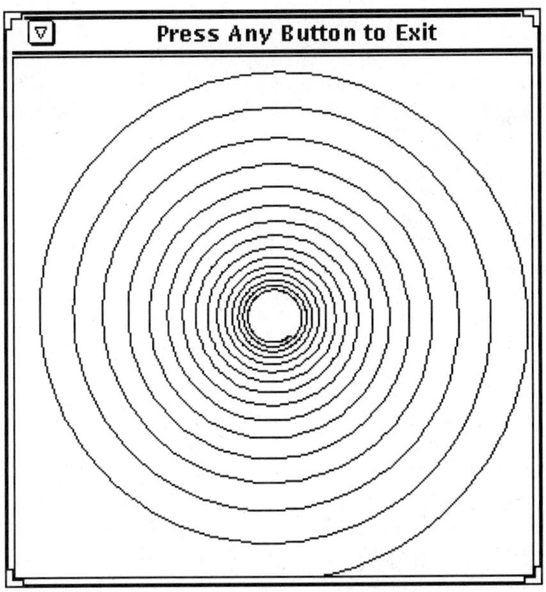

The complexity of the program lies in the creation of the spiral, with only two calls going to graphic routines. By using the `put_line()` function and, possibly, a few others from Sections 1.4.2 and 1.4.3, you can create complex displays of plane geometric figures, limited only by your knowledge of geometry.

1.5.3 Visualization of Data

Listing 1.4 shows a program that reads a list of numbers from the standard input and then displays a histogram. Figure 1.9 shows an example of the program's output.

Listing 1.4: Histogram Plot — `File hist.c`

```
/*   Histogram Display  */
#include <stdio.h>

#define MAX_EL      32        /* maximum number of histogram values */
#define MAX_HH     400        /* maximum width available for display */
#define HORZ_SP     30        /* basic unit for horizontal display */
#define VERT_SP     20        /* basic unit for vertical display */

static int hist[MAX_EL];      /* histogram values */
static int hmax, hmin;
static int lengths[MAX_EL]; /* lengths of lines representing
                    histogram values */
static int n = 0;
static char bf[64];           /* buffer for character strings */

void read_histogram()
{
     double hrange, hscale;
     register i;
     /*   read values from standard input */
     while( gets(bf) && n<(MAX_EL-1) ) hist[n++] = atoi(bf);
     /*   Compute range of histogram */
     hmax = hmin = hist[0];
     for(i=1; i<n; i++){
          if(hist[i]>hmax) hmax =  hist[i];
          else if(hist[i]<hmin) hmin =  hist[i];
     }
     hrange = hmax - hmin;
     /*   Compute lengths of display by scaling histogram     */
     /*   values according to their range             */
     hscale = MAX_HH/hrange;
     if(hscale >1) hscale = 1;
     for(i=0; i<n; i++) lengths[i] = hscale*(hist[i]-hmin) + 1.5;
}
```

```
void show_histogram()
{
     register i;
     int y;
     put_text( sprintf(bf,"hmin = %4d ", hmin ), 2, 20);
     for(i=0; i<n; i++) {
          y  = (i+2)*VERT_SP;
          put_text( sprintf(bf,"%4d ", hist[i] ), 2, y+VERT_SP/2);
          fill_rectangle(HORZ_SP, y, lengths[i], VERT_SP-4);
     }
}

main()
{
     read_histogram();
     vis_window(show_histogram, MAX_HH + HORZ_SP, VERT_SP*(n+5) );
}
```

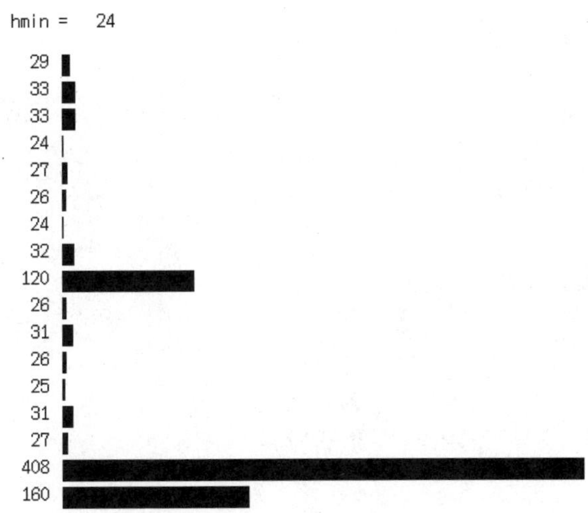

Figure 1.9 Display generated by the program of Listing 1.4.

The function `read_histogram()` not only reads the data but also computes their range to make the window an appropriate size. The structure of this program and that of Section 1.5.2 show how to convert existing visualization programs to run on the X Window System with the help of the Starter Toolkit.

The simplicity of the spiral and histogram programs reflects our limiting them only to line or text output and not making any demands on them about color or style of the lines drawn. Programs will become more complex as we add more requirements, but complexity will be introduced only as necessary.

Interactive programs that handle user input are somewhat more complicated and are discussed in Chapter 2.

1.5.4 Using Font Information

Listing 1.5 and Figure 1.10 illustrate the use of `get_font_height()` and `put_rectangle()`. This example also features the Unix function `cuserid()`, which returns a pointer to a character string with the login name of the user.

Listing 1.5: Using Font Dimensions — `File hello.c`

```
/*   Greeting Program    */
#include <stdio.h>
#include <string.h>

static char user_name[256]; /* Choose a big size to be safe */

show()
{
     int corner_x = 30;
     int corner_y = 30;
     int h, x, xmax;

     h = get_font_height();
     xmax = put_text("Good Morning", corner_x, corner_y);
     x = put_text(user_name, corner_x, corner_y+h);
     if(x>xmax) xmax = x;

     put_rectangle(corner_x-4, corner_y-h,
            xmax+8, 2*h+4);
}

main()
{
     strcpy(user_name, cuserid(NULL));
     vis_window(show, 200, 100);
}
```

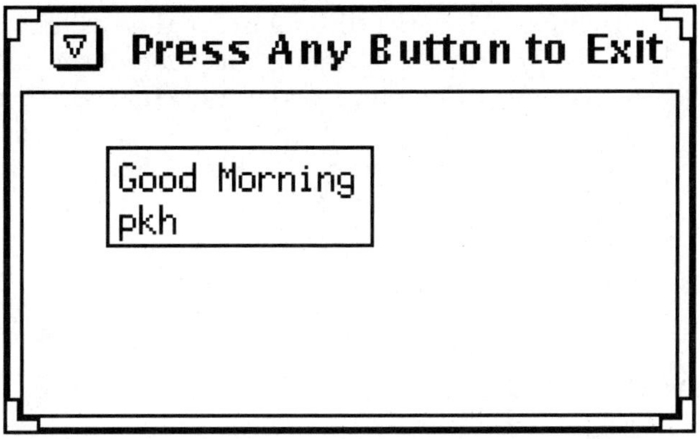

Figure 1.10 Display generated by the program of Listing 1.5. Here, ''pkh'' is the login name of the user running the program.

Calling `get_font_height()` from inside `show()` seems wasteful but is necessary. Among other things, `vis_window()` selects a font, and no inquiry about a font height can be made until a font has been selected. Other functions of the Starter Toolkit allow for a more efficient operation, as described in Chapter 3.

1.5 CONCLUSIONS

In this chapter we explained the basic hardware and software needed for creating graphic displays. We introduced the foundation of the X Window System and provided a strategy for managing its complexity. This strategy is based on the observation that many applications do not need all the features of the system. If a program needs only one drawing window, we can provide the programmer with a library of simple functions that call the *Xlib* functions with default arguments. The programs of Listings 1.3 through 1.5 hide all the intricacies of the X Window System, and they are no more complex than a similar Unix *PLOT* program. The only difference is that all plotting must be done within a single function, and that function's name is passed as an argument to the window function.

The key feature is the modularity of the resulting program. Such programs deal only with the creation of the displays and essentially are independent of the window system. A separate module (in this case a function of the Starter Toolkit) deals with creation of the window and its relationship with the rest of the display. The link between the two modules is provided by the function pointers: `show_spiral` (in Listing 1.3), `show_histogram` (in Listing 1.4), or `show` (in Listing 1.5).

For the most part we focused on output. Of course, that is only half the story. One reason that computer graphics and, in particular, window systems are so popular is that they allow for new ways of human beings and machines to interact (the subject of the next chapter).

The X Window System is only one of several window systems available today. All offer human-computer interaction that is quite different from the norm of the early 1970s and before. The following book is a good source on the exciting history of this technology. Although it focuses on the development of the Macintosh, it covers a lot of background that is common to all window systems.

- S. Levy. *Insanely Great*. New York, Viking, 1994.

1.6 ASSIGNMENTS

Note: Assignments 1-9 can be done on a monochrome display.

1. (a) Familiarize yourself with the makefile needed to compile, link to the appropriate libraries, and run a program under the X Window System. (See Appendix C for an example.) (b) Copy the program of Listing 1.3 and try to compile and run it so that you obtain the display of Figure 1.8.
2. Modify the program of Listing 1.3 so that it displays two spirals side by side, one clockwise and the other counterclockwise. Enclose each spiral by a rectangle. Structure the program so that the spirals are displayed "in parallel" rather than one after the other. (The order may not be apparent in machines with a CPU fast enough to draw a spiral instantaneously.)

Figure 1.11 Display to be produced by the program of Assignment 3 (labels added).

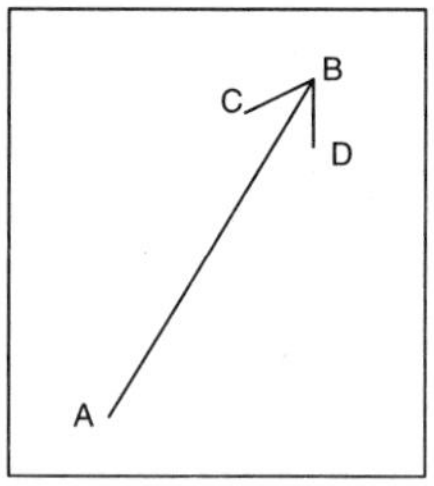

3. Write a program to display an arrow similar to that shown in Figure 1.11 (without the labels). The angle (expressed in degrees) of the line AB with the horizontal should be specified as the first argument of the

command line. The angle at the head of the arrow (`CBA` or `ABD`) should be specified as the second argument. For example, Figure 1.11 can be produced by `a.out 60 30`. (See the note at the end of the assignments on how to use command line arguments in C.)

4. Write a program to display an arrow similar to that shown in Figure 1.11 *with the labels*. See Assignment 3 for details.
5. Write a program to display a list of numbers as a plot with labeled axes. You may also add hash marks and arrows. Use lines of different styles and widths to plot many graphs simultaneously.
6. Write a program that reads a list of pairs of names and numbers and then creates a bar chart (in the same way the program of Listing 1.4 does) labeled with the names corresponding to the numbers. For example, the names could be those of countries and the numbers their populations.
7. Modify the program of Listing 1.5 so that the text is centered within the surrounding rectangle both horizontally and vertically.
8. Create a text display using different character sizes by calling the `select_font()` function from within the redrawing function.
9. Investigate how to run your programs on a different machine from the one controlling the display. Normally, the Unix shell variable `DISPLAY` contains the necessary information. (Type `echo $DISPLAY` to see the current destination. Most likely the answer will be `:0.0`, which stands for local display.) If you are sitting in front of a display controlled by a machine named `jupiter` and you want to run your program on a machine named `saturn`, the following sequence might work. (Bold characters denote the machine prompt.)

```
jupiter 12 % xhost +saturn
jupiter 13 % rlogin saturn
saturn 1 % setenv DISPLAY jupiter:0
saturn 2 % a.out
```

The details of this operation depend on the particular installation and you should ask for help from your instructor or system administrator if the above sequence does not work. (The third statement assumes a C shell command interpreter. Although it is the most commonly used in educational environments, it is not universal.)

Note: Assignments 10-12 must be done on a color display.

10. Repeat Assignments 2-8 by using colors. In particular the desired colors (foreground and background) of the display should be given as command line arguments — for example

```
a.out gold turquoise
```

Use the code of Section 1.4.3 for that purpose. (See also the note below.)

11. Carry out Assignment 5 using different colors rather than different line styles.
12. Create a straight rainbow, i.e. a sequence of rectangles, each having one of the colors appearing on a rainbow.

C language aside

The following code fragments show how to read command line arguments from inside a C program. First declare the main function as

```
main(int argc, char ** argv)
```

where `argc` is the number of command line arguments plus 1, and `argv` points to a set of strings, each corresponding to such an argument. The argument `argv[0]` contains the name of the command. The statement

```
angle0 = atoi(arv[1]);
```

converts the first argument into an integer and stores it in `angle0`. The statement

```
fore_color(arv[1]);
```

sets the foreground color to the color named by the first argument.

2

Event Driven Computing

Scope of the Chapter

Interrupts and events • Means of handling user input or other external actions (event handling) • Functions of the Starter Toolkit for handling input from the mouse and keyboard • Example programs: Painting with Pixels; Drawing Lines ("rubber banding"); Typing words at positions pointed to by the mouse; Using a Color Palette

2.1 BASIC CONCEPTS

2.1.1 Introduction

In Chapter 1 we focused on the technology used to create graphic window displays without saying anything about the structure of the programs running in such a system, especially how they handle user input. We explain that structure in this chapter, starting with an example outside the field of graphics, then discussing the specific mechanisms under the X Window System, and finally offering some sample graphics programs.

The programs running in a window system are quite different from the typical program discussed in programming courses where the emphasis is on internal computations. Such a program will have an input statement, followed by a sequence of calculations on the input and an output statement. For example,

```
Read an array of integers.
Sort them, largest first.
Print the sorted array.
```

A different style of programming is needed for programs that must respond to user requests. Such programs include not only those running on a window system but also many of the programs used in communications, banking, and other activities.

Because most people have used an automatic teller machine (ATM), we use that system as an example. The program controlling an ATM is idle until a person inserts a card and then proceeds with a sequence of operations. When these are completed the program returns to the idle state. The following might be a fragment of code written in some high-level language.

```
W: wait for a signal that a card has been inserted.
   Take care of the transaction.
   Go to W.
```

The sequence of instructions executed is determined largely not by what happens inside the program but by what happens outside. This type of operation is called *interrupt driven* computing, where the term *interrupt* denotes the signal that is produced when a physical event is sensed by one of the peripherals of the machine. (For example, inserting a card in an ATM or hitting one of the keys on a keyboard.) The main routine of such a program can be very simple:

```
If an interrupt occurs
     call interrupt_handler(kind_of_interrupt).
Repeat above.
```

The variable `kind_of_interrupt` contains information of the type of interrupt that occurred and the function `interrupt_handler` executes the appropriate code depending on the argument passed to it.

The geometric aspects of the display are secondary to the internal organization of the program. The important feature is that the program waits for signals, each associated with an action and, when the appropriate signal arrives, the action is taken.

2.1.2 Events

When a program is running under an operating system such as Unix (or any other), it cannot sense directly the physical interrupts. Interrupt handling (or servicing) is one of the tasks of the operating system. The operating system may do one of two things: signal the application program immediately or store the information about interrupts in a place that can be checked by the application programs.

In the X Window System, as well as in other window systems, the term *event* is used for the structure containing information about the physical interrupts (e.g., moving the mouse or hitting a key on the keyboard) and the term *event queue* for the place where all such structures are stored. Thus we usually talk about *event driven computing* rather than interrupt driven computing.

Of course, once an event queue has been established, programs may add elements to it for reasons other than the occurrence of a physical interrupt (which is exactly what the X Window System does). Thus the concept of event driven computing actually is more general than interrupt driven computing.

The following is a simple (but far from the best) implementation of this concept. Let `E[]` be an array of event structures. Let `Head` and `Tail` be two indices, both referring to the start of `E[]` in the beginning (meaning that both are zero). Information is stored by the operating system by a statement of the form

```
E[Tail++] = ...
```

Then the applications program given in Section 2.1.1 becomes

```
if(Head<Tail) {
     call E_handler(E[Head])
     increment Head by 1
}
repeat above
```

The program does nothing unless there is an entry in the array `E[]`, which will happen when an interrupt has occurred. From the viewpoint of the applications programmer there is very little difference between the two programs. As a matter of fact the functions `interrupt_handler` and `E_handler` can be identical. As we are using high-level descriptions for our programs, we may drop the details in the first part of the preceding pseudocode and describe the program as

```
Check whether an event has occurred
 and if it has, then call event_handler(kind_of_event)
repeat above
```

Then the similarity between event and interrupt handling becomes more evident.

Even though there is little practical difference between sensing interrupts and checking an event queue for simple programs that do little else, there is a major difference for programs that perform significant other computations. An interrupt does what its name says: It causes the execution of a procedure that services the interrupt instead of executing the next instruction of the program. An event will not be detected unless the program checks the queue. We return to this point in Chapter 3 when we discuss video games.

2.1.3 Two programming styles for event handling

Clearly, the response to the same event needs to be different in different circumstances. An ATM needs to differentiate the action when a user enters a personal identification number (PIN) from when the user enters a withdrawal amount. Both actions produce events indicating typing on the keyboard. There are two basic ways to handle the necessary distinction: by using nested event handlers or a state variable. We illustrate both methods for the ATM example.

Nested Event Servers

The following is a fragment of pseudocode that has each handler call another for the next user action.

```
main()
{
     W: Check whether an event has occurred
          and if it has, then call card_handler();
     Go to W;
}

card_handler() {
     if the event is other than card insertion return;
     Read and verify card number;
     If not a valid card number return;
     Prompt user to enter PIN;
     W: Check whether the ENTER key has been hit
          and if it has, then call PIN_handler();
     Go to W;
}

PIN_handler() {
     If event is other than ENTER key return;
     Read the buffer where the values of keys hit before
          ENTER are kept and form a number N;
     If N is not a valid PIN return;
     Prompt user to enter type of transaction;
     W: Check whether an event has occurred
          and if it has, then call trans_handler();
     Go to W;
}
```

Note that each procedure of the program executes an infinite loop while waiting for an event to occur.

Selection of Event Server by a Flag (State Variable)

Let `S` be a variable that takes integer values. Then the main program executes an infinite loop, the *main event loop*, and calls different handlers depending on the value of `S`. Think of `S` as a flag that signals to the system how to handle an event. The variable `S` is called a state variable because it indicates the state of the program. The following is the pertinent fragment of pseudocode.

```
main() {
     S = 0;
     W: Check whether an event has occurred
          and if it has execute {
          switch(S) {
          case 0: call card_handler(); break;
          case 1: call PIN_handler(); break;
          case 2: call trans_handler(); break;
          etc.
          }
     }
     Go to W;
}

card_handler() {
     if event is other than card insertion return;
     Read and verify card number;
     If not a valid card number return;
     Prompt user to enter PIN;
     S = 1;
}

PIN_handler() {
     If event is other than ENTER key return;
     Read the buffer where the values of keys hit before
     ENTER are kept and form a number N;
     If N is not a valid PIN return;
     Prompt user to enter type of transaction;
     S = 2;
}
```

The use of nested event handlers seems more natural for the programmer. The application determines the control of the program, and infinite loops waiting for an event are inserted whenever needed. However, such statements tend to depend on the window system under which the application is running. Having all the code dealing with events in one place, the *main event* loop, helps portability. Only one procedure will have to be changed when a program is moved to another system.

Another advantage of having one main event loop is that writing code dealing with unexpected events is easier. Most events are generated by users, who can be unpredictable.

The X Toolkit (see Section 1.3.3) uses a main event loop so that those intending to write programs for the X Window System have one more reason for becoming familiar with this style.

For simple programs there is little difference between the two styles, but for complex programs the organization can be quite different. In particular, using the state variable (flag) encourages modular programming.

2.1.4 Using Function Pointers

You have already encountered function pointer variables as used in C in the simple window program in Section 1.5.1. We use them again here because they let us simplify the code of event handling by removing the need for an explicit state variable. Instead we have a variable *handler*, declared as

```
    void (*handler)();
```

Now the last pseudocode fragment becomes

```
main() {
    handler = card_handler;
    W: Check whether an event has occurred
         and if it has execute {
              if(handler) handler();
         }
    Go to W;
}

card_handler() {
    if event is other than card insertion return;
    Read and verify card number;
    If not a valid card number return;
    Prompt user to enter PIN;
    handler = PIN_handler;
}

PIN_handler() {
    If event is other than ENTER key return;
    Read the buffer where the values of keys hit before
    ENTER are kept and form a number N;
    If N is not a valid PIN return;
```

```
        Prompt user to enter type of transaction;
        handler = trans_handler;
    }
```

This program is certainly more efficient (avoiding execution of the switch) and, arguably, easier to write and read than the previous version. Note the use of *defensive programming* in checking that `handler` is not null before calling the function. Since `handler` is a variable, there is always the chance that it may not have been set properly.

2.2 EVENT HANDLING UNDER THE X WINDOW SYSTEM

2.2.1 Types of Events and Event Handling

Interrupts occur at the physical device that contains the display screen and peripherals such as the mouse. Hence the display (server) has the information needed to create the event structures and place them in the event queue. In addition, the server places other information about local happenings that might be of interest to the applications (clients) in the event queue. For example, if the window manager running the display causes a window to be exposed, the application program that created the window must be notified so that it can redraw the contents of the window.

The following are some of the actions that result in the creation of an event.

- A key on the keyboard has been pressed or released.
- A mouse button has been pressed or released.
- The mouse has moved (obviously, a frequent event).
- The pointer (mouse controlled) cursor entered or left a window.
- A window has been exposed and needs to be redrawn.

Application programs need not keep track of all events. For example, they may ignore the mouse motion and check its position only when a button is pressed. Informing the display (server) about which events must be tracked is possible because the display maintains separate event queues for each application (client). In Chapter 6 we discuss how such selections are made, but for the initial simple applications discussed in this and the nonstarred chapters we use a default selection.

Because the event queue is kept in the display (server), the application (client) must make a request (using the X protocol) to check the queue and retrieve an event from it. The main part of an event driven program is a loop of the following form.

```
... reply;          /* declaration of structure for
                       holding event information */
int (*handler)();   /* declaration of function pointer */
keep_going = 1;
do {
     /* wait until there is an event in the queue and
        then store its structure in reply and continue */
     keep_going = handler(&reply);
} while(keep_going);
```

The call to `handler` processes the data contained in `reply`. Besides creating a window and initializing, this code is all that is needed for the main procedure of an event driven program. The simplicity of the code hides the fact that all the work is done by the `handler` function.

This code is written so that if the event handler returns a nonzero value, the program stops checking for events. (It usually exits after that.) This requirement is rather unreasonable because it affects any applications programmer who writes an event handler. A better approach is to have an infinite loop,

```
while(1) { .... }
```

and provide an exit function that event handlers may invoke to cause termination of the program. Such event handlers should be declared `void`.

2.2.2 Event Interpretation by the Starter Toolkit

In order to manage the complexity of the X Window System writers of simple application programs should not have to worry about handling the large number of events not directly related to the basic functions of the program.

The Starter Toolkit separates events into three categories. Events that are of no potential interest to graphics applications are ignored. Events requiring a response that is the same in all graphics applications are processed immediately by a fixed event handler. The remaining events are those that potentially are of direct interest to the application. The Starter Toolkit stores information about such events in a simple data structure and then calls the event handler specified by the particular application with a pointer to that structure as an argument.

An assumption in the X Window System is that a pointing device, the *pointer*, controls the location of the cursor (see Chapter 6 for details). In most systems the device is a mouse but it may also be a trackball or a stylus. A further assumption is the existence of up to six buttons associated with that device. The same assumptions exist in the Starter Toolkit, except that the number of buttons is fixed at three. The structure where the reduced information about the event is stored is called `pEvent`, and it is defined in Listing 2.1.

Listing 2.1: Event Structure of the Starter Toolkit — `File include/Starter.h (part of)`

```
typedef struct {
    int x, y;       /* location of the cursor */
    int kind;       /* what kind of event occurred */
    char key;       /* secondary information about the event */
    long origin;    /* place for storing widget information */
} pEvent;
```

The member `kind` contains a code that indicates whether a mouse button has been pressed or released, whether a key has been struck on the keyboard, and so on. Depending on the event, `key` contains the number of the button, the ASCII code of the key, and the like. Simple programs have no use for the last member, `origin`, and it is intended only for certain advanced applications of the Starter Toolkit. The events in Listing 2.2 are used in the rest of the application program.

Listing 2.2: Event Types of the Starter Toolkit — `File include/Starter.h (part of)`

```
/*   Simple events relying on the value of kind    */
#define LEFT              1 /* Left button pressed/released/dragged */
#define MIDDLE            2 /* Middle button pressed/released/dragged */
#define RIGHT             3 /* Right button pressed/released/dragged */
#define BTN_PRESS         4 /* Left button pressed */
#define BTN_RELEASE       8 /* Button (any) released */
#define MOVE             12 /* The pointing device moved */
#define DRAG             16 /* Pointing device moved with a button pressed */
#define KEY_RETURN       20 /* A return or new line  key was pressed */
#define KEY_ERASE        24 /* A back-space or delete key was pressed */
#define ESCAPE           28 /* The ``escape'' key was pressed */
#define KEY_NORMAL       32 /* A printable key was pressed on the keyboard */
#define NULL              0 /* Default (action of no interest to the program) */
/*   Composite events relying on the value of kind+key   */
#define LEFT_PRESS        5 /* Left button pressed */
#define MIDDLE_PRESS      6 /* Middle button pressed */
#define RIGHT_PRESS       7 /* Right button pressed */
#define LEFT_RELEASE      9 /* Left button released */
#define MIDDLE_RELEASE   10 /* Middle button released */
#define RIGHT_RELEASE    11 /* Right button released */
#define LEFT_DRAG        17 /* Pointing device moved with Left button pressed */
#define MIDDLE_DRAG      18 /* Pointing device moved with Middle button pressed */
#define RIGHT_DRAG       19 /* Pointing device moved with Right button pressed */
```

Note that the event types offer a certain flexibility for application programs. Those who do not care about which mouse button was pressed could use code such as

```
switch(p->kind) {
case BTN_PRESS:   /* etc */
```

Those who care about specific buttons could use

```
switch(p->kind+p->key) {
case LEFT_PRESS:   /* etc */
```

The variable `key` always takes a value between 0 and 3 unless `kind` is `KEY_NORMAL`. Then `key` contains the ASCII code of the key pressed.

2.2.3 An Event Handler of the Starter Toolkit

In Section 1.5.1 we used a function, `vis_window()`, that created a single window and then displayed graphic output produced by a routine written by the applications programmer. The Starter Toolkit has another function, `draw_window()`, which allows the application programmer to specify an event handler. This function takes more arguments than `vis_window` and is specified as

☛
```
void draw_window( void (*f)(), void (*g)(pEvent *),
                  int width, int height, char *label)
```
where `f` is a pointer to a drawing function, as in `vis_window`, `g` is a pointer to the event handler, `width` and `height` are the width and height of the window, and `label` is the label displayed on the frame of the window. ☜

Listing 2.3 shows a possible implementation of `vis_window` in terms of `draw_window`.

Listing 2.3: Visualization Window

```
#include <Starter.h>

void quit(pEvent *p)
{
    if(p->kind==BTN_PRESS) exit();
}

void vis_window( void (*f)(), int w, int h)
{
    draw_window(f, quit, w, h, "Press Any Button to Exit");
}
```

The function `quit()` is the event handler used by `draw_window()` and is very simple. When a pointer button is pressed the program exits.

Note the use of *modular programming* to divide the application program into two parts: a specific module that deals with a particular set of interactions and a generic window module that deals directly with the display (server). The two modules communicate in a restricted way. The specific application module informs the window module about the name of a function. When an event occurs, the window module calls that function without knowing anything about what the function does. The cost of insulating the two parts is two procedure calls.

2.3 PAINTING WITH PIXELS

2.3.1 Using a Pointer to Paint the Display Screen

We can illustrate event driven programming with a simple painting program that allows the user to point to pixels and give them a new color. To keep things simple in the beginning we will attempt to paint only black and white pictures. The function `fill_rectangle()` is one of the fastest operations in window systems, so we define the following macro in our program.

```
#define put_pixel(X, Y) fill_rectangle(X, Y, 1, 1)
```

The following simple *event handler* assigns the foreground color (see Section 1.4.3) to the pixel pointed to by the cursor anytime we press a button.

```
#include <Starter.h> /* The file of Listing 2.1 and 22 */
void paint_pixel(pEvent *p)
{
    if(p->kind==BTN_PRESS) put_pixel(p->x, p->y);
}
```

The main program can be as simple as

```
main()
{
    draw_window(0, paint_pixel, 400, 400, "Paint Pixels");
}
```

The first argument is 0 because there is no prepared display. The only display is what we paint with the pointer (mouse).

We can enhance this simple program in many ways. For example, we can provide means for terminating the painting by pressing another button. If we assume a three button mouse, we may use the left button to paint, the middle to erase, and the right to exit. Listing 2.4 shows the resulting program.

Listing 2.4: Simple Pixel Painting — File `paint0.c`

```
#include <Starter.h>
#define put_pixel(X, Y) fill_rectangle(X, Y, 1, 1)

void paint_pixel(pEvent *p)
{
     switch(p->kind+p->key){
          case LEFT_PRESS:   /* draw */
               put_pixel(p->x, p->y);
               return;
          case MIDDLE_PRESS: /* erase */
               clear_screen(p->x, p->y, 1, 1);
               return;
          case RIGHT_PRESS:  /* finish */
               exit();
     }
}

main()
{
     draw_window(0, paint_pixel, 400, 400, "Paint Pixels");
}
```

Why not use exclusive OR to erase? The reason is that in a program of this type the user should feel free to go over pixels without worrying about whether they already have been assigned a color. Actually we need to add a statement to make sure that the replacement mode is in effect. This addition is part of the extensions of this program discussed in the next section.

2.3.2 Changing the Size of Pixels

If we try to run the program of Listing 2.4 on a high-resolution screen, the pixels are barely visible and painting a small area takes a long time. We can solve this problem by creating a coarser grid with bigger pixels.

We achieve the effect of grid size `d` with the simple expressions

```
x = (x/d)*d;   y = (y/d)*d;
```

provided that `x` and `y` have been declared as integers. In this way the values of the coordinates are converted to multiples of `d`. Then rather than draw a filled rectangle of size 1, we draw a filled rectangle of size `d`.

The program of Listing 2.4 paints the screen only when the left mouse button is pressed, not when the mouse is moving with the button pressed. We can ease the stress on the user's hand by making drawing possible without having to release the button. We do so by checking for the DRAG events. Listing 2.5 is a modification of the program of Listing 2.3 that paints rectangles rather than pixels. Figure 2.1 shows the appearance of a window during use of this program

Listing 2.5: Painting with Magnified Pixels — File paint1.c

```
#include <Starter.h>

static int d = 16;  /* It may also used by other functions */

void paint_pixel(pEvent *p)
{
     int x, y;

     use_replace_mode();
     x = (p->x/d)*d;
     y = (p->y/d)*d;

     switch(p->kind+p->key){
          case LEFT_PRESS:   /* draw */
          case LEFT_DRAG:
               fill_rectangle(x, y, d, d);
               return;
          case MIDDLE_PRESS: /* erase */
          case MIDDLE_DRAG:
               clear_screen(x, y, d, d);
               return;
          case RIGHT_PRESS:  /* finish */
               exit();
     }
}

main()
{
     draw_window(0, paint_pixel, 400, 400, "Paint Pixels");
}
```

Figure 2.1 Sketch produced with the program of Listing 2.5.

2.3.3 Creating a Backup

The program of Listing 2.5 does not save any data, so whatever we drew is lost when we exit the program. The drawing is lost also whenever the drawing window is obscured for some reason. We can save the drawing by creating a two-dimensional array whose elements correspond to the painted rectangles on the screen. The following declaration provides such an array.

```
#define MAX_HEIGHT 32
#define MAX_WIDTH  32
static char pix[MAX_HEIGHT][MAX_WIDTH];
```

These values are used to create a window of appropriate size by passing `MAX_WIDTH*d` and `MAX_HEIGHT*d` as arguments to `draw_window()`. The complete program is shown in Listing 2.6.

Listing 2.6: Backing Up The — `File paint2.c`

```
#include <Starter.h>

#define MAX_HEIGHT 32
#define MAX_WIDTH  32
static char pix[MAX_HEIGHT][MAX_WIDTH];

static int d = 16;  /* It may also used by other functions */

void paint_pixel(pEvent *p)
{
     int x, y;
     int ix, iy;
```

```
    use_replace_mode();
    x = (ix=p->x/d)*d;      y = (iy=p->y/d)*d;
    if(ix>=MAX_WIDTH || iy>=MAX_HEIGHT) return;

    switch(p->kind+p->key){
        case LEFT_PRESS:   /* draw */
        case LEFT_DRAG:
            fill_rectangle(x, y, d, d);
            pix[iy][ix] = 1;
            return;
        case MIDDLE_PRESS: /* erase */
        case MIDDLE_DRAG:
            clear_screen(x, y, d, d);
            pix[iy][ix] = 0;
            return;
        case RIGHT_PRESS:  /* finish */
            exit();
    }
}

void redraw_pixels()
{
    register iy, ix;

    for(iy=0; iy<MAX_HEIGHT; iy++)
        for(ix=0; ix<MAX_WIDTH; ix++)
            if(pix[iy][ix]) fill_rectangle(ix*d, iy*d, d, d);
}

main()
{
    draw_window(redraw_pixels, paint_pixel,
        MAX_WIDTH*d, MAX_HEIGHT*d, "Paint Pixels");
}
```

Adding code to write the array to a prespecified file, as well as to read such an array when the program starts, is easy to do. We might also add a grid to guide the drawing by including the code in `redraw_pixels()`. Note that the redrawing routine always is called after the window has been created, so there is no need for special initialization. With the addition of such features the program of Listing 2.6 can be turned into a *pixel editor*. Such a pixel editor forms the core of the `bitmap` program, which is part of the X Window System utilities. We return to this topic in Chapter 3.

2.4 DRAWING POLYLINES

The pixel painting program of Section 2.3 draws one pixel at a time which may be limiting for some applications. If we want to draw a cartoon or, more likely, produce a technical drawing, we prefer to use line segments as the elementary building blocks. The term *polyline* describes a set of segments attached to each other, and *polygon* means a closed polyline; that is, one where the first and last point coincide, as shown in Figure 2.2.

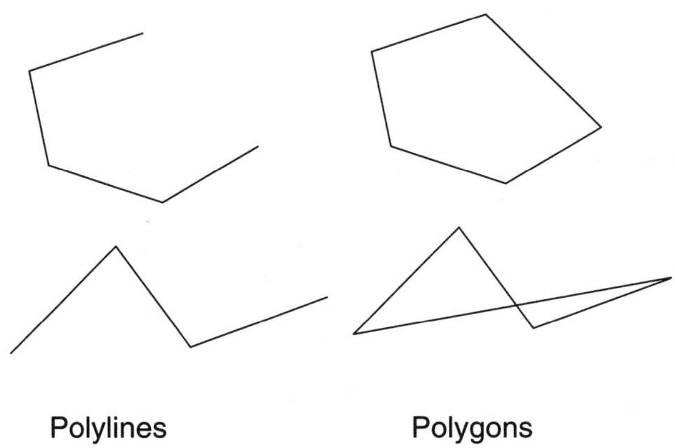

Figure 2.2 Examples of polylines and polygons.

2.4.1 An Event Handler for Drawing Polylines

Rather than draw lines explicitly, we can pick their endpoints and let the graphic primitive function draw the line between. However, this method may produce surprises because the location of a line is not always obvious from the location of its endpoints. For example, in Figure 2.3 we cannot tell whether the line joining A and C passes above or below point B without actually drawing such a line.

Figure 2.3 Does the line joining points A and C pass above or below point B?

Therefore having the program draw *tentative* lines is important. When satisfied with a particular location, the user can select it by clicking a mouse button. Listing 2.7 shows the event handler for such a program. This way of drawing is often called *rubber banding* because the tentative lines give the impression of rubber bands being stretched by the mouse. The program uses the exclusive OR mode for erasing.

Listing 2.7: Polyline Drawing (First Version) — `File polydraw1.c`

```
/*   Rubber Band Program - Version 1  */
#include <Starter.h>

void poly_draw(pEvent *p)
{
     static int initialized = 0;
     static int x0, y0, x1, y1;

     use_xor_mode();
     switch (p->kind+p->key) {
     case MOVE:                          /* rubber band */
          if(initialized){
               put_line(x0, y0, x1, y1);     /*erase*/
               x1 = p->x;         y1 = p->y;
               put_line(x0, y0, x1, y1);     /*draw*/
          }
          return;
     case LEFT_PRESS:              /* add points to polyline */
          x0 = x1 = p->x;     y0 = y1 = p->y;
          initialized = 1;
          return;
     case MIDDLE_PRESS:
     case RIGHT_PRESS:
          if(initialized) {
               put_line(x0, y0, x1, y1);     /*erase*/
               initialized = 0;
               return;
          }
          else exit();
     }
}

main()
{
     draw_window(0, poly_draw, 300, 300, "Rubber Band");
}
```

When an event occurs, `poly_draw` is called with a pointer to a `pEvent` structure as argument. If the variable `initialized` is 0, nothing happens unless the left mouse button has been pressed. In that case there is some action. The location of the cursor is stored in two pairs of coordinates: `x0, y0` and `x1, y1`, and the variable `initialized` is set to 1.

Now control returns to the main event loop (which is inside the `draw_window()` function) but the next time an event occurs, `poly_draw` will be called and, as `initialized` is nonzero, all parts of the routine are exercised. In particular:

(1) If the *mouse has moved (but no button has been pressed)*, two line segments are drawn from `x0, y0`, first to the point with coordinates equal to the old values of `x1, y1`, and then to the point with coordinates equal to the new values of `x1, y1`, which correspond to the coordinates of the cursor. These operations have the effect of creating a "rubber band" between the last point where the left button was pressed and the cursor location. Indeed the first time a motion is sensed after the left button is pressed, the first line is not drawn because `x0, y0` and `x1, y1` are the same. The second line joins the old cursor location with the new one. When this part of the code is run again, the first line drawn is the same as the second line drawn the previous time. Because we are plotting in the exclusive OR mode (XOR) that line is erased! The only visible line will be the one drawn to the new position of the cursor. The point with coordinates `x0, y0` acts as an anchor point where the rubber band is pinned.

(2) If the *left button is pressed*, the old line is not erased and the anchor point `x0, y0` is moved to the new cursor position, which will serve now as the start of the rubber band.

(3) If a *button other than the left one is pressed*, the last line is erased and the variable `initialized` is set to 0. This action terminates the drawing of that polyline, and the program is ready to start a new one. However if the middle or right button is pressed again before the left button, the program exits.

2.4.2 Using Two Event Handlers

The program of Listing 2.7 uses an explicit state variable, `initialized`, rather than change event handlers to reflect a change in state. This approach is similar to the one mentioned in Section 2.1.3. We can write a program using the approach of Section 2.1.4 by eliminating the variable `initialized` and, instead, using different event handlers. The Starter Toolkit provides a function `set_handler()` that lets application programmers specify event handlers explicitly.

☛ **`void set_handler(void (*f)(pEvent *))`**
This function takes a function pointer, `f`, as its argument. The function pointed to by `f` takes exactly one argument, a pointer to a `pEvent` structure. When an event occurs, the event handler of the window system calls the function pointed to by `f`. ☜

The program of Listing 2.8 draws polylines by using two event handlers: one to select the initial point and another after the point has been selected.

Listing 2.8: Polyline Drawing (Second Version) — `File polydraw2.c`

```
/*   Rubber Band Program - Version 2  */
#include <Starter.h>

extern void rubber_band();
extern void pick_point();

static int x0, y0, x1, y1;

void pick_point(pEvent *p)
{
     switch(p->kind+p->key) {
     case LEFT_PRESS:
          x0 = x1 = p->x;
          y0 = y1 = p->y;
          set_handler(rubber_band);
          return;
     case MIDDLE_PRESS:
     case RIGHT_PRESS:
          exit();
     }
}

void rubber_band(pEvent *p)
{
     use_xor_mode();                    /* make sure */
     switch (p->kind+p->key) {
     case MOVE:                    /* rubber band */
          put_line(x0, y0, x1, y1);    /*erase*/
          x1 = p->x;
          y1 = p->y;
          put_line(x0, y0, x1, y1);    /*draw*/
          return;
     case LEFT_PRESS:                   /* add points to polyline */
          x0 = x1 = p->x;
          y0 = y1 = p->y;
          return;
```

```
        case MIDDLE_PRESS:
        case RIGHT_PRESS:
            set_handler(pick_point);
            return;
        }
}

main()
{
        draw_window(0, pick_point, 300, 300, "Rubber Band");
}
```

The external behavior of the programs in Listings 2.7 and 2.8 is identical. Which one to use is purely an engineering decision. The first solution requires less code, whereas the second provides a general rubber band routine that may be used for operations other than polyline drawing.

This program does not save its data but can be easily modified to do so. We can create two integer arrays for storing the `x` and `y` coordinates anytime the left mouse button is pressed. This modification can be done in either the program of Listing 2.7 or that of Listing 2.8. (In Listing 2.8 it should happen in both event handlers.) When the right mouse button is pressed, special values of `x` and `y` should be added (for example, −1) to serve as flags to indicate the end of a polyline.

2.5 HANDLING OF TEXT

2.5.1 A High-Level Event Handler for Typed Input — Preliminaries

The X Window System server adds an event to the queue anytime a key is struck. Typing a string of characters generates many events, and the event handler returns after each event. The Starter Toolkit includes a high-level event handler, `collect_text()`, that changes the state of the program only when the user signifies (by hitting the RETURN or ESCAPE key) that the whole string has been typed.

This handler uses an underscore as a prompt, erases characters by backspace, and normally terminates the input with the ESCAPE key. This method allows multiline input without another invocation of the handler. The program uses static variables to store the intermediate results because the different functions are called from another module.

The different parts of the program are shown in Listing 2.9. Listing 2.9.1 shows the static variables and an initialization function that must be called before we type any text.

Listing 2.9.1: Text Initialization — `File lib/p_util.c (part of)`

```
/*   Initialization of Text Collection Module */

#define MAX_TEXT_LENGTH256

static int name_started = 0;
static char str_buffer[MAX_TEXT_LENGTH];
static char * bfp; /* first available location in buffer */
static char * nlp; /* start of last line of text */
static char *prompt = "_";
static int x0, x1, y0, y1;
static int end_with_return = 0;

void init_text(int x, int y, int k)
{
     if(name_started) return;     /* No need to initialize */
     name_started = 1;
     nlp = bfp = str_buffer;
     x1 = x0 = x;  y1 = y0 = y;
     end_with_return = k;
     put_text(prompt, x1, y1);    /* Display prompt character */
}
```

The typed characters and the pointers are saved in `str_buffer`. `bfp` and `nlp` are used to track the first available position and the first position after a new line (or the start of the buffer), respectively. The flag `name_started` is set to 1 by `init_text()` and is set to 0 when the terminating key (normally escape) is struck. It indicates to the other functions of the module that text input is expected. The variable `x0` equals the leftmost place where the text may be placed, and `y0` is the location of the top baseline.

The first two arguments of `init_text()` are used to signify the location in the window where the first typed character is displayed. The third argument is copied to the variable `end_with_return`. If it is nonzero, then only single lines of text can be entered. The function `init_text()` performs the initialization and then displays a prompt.

The function `init_text()` can be used in two ways. If the location of the typed text is defined by the application program, `init_text()` is called directly and is followed by

```
set_handler(collect_text);
```

If the location of the typed text is to be defined by the user, the applications program must provide an additional event handler to call `init_text()`

(see Section 2.5.3 for an example). Listing 2.9.2 shows another auxiliary function.

Listing 2.9.2: Specifying the Use of Typed Text — `File lib/p_util.c (part of)`

```
static void (*use)(char *);

set_string_use( void (*f)(char *) )
{
     use = f;
}
```

When the terminating key is struck, the function `use()` is called with the collected string of characters (stored in `str_buffer`) as its argument. The function `use()` is defined by the application, determines what to do with the character string, and is set with the "messenger" function `set_string_use()`.

2.5.2 A High-Level Event Handler for Typed Input — The Main Part

Note: This section may be skipped for now. Most programs relying on the Starter Toolkit are not concerned with the implementation of the `collect_text()` function.

Listing 2.9.3 shows the main function of the module. We distinguish four types of keys: normal keys (alphanumerics, space, and punctuation symbols), erasing keys (backspace or delete), return keys (return or line feed), and the escape key. If the variable `end_with_return` is nonzero, then a return key is treated like the escape key. When the string buffer is full, no matter what key has been struck, it is replaced by an escape so that collection of text terminates.

Listing 2.9.3: Event Handler for Text — `File lib/p_util.c (Part of)`

```
/*   Event handler for collecting strings of text   */

void collect_text(pEvent *p)
{
     if(!name_started) return;
     /*   Simulate termination if the buffer is full */
     if(bfp-str_buffer >= MAX_TEXT_LENGTH) p->kind = ESCAPE;

     switch(p->kind) {
     case KEY_NORMAL:
          put_text(prompt, x1, y1);    /* erase prompt */
```

```
        *bfp++ = p->key;
        *bfp = 0;
        x1 += put_text(bfp-1, x1, y1);   /* display new text */
        put_text(prompt, x1, y1);
        return;
    case KEY_ERASE:                        /* backspace */
        if(bfp <= nlp) return;        /* do not erase past a new line */
        put_text(prompt, x1, y1);     /* erase prompt */
        put_text(nlp, x0, y1);        /* erase all text in the line */
                                      /* see note in end of section */
        bfp--;
        *bfp = 0;
        x1 = x0 + put_text(nlp, x0, y1); /* redisplay text */
        put_text(prompt, x1, y1);
        return;
    case KEY_RETURN:                                /* new line */
        if(!end_with_return) {
            put_text(prompt, x1, y1);   /* erase prompt */
            *bfp++ = '\n';
            nlp = bfp;                  /* mark new line position */
            x1 = x0;
            y1 += get_font_height()+3;
            put_text(prompt, x1, y1);
            return;
        }
    case ESCAPE:                               /* text entry completed  */
        put_text(prompt, x1, y1);    /* erase prompt */
        *bfp = 0;
        name_started = 0;
        bfp = str_buffer;
        if(use) use(str_buffer);
        return;
    default:
        return;
    }
```

The code of Listing 2.9.3 uses four static variables declared in Listing 2.9.1. `x0` and `y0` are the coordinates of the top left corner of the text block, and `x1` and `y1` are the coordinates of the beginning of the current line of text. In this implementation `x1` always equals `x0`; however, the handler could be modified to accept other arrangements. The function `get_font_height()` returns the maximum possible height of the typed text, as discussed in Section 1.4.4. The new value of `y1` is incremented by 3 to make sure there is a gap of at least 3 pixels between lines of text.

Note that when a user erases the last character, the entire line of text is erased and redisplayed without the last character. The reason is that the width of the last character is unknown.

2.5.3 Using Typed Text

Listing 2.10 shows an example of an intermediate event handler for typed text. It is useful when a user wants to type text strings in various parts of the screen as defined by the position of the cursor.

When the left mouse button is pressed, the text collection is initialized by calling `init_text()`. The typed string is displayed, starting at the location of the cursor. The third argument is 0 indicating that only the ESCAPE key will terminate a string entry. If the third argument is nonzero, hitting the RETURN key also terminates entry. If the text collection has been initialized already, `init_text()` returns immediately.

Listing 2.10: High-Level Event Handler for Text — `File lib/p_util.c (Part of)`

```
void get_string(pEvent *p)
{
     switch(p->kind+p->key) {
     case LEFT_PRESS:
          init_text(p->x, p->y, 0)
          return;
     case MIDDLE_PRESS: case RIGHT_PRESS:
          exit();
     default:
          collect_text(p);
     }
}
```

Any event other than pressing mouse buttons is passed to the `collect_text()` function, which returns immediately if there has been no initialization. Thus different events may be ignored, depending on the state of the program as shown in Table 2.1. The following one-line main program can be used to let the user type text at any screen location and confirm the types of response described in the table.

```
draw_window(0, get_string, 400, 400, "Text Entry");
```

Listing 2.11 shows a text entry program that is a little more interesting because it specifies a text usage function.

Table 2.1: Response to a Sequence of Events of the Programs of Listings 2.9 and 2.10

	Event	Response
1	Left mouse button is pressed at x, y	Text collection initialized
2	Key **A** is struck	**A** is displayed at x, y
3	Key **b** is struck	**b** is displayed to the right of **A**
4	Left mouse button is pressed	Ignored. Text is still being collected
5	Key **l** is struck	**l** is displayed to the right of **b**
6	Key **e** is struck	**e** is displayed to the right of **l**
7	**Esc** is stuck	Text collection terminates
8	Key **i** is struck	Ignored. Text collection must be initialized again through the mouse.

Listing 2.11: Text Entry — `File count.c`

```
/*   Count characters of typed text    */
#include <Starter.h>

extern void get_string(pEvent *);

static int kount = 0;

void count(char *s)
{
     kount += strlen(s);
     printf("%d chars typed so far\n", kount);
}

void g(pEvent *p)  /* initial event handler */
{
     if(p->kind+p->key == LEFT_PRESS) {
          set_string_use(count);
          set_handler(get_string);
          get_string(p);
     }
}
```

```
main()
{
    draw_window(0, g, 400, 400, "Text Entry");
}
```

This program counts the total number of characters typed and displays the result every time a string is typed. To place the display of the result under user control you must modify the `get_string()` function (see Assignment 8).

In this section we illustrated another important concept of the X Window System: that of using "cascaded" event handlers. The first event handler called by the system is `get-string()`. If the event is anything other than pressing a mouse button, a second event handler, `collect_text()`, is called.

2.6 PAINTING WITH COLOR

2.6.1 Subdividing a Window

Painting with colors is more interesting than painting in black and white, and we next modify the program of Listing 2.6 to use a palette of colors. For this reason we divide the window into two subwindows: a *palette* subwindow to display the available colors and a *canvas* subwindow where we actually do the drawing.

Note: *In Chapter 7 we show how to use facilities of the X Window System to deal with multiple windows. The material of Section 2.6 illustrates some of the internals of a window system by letting application programmers manage explicitly a subwindow.*

The program of Listing 2.12 is similar to the program of Listing 2.6 but has an important addition in the event handler. The first action of the event handler is to determine in which of the two subwindows the event has occurred. This decision is made by the procedure `region()` which returns 1 if the event occurred in the palette, 2 if it occurred in the canvas, and 0 if it occurred in the boundary between the two. The event is ignored in the latter case. (The operating system guarantees that the event occurred somewhere in the window of this program. Otherwise the event handler would not have been called.)

Listing 2.12.1: Coloring Pixels (Part 1) — `File paint3.c`

```
/*   Painting with Color - Part 1      */
#include <Starter.h>

#define MAX_HEIGHT 32
#define MAX_WIDTH  32
static char pix[MAX_HEIGHT][MAX_WIDTH];

#define MARGIN 2

static int ypalet, xpalet;
static int w_width, w_height;

int region(int x, int y)
{
     if( y < ypalet-MARGIN) return(1);
     else if( y > ypalet+MARGIN) return(2);
          else return(0);
}

static int d = 16;

void paint_pixel(pEvent *p)
{
     int x, y;
     int ix, iy;
     static int color;

     use_replace_mode();
     x = (ix=p->x/d)*d; y = (iy=p->y/d)*d;
     if(ix>=MAX_WIDTH || iy>=MAX_HEIGHT) return;

     switch( region(x,y) ) {
     case 1:   /* palette subwindow */
          if(p->kind == BTN_PRESS) color = get_palet(x, y);
          return;

     case 2:   /* canvas subwindow */
          switch(p->kind+p->key) {
          case LEFT_PRESS:   /* draw */
          case LEFT_DRAG:
               fill_rectangle(x, y, d, d);
               pix[iy][ix] = color;
               return;
          case MIDDLE_PRESS: /* erase */
          case MIDDLE_DRAG:
```

```
                clear_screen(x, y, d, d);
                pix[iy][ix] = 0;
                return;
            case RIGHT_PRESS:  /* finish */
                exit();
            }
            return;
    }
}
```

The function `get_palet()` returns the color value that is to be assigned to elements of the `pix[][]` matrix. The function itself sets the appropriate foreground color, as described in Section 2.6.3. The variable `color` is declared static because it is assigned a value in one call of the procedure `paint_pixel()` and then is used in a *different* call. This procedure is an example of the type of considerations that are important in event driven programming. *The event queue controls the flow of execution rather than the programmer!*

The procedure `region()` is called with two arguments, even though only one of them is used. In this way the `paint_pixel()` procedure does not depend on subwindow geometry. Having procedures that are as independent as possible makes a program easier to modify in the future.

2.6.2 Making a Palette of Colors

We are left with the task of creating the palette subwindow and implementing the function `get_palet()`, which returns the chosen color, and the function `init_palet()`, which creates the color display. The function `init_palet()` creates a set of squares near the top of the screen, each with a different color. When one of the squares is pointed to, its color is used to paint the lower part of the screen.

For this type of program storing the values corresponding to each color and then using the `set_foregr()` function is better than incurring the higher overhead of the functions `fore_color()`. The latter relies on a function that searches a color database in the X Window System and returns a value to be used for foreground. Here is the description of the function that converts color names to color values.

☛ **`int add_named_color(char *cname)`**
Find the named color in the database of the X Window System and check whether its red, green, and blue values are in the color map used by the application. If not, make a new entry in the colormap as long as there is space. In either case return the index, `k`, of the colormap entry. This value should be assigned to pixels that must have the specified color. For

example,

```
purple_value = add_named_color("purple");
     ....
pix[y][x]    = purple_value;
```

If the name is not found in the database, or if it is found but there is no space for the new color, the function returns – 1. ☜

Listing 2.12.2 contains the initialization routine.

Listing 2.12.2: Coloring Pixels (Part 2) — `File paint3.c`

```
#define MAX_NCOLORS     32
#define Margin           1

static int colors[MAX_NCOLORS];
static char *color_names[] = { "black", "purple", "blue", "skyblue",
     "green", "yellow", "orange", "red", "brown", "white", 0};
static int Ncolors;
static int xx;

int init_palet()
{
     register i;

     /* find color values */
     for(i=0; color_names[i]; i++)
          colors[i] = add_named_color(color_names[i]);
     Ncolors = i;

     ypalet = xpalet = 32;
     for(i=0, xx=0; i<Ncolors-1; i++, xx+=xpalet) {
          set_foregr(colors[i]);
          fill_rectangle(xx + Margin, Margin,
                    xpalet-MARGIN, xpalet-MARGIN);
     }
     /* now i equals Ncolors-1, i.e. white */
     set_foregr(colors[0]); /* draw outlines with black */
     put_rectangle(xx + Margin, Margin, xpalet-MARGIN, xpalet-MARGIN);

     put_line(w_width-xpalet*2, Margin, w_width-xpalet*2, ypalet-Margin);
     put_text("Exit", w_width-xpalet*2+8, ypalet -8);
     put_line(0, ypalet+MARGIN, w_width, ypalet+MARGIN);
     xx += xpalet+MARGIN;
     return(ypalet+MARGIN);
}
```

This program creates eight colored squares and, in addition, delineates a square at the right end of the subwindow to be used for exiting the program. The background is white, so the white square is outlined rather than filled. A horizontal line is drawn at the subwindow boundary. Listing 2.12.3 shows the calling program.

Listing 2.12.3: Coloring Pixels (Part 3) — `File paint3.c`

```
void redraw_pixels()
{
     register iy, ix;

     for(iy=0; iy<MAX_HEIGHT; iy++)
          for(ix=0; ix<MAX_WIDTH; ix++)
               if(pix[iy][ix]) {
                    set_foregr(pix[iy][ix]);
                    fill_rectangle(ix*d, iy*d, d, d);
               }
}

redraw()
{
     init_palet();
     redraw_pixels();
}

main()
{
     w_width  = MAX_WIDTH*d;
     w_height = MAX_HEIGHT*d;
     draw_window(redraw, paint_pixel, w_width, w_height, "Paint Pixels");
}
```

Note that the palette initialization is called only when the window is redrawn. This call always happens when the program starts, so there is no need to add an explicit call to `init_palet()`. The small constants in Listing 2.12.2 have been determined empirically to yield a "good-looking" display.

2.6.3 Using the Palette of Colors

The routine `get_palet()` in Listing 2.12.4 checks on whether the event has occurred over the rightmost part of the palette and then exits. Otherwise it returns an index to the chosen color. An index to white is returned even if the pointer is past the white square.

Listing 2.12.4: Coloring Pixels (Part 4) — `File paint3.c`

```
int get_palet(int x, int y)
{
     int pick;

     if(x > w_width-xpalet*2) exit();
     pick = x/xpalet;
     pick = pick > Ncolors-1 ? Ncolors-1: pick;
     set_foregr(colors[pick]);
     return(colors[pick]);
}
```

The design of the palette subwindow should make the program as easy to use as possible. The only user instruction needed is: "Point to a color and use it to paint below." The program can be used without a manual. Plate 1 (in the color insert) shows the appearance of the screen of the painting program in the midst of creating a picture. As we can exit the program by pointing to an area in the palette and can erase by using white color, we can simplify the `paint_pixel()` function of Listing 2.12.1 as shown in Listing 2.13.

Listing 2.13: Coloring Pixels (Modification of Part 1)

```
     /* .... as in Listing 2.12.1     */
     case 2:   /* canvas sub-window */
          switch(p->kind) {
          case BTN_PRESS:
          case DRAG:
               fill_rectangle(x, y, d, d);
               pix[iy][ix] = color==WHITE? 0: color;
          }
          return;
     /* .... as in Listing 2.12.1     */
```

The last set of changes eliminated the need for three mouse buttons so that the program can work with a one-button mouse or a stylus.

2.7 CONCLUSIONS

In this chapter we explained the basic structure of user driven programs. User actions, such as pressing a mouse button or key on the keyboard, are translated by the system into events in a queue that is checked periodically by the program. The Starter Toolkit provides a simple function that creates a window and then enters into a loop waiting for events. Application programmers need supply only the names of the functions that do the event handling and the redrawing of the screen.

We described in detail four programs (simple pixel painting, drawing polylines, input of text, and pixel painting with color) that perform event driven computing. We describe additional programs of this type in the rest of the text, starting with a video game in Chapter 3. Event driven programs also can be used for a purpose that has nothing to do with visualizing data or creating art work: to let a user communicate with a computer in an intuitive way. For example, pointing the mouse to a labeled area of the screen, instead of typing the program name, can cause the execution of a program. Such a style of *graphical computing* has been popularized by Apple Computers products and more recently by various PC window systems. Graphical computing is the topic of Chapter 7.

2.8 ASSIGNMENTS

Note: Assignments 1-8 can be done on a monochrome display.

1. Implement one of the pixel painting programs given in this chapter and modify it to accept input from the keyboard so that different pixels can be labeled with letters. One way to do so is to save in a special place the coordinates of the last point where the left mouse button was pressed and, when a key from the keyboard is struck, the corresponding letter is drawn on that spot. This method requires adding a case for `KEY_NORMAL` in the event handler.
2. A more ambitious version of Assignment 1 is to keep track of all painted pixels and use them to store text typed on the keyboard later. Allow for corrections.
3. Implement one of the polyline drawing programs given in this chapter (for example that of Listing 2.7) and modify it so that it prints out the coordinates of the points it has collected anytime you finish drawing a polyline.
4. Implement one of the polyline drawing programs given in this chapter and modify it by assigning a role to the middle mouse button. Doing so could change the thickness or the style of the lines used. (You could switch between thick and thin lines or between solid and dashed.)
5. Use the keyboard to provide information about the thickness or line style used. To do so you could add a case for `KEY_NORMAL` in the `pick_point` handler of Listing 2.8. For example, typing "d" would cause the next polyline to be drawn as dashed.

6. The polyline drawing programs listed in this chapter draw lines while the left mouse button is not pressed. When you move the mouse with the left button pressed, nothing is drawn. Modify one of these program so that this behavior is reversed: The program should draw lines while the left button is pressed, but when you move the mouse without pressing the left button nothing should be drawn.

   Note: This method requires a major modification of the program. If you understand the program thoroughly before attempting to modify it, the task is simple; otherwise it may take forever. Basically you need to replace the cases for `MOVE`, `LEFT_PRESS`, and `RIGHT_PRESS`, by cases for `BTN_RELEASE`, `LEFT_DRAG`, and `LEFT_PRESS` in some new order. Having a truly symmetrical behavior is important. In particular, the new program should draw polylines with more than two points.

7. Write a program for picking two points with the mouse and then drawing an arrow connecting the two points. Try to reuse as much as possible of the code of Assignment 3, Chapter 1.

8. Modify the `get_string()` function of Listing 2.10 to provide the number of characters typed so far when the middle mouse button is pressed.

Note: Assignments 9-14 require a color display.

9. Write a program for entering text in various parts of the screen and provide a `use` function that interprets the typed text as color. The function should draw a solid rectangle of that color covering all the typed text. You should provide for interpreting both words (e.g., "purple") and numbers as colors. Provide a command line flag that determines whether the typed text remains visible.

   Hint: Rename and modify the function `get_string()` described in Section 2.5.3.

10. Implement the color painting program of Listing 2.12.

11. Modify the pixel painting program of Section 2.6 to read the colors to be used from a file. This approach lets the user rather than the applications programmer select the colors of the palette.

12. The program of Listing 2.12 stores in the array `pix[][]` the bit patterns corresponding to a particular color. Such bit patterns may differ from system to system or even from time to time in the same system. Assigning values that correspond to the color name itself is better. Devise a way to do so and modify the program of Listing 2.12 accordingly.

13. The X utility `showrgb` displays the color name database. Its output consists of three numbers (the red, green, and blue values) and the

name of the color. The following Unix shell script strips the RGB values, packs spaces, and eliminates duplicate entries

```
showrgb  | awk '{print substr($0,14) }' |
sed "s/ //g" | sort -u
```

(The code assumes that the color names start after the fourteenth location.) Write a program to display some of the names next to a solid rectangle with the corresponding color. Plate 2 shows what the output of your program should look like.

Hints: Your program should read its standard input and store the color names in a two-dimensional `char` array. (You may assume that no color name is longer than 32 bytes.) A good way to select colors is to use the Unix `grep` or `egrep` commands before your program. If you name your program, say, `show_color`, then the following pipe will produce an output similar to Plate 1a

```
showrgb  | awk '{print substr($0,14) }' |
sed "s/ //g" | sort -u | grep red | show_color
```

14. Modify the program of Assignment 13 so that when you click a mouse button on a color, the color name is printed in the standard output and the color name is shown in reverse video. If you also have completed Assignment 11, you can put the pixel painting program at the end of a pipe following the program of the current assignment. With such a program the user could construct the palette by pointing to colors.

3

Icons and Games

Scope of the Chapter

Creating and using icons • Cursor icons and icon masks • Animation and video games built with icons • Introduction to object-oriented programming.

3.1 INTRODUCTION

3.1.1 Some Definitions

You probably are familiar with *icons*, the small pictures used in computers to convey information concisely. We showed some examples of icons in Figure 1.1. The word *icon* comes from the Greek *eikona*, which means picture. Eventually the word came to refer to a religious picture, especially one of Byzantine origin. An *eikonomachos* was a person who opposed the use of religious icons and an *eikonolatris* was one who worshiped them. (The issue of icon worship was a cause of civil wars in the ninth century Byzantine Empire.)

The word was first used in English with the religious connotation but, according to *Webster's New World Dictionary*, its first meaning now is "a stylized figure, as displayed on a microcomputer screen, representing available functions or resources." People now probably spend far more time staring at icons on a computer screen than the most devout Byzantine icon worshipers ever spent in front of their sacred images.

An icon is used to convey information about the contents of a file, the location of the cursor, the nature of a menu entry or a panel button, the status of a program, and the like. For example, in Figure 1.1 a picture of an envelope in a tray marks the window of a mailtool, and the image of a page of text identifies a file that contains plain text. Figure 3.1 shows close-ups of some icons.

Figure 3.1
Examples of icons: a cup, a sailboat, a telescope, and an arrow.

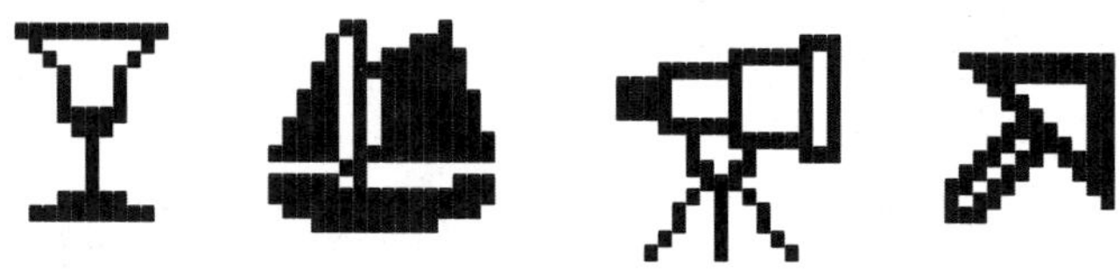

A computer icon is nothing more than an array of pixels with a few distinct colors, in other words a flat picture (see Section 1.1.2). In practice the term is limited to small pictures (rarely larger than 64 pixels square) with only two colors.

Definition An *icon* is a small flat picture, usually with only two colors, stored in a form that it is convenient to use in computer programs. *Texture* is an icon that is used repeatedly to fill a given area. A *cursor* is an icon that marks the position of the pointer on the screen.

In this chapter we describe how to create icons, discuss the form that is used to store icons, and demonstrate how to incorporate such data into programs. Then we show how to write video game programs using icons.

3.1.2 Icon Editors

We can use the pixel painting program of Section 2.3 to create icons. (Figure 2.1 certainly qualifies as an icon if drawn at the proper scale.) Because icons are used in so many other programs, the format of the file where icons are stored is strictly specified. Therefore the main task for converting a pixel painting program into an icon editor is to use the proper format for storing the results. Building our own is possible, but finding an existing program is better.

Warning *Converting a prototype program into a commercially viable program may require as much effort as converting the blue-print of a car into a real car.*

Lack of understanding of this point has led to the belief that software development is highly unpredictable and costly. In the case of hardware, the difference between the blue-print and the metal final product is easy to see. More difficult is to discern that difference in software because both versions consist of lines of code.

Most installations have an icon editor. You should use that facility to create icons for other programs, rather than try to expand the pixel editor of Chapter 2. A program called `bitmap`, which is part of the X Window System utilities, provides some rudimentary facilities for icon creation. Try the command

```
man bitmap
```

to read its documentation. Other, better programs also are available and your installation may have one of them.

3.2 USING ICONS

3.2.1 File Format

Icon files are represented by printable characters so that the data can be included easily in a C program. In particular, pixel values are expressed by *hexadecimal numbers*, for example `0x700E`. Each hexadecimal digit has four bits, so its value represents a particular bit arrangement. Thus `0x700E` represents the bit array

```
0111 0000 0000 1110
```

and `0xD3CB` represents

```
1101 0011 1100 1011
```

Such values can be stored in an array of `short` (two byte) integers. For example, the expression

```
static short my_icon[] = {
    0x0000,0x3FF8,0x1010,0x0820,0x0440,0x0440,0x0440,0x07C0,
    0x0380,0x0100,0x0100,0x0100,0x0100,0x07C0,0x1FF0,0x0000
};
```

corresponds to the first icon (cup) shown in Figure 3.1.

This 16 bit arrangement was used in early versions of the X Window

System, as well as in icon editors of other window systems. However the current X standard requires 8 bit patterns that can be stored in a byte (`char`) array. The program `bitmap` always requires an argument, which is used to produce a file that can be included in a C program. For example, if we invoke

```
bitmap cute.icon,
```

draw an icon, and save it, the file `cute.icon` will contain data of the form.

```
#define cute_width 16
#define cute_height 16
static char cute_bits[] = {
   0x00, 0x00, 0xfc, 0x0f, 0xf8, 0x0f, 0x38, 0x08,
   0x38, 0x08, 0x38, 0x00, 0x38, 0x01, 0xf8, 0x01,
   0xf8, 0x01, 0x38, 0x01, 0x38, 0x00, 0x38, 0x08,
   0x38, 0x08, 0xf8, 0x0f, 0xfc, 0x0f, 0x00, 0x00};
```

Then the image can be included in a C program with the statement

```
#include <cute.icon>
```

Converting this format into a pixel array and vice versa is a straightforward process but requires some careful writing of code. The X Window System has functions that create icons directly from such descriptions, and we present the respective functions of the Starter Toolkit in Section 3.2.3. However, in certain cases we may want to modify an icon and, if so, we must extract the pixel array from the character vector. We show next how this can done.

3.2.2 An Example of Icon Processing — Cursor Masks

Listing 3.1 provides a function that creates a pixel array (bit matrix) from a byte (`char`) vector. With slight modifications this function might be useful for creating new icons from old ones.

Listing 3.1: Icon to Bit Matrix — `File lib/p_util.c (part of)`

```
/*  Construct a bit matrix from an icon  */
#define MAX_WIDTH   64
#define MAX_HEIGHT  64
static char pix[MAX_HEIGHT][MAX_WIDTH];
static int hmask[] = { 01, 02, 04, 010, 020, 040, 0100, 0200 };

void make_bit_matrix(unsigned char bits[], int n, int width)
{
    int y = 0, x = 0, xv, k, j;
```

```
	for(j=0; j<n; j++) {
		xv = bits[j];
		/*  See below for explanation of the & operator   */
		for(k=7; k>=0; k--, x++) pix[y][x] = hmask[k]& xv ? 1: 0;
		if(x >= width) { x = 0;y++; }
	}
}
```

The array `hmask[]` is used to extract the bit values from the byte representation. The inverse function, creating a `char` vector from a pixel array (bit matrix), is shown in Listing 3.2.

Listing 3.2: Matrix to Icon — `File lib/p_util.c (part of)`

```
void make_char_vector(unsigned char bits[], int width, int height)
{
	int y = 0, x = 0, xv, k, j = 0;
	do{
		xv = 0;
		/*  See below for explanation of the | operator   */
		for(k=7; k>=0; k--, x++) if(pix[y][x]) xv |= hmask[k];
		bits[j++] = xv;
		if(x >= width) { x = 0;y++; }
	} while(y <h eight);
}
```

C language aside Programs that deal with icons often using the bit operators | (OR) and & (AND) of C, as well as octal notation for numerical values because it is easier to see the connection with bit patterns that way. For example, octal `020` is the bit pattern `00 010 000`. Thus in Listing 3.1 the elements of `hmask[k]` all start with 0 and therefore are interpreted as *octal* values. In the same listing the expression

`hmask[k] & xv`

is the bitwise AND operation on `hmask[k]` and `xv`. Only one bit of `hmask[k]` is nonzero, so the result will be nonzero only if the respective bit of `xv` also is nonzero. In Listing 3.2

`xv |= hmask[k]`

performs a bitwise OR operation between the value `xv` and `hmask[k]` and stores the result back to `xv`.

These functions come in handy for creating cursor masks. When the cursor is displayed over an area with the same color as its own, it becomes invisible. To avoid this problem you may create a cursor mask that has a slightly bigger area and is shown in a different color. Then you can always see at least part of the cursor. Although better results are obtained when both the cursor and its mask are designed individually, automatically generated cursor masks can be adequate for prototype programs. Listing 3.3 shows a function that does this task.

Listing 3.3: Cursor Mask Generation — `File lib/p_util.c (part of)`

```
make_cursor_mask(unsigned char cursor_image[],
     unsigned char mask_image[], int height, int width)
{
     register y, x;

     make_bit_matrix(cursor_image, (height*width)/8, width);

     for(y=0; y<height; y++) {
          for(x=0; x<width; x++){
               if(pix[y][x]) continue;
               if(x>0)
               if(pix[y][x-1]==1) { pix[y][x] = 2; continue; }
               if(x<width-1)
               if(pix[y][x+1]==1) { pix[y][x] = 2; continue; }
               if(y>0)
               if(pix[y-1][x]==1) { pix[y][x] = 2; continue; }
               if(y<height-1)
               if(pix[y+1][x]==1) { pix[y][x] = 2; continue; }
          }
     }

     make_char_vector(mask_image, width, height);
}
```

This function marks (with the value 2) all white pixels that have a black pixel above them or below them or to their right or to their left. During the double loop, pixels with value 2 are still interpreted as white. However the code of `make_char_vector()` interprets such pixels as black so that the bigger mask is created. Figure 3.2 illustrates construction of the mask.

Figure 3.2 Creation of an icon mask: Original bit matrix (left) and matrix after execution of the double loop in `make_cursor_mask()` (right).

```
0000000000000000    0000000220000000
0000000110000000    0000002112000000
0000001111000000    0000021111200000
0000011111100000    0000211111120000
0000111111110000    0002111111112000
0001111111111000    0021111111111200
0011111111111100    0211111111111120
0000001111000000    0022221111222200
0000001111000000    0000021111200000
0000001111000000    0000021111200000
0000001111000000    0000021111200000
0000001111000000    0000021111200000
0000001111000000    0000021111200000
0000001111000000    0000021111200000
0000001111000000    0000021111200000
0000000000000000    0000002222000000
```

3.2.3 Making Icons Useful

The compact description of the icon format is not suitable for display. A bitmap that can be copied into the refresh memory must be created. The Starter Toolkit provides facilities for creating icon bitmaps directly from the hexadecimal character vectors. A pointer to the bitmap and the dimensions of the icon are placed in a structure that can be used to display the icon at various locations of the screen. The structure contains two more members: numbers representing the offset of the icon's center with respect to the coordinates of the display point. The following function does this work.

☛ **`int make_icon(unsigned char iconbits[], int width, int height, int cx, int cy)`**

The array `iconbits` contains the pixel description, `width` and `height` are the width and height of the icon respectively, `cx` and `cy` are the coordinates of the center with respect to the upper left corner. The center is used to display the icon in a particular location. The function returns an integer that is used to reference the icon from the applications program. The function returns a negative value when not enough memory is left to create the structure. ☜

Another function of the Starter Toolkit displays the icon by using the value returned from `make_icon()`.

☛ **void draw_icon(int k, int x, int y)**
Display the icon pointed at by `k` at location `x, y`. ☜

Thus to create an icon bitmap from the data contained in the file `cute.icon` created by the `bitmap` program we need the following code fragment

```
#include <cute.icon>
    /* ... */
int cute;
    /* ... */
cute = make_icon(cute_bits, cute_width, cute_height, 0, 0);
```

We can display it later with

```
    draw_icon(cute, x, y);
```

The structure used for icons is *private* to the Starter Toolkit and programmers cannot access its members except through the two functions just described. The structures are stored in an array, and their index in that array is the only way that programmers can refer to them.

Icons that are used for cursors must be 16 by 16 pixels and are created by the following Starter Toolkit procedures.

☛ **int make_cursor(unsigned char iconbits[], int hx, int hy)**
Create a 16 by 16 cursor icon using the array `iconbits`. Here, `hx` and `hy` are the coordinates of the "hot spot" of the cursor, the point whose coordinates are returned by the event handler. The upper left corner of the icon is 0, 0. The function returns an integer that is used to reference the cursor from the applications program. The function returns a negative value when not enough memory is left to create the structure. There is no need to supply a mask; it is created automatically by the method of Section 3.2.2. The cursor is black and the mask is white. ☜

The same structure is used to store all icons whether they are used by a cursor or not. The cursor is not displayed until it is activated by the following Starter Toolkit procedure.

☛ **void active_cursor(int n)**
Make the visible cursor be the one whose index in the icon array is `n`, which is the number returned by a previous call to `make_cursor()`. The program will fail if the argument used is nonnegative but not one returned by such a call. If `n` is negative the default cursor is restored. ☜

Important Point: *Icons are always drawn in the foreground color, but cursors are not. Their color must be specified when they are created.*

Because of this restriction the Starter Toolkit provides a second function for creating cursors with specified colors.

☛ **`int make_color_cursor(unsigned char iconbits[], int hx, int hy, char *color, char *mask_color)`**

Same as `make_cursor()` except that the cursor has `color` color and the mask has `mask_color` color. As a matter of fact `make_cursor()` calls `make_color_cursor(iconbits, hx, hy, "black", "white");` ☜

At this point we must introduce some additional functions of the Starter Toolkit because `vis_window()` and `draw_window()` are not sufficiently flexible. Normally, `draw_icon()` can be called from inside the redraw function (the first argument of `vis_window()` and `draw_window()`) but how about `make_icon()`? It cannot be called before `draw_window()` because of the need to access certain structures of the X Window System that are initialized by `draw_window()`. We could call it from inside the redraw function the first time it is invoked but that is rather awkward.

3.3 SOME NEW FUNCTIONS OF THE STARTER TOOLKIT

3.3.1 Definitions of the New Functions

In order to write programs that are more complicated than the examples of Chapters 1 and 2 we need to access the components of `draw_window()`. Listing 3.4 shows an implementation of `draw_window()` through five other functions of the Starter Toolkit. (The actual implementation is different for the sake of efficiency.)

Listing 3.4: An Implementation of draw_window()

```
void draw_window( void (*f)(), void (*g)(pEvent *), int width,
     int height, char *label)
{
     begin_display(width, height, label);
     complete_display();
     set_redraw(f);
     set_handler(g);
     wait_for_event();
}
```

We have already described and used one of them, `set_handler()`, in Section 2.4.2. The definitions of the other functions are as follows.

☛ **`void begin_display(int w_width, int w_height, char *window_label)`**
Start the program by connecting to the display (server) (see Section 1.3.2) and initialize internal data structures to allow the creation of a drawing window with width equal to `w_width` and height equal to `w_height`. The string `window_label` is used as a label in the frame of the window. This function should be called *before* any other function of the Starter Toolkit. The only exceptions are `vis_window()` and `draw_window()` that contain, in effect, the code of `begin_display()`. ☜

☛ **`void complete_display()`**
Creates and displays a drawing window, as well as any other windows that have been requested. (We present examples of programs with many windows in Chapter 7.) ☜

☛ **`void wait_for_event()`**
Goes into an infinite loop, but at each iteration checks whether an event has occurred (for example, the mouse moved) and calls the appropriate event handler. ☜

☛ **`void set_redraw( void (*f)() )`**
Here, `f` is the name of a function that takes no arguments and should be called whenever there is a need to redraw a window. ☜

3.3.2 Changing the Cursor Icon

We illustrate the use of the Starter Toolkit functions introduced so far by writing a simple program that allows user actions to change the cursor icon. To use the program of Listing 3.5 we first need to draw two 16 by 16 icons by using `bitmap` (or an equivalent program). Let `mouse.icon` and `cat.icon` be the names of the files where the icons have been stored. These files are included in the program of Listing 3.5, and usable icons are created by the calls to `make_icon()`, whereas usable cursor icons are created by the calls to `make_cursor()`.

Listing 3.5: Varying the Cursor Icon — `File icon_demo.c`

```
/*   Creating Icons and Cursors   */
#include <Starter.h>
#include <mouse.icon>
#include <cat.icon>

static int icursor[2], image[2], j=0;

void ff()
```

```
{
     draw_icon(image[j], 80, 20);
}

void gg(pEvent *p)
{
     if(p->kind==BTN_PRESS) {
          draw_icon(image[j], 80, 20);     /* erase */
          j = 1 - j;
          draw_icon(image[j], 80, 20);
          active_cursor(icursor[j]);
     }
}

main()
{
     begin_display(200, 200, "Icon Test");
     complete_display();
     icursor[0] = make_cursor(cat_bits, 0, 0);
     icursor[1] = make_cursor(mouse_bits, 0, 0);
     image[0]   = make_icon(mouse_bits, mouse_width, mouse_height, 0, 0);
     image[1]   = make_icon(cat_bits, cat_width, cat_height, 0, 0);
     set_redraw(ff);
     set_handler(gg);
     active_cursor(icursor[j]);
     wait_for_event();
}
```

The program stores the fixed icon identifiers in the array `image[]` and the cursor icon identifiers into the array `icursor[]`. The variable `j` is used to index both arrays, and, whenever a button is pressed, its value switches from 0 to 1 and vice versa. The old icon is erased and the new one is drawn. There is no need for explicit redrawing of the cursor icon. The call to `active_cursor()` takes care of that.

Question to the Reader: What is the effect of reversing the indices of the icons in arrays `icursor[]` and `image[]` in the `main()` function?

3.4 USING ICONS FOR GAMES

Programs for commercial video games are very elaborate and take full advantage of the features of the computing and display hardware and produce impressive displays (see color insert). Quite often special purpose hardware is used. A game developed on a generic platform by a beginning programmer is not likely to be a match for commercial products. But interesting games can be produced with relatively simple programs, and we show you how to do so in this and the next section.

3.4.1 Creation of Game Objects

We use the term "graphin" to refer to an object that is represented by a drawn icon and also has other attributes that make it a component for a game. Such an object is given by the structure of Listing 3.6. (If you are unfamiliar with object-oriented programming, you should read the brief overview in Appendix A.)

Listing 3.6: Graphin Structure — `File graphin.h`

```
#ifndef GRAPHIN
typedef struct _graphin {
     int icon;                                /* what it looks like */
     int color;                               /* for the icon */
     int x, y;                                /* its location */
     int dx, dy;                              /* its motion */
     int status;                              /* for future expansion */
     int nature;                              /* for future expansion */
     void (*draw_me)(struct _graphin *);      /* function to draw a graphin */
     void (*move_me)(struct _graphin *);      /* function to move a graphin */
} graphin;
#define GRAPHIN
#endif
```

The integer `icon` is returned by a call to the `make_icon()` function discussed in Section 3.2.3. The integer `color` is useful for storing information about the icon color and can be used as the argument of the `set_foregr()` function. The structure members `dx` and `dy` determine the direction of the motion by their ratio `dy/dx` and the speed of the motion by the module `sqrt(dx*dx + dy*dy)`

The functions `draw_me()` and `move_me()` take as an argument a pointer to a graphin structure, and they draw and move the graphin. In its simplest form `draw_me()` calls the function `draw_icon()` discussed in Section 3.2.3. In the terminology of object-oriented programming, they are the *methods* of the graphin object.

The C preprocessor statements (with the # as first characters) are used to allow multiple inclusions of the `graphin.h` file in C programs. If `GRAPHIN` is already defined, the contents of the file are ignored.

Listing 3.7.1 shows the creation of a graphin with a predrawn icon file, `gremlin.icon`. The initial location is arbitrary.

Listing 3.7.1: Example of Programming with Graphins (Part 1) — `File graphin0.c`

```
#include <graphin.h>

void simple_draw(graphin *mp)
{
     draw_icon(mp->icon, mp->x, mp->y);
}

void simple_move(graphin *mp)
{
     mp->draw_me(mp);    /* erase old position */
     mp->x += mp->dx;
     mp->y += mp->dy;
     mp->draw_me(mp);    /* draw new position */
}

#include <gremlin.icon>

static graphin Gremlin;

void create_object()
{
     Gremlin.icon = make_icon(gremlin_bits,
          gremlin_width, gremlin_height,
          gremlin_width/2, gremlin_height/2);
     Gremlin.x = Gremlin.y = 120;
     Gremlin.dx = 2;    Gremlin.dy = 1;
     Gremlin.draw_me = simple_draw;
     Gremlin.move_me = simple_move;
}
```

3.4.2 Animating a Graphin

In order to have a graphin moving around regardless of user actions, we need to add some code in the infinite loop that checks for events so that, when there are no events in the queue, the graphin will move around. The Starter Toolkit provides a function that can be used for that purpose.

☛ **`int add_work( int (*f)() )`**
The function `f()` will be called when no events are waiting in the queue, and it must have no arguments. The return value of `f()` is important. If it is nonzero the function is removed from the system. The function `f()` usually is called a *background* function because it runs whenever there is no user interaction. ☜

Because the event queue is not checked until the function `f()` returns, extensive computation within `f()` must be avoided; otherwise user actions will lag behind the motion of the graphins. The opposite is also possible: The motion could be too fast to be observed. In that case a delay in the program must be introduced by calling `idle()` just before return. This function has the following specification.

☛ **`void idle(int n)`**
Suspend execution (sleep) for (approximately) `n` microseconds. ☜

The proper value of the argument depends on the speed of the computer in which the program is running and the number of objects. The slower the machine the shorter is the time that it must sit idle and therefore the smaller is the value of `n`. The number should also be adjusted according to the computation performed by the background function. Trial and error usually is necessary to arrive at an appropriate value.

Listing 3.7.2 shows how these functions can be used.

Listing 3.7.2: Example of Programming with Graphins (Part 2) — `File graphin0.c`

```
#define DELAY 10000     /* system dependent constant */

move()
{
     Gremlin.move_me(&Gremlin);
     idle(DELAY);
     return(0);     /* zero return means that the system     */
                    /* should continue calling the function. */
}

void plot()
{
     Gremlin.draw_me(&Gremlin);
}

main()
{
     begin_display(400, 400, "Game");
     complete_display();
     create_object();
     set_redraw(plot);
     add_work(move);
     use_xor_mode();
     wait_for_event();
}
```

The main program starts with the two statements necessary to create a window. The function `create_objects()` contains the initialization of the structure for the graphin, as shown in Listing 3.7.1. The intermediate functions `plot()` and `move()` are needed because we cannot use

```
set_redraw(Gremlin.draw_me);
```

The functions passed as arguments either to `set_redraw()` or to `add_work()` cannot have arguments of their own, but the function `Gremlin.draw_me()` does.

Running the program of Listings 3.7.1 and 3.7.2 will show that the graphin moves quickly outside the window. We can keep the graphin inside the window by changing the values of `dx` and `dy` so that the motion is reversed when the graphin is about to go outside a window. Adding a few statements inside the function `move()` will do that (see Assignment 2).

3.4.3 Animating a Population of Graphins

A simple way to handle many objects is to create an array. To do so requires changing the program of Listings 3.7.1 and 3.7.2 only slightly by adding loops inside the functions `create_object()`, `move()`, and `plot()`, as shown in Listing 3.8.

Listing 3.8: Animation of Population — `File graphin1.c`

```
/*   The file graphin1.c contains only a collection of functions to be */
/*   used with other programs. It is not executable by itself        */
#include <graphin.h>
#define DELAY     10000 /* system dependent */
#define FUDGE       200 /* system dependent */
#define TOO_MANY     50 /* should equal DELAY/FUDGE */
#define MAX_NUMBER 100

static graphin population[MAX_NUMBER];
static int how_many;    /* number of graphins */

move()
{
     register i;
     register graphin *mp;

     for(i=0, mp=population; i<how_many; i++, mp++) mp->move_me( mp );
     if(how_many<TOO_MANY) idle(DELAY - how_many*FUDGE);
     return(0);
}
```

This code also illustrates how the delay can be adjusted according to the number of objects. Note that the number of icons and graphins need not be the same. The same icon may be used for more than one graphin.

3.4.4 Objects with Erratic Motion

A predictable motion is not very interesting, so a *random number* generator can be used to make the motion appear erratic. The C library function `random()` returns a pseudo-random number in the range 0 to $2^{31}-1$. To generate a random number with a smaller range we can mask some of the bits. By masking different numbers of bits we can create graphins with different degrees of randomness in their motion. Listing 3.9 contains a set of functions that produce an apparently erratic motion.

Listing 3.9: Random Motion — `File graphin1.c`

```
/*   See Listing 3.8 for comment on file graphin1.c*/
/*   Random Graphin Motion */
#include <graphin.h>

void randomize(int *u, int *v, int mask)
{
     int rn, tmp;

     rn = random()&mask;
     switch(rn) {
     case 1:          /* bounce off an imaginary vertical wall */
          *u = - *u;
          break;
     case 3:          /* bounce off an imaginary horizontal wall   */
          *v = - *v;
          break;
     case 5:          /* turn by a right angle */
          tmp = *u; *u = *v; *v = - tmp;
          break;
     }
}

/*   probability of change 3/128 (octal 177 equals 127 decimal)   */
void slightly_random_motion(graphin *mp)
{
     mp->draw_me(mp);   /* erase old position */
     randomize( &(mp->dx), &(mp->dy), 0177 );
     mp->x += mp->dx;
     mp->y += mp->dy;
     mp->draw_me(mp);   /* draw new position */
```

```
}

/*   probability of change 3/8 */
void highly_random_motion(graphin *mp)
{
     mp->draw_me(mp);    /* erase old position */
     randomize( &(mp->dx), &(mp->dy), 07 );
     mp->x += mp->dx;
     mp->y += mp->dy;
     mp->draw_me(mp);    /* draw new position */
}
```

If we declare

```
graphin Normal, Erratic;
```

the assignment

```
Normal.move_me = slightly_random_motion;
```

will result in a graphin with 3 chances in 128 that the direction of its motion will change at each iteration. On the other hand, the assignment

```
Erratic.move_me = highly_random_motion;
```

will result in a graphin with 3 chances in 8 that the direction of its motion will change at each iteration.

Undoubtedly, you can think of many other ways that the direction and size of each motion step can be changed. You can implement them easily by adding cases to the switch of `randomize()`.

3.5 SEA WORLD: AN EXAMPLE OF SIMPLE ANIMATION

This section integrates the functions described in Sections 3.4.2 and 3.4.3 into a single program that performs simple animation.

3.5.1 Preparing the Graphins

Figure 3.3 shows some icons that are (rather crude) depictions of sea life. A simple animation that uses them (and a few other similar icons) is given in Listing 3.10.

Figure 3.3 Some icons that can be used in a "sea life" simulation.

Listing 3.10.1: Sea World (Part 1) — `File sea.c`

```
#include <graphin.h>

#include <crab.icon>
#include <r_crab.icon>
#include <fish.icon>
#include <small_fish.icon>
#include <tooth_fish.icon>
#include <r_small_fish.icon>

static int  small_fish, tooth_fish, r_small_fish, Fish, R_crab, Crab;

void make_icons()
{
     small_fish   = make_icon(small_fish_bits, small_fish_width,
                              small_fish_height, 8, 8);
     tooth_fish   = make_icon(tooth_fish_bits, tooth_fish_width,
                              tooth_fish_height, 8, 8);
     r_small_fish = make_icon(r_small_fish_bits,
                    r_small_fish_width, r_small_fish_height, 8, 8);
     Fish         = make_icon(fish_bits, fish_width, fish_height, 8, 8);
     R_crab       = make_icon(r_crab_bits, r_crab_width, r_crab_height, 8, 8);
     Crab         = make_icon(crab_bits, crab_width, crab_height, 8, 8);
}

void simple_draw(graphin *mp)
{
     set_foregr(mp->color);          /* if color is used */
     draw_icon(mp->icon, mp->x, mp->y);
}
```

```
void simple_move(graphin *mp)
{
     int r, tmp;

     mp->draw_me(mp);    /* erase old position */

     r = random() & mp->nature;
     if(r==3) {     /* turn by 90 degrees */
          tmp = mp->dx; mp->dx = mp->dy;   mp->dy = tmp;
     }

     mp->x += mp->dx;
     mp->y += mp->dy;
     mp->draw_me(mp);    /* draw new position */
}
```

Rather than use the `randomize()` function of Listing 3.9, we have a single-motion function that uses as a mask for the result of `random()` a member of the graphin structure. If `mp->nature` is a two bit mask, the number 3 will appear on average 1 in 4 times, so the motion will change direction a lot. If the mask has many bits, the number 3 will appear infrequently and the motion will be along a constant direction.

3.5.2 Creating the Graphins

The group of functions in Listing 3.10.2 create the graphins while taking into account the dimensions of the display screen.

Listing 3.10.2: Sea World (Part 2) — `File sea.c`

```
static int S_WIDTH  = 400;
static int S_HEIGHT = 400;

void init_object(graphin *mp)
{
     mp->x = S_WIDTH/8 + (int)(random()&0377);
     mp->y = S_WIDTH/8 + (int)(random()&0377);
     mp->dx = 1 + (int)(random()&01);
     mp->dy = 1 + (int)(random()&01);
     mp->nature = 017;
     mp->draw_me = simple_draw;
     mp->move_me = simple_move;
}

void bounce_object(graphin *mp)
```

```
{
     if(mp->x + mp->dx <0 || mp->x + mp->dx >= S_WIDTH)
               mp->dx = -mp->dx;
     if(mp->y + mp->dy <0 || mp->y + mp->dy >= S_HEIGHT)
               mp->dy = -mp->dy;
}
```

The function `init_object()` creates a single structure by using random initial location and speed. The mask for motion randomization is set to four bits, giving 1 chance in 16 of a turn, according to the code of `simple_move()`. The function `bounce_object()` is needed to keep the graphins inside the screen.

The function `create_objects()` calls the functions that make the icons and initialize the objects. Finally, it assigns an icon and a color to each graphin. It can be changed to enhance the individuality of the graphins (for example, by assigning different values to `nature` and other members of the graphin structure).

Listing 3.10.3: Sea World (Part 3) — `File sea.c`

```
/*   Colors Names Selected from the X Database */
#define N 64
static graphin F[N];
static int how_many = N;

void create_objects()
{
     int i, color;

     for(i=0; i<how_many; i++) init_object(F+i);
     make_icons();
     color = add_named_color("brown"); /* use only for color displays */
     for(i=0; i<6; i++) {
          F[i].icon = Crab;
          F[i].color = color;     /* use only for color displays */
     }
     color = add_named_color("sandybrown");
     for(;i<12; i++)     {
          F[i].icon = R_crab;
          F[i].color = color;
     }
     color = add_named_color("green3");
     for(;i<18; i++)     {
          F[i].icon = tooth_fish;
          F[i].color = color;
```

```
    }
    color = add_named_color("red");
    for(;i<24; i++)     {
        F[i].icon = Fish;
        F[i].color = color;
    }
    color = add_named_color("gold");
    for(;i<44; i++)     {
        F[i].icon = r_small_fish;
        F[i].color = color;
    }
    color = add_named_color("gold3");
    for(;i<N; i++)      {
        F[i].icon = small_fish;
        F[i].color = color;
    }
}

void plot_objects()
{
    register i;
    for(i=0; i<how_many; i++) F[i].draw_me(F+i);
}
```

In this example we create two sets of 6 graphins having a crab icon (facing opposite ways), two more sets of 6 graphins for two kinds of big fish, and another 40 graphins that have icons of a small fish, half facing to the left and half to the right. The rest of the program is given in Listing 3.10.4. It consists of the function that moves the graphins and the main function.

Listing 3.10.4: Sea World (Part 4) — `File sea.c`

```
#define DELAY 10000
static int play = 0;

int move_objects()
{
    register i;

    for(i=0; i<how_many; i++) {
        bounce_object(F+i);
        F[i].move_me(F+i);
    }
    idle(DELAY);
    return(0);
```

```
}

main()
{
/*1*/     srandom(time(0));
/*2*/     begin_display(S_WIDTH, S_HEIGHT, "Sea World");
          complete_display();
/*3*/     create_objects();
/*4*/     set_redraw(plot_objects);
          use_xor_mode();
/*5*/     add_work(move_objects);
/*6*/     wait_for_event();
}
```

The `main` procedure does the following:

1. It seeds the random number generator with the time of the day, a necessary step for providing the illusion of randomness.
2. It creates the display window.
3. It creates the graphins.
4. It informs the system about the function that redraws the window.
5. It informs the system about the function that should be called when there are no events in the queue.
6. It goes into an infinite loop waiting for events while moving the graphins between events.

Figure 3.4 shows a snapshot of the screen while the program of Listing 3.5 is running.

3.6 INTERACTION AMONG OBJECTS

The interactions among objects can be specified by a function that first checks on whether the objects are close to each other and then takes an action specified by the function `proximity()`. The first function must be called by the `move_objects()` function. An example of such an arrangement is shown in Listing 3.11.

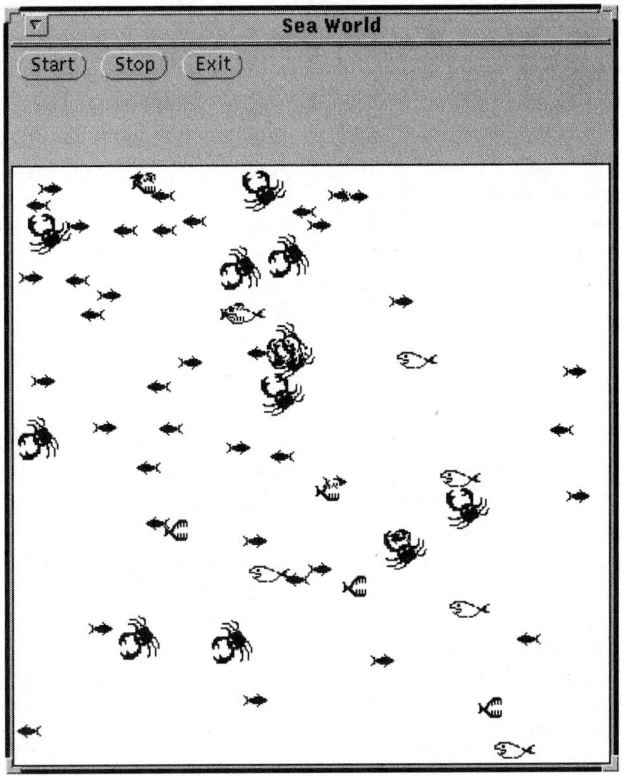

Figure 3.4 Snapshot of the screen while the program of Listing 3.5 is running.

Listing 3.11: Graphin Interaction

```
#define NEAR  8    /* comparable to icon size */

int graphin_meeting(graphin *mp1, graphin *mp2)
{
     if(abs(mp1->x - mp2->x) > NEAR) return(0);
     if(abs(mp1->y - mp2->y) > NEAR) return(0);
     /*  *mp1 and *mp2 are near each other */
     proximity( mp1, mp2);
     return(1);
}

void move_objects()
{
```

```
    register i, j;

    if(!play) return;
    for(i=0; i<how_many; i++) {
        bounce_object(F+i);
        F[i].move_me(F+i);
    }
    for(i=0; i<how_many-1; i++)
        for(j=i+1; j<how_many; j++)
            graphin_meeting( F+i, F+j );
}
```

There are many possibilities for the type of action that occurs when two objects are close to each other. Graphins may eat one another, spawn others, bounce off each other, and so on. The member `status` can be used to denote whether a graphin is alive. Listing 3.12.1 contains the necessary modifications for some of the functions of Listing 3.10, and Listing 3.12.2 shows a `proximity()` function.

Listing 3.12.1: Modifications of Sea World Functions

```
#define ALIVE 2
#define NUMB  1
#define DEAD  0

void init_object(graphin *mp)
{
    mp->x = S_WIDTH/8 + (int)(random()&0377);
    mp->y = S_WIDTH/8 + (int)(random()&0377);
    mp->dx = 1 + (int)(random()&01);
    mp->dy = 1 + (int)(random()&01);
    mp->nature = 017;
    mp->status = ALIVE;
    mp->draw_me = simple_draw;
    mp->move_me = simple_move;
}

void plot_objects()
{
    register i;

    for(i=0; i<how_many; i++)
        if(F[i].status != DEAD)
            F[i].draw_me(F+i);
}
```

```
void move_objects()
{
     register i;

     if(!play) return;
     for(i=0; i<how_many; i++) {
          if(F[i].status != ALIVE) continue;
          bounce_object(F+i);
          F[i].move_me(F+i);
     }
     for(i=0; i<how_many-1; i++)
          if(F[i].status==ALIVE)
               for(j=i+1; j<how_many; j++)
                    if(F[j].status==ALIVE)
                      graphin_meeting( F+i, F+j );
}
```

The function of Listing 3.12.2 determines the interaction on the basis of the type of graphins that meet. A "tooth_fish" immobilizes any other graphin. Big fish eat the small fish, and crabs bounce off each other. There is a lot of room for improvement in this function (see Assignment 6).

Listing 3.12.2: Additional Function for Sea World

```
/*   What happens when graphin meets graphin   */

void proximity(graphin *mp1, graphin *mp2)
{
     /* graphin goes numb when it encounters a tooth fish */
     if( mp1->icon==tooth_fish ) {
          mp2->status = NUMB;
          return;
     }
     if( mp2->icon==tooth_fish ) {
          mp1->status = NUMB;
          return;

     }
     /* small fish are eaten by big fish */
     if( mp1->icon==Fish &&
          (mp2->icon==small_fish || mp2->icon==r_small_fish) ) {
          mp2->draw_me( mp2 );    /* erase */
          mp2->status = DEAD;
          return;
     }
```

```
    if( mp2->icon==Fish &&
        (mp1->icon==small_fish || mp1->icon==r_small_fish) ) {
        mp1->draw_me( mp2 );    /* erase */
        mp1->status = DEAD;
        return;
    }
    /* crabs just bounce off each other */
    if( (mp1->icon==Crab || mp1->icon==R_crab) &&
        (mp2->icon==Crab || mp2->icon==R_crab) ) {
            mp1->dx = -mp1->dx;    mp1->dy = -mp1->dy;
            mp2->dx = -mp2->dx;    mp2->dy = -mp2->dy;
            return;
    }
    /* other interactions remain to be specified */
}
```

3.7 A SIMPLE VIDEO GAME

The simple animation program just described can be converted into a video game without too much trouble. An icon for the cursor and an event handler must be added. Both operations are placed in a single function shown in Listing 3.13.1. Having everything related to a player in a single function makes it easy to add an option to a program allowing the user to select one of several different characters. For example, able to catch fish easily but vulnerable to bites, or having a tough time catching fish but immune to bites. The selection can be made either by command line arguments (see the note after the Assignments in Chapter 1) or by pointing to areas of the screen that have been prepared in a way similar to the palette of colors described in Chapter 2. A systematic way for doing the latter is described in Chapter 7.

Listing 3.13.1: Interactive Sea World (Part 1)

```
#include <player.icon>
static int player_cursor;
void player_handler();

void create_player()
{
    player_cursor = make_cursor(player_bits, 8, 8);
    active_cursor(player_cursor);
    set_handler(player_handler);
}
```

After the game starts, when the player presses a button a special proximity function is called for all graphins that are nearby. The simple function of Listing 3.13.2 kills all creatures that are near the player's icon.

Listing 3.13.2: Interactive Sea World (Part 2)

```
static int score = 0;

void player_handler(pEvent *p)
{
     register i;

     switch(p->kind) {
     case BTN_PRESS:
          for(i=0; i<how_many; i++) {
               if(F[i].status    != ALIVE) continue;
               if(abs(p->x-F[i].x) > NEAR) continue;
               if(abs(p->y-F[i].y) > NEAR) continue;
               F[i].draw_me(F+i); /* erase */
               F[i].status = DEAD;
               score++;
          }
          break;
     }
}
```

A more interesting form of player-graphin interaction is offered by the program of Listing 3.14. It counts how many graphins are near the player's icon. If there are more than two, they overwhelm the player and the game ends. You may wish to replace the call to `exit()` with an elaborate obituary to the player.

Listing 3.14: Modified Interactive Sea World

```
#define TOO_MANY 2
static int score = 0;
static graphin *nearby[N];

void player_handler(pEvent *p)
{
     register i;
     int count = 0;

     switch(p->kind) {
     case BTN_PRESS:
```

```
            for(i=0; i<how_many; i++) {
                if(F[i].status    != ALIVE) continue;
                if(abs(p->x-F[i].x) > NEAR) continue;
                if(abs(p->y-F[i].y) > NEAR) continue;
                nearby[count++] = F+i;
            }

            if(count > TOO_MANY) exit(0);
            else {
                for(i=0; i<count; i++)
                nearby[i]->draw_me(nearby[i]);    /* erase */
                nearby[i]->status = DEAD;
                score++;
            }
            break;
        }
}
```

3.8 CONCLUSIONS

In this chapter we started with the description of icon files and the Starter Toolkit functions that convert such data into icons and/or cursors that can be used for animation and in interactive programs. Next we introduced a group of functions of the Starter Toolkit, which together perform the task of the simple function `draw_window()`. In this way we can separate initialization (for example, calls to `make_icon()`) from the normal operation (for example, calls to `draw_icon()`).

Then we showed how to do simple animation with icons. This procedure requires the creation of an object (`graphin`) and the introduction of a Starter Toolkit function that allows for background execution of functions. Finally we combined the animation program with a simple event handler to create a video game.

You can improve the game in many ways but we should point out the simple version consists of less than 300 lines of C code. This small amount of code was possible because we relied extensively on the Starter Toolkit. In later chapters we show how to enhance the game by adding ways to select options, obstacles, or hiding places.

3.9 ASSIGNMENTS

Note A: All assignments can be implemented on a monochrome display. If a color display is available, the color member of the graphin structure may be used as illustrated in Listings 3.10.1 and 3.10.3. Keep in mind that each icon can have only one color (that of foreground). Multicolor graphins can be made with the methods detailed in Chapter 20.

Note B: Except for the first assignment all others can be used as the first part of a game program, which can be enhanced by adding features introduced in later chapters.

1. The left figure in Figure 3.5 shows part of a cursor, while the figure in the middle shows the results of the mask generator program of Section 3.2.2. (The mask pixels are shown in gray while the cursor pixels are shown in dark gray and the background in light gray.) This program does not change pixels that touch the original icon only at a corner. Modify it so that the result will be similar to the one on the right. In other words, pixels touching the original icon only at a corner should also be included in the mask.

Figure 3.5 Pixel arrangement during cursor mask construction.

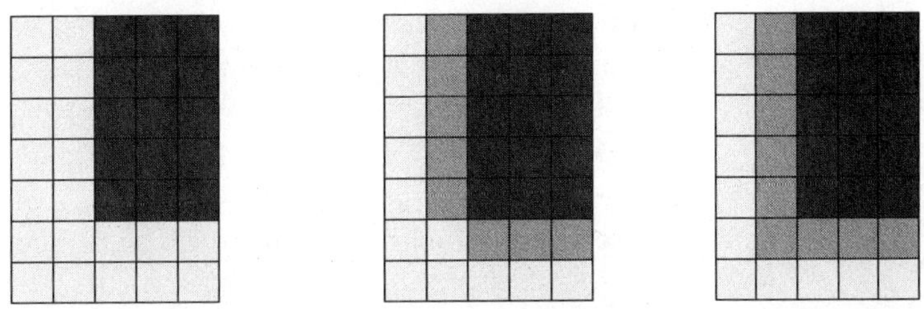

2. (a) Modify the program of Section 3.4.2 so that the graphin always stays within the screen.
(b) Modify this program further by using two icons for the graphin, one facing left and the other right. Select the icon to be displayed according to the direction of the motion.
3. (a) Use the program of Assignment 2 as a starting point and write a new program that displays a rectangle, and make it the object of the user to keep the graphin within that rectangle. The way to do that is to add an event handler so that when the user hits a particular key or presses a particular mouse button ("sends a signal") the motion of the graphin is reversed. The program should ignore such events if the graphin is outside the box.
(b) Make the game more interesting by modifying the event handler as follows: (1) Add code so that it ignores the user signal unless the cursor is near the graphin; and (2) define a static variable, say, `dir`, that is

initialized to 0 and, any time the user sends a signal, it flips, i.e.,

```
dir = 1 - dir
```

Reverse the horizontal motion if `dir` is 0 and reverse the vertical motion otherwise.
(c) Have more than one graphin that the user must keep inside the rectangle.

4. Enhance the program of Assignment 3 by adding a scoring system as follows. When the graphin reverses its motion in response to a user signal, compute its distance from the nearest box side. Let that distance be `near`. If `near` is 0, add 100 points to the score. Otherwise add `50/near`. Anytime the graphin crosses the box boundary and goes outside the box, subtract 100 points. Display the score on the screen.
5. You can create lively graphins by using many icons to represent different graphin forms. For example, if the graphin is a bird you can program it to flap its wings. One way of doing so is to modify the structure of Listing 3.6 as follows: (a) Replace the `icon` member by an array whose elements point to the different icons; (b) add a member that equals the number of different icons, say, `n_icons`; and (c) add a counter `own_time`. Then at each cycle of the program the `own_time` will be incremented modulo `n_icons`. You must also modify the `simple_draw` function by using `mp->icon[mp->own_time]` rather than `mp->icon`.
6. Implement the animation program of Sections 3.4 and 3.5 and enhance it by completing the function of Listing 3.12.2 for all possible encounters.
7. Implement a game wherein the player shoots missiles at the graphins. Because the missiles must move much faster than the other objects on the screen, you must call the `move` function more frequently for them than for other objects.
8. Design a game and start implementing it. It can be an imitation of an existing game or a completely new one. At this stage you should create icons for some of the characters, implement their motion, and generally complete the graphin structures. Add simple animation and encounter rules. Later you can enhance the game with material from subsequent chapters. (This assignment is an open-ended alternative to Assignments 2-4.)

4

Fundamentals of the X Window System*

Scope of the Chapter

Major features of the X Window System, especially those pertinent to creating graphic displays • X Protocol and Xlib • Clients and Servers • Window Managers • Window creation, mapping, and reparenting • Attributes, Properties, and Atoms

4.1 INTRODUCTION

4.1.1 Clients and Servers

A primary motivation for the development of the X Window System was the need for a system that could do graphics over a network. The graphics setups of the 1970s and earlier usually required two machines, one in which the graphics were computed and the other in which they were displayed. The first machine sent a sequence of instructions (''graphics metafile'') to the second, which first translated them into primitive graphics instructions and then executed them.

* **This chapter may be skipped by those who want to use only the Starter Toolkit.**

However, the spread of personal computers and workstations in the early 1980s changed the situation. Such machines combined the computer and the graphics device in one unit, with the same CPU running the applications program and the graphics display. Therefore the graphics file was an "internal affair." Although such integration simplified some things, it did not allow application programs to do the computation on a different machine than that controlling the display.

The X Window System reestablished the distinction between the device that does the computation of the applications program and the device that displays the graphics. The first is called the *client*, and the second is called the *server*. These names are rather unfortunate and cause confusion for beginners.

Most people are familiar with file servers, which are remote machines supporting client workstations (the machines in front of each user). In X the situation is reversed. The server is the machine in front of the user, and the client is whatever machine is running the application program, not necessarily the same as the server. The client may be a supercomputer in New Jersey running, for example, a weather prediction program and the server a graphics device in California displaying a visualization of the results.

In this book we use the more intuitive term *display* to refer to the server and *application* to refer to the client. The original terms usually are added in parentheses to help you refer to other literature on the X Window System.

Because the two machines can be quite far from each other, development of the X Window System had to go beyond a graphics file specification and design a network protocol for their communication.

4.1.2 X Protocol and Xlib

The *X Protocol* is a set of messages that are exchanged between the applications program (client) and the graphics display (server). A particular device can be used for X if it is able to translate such messages into graphic displays and generate the appropriate messages for communicating back to the application.

Writing a program to generate such messages explicitly would be quite laborious, so a set of functions has been written that do the task. The set of such functions for the C language is known as *Xlib*.

The functions of *Xlib* are parallel to the set of functions of *PLOT(3)* but there are many more of them and, usually, they have a more complex call. For example, the counterpart of

```
line(x1, y1, x2, y2)
```

is

```
XDrawLine(a1, a2, a3, x1, y1, x2, y2)
```

The increased complexity is a consequence of the requirement that the X protocol should anticipate all conceivable graphics operations. Therefore a large number of message types is needed (there are over 100 of them in comparison to just ten of *PLOT(5)*). The current specifications still do not cover all graphics operations (e.g., plotting curves besides circular and elliptic arcs).

Let's now look at the extra arguments. The *PLOT(3)* functions write always in the standard output. The *Xlib* functions can have varied destinations, and the first two arguments are used for that purpose. The situation is analogous to the

```
printf( " ... ", ... )
```

and

```
fprintf(stderr, " ... " , .... )
```

C Library functions.

The third argument contains information, among other things, about the color and the style (solid, dashed, etc.) of the line segment. In many earlier systems such information was set globally, and all lines drawn after a setting had the same color, style, and other features. However global variables pose serious problems in programming and associating information locally is best. Therefore the extra three arguments are necessary to deal with the generality of the system.

It is beyond the scope of this text to discuss whether the generality of X is worth the price paid in increased complexity. But even if such complexity is necessary, it should be hidden from people who do not want or need to use the full power of the system. Thus the challenge is to manage properly its size and complexity. One way to do so is to think of *Xlib* as the equivalent of a low-level programming language and develop other libraries on top of it, which is what the Starter Toolkit is. We return to this topic in Chapters 8 and 9.

4.1.3 An Example of an X Protocol Message

As this book is not intended for systems programmers, we do not discuss the X Protocol again, but you may be interested seeing an example of its structure. Table 4.1 is the counterpart of Table 1.1.

Table 4.1: The *X Protocol* Graphics Primitive for Drawing a Group of Line Segments

Bytes	Value	Description	Comments
First	0102	Operation Code	[1]
Second	—	Unused	
3 & 4	(short integer)	Length of the Request	[1]
5 to 8	(long integer)	Reference number	[2]
9 to 12	(long integer)	Reference number	[3]
13 & 14	(short integer)	Value of x1	[4]
15 & 16	(short integer)	Value of y1	[4]
17 & 18	(short integer)	Value of x2	[4]
19 & 20	(short integer)	Value of y2	[4]
21 on	...	...	[5]

[1] The X protocol allows sending messages for groups of line segments, not just one. Message lengths always are multiples of four bytes, and the length of the request states how many 4 byte words are contained. If N segments are to be drawn, each requires four pairs of bytes, or two 32 bit words, so the total length is $3 + 2N$. (For `XDrawLine()` this sum is 5.)

[2] Reference number to the part of the display screen where the line will be drawn (corresponding to the second argument of `XDrawLine()`).

[3] Reference number to the data structure containing information about style, color, etc. (corresponding to the third argument of `XDrawLine()`).

[4] Endpoints of first segment (fourth to seventh arguments of `XDrawLine()`).

[5] Endpoints of the second segment followed by the rest (absent from `XDrawLine()`).

One important feature of the message is that the part of the display screen where the segments are drawn and the data structure are described not by pointers but by reference numbers. This feature is essential for communication between different machines because pointers have meaning only within a single machine.

The message for drawing a single line segment consists of 20 bytes compared with only 9 for the *PLOT* graphics file, so it is about twice as long. However, the message for drawing, say, 100 segments is 812 bytes long, which is less than the 900 bytes of the *PLOT* graphics file. Besides the `XDrawLine()` function, which sends a segment drawing request with

$N = 1$, *Xlib* has another function, `XDrawSegments()`, which can be used to draw an arbitrary number of segments by sending a single message. (These are the only two functions that generate the request with operation code 0102 (octal).)

The need to draw a large number of segments at once is not that unusual. Besides being the result of a buffering operation, it occurs when we need to draw a curve. If the segments are small enough, the curve arc can be replaced by an approximating straight line segment.

This message could not have been made simpler because no piece of information in it is redundant. See Section 4.5 for suggestions on additional reading.

4.2 WINDOWS

4.2.1 What Is a Window?

So far we have described the X Window System as a communications protocol between application programs (clients) and programs controlling graphic display devices (servers). You may be wondering about our use of the word *windows.* The reasons are that the system can be used in a window environment and that a large part of the X Protocol (and *Xlib*) are devoted to window operations that go well beyond graphics primitives.

Window systems have existed since the late 1970s, well before the X Window System was introduced. The major new feature of X is the use of the client-server concept and the provision of a protocol for the communication between them so that window programs can be run over a network.

Definition A *window* is a rectangular area of the screen (refresh memory). Internally, it may be represented by two pairs of coordinates, those of its top left and bottom right corners. An alternative representation (used in X) is by the coordinates of its top left corner, its width, and its height. In practice the data structure for a window has many additional members that are described later in this chapter.

The following are some common terms.

Definition A window is *created* when the data structure is allocated and initialized. There is no change yet in the refresh memory and nothing is visible on the display screen.

Definition A window is *mapped* when the screen area corresponding to the window rectangle is painted with a background color or whatever other means have been chosen by the program.

Definition Because a display can have *overlapping* windows, mapped windows may be *visible*, *partially visible*, or *obscured*.

4.2.2 Windows and Multitasking

What makes windows so useful is that each can be associated with a program and used as its output area. Unix and some other operating systems allow *multitasking*: having many programs running at the same time. Of course this is not literally true as there is only one CPU.

What happens in multitasking is that a piece of the computer memory is devoted to each program and every, say, 1 millisecond a program is given access to the CPU. For example, if ten programs were running, each would run for 1 millisecond and be idle for 9. Because run/idle cycle times are so short, users have the illusion of many programs running simultaneously with continuous access to the system. (Of course, when many programs are running, the computer seems to be sluggish.) The word *process* is used to describe the memory holding the information about a program that is in a run/idle cycle. (*Note:* This is a simplified description of what actually goes on, and anyone interested in this topic should consult an operating systems text.)

Although sharing the CPU is easy, sharing the input device (keyboard) and output area (screen) is a bit more difficult because I/O processes take considerably more time than computation. Unix solved this problem by having processes run in *background* and by the *redirection* of input and output. For example, typing

```
sort < file1 > file2 &
```

causes the start of a sorting program that takes its input from `file1` and places its output in `file2`. In the meantime the user may run other programs, such as a text editor, that have complete control of the terminal.

If a system has windows, a natural approach is to assign a window for each process to be used for output without having to redirect the output. The system also may provide means for deciding which window takes input from the keyboard. If the process associated with a window is a shell (command interpreter), the user has the illusion of multiple terminals to a machine. Then new programs may be started on each window. For example, the window at the lower right corner of Figure 1.1 indicates that the user has just run a `ls -l` command.

You can use such a *shell window* to start programs that create their own windows (rather than use the existing window) to which they direct all their output. That is the case with the clock program of Figure 1.1 and the picture display program of Figure 1.2. If a program creates its own window, it should be run in background mode so that the original shell window will be available for other uses.

In a multitasking system the refresh memory is another resource to be shared among processes. Each process may create its own window or use an existing window for output. There is no theoretical limit on the number of windows a process can create. Figure 1.2 depicts a program that creates a control panel containing the names of image files and then creates additional windows in response to user requests to display individual pictures. Sharing of input facilities (for example, the keyboard) is discussed in the next section.

4.2.3 Window Managers

Typing the name of a program in a shell window starts an application (or client). If this program requires its own window, it asks the server for a rectangle in the refresh memory. The server creates the appropriate data structure and adds it to the list of the windows it maintains. This list contains information not only about the geometry of the windows but also their *stacking order*, that is, their relative order with respect to the display screen. Windows may obscure other windows that are behind them in the stacking order.

When the application (client) asks for a window to be mapped (i.e., take actual control of the allocated piece of refresh memory), the server does not do the display but asks the window manager to do it.

Definition A *window manager* is an application (client) program that displays the windows of other applications (usually with added "decorations") and, in addition, modifies the size, position, and relative placement of the windows on the basis of user actions. The window manager also mediates the allocation of unique resources such as the *keyboard* and the *video lookup table* (see Figure 1.3).

Usually, the window manager tracks the position of the mouse-controlled cursor. When the cursor is inside a window, the process associated with that window takes control of the keyboard and the video lookup table. Control of the keyboard by a process means that all typed input is sent to the standard input of that process. That window usually is called the *active window*.

Like any other application, the window manager sends messages to the server to implement any of those operations. Figure 4.1 illustrates what is happening when a user asks the program shown in Figure 1.2 to display a particular picture. The program reads the picture file, computes the dimensions of the window, and then asks the server to create the window data structure (message 1). Then it asks the server to map (display) the window (message 2). The server passes the request to the window manager (message 3), which must decide where and how to position the window relative to other windows on the screen. After doing so it asks the server to execute the appropriate graphics primitives (message 4).

Figure 4.1 Interaction among an application program, the server, and the window manager. For clarity, only major messages are shown. Confirmation messages are omitted.

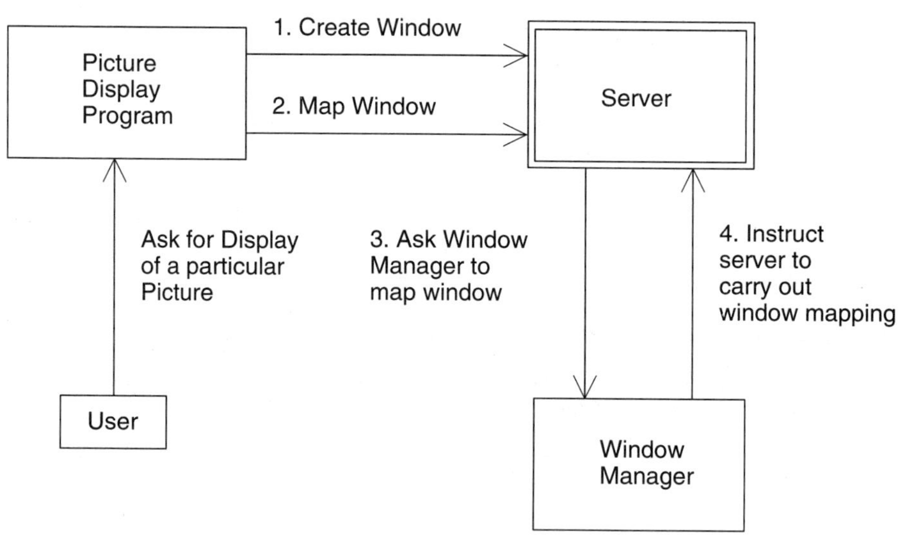

Having the window manager as a program distinct from the server is a characteristic of the X Window System. (Actually, you can run programs, albeit awkwardly, without a window manager.) Such a separation is not a requirement for window systems. It is possible to write a server that also manages the windows. Having the functions in two separate programs has two advantages:

1. It allows users to vary the "look and feel" of the window system because that depends on the window manager.
2. It makes the server a simpler program. Servers must translate the protocol messages to machine instructions and therefore are hardware dependent. In order to make a new device conform to the X standard the manufacturer must provide a server. Making that task easier helps the establishment of the standard.

This separation also has a disadvantage. A large part of the protocol (and as a consequence of *Xlib*) has to do with communication between server and window manager. Some of the *Xlib* functions are reserved for window managers only (although there is no automatic way to enforce that). The window manager is indeed a very important client!

A further discussion of trade-offs between the two possible designs is beyond the scope of the text. Our focus is on graphics rather than systems.

Because the two programs are distinct, we must invoke both when we want to work on a machine with the X Window System. The typical sequence is to invoke the program `xinit`, which starts a server (given as an argument) and a single client. For example SUN workstations use the `xnews` server, and the first client is the *Open Look* window manager `olwm`. Rather lengthy shell scripts are necessary, but in a well-maintained system the average user needs to invoke only one script to start the whole process.

One possibility is to have X handle the login process so that the server and window manager are started only once and users find themselves immediately in an X environment after login.

4.2.4 Backing Up Windows

So far we have described how different processes share limited resources: the CPU (Section 4.2.2), the keyboard, and the video lookup table (Section 4.2.3). When windows overlap, processes also must share the refresh memory. The key issue is what to do with the contents of the memory that is allocated to another process. The server can be asked to copy the contents into another part of the (nonrefresh) memory and restore it later.

Unfortunately, this simple solution is not supported by the X Window System. The decision was made not to place the responsibility for backing up obscured windows on the display device (server). That was too much to ask because it went well beyond the main task of interpreting network messages and mapping them into the refresh memory.

When a window is obscured, nothing happens. When a window becomes visible, the display device sends a message to the applications program, informing it about the need to redraw the display. Such messages are placed in the queue as *exposure* events, and applications programs must provide an appropriate function for the event handler to call. That is the role of the function used as first argument in the function `vis_window()` discussed in Section 1.5.1.

Although not required by the specifications of the X Window System, many servers offer a backup facility. Because it is not guaranteed to be there, each application should have a "redraw" function. (In Section 4.4.2 we discuss how to determine whether a particular server supports backing storage.)

However, there are situations where an automatic backup is not desirable. Suppose that we have an application that scales a drawing to fill a window. If the user reduces the window size, then an automatic backup will leave some of the drawing invisible because it will not fit in the new window. The correct solution is to redo the drawing using a smaller scale. If the user increases the window size, an automatic backup will leave empty areas. A better solution is to redraw the drawing using a larger scale.

4.2.5 Server Resources

The two-part structure of graphics programs requires that we distinguish between resources of the application (client) and resources of the display (server). Thus refresh memory clearly is a server resource. The term also is used with a more specific meaning to denote any data stored in the server — for example, structures defining areas of the memory, color maps, graphics context (see Section 1.4.3), and others.

4.3 A SIMPLE WINDOW PROGRAM

4.3.1 The Simplest Possible Window Program

Listing 4.1 shows what is probably the simplest X program. It does nothing but display an empty window for 5 seconds and then exit. The program consists of six statements, five of them calls to *Xlib* functions. It (1) establishes a connection to the server; (2) asks the server to create the structure for the window with dimensions and colors given by the numerical arguments; (3) asks the server to allocate refresh memory to the window and pass it to the window manager for display; (4) flushes the output buffer, which causes the window to appear on the screen; (5) sleeps for five seconds; and (6) closes the connection to the server and exits. The fourth statement is needed because communication with the server is asynchronous.

We discuss the calls to the *Xlib* functions in more detail in the following sections.

Listing 4.1: The Simplest Possible *Xlib* Program — `File window.c`

```
#include <X11/Xlib.h>

main()
{
         Display *Dp;
         Window w;

/*1*/    Dp = XOpenDisplay("");
/*2*/    w = XCreateSimpleWindow(Dp,
              DefaultRootWindow(Dp),
              0, 0, 256, 256, 4, 1, 0);
/*3*/    XMapWindow(Dp, w);
/*4*/    XFlush(Dp);

/*5*/    sleep(5);

/*6*/    XCloseDisplay(Dp);
}
```

4.3.2 Connecting to the Server (Display)

Statement 1, the call to `XOpenDisplay()`, establishes a connection of the application (client) to the display device (server). Normally its argument would be a string with the name of the server but, unless you plan to write a program allowing the use of different displays at the same time, you would not have to worry about this issue. When the function is called with an empty string ("") as an argument, it takes its destination from the Unix shell environment variable DISPLAY. If that is not set in your environment, try ":0". That should connect your application program to another process in the same machine. (See Assignment 9 of Chapter 1 for how to run a program on different machines.)

The function returns a pointer (`Dp`) to a `Display` structure, which contains all the information needed both for communication with the server and for creating graphics displays in the server. This structure is quite large (more than 50 members, some of them large vectors), and a set of macros is provided for accessing its members.

One of the members is the identity of the root window of the server. The server process always creates a root window, and all other windows are created as subwindows of the root window. Therefore we need that information as an argument to the function that creates the window. The macro `DefaultRootWindow()` (used in Statement 2 of Listing 4.1) does exactly that. A server can have more than one display screen (refresh memory), but in this text we do not deal with such systems.

The pointer returned by `XOpenDisplay()` appears as the first argument of all *Xlib* functions and macros, with different functions using different members of the structure. Most of the functions use the member that is a *file descriptor* to write in the channel to the server. However, most macros access some other member of the structure. For most simple application programs you can reasonably think of this pointer (`Dp` in Listing 4.1) as a file descriptor, even though it is not exactly that.

The statement `XCloseDisplay()` closes the connection and need not be called explicitly in most programs because the connection is closed automatically upon exit.

4.3.3 Creating and Mapping a Window

Statement 2 of Listing 4.1 creates the server data structure for the drawing window. In general, the statement has the form

```
XCreateSimpleWindow( display_pointer, parent_window,
     x_of_left_side, y_of top_side,  width, height,
     border_width, border_color, background_color);
```

All the arguments, except the first two, are integers. The first two and last three arguments are self explanatory. The four in the middle also appear to be obvious, except for one factor: It is not certain that the window will have the requested location and size.

These parameters are called *hints* because the window manager uses them only as suggestions. This role is particularly true for the location of the upper left corner but less so for the width and the height. The main reason that the window manager ignores the location is to avoid windows that are stacked directly on top of each other. That will happen if the same application is called twice and the positional parameters are used without any change. You can confirm the desirability of ignoring exact positioning by running one program in the background twice. Figure 4.2 illustrates the situation.

The arguments of `XCreateSimpleWindow()` constitute a minimal set of parameters with the remaining parameters of the window copied from the root window. We can modify the implicit attributes by using other *Xlib* calls or by creating the window with another function, `XCreateWindow()`.

In Statement 3 the function `XMapWindow()` passes, in effect, the window from the server to the window manager. Whether the window will actually be displayed depends on the window manager. For example, other windows may be obscuring it. If the window can be displayed the window manager sends the appropriate graphics commands to the server.

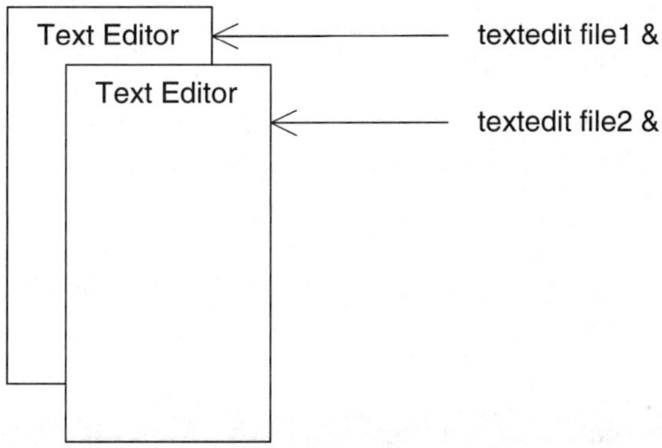

Figure 4.2 Screen arrangement when two invocations of the same application are running at the same time.

4.3.4 X Identity Numbers (XID)

Listing 4.1 shows that the return of the function `XCreateSimpleWindow()` has been declared of `Window` type. Is `Window` a pointer to a structure or a structure? *It is neither.* There is a window structure, but it resides in the server. As pointers to structures make no sense across CPUs, we cannot pass a pointer to the client. Instead we pass a long integer called an *X Identity Number*, which can be used to reference structures across machines. Such identity numbers are used widely in X to communicate between server and client. The type name is `XID` so that the *Xlib* header files include declarations such as

```
typedef XID Window;
```

The type `XID` itself has been declared by the statement

```
typedef unsigned long XID;
```

You can insert in the program of Listing 4.1 the statement

```
printf("Window XID = %o\n", w);
```

to see what this number looks like. A long integer can be translated into a structure pointer in one of many ways. How the translation is done is beyond the scope of this text because the topic is of interest only to writers of server programs.

Such identity numbers sometimes are called *handles,* but we would rather avoid that name because it sounds too much like "handler." The concept is by no means restricted to X or even to graphics. Identity numbers offer one way to enforce information hiding in object-oriented programming (see Chapter 3 where such numbers are used by the Starter Toolkit to identify icons).

4.3.5 Dealing with Asynchrony

Statement 4 of Listing 4.1 flushes the message queue to the server because the interaction between client and server is asynchronous.

Important Point *Always be aware that the statements in an application program never do any graphics operations themselves. Instead they send messages to the server.*

For example, `put_line()` does not draw a line. It calls an *Xlib* function that creates a message of the form shown in Table 4.1. This message is not sent immediately to the server but is buffered. Usually the buffered messages are not sent until the application requests some input from the server.

Being aware of the asynchrony between client and server is very important in debugging a program.

4.3.6 Reparenting and the Obligations It Imposes

If you compile and run the program of Listing 4.1, you will observe that the displayed window has a fancy frame, similar to other windows on the screen. Who inserted all these decorations? Actually no one did anything to the window your program created. However, the window manager has inserted a new window (with "decorations") between the root window and the one just created. This process is called *reparenting*.

The reason for reparenting is that the window manager allows a user to move and resize its windows, and offering the same facilities to any window created by an application is a good practice. Because forcing all applications programmers to do that would be almost impossible, the window manager solves the problem by inserting a window of its own (with all the desired facilities) between the root and the top application window.

Reparenting imposes various obligations on the applications programmer. The program must respond in a graceful way when the user operates on the (new) top window. How does the program know that the new parent has been manipulated? The server generates events when the window is moved or resized and the program must make provisions to look for them in the event queue and act accordingly. Because the program of

Listing 4.1 does not do anything useful, it may ignore most of these events. Hence we postpone discussing them until Chapter 5, where we illustrate them with a nontrivial program.

However, one event cannot be ignored, even by the current trivial program. If the user terminates the top window, everything disappears from the screen. However the program of Listing 4.1 continues running, at least for five seconds. To act properly in the window environment the program must exit when its parent exits. We describe the mechanism for making it do so in Sections 4.4.3 and 6.1.5, after we introduce certain needed background.

4.4 FEATURES OF WINDOWS

4.4.1 Overview

Each window has many features and a large amount of data associated with it. We have already mentioned some of them in Section 4.3.3: location (`x_of_left_side` and `y_of_top_side`), width, height, border width, and so on. Such data are divided into two classes: *attributes* and *properties*.

Definition *Attributes* are features that are intrinsic to the window, such as border width and color.

Definition *Properties* are an X mechanism for communication between applications (clients). Properties have an ASCII name and can contain arbitrary information. They are most commonly used to communicate with the window manager and contain information such as location, width, and height.

In addition, a server structure describes how the window relates to user actions by having a list of events that must be sent to the window. These events are defined by a call to the `XSelectInput()` function, which we discuss in Section 6.1.4 together with other event-related issues.

4.4.2 Attributes

Attributes are members of a structure, with their type being defined as `XSetWindowAttributes`. They can be set by a call to the *Xlib* function `XChangeWindowAttributes()`. This function takes as arguments a `Display` pointer, a window XID, a *value mask*, and a pointer to an

XSetWindowAttributes structure. The value mask is an integer of type unsigned long, whose bits correspond to attributes. If a bit is set to 1, the corresponding attribute is used in XSetWindowAttributes(). For example, to request the server for automatic backup of all window contents we can use the following code fragment.

```
if( DoesbackingStore( DefaultScreenOfDisplay( Dp) ) ==
     Always) {
     XSetWindowAttributes attr;
     unsigned long valuemask = CWBackingStore;

     attr.backing_store = Always;
     XChangeWindowAttributes(Dp, w, valuemask, &attr);
}
```

The macro DefaultScreenOfDisplay() returns a pointer to the screen (refresh memory) of the server, and the macro Doesbacking-Store() returns an integer with information about the availability of memory backups in the server. Both Always and CWBackingStore are predefined constants (1L<<6 for the latter). Because of this setting, the XChangeWindowAttributes() call tells the server to ignore all other members of the attr structure and update only the one determining the backup of window contents. In this example that attribute is set to the predefined constant Always asking the server to always make a copy of the window contents.

4.4.3 Properties and Atoms

Note: This section deals with more difficult material than the rest of the chapter and can be skipped for now.

Properties have names that are character strings. For example, "WM_NORMAL_HINTS" is the name of the property that contains information about the size of the window in a structure of type XSizeHints. "WM_HINT" property corresponds to a structure of type XWMHints that contains a rather odd assortment of data, including information about how to direct keyboard input to a window.

Definition The names of window properties are converted into integers called *Atoms*, which are used in the communications between server and client (and hence between client and client).

For example, "WM_HINT" is converted into the atom XA_WM_HINTS, which actually is the integer 35. The atom for "WM_NORMAL_HINTS" is

`XA_WM_NORMAL_HINTS` (or 40).

Not all properties have predefined atoms. We illustrate a case in point by describing the mechanism for informing a window that its parent has been destroyed. (We pointed out the need for such information in Section 4.3.6.)

There is a type of event, `ClientMessage`, which is placed in the event queue by the window manager, provided that the application has selected for it. It is not a true user input event, so it cannot be selected with the `XSelectInput()` function described in Section 6.1.4. (The user-generated event, if any, was handled by the window manager, which then destroyed the window.)

This event can be selected through the WM_PROTOCOLS property, which is a list of atoms and which is set with the `XSetWMProtocols()` function. This function takes as an argument a list of protocols. The list includes WM_DELETE_WINDOW, which causes the window manager to send a `ClientMessage` when the parent window is destroyed, as shown by the following code fragment.

```
static Atom quit_atom;
     ....
quit_atom = XInternAtom(Dp, "WM_DELETE_WINDOW", False);
XSetWMProtocols( Dp, w, &quit_atom, 1);
```

The call to the function `XInternAtom()` converts the string WM_DELETE_WINDOW to an atom. The third argument controls the return of the function if the property does not exist. Setting it to `False` requires the function to create the atom if it does not already exist. If it were set to `True`, it would return the atom value only if the atom already existed. Here `w` is the XID of the window that is going to receive the message. The number 1 is simply the number of atoms in the list.

In Section 6.1.5 we demonstrate the use of this property to make the window of the simple program of Listing 4.1 exit gracefully.

4.4.4 Convenience Functions

Things are a little easier for properties with predefined atoms. There are many *convenience functions* in *Xlib* that hide the distinction between properties and attributes so that for most of the time the applications programmer does not have to worry about atoms or property names.

Because there are many property structures — and each has many members — a mechanism similar to the value mask used for attributes is needed. Indeed, each property structure contains a member, `flag`, declared as `long`, which is used for that purpose. For example, the following code fragment tells the window manager to direct keyboard input to window `w` when the mouse-controlled cursor is located in that window.

```
XWMHints wmhints;
...
wmhints.flags = InputHint;
wmhints.input = True;
XSetWMHints(Dp, w, &wmhints);
```

Here, `InputHint` is a predefined constant and `XSetWMHints()` is a convenience function.

4.5 CONCLUSIONS

We have provided an overview of the X Window System, emphasizing features that are useful for graphics programs. Many sources are available for those desiring to learn more about the subject. If you plan to write programs using *Xlib* directly you must consult one of the sources below because details about *Xlib* functions have been left out of this text. The following book has been written by the architects of the X Window System (the protocol and *Xlib*, respectively) and is recommended for those wanting to explore the subject further.

- R. W. Scheifler and J. Gettys. *X Window System*, 3rd ed. Burlington, Mass.: Digital Press, 1992.

A series of books published by O'Reilly & Associates contain extensive information on the X Window System. Volume 2 of the series contains an alphabetic listing of all functions of *Xlib*. It is recommended for those wanting to write new programs in X using *Xlib* functions.

- A. Nye (ed.). *Xlib Reference Manual*, Vol. 2, 3rd ed. Sebastopol, Calif.: O'Reilly & Associates, 1992.

Those interested in finding out more about the protocol should consult one of the specialized sources, either the book by Scheifler and Gettys cited or the following.

- A. Nye (ed.). *X Protocol Reference Manual*, Volume 0. Sebastopol, Calif.: O'Reilly & Associates, 1990.

Our discussion so far should convince you that creating windows with *Xlib* can be difficult for programs that have any real use (as opposed to the trivial program of Listing 4.1). As a matter of fact the X Window System has facilities that create windows with properties defined at a higher level. (We discuss them in Chapters 8 and 9.) The reason for Section 4.4.4 is to provide you with some insight into the properties of windows as opposed to widgets, which, in effect, are windows "packaged" with a group of functions and various parameters.

4.6 ASSIGNMENTS

1. Locate the shell script that starts X in your system and try to identify the statments that refer to the server and the window manager.
2. Modify the program of Section 4.3.1 to provide information on whether the server has backing store or not. (You must also search for the definition of the symbolic names returned, so the program should print out an ASCII string rather than a number.)
3. Write a program that creates a window in each of several displays. You must modify Listing 4.1 by enclosing the first four statements in a loop and replacing the empty string in statement 1 by the appropriate machine name. In order to execute your program you must secure appropriate permission for each machine.

5

Drawing with the X Window System*

Scope of the Chapter

Drawables • Pixmaps • Graphics Context • Primitive graphics functions of Xlib • Icons • Color • Fonts

5.1 THE BASICS OF DRAWING

5.1.1 Drawables and Pixmaps

Because a window corresponds to an area of the refresh memory, it can serve as the destination for graphics output. The X Window System defines `Drawable` as a server resource that can be mapped to the refresh memory. Besides the `Window` type there is another drawable type: `Pixmap`. Here, the term has a slightly narrower meaning than that given in Section 1.2.5: It refers to a specific part of memory rather than to a type of memory.

Definition An X Pixmap is a region in the memory of the server (a *server resource*) that is NOT part of the refresh memory but can be copied there. The type `Pixmap` is the XID used to address that region.

---

* **This chapter may be skipped by those who want to use only the Starter Toolkit.**

Windows can be copied into Pixmaps and vice versa. Note that the application (client) does not have a pointer to the window server structure or the pixmap but does have an XID number. All drawing functions take a `Drawable` as second argument, after the `Display` pointer. They can be invoked either with a window or pixmap XID in that place.

There are several good reasons for drawing on a pixmap rather than in a window. Pixmaps are always maintained. But if windows become obscured, what is drawn in them is lost. If a particular drawing requires extensive computation, drawing it on a pixmap and then copying it to a window whenever necessary makes sense. That is a straightforward case of time versus space trade-off. For example, in the program of Listing 1.3 (visualization of a spiral) we could have not only precomputed the points of the spiral but also drawn it on a pixmap which would be copied by a single statment in the `show_spiral()` function.

Besides speed, there is another reason for using a pixmap. If we use the exclusive OR mode, whenever a self-intersecting figure is drawn, parts of it are erased. Deletion is likely to happen for the innermost part of the spiral. Theoretically the spiral does not intersect itself, but truncated values may coincide. If the figure is drawn on a pixmap, using the replacement mode, that problem does not occur. Then the pixmap can be copied in the window by using the exclusive OR mode.

5.1.2 Pixmap Manipulation Functions

Pixmaps are created with the function `XCreatePixmap()`, which takes the arguments shown below

```
XCreatePixmap( Display *Dp, Drawable dr, int width,
               int height, int depth)
```

The `Dp`, `width`, and `height` arguments are self-explanatory. The `Drawable` argument may appear strange because we want to create a drawable. The argument is used only to find the refresh memory (`screen`) where the pixmap might be eventually copied and the root window can be used safely for that purpose. The `depth` argument refers to the number of bits per pixel and, again, information from the display structure can be used safely. The following is a typical call to the function.

```
Pixmap pxmp;

pxmp = XCreatePixmap(Dp,  DefaultRootWindow(Dp), width,
    height, DefaultDepth(Dp, DefaultScreen(Dp)) );
```

Because the piece of memory obtained in this way may contain data, it must be cleared first. The following combination does the job.

```
XSetFunction(Dp, gc, GXclear);
XFillRectangle(Dp, pxmp, gc, 0, 0, w, h);
XSetFunction(Dp, gc, GXcopy /* or GXxor, etc */);
```

where `gc` is a graphics context (see next section). The `GXclear` flag causes all locations of the destination to have values of 0. (Normally `XFillRectangle` assigns the foreground values.)

After a pixmap has been created, it can be copied in whole or in part into another pixmap or a window by the function `XCopyArea()`. This function copies a rectangle from one drawable into a rectangle of another and has the following arguments.

```
XCopyArea(Display *Dp, Drawable source, Drawable destination,
    GC gc, int x_source, int y_source,
    int width, int height, int x_dest, int y_dest)
```

The function copies a rectangle of width `width` and height `height` with upper left corner at `x_source, y_source` in drawable `source` into a rectangle with similar dimensions and upper left corner at `x_dest, y_dest` in drawable `destination`.

The decision between drawing directly in a window or on a pixmap, which then is copied to the window, involves a time-space trade-off. If we draw on the pixmap, we use a (possibly) significant piece of memory of the server. But to redraw in response to an expose event we need only send the short X protocol message generated by the `XCopyArea()` function. If we draw directly in a window, we must send X protocol messages corresponding to all drawing instructions each time an expose event occurs.

The Starter Toolkit uses intermediate pixmaps only in two cases: When the amount of data to be drawn is very large (for example, a full picture); and in order to circumvent the problems with exclusive OR mentioned in Section 5.1.1.

5.1.3 Graphics Context

A drawing may contain lines of different color, thickness, and style. (The word *style* refers to whether the line is solid, dashed, dotted, etc.) Similarly, text may be displayed with different sizes of characters and fonts. Passing all these parameters as part of the line drawing or text display routines is not practical because there are so many of them and only a few at a time are pertinent. The X Window System uses a data structure in the server where the values of all such pertinent parameters (more than 20 of them) are stored. It is called the *graphics context*; we described some of its elements in Section 1.4.3.

There is an *Xlib* function that creates a graphics context structure for a given drawable and returns a pointer to a structure that contains an XID number and a cache of the server structure. However, the drawable does not acquire ownership of the structure, so it can also be used with other drawables, *provided all of them correspond to a refresh memory with the same number of bits per pixel as the original.*

The following code fragment illustrates the use of the function.

```
GC gc;
XGCValues  values;
static unsigned long valuemask = GCForeground | GCBackground;
values.foreground = BlackPixel(Dp, DefaultScreenOfDisplay(Dp));
values.background = WhitePixel(Dp, DefaultScreenOfDisplay(Dp));
gc = XCreateGC( Dp, w, valuemask, &values);
```

The structure with type `XGCValues` contains all the graphics context information on the client side. Here, `valuemask` plays the same role as the argument with the same name in the `XChangeWindowAttributes()` we previously discussed in Section 4.4.2. In the preceding example `BlackPixel` and `WhitePixel` yield the values used by the particular server. The preceding code creates a graphics context appropriate for window `w`, with default values for all its members except the foreground and background colors. Instead of returning an XID, `XCreateGC()` returns a pointer to an application structure, whose members include an XID and an `XGCValues` structure. The type `GC` is a pointer to an `_XGC` structure. The arrangement is shown in Figure 5.1. The members of the structure contain the same values as the server structure and thus serve as a cache.

Figure 5.1 Arrangement of graphics context between client and server.

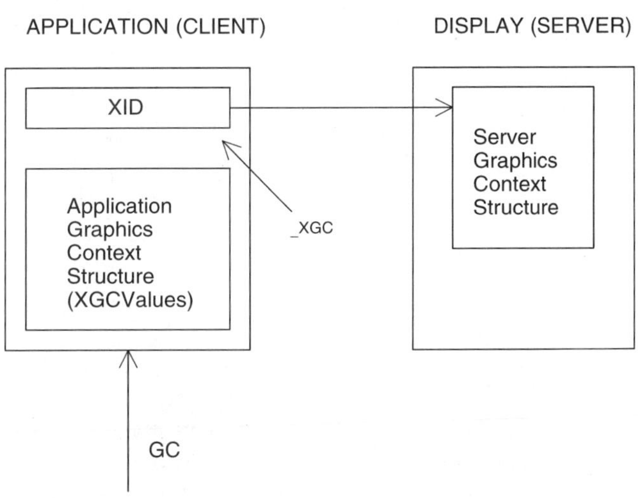

In summary, `XCreateGC()` performs the following tasks: (a) It creates (silently) the `_XGC` type structure; (b) it copies the appropriate values; (c) it sends the structure values to the server; (d) it receives from the server an XID for the server structure; (e) it stores that XID in a member of the `_XGC` type structure; and (f) it returns a pointer to the latter structure (`gc`).

5.2 FUNCTIONS FOR PLOTS

5.2.1 Drawing Primitives

In Section 1.4.2 we described a set of drawing primitives of the Starter Toolkit. Table 5.1 shows the correspondence between them and *Xlib* functions. The Starter Toolkit functions are not macros because some of them perform error checking for their arguments. In Section 4.1.2 we pointed out that *Xlib* functions have three additional arguments but we did not discuss their nature. The first is a pointer to a `Display` structure denoted `Dpy` in the table. The second argument is a pointer to a `Drawable` where the actual drawing is done. For many applications this is a window identifier (`Window` type) and is denoted `c_window` in the table. The third argument is a graphics context identifier (`GC` type) and is denoted `c_gc`.

Table 5.1: Drawing Function Correspondence

Starter Toolkit	Xlib
`put_line(x1, y1, x2, y2)`	`XDrawLine(Dpy, c_window, c_gc, x1, y1, x2, y2)`
`put_rectangle(x, y, w, h)`	`XDrawRectangle(Dpy, c_window, c_gc, x, y, w, h)`
`fill_rectangle(x, y, w, h)`	`XFillRectangle(Dpy, c_window, c_gc, x, y, w, h)`
`put_text(text, x, y)`	`XDrawString(Dpy, c_window, c_gc, x, y, text, strlen(text) )`
`clear_screen(x, y, w, h)`	`XClearArea(Dpy, c_window, x, y, w, h, False)`
`clear_screen(-1)`	`XClearWindow(Dpy, c_window)`

The `put_text()` function also invokes a second *Xlib* function, `XTextWidth()`, which computes the width of the drawn text in pixels. This information is returned to the calling program where it can be used to place additional strings on the screen. The function `XTextWidth()` uses a data structure describing the font used. We discuss it in Section 5.5.

The variables Dpy, c_window, and c_gc are external static variables in the module that contains the drawing functions of the Starter Toolkit. The Starter Toolkit function, set_default_args(), allows another module to set these variables and the function, get_default_args(), reads them. They are shown in Listing 5.1.

Listing 5.1: Xlib Defaults of the Starter Toolkit — File lib/paper_use.c (in part)

```
static Display *Dpy;
static Window c_window;
static GC c_gc;

void set_default_args( Display *d, Window w, GC g)
{
     Dpy      = d;
     c_window  = w;
     c_gc     = g;
}

void get_default_args( Display **dp, Window *wp, GC *gp)
{
     *dp = Dpy;
     *wp = c_window;
     *gp = c_gc;
}
```

You should use get_default_args() when a window has been created with the Starter Toolkit and you want to use *Xlib* functions that are not covered by the Starter Toolkit (see Section 18.1 for examples). The use of set_default_args() requires special caution. You can use it when you want to draw with the simple graphics functions of the Starter Toolkit in a window created by means other than the Starter Toolkit. You should *never* mix it with functions of the Starter Toolkit that create windows, set event handlers, and the like.

5.2.2 Graphics Context Functions

Table 5.2 shows the correspondence between three Starter Toolkit and *Xlib* functions that deal with the graphics context. Three other functions described in Section 1.4.3 use the same *Xlib* function, XChangeGC(), but with different argument values. They are shown in Listing 5.2. Arguments GCLineStyle and GCLineWidth are bit patterns that determine which of the values of the vv structure will be looked at.

Table 5.2: Graphics Context Function Correspondence

Starter Toolkit	Xlib
set_foregr(c)	XSetForeground(Dpy, c_gc, c)
use_xor_mode()	XSetFunction(Dpy, c_gc, GXxor)
use_replace_mode()	XSetFunction(Dpy, c_gc, GXcopy)

Listing 5.2: Graphics Context Functions — `File lib/paper_use.c (part of)`

```
static XGCValues vv;    /* intermediate storage */

void make_dash()
{
     vv.line_style = LineOnOffDash;
     XChangeGC(Dpy, c_gc,  GCLineStyle, &vv);
}

void make_solid()
{
     vv.line_style = LineSolid;
     XChangeGC(Dpy, c_gc, GCLineStyle, &vv);
}


void set_line_width(n)
{
     vv.line_width = n;
     XChangeGC(Dpy, c_gc, GCLineWidth, &vv);
}
```

5.3 COLOR

5.3.1 Colormaps and Color Cells

Handling of colors in the X Window System is a rather complex process because an effort is made to share a unique resource, the video lookup table, among different programs. (Recall that the video lookup table, "hardware colormap," gives the red, green, and blue values for various bit patterns.) We discuss the handling of color in detail in Chapter 22 in connection with the display of full pictures (see Section 1.1.2). Here we deal only with issues that affect displays of only a few colors, namely, those that contain line drawings or flat pictures.

The server maintains "logical colormaps," which are arrays of red, green, and blue values that are loaded in the video lookup table by the window manager under certain conditions. If a program is going to use only a few colors, you should *not create a new colormap* but should instead use colors from the existing *default colormap.*

A general rule of thumb is that new colormaps should be created only when full pictures are to be displayed. All other programs should obtain a colormap XID either from the X Toolkit (see Chapter 22) or through the following code fragment.

```
    Display  *Dpy;
    Colormap cmap;
    /* ... */
    cmap = DefaultColormap(Dpy, DefaultScreen ( Dpy ) );
```

The macro `DefaultColormap()` obtains the information from the `Display` structure.

The basic data structure for dealing with color in the X Window System is `XColor`, which is declared as follows

```
typedef struct {
    unsigned long pixel;
    unsigned short red, green, blue;
    char flags;
    char pad; /* to provide an even number of bytes */
} XColor;
```

The structure corresponds to a *color cell,* which simply is an entry in the colormap to be loaded in the video lookup table. The `pixel` member is the bit pattern and is used as an index into the table. The `red`, `green`, and `blue` members are the color mix associated with it. The member `flags` is used to allow selective resetting of colors. If you want to change all of them, `flags` should have the value `DoRed | DoGreen | DoBlue`.

Two functions can be used to create a colormap entry from an `XColor` structure: `XAllocColor()` and `XStoreColor()`. Both functions have the same argument structure

```
Boolean XAllocColor(Display *Dpy, Colormap cmap,
                    XColor *color_cell_ptr)
Boolean XStoreColor(Display *Dpy, Colormap cmap,
                    XColor *color_cell_ptr)
```

The arguments are self-explanatory, but there is a major difference in the way the `pixel` member of `color_cell_ptr` is treated. The function `XAllocColor()` ignores the `pixel` value given and looks for an existing color cell with the given RGB values. Then it assigns to `pixel` the value from that cell and returns. If it does not find one, it attempts to create a new cell and, if successful, it places in `pixel` the value that corresponds to the first available place. The value assigned by this function must be used for all subsequent references to that particular RGB color. This function also ignores the values of the given flags.

The function `XStoreColor()` creates a color cell with the given pixel value and changes the colors according to the given flags. This function *cannot* be used with the default colormap, and we mention it here only because of its similarity with `XAllocColor()`. The use of `XStoreColor()` is discussed in Chapter 22.

Both functions return `False` (0) if they fail to accomplish their task. Failure usually is the result of lack of space in the colormap.

5.3.2 Using Colors by Name

The X Window System maintains a database of colors so that writing programs with colors described by name is possible. The function `XParseColor()` returns the red, blue, and green values corresponding to the named color from the database. The color names may be composite and contain spaces that are ignored. Most common as well as many uncommon colors are likely to be in the database. However, the database is server dependent, and you should be careful in looking for unusual colors. One server contained colors such as "snow" (RGB values 255, 250, 250), "ghost white" (248, 248, 255), and "olive drab" (107, 142, 35) but not "olive green." The function has the following argument structure.

```
Boolean XParseColor( Display *Dpy, Colormap cmap,
          char * color_name, XColor *color_cell_ptr )
```

Here, the character string `color_name` is the given name and `color_cell_ptr` is a pointer to the structure where the RGB values are copied from the database. If the color cannot be found, the function returns 0. Listing 5.3 shows a first attempt at implementing the function `fore_color()` described in Section 1.4.3.

Listing 5.3: Converting Color Names to Pixels - A — `File lib/paper_use.c (part of)`

```
int fore_color(char *color_name)
{
    Xcolor color_cell;
    XParseColor( Dpy, cmap, color_name, &color_cell );
    XAllocColor( Dpy, cmap, &color_cell)
    set_foregr(color_cell.pixel);    /* Call to Starter Toolkit function */
}
```

This implementation is wrong because it does no error checking. It also is quite inefficient because it checks the color database each time it is invoked. The X Window System provides a function for converting character strings into quantities (integers) that can be compared faster than strings. Converting each color name into such a quantity and saving it in a structure together with the pixel value yields a more efficient program. Listing 5.4 below shows the implementation of the function called `add_named_color()` (see Section 2.6.2) which can then be used to implement `fore_color()` and `back_color()`.

Listing 5.4: Converting Color Names — `File lib/p_fullpix.c (part of)`

```
typedef struct {
     int cv;          /* color value */
     XrmQuark q;        /* color name  */
     } color_pair;

#define MAX_C_N         256
static color_pair cp[MAX_C_N];
static int cpi = 0;

int add_named_color(char *color_name)
{
     XColor color_cell;
     XrmQuark q;
     register i;

     /* return -1 if server does not support color */

     q = XrmStringToQuark(color_name);
     for(i=0; i<cpi; i++) if(cp[i].q == q) return(cp[i].cv);

     if( ! XParseColor(Dpy, cmap, color_name, &color_cell) ) {
          cp[cpi].q = q;     cp[cpi].cv = -1;   cpi++;
          return(-1);
     }
     if( ! XAllocColor(Dpy, cmap, &color_cell) ) {
          cp[cpi].q = q;     cp[cpi].cv = -1;   cpi++;
          return(-1);
     }
     else {
          cp[cpi].q = q;
          cp[cpi].cv = color_cell.pixel;  cpi++;
          return(color_cell.pixel);
     }
}
```

The function `XrmStringToQuark()` converts the color name into a `XrmQuark` (an integer), and the array `cp` is then searched for the same value. If found, the corresponding color value member is returned. If not, the function calls `XParseColor()`. The function always returns a pixel value. A negative value indicates a failure to allocate the color.

5.4 ICONS

5.4.1 Creating Icons

Icons are bitmaps, but the X Window System does not have a separate data type for bitmaps; they simply are pixmaps of depth 1. However, the word `Bitmap` is used in the names of functions, if the result is a pixmap of depth 1. The function `XCreateBitmapFromData()` creates a pixmap of depth 1 where the bit pattern corresponds to that of an icon file created with the `bitmap` program or similar (see Section 3.1.2). It has the following argument structure.

```
Pixmap XCreateBitmapFromData( Display *Dp, Drawable dr,
     char * iconbits, int width, int height )
```

All the arguments except `iconbits` have the same meaning as the arguments for `XCreatePixmap()` (discussed in Section 5.1.2). In particular, the role of `dr` is exactly the same. The member `iconbits` is a pointer to a `char` array where the icon data are stored, as described in Section 3.1.2. If the program contains the statement

```
#include <spacecraft.icon>
```

where the file `spacecraft.icon` is output of the `bitmap` program, then the call should be

```
Pixmap spacecraft_icon;
spacecraft_icon = XCreateBitmapFromData(Dp, window_name,
     spacecraft_bits, spacecraft_width, spacecraft_height);
```

The Starter Toolkit hides these details by having a structure which contains all the relevant information about an icon, as shown in Listing 5.5.1.

Listing 5.5.1: Creation of Icons (Part 1) — `File lib/paper_use.c (part of)`

```
typedef struct Icon_set {
     Pixmap pixels;
     int w, h;
     int cx, cy;
} Icon_set;
```

The coordinates cx and cy are relevant when an icon is used as a cursor (discussed in Section 5.4.2). The Starter Toolkit also maintains an array of such objects and an index to it, as shown in Listing 5.5.2.

Listing 5.5.2: Creation of Icons (Part 2) — File lib/paper_use.c (part of)

```
#define NICON   64
static Icon_set u_icon[NICON];
static int n_icon = 0;
```

The functions make_icon() and draw_icon() introduced in Section 3.2.3 are implemented as shown in Listing 5.5.3.

Listing 5.5.3: Creation of Icons (Part 3) — File lib/paper_use.c (part of)

```
int make_icon(unsigned char iconbits[], int w, int h, int cx, int cy)
{
     if(n_icon>(NICON-1)) return(-1);

     u_icon[n_icon].pixels = XCreateBitmapFromData(Dp,
          c_window, iconbits, w, h);
     u_icon[n_icon].w = w;
     u_icon[n_icon].h = h;
     u_icon[n_icon].cx = cx;
     u_icon[n_icon].cy = cy;
     n_icon++;
     return(n_icon-1);
}

void draw_icon(int k, int x, int y)
{
     if(0<=k && k<NICON)
     XCopyPlane(Dp, u_icon[k].pixels, c_window,
          c_gc, 0, 0, u_icon[k].w, u_icon[k].h, x, y, 1);
}
```

Because spacecraft_icon is a pixmap of depth 1, draw_icon() cannot use the XCopyArea() function. It must use XCopyPlane(), which takes the same arguments as XCopyArea() and an eleventh argument that represents a bit pattern with one bit set to 1. For the present purpose that argument should equal 1.

5.4.2 Creating Cursors from Icons

A cursor is a special icon that is used to mark the position of the point controlled by the mouse. The X Window System has a type `Cursor`, an XID for an object in the server. The function `XCreatePixmapCursor()` returns a cursor XID and builds a cursor image from two icons. One icon has the shape of the cursor (for example, an arrow), and the other is slightly larger and is used to outline it against the rest of the window. This outline is particularly useful when the cursor is displayed against an area of similar color. The function has the following argument structure.

```
Cursor XCreatePixmapCursor( Display *Dp, Pixmap Cursor_icon,
     Pixmap Cursor_mask, XColor *foreground,
     XColor *background, int hx, int hy )
```

Normally, `Cursor_icon` and `Cursor_mask` are created through the `XCreateBitmapFromData()` function, and both must have the same size. In the call to `XCreatePixmapCursor()` there is no need to specify the size because that information is contained in the cursor server structure. Here, `foreground` is a pointer to a structure containing the color of the cursor (see Section 5.3.1) and `background` is a similar pointer for the color of the mask. Members `hx` and `hy` are the coordinates of the *hot spot* of the cursor relative to the upper left corner of the icons, the point whose coordinates are tracked by the mouse.

Creation of a cursor does not necessarily mean that it will be used. It appears on the screen only after a call to `XDefineCursor()`, which has following argument structure.

```
XDefineCursor( Display *Dp, Window w, Cursor cursor_xid)
```

The first two arguments are self-explanatory; the third argument is an XID returned by a call to `XCreatePixmapCursor()`. The third argument may also have the value `None`, in which case the cursor used for the window is the same as the cursor of the parent window.

The Starter Toolkit maintains an array of cursor XIDs and has three functions for cursor manipulation, as shown in Listing 5.6.

Listing 5.6: Creation of Cursors — `File lib/paper_use.c (part of)`

```
/*   Cursor Creation and Use*/
#define BL      512 /* more than enough space for mask bits */

static Cursor u_cursor[NICON];   /* NICON defined in Listing 5.2.2 */
static int n_cursor;

int make_color_cursor(unsigned char iconbits[], int hot_x, int hot_y,
```

```
    char *color, char *mask_color)
{
    XColor Ccursor, Cmask;
    unsigned char maskbits[BL];
    int default_cursor_color = 0, default_mask_color = 0177777;
    static Pixmap Cursor_icon;
    static Pixmap Cursor_mask;

    if(n_cursor > NICON-1) return(-1);

    make_cursor_mask(iconbits, maskbits, 16, 16);
    Cursor_icon = XCreateBitmapFromData(Dp,
        c_window, iconbits, 16, 16);
    Cursor_mask = XCreateBitmapFromData(Dp,
        c_window, maskbits, 16, 16);

    get_color_cell( &Ccursor, color, default_cursor_color);
    get_color_cell( &Cmask, mask_color, default_mask_color);

    u_cursor[n_cursor++] = XCreatePixmapCursor(Dp,
        Cursor_icon, Cursor_mask, &Ccursor, &Cmask, hot_x, hot_y);

    return(n_cursor-1);
}

void active_cursor(int n)
{
    if(n<0 || n>=NICON) XDefineCursor(Dp, can_win, None);
    else XDefineCursor(Dp, c_window, u_cursor[n]);
}

int make_cursor(unsigned char iconbits[], int hx, int hy)
{
    return make_color_cursor(iconbits, hx, hy, "black", "white");
}
```

The function `make_cursor_mask()` automatically creates an icon for the surrounding area of the cursor shape, as described in Section 3.2.2. Both icons are forced to be 16 by 16. The function `get_color_cell()` stores in its first argument the RGB values corresponding to the color name of its second argument. If that cannot be done for some reason, the function stores the value of the third argument in each color location. In the implementation of Listing 5.6, this results in black color for the cursor and white for the mask.

5.5 FONTS

The term *font* denotes a set of bitmaps, usually with character images, that are stored with a header structure. Fonts are found in files whose names indicate the font name and size plus certain suffixes. For example, `timeR10.fb` is the name of the binary file of the 10 point size Times Roman font. The `fonts` directory is usually a subdirectory of the `lib` directory.

Fonts are kept in the display machine (server) and copying them into the application (client) machine is wasteful. Instead, an *Xlib* function extracts an *information structure* that is made available to the application. Such structures are used widely in the X Window System. They describe certain aspects of the server but do not point to any actual server data. (We showed an example of such a structure when we discussed the graphics context.)

The font information structure contains data that can be used to compute the font height and the width of strings of characters. These parameters are essential for laying out text. Listing 5.7.1 shows the functions used by the Starter Toolkit for handling fonts.

Listing 5.7.1: Font Functions (Part 1) — `File lib/paper_use.c (part of)`

```
static XFontStruct *font_info;

/*   Find the font of the graphics context and try to    */
/*   access its information structure. If this is not    */
/*   possible, select the fixed font.           */

static void find_font(GC gc)
{
     XGCValues v;
     XFontStruct *font_info_t;

     XGetGCValues(Dpy, c_gc, GCFont, &v);
     font_info_t = XQueryFont(Dpy, v.font);
     if(!font_info_t) select_font("fixed");
     else  font_info = font_info_t;
}

/*   Select a font by accessing its information structure    */
/*   and assigning to the graphics context.             */

int select_font(char *s)
{
     XFontStruct *font_info_t;
```

```
    font_info_t = XLoadQueryFont(Dpy, s);
    if(font_info_t) {
        font_info = font_info_t;
        XSetFont(Dpy, c_gc, font_info->fid);
        return(1);
    }
    else {
        /* issue error message */
        return(0);
    }
}
```

Both `find_font()` and `select_font()` rely on the *Xlib* function `XLoadQueryFont()` that does two things, if it finds a font:

[1] It loads the font from the off-line storage into the appropriate memory of the *server*. Note that there is no reference to a screen because fonts, once loaded in memory, can be used on any screen.

[2] It stores information about the font in the *client* in a structure of type `XFontStruct` and returns a pointer to that structure.

Note that `find_font()` has been declared as `static`, so it cannot be called from other modules. This function is used only internally. By hiding it, we do not reserve its name. Applications using the Starter Toolkit can call only `select_font()`.

Listing 5.7.2 shows the implementation of the two messenger functions, `get_font_height()` and `fontlength()`, used in earlier chapters.

Listing 5.7.2: Font Functions (Part 2) — `File lib/paper_use.c (part of)`

```
int get_font_height()
{
    if(font_info) return(font_info->ascent + font_info->descent);
    else return(20);
}

int fontlength(char *s)
{
    if(font_info) return( XTextWidth(font_info, s, strlen(s)) );
    else return( strlen(s)*12);
}
```

These functions return the font height and string width, respectively. Both are measured in pixels. If the font information is null, these two functions return reasonable guesses.

The Starter Toolkit does not provide facilities for keeping more than one font. Thus `select_font()` must be called each time a program needs a new font. However, writing code with *Xlib* functions that allow for multiple fonts is easy. We need (1) an array, say, `FIF`, of `XFontStruct` pointers; (2) a variable, say, `cf`, indicating the *current font* that will be an index to that array and will be used by the (modified) functions `get_font_height()` and `fontlength()`; and (3) a function specifying the current font. The function should not only change the value of `cf` but also should invoke the `XSetFont()` function.

5.6 CONCLUSIONS

The programs described in Chapter 4 can be implemented in a simpler way (using the X Toolkit introduced in Chapter 8), but there is no such relief for the drawing functions. You must deal directly with *Xlib*.

In this chapter we covered the basic drawing operations, using the implementation of the Starter Toolkit to illustrate how various *Xlib* functions can be used in application programs. We describe more advanced operations in Chapter 18.

5.7 ASSIGNMENTS

1. Modify Assignment 3 of Chapter 4 by drawing a rectangle (using `XDrawLine()` or `XDrawRectangle()`) on the created window. You must create a graphics context using code similar to that of Section 5.1.3 and then pass that context as argument to the *Xlib* functions that need it. You must also use `XFlush()` for the drawing operations to appear. You will need to insert a `sleep()` statement both before and after the drawing operations. (The first `sleep()` statement guarantees that you draw only after the window manager has completed the mapping of the window.)
2. Repeat Assignment 1 to display on each window a message such as "Greetings from U," where U is the login name of the person executing the program (see Section 1.5.4).

6

Event Handling in the X Window System*

Scope of the Chapter

Dealing with the event queue • the `XEvent` structure • Types of Events: generated by direct user action or by the window manager • Event Selection • Implementation of a simple program for visualization and drawing.

6.1 INTRODUCTION

6.1.1 Checking for Events

An event is a structure placed in a queue in response either to a physical interrupt or the action of some program. The event queue is formed by the server and is polled by the application (client). It is the main way that X applications use to communicate with the users and other applications. The simple program of Listing 4.1 ignores all events and simply sleeps. To make it responsive to user actions we must replace the `sleep(5)` statement with statements that check the event queue. Most event driven programs have the following structure.

* **This chapter may be skipped by those who want to use only the Starter Toolkit.**

```
while(1) {
     /* get an event from the queue */
     /* execute a function depending on the event type */
}
```

Xlib has many functions that examine the queue. Some of them are *blocking*: If the queue is empty, they wait for an event to occur. Others are *nonblocking*: If there is no event in the queue, execution continues. For the simple loop shown, there is no difference. However, certain programs (e.g., the video games of Chapter 3) must perform other calculations while waiting for an event. In those cases you must use an nonblocking function so that the structure of the program becomes:

```
while(1) {
     /* get an event from the queue */
     /* execute a function depending on the event type */
     /* perform other calculations */
}
```

This arrangement has the disadvantage that if more than one event occurs while the program is busy with the calculations, events will pile up in the queue. The following is a better way to structure the program.

```
while(1) {
     while(/*queue is not empty*/) {
          /* get an event from the queue */
          /* execute a function depending on the event type */
     }
     /* perform other calculations */
}
```

Functions that check the event queue include `XNextEvent()`, which is blocking and `XCheckIfEvent()`, which is nonblocking. In addition, the X Toolkit has higher-level functions for manipulating the event queue, and these functions are sufficient for most applications. We describe the use of the X Toolkit functions in Chapters 8 and 9, so we limit the discussion in this chapter to `XNextEvent()`. This function takes two arguments: a pointer to a `Display` structure and a pointer to an `XEvent` structure so that a program using it has the form:

```
XEvent activity;
while(1) {
     XNextEvent(Dp, &activity);
     /* execute a function depending on the event type */
}
```

We describe next the `XEvent` structure and then discuss various responses to events.

6.1.2 The `XEvent` Data Structure

The second argument of the function `XNextEvent()` is a pointer to a data structure that contains all available information about the event. Because events can be quite different, `XEvent` is a union of structures. Here is a partial listing of its definition.

```
typedef union _XEvent {
        int type;
        XAnyEvent xany;
        XButtonEvent xbutton;
        ...
        XExposeEvent xexpose;
        ...
        XKeyEvent xkey;
        ...
        XMotionEvent xmotion;
        ...
} XEvent;
```

The reason for this arrangement is that what is relevant information depends on the type of event. For example, if we strike a key we want to know the corresponding character. However, that information is of no interest if we are tracking the motion of the mouse. Because some information is of interest to many events, information is stored in a "most common first" order.

The first member of all event structures is the integer `type`, which also is a member of the union. That makes possible writing the following code.

```
XEvent activity;
while(1) {
        XNextEvent(Dp, &activity);
        switch(activity.type) {
                /* execute a function depending on the event type */
        }
}
```

This code is guaranteed to be correct because the server always stores the `type` first, regardless of the type of event. Once you know the type, then you can select the appropriate structure for the rest of the information contained in `activity`.

The next four members in all event structures are:

```
        unsigned long serial;
        Bool          send_event;
        Display       *display;
        Window        window;
```

Together with type, they are the members of the XAnyEvent structure. The last two members refer to the display (server) and the window where the event originated. The member serial is the number of the last message sent to the server and it is often used for debugging, and send_event indicates whether the event was produced by another application. Clearly, all such information is meaningful regardless of event type, and it is always contained in the structure. This member of the union is useful for writing a procedure that tries to find from a list the window where the event occurred. The function that does this job takes as argument a pointer to an XAnyEvent type structure, as shown in the following code fragment.

```
window_of_event( window_list, event_pointer)
     Window    window_list[];    /* last entry is 0 */
     XAnyEvent *event_pointer;
{
     register i=0;
     while(window_list[i]){
          if(window_list[i] == event_pointer->window)
                                   return(i);
          i++;
     }
     /* event did not occur in a window on the list */
     return(-1);
}
```

For Expose events there are a few additional pieces of information: the coordinates of the top left corner of the exposed rectangle (x and y) and its dimensions (width and height) and an integer count, whose meaning is discussed in Section 6.2.5. Therefore the organization of the structure appears as in Figure 6.1. Related events (mouse motion and mouse button events) may share additional members.

6.1.3 Analyzing Mouse Events

Once we have found an event type we can use the corresponding structure to extract additional information. For example, if the event taken from the queue corresponds to mouse motion, we use the xmotion member (of type XMotionEvent) of the event structure. It contains a state member indicating which, if any, mouse buttons were pressed during the motion. This procedure may look too complicated, but it has to be. The button indicator refers to an *old* event rather than the current one. The state variable holds previous history. Of course, we can hide such complexity by creating a new structure (e.g., pEvent of the Starter Toolkit) where user actions are described in a more intuitive way.

Figure 6.1 Information layout in the `XEvent` union. The first few individual members of each member of the union are the same. Other members differ, depending on the type of the event.

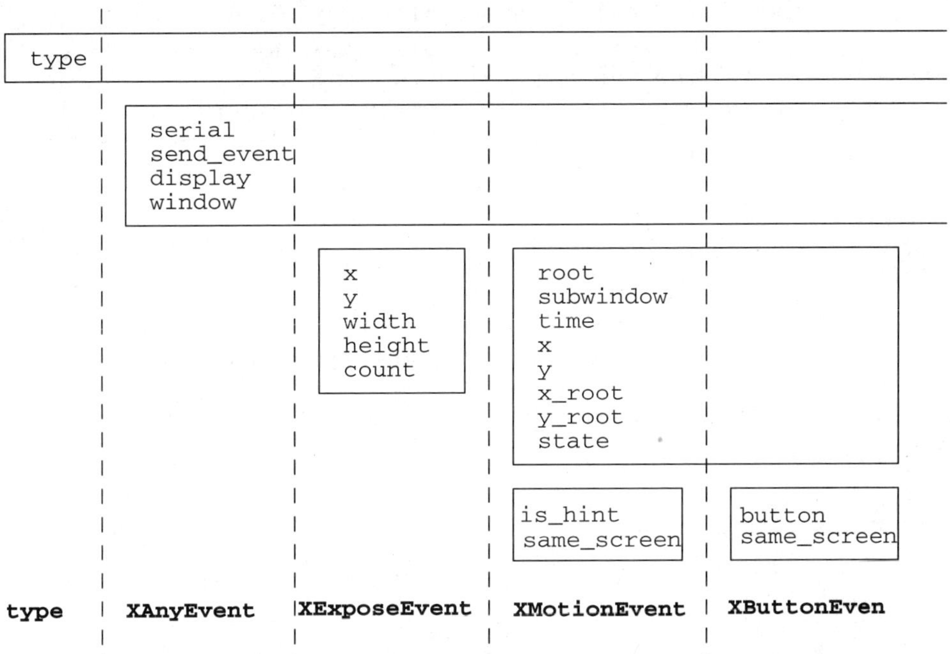

Only one type of event is generated when a button is pressed, and the information about which particular button was pressed is stored in a member of the `xbutton` structure (of type `XButtonEvent`) called `button`. Whereas such a two-step approach was necessary for motion events, here it is a result of a design decision. Related events (pressing a mouse button) were given the same type with details (which particular button was pressed) stored in an "auxiliary" variable (`button`). Such complexity is hidden from the programmer who is using the Starter Toolkit because the `pEvent` structure has three distinct `PRESS` types. We discuss the translation process in Section 6.4.

6.1.4 Input Selection

We can modify the simple program of Listing 4.1 to check for events and exit when the user presses any mouse button. However, if we add only the event loop and compile the program, nothing different happens. The reason is that the server does not place events in the queue unless the application has selected for them. That is done by calling the function `XSelectInput()`, which takes three arguments: `Display` pointer, window (not just any drawable), and a bit mask that selects the events. Listing 6.1 shows the modified program of Listing 4.1.

Listing 6.1: Not Quite the Simplest *Xlib* Program — `File window1.c`

```
#include <X11/Xlib.h>

main()
{
     Display *Dp;
     Window w;
     XEvent activity;

     Dp = XOpenDisplay("");
     w = XCreateSimpleWindow(Dp,  DefaultRootWindow(Dp),
          0, 0, 256, 256, 4, 1, 0);
     XSelectInput(Dp, w, ButtonPressMask);

     XMapWindow(Dp, w);

     while(1) {
          XNextEvent(Dp, &activity);
          if(activity.type==ButtonPress) break;
     }
     XCloseDisplay(Dp);
}
```

Both `ButtonPressMask` and `ButtonPress` are predefined constants. Note also that we have dropped the `XFlush()` statement. Now the function `XNextEvent()` flushes the buffer if the queue is empty, so a separate call is not needed.

This program still has the problem described in Section 4.3.6: When the parent window (installed by the window manager) is destroyed, the program still runs. Because the connection to the server has closed, the call to `XNextEvent()` causes an error with a diagnostic statement similar to

```
XIO: fatal IO error 32 (Broken pipe) on X server ":0.0"
     after 5 requests (2 known processed) with 0 events remaining.
     The connection was probably broken by a server shutdown or KillClient.
```

We need one more fix, which we describe in the next section.

6.1.5 Dealing with Window Manager Events

Note: This section depends on Section 4.4.3 and should be skipped if you also skipped that section.

The remedy for the last remaining problem is to give the window of our simple program the property WM_DELETE_WINDOW discussed in Section 4.4.3 and then provide a response for an event of `ClientMessage` type. The code is given in Listing 6.2. The `data` member of `xclient` is a union, and in this listing we address the beginning of the location, interpreting it as a long integer.

Listing 6.2: The Simplest Well-behaved *Xlib* Program — `File window2.c`

```
#include <X11/Xlib.h>

main()
{
    Display *Dp;
    Window w;
    XEvent activity;
    Atom wm_quit;
    int keep_going = 1;

    Dp = XOpenDisplay("");
    w = XCreateSimpleWindow(Dp,  DefaultRootWindow(Dp),
        0, 0, 256, 256, 4, 1, 0);
    XSelectInput( Dp, w, ButtonPressMask);
    wm_quit = XInternAtom(Dp, "WM_DELETE_WINDOW", False);
    XSetWMProtocols(Dp, w, &wm_quit, 1);
    XMapWindow(Dp, w);

    while(keep_going) {
        XNextEvent(Dp, &activity);
        switch(activity.type) {
        case ClientMessage:
            if(activity.xclient.data.l[0] != wm_quit) continue;
            printf("Exit because of Window Manager action\n");
            keep_going = 0;
            continue;
        case ButtonPress:
            printf("Exit because of user action\n");
            keep_going = 0;
            continue;
        }
    }
    XCloseDisplay(Dp);
}
```

We have made two minor and two major changes in the program of Listing 6.1. We replaced the "if equal" statement with a switch and introduced the auxiliary variable, `keep_going`, because we cannot use `break` to exit from the loop. The major changes — setting the window manager protocol property and handling the `ClientMessage` — are highlighted.

6.2 CATEGORIES OF EVENTS

6.2.1 Overview

The program in Listing 6.2 illustrates two different types of events: those generated by the window manager or the server and those generated directly by the user. It is beyond the scope of this text to discuss all event types (there are about 40). Instead, we focus on events that are particularly relevant for graphics programs.

We say that an event type has been *selected* for a window `w` if the server has been asked to insert in the event queue events of that type when the pointer is within window `w`. Most event types are selected by a call to the *Xlib* function `XSelectInput()`, but for some of the event types generated by the window manager or server the selection is a bit more complicated.

6.2.2 Events Generated by Immediate User Action

Besides `ButtonPress`, symbolic names for events generated by the user include `MotionNotify` (the mouse moved), `KeyPress` (a keyboard key was pressed), `ButtonRelease`, and `KeyRelease`. These events are all selectable through the `XSelectInput()` function with respective masks. Thus the call

```
XSelectInput( Dp, w, ButtonPressMask | PointerMotionMask
     | KeyPressMask );
```

tells the server that, when a mouse button is pressed, the mouse moves, or a key is struck while the pointer is within window `w`, an appropriate event should be inserted in the queue.

6.2.3 Events That Always Are Selected

Some events always are selected. Of interest to us is `ClientMessage`, which we discussed previously, and `MappingNotify`, which is generated when another client does one of the following: (1) changes the codes of one or more of the keyboard modifier keys (SHIFT, CONTROL, etc.) or the encoding of other keys; (2) changes the mapping of the mouse buttons. Normally, the buttons are numbered 1, 2, 3 from left to right but can be changed. Although an unlikely event (it is NOT generated by such actions as capital or numeric lock), it can have drastic effects on the operation of a program. In spite of its name, *it has nothing to do with window mapping.*

6.2.4 Events Selected Through the Graphics Context

Two events cannot be selected by `XSelectInput()`. Instead, they must be selected through the graphics context. These events are `GraphicsExpose` and `NoExpose`. The first is generated when a part of the refresh memory could not be copied onto another, and the second is generated when the copying was successful. Some programs, such as video games, perform the copying operation many times and they can "flood" the event queue with `NoExpose` events. Unfortunately, to select for `GraphicsExpose` but not for `NoExpose` is not possible. Hence we recommend including the following call right after the graphics context is created.

```
XSetGraphicsExposures(Dp, gc, False);
```

6.2.5 Events Generated by the Server or the Window Manager and Selected by `Select_Input()`

The following event types are of particular interest for graphics programs.

The event `Expose` is generated when a window becomes visible and must be redrawn. If we have opted for server backup, such events are not generated (with one exception that we explain shortly). Because a window may be covered by many others, there will be cluster of `Expose` when that window is moved in front of the others. To keep redrawing it is wasteful, so the `XEvent` structure for exposures, `xexpose`, contains a member, `count`, with the number of remaining exposure events for that window. Waiting for that number to become 0 before redrawing is a good idea. The event type is selected with the `ExposureMask`.

The event `ConfigureNotify` is generated when the window moves or it is resized. It is selected with the `StructureNotifyMask`, and information about it is stored in the structure `xconfigure`. When the window is resized it also generates an `Expose` event *unless* we provide a hint about how the old window area should be copied into the new one. This hint is provided by a window attribute called *gravity*. It determines the side and corner toward which the contents gravitate when the window size changes. The following code, which is a modification of the code fragment shown in Section 4.4.2, selects the server backup and also specifies the gravity.

```
if( DoesBackingStore( DefaultScreenOfDisplay( Dp) ) ==
     Always) {
     XSetWindowAttributes attr;
     unsigned long valuemask =
          BackingStore | CWBitGravity;
```

```
        attr.backing_store = Always;
        attr.bit_gravity = NorthWestGravity;
        XChangeWindowAttributes(Dp, w, valuemask, &attr);
    }
```

The attribute NorthWestGravity specifies that the contents should gravitate toward the top left corner of the window.

The events EnterNotify and LeaveNotify are generated when the pointer enters or leaves a window. These events are selected by the masks XEnterWindowMask and XLeaveWindowMask, respectively, and information about them is stored in the XEvent union member xcrossing. Handling these events is complicated because they are generated for all the windows in the hierarchy when the pointer moves from an origin window to a destination window. A member of the xcrossing structure, detail, contains the relevant information. Tracking these events is useful for programs that are to grab a resource when the pointer is inside one of their windows and relinquish it when the pointer leaves. This procedure is not necessary for most simple graphics programs, so we do not discuss these events further. Instead we rely on the window manager to do such resource allocation.

6.3 IMPLEMENTATION OF THE draw_window() PROCEDURE

6.3.1 Structure of the Function

You now have all the tools needed to write a program that implements the function draw_window described in Section 2.2.3. It probably is the simplest *useful* X Window System program for graphics. However, be aware that the *actual* implementation of this function is based on the X Toolkit rather than *Xlib* and has little in common with what is given here. In particular the code that follows *cannot* be linked safely with the Starter Toolkit. Hence we pass a pointer to the full XEvent structure rather than pass a pointer to the reduced structure pEvent.

Recall that draw_window is called with the following arguments: (1) a pointer to a function that redraws the window; (2) a pointer to a function that handles events; (3) the width of the window; (4) the height of the window; and (5) a label for the window.

Clearly, the program has two parts: (a) creation of the window, creation of graphics context, selection of input masks, and mapping of the window; and (b) the loop for checking the event queue. It is a good idea to keep an eye to the future and try to write reusable code. For example, at some point you may want to have more than one drawing window, so the code for creating and initializing the window should be a separate procedure. All operations related to a window could be assigned to one function, but the graphics context should be constructed separately because it is connected to a window only in a very loose way (see Section 5.1.3).

We also removed the variable `keep_going` used in Listing 6.2 for terminating the execution of the program. As exit is now selected from within the function `g()`, we need a policy that all event handlers provided by applications must return 0 for continuing execution and 1 for terminating. This is an unreasonable load for writers of applications (especially beginners), so instead we provide an `own_exit()` function to be called from within event handlers. Listing 6.3 shows the basic arrangement of the `draw_window()` function.

Listing 6.3: The Draw Window Function (Part 1) — `File draw_w.c`

```
#include <X11/Xlib.h>
#include <X11/Xutil.h>
static Display *Dp;
static Window w0;
static GC gc;
extern Window create_canvas();
extern GC     create_gc();

draw_window(void (*f)(), void (*g)(XEvent *), int width, int height, char *s)
{
     XEvent   activity;

     Dp = XOpenDisplay("");
     w0  = create_canvas( (Window)0, width, height, s); /* Listing 6.4 */
     gc = create_gc(w0);                              /* Listing 6.5 */
     XMapWindow(Dp, w0);
     while(1) {
          XNextEvent(Dp, &activity);
          process_event(&activity, f, g);             /* Listing 6.6 */
     }
}

own_exit()
{
     XCloseDisplay(Dp);
     exit(0);
}
```

For simplicity we omitted error checking from the listings. Such code should be added before compiling the program.

The word *canvas* is widely used in windows literature (and not just in the X Window System) to denote a window that is used mainly for drawing. We have given a window XID as first argument to the function `create_canvas()` to allow for future reuse where there may be a parent window containing one or more canvases as well as other windows.

6.3.2 The Function `create_canvas()`

Listing 6.4 contains the function `create_canvas()`, which creates a simple drawing window from fragments of code described earlier in this chapter and in Chapter 4. The only purpose of this code is to demonstrate certain aspects of window creation. It is *not* the real implementation of the function used in `draw_window` in the Starter Toolkit. Comments refer to the listing or section in which the code was first introduced.

Listing 6.4: The Draw Window Function (Part 2) — `File draw_w.c`

```
#define B_WIDTH    1
#define BLACK      1
#define WHITE      0

static Atom wm_quit;

Window create_canvas(Window parent, int width, int height, char *label)
{
      Window w;
      XWMHints wmhints;
      XSetWindowAttributes attr;

      /*  Listing 4.1 and Section 4.3.3     */
/*1*/ w = XCreateSimpleWindow( Dp,
           parent? parent: DefaultRootWindow(Dp),
           0, 0, width, height, B_WIDTH, BLACK, WHITE);

/*2*/ if(!parent) {
           /*  Section 4.4.3 and Listing 6.2    */
           wm_quit = XInternAtom(Dp, "WM_DELETE_WINDOW", False);
           XSetWMProtocols( Dp, w, &wm_quit, 1);
      }

      /*   Sections 6.2.2 and 6.2.5     */
/*3*/ XSelectInput( Dp, w, ExposureMask | StructureNotifyMask |
           ButtonPressMask | PointerMotionMask | KeyPressMask);

      /*   Section 4.4.4 */
/*4*/ wmhints.flags = InputHint; wmhints.input = True;
```

```
    XSetWMHints(Dp, w, &wmhints);

    /*  Used for the first time*/
/*5*/ if(strlen(label)>1) XStoreName(Dp, w, label);
    return(w);
}
```

The function is called with four arguments: the parent, width, height, and label of the window. It does the following:

1. It creates the data structure for the window with the default root window as parent if the first argument was 0.
2. If it is a child of the root window of the display (which means that it will be reparented by the window manager), it is given the property that will allow it to receive client messages. To do so for all windows of an application will be wasteful.
3. It selects the type of events that the server will insert in the input queue.
4. It tells the window manager that, whenever the mouse points to this window, input from the keyboard should generate events to be placed in the queue of this program.
5. It asks the window manager to display the character string `label` in the margin of the inserted parent, but only if the passed string has more than one character.

6.3.3 The Function `create_gc()`

Listing 6.5 contains the function `create_gc()` which creates a graphical context appropriate for drawing windows.

Listing 6.5: The Draw Window Function (Part 3) — `File draw_w.c`

```
GC create_gc(Window w)
{
    XGCValues  values;
    GC  gc;

    /*  Section 5.1.3 */
/*1*/ values.foreground = BLACK;
    values.background = WHITE;
    values.line_width = 0;
    values.line_style = LineSolid;

    /*  Section 5.1.3 */
```

```
/*2*/ gc = XCreateGC( Dp, w,
          ( GCForeground | GCBackground
          | GCLineWidth | GCLineStyle),
          &values);

     /*   Used for the first time*/
/*3*/ XSetFunction(Dp, gc, GXxor);

     /*   Section 6.2.4 */
/*4*/ XSetGraphicsExposures(Dp, gc, False);
     return(gc);
}
```

The function does the following:

1. It assigns to members of the `values` structure values for the foreground, background, width of line segments, and style of line segments. Width 0 is interpreted as 1 pixel width.
2. It creates a graphics context that is appropriate for window `w` but can also be used for other windows.
3. It sets the drawing mode to exclusive OR. The *Xlib* function `XSetFunction()` sets the mode according to its third argument.
4. It asks the server to ignore events generated during copying of one part of the refresh memory onto another.

6.3.4 The Function `process_event()`

This function probably is the most important function of the program because it responds to the direct and indirect actions of users. (Again, the real `process_event()` of the Starter Toolkit is different.) It is contained in Listing 6.6.

Listing 6.6: The Draw Window Function (Part 4) — `File draw_w.c`

```
process_event(XEvent *ep, void (*f)(), void (*g)(XEvent *))
{
     switch(ep->type){
/*1*/ case ClientMessage:
          if(ep->xclient.data.l[0] == wm_quit) own_exit();
/*2*/ case Expose:
          if(ep->xexpose.count) return;
          if(f) f();
          return;
/*3*/ case ButtonPress:
```

```
    case MotionNotify:
    case KeyPress:
         if(g) g(ep);
         return;
    }
}
```

The events have been divided into two classes: The first two events are handled within the function, and the last three are passed to the function that was passed as the second argument to `draw_window()`. This division may be followed in other programs as well. The response to some events does not depend on the particular graphics application, but for others it is quite specific to the application.

Listing 6.6 concludes one possible implementation of the function `draw_window()`. We used more than 100 lines of C code for minimal functionality — the program will not do anything interesting until we provide an event handler and/or drawing function. There are simpler ways to create a window with the X Toolkit. However, this program illustrates what must be done in terms of basic graphics operations.

6.4 EVENT TRANSLATION BY THE STARTER TOOLKIT

In order to simplify application programs, the Starter Toolkit copies some members of the `XEvent` structure into the `pEvent` structure defined in Section 2.2.2. Listing 6.7 shows the translation of motion events. (In contrast to the implementation of the previous three sections, the code given here is similar to the actual code of the Starter Toolkit.)

Listing 6.7: An Event Translator — `File lib/paper_use.c (part of)`

```
#include <Starter.h>
/*   XEvent *ep    */
/*   pEvent *p;    */
     case MotionNotify:
          switch(ep->xmotion.state){
          case 0:  p->kind = MOVE; p->key = NULL;
               break;
          case Button1Mask: p->kind = DRAG; p->key = LEFT;
               break;
          case Button2Mask: p->kind = DRAG; p->key = MIDDLE;
               break;
          case Button3Mask: p->kind = DRAG; p->key = RIGHT;
               break;
```

```
        default: p->kind = NULL;
        }
        p->x =  (ep->xmotion).x;
        p->y =  (ep->xmotion).y;
        return;
```

When the mouse moves, the event `MotionNotify` is entered into the queue. In many applications we want to distinguish motion occurring with a mouse button pressed from motions without any button being pressed. As the `MotionNotify` event occurs regardless of the status of the button, we must check an element of the event structure, the `xmotion.state`.

In this way the Starter Toolkit has split the pointer motion event into two others: `MOVE` and `DRAG`. However, an inspection of Listing 2.2 reveals that an alternative split, into four events, also is available. For example, `LEFT_DRAG` is the sum of `DRAG` and `LEFT`. Applications programmers have access to either partition by selecting `p->kind` or else the sum of `p->kind` and `p->key` as switch arguments.

Keyboard events require special attention as shown in Listing 6.8. The function `XLookupString` places the codes for one or more struck keys in a buffer and returns the number of keys. The variables `keysym` and `compose` are used for the translations of alphabets other than Latin. Both arguments can be `NULL` if you are not interested in the information. They are provided here for your use in extending the Starter Toolkit for other alphabets, if you so desire.

Listing 6.8: An Event Translator — `File lib/paper_use.c (part of)`

```
#include <Starter.h>
/*   Pertinent Definitions
     static char buffer[KEY_BUF_SZ];
     KeySym keysym;
     XComposeStatus compose;
*/
     case KeyPress:
          p->x =  (ep->xkey).x;
          p->y =  (ep->xkey).y;
          nc = XLookupString(ep, buffer, sizeof(buffer),
               &keysym, &compose);
          if(nc) {
               switch(buffer[0]){
               case '0: p->kind = KEY_RETURN;
               case '
                    return;
               case 127: /*DEL*/
```

```
        case 8: /*BS*/     p->kind = KEY_ERASE;
             return;
        case 033: /*ESC*/ p->kind = ESCAPE;
             return;
        default: if(' '<=buffer[0]&& buffer[0] <='~'  ) {
                    /* 32 to 126 */
                    p->kind = KEY_NORMAL;
                    p->key = buffer[0];
             }
             else p->kind = 0;
             return;
        }
   }
```

A KeyPress is translated into one of four application events. This implementation is based on the assumption that nc equals 1, which normally is the case.

The entire event translation function is shown in Listing 6.9.

Listing 6.9: An Event Translator — File lib/paper_use.c (part of)

```
#include <Starter.h>
#define KEY_BUF_SZ 256

translate_events(XEvent *ep, pEvent *p)
{
    static char buffer[KEY_BUF_SZ];
    KeySym keysym;
    XComposeStatus compose;
    int nc;

    p->kind = NULL;
    switch(ep->type) {
    /*  Include Listing 6.7          */

    case ButtonRelease:
        p->kind = BTN_RELEASE;
        switch((ep->xbutton).button) {
        case 1:  p->key = LEFT;      break;
        case 2:  p->key = MIDDLE; break;
        case 3: p->key = RIGHT; break;
        }
        p->x =  (ep->xbutton).x;
        p->y =  (ep->xbutton).y;
        return;
```

```
    case ButtonPress:
        p->kind = BTN_PRESS;
        switch((ep->xbutton).button) {
        case 1:  p->key = LEFT;      break;
        case 2:  p->key = MIDDLE; break;
        case 3: p->key = RIGHT; break;
        }
        p->x =  (ep->xbutton).x;
        p->y =  (ep->xbutton).y;
        return;

    /*  Include Listing 6.8         */
    }
}
```

The translations of the `ButtonRelease` and `ButtonPress` events are similar to the translation of the `MotionNotify` event. Application programs can choose between one or three event types depending on the switch argument (see Listing 2.2).

6.5 CONCLUSIONS

In this chapter we discussed some of the event types in the X Window System and described some simple programs that created an interface for application programs. A basic system such as the X Window System must provide significant flexibility for event handling. However, if you are dealing with a class of application programs that use only a few types of events, hiding most of them from the applications programmer makes sense.

The functions `draw_window()`, `collect_text()` (described in Section 2.5), and the three initialization functions of Listing 6.6 allow the writing of many display and drawing programs without having to worry about the large range of options available under the X Window System.

This approach can be used for other applications besides the writing of graphics programs. Any class of simple applications is unlikely to involve more than a few events, and many of them could be handled in a uniform way. Thus the organization of the functions shown in Listings 6.6 and 6.9 could be adapted to the needs of other application classes.

This is probably the place to mention one concept commonly used in the X Window System (as well as other window systems): *callbacks*. Operationally, a callback is defined as a function called in response to a particular event. At the programming level of this chapter, a callback is a function called by a particular event. For example, suppose that a toolkit provides callbacks for each of the three mouse buttons. Listing 6.10 shows a possible implementation.

Listing 6.10: Illustration of Callbacks

```
static void *(left_callback)();
static void *(middle_callback)();
static void *(right_callback)();

set_left_callback( void (*f)())
{
     left_callback = f;
}
/* ... */
     case  ButtonPress:
          switch((ep->xbutton).button) {
          case 1:   left_callback();   break;
          case 2:   middle_callback(); break;
          case 3: right_callback();    break;
          }
/* ... */
```

Additional reading on the subject of event handling can be found in the books cited in Section 4.5.

Finally, a warning. In spite of its relative complexity, the implementation of `draw_window()` described in Listings 6.3-6.6 is incomplete because it does not satisfy the X Window System *Inter-Client Communication Conventions Manual (ICCCM)*. The manual requires that X Window System programs provide facilities that enable other applications programs to communicate with them. Compliance to the conventions is guaranteed when a program is written using the X Toolkit library (rather than *Xlib*). This is one of the reasons the Starter Toolkit was built using the X Toolkit facilities rather than *Xlib*.

6.6 ASSIGNMENTS

1. Find the file `X.h` that contains the event definitions. Use that information to write a program that prints for each event its symbolic name (e.g., when you press a button, it should print `ButtonPress`).
2. Expand the program of Assignment 1 to print also the contents of the `XEvent` structure.
3. Modify the `draw_window()` function described in Section 6.3 to include a background procedure. To do so you should: (a) add an

argument with the pointer to that background procedure; (b) replace `XNextEvent()` with `XCheckIfEvent()`; and (c) modify the infinite loop of Listing 6.3 as suggested in Section 6.1.1. The new function `XCheckIfEvent()` takes four arguments. The first two are the same as in `XNextEvent()`. The third is a pointer to a function, which for this assignment is trivial, and should return always `True`. The fourth should be the string ``` ``True.'' ```

4. Add events handling capabilities in the programs of Assignment 3 of Chapter 4 and to Assignments 1 and 2 of Chapter 5.

7

Graphical Computing

Scope of the Chapter

Graphics as a means of human-computer communication • Menus, Buttons, and Panels • Programs with more than one window • Facilities of the Starter Toolkit for constructing selection panels • Examples of using panel buttons to select the event handler or to select the values of parameters • Use of pipes for graphic interfaces to existing programs.

7.1 INTRODUCTION

Computer Graphics is not only a means for composing and displaying pictures on a computer. It also offers the possibility of new ways of computing, especially for applications that require a large amount of user interaction. Rather than typing, the user may point to menu items or write on a tablet with a stylus.

Currently, the most popular pointing device is a mouse, because it costs less than a tablet and stylus combination. However, development of touch sensitive screens means that the mouse may disappear someday. Because of this possibility, we also describe alternatives to the mouse when discussing graphical computing.

Touch sensitive screens offer the possibility of replacing not only the mouse but also the keyboard. Indeed, there is a great deal of excitement about computer programs that are supposed to recognize handwriting so users may communicate with their machines in a way similar to writing notes on a piece of paper.

Unfortunately, handwriting recognition by computers leaves much to be desired. And recognition of cursive (free form) handwriting is likely to remain an elusive goal for a long time for the simple reason that *humans themselves have difficulty recognizing cursive handwriting!* Most people can read only the handwriting of people they have known for some time, and some people cannot even read their own handwriting if they look at something they wrote a long time ago.

Communicating with a computer via speech is another method depicted in many science fiction movies. Although making a computer "talk" (speech synthesis) is feasible today, having a computer "listen" (speech recognition) is much more difficult. Currently, systems that recognize a limited vocabulary have been developed but no system can recognize connected speech from *any* speaker. It is beyond the scope of this text to discuss the reasons for the underlying difficulties or the future prospects of such technology.

The recognition of speech or handwriting by computer can be simplified if we insist on stylized input. For example, we may insist that users use only words from a limited vocabulary. In the case of speech such words should be pronounced with a clear pause between them. Letters should be written in "guide" boxes, with the writer following certain rules about the sequence of strokes.

Whereas, machines have trouble recognizing continuous speech or cursive handwriting, there are other ways to cut down on typing. One possibility is a simulated keyboard, whereby users touch a point on the screen to enter a character. Another possibility is to encourage users to write with stylized handprinting. Figure 7.1 shows three different ways of entering text through a touch sensitive screen. In any case, entering text will still be a stylized process, and we assume so in this text. This assumption implies that the primary means of graphical human/computer interaction are through menus. We devote most of this chapter to the creation and use of menus.

7.2 COMPUTING WITH MENUS

7.2.1 What Is a Menu?

There are two fundamental ways for communicating with a computer: through typed *commands* or through *menu selections*. When you use an

Figure 7.1 Examples of entering text through a touch sensitive screen: simulated keyboard (top), cursive handwriting (middle), and stylized handprinting (bottom).

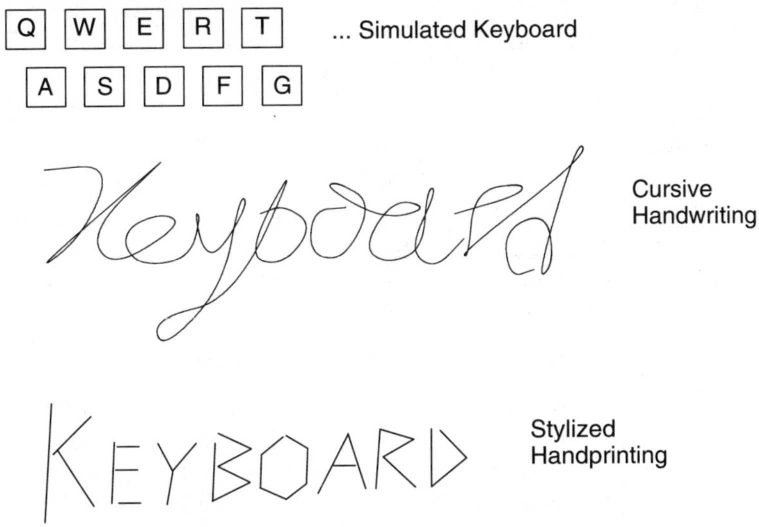

automatic teller machine (ATM) you do both. You type your personal identification number (PIN) and the amount you wish to withdraw. You select the action (e.g., your savings or checking account) by typing a digit from a choice offered by the machine (1 for savings, 2 for checking, and so on). When you dial an airline's 800 number you initially deal only with menu selections. For example, you may hear something like:

> To check estimated arrival times, press 1.
> For domestic reservations or ticket price information, press 2.
> For international reservations or ticket price information, press 3.
> Or, to speak to an agent, press 0.

This example shows the major limitation of menus: the list of choices may not always anticipate all potential selections that a customer may want to make. Therefore an escape mechanism must be provided.

Menus are becoming increasingly popular ways of communicating with a machine. They have the following major advantages.

1. They save typing. (Imagine if you had to type "reservations" through the telephone keys rather than just pressing 1.)
2. They force the user to enter commands that are meaningful to the program.

These advantages tend to overcome the disadvantage of limited choices. That limitation also can be overcome by having an *escape* option in the menu that allows the user some other way to communicate: talking to a human operator as in the airline example, typing a command line, and so on. Distinguishing between the concept of the menu and the way it is implemented is important. The basic idea is:

The user of a program is asked to select one item from a set of choices, exactly as a person orders a meal in a restaurant.

Menus may be implemented in many ways. In the airline and the ATM examples the user is presented with a list of choices and numbers and makes the selection by pressing a number key. When a large computer screen is available the choice may be made by pointing to a particular area of the screen and then pressing a key.

7.2.2 Pointing to an Item on a Computer Screen

Figure 7.2 shows a possible display for an ATM. To make a selection we must have a way to point to the screen surface. If a touch sensitive screen is available, we can use a stylus or a finger and simply press on a point. The touch sensor need not be mechanical. It could also be electromagnetic but the hardware behind the stylus-screen interaction is not of immediate concern for most applications.

Touch sensitive screens are not yet commonplace, and pointing today is done by means of a cursor controlled by a mouse or by a trackball. (Recall Section 1.2.6.) In Figure 7.2 the cursor is an arrow. The user can move it with a mouse and, once it is on the desired area, can press a button of the mouse to make the selection. The cursor also may be moved onto the boxes with the digits to form a number, which is shown in the window at the top of the screen.

7.2.3 Types of Graphical Menus

The layout in Figure 7.2 has the disadvantage of occupying the entire screen and not leaving room for much else. That may be fine for a single purpose computer, such as an ATM, but it is not practical for most other applications. One solution is to use menus that appear on the screen only on demand. The two most common kinds are *pull down* and *pop up* menus.

Pull-Down Menus: A small menu is always on display, usually at the top of the screen. When a user makes a selection, the single item is replaced by a longer menu, which disappears after the selection has been made. In Figure 7.3 the permanent menu has three items: `File`, `Print`, and `Edit`. When `Print` is selected, three new items appear, allowing the user to select the particular printer to be used.

Figure 7.2 A possible touch screen layout for an ATM machine.

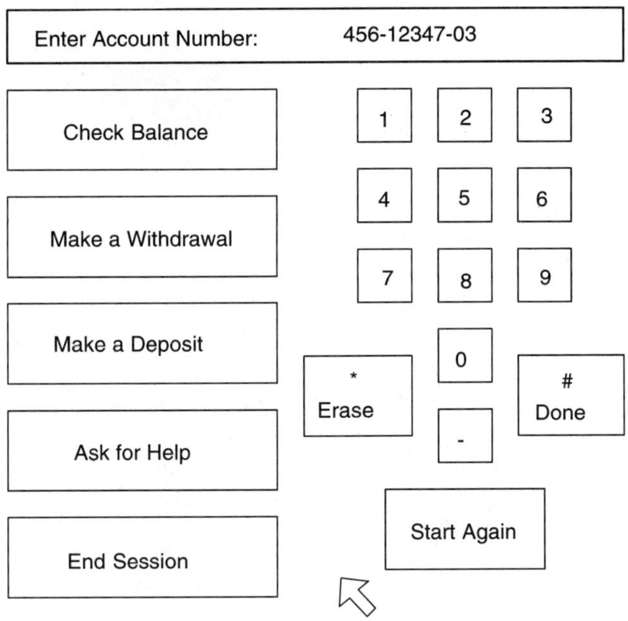

Figure 7.3 Example of pull-down menu.

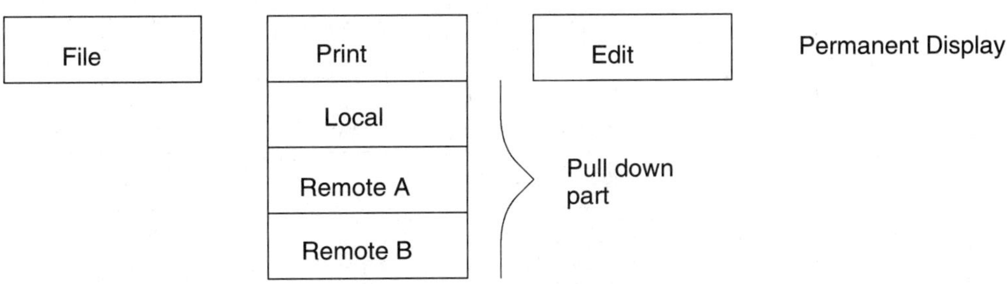

Pop-Up Menus: The menu is always hidden. It appears in response to a particular user action — for example, pressing the right button of the mouse. It stays visible only until the user has made a choice. Sometimes a choice may cause another menu to appear, as shown in Figure 7.4.

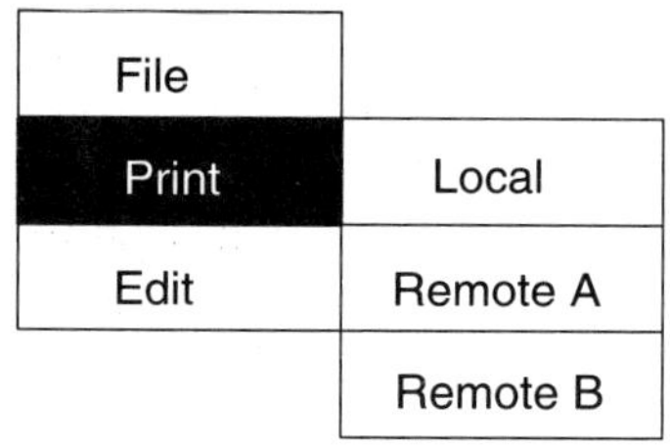

Figure 7.4 Example of pop-up menu.

The use of such temporary menus is so widespread that the term menu often is reserved only for them. An additional type of menu is panels.

Panels: The menus are permanently displayed. There are no limits on the way selection items are presented. The term *button* denotes a specially outlined area marked with the selection. The marking can be a text label or an *icon*. Figure 7.5 shows a panel with text labels, and Figure 7.6 shows the same panel with icons. Note that, although *icons are cute, they also can be puzzling.*

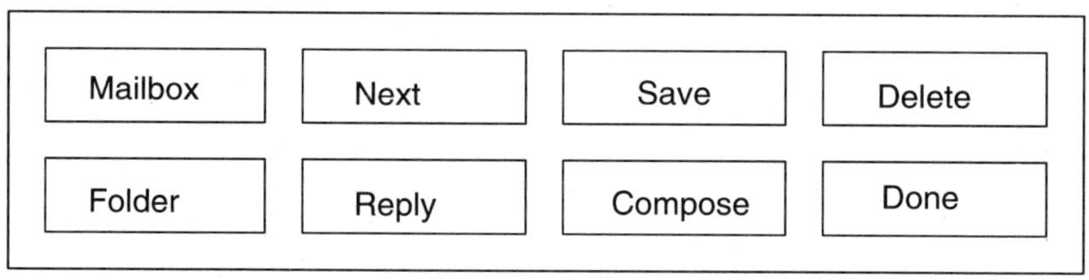

Figure 7.5 Panel with text labels for an electronic mail command.

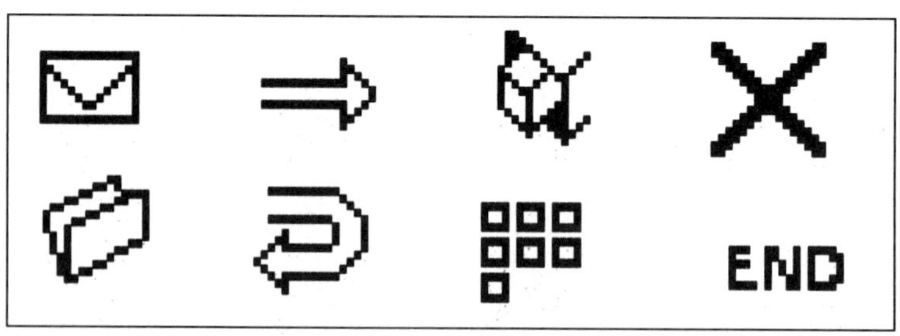

Figure 7.6 Panel with icons for the same command as Figure 7.5.

In the examples and exercises of this text we use panels rather than pop-up or pull-down menus. The main reason is that, with panels, users always have in front of them a list of all possible selections. The disadvantage of occupying a large display area is not so serious in the case of workstations with large screens. Also, panels and pop-up menus can be combined: When users make a selection on the panel, a menu becomes available, enabling them to narrow their selection.

7.2.4 Sliders and Scrollbars

Another way of communicating with a computer is through *sliders*. Menus offer the user a choice of *discrete* options, whereas sliders offer a choice from a *continuous range*. Sliders frequently are used for scrolling windows. Such sliders are called *scrollbars*. Figure 7.7 shows a scrollbar that defines the visible part of a document. The shaded box represents the entire document (text or drawing), which is taller than the window. The scrollbar specifies the portion of the document that will be seen at the top of the window. This correspondence is shown by a dashed line, and, as the size of the window is fixed, it automatically defines the part of the document that will appear at the bottom of the window. In many implementations the scrollbar also shows (shaded part) the relative size of the document that is visible.

Figure 7.7 Example of a Scrollbar.

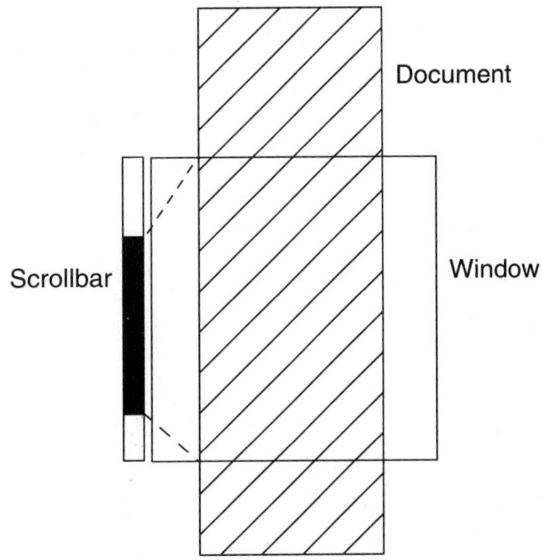

The core of the program for selecting a value from a scrollbar is quite simple. Suppose, for example, that the scrollbar is horizontal and that the two extreme values are `v1` and `v2` displayed at `x1` and `x2`, respectively. Then for a value `x`, from the cursor position, a new value `v` is computed as follows:

```
v = v1 + (x-x1)*(v2-v1)/(x2-x1);
```

7.3 GRAPHICAL MENU PROGRAMS

7.3.1 Overview

Clearly, the creation and use of a menu involves two parts: (1) the geometric layout during creation and the location check during use; and (2) the pairing of labels and actions. Certain areas of the window are marked with a label (it need not be text; it may be an icon) and the program keeps a list of them. The list also contains information linking each area with a function that is executed when an area is selected.

In effect, menu programs are event handlers. When an event that corresponds to selection (e.g., clicking a mouse button) occurs, the location of the pointer (mouse controlled cursor) is compared with all the areas in the list. If the pointer is inside one of the areas, the type of event is examined and a function corresponding to this type is executed. These functions often are called *callback functions* or, simply, *callbacks*. We return to them in Section 7.5. Listing 7.1 shows the first part of such a program.

Listing 7.1: Selection Menu (Part 1)

```
extern check_bal(), withdrawal(), deposit(), help(), restart();

struct ActionMenu {
     int x1, y1, x2, y2;
     char *label;
     int (*fun)();
};

struct ActionMenu choices[] = {
     10,  10, 70,  30, "Check Balance",      check_bal,
     10,  40, 70,  60, "Make a Withdrawal", withdrawal,
     10,  70, 70,  90, "Make a Deposit",     deposit,
     10, 100, 70, 120, "Ask for Help",       help,
     10, 130, 70, 150, "End Session",        restart,
     0
};
```

The structure `ActionMenu` has as members the coordinates of two points that can serve as opposite corners of a rectangle, a label that is placed in the rectangle, and a pointer to a function that is called when the selection point is within the menu area. (We have already discussed such pointers in Section 1.5.1.) An array of such structures, `choices`, is initialized for later use.

The other relevant part of the program is a simple event handler, shown in Listing 7.2. It performs operations similar to those performed by the color selection program of Section 2.6. Indeed, the color palette of that program is a special case of a menu.

Listing 7.2: Selection Menu (Part 2)

```
#include <Starter.h>

void select(pEvent *p)
{
    struct ActionMenu *b;

    if(p->kind != BTN_PRESS) return;

    for(b=choices; b->x1; b++) {
        if(p->x>b->x1 && p->x<b->x2 && p->y>b->y1 && p->y<b->y2) {
            b->fun();
            return;
        }
    }
}
```

The program of Listings 7.1 and 7.2 mixes the menu declarations with the mechanism used for selecting an action. This mixture is undesirable because the mechanism can be used repeatedly for different types of labels and selections. The X Window System as well as most other systems provide libraries that take care of the selection process so that the user has to provide only the label-function pair.

7.3.2 A Starter Toolkit Function for Action Panels

The Starter Toolkit provides a mechanism for creating and using panel menus. Such panels are created as *separate windows*, and selection events are sent directly to them so that the event handlers of the drawing area can ignore them completely. For example, we may want to select the color or line thickness used in the rubber band programs of Listing 2.7 or 2.8. Nothing will change in the event handler. However, because the program now has more than one window, we cannot use the simple function `draw_window()` any longer. Instead, we must use `begin_display()` and the other functions introduced in Section 3.3.1. We show how this is done in Section 7.4.

The Starter Toolkit defines the following structure to be used in creating menus.

```
typedef struct {
     char *label;  /* item label */
     int (*fun)(); /* callback function */
} pAction;
```

It also has a function that has as an argument a pointer to such a structure and a pointer to another function.

☛ **`void setup_a_panel(char *name, pAction a[], void (*rfun)(), char *icdata[])`**

This function sets up a panel with button labels and callbacks as specified by the array `a[]`. The last element of the array must be a structure with a null label. If `a[].fun()` returns a nonzero value for some entry, the panel button pops back up after that entry is selected; otherwise, it stays depressed. The argument `name` is used to identify the class of actions of the panel. The function `rfun`, if provided, is called before each callback. Its purpose is to collect in one place operations that may have to be performed by each selection before proceeding with the particular task. One example of such operations is cleaning up the results of an earlier selection. The array of character strings `icdata[]` is used for setting panels with icons rather than text labels. Each element of the array should be the name of an icon byte array, as described in Section 3.2.1. See Section 7.5.2 for more on this topic. The argument `icdata` can be omitted for panels having only text labels. As only one selection can be made at any one time, the panel behaves like a "radio box." ☜

Listing 7.3 shows a possible menu for the programs of Chapter 2.

Listing 7.3: Very Simple Drawing Program

```
extern paint_pixel, poly_draw(), exit();

p_paint() {
     set_handler(paint_pixel);
}

r_paint() {
     set_handler(poly_draw);
}
```

```
line_thickness1(){
     set_line_width(1);
}

line_thickness2() {
     set_line_width(2);
}

pAction user_actions[] = {
     "Pixel Paint",     p_paint,
     "Rubber Band",     r_paint,
     "Exit",        exit,
     "Thickness 1",     line_thickness1,
     "Thickness 2",     line_thickness2,
0};

/*   other code    */
     setup_a_panel("", user_actions, 0);
/*   other code    */
```

Because there is only one panel and the actions are self-explanatory, we provide no name for this panel.

7.3.3 A Starter Toolkit Function for Value Panels

The code fragment of Listing 7.3 has an obvious weakness. We need to define a series of callback functions for each line thickness, but all they do is call a primitive function with different arguments. In order to avoid this problem, the Starter Toolkit provides for *value* menus that are pairs of labels and integers:

```
typedef struct {
     char *label;  /* item label */
     int value;    /* value returned when selection is made */
} pValue;
```

When a selection is made, a common callback function is invoked with an argument that is the `value` member corresponding to the `label` of the selected button. This type is the most general menu structure because the `value` member can be an index to an array of any type. The function for setting up such menus is:

☛ **`void setup_v_panel(char *name, pValue v[],`**
`int (*cfun)(int), char *icdata[])`

This function sets up a panel with button labels and values as specified by the array `v[]`. The last element of the array must be a structure with a null label. The function `cfun` pointer *always* must be provided, and it is the common callback function. It is called with an argument that is the `value` member corresponding to the selection. If it returns a nonzero value, the panel button pops back up after each selection; otherwise it stays depressed. The argument `name` is a label for the panel. The array of character strings `icdata[]` is used for setting up panels with icons rather than text labels. Each element of the array should be the name of an icon byte array, as described in Section 3.2.1. See Section 7.5.3 for more on this topic. The argument `icdata` can be omitted for panels having only text labels. As only one selection can be made at any one time, the panel behaves like a "radio box." ☜

Note that, although the function argument can be 0 for the function `setup_a_panel()`, the corresponding argument for `setup_v_panel()` is essential because it is the only callback function. As it is the same for all selections, it may include any operations that the function given as an argument to `setup_a_panel()` does. For example, we may want to print a message any time a panel selection is made. For an action panel we can use the function

```
void say_hello() {
     printf("An item was selected from a panel\\n");
}
```

and pass its name as argument

```
     setup_a_panel(a, say_hello);
```

In a value panel `say_hello()` would be called from inside the callback function:

```
common_callback() {
     say_hello();
     /* ... */
}
     /* ... */
     setup_v_panel("Title", v, common_callback);
```

We can eliminate the last two entries of the array `user_actions` in Listing 7.3 (Section 7.3.2) and instead create a value panel with more choices:

```
pValue user_choices[] = {
     "1", 1,
     "2", 2,
     "4", 4,
     "8", 8,
0};
```

```
void line_thickness(nv)
{
     set_line_width(nv);
}

/*   other code    */
     setup_v_panel("Line Thickness", user_choices, line_thickness);
/*   other code    */
```

Figure 7.8 shows the appearance of the two panels of this example.

Figure 7.8 Two panels created by calls to `setup_a_panel()` and `setup_v_panel()`.

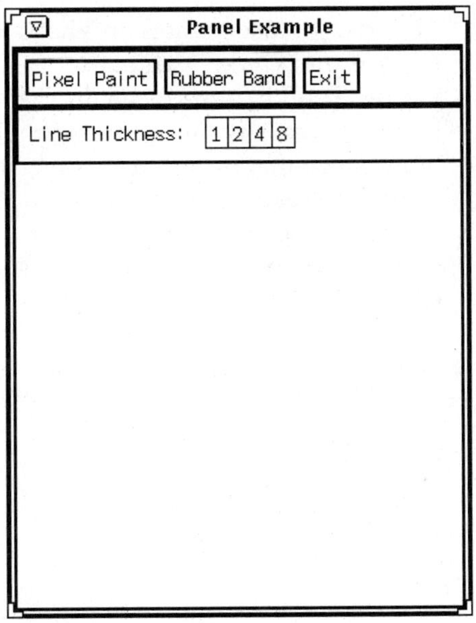

Note that value menus offer more flexibility than a slider. A slider assumes contiguous values — for example the vertical position along a window. However, in many applications we may want to select from values that have gaps between them or that are not even numeric. For example we can use a value menu to specify the style of a line in the following manner:

```
pValue user_choices[] = {
     "solid",  1,
     "dashed", 2,
0};

void set_style(n)
```

```
{
     switch(n){
     case 1: make_solid(); break;
     case 2: make_dash(); break;
     }
}
```

7.4 CREATING AND USING PANELS

7.4.1 A Simple Program Using Panels

In order to use panels in the painting program of Chapter 2 we must replace the `draw_window()` function with the group of functions of the Starter Toolkit introduced in Section 3.3.1. We must start with a call to `begin_display()` and then invoke the panel setup functions. These functions compute the layout and build the necessary data structures but do not actually create any windows. Windows are created by the function `complete_display()`. To write such a program we must include the structures shown in Listing 7.4. The main program takes the form shown in Listing 7.5.

Listing 7.4: Structures for Selection Panels — `File include/Starter.h (part of)`

```
typedef struct {
     char *label;  /* item label */
     int (*fun)(); /* callback function */
} pAction;

typedef struct {
     char *label;  /* item label */
     int value;    /* value returned when selection is made */
} pValue;
```

Listing 7.5: Simple Drawing Program — `File quick_draw.c`

```
#include <Starter.h>

extern void paint_pixel(), poly_draw();
extern exit();

p_paint() {
     set_handler(paint_pixel);
```

```
    return(0);
}

r_paint() {
    set_handler(poly_draw);
    return(0);
}

pAction user_actions[] = {
    "Pixel Paint",     p_paint,
    "Rubber Band",     r_paint,
    "Exit",        exit,
0};

pValue user_choices[] = {
    "1", 1,
    "2", 2,
    "4", 4,
    "8", 8,
0};

line_thickness(nv){
    set_line_width(nv);
    return(0);
}

void paint_pixel(pEvent *p)
{
    /* From Listing 2.6  or similar */
}

void poly_draw(pEvent *p)
{
    /* From Listing 2.7  or similar */
}


main()
{
    begin_display(300, 300, "Drawing Program");
    setup_a_panel("", user_actions, 0);
    setup_v_panel("Line Thickness: ", user_choices, line_thickness);
    complete_display();
    wait_for_event();
}
```

The Starter Toolkit imposes a window arrangement: Panels and the drawing window are stacked vertically, in the order in which they are created. Because the drawing window is created last (by the call to the function `complete_display()`), it will be placed at the bottom, as shown in Figure 7.8. We can place the drawing window in any location by using the following function of the Starter Toolkit.

☛ **void setup_canvas(int width, int height)**
Creates a drawing window of the given dimensions. ☜

The function `complete_display()` will not create a drawing window, if one has been created already. For example, to place the drawing window between the panels we should modify the last part of the code of Listing 7.5 as follows:

```
main()
{
     begin_display(300, 300, "Drawing Program");
     setup_a_panel("", user_actions, 0);
     setup_canvas(400, 300);
     setup_v_panel("Line Thickness: ", user_choices,
                                                 line_thickness);
     complete_display();
     wait_for_event();
}
```

If `setup_canvas()` is called, its arguments take precedence over those of `begin_display()`. Thus in the preceding example the drawing window will have a width of 400 pixels.

7.4.2 Constructing a Value Panel from an Integer Array

Many times either the labels or the values are given and we want to compute the other member of the pair without going through an initialization statement. For example, instead of an array of label-value pairs, we may have only an array of integers representing dollar amounts, such as:

```
int values[] = { 200, 100, 50, 20, 10, 5, 2, 1, -1 };
```

The program of Listing 7.6 creates the `pValue` structure from the integer array. It also creates at the end a cancellation option.

Listing 7.6: Value Panel from an Array

```
struct pValue vchoices[64];

char tmp[16]; /* buffer for value strings */
```

```
for(i=0; values[i]>0; i++) {
     vchoices[i].value = values[i];
     sprintf(tmp,"$%d",values[i]);
     mk_label( &(vchoices[i].label), tmp );
}
vchoices[i].value = 0;
mk_label( &(vchoices[i].label), "cancel" );
i++; vchoices[i] = 0;   /* last element */
```

This code uses a procedure `mk_label()` that allocates memory to a string pointer (its first argument) and then copies its second argument to that memory. Listing 7.7 is one possible implementation and is part of the Starter Toolkit.

Listing 7.7: Construct Label — `File lib/p_util.c (part of)`

```
mk_label(char **s1p, char *s2)
{
     *s1p = (char *)malloc( strlen(s2)+1 );
     strcpy(*s1p, s2);
}
```

The reason we have to use an extra indirection for the first argument is that `mk_label()` does the memory allocation and needs to return the address of the allocated memory.

7.4.3 Computing a Value Panel from a String Array

Sometimes the labels are given first — for example, as arguments to a program. Listing 7.8 shows an example.

Listing 7.8: Value Panel from Strings

```
#include <Starter.h>

void make_value_pairs();

static pValue *vp;

use_arguments(n)
{
     /* what to do with the selected value */
}
```

```
main(int argc,  char **argv)
{

     if(argc<2) exit(1);
     begin_display( ... );
     make_value_pairs(argc-1, argv+1);
     setup_v_panel("Arguments", vp, use_arguments);
     /* other panels */
     complete_display();
     wait_for_event();
}

void make_value_pairs(int n, char ** labels)
{
     register i;

     vp = (pValue *)malloc( (n+1)*sizeof(pValue) );
     for(i=0; i<n; i++) {
          (vp+i)->value = i+1;
          mk_label( &( (vp+i)->label ), labels[i] );
     }
     (vp+i+1)->label = 0;
}
```

We use this function in Section 7.7.1 in a complete example.

7.5 PIXEL PAINTING REVISITED

We can enhance the painting programs discussed in Chapter 2 by adding panels for color selections, ways to save files, and the like. This task gives us the opportunity to discuss various types of panels and how to use the Starter Toolkit to implement them. For simplicity we consider pixel painting only without drawing lines. In Chapter 14 we discuss more general drawing programs.

7.5.1 Panels for Color

We can use an array of color names to create directly a panel that provides for color selection. The Starter Toolkit has a function that fills the second members of the `pValue` structure without going through the creation of a panel. Its specification is:

- **void add_colors_by_name(pValue clist[])**
Only the labels of the value pair list need be initialized, and each name must be preceded by a "-" (for example `-white`). Then the function `add_named_color()` is called for each named color (after skipping the first character) and the returned value is stored in the corresponding value member of the structure. If the value returned by `add_named_color()` is negative, the value of the previous entry is copied except for the first element when the value is set to 0. The function returns when a 0 label is found in `clist[]`.

Because of the way `add_colors_by_name()` operates, we need to (a) start with a common color that is certain to be found in the database and the default colormap; and (b) list less common colors (e.g., olive green) after a similar color. Thus, if they cannot be found in the data base, they will be replaced by a similar color. This function, shown in Listing 7.9, may be modified if you so desire.

Listing 7.9: Color List — `File lib/p_util.c`

```
#include <Starter.h>

add_colors_by_name(pValue ll[])
{
	pValue *lp;

	for(lp = ll; lp->label; lp++) {
		if(*lp->label != '-') continue;
		lp->value = add_named_color(lp->label+1);
		if(lp->value<0) {
			lp->value = lp>ll? (lp-1)->value: 0;
		}
	}
}
```

Using this function we can create a color palette by starting with a `pValue` array that has arbitrary entries for its second members. First we call `add_colors_by_name()`, which provides correct values for the second members, and then we call `setup_v_panel()`. The two functions that set up panels always check the first character of labels. If it is `-`, they create a button, not with the text of the label, but with a solid area of the named color. Listing 7.10 shows the relevant code.

Listing 7.10: Value Panel from a Color List — `File color.c`

```
/*   Creation of a color palette */
/*   The program does nothing else    */

#include <Starter.h>

static pValue color_labels[] = {
     "-white", 0,
     "-black", 1,
     "-red",   1,
     "-green", 1,
     "-blue",  1,
     "-yellow",     1,
     "-cyan",  1,
     "-purple",     1,
     "-tan",   1,
     0};

extern   set_foregr();

main()
{
     begin_display(400, 400, "Paint Pixels");
     add_colors_by_name(color_labels);
     setup_v_panel("Colors:", color_labels, set_foregr);
     complete_display();
     wait_for_event();
}
```

7.5.2 Panels with Icons

Sometimes labeling a button in a selection panel with an icon rather than with a text label or color is desirable. The Starter Toolkit provides a way of doing so by using the last argument of the functions `setup_a_panel()` and `setup_v_panel()`, as mentioned in Sections 7.3.2 and 7.3.3. The only restriction imposed is that the icons used must be square.

The panel can be either action or value. The labels must start with the '@' character followed by a number indicating the size of the icon. (Spaces between the '@' and the number are allowed but are not necessary.) The last argument (which is a pointer to an array of pointers to character strings) is used to store the addresses of the character bit vectors.

Suppose that we want to create a panel with icons in the files `icon1`, `icon2`, `icon3`, and `icon4`. If they were created with the `bitmap` program, we know that their form will be stored in the character arrays `icon1_bits`, `icon2_bits`, and so on. Then we can set up the panel with the following code fragment.

Listing 7.11: Panel with Icons

```
#include <icon1>
#include <icon2>
#include <icon3>
#include <icon4>

static pValue icon_panel[] = {
    "@ 16",  5,   /* extra space after @ is OK */
    "@16",   6,
    "@24",   7,
    "@32",   8,
    0};

report(int n)
{
    /* callback function for the panel */
}

main()
{
    ...
    char *icons[4];
    ...
    icons[0] = icon1_bits;
    icons[1] = icon2_bits;
    icons[2] = icon3_bits;
    icons[3] = icon4_bits;
    ...
    begin_display( ... );
    ...
    setup_v_panel("Test Panel", icon_panel, report, icons);
    ...
    complete_display();
    ...
}
```

A value panel is used in Listing 7.11. An action panel can be handled in a similar way.

Buttons labeled with text, color, and icons can be mixed. This is possible because the functions of the Starter Toolkit look at the first character of the label to decide about the button type. For example, the function `add_colors_by_name()` does not change the values of entries whose labels do not start with the '-' character. Hence we can call this function safely for a panel with different kinds of buttons.

7.5.3 Varying the Cursor to Match a Panel Selection

For many applications changing the cursor is desirable when a panel selection is made so that the cursor icon reflects the action expected by the user. For example, if a program offers the option of drawing with the mouse or typing, we create two icons, one representing a pencil and the other the word "type," as shown in Figure 7.9. Listings 7.12 and 7.13 show the contents of the two icon files.

Figure 7.9 Left: The icon used for the painting cursor. Right: The icon used for the typing cursor.

Listing 7.12: Pencil Icon — File `pencil.icon`

```
#define pencil_width 16
#define pencil_height 16
static char pencil_bits[] = {
   0x00, 0x00, 0x00, 0x00, 0xe0, 0x03, 0x20, 0x02,
   0x20, 0x02, 0x20, 0x02, 0x20, 0x02, 0x20, 0x02,
   0x20, 0x02, 0x20, 0x02, 0x20, 0x02, 0xe0, 0x03,
   0xc0, 0x01, 0x80, 0x00, 0x00, 0x00, 0x00, 0x00};
```

Listing 7.13: Typing Icon — File `type.icon`

```
#define type_width 16
#define type_height 16
static char type_bits[] = {
   0x00, 0x00, 0x00, 0x00, 0x1f, 0x00, 0x04, 0x00,
   0x04, 0x00, 0xa4, 0xee, 0xa4, 0xaa, 0xa4, 0xea,
   0xa4, 0x2a, 0xe4, 0xee, 0x80, 0x02, 0x80, 0x02,
   0x80, 0x02, 0x60, 0x02, 0x00, 0x00, 0x00, 0x00};
```

Listing 7.14 shows part of a program in which the icons are used to mark the panels and, when a selection is made, are also used for the cursor.

Listing 7.14: Using Icon Panels — `File tpaint.c`

```
#include <Starter.h>

int draw_pixels(), type_text();
extern void paint_pixel(), get_string();

static pAction Actions[] = {
     "@16", draw_pixels,
     "@16", type_text,
     0 };

#include <pencil.icon>
#include <type.icon>

static char * icons[2];
static int pencil_icon;
static int type_icon;

int draw_pixels()
{
     active_cursor(pencil_icon);
     set_handler(paint_pixel);
     return(0);
}

int type_text()
{
     active_cursor(type_icon);
     set_handler(get_string);
     return(0);
}

void paint_pixel(pEvent *p)
{
     /* copy from Listing 2.6 or similar */
}

main()
{
     icons[0] = pencil_bits;
     icons[1] = type_bits;
```

```
    begin_display(600, 600, "Paint and Type");
    setup_a_panel("Medium", Actions, 0, icons);
    complete_display();
    pencil_icon = make_cursor(pencil_bits, 7, 15);
    type_icon = make_cursor(type_bits, 7, 7);
    use_xor_mode();
    wait_for_event();
}
```

Any time we make a panel selection by clicking a mouse button over an icon, the cursor changes to the selected icon as it is moved in the drawing area. (When the cursor is over the panel, its shape is not controlled by the Starter Toolkit.)

7.5.4 A Dialogue Panel

Menu selections can be used for many instructions, but typing information, such as file names, often is necessary. The Starter Toolkit provides a special type of panel for that, which we describe here and give an example of its use.

In contrast to action and option panels that must be created explicitly, the dialogue panel is a *pop-up* window created on demand anytime that the function described next is called. The applications programmer must provide an array of `pAction` structures, say, `ad[]`, to use as an argument to the function `start_dialog()`. When this function is called, the dialogue panel appears and displays a message that is the same as the first label of the array, `ad[0].label`. The underscore character also is displayed, prompting the user for a message. The string typed by the user is used as an argument by `ad[0].fun`, which is then executed. Then the dialogue panel displays `ad[1].label` and so on until a 0 entry is found for a label. Suppose for example that we have the following array of structures.

```
static pAction dialog[] = {
    "Enter file name:",     save_file,
    "Hit Esc/Ret to proceed", end_dialog,
    0 };
```

We can arrange for the `save()` callback function of the painting program to be

```
save()
{
    start_dialog(dialog);
}
```

Then when `Save` is selected from the panel, the dialogue panel appears with the message

```
Enter file name: _
```

After the user types the file name (e.g., `mypicture`) the program makes a call equivalent to `save_file("mypicture")` and then displays the second label in the dialogue panel, which will appear as

```
Enter file name: mypicture
Hit Esc/Ret to proceed _
```

Hitting the ESCAPE or RETURN keys ends the display of the dialogue window. The function called can write a message on the dialogue panel by passing a string to the function `to_dialog()`. For example, if the function `save_file()` contains a statement `to_dialog(''File saved'')`, the dialogue panel displays:

```
Enter file name: mypicture
File saved
Hit Esc/Ret to proceed _
```

The following is the documentation of the three functions that deal with the dialogue panel.

☛ **`void start_dialog(pAction messages[])`**
Cause a dialogue panel to appear and display `messages[0].label` plus an underscore. The user is expected to type a string ending with RETURN or ESCAPE. (Errors can be corrected simply by backspacing.) Then `messages[0].fun()` is called with the typed string as an argument. If `messages[0].fun()` contains any `to_dialog()` calls, their strings are displayed before `messages[1].label` is displayed. The process continues in this way until a 0 label is found. ☜

☛ **`void to_dialog(char *s)`**
Display the string `s` in the dialogue panel. ☜

☛ **`void end_dialog()`**
Erase the dialogue panel and wait for another panel selection. ☜

In contrast to the dialogue boxes of other window systems, the dialogue panel of the Starter Toolkit can handle any number of exchanges (the argument passed to `start_dialog` can have any length). However, the window displayed is rather small, and having more than two or three message exchanges is not a good idea.

7.5.5 Saving a File

The dialogue scenario of Section 7.5.4 has one weakness: The user cannot correct a string after hitting RETURN or ESCAPE. However, a confirmation function can be provided. Listing 7.15 shows a possible implementation of such a feature.

Listing 7.15: Saving a File — `File paint4.c`

```
#include <Starter.h>

static char bf_save[256];
void save_file();

int save_name(char *s)
{
     strcpy(bf_save, s);
}

int confirm(char *s)
{
     if(*s=='y') save_file(bf_save);
     else to_dialog("Data not saved");
}

void save_file(char *s)
{
     static char bf[256];
     int error_code;

     /* Code to access the file whose name is in array
     bf_save, write the data there, and obtain an error code */

     if(!error_code) sprintf(bf, "Data saved in %s", s);
     else sprintf(bf, "Could not save data");
     to_dialog( bf );
}

extern end_dialog();

static pAction dialog[] = {
     "Enter file name:",     save_name,
     "OK? (y/n)",       confirm,
     "Hit Esc/Ret to proceed", end_dialog,
     0 };

void save()
{
     start_dialog(dialog);
}
```

When a user enters a file name, it is not used immediately but is saved in the buffer `bf_save[]`. Then the dialogue panel displays the message `OK?`(y/n) and the function `confirm()` is called with the user's response as an argument. If the first letter of the response is `y`, the function `save_file()` is called; otherwise the message `Data not saved` is displayed and, after the user hits RETURN or ESCAPE, the dialogue ends. The user must again select `Save` to attempt to save the data.

To implement the `save_file()` routine in Listing 7.15, we must decide how to save a picture as a file. What data should be stored on disk? Suppose that we store the values of the matrix `pix[][]`. Is that enough? The answer is *no* because the numbers stored in the elements of this matrix can be translated into the desired colors only through the default colormap on the display (server) used to create the picture. There is no guarantee that the same colors will appear when the program is run on another display (server). Storing the color string (e.g., `yellow`) requires far more space than for storing the numbers (pixel values).

A good to way to preserve color information is to use a slightly more complex mechanism for color than that described in Section 7.5.1. The values of the array with the color names are numbers in increasing order. For example:

```
pValue palette[] = {
     "-white",  0,
     "-black",  1,
     "-brown",  2,
     "-red",    3, /* etc */
```

We also create an integer array, `ColorList[]`, which is filled by statements such as

```
     pValue *lp;

     for(lp=palette; lp->label; lp++) {
          ColorList[lp->value] = add_named_color(lp->label+1);
     }
```

The callback function saves the selected value in a static variable and sets the foreground color indirectly.

```
static int selected_color;
select_color(n)
{
     selected_color = n;
     set_foregr(ColorList[n]);
     /* ... */
}
```

When a pixel is assigned a color we use the statement

```
pix[ ... ] = selected_color;
```

If the pixel matrix has been prepared in this way, we can save `pix[][]` *and* the `palette[]` entries preserving all color information in a portable way. (We should also store other information besides color, such as the dimensions of the picture.)

Plate 3 (color insert) shows an example of pixel painting produced by a program integrating the code described in Chapter 2 and in Sections 7.5.1-7.5.5. (See Assignment 12.)

7.6 VIDEO GAMES REVISITED

Panels offer the possibility to enhance the video games described in Chapter 3 by adding options for specifying game parameters. We can also have selections from a continuous range by using sliders. A set of functions of the Starter Toolkit is useful in this context.

☛ **`void slider(void (*usage)(double), char *label)`**
Create a window with a slider that displays a scale between 0 and 100. Users may select a value by pressing the left mouse button on top of the slider box and then moving the mouse with the button pressed down until the box is in the desired location. When a selection is made, the function `usage()` is called with the selected value as an argument. The value is displayed near the upper left corner of the window, and `label` is displayed near the right side of the window; it is truncated to 14 characters if it is longer than that. There is no way to change the dimensions of the slider. ☜

The slider is useful for controlling such things as the speed of graphins. Figure 7.10 shows two sliders created by the preceding function for a video game. The slider marked `Speed` determines how fast the graphin moves (in this case, it is 46 percent of the maximum). The slider marked `Grasp` determines how far the player icon can be from the target icon and the player still score a hit (in this case, it is 65.67 percent of the maximum). This particular game has been set up to be fair when the two sliders line up. The setting of the illustration is a bit on the easy side because the selected graphin speed is relatively low to the selected grasp of the player.

The following code fragment shows the parts of the game program that must be modified for a slider to control the speed of the graphins.

Figure 7.10 Example of the use of the slider widget prototype.

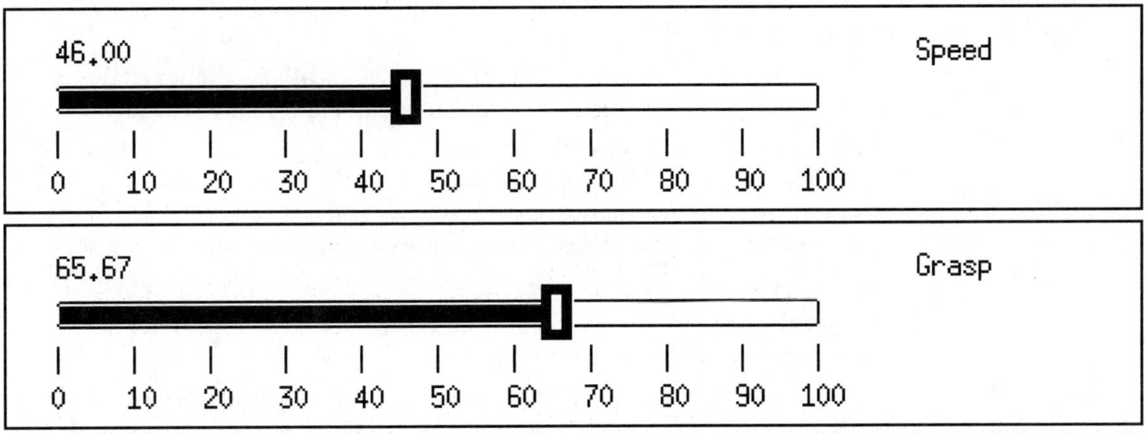


```
#define DELAY 10000
#define FUDGE   100

static int delay = DELAY;
    ...
void set_speed(double x)
{
     delay = DELAY - x*FUDGE;
}
     ...
/* inside the background process */
     idle(delay);
     ...
/* inside main() */
     ...
     slider(set_speed, "Speed");
     ...
```

Normally the slider is black on a white foreground, but other colors can be selected with the following function.

☛ **`void color_slider(void (*usage)(double), char *label, char *fore_color, char *back_color)`**
Create a slider window with background color `back_color` and foreground color `fore_color`. Otherwise the operation is the same as for `slider()`. ☜

There are two other functions that must be called whenever we have a background process (executed between events) and many windows.

☛ **`void grab_draw_area()`**
This function should be called before any graphics operations in a background function (one that is passed as an argument to `add_work()`). To do so is important if the application has more than one window. ☜

☛ **`void release_draw_area()`**
This function should be called after all graphics operations in a background procedure and BEFORE calling `idle()`. ☜

These functions are needed because the drawing functions of the Starter Toolkit (e.g., `put_line()`) do not take a window as an argument. If there is only one window (as in all programs of Chapters 1, 2, and 3), that is not a problem. When there are many windows, the Starter Toolkit draws in the window where the event causing the action has occurred. This method works fine when an output is caused by user action but it fails in the case of a background process. The `grab_draw_area()` function tells the Starter Toolkit to draw in the window where the background process occurs. `release_draw_area()` tells the Starter Toolkit to draw in whatever window it was drawing before `grab_draw_area()` was called.

Calling these functions does not hurt anything, so using them in background processes is a good practice. Note that creation of windows with the Starter Toolkit is a tightly controlled process. There can be only one window whose appearance is controlled by the application or the user. All other windows have a fixed functionality: panels, sliders, dialogue windows, and the like. Programs that need more flexibility must use directly the X Toolkit functions described in Chapters 8 and 9.

7.7 PIPES

The pipe mechanism of Unix is useful for creating graphical user interfaces (GUIs) for existing programs. Although most GUIs require two-way pipes, we first describe the simpler one-way pipes because they also are useful in certain applications.

7.7.1 One-Way Pipes

Many times we would like to direct the output of a program to a graphics display. In Section 1.5.3 we showed how to read a list of numbers and construct a histogram. If `analyze` is the name of the program creating the histogram and `hist_display` is the name of the program displaying the histogram, we can run them together as

```
analyze | hist_display
```

piping the output of the first through the second. That solution is based on the assumption that all the data can be produced and displayed at a pace controlled by the first program. That is not always possible. For example, we may want to plot a diagram of part of the data and later plot additional diagrams in response to user actions.

The Starter Toolkit provides a function that registers a file descriptor with the X Window System so that a program may receive input from that descriptor while also monitoring the event queue.

☛ **`void take_from_file(int fid, int (*fun)(long, int *))`**
Here, `fid` is a file descriptor and `fun` is the function called to read data from the file descriptor when such data become available. ☜

Listing 7.16 shows a program that uses this function.

Listing 7.16: One-Way Pipe — `File one_way.c`

```
#include <stdio.h>
#include <Starter.h>

void read_from_child();/* below */

void graphic_input(pEvent *p)
{
     /* any interactive operations */
}

static FILE *fd;

main()
{
     begin_display(200, 60, "Background Gossip");
     complete_display();
     fd = popen("./gossip", "r");
     take_from_file(fileno(fd), read_from_child);
     set_handler(graphic_input);
     wait_for_event();
}
```

```
#define BFSIZE     32

static int x = 10, y = 20;

void read_from_child(long unused, int *source)
{
     int n;
     static char read_bf[BFSIZE];

     n = read(*source, read_bf, BFSIZE);
     if(n>0) {
          read_bf[n-1] = 0;
          x += put_text(read_bf, x, y);
     }
}
```

This is a trivial program. Whenever a program called `gossip` has any output, it is read and displayed in the window. Listing 7.17 shows such a program. In the meantime the user can interact with the program through the event handler. (It can be any of the routines discussed earlier — for example, one from a pixel painting program.) Note that there is no way for the program of Listing 7.16 to "talk" to the `gossip` program. For that we need a two-way pipe.

Listing 7.17: Program that Provides Input to a Pipe — `File gossip.c`

```
#include <stdio.h>

main()
{
     do{
          printf("Hello\n");
          fflush(stdout);
          sleep(5);
     } while(1);
}
```

The unused first argument in the `read_from_child()` function is necessary because this function is called by other functions of the X Window System that supply the arguments. Therefore we must obey a certain argument discipline. (See Section 9.3.4 for more on this topic.)

7.7.2 Two-Way Pipes

In some applications the user must provide input not only to the display program but also to the program generating the data. For example, we may create a graphical calculator whereby users enter numbers by clicking a mouse button when the cursor is over the number and then have the numbers displayed in a special window. Because many calculator programs are available, we can use one of them rather than write our own number cruncher. The arrangement is shown in Figure 7.11.

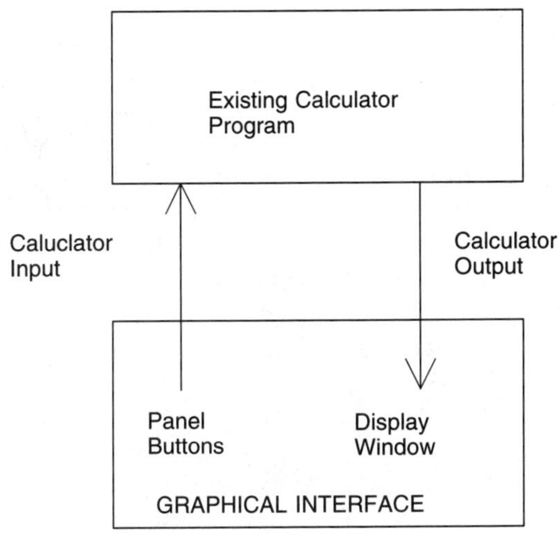

Figure 7.11 Interaction between an existing program and a graphical interface for it.

The Starter Toolkit provides a utility function for such programs.

☛ **`void two_way_pipe(char *cmd, int *to_child_p,`**
`int *from_child_p)`

Start execution of the Unix command `cmd` and return pointers to two file descriptors: `to_child_p` for providing input to the command and `from_child_p` for taking output from the command. ☜

Listings 7.18.1-7.18.3 show the three parts of a sample program.

Listing 7.18.1: Using Two-way Pipes (Part 1) — `File two_way.c`

```
#include <Starter.h>

static   int to_child, from_child;
extern read_from_child();
```

```
void graphic_input();

main()
{
     begin_display(200, 60,"Trial");
     complete_display();

     two_way_pipe("./cap", &to_child, &from_child);
     take_from_file(from_child, read_from_child);
     set_handler(graphic_input);

     wait_for_event();
}
```

The main procedure creates a window and opens a two-way pipe to a program called `cap` in the same directory. Then it informs the system that, when there is input from the child process, it should be processed by the function `read_from_child()`, and, when there are events in the queue, they should be processed by the function `graphic_input()`. Listing 7.18.2 shows these two functions.

Listing 7.18.2: Using Two-way Pipes (Part 2) — `File two_way.c`

```
#define BFSIZE     8

static int x = 10, y = 20;

read_from_child(long client_data, int *source)
{
     int n;
     static char read_bf[BFSIZE];

     n = read(*source, read_bf, BFSIZE);
     if(n>0) {
          read_bf[n-1] = 0;
          x += put_text(read_bf, x, y);
     }
}
```

The arguments of `read_from_child` are specified by the X Window System Toolkit. In this case `client_data` is ignored. The function truncates the string read by one character (dropping the new line ending the string in this case) and displays it.

Listing 7.18.3: Using Two-way Pipes (Part 3) — `File two_way.c`

```
void graphic_input(pEvent *p)
{
	static char bf[BFSIZE];
	if(p->kind==KEY_NORMAL) {
		sprintf(bf, "%c\n",p->key);
		write(to_child, bf, 2);
		bf[1] = 0;
		put_text(bf, x, y+30);
	}
}
```

The event handler is trivial. When the user presses a key other than RETURN, ESCAPE, or any other special key, a new line is appended and the string is sent to the child process while the character is displayed in the screen.

The `cap` program also is trivial. It simply echoes what it receives, but if it is a lowercase letter, it converts that to uppercase. The code is shown in Listing 7.19.

Listing 7.19: Word Capitalization — `File cap.c`

```
#include <stdio.h>

main()
{
	char bf[8];
	while(gets(bf)){
		if('a'<=*bf && *bf<='z') *bf += 'A'-'a';
		puts(bf);
		fflush(stdout);
	}
}
```

The combination acts as a letter translator. An uppercase version of the text typed by the user appears in the line above it. However, the program shows all the elements necessary for a two-way pipe. The "back" program must not buffer its output, which is the reason for the `fflush()` statement in Listing 7.19.

Instead of the event handler, the function "talking" to the child process could be a panel callback function, which is a good solution for a calculator program. Incidentally, the Unix calculator program, `dc`, flushes its output when the user types `p` followed by a new line.

7.8 CONCLUSIONS

The subject of menus and related topics is central to the design of *Graphical User Interfaces* (GUIs). As this text focuses on graphics, our coverage of GUIs is by necessity limited. We described: (a) creation of selection panels from lists supplied by the applications programmer; (b) examples of the use of such panels in a pixel painting program; (c) creation of a dialogue window and an example of its use for saving data from a program into a file; and (d) creation of a window with a slider and its use with a game program. We also discussed how to set up pipes to allow attaching graphical interfaces to existing programs.

The first four topics covered dealt with widgets: windows with a functionality attached to them. We deal with widgets in more depth in Chapters 8 and 9 where we discuss implementation of some of the tools described in this chapter. In those chapters we also describe various toolkits that are available for creating panels with functionality beyond that provided by the Starter Toolkit.

7.9 ASSIGNMENTS

1. Identify a program that uses menus that you encounter in your daily life, e.g. an ATM, or a program that lets you check your bank balance over the phone. Make a diagram of its menus and identify which choices correspond to actions and to selection of a value.
2. Implement the program of Section 7.3.3, using also the code from the assignments of Chapter 2. Add a facility for entering text by creating a panel button labeled "Text." The event handler should be similar to the `get_string` function of the Starter Toolkit (Listing 2.9) that does the following. When the user presses a mouse button, the program prompts with an underscore (_), and the user may then type one or more lines of text. Hitting the ESCAPE key terminates the entry of text.
3. Rather than define the elements of a menu by initializing a structure (as was done in Listing 7.5, for example), write a program to read them from a file. This task is easy for value menus, but you have to be careful with action menus because function pointers have no meaning in a file.
4. Complete the `save_file()` function according to the suggestions of Section 7.5.5.
5. Add a facility to the pixel painting program to read pictures from earlier sessions. In particular, write a function that replaces the values of the pixel array by new values that you obtain from calls to `add_named_color()`.

6. Make the cursor match the menu selection in the pixel painting program. For example, if the button is marked with an icon, that icon should be used by the cursor. If the button displays a color, the cursor should be displayed in that color. (You must create in advance as many cursors as there are colors in the palette.)
7. (a) Add a slider to the game program to control the speed with which the graphins move. (b) Add more sliders for any continuous parameters such as the number used to decide when two graphins are near enough to interact.
8. Add a panel to the game program with buttons to start and stop the game. Also add a button labeled "Help" that suspends the game and displays the documentation of the program instead.
9. Add a panel with buttons labeled with icons, each one representing a character for the player. When a selection is made the cursor icon should match the one on the button.
10. Write a slider program. Your slider will be using the main drawing window, so it cannot be used with a game. Thus the purpose of this assignment is to help you understand the basic graphics operations involved. You should display a ruler and dark square (indicator) on top of the selected value (see Figure 7.12). You need an event handler that relies on a static variable, say, `pick`, and operates as follows. When you press a button (or drag the mouse), the value of `pick` is checked. If it is 0 *and the event occurred near the indicator*, set `pick` to 1. Otherwise erase the indicator and display it in the location of the cursor. (The program acts like a one-dimensional rubber band.) When the button is released the value of `pick` is checked again. If it is 0, the event is ignored. If it is 1, `pick` is set to 0 and the position of the indicator is reported. In this way you achieve the following functionality: When you press the left mouse button near the square, you grab it and can move it along the line as long as you hold the mouse button down. When you release the mouse button, the indicator stops moving and the corresponding value is printed on the screen.
11. Write a two-dimensional slider by which you move a point on the plane against two scales. The basic user interaction is the same as in Assignment 10; only the drawing details change.
12. Integrate the material of Chapter 2 and Section 7.5 to construct a pixel painting program that uses a selection panel for colors, changes the cursor according to the color selection, and uses a dialogue panel to save the file. If the program is called with an argument, the program should interpret it as a file name and attempt to read the file.

8

The X Window System Toolkit*

Intrinsics and Widgets

Scope of the Chapter

Window objects • Associating events with window objects • The X Window System Toolkit: Intrinsics and Widgets • Relationship between the X Toolkit, *Xlib*, and Widget Sets such as *Motif* • Widget Class Hierarchy and Widget Trees • Resources • Callbacks • Event Handlers

8.1 INTRODUCTION

8.1.1 Window Objects

In Chapters 4-6 we discussed various features of the X Toolkit and gave examples of simple programs. All such programs had only one window because we used them to explain the structure of the programs of Chapters

---

* **This chapter may be skipped by those who want to use only the Starter Toolkit.**

1-3 which also had only one window. In contrast, the programs of Chapter 7 contain many windows; besides the drawing window they also have panels and buttons. The Starter Toolkit supports applications with multiple windows, but with certain limitations. For example, it allows for only one drawing window and for only one type of selection panel ("radio boxes").

In this chapter we describe some of the facilities of the X Toolkit for writing applications with multiple windows, using the functions of the Starter Toolkit as case studies. Mixing functions of the Starter Toolkit and the X Toolkit, gradually trading off programming simplicity versus generality, is also possible.

The two primary concerns for multiple window programs are: the *window tree* and the *grouping* of windows with certain parameters and functions associated with them. The window tree describes the relationship of each window with other windows — in particular, which window contains a window `w` (the parent window of `w`) and the windows contained in `w` (the children windows of `w`). The second is the more complex and also the more important of the two. We need to create *objects* that consist of a window and all related functions and information, including the position of the window in the window tree.

We have already introduced a basic concept of *object-oriented programming* in the preceding chapters. The graphins are objects that correspond to a structure that includes not only information about their form (`icon`) and position (`x` and `y`) but also pointers to functions that were used for their display and motion. That simplified considerably the rest of the program. For example, the population motion function (Listing 3.8) had only one statement in the loop

```
mp->move_me( mp );
```

We did not have to check the particular type of motion of each graphin. That is settled during initialization with a statement such as

```
mp->move = simple_move;
```

We could do the same thing with a window. If we created a structure whose members included a function to redraw a window after an `Expose` event, we could simply call a statement such as

```
wp->redraw_me ( wp );
```

or, simply,

```
wp->draw ( wp );
```

Listing 8.1 shows a rudimentary window object.

Listing 8.1: A Simple Window Object

```
typedef struct window_object {
     int       x, y, width, height;
     char      *label;
     Window    win;
     GC        gc;
     int       (*draw)();
     int       (*user_events)();
     struct window_object *parent;
     struct window_object **children;
     int       number_of_children;
} window_object;
```

The structure contains information about the geometry of the window (`x, y, width, height`), a label, the XID of the window (`win`), a graphics context (`gc`), and two function pointers: one for redrawing the window and the other for handling user-generated events (either from the mouse or the keyboard). In addition it includes pointers to similar structures in a tree of such objects that corresponds to the tree of the respective windows.

8.1.2 Creating Window Objects

After we define a `window_object`, the function `draw_window()` (discussed in Section 6.3) appears in a different light. This function creates a window object, but it also monitors the event loop. Hence we may want to separate these two parts because, in a multiwindow application, there may be many window objects but only one event loop. Rather than invoke `f()` and `g()` from the `process_event()` function (as we did in Section 6.3.4) we should make them members of the window object. The `process_event()` function should first identify the window object and then examine the type of event and invoke the appropriate function. Listing 8.2 shows one possible variation of Listing 6.3.

Listing 8.2: Window Object Creation

```
#include <X11/Xlib.h>
#include <X11/Xutil.h>

Display *Dp;  /* only global variable */
window_object *draw_window_object(window_object *parent,
     int (*f)(), int (*g)(), int width, int height,
     char *s)
{
     window_object *wp;
```

```
    wp = (window_object *)malloc(sizeof(window_object));

    if(!parent) Dp = XOpenDisplay("");

    wp->width  = width;
    wp->height = height;
    mk_label(wp->label, s);
    wp->draw = f;
    wp->user_event = g;
    wp->parent = parent;
    *(parent->children++) = wp;

    return   wp;
}
```

We have changed the function name to reflect its new role and have introduced some other changes. With a window tree we must also have a window object tree, so we have added one argument to the function that is a pointer to a parent window object. If it is null, we call `XOpenDisplay()`. The function `mk_label()` allocates sufficient memory to its first argument and then copies on it the string pointed to by the second argument (see Listing 7.7). The rest of the code is self-explanatory.

We have omitted many of the original statements in Listing 6.3 in order to separate the creation of window objects from the creation of windows. Also, the infinite event checking loop will be called after all windows have been created.

8.1.3 Creating Windows

The X Window System clips all children windows to the size of the parent window. To be sure that all windows are displayed, each parent must be big enough to contain its children. Thus if we want to have two drawing windows, each of size 400 by 400 and side by side, we must create a parent of size 800 by 400. We have the following conflict.

A child window cannot be created until its parent window has been created.

The dimensions of a parent window must be determined from the dimensions of its children windows.

The order of operations is

```
layout computation:    buttons -> panel(s) -> top window
window creation:       top window -> panel(s) -> buttons
```

During the layout computation we must create the window objects; their data structure can be used to store information about both the geometry as well as the window tree.

Precomputing all the dimensions in advance is possible. Although easily done for the applications with 3 or 4 windows, it becomes complicated for applications with many windows and complex arrangements. A systematic approach is to include a geometry layout function in the window object and invoke it after all the children objects have been created. Then the object definition becomes that presented in Listing 8.3.

Listing 8.3: Modified Simple Window Object

```
typedef struct window_object {
     int  x, y, width, height;
     char      *label;
     Window    win;
     GC   gc;
     int  (*draw)();
     int  (*user_events)();
     int  (*geometry_layout)();
     struct window_object *parent;
     struct window_object **children;
     int  number_of_children;
} window_object;
```

For purposes of the current discussion we need not be concerned with implementation of the `geometry_layout()` function. We assume that it computes `width` and `height` (as well as `x` and `y`) for all the window objects so that they contain the windows of their children objects. After creating all the window objects we are left with the window object tree. We can traverse this tree by starting at its leaves. After the geometry of a set of siblings that are leaves of the tree has been determined, the `geometry_layout()` of their parent node is called. This fills the `x` and `y` for each of the children and the `width` and `height` of the parent. We repeat the process by going up the tree until we reach the top node. At the end of the process we will have the dimensions of all windows and the position of all windows except the topmost. Its position will be determined by the window manager. Implementation of the tree traversal is simple with the use of the recursive procedure of Listing 8.4.1.

Listing 8.4.1: Creating a Window (Part 1)

```
compute_dimensions(window_object *wp)
{
    register i;

    for(i=0; i<wp->number_of_children; i++)
        compute_dimensions(*(wp->children+i));

    wp->geometry_layout(wp);
}
```

After completing this *bottom up* computation of the geometric layout of the windows, we proceed with the *top down* creation of the windows by calling the `create_canvas()` function of Listing 6.4. (This function already has provisions for creating a window without a parent, which will be the case at its first invocation.) The recursive function for this operation is given in Listing 8.4.2.

Listing 8.4.2: Creating a Window (Part 2)

```
extern Window make_canvas();
extern GC     create_gc();

extern Display *Dp;

create_windows(window_object *wp)
{
    register i;

    wp->win = create_canvas(wp->win, wp->width, wp->height, wp->label);
    XMapWindow(Dp, wp->win);

    for(i=0; i<wp->number_of_children; i++)
        create_windows(*(wp->children+i));
}
```

The top window object of the application is stored in an external variable, say, `top_window_object`, and both of the functions of Listings 8.4.1 and 8.4.2 are called explicitly with that window object as argument.

8.1.4 Processing Events

The recursive functions of Listings 8.4.1 and 8.4.2 suggest a way for modifying the event loop of Listing 6.3. Because `window` is a member of the `XAnyEvent` structure, the implementation of Listing 8.5 is valid.

Listing 8.5: Event-Window Correspondence

```
int dispatch_event(window_object *wp, XEvent *ep)
{
     register i;

     if(wp->win == ep->xany.window) {
          process_event(ep, wp);
          return 1;
     }

     for(i=0; i<wp->number_of_children; i++)
          if( dispatch_event(*(wp->children+i), ep) ) return 1;
     return 0;
}

wait_for_event()
{
     XEvent activity;
     while(1) {
          XNextEvent(Dp, &activity);
          dispatch_event(top_window_object, &activity)
     }
}
```

The `process_event()` function is similar to that of Listing 6.6, with the obvious modifications of replacing `f` and `g` with `wp->draw()` and `wp->user_events()`, respectively. Of course, we pass only `wp` as argument to the function rather than the individual function pointers.

8.2 COMPONENTS OF THE X WINDOW SYSTEM TOOLKIT

8.2.1 Introduction

The object and functions we described in Section 8.1 offer more options than the `draw_window()` function of Section 6.3, but they still are rather limited for general applications. For example, they allow for only two event handling functions, and some applications must deal with a few more — for example, responding to the resizing of a window.

The implementation also is rather wasteful. In particular there is only one type of a window object, which must have enough members for any possible window application. Although a core of members must exist in any window objects (e.g., the dimensions and the XID of the window), others are not necessary in most cases. For example, a window that serves as a panel button need not have any children. Or a panel window that serves as a container for the button windows need not have any user event handling function.

Therefore introducing different types and a hierarchy of window objects is desirable. In addition, generalizations of the functions that create objects and process events also are desirable.

Definition A collection of window objects and functions is called a toolkit.

As mentioned in Section 1.3.3, in addition to *Xlib*, the X Window System provides a toolkit, known as the X Window System Toolkit (often called simply the X Toolkit). This toolkit has two components: a set of window objects, called *widgets*, and a set of functions called the *Intrinsics*. The terminology is somewhat confusing because the X Toolkit has a rather limited set of widgets, which must be augmented for any nontrivial applications. Thus it is often said that the X Toolkit provides a widget framework rather than a widget set. Useful widget sets are built on top of that framework, and well-known examples of such sets include the *Athena*, *Motif* and *OLIT* sets. (*OLIT* stands for OPEN LOOK Intrinsics Toolkit.)

Because the X Toolkit must address a large range of applications, it has a rather complex structure. Therefore we do not deal at all with the internal structure of the widgets and the intrinsics. Essentially they are similar to the window object and the functions defined in Section 8.1.

The C language type `Widget` is defined as a pointer to object structures. Application programs never deal with the structures themselves. Window objects are created with the function `XtCreateManagedWidget()`, which can be thought of as a counterpart of `draw_window_object()` of Listing 8.2. The function `XtRealizeWidget()` subsumes the functions `compute_dimensions()` and `create_windows()` of Listings 8.4.1 and 8.4.2. Finally, there is an `XtDispatchEvent()` function and an `XtMainLoop()`, which is equivalent to `wait_for_event()` of Listing 8.5.

Different types of window objects are called *widget classes*, which follow a class hierarchy explained in Section 8.2.3. Subsequent sections explain other parts of the X Toolkit.

Most programming in X dealing with the creation and manipulation of windows, as well as that dealing with the event queue, is done through the X Toolkit, not through *Xlib*.

8.2.2 Relationship between *Xlib*, Toolkit, Widget Sets, and the Starter Toolkit

The X Window System Toolkit offers a wide range of facilities for creating window-based objects such as menus, panels, and scrollbars, but it provides few facilities for other graphics applications. In particular, applications programmers must still use *Xlib* functions for all drawing operations.

Because the X Window System Toolkit provides only skeletal widgets, an application program must use some *Xlib* functions, some *Xt Intrinsics*, and a widget set, such as *Motif*. Figure 8.1 shows the dependency of application programs on the various libraries.

Figure 8.1 Dependency of application programs on various libraries.

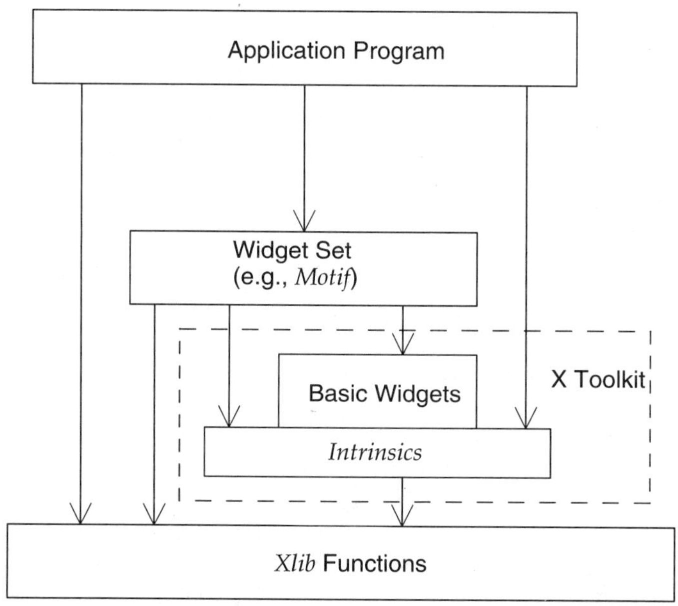

Consider, for example, the pixel painting program of Chapter 7. The functionality expected from the functions `begin_display()` and `setup_a_panel()`, among others, must be provided through a widget set such as *Motif* (middle arrow). The function `wait_for_event()` corresponds to an *Intrinsic* function (right arrow), and all the rest to calls to *Xlib* (left arrow). The statement that "you never have to use *Xlib* if you are using the X Window System Toolkit" is valid only for programs that consist only of menus, selection panels, windows for entering text, and a few other highly stylized windows. It is *not* valid for programs that make wide use of color, draw arbitrary geometric shapes, use a wide range of fonts, or display either scanned or synthesized images — in other words, for most graphics programs.

The Starter Toolkit includes a widget class, `PaperWidgetClass`, specifically designed to support graphics operations by the user. In contrast to most other classes, widgets of this class appear blank until the user draws on them or calls a function that creates a drawing. Various widgets sets include widgets that allow drawing operations, but they still impose some restrictions on applications programmers and the users because their drawing widgets have limited access to the resources of the graphics display. In addition, selecting a drawing widget from a particular set would make the Starter Toolkit depend heavily on a commercial set. The "paper widget" minimizes such dependence.

Most of the functions of the Starter Toolkit are "wrappers" either of *Xlib* or *Intrinsic* functions with a few functions accessing a widget set such as *Motif* so that the relationship is as shown in Figure 8.2.

Figure 8.2 Dependency of the Starter Toolkit and application programs using it on various libraries.

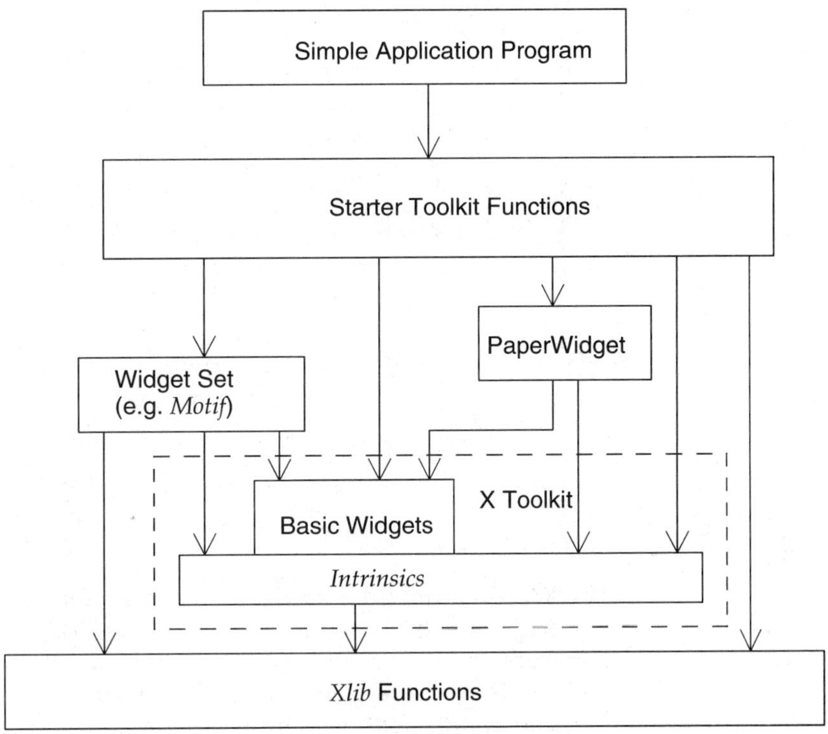

Because the Starter Toolkit is based on the X Toolkit, application programs using it are not limited to it but then access directly other parts of the X Window System if needed. This allows a *gradual migration* from the simple world of the Starter Toolkit to the complete facilities of the X Window System. The relationship is shown in Figure 8.3. The dashed arrows correspond to the extended dependencies.

Figure 8.3 Dependency of complex application program on the Starter Toolkit and various other libraries.

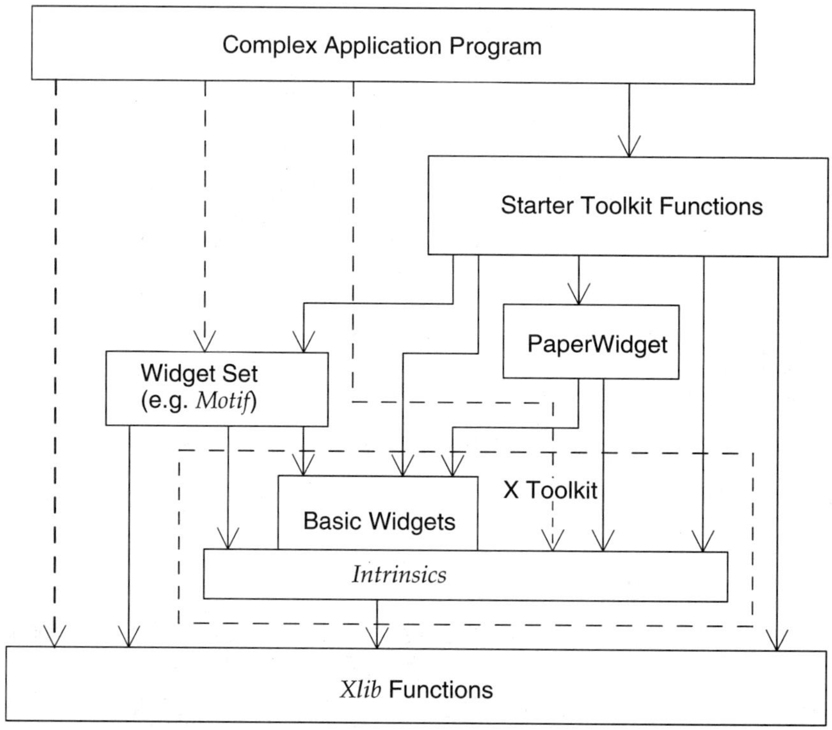

8.2.3 Widget Classes

The X Toolkit provides a *Core* widget class that contains all the information necessary for any widget. Other widget classes are built by adding members to the structure of the core widget. The internal structure of widgets is of interest mainly to widget writers and therefore well beyond the scope of this text, which focuses on graphics applications. Constructing an analogy with the structure of the window object of Listing 8.1 is probably easier. Listing 8.6 shows a core window object.

Listing 8.6: Core Window Object

```
/* Illustration of the Concept. NOT the core widget */

typedef struct core_window_object {
     int x, y, width, height;
     char      *label;
     Window    win;
     GC   gc;
     int  (*draw)();
     int  (*user_events)();
     struct window_object *parent;
} core_window_object;
```

Definition Widget class B is derived from widget class A, or B is a subclass of A, if the structure of B contains all members of A, in addition to other members of its own class.

Thus the X Toolkit has a *Composite* widget class derived from the Core class by adding members that deal with children. In that sense, the window object of Listing 8.1 is a composite window object. According to the preceding definition the Composite class is a *subclass* of the Core class. The term *subclass* seems counter-intuitive because the Composite class has more members than the Core class, but it makes sense in terms of a *class hierarchy*.

Two classes are derived from the Composite class: *Constraint* and *Shell*. Constraint widgets can have many children and have means to control their layouts, somewhat similar to the function `geometry_layout()` of Listing 8.3. Shell widgets can have only one child but they have means for interacting with the window manager. These four classes are some of the *base classes* of the X Toolkit. Figure 8.4 illustrates the relationship between their structures and Figure 8.5 illustrates the hierarchy.

The base classes are incomplete and additional work is needed to construct widget classes that can be used by application programs. This is the point at which systems such as *OLIT* and *Motif* come into play. Such systems provide many widget classes that can be used by application programs. Each widget class has a name that is used to refer to it in application programs — for example, `OblongButtonWidgetClass`. The names are actually pointers to structures (somewhere in the code of the system there is a definition

```
typedef struct ... *        OblongButtonWidgetClass; )
```

Figure 8.4 Relationship among the Core, Composite, Constraint, and Shell class structures.

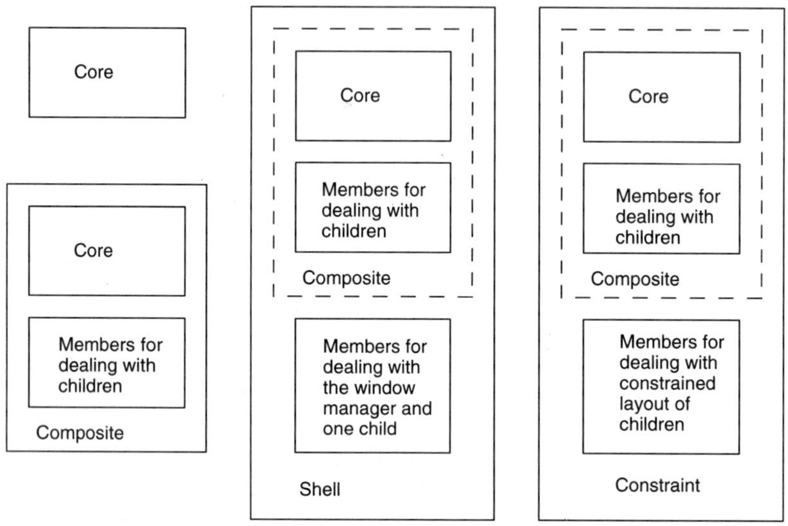

Figure 8.5 The widget class hierarchy for the base classes.

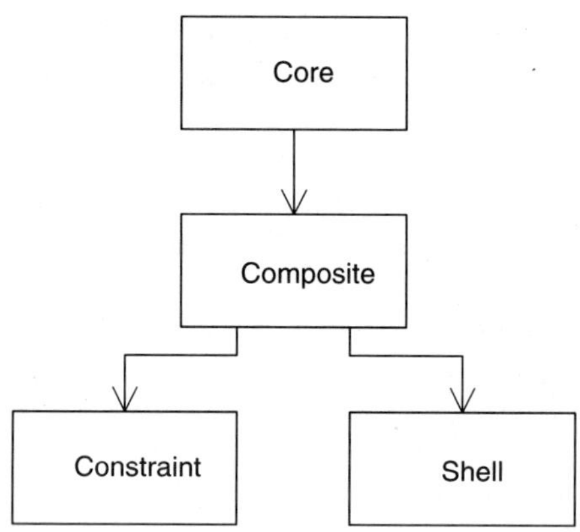

but application programs are not supposed to access the members of the structures directly.

New widget classes can be added any place in the class hierarchy, not just below its lowest members. In particular, both *OLIT* and *Motif* have a *Primitive* class derived directly from the Core widget, which is used as the basis for building childless widgets, mostly various types of buttons. The

Paper widget class of the Starter Toolkit also is a direct subclass of Core. Figure 8.6 shows parts of the class hierarchy for various widget sets.

Figure 8.6
Part of the widget class hierarchy for various toolkits.

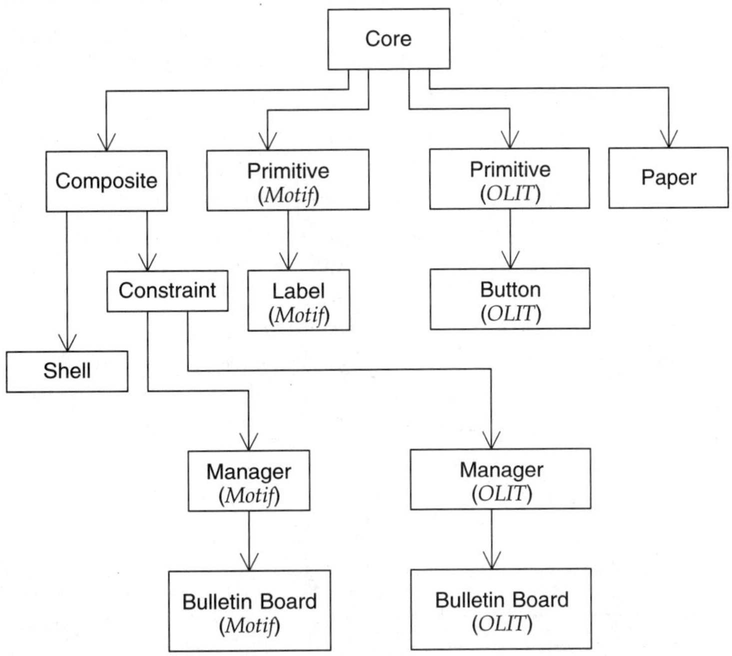

Can widgets from different parts of the hierarchy be used? The answer in general is *no* because of the need to initialize widget structures so that a widget class can be used only if the classes above it in the hierarchy are also used. Because *Motif* and *OLIT* widgets are all descendants of the respective Primitive and Manager classes, they cannot be mixed. However, the Paper widget class is a direct descendant of the core class and therefore can be used with any other widget set.

8.2.4 Widget Class Hierarchy, Widget Tree, and Instances

Do not confuse the class hierarchy with the widget tree of the application. The first describes how classes are derived from one another. The latter describes which window includes another. The distinction becomes clearer if we distinguish between a widget class and an *instance* of a widget.

A widget class is a structure definition such as shown in Listing 8.1. An instance of a widget is a particular object whose type is that of the class.

Thus in Listing 8.2 the variable `wp` points to an instance of the window object. The situation can also be seen from a statement such as

```
int n, m;
```

`int` is a type of variable while `n` and `m` are instances of that variable.

Important Point: *The class hierarchy deals with the classes themselves, whereas the widget tree consists of instances of widgets.*

Figure 8.7 shows the window layout and the widget tree for an application with a selection panel with buttons and a drawing window. The top widget of the widget tree always is a shell widget because it must deal with the window manager. A shell widget can have only one child, so that child must be a composite widget, or, even better, a constraint widget. A constraint widget is preferable because it can manage dynamically the layout of its children. It can have two children: a panel widget (a subclass of Composite) and a drawing widget (which may be a subclass of Core). The panel widget has as many children as buttons.

Figure 8.7 A window layout and the respective widget tree.

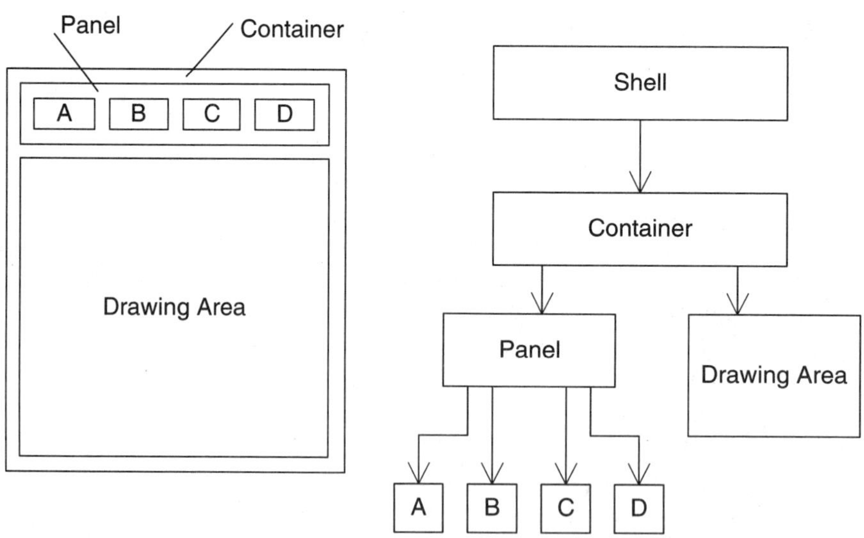

In general, the class hierarchy is primarily of interest to widget writers, and most application programs do not have to deal with it. However, the widget tree is of obvious interest: With one exception, it determines the containment relationship of the windows of an application.

Popup widgets are the exception to the containment rule. The window of a popup widget always is a child of the root window, but the widget itself can be the child of any widget in the tree, including the top shell widgets. (The rule that shell widgets must have only one child does not apply to popup widgets.) We discuss popup widgets in more detail in Section 9.2.

8.2.5 Resources

A major feature of the X Window System in general and the X Toolkit in particular is the concept of a *Resource*. A resource database stores information about the parameters of various widget classes.

Certain members of the widget are defined as resources by associating with them a structure (type `XtResource`) that contains members such as a default value but also a *resource name*. The name is an ASCII string, but it is also defined in a header file by a symbolic name that is used in programs. For example, `XtNwidth` is the symbolic name for widget width, and `XtNheight` is the symbolic name for widget height. To specify that the window of a widget must have width 200 pixels and height 100 pixels we may make the following call.

```
XtVaSetValues(new_widget, XtNwidth, 200, XtNheight, 100, NULL);
```

The function `XtVaSetValues()` takes as arguments a widget and a null terminated list of pairs, the first of which is a resource name and the second a resource value. When `XtVaSetValues()` is called in the preceding example, the resource database of `new_widget` is searched for the name `XtNwidth`. When it is found in a record the value `200` is stored in an address pointed to by another member of the record. That address is the member of the widget that contains the width of the window. This method is more complex than the one used by *Xlib* to define the use of arguments (for the graphics context functions, for example) but also allows for more flexibility.

This arrangement offers flexibility for assigning values to members of widgets. Without resource names we would need special functions for setting them, for example — `SetWidth(new_widget, 200)`.

Probably, the most important feature of the resource database is that it can be kept in a file that is read when a program is run. In this way users (as opposed to program writers) can select values for the various members of the widget. For example, the following entry might be found in the `.Xdefaults` file in the user's home directory.

```
OpenWindows.ScrollbarPlacement: left
```

The string `OpenWindows` refers to the window manager that looks at this file when it creates a new window. `ScrollbarPlacement` is a parameter in that program and the resource assigns it the value `left`.

Alternative ways of specifying parameters include command line arguments, but they can be quite cumbersome for programs with many parameters. In addition the resource file can be modified at any time while the program is running, something that is impossible to do with command line arguments. Placing all parameters in a resource file allows individual users to customize programs to a high degree.

Unfortunately, this approach has some disadvantages. Using a text editor to modify a resource file is an awkward and error-prone way of doing things. Instead, applications programs (or families of application programs) should provide a tool for modifying the resource file. Therefore users must be familiar with two programs rather than one. This requirement probably is reasonable for basic programs such as window managers (where the resource modification program can be invoked from a menu) but less so for infrequently used programs.

The following is a good rule for writers of application programs: *If a program is going to rely on a resource file, the program should include simple means for editing that file.* For example, one of the panel buttons might be labeled "Properties" or "Resources," and selecting it might cause a new panel to appear from which parameter selections may be made.

Another potential problem has to do with software maintenance. When a new version of the program is distributed, a new version of the resource file also must be distributed and installed in the right place. Making sure that the versions of two program are in synchrony is not a problem in an ideal world but it is very much a problem in the real world.

Because this text is aimed at beginners, we will not dwell on resources, except when they are used as arguments to functions. Most programs written in a classroom environment are used only by the person who wrote them, so there is little need to distinguish parameter setting by a user from parameter setting by the programmer.

8.3 CALLBACKS AND EVENT HANDLERS

8.3.1 Introduction

In Chapter 6 we described how to handle events using *Xlib* functions, and in Section 8.1.4 we gave the basic structure of a program for handling events with a window object structure. Application programs are likely to treat various events differently. The response to pressing a button is more likely to be customized than is the response to a window manager event. The Intrinsics contain a basic event handler and provide facilities for application programs to specify their response to selected events.

The simplest interaction is through *callbacks*, which are functions that are called in response to a specific event (e.g., window exposure), as discussed in Section 6.5. If the application is interested in a group of events (e.g., both pressing and releasing mouse buttons), it can specify *event handlers*. In the case of the simple window objects described in Section 8.1, `draw()` is a callback (called in response to an expose event), and `user_events()` is an event handler (called in response to any of a group of events).

The X Toolkit provides a more general mechanism for dealing with such functions. Each widget can have a *list* of callbacks and a *list* of event handlers. The need for such a sequence was demonstrated in Section 2.5. There the function `get_string()` was an event handler that was called first, and `collect_text()` was an event handler that was called second. Although `collect_text()` was called from inside `get_string()`, both can be called from another program.

8.3.2 Callbacks

The following function adds a callback to a widget's callback list.

```
XtAddCallback( Widget w, char * name, (void *)f(),
               XtPointer client_data )
```

The `name` argument is that of a resource corresponding to the callback list of the widget. The resource in turn corresponds to an event. For the reasons discussed in Section 8.2.5 we use a symbolic name for accessing a member of the widget. Argument `f()` is the callback function to be added to the list of `w` identified by `name`. Finally, `client_data` is a pointer to (usually) a structure that will be passed as argument to the callback function.

Callback functions should have the following argument structure.

```
void f( Widget w, XtPointer client_data, XtPointer call_data)
```

The value of `call_data` is supplied by the widget. For the simple graphics applications discussed in this text there usually is no need to examine the arguments.

The X Toolkit contains additional functions to deal with callback lists of which only one is of interest here.

```
XtRemoveAllCallbacks( Widget w, char * name);
```

The use of these functions is illustrated in Listing 8.7, which contains a possible implementation of the `set_redraw()` function. (The actual implementation of the Starter Toolkit function found in the named file is slightly different.)

Listing 8.7: The set_redraw( ) Function — `File lib/paper_mate.c (part of)`

```
static Widget ws;

set_redraw(void (*f)())
{
     XtRemoveAllCallbacks(ws, XtNredrawCallback);
     XtAddCallback(ws, XtNredrawCallback, f, NULL);
}
```

As we mentioned in Section 7.6, the Starter Toolkit identifies a particular widget as the one to which all graphics output is directed. This widget is stored in the variable `ws` and it is the one where the redraw function set by `set_redraw()` is assigned. We discuss this topic further in Section 9.4. Argument `XtNredrawCallback` is the symbolic name for a resource of the Paper widget class. No client data are passed; therefore the fourth argument is `NULL`. Because the Starter Toolkit allows for only a single redrawing function and the X Toolkit keeps a list of them, all the earlier ones must be removed.

8.3.3 Event Handlers

The following function adds an event handler to a widget's list.

```
XtAddEventHandler( Widget w, EventMask event_mask,
   Boolean nonmaskable, (void *)g(), XtPointer client_data )
```

Here, `EventMask` is a type defined by the *Intrinsics* as `unsigned long`, and `event_mask` is a bit pattern similar to that used in Statement 3 of Listing 6.4. Argument `nonmaskable` is set to `True` if the event handler should be called in response to a nonmaskable event (such as those described in Section 6.2.3), `g` is the event handler, and `client_data` is a pointer to user-defined data.

Event handlers are expected to have the following argument structure.

```
void g( Widget w, XtPointer client_data, XEvent *event,
     Boolean * continue_to_dispatch )
```

The first three arguments are self-explanatory; the fourth one is a pointer to flag that is set to `False` if we do not want other event handlers to be called by the *Intrinsics*. As the *Intrinsics* always set it to `True` before calling an event handler, it usually can be ignored.

The Starter Toolkit uses a basic event handler, `own_handler()`, which does the event translation described in Section 6.4 and then calls the user-defined event handler. The latter is passed as client data! The following is the core of the implementation of `set_handler()`.

```
set_handler(void (*g)())
{
     XtAddEventHandler(ws,
     ButtonReleaseMask | ButtonPressMask | KeyPressMask |
     PointerMotionMask | EnterWindowMask | LeaveWindowMask,
     False, own_handler, g);
}
```

Widget `ws` is where the Starter Toolkit directs drawing output; the remaining arguments are self-explanatory. This code is deficient because it adds a handler without removing the previous ones. The *Intrinsics* have the following function for removing event handlers.

```
XtRemoveEventHandler( Widget w, EventMask event_mask,
   Boolean nonmaskable, (void *)g(), XtPointer client_data )
```

The arguments are exactly the same as for `XtAddEventHandler()`, which means that we must specify the same client data that were used when the event handler was added. The Paper widget class has a resource with the symbolic name `XtNuserHandler`, which keeps track of such data, so the complete code of `set_handler()` is as shown in Listing 8.8. (Again, the actual implementation is slightly different.)

Listing 8.8: The set_handler( ) Function — `File lib/paper_mate.c (part of)`

```
static Widget ws;

set_handler(void (*g)(void *));
{
     void (*h)();

     XtVaGetValues(ws, XtNuserHandler, &h, NULL);
     XtRemoveEventHandler(ws, XtAllEvents, True, own_handler, h);

     XtAddEventHandler(ws,
          ButtonReleaseMask | ButtonPressMask | KeyPressMask |
          PointerMotionMask | EnterWindowMask | LeaveWindowMask,
          False, own_handler, g);
     XtVaSetValues(ws, XtNuserHandler, g, NULL);
}
```

First, the function finds the current client data, stores its value in `h`, and removes the basic handler with client data `h` from the list of event handlers. Then it adds the new handler and saves the client data. Listing 8.9 shows part of the implementation of the generic event handler.

Listing 8.9: Basic Event Handler of the Starter Toolkit — `File lib/paper_mate.c (part of)`

```
void own_handler(Widget w, XtPointer client_data,
     XEvent *ep, Boolean *disp)
{
     struct pen Pen;
     int (*h)();

/*1*/     h = (int (*)())client_data;
     /* ... */

     switch(ep->type) {
/*2*/     case EnterNotify:
          XSetInputFocus(XtDisplay(w), XtWindow(w),
                         RevertToParent, CurrentTime);
          return;
     /* ... */

/*3*/     case ButtonPress:
     case ButtonRelease:
     case MotionNotify:
     case KeyPress:
          if(h) {
               translate_events( ep , &Pen);
               h(&Pen);
          }
          return;
     }
}
```

Statement 1 obtains the pointer to the Starter Toolkit handler from the client data. The casting is necessary only for avoiding compiler warnings. Statement 2 assigns the keyboard to the window where the cursor is located. Statement 3 performs the event translation for the Starter Toolkit structure and calls the event handler specified by the Starter Toolkit user. The code associated with Statement 3 is similar to that of Listing 6.6.

8.3.4 While Waiting Between Events

The X Toolkit provides two functions that allow a program not to be idle while waiting for events. One of them, `XtAddWorkProc()`, registers a function with the *Intrinsics*, which is executed when no events are in the queue. The other, `XtAppAddInput()` registers a file descriptor and a function with the *Intrinsics*; when there is input in the file descriptor, the function is called.

The use of these functions is illustrated by the listings of the respective function wrappers of the Starter Toolkit, which are shown in Listing 8.10.

Listing 8.10: Adding a Background Process — `File lib/paper_mate.c (part of)`

```
add_work(int (*f)())
{
        XtAppAddWorkProc(app, f, NULL);
}

take_from_file(int fid, int (*fun)(XtPointer, int *))
{
     XtAppAddInput(app, fid, XtInputReadMask, fun, NULL);
}
```

Argument `app` is the applications context that is returned by the process starting an application, and its meaning is explained in Section 9.3.2. Its presence as the first argument of both functions serves to tell the system which event queue to look for. The second argument of the function `XtAppAddWorkProc()`, `f()`, is the function to be invoked when no events are pending. If this function has a nonzero return, then it is removed from the system. The third argument is a pointer to data that are passed as argument to `f()` when it is invoked by the *Intrinsics*. This feature is not used by the Starter Toolkit; therefore the third argument is `NULL`.

The function `add_work()` was introduced in Section 3.4.2 in order to animate the graphins. More than one such function may be added. They are invoked in the reverse order in which they were added.

The second argument of `XtAppAddInput()`, `fid`, is a file descriptor returned from an `open()` call. The fourth argument, `fun()`, is the function that reads the data corresponding to the file descriptor. The third argument is a symbolic constant that, in this case, states that the file descriptor will be used for reading. The last argument is a pointer to structure that is used as the first argument of `fun()` when the latter is invoked by the *Intrinsics*. Because the Starter Toolkit does not use the first argument of the function that reads the input (see Listing 7.16 in Section 7.7.1), the last argument of `XtAppAddInput()` is `NULL` here.

8.4 CONCLUSIONS

The implementation of the X Window System Toolkit is complex. For this reason we present a simplified version in Section 8.1 so that you can get at least a general idea of what the X Window System Toolkit functions do.

Because the X Window System was developed in a decentralized fashion, the relationships between its various parts also are quite complex, as we explained in Section 8.2. There we also discussed the concepts of widget class hierarchy and widget tree. Section 8.3 deals with event handling.

The following texts are recommended for additional reading.

For the X Window System Toolkit in general:

- P. J. Asente and R. R. Swick. *X Window System Toolkit*. Newton, Mass.: Digital Press/Butterworth-Heinemann, 1990.
- D. Flanagan (ed.). *X Toolkit Intrinsics Reference Manual*, vol. 5, 3rd edition for X11, Release 4 and Release 5. Sebastopol, Calif.: O'Reilly & Associates, 1992.

For programming with the X Window System Toolkit and the *Motif* widgets:

- A. Nye and T. O'Reilly. *X Toolkit Intrinsics Programming Manual*, vol. 4, OSF/Motif 1.2 edition. Sebastopol, Calif.: O'Reilly & Associates, 1993.
- D. A. Young. *The X Window System: Programming and Applications with Xt — OSF/Motif Edition*, Englewood Cliffs, NJ: Prentice-Hall, 1990.

For programming with the X Window System Toolkit and the *OLIT* Widgets:

- D. A. Young and J. A. Pew. *The X Window System: Programming and Applications with Xt — Open Look Edition*. Englewood Cliffs, NJ: Prentice-Hall, 1992.

The following contains examples of advanced programming with the X Window System Toolkit using either the *Athena* or the *Motif* widget sets.

- P. E. Kimball. *The X Toolkit Cookbook*. Englewood Cliffs, NJ: Prentice-Hall, 1995.

8.5 ASSIGNMENTS

1. Locate the files `CoreP.h` and `Core.h`, which describe the core widget of the X Toolkit and try to understand the meaning of each member of `CorePart`. (First you have to find out whether your installation has a separate `include` directory for all X related files. Then look for a subdirectory named `X11` or `X11R5` or something similar.)

2. The Starter Toolkit does not maintain a handler list. Thus the use of two handlers (as in Section 2.5.3) must be done explicitly. Provide an alternative design where instead of `set_handler()` there will be two functions: `add_handler()` and `remove_handler()`. Discusses the advantages and disadvantages of this solution.
3. The Starter Toolkit relies on existing widget sets for its selection panels. Use the example in Section 2.6.1 as a starting point and design an alternative set of panels that do not rely on another widget set.

9

Using Toolkits*

Scope of the Chapter

Program structure with the X Toolkit • Advanced use of the Starter Toolkit (widget prototypes) • Creating Widgets with the X Toolkit • *Motif* and *OLIT* widget sets • The Tk Toolkit

9.1 INTRODUCTION

9.1.1 Toolkits

In this chapter we explain how to use of the facilities of the *X Toolkit* (abbreviated *Xt*) to create application programs. Frequently, we use the functions of the Starter Toolkit as case studies. In addition, we describe the Tk Toolkit, which is independent of the X Toolkit because it relies directly on *Xlib*. However, it provides excellent facilities for creating graphical user interfaces.

The X Toolkit cannot be used by itself but only in conjunction with a widget set such as *Motif* (see Section 8.2). While the particular features of the widgets are important for the precise look of the program, the overall design and organization is independent of them as demonstrated in the next section.

---

* **This chapter may be skipped by those who want to use only the Starter Toolkit.**

9.1.2 Simple Examples

The widget tree of simple programs, such as those discussed in Chapters 1 and 2, has only two elements: the shell and a drawing widget. The code of Listing 9.1 is one possible implementation of the `draw_window()` function in terms of the X Toolkit. (We omit most of the function arguments for the time being.)

Listing 9.1: Creating a Single Drawing Window

```
#include <X11/StringDefs.h>
#include <X11/Intrinsic.h>
#include <X11/Shell.h>
#include <Paper.h>

draw_window(void (*f)(), void (*g)(pEvent *),
     int width, int height, char *label)
{
     Widget toplevel, draw_widget;

     toplevel     = XtAppInitialize(...);

     draw_widget = XtCreateManagedWidget( ... ,
          paperWidgetClass, toplevel, .... );
     if(f) XtAddCallback(draw_widget, ... , f, NULL);
     if(g) XtAddEventHandler(draw_widget, ... , g);

     XtRealizeWidget(toplevel); /* create and map windows */

     XtMainLoop(); /* infinite loop checking event queue */
}
```

This program is much simpler than either the one in Section 6.3 or the one in Section 8.1. It remains simple, even after the code for creating a shell window and the code dealing with the parameters has been added. This is possible because the *Intrinsics* take care of most of the operations described in Section 8.1. For programs with many windows you must use a widget set such as *Motif, OLIT*, or *Athena*. The program whose window layout was shown in Figure 8.7 can be implemented in three ways, depending on the widget set use. Listings 9.2, 9.3, and 9.4 shows the implementation using *Motif, OLIT*, and *Athena* widgets, respectively.

Listing 9.2: Creating a Drawing Window with *Motif* widgets

```
main()
{
     Widget toplevel, container_widget, panel_widget, draw_widget;

     /* ... */
     toplevel = XtInitialize( ... );

     /* Create Container Widget */
     container_widget = XtCreateManagedWidget( ... ,
          xmRowColumnWidgetClass, toplevel, ... );

     /* Create Panel and Button Widgets */
     panel_widget = XtCreateManagedWidget( ... ,
          xmRowColumnWidgetClass, container_widget, ... );
     for(i=0; i<number_of_buttons; i++)
       XtVaCreateManagedWidget( ... , XmNarmCallback, panel_widget, ... );

     /* The code below is Common in all implementations  */
     /* Create Draw Area Widget */
     draw_widget = XtCreateManagedWidget( ... ,
          paperWidgetClass, container_widget, .... );
     XtAddCallback(draw_widget, ... , redraw_function, NULL);
     XtAddEventHandler(draw_widget, ... , event_handler);

     /* Create and Map Windows */
     XtRealizeWidget(toplevel);

     XtMainLoop(); /* infinite loop checking event queue */
}
```

Note that the code dealing with the drawing window is similar to that of Listing 9.1 (the redraw and event handler functions have been renamed). The code of Listings 9.3 and 9.4 is almost identical to the code of Listing 9.2. The main changes are in the names of the widget classes. The Paper widget is used for the drawing area in all cases. As it is a direct subclass of the `Core` class, its instances can be children of the *Motif, OLIT,* or *Athena* subclasses.

Listing 9.3: Creating a Drawing Window with *OLIT* widgets

```
main()
{
     Widget toplevel, container_widget, panel_widget, draw_widget;
```

```
    /* ... */
    toplevel = OlInitialize( ... );

    /* Create Container Widget */
    container_widget = XtCreateManagedWidget( .... ,
         controlAreaWidgetClass, toplevel, ... );

    /* Create Panel and Button Widgets */
    panel_widget = XtCreateManagedWidget( ... ,
         exclusivesWidgetClass, container_widget, ... );
    for(i=0; i<number_of_buttons; i++)
      XtVaCreateManagedWidget( ... , rectButtonWidgetClass, panel_widget,
                ... );
    /* Repeat code labeled as Common from Table 9.2 */
}
```

The container widget class has the following names in the various widget sets.

`xmRowColumnWidgetClass`	in *Motif*,
`controlAreaWidgetClass`	in *OLIT*, and
`boxWidgetClass`	in *Athena*.

The panel widget for the *Motif* and *Athena* implementations is the same as the container widget but with a different set of parameters (not shown in these listings). The *OLIT* implementation uses a different widget, `exclusivesWidgetClass`, for the panel. Each implementation uses a different widget for the selection buttons of the panel.

Listing 9.4: Creating a Drawing Window with *Athena* widgets

```
main()
{
    Widget toplevel, container_widget, panel_widget, draw_widget;

    /* ... */
    toplevel = XtInitialize( ... );

    /* Create Container Widget */
    container_widget = XtCreateManagedWidget( .... ,
         boxWidgetClass, toplevel, ... );

    /* Create Panel and Draw Area    */
    panel_widget = XtCreateManagedWidget( ... ,
         boxWidgetClass, container_widget, ... );
    for(i=0; i<number_of_buttons; i++)
      XtVaCreateManagedWidget( ... toggleWidgetClass, panel_widget, ... );
```

```
    /* Repeat code labeled as Common from Table 9.2 */
}
```

9.2 ADVANCED USE OF THE STARTER TOOLKIT

9.2.1 Using the Starter Toolkit and the X Toolkit Together — 1

The functions of the Starter Toolkit that start an X application and create windows such as `draw_window()` or `begin_display()` may be too confining in some cases. For example, you cannot create two drawing windows with them. On the other hand the implementations of Section 9.1 represent a major increase in complexity.

The Starter Toolkit provides facilities for an intermediate level of programming. Applications programmers must be aware of the X Toolkit and the widget classes but need make only limited use of the X Toolkit functions. In particular, there is a simplified call for creating a drawing window.

☛ **`Widget create_paper_widget(int (*redraw)(), int (*handler)(pEvent *), int width, int height, int relationship, char *window_name)`**
Create a paper widget that provides a drawing window of dimensions `width` and `height` with frame label `window_name`. The function `redraw()` is called in response to exposure events and the function `handler()` is called in response to mouse and keyboard events. The argument `relationship` is a flag that can have one of the predefined values: `NormalChild`, `PopupChild` and `IndependentChild`. When this function is used, files `<X11/StringDefs.h>` and `<X11/Intrinsic.h>` must be included. ☜

The flag `NormalChild` is used when the drawing window is contained within an application in an arrangement similar to that of Figure 8.7. In such a case the call

```
create_paper_widget(redraw_function, event_handler,
... , NormalChild, ... );
```

replaces the following group of statments in Listing 9.2.

```
draw_widget = XtCreateManagedWidget( ... ,
    paperWidgetClass, container_widget, .... );
XtAddCallback(draw_widget, ... , redraw_function, NULL);
XtAddEventHandler(draw_widget, ... , event_handler);
```

There is no need to save the return of `create_paper_widget()` in this case because the widget has been placed in the widget tree during its creation. Note also that the arguments of `create_paper_widget()` do not contain information about a parent; it is provided by the Starter Toolkit depending on the value of the `relationship` flag. Therefore the following sequence of calls is allowed.

```
    begin_display( ... );
    create_paper_widget( ... , NormalChild, ... );
```

The flag `PopupChild` is used for windows that are displayed outside the main window of the application, usually for a brief period. The dialogue panel introduced in Section 7.5.4 is created in this fashion.

The flag `IndependentChild` is used when the drawing window is the only window of the application. For example, the implementation of the function `draw_window()` consists mainly of the following code.

```
static XtAppContext app;

draw_window(void (*redraw)(), void (*handler)(),
      int width, int height, char *label)
{
      Widget w = create_paper_widget(redraw, handler,
            width, height, IndependentChild, label);
      XtRealizeWidget(XtParent(w));
      /* ... */
      XtAppMainLoop(app);
}
```

The set of widget creation functions provides a succession of functions, each simpler to use than the preceding one. At the first level is the most general call (`XtCreateManagedWidget()`, in this case). Next is `create_paper_widget()`, then comes the pair `begin_display()` and `complete_display()`, and finally functions such as `draw_window()`. A well known example of a similar organization is offered by the I/O functions of Unix. A principal difference between Unix and the X Window System is that while Unix provides a full range of functions, X usually provides no more than two levels (*Xlib* and the X Toolkit). The remaining levels must be supplied by new toolkits.

9.2.2 Using the Starter Toolkit and the X Toolkit Together — 2

Besides the widget creation function, another group of functions may be used for programs that deal directly with widgets. The following function directs output to the window of the widget.

☛ **`void draw_area(PaperWidget w)`**
Copy the display pointer, window, and graphics context associated with `w` to the static variables of the module that contains the drawing functions of the Starter Toolkit, such as `put_line()` or `fore_color()`. ☜

When an event occurs the Starter Toolkit invokes this function for the widget where the event occurred. It does so by storing that widget in the `origin` member of the `pEvent` structure. The member `origin` has been declared as `long` so that programs using the `pEvent` type can be compiled without the X Toolkit definitions. However, the space is enough to store the `Widget` type, which is a pointer to a structure. For example, we may use the statement

```
draw_area((PaperWidget)p->origin);
```

(The Starter Toolkit normally executes an equivalent call when an event occurs so there usually is no need for an explicit call.)

Another "hidden" feature of the Starter Toolkit is that a function that redraws a window may take a widget as an argument. When the function is called later in response to an expose event, the system passes to it as the first argument the widget where the event occurred. Applications writers have the option of ignoring that argument, as done in Chapters 1-3 and 7.

The Starter Toolkit remembers the Paper widget that was used as drawing area last. It can be recovered by the following function.

☛ **`void restore_destination()`**
Restore the previous widget for destination of the output of the Starter Toolkit graphics functions. ☜

Suppose, for example, that whenever a certain event occurs we want to print a message in some particular window and then continue processing. The following code will do it.

```
handler(pEvent *p)
{
     /* ... declarations ... */

     if(p->kind==BTN_PRESS) {
          draw_area(memo_widget);
          put_text("Button was pressed", 100, 20);
          restore_destination();
     }
}
```

The following is another related function of the Starter Toolkit whose use is illustrated in later examples.

☛ **void default_destination()**
Restore the widget of the main drawing window for destination of the output of the Starter Toolkit graphics functions. ☜

Popup widgets do not appear automatically after they are created. Their appearance is manipulated by the following functions.

☛ **void popup(Widget w, int easy)**
Cause the window of `w` to appear. If the flag `easy` is zero, all keyboard and mouse input is ignored unless directed to that widget. This setting is appropriate for dialogue widgets. ☜

☛ **void popdown(Widget w)**
Cause the window of `w` to disappear. ☜

With a bit more work we can create *prototype widgets*. Suppose that we write a slider program (e.g., the one in Assignment 10 of Chapter 7) and that we want to use two copies of it from within another program. Storing the state of the slider in static variables will not work any more unless we follow the ugly solution of having two sets of them. A better solution is to associate the state with the widget. That can be done with the following function of the Starter Toolkit.

☛ **XtPointer * paper_hanger(PaperWidget w)**
Return a pointer to a pointer associated with the widget `w`. ☜

Let `slider_state` be a type which is a structure holding the state of a widget. The following sequence initializes the storage

```
extern slider_state   ** paper_hanger();
     /* ... */
     slider_state *slp;

     sl_widget = create_paper_widget( /* ... */ );
     *paper_hanger(sl_widget) = slp =
          (slider_state *)malloc(sizeof(slider_state));

     /* statements of the form slp-> ... = ... */
```

The first statement keeps the compiler happy. After creating the widget, we store the address of the block of memory returned by `malloc()` inside the structure of the widget. `slp` is only a convenient local variable that places data in that block.

The following code extracts the widget state from within an event handler and a redraw function.

```
handler(pEvent *p)
{
     slider_state *sp;
```

```
        sp = *paper_hanger( (Widget)p->origin );
        /* ... */
}

redraw(Widget w)
{
        slider_state *sp;

        sp =  *paper_hanger(w);
        /* ... */
}
```

We discuss the implementation of a slider widget prototype in Section 9.2.4.

9.2.3 The Dialogue Window of the Starter Toolkit

Let's now consider the implementation of a popup window using the X Toolkit and a Paper widget. This window is the dialogue window of Sections 7.5.4 and 7.5.5. The `start_dialog()` function checks on whether the `d_widget` has been created and, if not, this function creates it as a popup widget. It is shown in Listing 9.5.1.

Listing 9.5.1: Dialogue Widget (Part 1) — `File lib/dialog.c (part of)`

```
/*   Pop up a window (create it if need be) for dialogue */
#include <X11/StringDefs.h>
#include <X11/Intrinsic.h>
#include <Starter.h>

extern Widget create_paper_widget();
extern void collect_text();       /* See Section 2.5.2 */
static void d_draw();             /* See Listing 9.5.2 */

static Widget d_widget = 0;
static int d_x0 = 10, d_y0 = 20, d_width = 256, d_height = 128;
static int dx_gap = 5, dy_gap = 24;
static pAction *scenario, *scenario_start;
static int dialog_active = 0;
static char *reply[64]; /* well above maximum number expected */
static char **rp;
static int x, y;

void start_dialog(pAction messages[])
{
     scenario = scenario_start = messages;
     rp = reply;
```

```
    dialog_active = 1;

    if(!d_widget) d_widget = create_paper_widget(d_draw, collect_text,
            d_width, d_height, PopupChild, "Dialogue");
    popup(d_widget, 0);
    draw_area(d_widget);

    set_string_use(cont_dialog);
}
```

The function initializes certain pointers (their role will become clear later), creates the widget (if it has not been created), and then causes it to appear by the call to `popup()`. Because the second argument is 0, the widget grabs all input (see the documentation of the function `popup()` in Section 9.2.2). The call to `draw_area()` directs all output from the Starter Toolkit graphics functions to the window of the `d_widget`. The call to `set_string_use()` ensures that any string typed on that window will be passed as an argument to the function `cont_dialog()`.

The function `d_draw()` is the one called when an expose event occurs, and therefore it is also called the first time the window pops up. It paints the window with a light gray background and sets the foreground to a value that will yield 1 when it is XOR'ed with the background color. The procedure is shown in Listing 9.5.2.

Listing 9.5.2: Dialogue Widget (Part 2) — `File lib/dialog.c (part of)`

```
static void d_draw()
{
    register j;
    pAction *ap;
    char **cp;

    set_foregr(beige('l'));
    use_replace_mode();
    fill_rectangle(0, 0, d_width, d_height);
    set_foregr(beige('l')^01);
    use_xor_mode();

    ap = scenario_start;
    for(y=d_y0, cp=reply ; ap<=scenario; ap++, y+=dy_gap, cp++) {
        x = d_x0;
        x += put_text( ap->label, x, y) + dx_gap;
        if(cp<rp) if(*cp) put_text(*cp, x, y);
    }
```

```
    y -= dy_gap;
    init_text(x, y, 1);
}
```

The main loop displays the labels of the array of structures that was the argument of `start_dialog()` and, possibly, additional text from the `reply` array.

The function `cont_dialog()` operates on the string typed by the user. This procedure is shown in Listing 9.5.3.

Listing 9.5.3: Dialogue Widget (Part 3) — `File lib/dialog.c (part of)`

```
/* Process the string typed by the user     */
/* scenario points to the pAction array that was */
/* passed as argument to start_dialog() */
#define CAUTION(A) if( !(A) ) { end_dialog(); return; }

void cont_dialog(char *s)
{
    if(!dialog_active) return;
    CAUTION(scenario);
    CAUTION(scenario->label);

    scenario->fun(s);           /* act upon the typed message */
    mk_label(rp, s);   rp++;
    if(!dialog_active) return;  /* it may have been reset by fun() */
    scenario++;
    CAUTION(scenario->label);

    draw_area(d_widget);
    y += dy_gap;   x = d_x0;
    x += put_text( scenario->label, x, y) + dx_gap;
    init_text(x, y, 1);     /* get ready for another line of input */
}
```

This function does some error checking and then invokes a member of the array of structures that was the argument of `start_dialog()` corresponding to the last displayed label. The typed text is saved so that it can be available for redrawing. Because we are invoking a function about which we know nothing, defensive programming dictates that we check the status flags and redirect output to the window of the dialogue widget. Finally, the next label is displayed and text collection is initialized.

The dialogue ends by popping down the window and restoring a ground state.

Listing 9.5.4: Dialogue Widget (Part 4) — `File lib/dialog.c (part of)`

```
void end_dialog()
{
     dialog_active = 0;
     popdown(d_widget);
     default_destination();
     set_string_use((int *)0);
     while(--rp>=reply) free(*rp);
}
```

One more function, which lets other parts of the program post messages on the dialogue window, is needed. It is given in Listing 9.5.5.

Listing 9.5.5: Dialogue Widget (Part 5) — `File lib/dialog.c (part of)`

```
void to_dialog(char *s)
{
     draw_area(d_widget);
     y += dy_gap;  x = d_x0;
     put_text( s, x, y);
}
```

In the example in Section 7.5.5, `to_dialog()` is invoked by the function that attempts to save the file. It informs the user whether the file was saved.

The implementation presented in Listing 9.5.5 has one bug: Messages displayed as a result of a call to `to_dialog()` are not made available to the function that redraws the window in response to an expose event. That can be corrected by generalizing the `reply` array (see Assignment 2).

Another limitation of the program is that an application can have only one dialogue window open at any given time because only one widget supports the operation. An application may have mechanisms for selecting more than one dialogue panel but they have to be invoked one at a time. This restriction is imposed by the second argument of the `popup()` function in Listing 9.5.1. It specifies that all input be directed to the popup window, so the user cannot make another selection as long the dialogue window is open.

9.2.4 A Prototype for a Slider Widget

The various parts of Listing 9.6 contain most of the code for the prototype slider widget described in Section 7.6. We omit only the selection of specific parameters and the details of the drawing because they were the subject of Assignment 10 in Chapter 7. The program starts with the definition of a structure that holds the state of the slider. In Listing 9.6.1 `x1` is the position of the slider indicator; `pick` is a flag set to 1 when the user presses the left button and is set to 0 when that button is released; `msg` and `bf[]` are auxiliary variables used for the display; and `use` points to a function provided by the application that is invoked when a slider position has been selected. It takes as an argument the position of the slider expressed as a percentage of its range. Finally, `name` is a label supplied by the application and indicates to the user the purpose of the slider.

Listing 9.6.1: Slider Prototype (Part 1) — `File lib/slider.c (part of)`

```
/*   Slider Widget Prototype*/

#include <X11/StringDefs.h>
#include <X11/Intrinsic.h>
#include <Starter.h>

typedef struct {
     int x1;
     int pick;
     int msg;
     int (*use)();
     char bf[16];
     char *name;
     } slider_state;

extern slider_state  ** paper_hanger();    /* actually XtPointer */
extern Widget create_paper_widget();
extern void handler(), redraw();
```

The prototype widget is created by calling the function `slider()` with two arguments: a pointer to a function that is called when a selection is made and a label that is displayed on the slider window. The function corresponding to the first argument takes as an argument a double precision floating number since this particular implementation returns a number between 0 and 1 which can be scaled by the calling program. Listing 9.6.2 shows the code of `slider()`.

Listing 9.6.2: Slider Prototype (Part 2) — `File lib/slider.c (part of)`

```
void slider(int (*usage)( double), char *label)
{
     Widget sl_widget = 0;
     slider_state *slp;
```

```
    sl_widget = create_paper_widget(redraw, handler,
                window_width, window_height, NormalChild, label);

    *paper_hanger(sl_widget) = slp =
                (slider_state *)malloc(sizeof(slider_state));
    slp->use = usage;
    slp->msg = slp->pick = slp->x1 = 0;
    mk_label(&(slp->name), label);
}
```

Here, `window_width` and `window_height` are static variables, local to the module. The argument `label` is used for two things: as a widget name and as a member of the state structure for labeling the window.

Listing 9.6.3 shows the function needed to draw the slider. We skip the actual details of the drawing. The function `mark()` draws the slider indicator. The flag `sp->msg` is set when a message with the slider value is displayed. The function `default_destination()` directs all drawing commands to the main drawing window of the application (see Section 9.2.2).

Listing 9.6.3: Slider Prototype (Part 3) — `File lib/slider.c (part of)`

```
redraw(wg)
    Widget wg;
{
    slider_state *sp;

    sp =  *paper_hanger(wg);

    /* draw slider using information from sp */

    mark(sp->x1 = sp->x1? sp->x1: /* default value */);
    default_destination();
}
```

Listing 9.6.4 shows the event handler, again omitting details of calculating the geometry. The two sliders of Figure 7.10 were created by this program.

Listing 9.6.4: Slider Prototype (Part 4) — `File lib/slider.c (part of)`

```
handler(pEvent *p)
{
    Widget w;
    double xresult;
    slider_state *sp;
```

```
    w = (Widget)p->origin;
    sp = *paper_hanger( w );

    switch(p->kind+p->key) {
    case LEFT_RELEASE:
        if(sp->pick) {
            /* compute the value to be returned, store
            it in xresult, and also display it */
            sp->pick = 0;
            if(sp->use) sp->use(xresult);
        }
        break;

    case LEFT_PRESS:
    case LEFT_DRAG:
        if(/* too far from slider area */) return;
        if(!sp->pick) {
            if(/* if close to the indicator */) sp->pick = 1;
            return;
        }
        else {
            mark(sp->x1); sp->x1 = p->x;    mark(sp->x1);
        }
        break;
    }
}
```

9.3 DIRECT USE OF THE X TOOLKIT

9.3.1 Creating Widgets

We discuss here the implementation of `create_paper_widget()` introduced in Section 9.2.1. In the process we present examples of direct use of the X Toolkit. They include three general cases of widget creation that can be used as models for other programs. Listing 9.7.1 show the first part of the paper widget creation function.

Listing 9.7.1: Creating a Drawing Widget (Part 1) — `File lib/paper_mate.c (part of)`

```
#include <X11/StringDefs.h>
#include <X11/Intrinsic.h>
#include <X11/Shell.h>
#include <Paper.h>
```

```
extern Widget base_widget();

Widget create_paper_widget(
     int (*redraw)(), int (*handler)(pEvent *),
     int width, int height, int relationship,
     char *window_name )
{
     Widget new_paper_w, parent_w;
     int dummy = 1;
     static char wgname[64];
     Position xpos = 0, ypos = 0;
```

The arguments were described in Section 9.2.1. All but the fifth are also self-explanatory. The argument `relationship` is a flag that determines the relationship of the new widget with the rest of the application. There are three broad possibilities.

1. The Paper widget is a child of a container widget such as those described in Section 8.2.3.
2. The application contains only the Paper widget and a Shell widget that interacts with the window manager.
3. The widget is a *popup*. It is not contained in the main application window and can be placed anywhere on the screen.

In the first and third cases the new widget needs a parent, which is provided by the function `base_widget()`. The main purpose of having such a function, rather than passing the parent widget as an argument, is to provide flexibility in using the function with other widget sets and in different circumstances. In the first case, `base_widget()` returns the container widget of the set that is used. If a different widget set is to be used, the module containing `create_paper_widget()` does not have to be recompiled, only relinked. If the application does not rely on such a set, a different implementation of the `base_widget()` function will return the Shell widget that is at the top of the application.

We set aside a discussion of the computation of the position of the window and focus instead on the code creating the parent widget shown in Listings 9.7.2 and 9.7.3 (on page 229).

Listing 9.7.2: Creating a Drawing Widget (Part 2) — `File lib/paper_mate.c (part of)`

```
switch(relationship) {
case NormalChild:
     parent_w = base_widget();
     break;
```

```
case PopupChild:
    parent_w = XtVaCreatePopupShell(window_name,
         topLevelShellWidgetClass,  base_widget(),
         XtNx,  xpos,  XtNy,  ypos,
         XtNtitle,  window_name,  NULL);
    break;
```

Finding the parent widget is easy in the case of a `NormalChild`. (It corresponds to the call of the function `create_paper_widget()` from `complete_display()`, among other cases.) We use `parent_w` later in the code when we create the Paper widget.

Things are more complicated when the Paper widget is a `PopupChild`. As mentioned in Section 8.2.4 popup widgets hold a position in the widget tree that does not correspond to the placement of their window with respect to other windows. Because their window is a child of the root window they require a Shell widget that must deal with the window manager. Thus before we create the paper widget we must create a Shell widget that will be its parent. But in order to access the popup widget through the widget tree, its Shell widget requires as parent some widget on that tree. In this case `base_widget()` provides the "grandparent" of the paper widget.

The first three arguments of the function `XtVaCreatePopupShell()` have the following meaning: (1) name of the widget, (2) class of the widget to be created, and (3) the parent widget. The name of the widget is used mainly for the resource database described in Section 8.2.5. The rest of the arguments are name value pairs as described in Section 8.2.5. The argument `XtNtitle` specifies the name to be placed in the window frame that is created by the window manager during the reparenting process (see Section 4.3.5). We do not provide dimensions for the Shell widget because such widgets compute their size from the size of their child.

The `topLevelShellWidgetClass` is part of the base widgets of the X Toolkit. Hence we do not have to worry what other widget set the application is using.

9.3.2 Starting an Application

We must start a new application when the value of the fifth argument of `create_paper_widget()` is `IndependentChild`. This is the case when this function is called from `draw_window()` or `vis_window()`. Then no other widget set is used, and the application consists only of a single drawing window.

Listing 9.7.3: Creating a Drawing — `File lib/paper_mate.c (part of)`

```
case IndependentChild:
     parent_w = XtAppInitialize(
          &app,  "StandAlonePaperWidget",
          (XrmOptionDescList)NULL, 0, &dummy, &window_name,
          (String *)NULL,    (ArgList *) NULL, 0);

     XtVaSetValues(parent_w,
          XtNtitle,  window_name,  XtNinput,  True, NULL);

     set_server( XtDisplay(parent_w) );
     init_color_map(parent_w);
     break;
default:
     error_exit();
}    /* end of the switch */
```

In this part of the program we ignore the function `base_widget()` (it would have returned a null value anyway). Instead, we invoke the function `XtAppInitialize()` that does what its name says: It initializes an application and returns the top shell widget. Initialization includes opening a connection to the server and the other operations shown in Listing 6.3.

The first argument, `&app`, requires special attention. It is a pointer to an *application context*, which is a structure containing all information needed to run the application. We have already demonstrated its use in Section 8.3.4 as argument to functions that needed to know a particular event queue. In the Starter Toolkit it is declared as

```
static   XtAppContext app;
```

All widgets created under a particular application contain a pointer to the structure and it can be extracted by the function

```
XtAppContext  XtWidegtToApplicationContext(Widget w);
```

This function is useful when you do not have access to all the code of an application.

The string `StandAlonePaperWidget` is the name of the widget to be used by the resource database, among others.

The other arguments refer to parameter values that might be set for this application. In this particular case we provide no parameter values, so most of the arguments are null. The pair `&dummy` and `&window_name` require an explanation. Normally, `XtAppInitialize()` expects the command line arguments in this place. Thus if we called the function directly from the main program we would have code such as

```
main(int argc, char **argv)
{
     /* ... */
     XtAppInitialize( /* ... first four arguments ... */,
          &argc, &argv, /* ... rest of the arguments */ );
     /* ... */
}
```

The argument line is parsed for flags recognized by the X Toolkit and corresponding parameters are set. This method gives the user a convenient way to customize the application (besides modifying the resource database file). Because the Starter Toolkit imposes certain constraints on applications, it does not allow that option. However, `XtAppInitialize()` expects the arguments, so we provide the address of an integer with value 1, which corresponds to no command line arguments. The `&window_name` is used as a conveniently available pointer to a character string.

The first argument of the function `XtVaSetValues()` is a widget, and the rest are pairs of resource names and values. You have already encountered `XtNtitle` in Section 9.3.1. The argument `XtNinput` refers to the keyboard input. By setting it to `True` we ask the window manager to direct keyboard input to this widget whenever the mouse-controlled cursor is in the window of the widget. In Section 4.4.4 we showed how this procedure is done through *Xlib* functions. The *Intrinsics* call these functions themselves.

The X Toolkit convenience function `XtDisplay` extracts the `Display` pointer from the widget. The Starter Toolkit function `set_server()` passes it to the module of the Starter Toolkit that needs the value for calls to *Xlib* functions. The function `init_color_map()` extracts the information about the colormap used by the top-level widget and passes it to the module of the Starter Toolkit dealing with color. This function is discussed in Chapter 22.

9.3.3 Creating a Drawing Widget

After creation of the parent, creation of the drawing widget itself is simple, as shown in Listing 9.7.4.

Listing 9.7.4: Creating a Drawing Widget (Part 4) — `File lib/paper_mate.c (part of)`

```
sprintf(wgname,"paper.%s", window_name);
new_paper_w = XtVaCreateManagedWidget(wgname,
     paperWidgetClass, parent_w,
     XtNwidth,  width,  XtNheight,  height,
     XtNborderWidth, 1,
     NULL);
```

The first statement creates a name for the widget. (Note that allocating `wgname` dynamically in Listing 9.7.1 would have been safer than using fixed storage.) The function `XtVaCreateManagedWidget()` is used to create widgets that are children of other widgets. Because `window_name` might have been used as a name for a Shell widget, we create a new name by prefixing it with the string "`parer.`" and use that as the first argument of the creation function. `paperWidgetClass` is defined in the definition file `Paper.h` and informs the *Intrinsics* about the class of the widget to be created. The other arguments are self-explanatory.

There is another function, `XtCreateManagedWidget()` (used in the examples in Section 9.1.2), that performs the same operations as `XtVaCreateManagedWidget()` but takes a different form of arguments. The code fragment of Listing 9.8 shows how to set parameters for it.

Listing 9.8: Alternative Argument Passing

```
Arg paperArgs[3];

XtSetArg(paperArgs[0], XtNwidth,    width);
XtSetArg(paperArgs[1], XtNheight,   height);
XtSetArg(paperArgs[2], XtNborderWidth, 1);

new_paper_w = XtCreateManagedWidget(wgname,
      paperWidgetClass, parent_w,
      paperArgs, 3);
```

Rather than pass the resource pairs explicitly, we store them first in an argument vector, `paperArgs` in this case, and then pass a pointer to the vector and the number of its components to the function that creates the widget, `XtCreateManagedWidget()`.

This version is convenient when many widgets with similar arguments have to be created. All *Xt* functions that contain the string `Va` in their names have a counterpart without it that uses the syntax of Listing 9.8 for passing the resource values (see Assignment 1).

9.4 CREATING *Motif* AND *OLIT* WIDGETS

9.4.1 Implementation of `begin_display()` and `complete_display()`

We now can revisit the examples in Section 8.1 and discuss in more detail the creation of *Motif* and *OLIT* widgets by using the case of `begin_display()`. The function is presented in Listings 9.9.1 and 9.9.2 (on page 232).

Listing 9.9.1: Starting an Application (Part 1) — `File lib/p_panel.c (part of)`

```
#include <X11/StringDefs.h>
#include <X11/Intrinsic.h>
#include <X11/Shell.h>

static Widget toplevel, base_w;

Widget  base_widget()
{
     return(base_w);
}

#ifdef OLIT
#include <Xol/OpenLook.h>
#include <Xol/ControlAre.h>
#define AP_INITIALIZE       OlInitialize
#define CONTAINER_CLASS     controlAreaWidgetClass
#define VERTICAL_STACK      XtNlayoutType,     OL_FIXEDCOLS
#endif

#ifdef MOTIF
#include <Xm/Xm.h>
#include <Xm/RowColumn.h>
#define AP_INITIALIZE       XtInitialize
#define CONTAINER_CLASS     xmRowColumnWidgetClass
#define VERTICAL_STACK      XmNorientation, XmVERTICAL
#endif
```

The first part contains declarations of two widgets as static variables, the function `base_widget()` that is called by other modules that create children of the base widget and two sets of conditional declarations. Which one is used depends on the C compiler flag:

```
cc -DMOTIF ...
```

compiles for *Motif*, whereas

```
cc -DOLIT
```

compiles for *OLIT*. By structuring the program in this manner, we facilitate its extension to other widget sets. Also, the main code uses names that are mnemonic.

Listing 9.9.2: Starting an Application (Part 2) — `File lib/p_panel.c (part of)`

```
static Display *Dpy;

begin_display(int w_width, int w_height, char *window_name)
{
     int dummy = 1;

     /* save w_width and w_height in static variables
        for later use by complete_display */

     toplevel = AP_INITIALIZE( window_name, window_name,
          NULL, 0, &dummy, &window_name);

     set_server( Dpy = XtDisplay(toplevel) );
     init_color_map( toplevel);

     base_w = XtVaCreateManagedWidget("base_w",
          CONTAINER_CLASS, toplevel,
          VERTICAL_STACK,
          XtNborderWidth, 2,
          NULL);
}
```

Motif starts an application by calling `XtInitialize()`, so the first few lines of `begin_display()` are similar to the code of Listing 9.7.3. *OLIT* uses another function, `OlInitialize()`, that has the same type of arguments.

The Starter Toolkit stacks major widgets vertically, so in creating a container widget we must pass arguments that ensure a vertical stack. The `CONTAINER_CLASS` for *Motif* is `xmRowColumnWidgetClass` and the pair of arguments for `VERTICAL_STACK` is

```
XmNorientation, XmVERTICAL
```

The `CONTAINER_CLASS` for *OLIT* is `controlAreaWidgetClass` and the pair of arguments for `VERTICAL_STACK` is

```
XtNlayoutType,     OL_FIXEDCOLS
```

See Section 9.3.2 for a discussion of the calls to `set_server()` and `init_color_map()`. The only difference here is that the pointer to the server structure also is saved in a static variable `Dpy` to be used by other functions of this module.

Distinguishing between the design of an interface and its implementation with a widget set is important. Listing 9.9.2 corresponds to the design phase. The declarations of Listing 9.9.1 correspond to the implementation phase. Once you know what you want to do in terms of the X Toolkit, you then have to read the manual for the widget set to be used and identify the widget class that will do the job and the type of parameters it takes.

A possible implementation for the function `complete_display()` is given in Listing 9.9.3. (The real implementation is a bit more complicated in order to take care of some special features of the Starter Toolkit.)

Listing 9.9.3: (Part 3) — `File lib/p_panel.c (part of)`

```
static Widget canvas;

complete_display()
{
	canvas = create_paper_widget(0, 0,
		w_width, w_height, NormalChild, "canvas");
	XtRealizeWidget(toplevel);
}
```

The drawing window is created last, so it appears below any panel windows. The function `XtRealizeWidget()` creates and maps windows not only for its argument but also for the widget tree that descends from its argument.

9.4.2 Implementation of the Panel Functions of the Starter Toolkit

The functions `setup_a_panel()` and `setup_v_panel()` are similar to each other, so we discuss only the first one here. When the *OLIT* is used, `setup_a_panel()` creates a `captionWidgetClass` widget which contains an `exclusivesWidgetClass` panel widget. When the *Motif* widget set is used, `setup_a_panel()` creates a `xmRowColumnWidgetClass` container widget that has as its first child a `xmLabelWidgetClass` widget for the label of the panel.

After these operations, the required push-button widgets are created as children of the panel widget. The difference in the treatment of text labels between the two widget sets causes some duplication of code. We show only part of the code for *OLIT* in Listing 9.10, omitting the details of some auxiliary operations such as `estim_columns()` which estimates the number of columns for the list of actions, and `beige()`, which returns a gray value for the panel background.

Listing 9.10.1: Selection Panels (Part 1) — `File lib/p_panel.c (part of)`

```
/*   Function that sets up an action panel using OLIT widgets     */

#define PUSH_BUTTON_ACTION  XtNselect
#define TEXT_LABEL(A)       XtNlabel,A

static char **iconhold;

int setup_a_panel(char *caption, pAction *a,
     int (*rfun)(), char **icons)
{
     pAction *ap;
     Widget cap, pex, bt;
     int newval, kols;
     register j;

     iconhold = icons;
     kols = estim_columns(a);

     cap = XtVaCreateManagedWidget(caption,
          captionWidgetClass, base_w,
          XtNbackground,  beige('1'),
          XtNborderWidth, 2,
          TEXT_LABEL(caption),
          NULL);

     pex = XtVaCreateManagedWidget("ExPanel",
          exclusivesWidgetClass, cap,
          XtNbackground,  beige('1'),
          XtNborderWidth, 2,
          XtNnoneSet, TRUE,
          VERTICAL_STACK,
          XtNmeasure,   kols,
          NULL);

     for(ap=a, j=0; ap->label; ap++, fap++, j++) {
          fap->f = rfun;
          fap->af = ap->fun;
          bt =  make_button(ap->label, pex, iconhold, j, &newval);
          if(ap->fun) XtAddCallback(bt, PUSH_BUTTON_ACTION, a_generic, fap);
     }

     return(j);     /* number of buttons created */
}
```

The auxiliary variable `iconhold` is used to avoid passing `icons` as argument to the function `make_button()` because the fourth argument of the functions that create panels may be omitted. (Another instance of defensive programming.)

To achieve greater flexibility the Starter Toolkit provides a generic callback, `a_generic`, which in turn calls the functions supplied with the call to `setup_a_panel()`. The function is shown in Listing 9.10.2.

Listing 9.10.2: Selection Panels (Part 2) — `File lib/p_panel.c (part of)`

```
typedef struct {
     int (*f)();
     int (*af)();
     } f_a_pair;
static f_a_pair fa[128];
static f_a_pair *fap = fa;

a_generic(Widget w, XtPointer client_data, XtPointer call_data)
{
     f_a_pair *p;
     int need_reset;
     p = (f_a_pair *)client_data;
     if(p->f) p->f();              /* common preparation */
     if(p->af) need_reset = p->af();
     if(need_reset) XtVaSetValues(w, XtNset, FALSE, NULL);
}
```

The X Window System callbacks have a specific argument structure: a widget and two pointers. One pointer, `client_data`, is to data specified during the registration of the callback (the call to `XtAddCallback()`), and the other, `call_data`, is to data specified during the creation of the widget (see Section 8.3.2). In this case, `client_data` is a pointer to the structure `f_a_pair`, which contains pointers to two functions: one for general preparation and the other the second member of the `pAction` structure. The Starter Toolkit uses the rule that whenever the latter function returns a nonzero value, the button pops up again. Otherwise it stays depressed.

9.4.3 Implementation of the Button Functions of the Starter Toolkit

The buttons are widgets of `xmToggleButtonWidgetClass` for *Motif* and `rectButtonWidgetClass` for *OLIT*. The first character of each label of the action or value pair arrays is examined to determine the parameters to be used for the creation of the appropriate widget. Listing 9.11 shows the function `make_button()`.

Listing 9.11: Selection Buttons — `File lib/p_panel.c (part of)`

```
#ifdef OLIT
#define PUSH_BUTTON_CLASS   rectButtonWidgetClass
#define ICON_LABEL        XtNlabelType,    OL_IMAGE
#define ICON_FOR_LABEL(I,Q) XtNlabelImage, icon_image(I, atoi(Q), atoi(Q), 1)
#endif

#ifdef MOTIF
#define PUSH_BUTTON_CLASS   xmToggleButtonWidgetClass
#define ICON_LABEL          XmNlabelType,    XmPIXMAP
#define ICON_FOR_LABEL(I,Q) XmNlabelPixmap, icon_pixmap(I, atoi(Q), atoi(Q), 1)
#endif

Widget make_button(char *label, Widget parent,
     char **iconhold, int pix_ix, int *newvp)
{
     char *cp;
     Widget bt;
     /* other variables for color buttons */

     cp = label+1; /* skip possible control character */

     switch(*label) {
          case '-':
               /* Omitted as too specific */
               break;

          case '@':
               bt= XtVaCreateManagedWidget(label,
                    PUSH_BUTTON_CLASS, parent,
                    ICON_LABEL,   ICON_FOR_LABEL(iconhold[pix_ix], cp),
                    XtNbackground,  beige('l'),
                    NULL);
               break;

          default:
               bt= XtVaCreateManagedWidget(label,
                    PUSH_BUTTON_CLASS, parent,
                    TEXT_LABEL(label),
                    XtNbackground,  beige('l'),
                    NULL);
     }
     return(bt);
}
```

The major difference between the *OLIT* and *Motif* versions is that the former creates buttons with icons stored as images on the client (application) site. In contrast, *Motif* buttons with icons must be given explicitly a representation in the server (display). (We describe the operation of the two functions `icon_image()` and `icon_pixmap()` in Section 22.3.5.)

9.5 THE Tk TOOLKIT

The Tk Toolkit is an X Window System toolkit based on the interpretive command language Tcl, both developed by John K. Ousterhout. It offers very simple methods for creating panels and other control structures. Because it does not rely on the X Toolkit it can interact with the Starter Toolkit only through the pipe mechanism discussed in Section 7.7.

The Tk command interpreter is called `wish`, and it can be invoked instead of a Unix shell. If the directory where `wish` resides (e.g., `/usr/local`) is in the search path of the user, typing `wish` gives a shell prompt (`%` normally). From then on, all typed input is used to construct a window. Thus, typing

```
button .b -text "Hello" -command exit
pack .b
```

creates a window with a single button labeled "Hello." When the user points to the button (by pressing the left mouse button when the cursor is over the control button), both the program and the command interpreter exit. Also `wish` scripts can be packaged into Unix shell scripts and run as regular Unix commands. Suppose that the following code is in an executable file called `run_tk`.

```
#!/usr/local/wish -f
button .a -text "Hello" -command { puts "How are you?" }
button .b -text "Exit" -command exit
pack .a .b
```

Typing `run_tk` (or `./run_tk`) will create a window with two buttons. Pointing to "Hello" will print in the standard output "How are you?" and pointing to "Exit" will terminate the program. The strings `.a` and `.b` are widget identifiers and the command `pack` does the layout, maps the windows, and starts a "wait for event loop." A slightly more general construction uses a function definition:

```
#!/usr/local/wish -f
proc echo { message } {
    puts $message; flush stdout
}
```

```
button .a -text "Hello" -command {echo "How are you?"}
button .b -text "Very well" -command {echo "Me too"}
button .c -text "Not so well" -command {echo "Sorry about that"}
button .x -text "Goodbye" -command exit
pack .a .b .c .x
```

The Tk commands are equivalent to the functions that set up panels in the Starter Toolkit and the equivalents of `complete_display` and the waiting loop are invoked by `pack`. Also an explicit initialization statement is not needed unless you intend to construct a group of panels. Then the button declarations should be preceded by a line of the form

```
frame .panel1
```

and the pack statement should be modified as

```
pack .a .b .c .x -in .panel1
```

Providing a more detailed description of Tk is beyond the scope of this text. If you are interested in a complete description, see the book cited in Section 9.6. The simplicity of Tk should be contrasted to the code for creating panels and buttons presented in Section 9.4.

It is possible to combine functions of the Tk and the Starter Toolkit by using two-way pipes (see Assignment 6).

9.6 CONCLUSIONS

We described how to use various Toolkits to create application programs. Writing a program is much easier once you comprehend its functions in an abstract way, focusing on what they do rather than how they will be implemented. For visualization, video games, or interactive drawing, the main part is the management of a drawing area. For simple programs, applications programmers need to specify in detail only two things: the display of what is drawn and how to handle events. The function `draw_window()` provides the environment for such programs.

For more complex programs, applications programmers also must provide the button callbacks. Again the construction of windows is hidden from them by providing such functions as `setup_a_panel()`.

Applications that have requirements for panels that go beyond those provided by the Starter Toolkit must either use directly a widget set such as *Motif* or use the Tk Toolkit.

The texts listed at the end of Chapter 8 provide additional reading on the X Toolkit. The following text is recommended for additional reading on the Tk Toolkit.

- J. K. Ousterhout. *Tcl and the Tk Toolkit*. Reading, Mass.: Addison-Wesley, 1994.

This chapter concludes our coverage of windows and widgets in the X Window System. (Chapters 18 and 22 cover various drawing functions of *Xlib*.) Because this text focuses on two-dimensional graphics, we have left out many features both of the X Window System *and* the Starter Toolkit. For example, we did not discuss *selections* (even though the Paper widget class supports them) because they do not involve any significant graphics.

9.7 ASSIGNMENTS

1. Modify the function `create_paper_widget()` by using
   `XtCreateManagedWidget()`
   instead of
   `XtVaCreateManagedWidget()`.
2. Modify the functions of the dialogue panel so that messages displayed as a result of a call to the `to_dialog()` function are saved and made available to the function that redraws the window.
3. Create a prototype widget for a two-dimensional slider (see Assignment 11 of Chapter 7).
4. Create a prototype widget with a background function such as that used for games. (For example, the widget may display a moving graphin bouncing on the window sides.) As there can be many copies of the widget in an application, you must provide a way for the background procedure to identify the correct widget. You can do so by using the third argument of `XtAppAddWorkProc()` described in Section 8.3.4.
5. Modify the program of Assignment 4 so that a background process is called only when the cursor is in the window of the widget. *Hint:* In this case you should not call explicitly the `draw_area()` or `grab_draw_area()` functions. Instead you should rely on the fact that when the cursor enters a window, the Starter Toolkit makes the widget of that window the destination of all the drawing functions. Calling `get_default_args()` yields the window ID of that widget, which you can compare with the window of a known widget by using the `XtWindow()` function.
6. Create a two-way pipe between a program written with the Starter Toolkit and a panel created by a Tk script. *Hint:* Use the programs of Section 7.7.2 as a starting point.

10

Plotting Lines and Circles

Scope of the Chapter

Plotting lines on bitmaps • Plotting of circular arcs on bitmaps • Plotting arcs through straight lines • Using of the plotting functions in the pixel painting program

10.1 INTRODUCTION

So far we have assumed the existence of certain graphics primitives, including a function that draws line segments between pairs of points. The Starter Toolkit provides the function `put_line(x1, y1, x2, y2)` which calls the corresponding primitive function of *Xlib*, `XDrawLine()`, after some additional arguments are supplied. Here, we describe how a function such as `put_line()` (or for that matter, `XDrawLine()`) can be built from scratch. Then, we will go on to describe plotting routines for circles.

We could argue that, as line segment drawing routines are available as primitives in all graphics devices, we should take them for granted and not worry about their implementation. However, when we want to draw a straight line in a style not supported by the X Window System, we need to use the basic plotting algorithm.

If we go beyond straight lines, the X Window System provides primitives only for circular and elliptic arcs, but not for other curves. Understanding the basic algorithms for displaying lines and curves is important because many types of curves are not available as graphics primitives.

The problem of drawing a straight line or any other curve on a *bitmap* appears deceptively simple. All we have to do is find the pixels closest to the curve we want to plot and assign to them the desired color. However, such a process can be computationally expensive. A better method is to find a way to locate the pixels on the line directly without having to use any floating point arithmetic. Writing a practically useful line segment drawing program can be quite a challenge.

In this chapter we describe in detail the routines for straight-line segments and circular arcs, but we postpone methods for drawing other curves until Chapter 17. Because geometric figures are rarely, if ever, drawn pixel by pixel on a window, we use a macro `put_pixel(x,y)` to denote that the pixel with coordinates `x` and `y` is given the *foreground* color. The definition of this macro depends on the exact line style we plan to use. In the simplest case it could be defined as in Section 2.3.1:

```
#define put_pixel(x, y) fill_rectangle(x, y, 1, 1)
```

10.2 PLOTTING STRAIGHT LINES

10.2.1 The Basics

Our goal is to develop simple and efficient programs to draw line segments that join two given pixels on a bitmap. Let the two pixels have coordinates `(x0,y0)` and `(x1,y1)`. Clearly, the easiest case is when the line segment is horizontal or vertical. Thus for horizontal lines we have

```
if(y0==y1) {
     if(x1>x0) dx = 1;  else dx = -1;
     x = x0 + dx;
     while(x != x1) {
          put_pixel(x, y0);
          x += dx;
     }
}
```

The code for vertical lines is similar.

For lines that are neither vertical nor horizontal we need to move in both directions: `|x1 - x0|` pixels along the horizontal and `|y1 - y0|` pixels along the vertical. Clearly, the best approach is to move along a diagonal as much as possible because it is the shortest distance and a straight line is the shortest path between two points. If `|x1 - x0|` and `|y1 - y0|` are equal, the plotting program is still very simple. It is almost the same as the program for a horizontal line, the main difference being an extra statement in the loop:

```
put_pixel(x, y);
x += dx; y += dy;
```

Difficulties occur when `|x1 - x0|` and `|y1 - y0|` are unequal. In Figure 10.1 they equal 10 and 7, respectively. Certainly we need five diagonal moves, but we also need three horizontal. The question is how to mix them. We could argue that the left side of Figure 10.1 offers a better solution than the right side, but what is the exact rule that must be used?

Figure 10.1 The solid squares are the two pixels that define a line segment. The gray pixels are candidates for pixels on the straight line segment joining the first two.

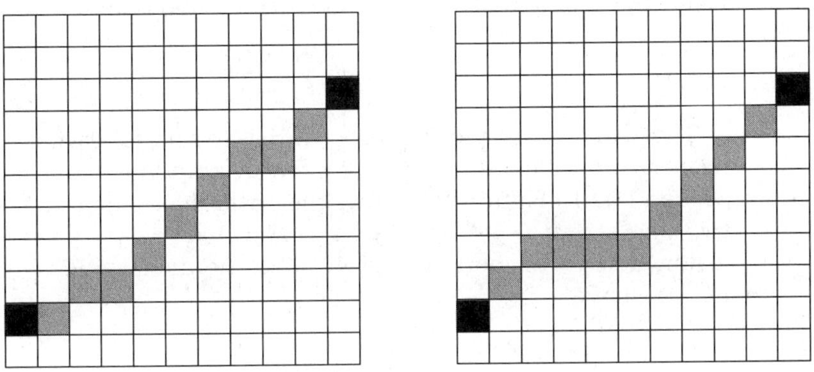

We now present Bresenham's method for plotting line segments in two stages. First, we provide a solution for the case when `y1` is greater than `y0`, `x1` is greater than `x0`, and the slope of the line is less than 1. (In other words, `y1 - y0` is less than `x1 - x0`.) Then we provide a solution for the general case.

The method proceeds by incrementing `x` from `x0` to `x1`, computing `y` at each point, and then finding the pixel nearest it.

10.2.2 Mathematical Foundations

In this section we use a subscript notation, so that x_0 stands for `x0`, and so on. The general equation for a straight line that is not vertical has the form

$$y = sx + b \tag{10.1}$$

where s is the *slope* of the line and b the point where it meets the y-axis. If the line passes through the point (x_0, y_0), then

$$y_0 = sx_0 + b \tag{10.2}$$

Subtracting Equation (10.2) from Equation (10.1) yields

$$y - y_0 = s(x - x_0) \tag{10.3}$$

As point (x_1, y_1) also is on the line, we have

$$y_1 - y_0 = s(x_1 - x_0) \tag{10.4}$$

We have assumed that the line is not vertical, so we are sure that $x_1 - x_0$ is not 0. Therefore we solve for the slope:

$$s = \frac{y_1 - y_0}{x_1 - x_0} \tag{10.5}$$

Substituting into Equation (10.4) and transferring y_0 to the right-hand side yields the equation of a straight line joining two points:

$$y = y_0 + \frac{y_1 - y_0}{x_1 - x_0}(x - x_0) \tag{10.6}$$

The goal of a line plotting procedure is to find for each x the y of the pixel nearest to the line. (Do not forget the assumptions we made at the end of Section 10.2.1.) Figure 10.2 shows the position of the line LM with respect to two pixels, A at $(x_0 + i + 1, y_0 + j)$ and B at $(x_0 + i + 1, y_0 + j + 1)$. The distance AD is proportional to AC, and the distance BE is proportional to BC. We have

$$AC = \frac{y_1 - y_0}{x_1 - x_0}(i + 1) - j \tag{10.7}$$

and

$$BC = j + 1 - \frac{y_1 - y_0}{x_1 - x_0}(i + 1) \tag{10.8}$$

Because of our assumptions, both quantities are positive and the line is closer to B than to A if $AC - BC$ is positive. The sign does not change if we multiply all terms by $(x_1 - x_0)$ to avoid the division. Then we find that

$$\begin{aligned} E(i, j) &= AC - BC \\ &= 2[(y_1 - y_0)i - (x_1 - x_0)j] + 2(y_1 - y_0) - (x_1 - x_0) \end{aligned} \tag{10.9}$$

Figure 10.2 Position of a line, LM, with respect to pixels A and B.

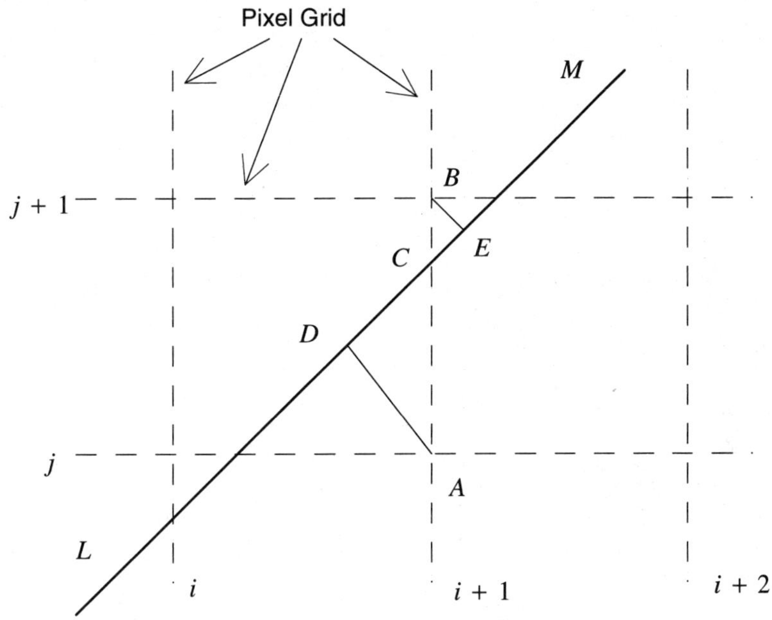

$E(i, j)$ is a quantity that tells which of the two points, A or B, is nearest the line. The nice thing is that $E(i, j)$ can be computed incrementally. If we move to A, then i should be replaced with $i + 1$ and j will stay the same so that

$$E(i + 1, j) = E(i, j) + 2(y_1 - y_0) \tag{10.10}$$

whereas if we move to B we must increment both i and j:

$$E(i + 1, j + 1) = E(i, j) + 2[(y_1 - y_0) - (x_1 - x_0)] \tag{10.11}$$

The initial value is

$$E(0, 0) = 2(y_1 - y_0) - (x_1 - x_0) \tag{10.12}$$

10.2.3 The Line Plotting Program

The analysis we just carried out leads to the program of Listing 10.1.

Listing 10.1: First Quadrant Line Segment Plot — `File line_plot1.c`

```
/*
     Segment Plotter  for First Quadrant
     Assume x1 > x0, y1 > y0, and x1 - x0 > y1 - y0
*/

void segment(int x0, int y0, int x1, int y1)
{
        register x, y;
        int P, Q, E;

        if(x1<=x0 || y1<=y0) return;
        P = y1 - y0;        Q = x1 - x0;
        if(P>Q) return;

        E = 2*P - Q;     y = y0;
        for(x=x0; x<x1; x++) {
                put_pixel(x, y);
                if(E>0) { y++;  E += 2*(P-Q); }
                else E += 2*P;
        }
        put_pixel(x, y);
}
```

Note that we decided to break ties ($E = 0$) in favor of the lower point. We could have broken them in favor of the higher point if the comparison in the inequality `E>0` had read `E>=0`.

We present next a program for plotting line segments whose endpoints do not satisfy the assumptions of Section 10.2.2. If the line has a slope greater than 1, the program of Listing 10.1 can be used after we modify it by switching `x` and `y`. If `x1` had been less than `x0`, we could also have used the same program with the following modifications: `x` would have to be decremented rather than incremented in the `for` loop, and `Q` would have to be replaced by its absolute value. Examination of the other cases suggests similar modifications, giving the general line segment plotting program shown in Listing 10.2.

Listing 10.2: Any Quadrant Line Segment Plot — `File line_plot2.c`

```
/*   General Segment Plotter      */
#define sgn(A)          A>0? 1: A<0? -1: 0;
#define max(A,B)   A>B? A: B
#define min(A,B)   A<B? A: B
```

```
void segment(int x0, int y0, int x1, int y1)
{
        register i, x, y;
        int P, Q, E;
    int dx, dy,  sx, sy, sx1, sy1, sx2, sy2;

        dy = y1 - y0;       dx = x1 - x0;
    sy = sgn(dy);    sx = sgn(dx);
    dy = abs(dy);    dx = abs(dx);
    P = min(dx,dy);       Q = max(dx,dy);
    if(dx > dy) { sx1 = sx; sy1 = 0; }
    else { sx1 = 0; sy1 = sy;}
    sx2 = sx;   sy2 = sy;

    E = 2*P - Q;  x = x0;   y = y0;
        for(i=0; i<Q; i++) {
         put_pixel(x, y);
         if(E>0) { E += 2*(P-Q);x += sx2;y += sy2;  }
         else  {   E += 2*P;     x += sx1;y += sy1;  }
        }
        put_pixel(x, y);
}
```

10.3 DIFFICULTIES OF GEOMETRY ON BITMAPS

The line drawing programs we just presented have some hidden flaws which we discuss next. We start with a simple numerical example. Let `x0` and `y0` both be 0, `x1` be 4, and `y1` be 1. Then `P` equals 1 and `Q` equals 4. When we execute the program, `E`, `x`, and `y` change as follows:

x	E	y
0	–2	0
1	0	0
2	2	1
3	–4	1
4	–2	1

Let's now reverse the endpoints of the line segment and repeat the calculation. We are simply replacing the increments in `x` and `y` by decrements. `P` and `Q` do not change because they are used for the calculation of the distance of a line from the pixels. We find:

x	E	y
4	−2	1
3	0	1
2	2	0
1	−4	0
0	−2	0

We have plotted a different line segment than before. The two segments are shown in Figure 10.3. There, the pixels of the segment from `(0, 0)` to `(4, 1)` are marked with horizontal lines, while the pixels of the segment from `(4, 1)` to `(0, 0)` by vertical lines. In this way pixels common to both segments appear with cross-hatching. There are two pixels that are not cross-hatched and those distinguish the two line segments.

Figure 10.3 Ambiguity in the plotting of a line segment (see text for explanation).

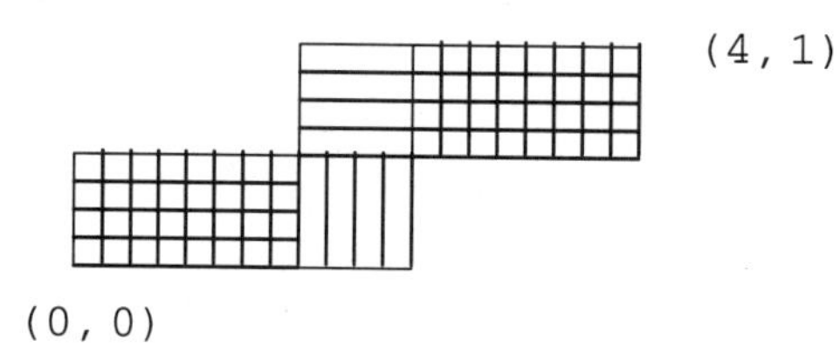

The reason for this fault is that we have decided to treat the value of `E` as positive when it is actually 0. Changing the program to treat it as negative will result again in an error so such a change is not a remedy. Clearly, we would like to have *retraceability,* in other words, to obtain the same line segment whether we traverse from the first point to the second or from the second to the first. After all, a straight line is supposed to be defined uniquely by any two of its points. Our programs do not provide retraceability.

One possible remedy is to insist on plotting a line always by incrementing `x`, swapping end points if necessary. This approach introduces other problems, though. Let us plot another segment where `x0` equals 0, `y0` equals 1, `x1` equals 4, and `y1` equals 0. `P` and `Q` stay the same. Then we have

x	E	y
0	−2	1
1	0	1
2	2	0
3	−4	0
4	−2	0

Putting these two line segments together, we observe the lack of symmetry shown in Figure 10.4. Also, the two line segments may have no common pixel.

Figure 10.4
Loss of symmetry in the plotting of a line segment (top) and lack of intersection (bottom).

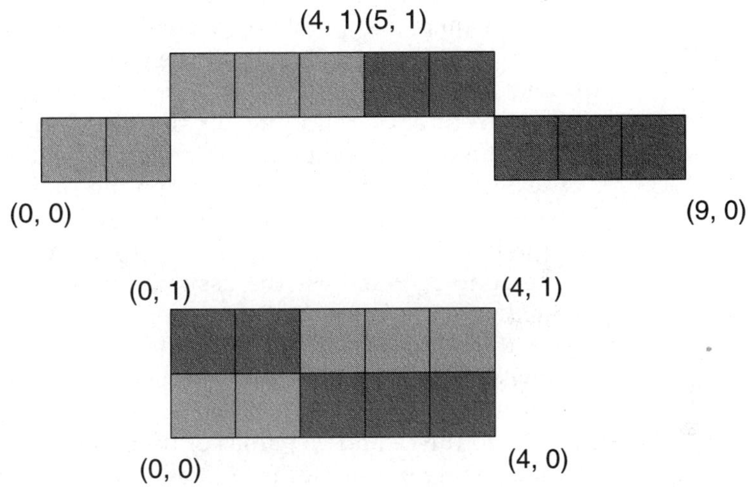

We can also construct examples of two line segments having more than one common pixel. That contrasts to the definition of plane geometry, which says that two straight lines always intersect at one point, unless they are parallel.

Unfortunately, these difficulties are not the result of weaknesses of the code we wrote. There are complex theoretical reasons why ordinary geometry cannot be transferred to bitmaps. A complete discussion of this topic is beyond the scope of this text, but the following simple argument gives some idea about the source of the problems.

Ordinary (Euclidean) geometry assumes infinite precision in the location of points. No matter how close two points are, there is a straight line segment joining them, and the middle of that segment always is a point different from either of the end points. On a bitmap, the precision of the location of points is limited. If two pixels are next to each other, the definition of a line segment becomes problematic. Certainly there is no other point between them.

10.4 PLOTTING CIRCULAR ARCS

Circular arcs probably are the most common geometric shape after straight lines and offer much greater possibilities for variations and for trouble. The difficulties we faced for straight line plotting suggest that the situation is far more complicated for circular arcs.

An arc is defined not only by its endpoints but also by the radius of the circle. We set aside for the moment the problem of finding the center of the circle that links two points by a given radius. This problem always has a solution in ordinary geometry (as long as the radius is greater than half the distance between the two points), but this may not be the case on the bitmap. Indeed, after rounding off the coordinates of the center to integer values, the second point may no longer lie on the chosen circular arc.

See Section 10.9 for some history on the subject. The following program is based on a method published nearly 20 years after the method for straight lines described in Section 10.2 was developed.

The code is based on the assumption that a center has already been selected, and it adjusts the location of the second point to make sure that it lies on the circle. The arc is traced clockwise if `dir` equals 1, and counterclockwise if `dir` equals -1. The procedure `onarc()` finds a point on the drawn arc that is near the intended endpoint. It takes as arguments pointers to the `x` and `y` values of that point, the coordinates of the center, and the square of the radius. Initially, the first two arguments point to the given values. When the procedure returns, these values have been replaced by those computed. Listing 10.3.1 shows the procedure.

Listing 10.3.1: Circular Arc Plot (Part 1) — `File circle_plot.c`

```
/*   Move a point on a Circle    */

void onarc(int *xp, int *yp, int x0, int y0, int rsq)
{
     int x, y, e, dr, dx, dy, exy;

     x = *xp - x0; y = *yp - y0;
     e = x*x + y*y -rsq;   /* distance of point from the circle */
     dr = -sgn(e);
```

```
    do {
        if(abs(y) > abs(x)) { dx=0; dy=sgn(y)*dr; }
        else if(x) { dx = sgn(x)*dr; dy = 0; }
            else { dx = 1; dy = 0; }
        exy = e + 2*(x*dx+y*dy) + 1;
        if(abs(exy)>abs(e)) break;
        x += dx; y += dy; e  = exy;
    } while(1);
    *xp = x;  *yp = y;
}
```

The first two steps inside the do loop check the coordinates of the correction and define the sign of the correction so as to move the point towards the circle, as shown in Figure 10.5. The new error is exy. The computation of exy uses the expansions

$$(x+dx)^2 = x^2 + 2xdx+(dx)^2$$

and

$$(y+dy)^2 = y^2 + 2ydy+(dy)^2$$

and the fact that $(dx)^2 + (dy)^2 = 1$.

Figure 10.5 Correction of the position of pixels with respect to a circle.

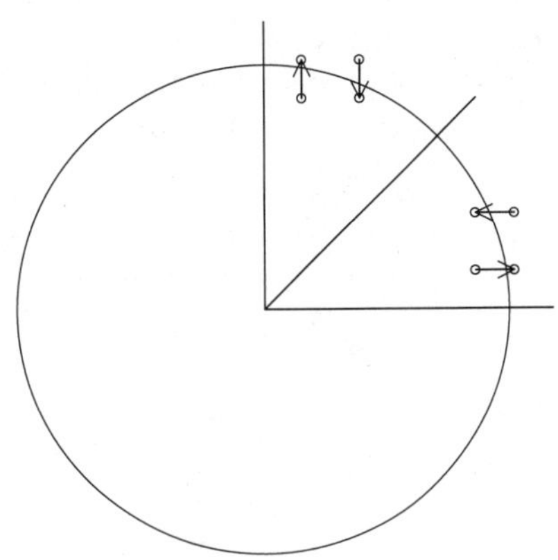

The main procedure starts by moving both endpoints onto the circle. The pixels are then plotted according to a principle similar to the one used for the line drawing algorithm. The plotted circular arc (or a circle if the two endpoints coincide) has pixels that lie as near the "analog" arc as possible. Listing 10.3.2 shows the procedure.

Listing 10.3.2: Circular Arc Plot (Part 2) — `File circle_plot.c`

```
/*
     Plot Arc from x1,y1 to x2,y2 with center at x0,y0,
     radius square rsq and direction dir
*/
/*   Essential Definitions   */
#define NEGATE e= -e; dxe= -dxe; dye= -dye; d2e= -d2e
#define sgn(x)   ( x<0 ? -1 : ( x==0 ? 0 : 1)  )
#define sgn2(x, y)   ( x!=0 ? sgn(x)  : sgn(y) )

/*   Definition needed only for testing    */
#define put_pixel(x, y) fill_rectangle(x, y, 1, 1)

void arc(int x0, int y0, int x1, int y1, int x2, int y2, int rsq, int dir)
{
     int e, ex, ey, exy, dxe, dye, d2e, dx, dy;

     onarc(&x1, &y1, x0, y0, rsq);
     onarc(&x2, &y2, x0, y0, rsq);

     dx= sgn2(-y1*dir, -x1); dy=sgn2(x1*dir, -y1);
     e = x1*x1+y1*y1-rsq; dxe=2*x1*dx+1; dye=2*y1*dy+1; d2e=2;
     if (dx*dy*dir>0) {NEGATE;}

     do {
          put_pixel(x0+x1, y0+y1);
          ex=e+dxe; ey=e+dye; exy=e+dxe+dye;
          if (-exy<ey) {x1 += dx; e+=dxe; dxe+=d2e; }
          if (exy<-ex) {y1 += dy; e+=dye; dye+=d2e; }
          if (x1 == 0) {dy = -dy; dye= -dye+d2e; NEGATE; }
          if (y1 == 0) {dx = -dx; dxe= -dxe+d2e; NEGATE; }
     } while ( ( x1 != x2 ) || (y1 != y2) );

}
```

10.5 PLOTTING ARCS WITH STRAIGHT LINES

10.5.1 The Basic Idea

A lot of work is needed to devise a plotting routine for any particular curve. An alternative is to compute points from the equation of the curve and join them with short straight lines. If the line segments are short enough, the overall curve will appear smooth.

This method is particularly important because the X Window System does not provide primitive drawing functions for curves other than straight lines or circular arcs.

There are various ways to implement the replacement of a curve with straight lines. If the curve is given in a *parametric* form

$$x = x(t) \qquad\qquad y = y(t)$$

we simply compute points for different values of t and then join them by lines. If the curve is given in an *implicit* form,

$$f(x,y) = 0$$

things are a bit more complicated. Let's examine the case of a circle with its center at the origin as a prime example of a curve given in the implicit form:

$$f(x,y) = x^2 + y^2 - r^2 = 0 \tag{10.13}$$

10.5.2 A Dangerous Solution

We now consider a point located at $(x+dx,\ y+dy)$ for some small distance dx and compute the expression $f(x+dx,\ y+dy)$ for it:

$$f(x + dx,y) = (x + dx)^2 + (y + dy)^2 - r^2$$

By expanding the terms $(x+dx)^2$ and $(y+dy)^2$ and subtracting Equation (10.13) from both sides, we obtain

$$f(x + dx,y) - f(x, y) = 2x\,dx + dx^2 + 2y\,dy + dy^2$$

If the motion is very small, we may choose to ignore dx^2 and dy^2 so that

$$f(x + dx, y) - f(x, y) = 2x\,dx + 2y\,dy \tag{10.14}$$

If the new point lies on the circle, the left-hand side of this equation will be 0. This result provides us with guidance about choosing dx and dy. If we select

$$dx = -2cy \quad \text{and} \quad dy = 2cx \tag{10.15}$$

for some constant c, the right-hand side of Equation (10.14) becomes 0, which is what we wanted. The expressions of Equation (10.15) lead to the following simple code fragment in which we replaced $2c$ with a single constant.

```
xold = x1;      yold = y1;
do {
      xnew = xold - step*yold;
      ynew = yold + step*xold;
```

```
        put_pixel(xnew, ynew);
        xold = xnew;   yold = ynew;
    } while(...)
```

This program certainly looks attractive. Unfortunately, it is wrong. If you look back at Listing 1.3, you will see that the equations yielding `xnew` and `ynew` from `xold` and `yold` are similar to the equations yielding `x` and `y` from `x0` and `y0` there. The program is plotting a spiral rather than a circle. We confirm that outcome by computing the square of the distance of the points from the center. By direct substitution we find that

$$\texttt{xnew}^2 + \texttt{ynew}^2 = (1 + \texttt{step}^2)(\texttt{xold}^2 + \texttt{yold}^2)$$

Therefore at each iteration the distance from the center increases by the square root of $(1 + \texttt{step}^2)$. In Listing 1.3 `step` was 0.05, so in this case the multiplying factor is

$$\sqrt{1 + 0.05^2} = 1.001249$$

Comparing this result to Figure 1.8 shows that even such a small increase (about 0.1 percent) is enough to yield a visible spiral. The approximation used to create a simple program has introduced systematic errors!

If we plot only a short arc, the problem is probably not visible. But it is likely to show when we try to plot a full circle — or when we decide to change `step` to a greater value. This is a classical example of a "booby-trapped" program. As long as we plot arcs with a small angle and with small values of `step`, everything is fine. But the moment we decide to plot a full circle of a significant radius, we find that the circle does not close upon itself.

10.5.3 A Remedy

We can fix this particular program by using a correction multiplier on the old values `xold` and `yold`. Because the curve spirals outward we select an *attenuation* factor with which to multiply those two variables to reduce (and possibly eliminate) the outward spiraling. We select the number *atten_factor* having the property

$$atten\_factor^2 + step^2 = 1 \tag{10.16}$$

and write the program as

```
    xold = x1;    yold = y1;
    do {
        xnew = atten_factor*xold - step*yold;
        ynew = atten_factor*yold + step*xold;
        put_pixel(xnew, ynew);
        xold = xnew;  yold = ynew;
    } while(...)
```

The selection of such a factor is possible only if step is less than 1. The squares of atten_factor and step add up to 1, so we define an angle ϕ such that $\sin(\phi)$ equals step and $\cos(\phi)$ equals atten_factor. Then the two assignment statements of the program become

```
xnew = cos(ϕ)*xold - sin(ϕ)*yold;
ynew = cos(ϕ)*yold + sin(ϕ)*xold;
```

If we square both sides of these equations and add them, the trigonometric terms drop and

```
xnew*xnew + ynew*ynew = xold*xold + yold*yold
```

Therefore the distance of the point with coordinates xnew and ynew from the origin does not change and the plotted points will lie on a circle. The arc between successive points equals ϕ. The selection of the value of step must be made so that ϕ is small and the points are sufficiently close to each other.

The Moral of the Story: Although we were able to fix the simple circular arc plotting program, that was not a simple task and required a certain degree of mathematical sophistication. Let this experience be a warning about programs that plot other complex curves.

10.6 PLOTTING FUNCTIONS FOR ARCS AND POLYLINES

This is probably the right place to describe some additional functions of the Starter Toolkit which call respective *Xlib* primitives.

☛ **void put_arc(int cx, int cy, int rx, int ry,**
int start_a, int length_a)

Plot a *circular* or *elliptical* arc with center coordinates cx and cy, starting at angle start_a (expressed in degrees) and spanning an angle of length_a degrees. If rx and ry are equal, the arc is circular with a radius of rx. Otherwise it is elliptical with its horizontal axis equal to rx and its vertical axis equal to ry. To plot a complete circle with radius r, the appropriate call is put_arc(cx, cy, r, r, 0, 360). The arc is drawn counterclockwise if length_a is positive and clockwise if it is negative. Starting angles are measured from the horizontal and can be either positive or negative. ☜

Figure 10.6 shows some examples of circular arcs drawn with put_arc(). Because the arcs are not directed, there are two possible choices for the pair start_a and length_a in each case.

Another function that is useful for plotting curves is the one that plots polygons. If we approximate a curve by a sequence of line segments, the number of the segments can be quite large. Sending each one as a single

Figure 10.6 Three arcs drawn with `put_arc()`. The starting angle and length are given underneath each plot.

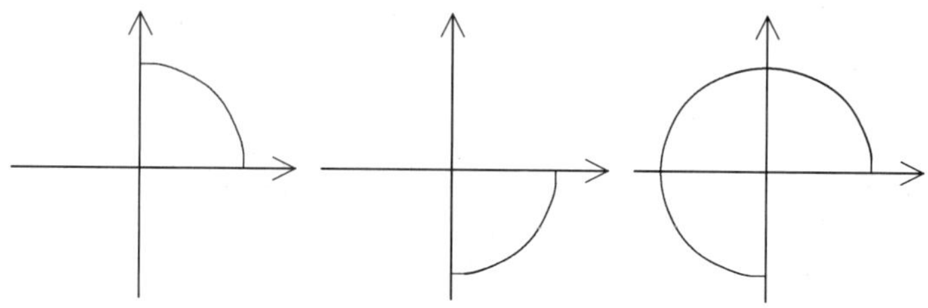

0°, 90° (or 90°, −90°) 0°, 90° (or −90°, 90°) 0°, 270° (or −90°, −270°)

segment from the application to the display (using the `put_line()` function) will create quite a bit of traffic. This function uses as an argument an array of structures defined as

```
typedef struct {
     short x, y;
     } pPoint;
```

This type is part of the Starter Toolkit and the `short` declaration is for compatibility with structures of the X Window System.

☛ **`void put_poly(pPoint v[], int n)`**
Plot a polygon with `n` vertices whose coordinates are stored in the array `v[]`. The value of `n` must be at least 1. ☜

10.7 ACCELERATING PIXEL PAINTING

10.7.1 Another Case of Planning

If you want to paint the pixels along a straight line in any of the pixel painting programs of Chapter 7, you must mark carefully all the points that are supposed to be on the line. A better approach would be to define only the end points and have the program fill in all the points between them with the line plotting routine of Section 10.2.

Other shapes also are defined by a few of their points: a rectangle by its two diagonally opposite corners; a circle by any three of its points, and so on. Such facilities could be provided easily by creating appropriate buttons in the control panel and then having the program prompt the user for the necessary geometric information. For example, for lines or rectangles it expects two points to be selected by the pointer (mouse) and then it uses them to determine the complete figure.

To avoid having a different event handler for each shape, you may use a single procedure to collect the points but with a variable function to call for a plot of a particular shape after enough pixels have been specified. The basic module is shown in Listing 10.4.

Listing 10.4: Collect an Array of Points — `File collect.c`

```
/*   point collection module (could be part of paint.c) */
#include <Starter.h>
#define put_pixel(x, y) fill_rectangle(x, y, 1, 1)
#define MAX_POINTS 32
static int xbf[MAX_POINTS], ybf[MAX_POINTS];
static int (*use)();
static int how_many;
static int i;

void set_xyc_use(int (*f)(int *, int *, int), int n)
{
     use = f;
     how_many = n;
     i = 0;
}

void get_points(pEvent *p)
{
     switch(p->kind+p->key) {
     case LEFT_PRESS:
     case MIDDLE_PRESS:
          fore_color("black");
          put_pixel(p->x, p->y); /* user feedback */
          xbf[i] = p->x;
          ybf[i++] = p->y;
          if(i>=how_many) {
               fore_color("white");    /* erase marked pixels */
               for(i=0; i<how_many; i++) put_pixel(xbf[i], ybf[i]);
               fore_color("black");
               use(xbf, ybf, how_many);
               i = 0;
          }
          return;
     case RIGHT_PRESS:
          reset_handler();
          return;
     }
}
```

The get_points() routine collects points and places them in the buffers xbf and ybf. When n points have been collected, it calls the plotting function through the variable use() and is ready to collect points for another plot of the same kind. As long as the user presses the left or middle buttons, points are collected for the chosen shape. Therefore you can draw more than one line segment without having to make a panel selection each time. (Unfortunately, the bitmap utility program is not as friendly.)

Pressing the right button changes the event handler. Rather than specify at this point which will be the next handler, we call a function reset_handler() and leave the specification to another part of the program. This method is another example of modular design. Low-level procedures (e.g., get_points()) should not deal with flow control issues.

The function set_xyc_use() is the messenger function. It specifies not only the variable use (as set_string_use() did) but also the parameter n. The first argument is expected to be a plotting function.

Next we present some examples, in each case giving the plotting and callback functions activated by panel buttons.

10.7.2 Straight Lines and Rectangles

For a straight line we make a selection from a panel button labeled "Line" with a callback paint_line(). The code is presented in Listing 10.5.1.

Listing 10.5.1: Plot a Line — File paint_plot.c

```
extern void get_points();
plot_line(int *x, int *y)    /* Plotting */
{
     put_line(x[0], y[0], x[1], y[1]);
     reset_handler();
}
paint_line() /* Callback */
{
     set_xyc_use(plot_line, 2);
     set_handler(get_points);
}
```

Note the flow of control. The callback function paint_line() sends a message to get_points that it should use plot_line() for its results. Then it tells the system that events are handled by get_points(). When get_points() is finished, it calls plot_line(), which completes the drawing and then informs the system that events are handled by the procedures that control the panel selections. You can think of this arrangement as *multiplexing*. Each of the `paint` procedures must eventually call the corresponding `plot` procedure by going through the common channel of the window system and the `get_points` procedure. The call to `set_xyc_use` is a way to tag the data coming through the channel.

The respective functions for a rectangle are shown in Listing 10.5.2.

Listing 10.5.2: Plot a Rectangle — `File paint_plot.c`

```
plot_rectangle(int *x, int *y)   /* Plotting */
{
     put_rectangle(x[0],y[0],x[1]-x[0]+1,y[1]-y[0]+1);
     reset_handler();
}
paint_rectangle() /* Callback */
{
     set_xyc_use(plot_rectangle, 2);
     set_handler(get_points);
}
```

The function `paint_rectangle()` is associated with a panel button labeled "Rectangle."

Keep in mind that both `put_line()` and `put_rectangle` color individual pixels rather than the enlarged pixels we have used for pixel painting. To have scale consistency, you should replace these functions with functions that implement the algorithms described earlier in this chapter.

10.7.3 Curves

Three points *A*, *B*, and *C* define a parabolic arc that passes through *A* and *C* and is tangent to lines *AB* and *BC*. As long as we have access to a routine that draws such arcs, the rest of the code will be similar to the code for lines or rectangles. The panel button may be labeled "Arc." In Chapter 17 we describe the routine `put_p_arc()`.

Listing 10.5.3: Plot an Arc — `File paint_plot.c`

```
plot_arc(int *x, int *y)
{
     put_p_arc(x[0],y[0],x[1],y[1],x[2],y[2]);
     reset_handler();
}
paint_arc()   /* callback */
{
     set_xyc_use(plot_arc, 3);
     set_handler(get_points);
}
```

Figure 10.7 shows how an arc is related to the three defining points. In the left figure only the three points and the arc are shown. In the right figure the lines joining the three points are also shown.

Figure 10.7 A parabolic arc defined by three points.

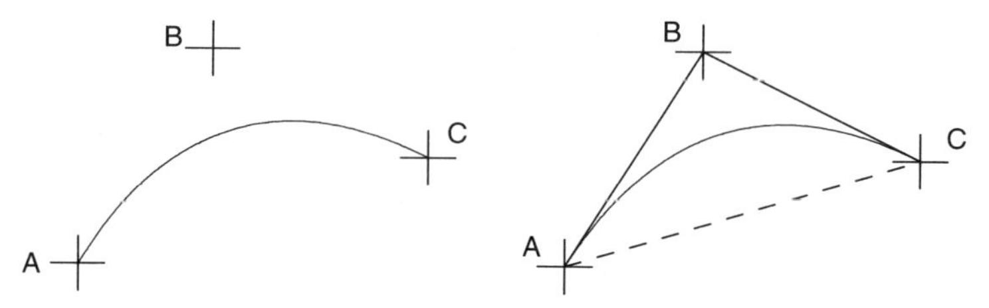

10.7.4 Resetting the Event Handler

Two choices for the event handler are available when the user has made no specific selection from the panel. One is to have a default handler — for example, painting individual pixels in the pixel painting program. The other is to ignore all events until another selection has been made from the panel. In the former case `reset_handler()` takes the form

```
reset_handler()
{
     * same as if the user has selected the paint option */
     paint();
}
```

In the latter case it is

```
reset_handler()
{
     set_handler((void (*)())0);
}
```

Note the rather cumbersome expression that is the argument of `set_handler()`. The term `(void (*)())` *casts* the constant `0` to be of the type pointer to a function that has no return. The Starter Toolkit event handler checks on whether the user defined handler is nonzero before calling it. If it is 0, all events are ignored. In such a case the user can interact with the program only through the panel.

10.8 WRITING USEFUL EVENT DRIVEN PROGRAMS

We have presented various pieces that could be added to the pixel editor of Section 7.5 to make it a practically useful editor. We start by making additional entries in the `user_actions[]` array to create a panel that includes buttons for drawing lines, rectangles, and arcs, as well as for reading a file. We should also add the code described in Sections 10.2.3 and 10.4. The program can be enhanced by changing the cursor icons for the panel selections made.

In programs having many event handlers, thinking of them as *filters* that interpret user input according to particular rules is useful. Some handlers ignore keyboard input (such as `paint_pixel()`); others handle only keyboard input (such as `get_string()`). There is a trade-off between the number of event handlers and the number of state variables that also influence how input is interpreted. We demonstrated that for the first time in the rubber band program of Chapter 2.

Another way to view the process is to think of the program as an aggregate of modules communicating with messages. When a value is selected through a panel, the panel module sends a message to the module where the value will be used. When a callback function is selected, it sends a message to the system saying which handler will be used and (possibly) a message to the handler module telling it what to do with its results.

The user sends messages to the handler module through events. Eventually that module sends its results to another module for processing. These relationships are shown in Figure 10.8 (on page 262). What is difficult to appreciate initially is that the main part of the program is rather simple. The complexity is in the rules for interaction, some of them well hidden in library procedures. Applications programmers must provide pieces that are joined by the hidden code.

10.9 CONCLUSIONS

We described two plotting routines and their use in the pixel painting program. The addition of different ways of pixel painting provided a motivation for looking at the structure of interactive graphics programs.

The method presented in Section 10.2 for plotting straight line segments was first proposed by Jack Bresenham in the following journal article.

- J. E. Bresenham. "Algorithm for Computer Control of a Digital Plotter." *IBM Systems J.*, January 1965, 25-30.

It is probably the most widely used line plotting method today.

Figure 10.8 Relationships between the modules of a pixel painting program. The dashed boxes represent switches that determine which path is operational.

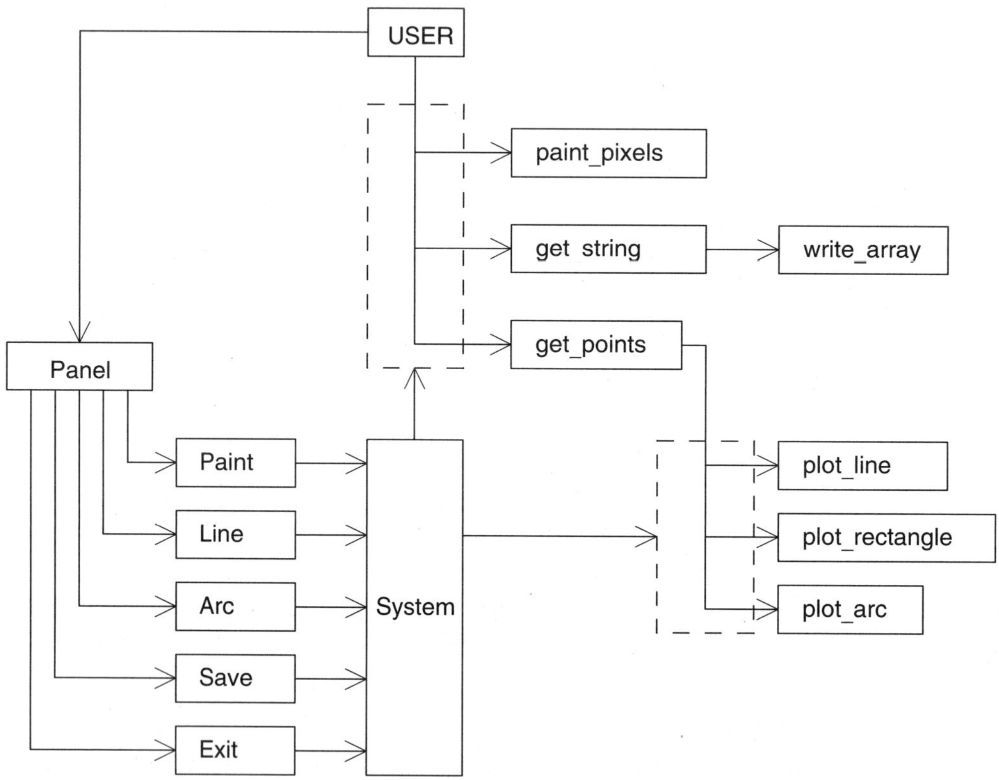

The method described in Section 10.4 for plotting circular arcs was proposed by Doug McIlroy in the following journal article.

- M. D. McIlroy. "Best Approximate Circles on Integer Grids." *ACM Transactions on Graphics,* 2, 1983, 237-363.

A measure of the slow progress in graphics is reflected in the dates of the two papers. Straight line plotting was of interest in the 1960s but circular arc plotting did not reach the same level of interest until nearly 20 years later.

We also discussed the incorporation of the line and circle plotting functions in a pixel painting program. A selection panel can be used to determine how to interpret user input. In some cases pixels selected by the user are given a new color immediately. In other cases pairs of pixels are collected and then all pixels in the line segment defined by each pair are given a new color. Such event driven programs can be considerably more complex than the programs discussed in Chapter 7.

10.10 ASSIGNMENTS

1. Implement the straight line segment plotting routine of Section 10.2.3, but instead of having it mark single pixels, have it mark squares of size `d`.
2. Select a square window size that is an integer multiple, say, `n`, of `d` and execute the following code. It is supposed to produce a group of straight line segments starting at the top left corner of the window and ending on the opposite sides.

   ```
   for(i=0; i<n/2; i++) {
   segment(0, 0, n-2*i, n);
   segment(0, 0, n, n-2*i);
   }
   ```

   Run the program for different values of `d` and `n` and observe the results. Look for a text on optics in your library and read about *Moiré Patterns*. Do they resemble the output of this program?
3. Modify Assignment 1 by using icons to mark pixels rather than squares and then write variants of the code given in Assignment 2 to create decorative patterns.
4. Add the code of Assignment 1 to the pixel painting program in the way described in Section 10.7.
5. Implement the circle plotting routine of Section 10.4 and compare the result with the circles plotted by the X Window System primitive (accessed through the `put_arc()` function described in Section 10.6).
6. Implement the method of Section 10.5.3 and use it to plot circular arcs of various angles and radii using the `put_poly()` function of Section 10.6. Compare the results with those obtained by using the X Window System primitive (accessed through the `put_arc()` function described in Section 10.6).
7. Add an option for circles and circular arcs in the pixel painting programs. A circle should be defined by its center and a point of its circumference; an arc should be defined by a sequence of three points. In either case, some computation will be necessary to extract the appropriate parameters for plotting.

11

Filling Areas

Scope of the Chapter

Filling the interior of an irregular area surrounded by pixels • Connectivity or flood filling

11.1 INTRODUCTION

In Chapter 10 we presented methods for plotting straight lines and certain curves. Here we address the problem of creating displays of regions. A region is defined by its outline, which can be a polygon, a curve, or just a set of pixels. Figure 11.1 shows some examples. The task is to find which pixels are inside a region and then assign to them a color or texture.

The outlines of a region may be as simple as those in the top row of Figure 11.1 or as complex as those on the bottom row. The process of filling is sometimes called *scan conversion* because it corresponds to mapping a mathematical entity (e.g., a polygon) to a set of pixels. If the outline of a region can be described mathematically, coming up with particularly efficient techniques for filling the interior is possible. We show how to do so for polygons in Chapter 12.

In this chapter we describe a general method for filling a region, given a pixel that is inside it. In such a case, filling is equivalent to finding all pixels *connected* to the given one. The initial pixel often is called a *seed*, and the process is called *seed filling*, *connectivity filling*, or *flood filling*. Such an operation is a useful addition to a pixel painting program.

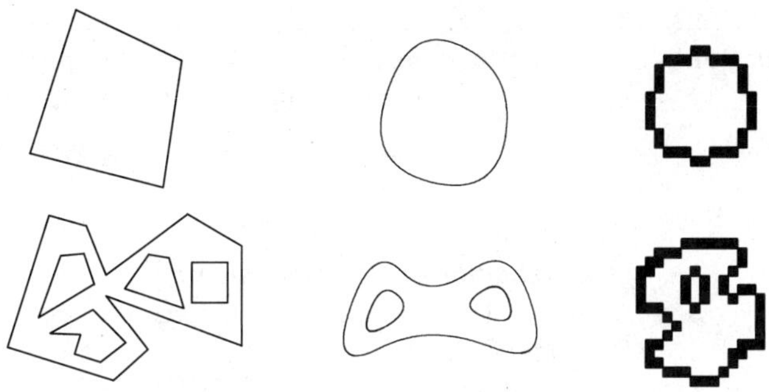

Figure 11.1 Examples of region outlines: polygon (left column), curve (middle column), pixels (right column).

A deceptively simple way to do seed filling with a recursive filling routine is shown in Listing 11.1. The program uses a call to `find_neighbors()` that fills an array `q[]` with pointers to all the neighbors of the given pixel pointed to by `p`. The details of such a routine do not concern us for now. Then if a neighbor does not already have the desired color, the procedure `fill()` is called for that neighbor.

Listing 11.1: Naive Connectivity Fill

```
typedef unsigned char pPixel;

fill(pPixel *p, int color)
{
     pPixel *q[NSIZE];
     register i;

     *p = color;
     find_neighbors(p,q);
     for(i=0; i<NSIZE; i++) {
          if(*q[i] != color) fill( q[i], color);
     }
}
```

Such a procedure does indeed solve the problem but requires very large *stack* memory. The `fill()` procedure is called recursively about as many times as the area of the region in pixels. The stack memory requirements are impractically large for any nontrivial application. What is needed is a procedure that traverses the area inside a region by coloring larger chunks than single pixels at a time.

In this chapter we describe a method that does seed filling using horizontal arrays of pixels as chunks.

Important Point *All our programs use the* `pPixel` *type for the arrays where the region to be filled lies. Depending on the application, this type may be defined as*

```
typedef unsigned char pPixel;
```

or

```
typedef unsigned long pPixel;
```

The rest of the code does not depend on how `pPixel` *has been defined. We use the term* `pPixel` *rather than* `Pixel` *because the latter is already defined in the X Window System.*

Another method for filling outlines is based on the *parity rule*. It is particularly appropriate for outlines that are polygons or curves, and we describe it in Chapter 12. When an outline is given as a set of pixels (such as the right-hand column of Figure 11.1), applying the parity rule is rather difficult, and connectivity filling is the preferred method.

11.2 CONNECTIVITY FILLING WITH LINE SEGMENTS

Connectivity or *seed* filling is based on the idea described in Section 11.1 but rather than color each pixel separately, we color groups of them to avoid having to make too many recursive calls. In the implementation we describe here we avoid recursion altogether and keep track of the stack explicitly. We outline our approach with reference to Figure 11.2.

Figure 11.2 Illustration of connectivity fill.

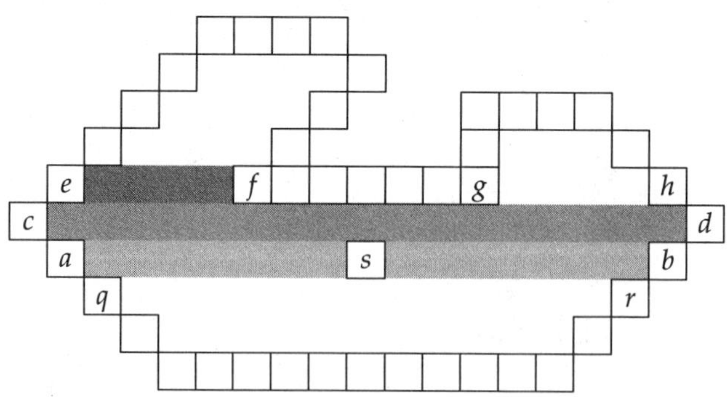

We work with groups of pixels that lie along a horizontal line segment between points of the contour to be filled. The seed is the point denoted by *s*. First, we fill the line *ab* by starting from *s* and coloring all pixels to its right until we reach a pixel with the contour color, *b*, and then by coloring all pixels to its left until we reach a pixel with the contour color, *a*.

Next, we find that this line segment has two neighboring segments, *cd* above it and *qr* below it, by looking at the pixel above *b* and the pixel below *b*. We will describe how to do so, but for now we simply note that we have found two new seed pixels, one in *cd* and another in *qr*. We can then process one of them, and therefore we need a way to keep track of seed pixels that have been found but not yet processed. A *stack* provides the desired mechanism. We can *push* both seeds onto the stack and then *pop* the stack to pick the next seed.

Suppose that we select a seed from *cd*. After it is colored, we find two seeds, one each from *ef* and *gh*. No seed is picked from *ab* because that has already been colored. If we select the seed from *gh*, we color all the line segments directly above it. Then we color all the line segments above *ef* and finally all the segments below *ab*. In this way the stack stays relatively small.

11.3 IMPLEMENTATION OF CONNECTIVITY FILLING

11.3.1 The Basics

We proceed now with a C implementation of the method just outlined. We present the code in the order in which it can be put into a file for compilation and execution. The module doing the filling consists of three short C routines, one to initialize the stack, and two to add and remove elements from the stack. To help you test them, we also provide a testing module consisting of the main program and an output routine. The code dealing with the stack is presented in Listing 11.2.1.

Listing 11.2.1: Local Stack — `File con_fill.c`

```
typedef unsigned char pPixel;    /* could be changed */
static pPixel ** pxstack;
static pPixel ** stp;
static int StackSize;

void init_stack(int pixwidth)
{
     StackSize = pixwidth;
     pxstack = (pPixel **) malloc( StackSize*sizeof(pPixel *) );
     if(!pxstack) exit(0); /* error messages should be added */
```

```
    stp = pxstack;
}

void push(pPixel *A)
{
    if(stp < pxstack+StackSize) *stp++ = A;
    else exit(0); /* error messages should be added */
}

pPixel *pop()
{
    if(stp > pxstack) return *(--stp);
    else return (pPixel *)0;
}
```

When the stack is empty, `pop` returns a null pointer. The size of the stack depends on the size of the image, and we use a heuristic to make it equal to the image width.

11.3.2 Calling the Filling Module

The filling module communicates with the rest of the program through the `fill()` routine and a `set_demo()` routine that can be used to animate the program. They are shown in Listing 11.2.2.

Listing 11.2.2: Connectivity Fill through Lines — `File con_fill.c`

```
void fill_line(pPixel *, pPixel, pPixel, int);

fill(pPixel *seed, pPixel border_color, pPixel fill_color, int width)
{
    pPixel * pxp;

    init_stack(width);
    push(seed);
    while(pxp = pop())
        fill_line(pxp, border_color, fill_color, width);
}

static int verbose = 0;

set_demo()
{
    verbose = 1 - verbose;
}
```

The stack is initialized and the seed is pushed onto it. Then, the program goes into a loop where seed pixels are popped from the stack and used as

Plate 2 Snapshot of a display showing color samples and their names in the X database (see Section 2.7)

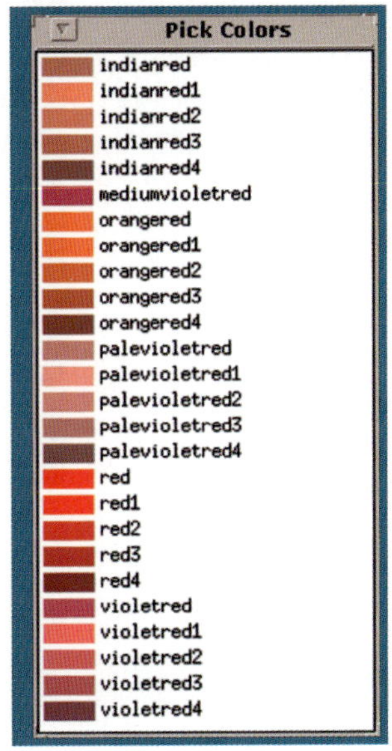

Plate 1 Snapshot of the pixel painting program of Section 2.6.3

Plate 3 Snapshot of the pixel painting program similar to that described in Section 7.5.5. The program has two windows with the *working* window using enlarged pixels.

Plate 4 A pie chart produced with the program of Section 18.2.2

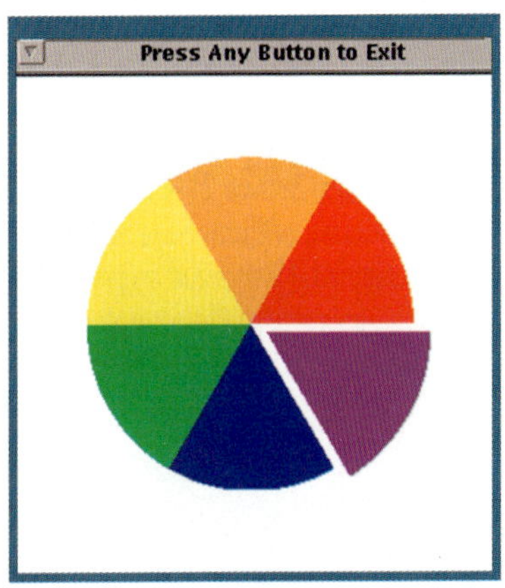

Plate 5 Snapshot of game using graphins of many colors. Generated by the method suggested in Assignment 8 of Chapter 20.

Plate 6 A composite 8-bit display from a 24-bit original without using halftoning. Note the contouring artifacts. (*Syntesized original courtesy of Professor Arie Kaufman, SUNY, Stony Brook.*)

Plate 7 A composite 8-bit display from a 24-bit original using error diffusion halftoning (described in Section 21.4.2). The contouring artificats have been eliminated. (*Syntesized original courtesy of Professor Arie Kaufman, SUNY, Stony Brook.*)

Plate 8 A composite 8-bit display from a 24-bit original without using halftoning. Note the contouring artifacts. (*Scanned original from Standard Color Image Data, ISO/ TC 130 courtesy of Professor Masayuki Nakajima, Tokyo Institute of Technology.*)

Plate 9 A composite 8-bit display from a 24-bit original using error diffusion halftoning (described in Section 21.4.2). The contouring artifacts have been eliminated. (*Scanned original from Standard Color Image Data, ISO/TC 130 courtesy of Professor Masayuki Nakajima, Tokyo Institute of Technology.*)

Plate 10
Daedalus,
courtesy of Virgin
Interactive Entertainment

Plate 11 *Daedalus*,
courtesy of Virgin
Interactive Entertainment

Plate 13 *X-WING*, © 1992, courtesy of LUCASARTS

Plate 12 *Dark Forces*, © 1995,
courtesy of LUCASARTS

Plate 14
SIMCITY 2000
(win, 4th zoom level, cover image), courtesy of Maxis

Plate 15
Magic: The Gathering, courtesy of MicroProse Software, Inc.

Plate 16
Dark Forces, © 1992, courtesy of LUCASARTS

Plate 17
Myst,
courtesy of
Broderbund
Software

Plate 18
Myst,
courtesy of
Broderbund
Software

Plate 19 *ECO East Africa*, courtesy of IVI Publishing, Inc. and Viridis Corporation

Plate 20 *ECO East Africa*, courtesy of IVI Publishing, Inc. and Viridis Corporation

Plate 21 *Across the Rhine*, courtesy of Microprose Software

Plate 22 *Fleet Defender Gold (F–14)*, courtesy of Microprose Software

Plate 23 *Aces of the Deep*, courtesy of Sierra On-line, Inc.

Plate 24
IndyCar Gold,
courtesy of Virgin
Interactive Entertainment

Plate 25
Ultimate Football '95,
courtesy of MicroProse
Software, Inc.

Plate 26 *Absolute Zero*, courtesy of Domark Software, Inc. 1995

Plate 27 *The Orion Conspiracy*, courtesy of Domark Software, Inc. 1995

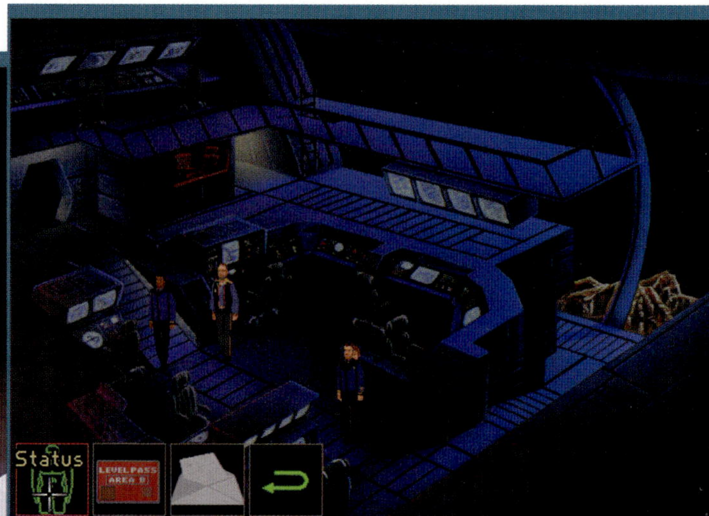

arguments in a procedure that fills line segments. The loop terminates when the stack is empty. The colors of the border and the interior pixels may or may not be the same. The program works correctly either way.

If the pixmap is displayed on a screen, the filling operation can be seen in real time. If not, a variable `verbose` can be used to control the calling of output statements from inside the filling routines. The variable `verbose` is hidden from other modules. They set it by calling the function `set_demo()`.

11.3.3 Filling a Line Segment

The code in Listing 11.3 does the actual filling (the two `while` loops) and then checks the lines above and below for new seeds.

Listing 11.3: Filling a Scanline — `File con_fill.c`

```
void check_line(pPixel *, pPixel *, pPixel , pPixel );

void fill_line(pPixel *seed, pPixel border_color, pPixel fill_color, int width)
{
    register pPixel *pxp;
    pPixel *pleft, *pright;

    pxp = seed;
    while( *pxp != border_color ) *pxp++ = fill_color;
    pright = pxp - 1;  /* last pixel colored */
    pxp = seed-1;
    while( *pxp != border_color ) *pxp-- = fill_color;
    pleft = pxp + 1;   /* last pixel colored */
    /* Check line above */
    check_line( pleft - width, pright - width,
                border_color, fill_color );
    /* Check line below */
    check_line( pleft + width, pright + width,
                border_color, fill_color );

    /*  show intermediate steps*/
    if(verbose) show_results();
}
```

The function `show_results()` (presumably) is provided by the main program. The filling program need not know anything about it.

The `check_line()` code is the only one that requires some attention. It shown in Listing 11.4.

Listing 11.4: Line Connectivity — `File con_fill.c`

```
void check_line(pPixel *pleft, pPixel *pright,
        pPixel border_color, pPixel fill_color)
{
    register pPixel *pxp;

    pxp = pright;
    while(1) {
/*1*/           while( (*pxp == border_color || *pxp == fill_color  )
                                    && pxp>pleft) pxp--;
        /* Check why we exited the loop */
/*2*/           if(*pxp==border_color || *pxp == fill_color) return;
/*3*/           push(pxp);
/*4*/           while(*pxp != border_color && *pxp != fill_color) pxp--;
/*5*/           if(pxp <= pleft) return;
    }
}
```

The program projects the two end pixels of a line segment to the lines above and below it, tries to find line segments that overlap the one just filled, and pushes a pixel onto the stack for each segment. The program alternatively traverses pixels on the border (or pixels that have already been filled) and uncolored pixels. The operation is illustrated in Figure 11.3.

Figure 11.3 Illustration of the operation of the code shown in Listing 11.4.

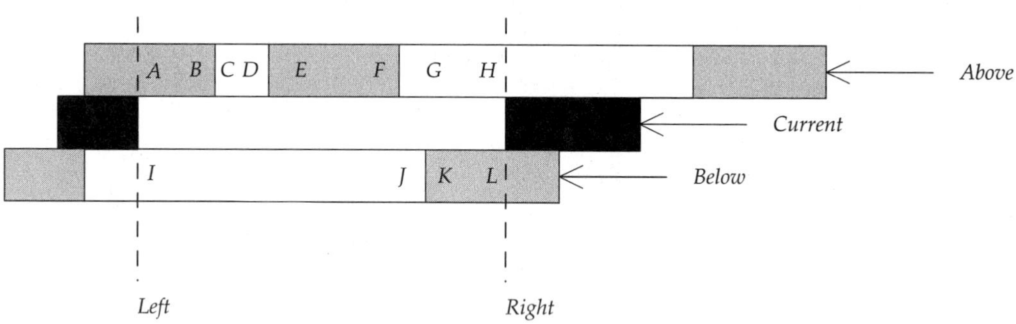

In the line labeled *Above* we start with pixel *H* and break right away from the loop of Statement 1 because *H* does not have a color. It is pushed onto the stack (Statement 3). We then move to *G* while executing Statement 4. When we reach *F*, we drop out of the inner loop (*F* has a color) and go to the top of the outside loop, executing Statement 1 while moving from *F* to *E*. When we reach *D*, we find that it is not colored, so we exit from the inner loop and *D* is pushed onto the stack. Statement 4 takes us to *C* and then to *B*. Subsequently, Statement 1 takes us from *B* to *A*. When we reach *A*, we exit from the inner loop because `pxp` equals `pleft`. Then Statement 2 causes a return and we have finished with the line *Above*.

In the line labeled *Below* we start at *L* and execute Statement 1 until we reach *K* and then *J*. Next, *J* passes the test of Statement 2 and is pushed onto the stack. Then we move from *J* to *I* while executing Statement 4. In this case we return because of Statement 5.

Figure 11.4 Sequence of steps in a connectivity fill.

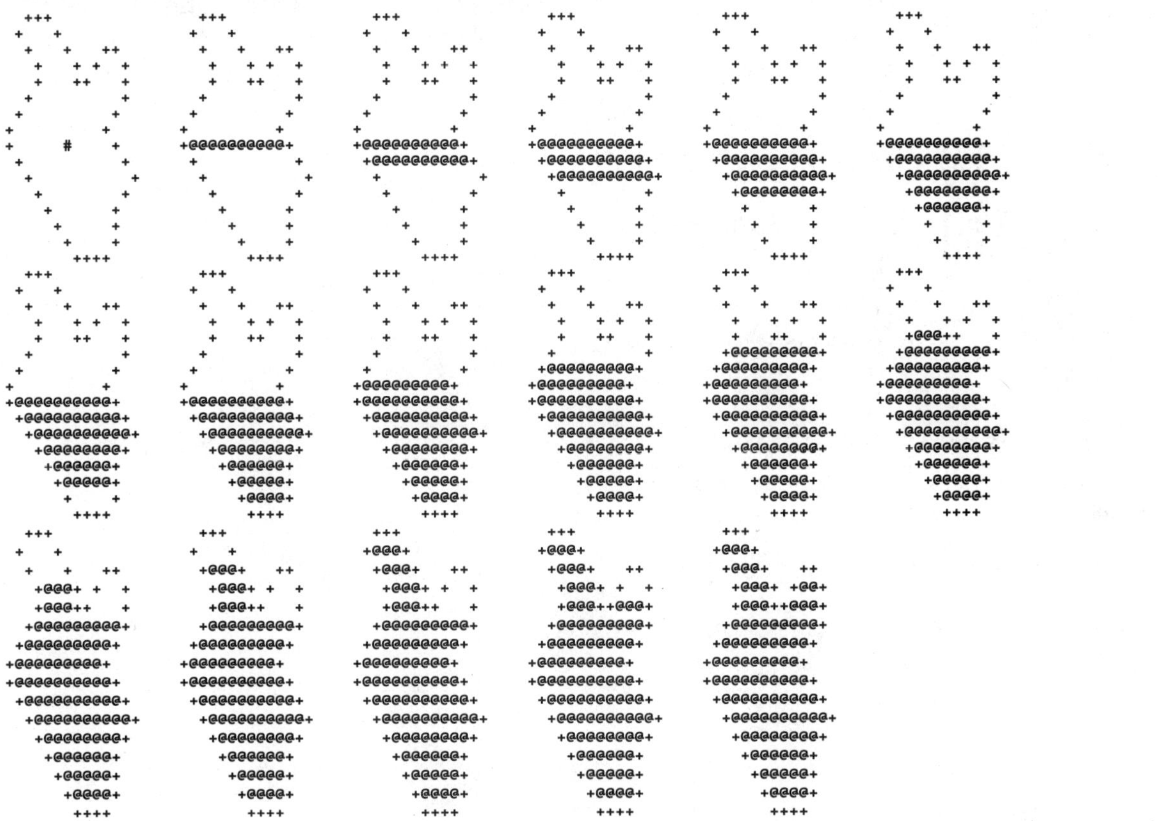

Figure 11.4 shows a sequence of pixmaps as the contour is filled. They were produced by running the procedures just described with the main and display programs described in Section 11.4.

11.3.4 Defensive Programming

The only crucial assumption of the filling method described is that a closed contour with color `border_color` surrounds pixels of a different color. If that is not true, color will "leak" out. This is not a major problem by itself because failure should be expected if there is no solution to the problem. Unfortunately, the way the program is written, not only does color leak but the program also crashes by going outside the pixmap boundary.

The first type of failure is acceptable, but the second is not. There are two ways to deal with it. One is to add checks for pixmap bounds in the filling routines. The other is to change the value of all pixels in the frame of the pixmap into the value used to mark the border. The second solution is preferable for two reasons: It does not slow down the execution; and it does not interfere with the graphics display because the filling is normally done in a buffer space rather than the refresh memory itself.

11.4 TESTING CONNECTIVITY FILLING

11.4.1 Stand Alone Testing

The simple program of Listing 11.5 can be used to test the procedures of Section 11.3. It reads from the standard input a character matrix that represents a pixmap and then calls `fill()` with a seed pixel and the colors as arguments.

Listing 11.5: Testing Program — `File fill_test.c`

```
/*   Demonstration of Connectivity Fill    */
typedef unsigned char pPixel;

#define PIXMAP_WIDTH   16

static pPixel m[PIXMAP_WIDTH][PIXMAP_WIDTH];
static int height;

static int demo   =   0;
static int bcolor = '1';
static int fcolor = '4';
static int scolor = '2';

main(int arc, char **arv)
{
     register i, j;
     char bf[PIXMAP_WIDTH+1];
```

```
    int seedfound = 0;
    pPixel *seed;

    while(arc>1 && arv[1][0]=='-') {
        switch(arv[1][1]){
        case 'b': bcolor = atoi(arv[1]+2); break;
        case 'd': set_demo();
                  demo = 1 - demo; break;
        case 'f': fcolor = atoi(arv[1]+2); break;
        case 's': scolor = atoi(arv[1]+2); break;
        default:;
        }
        arc--; arv++;
    }

    for(i=0; i<PIXMAP_WIDTH; i++){
        if( !gets(bf) ) break;
        for(j=0; j<PIXMAP_WIDTH; j++) {
            m[i][j] = bf[j];
            if(bf[j]==scolor) {
                seed = &(m[i][j]);
                seedfound = 1;
            }
        }
    }

    height = i;
    show_results();
    if(!seedfound) return;
    *seed = '0';
    fill(seed, bcolor, fcolor, PIXMAP_WIDTH);
    if(!demo) show_results();
}
```

The function of Listing 11.6 prints a character matrix representing the bitmap.

Listing 11.6: Display Function — `File fill_test.c`

```
show_results()
{
    register i, j;
    char bf[PIXMAP_WIDTH+1];
    pPixel tv;
```

```
        for(i=0; i<height; i++){
            for(j=0; j<PIXMAP_WIDTH; j++) {
                tv = m[i][j];
                bf[j] = tv=='0' ? ' ':
                    tv==bcolor ? '+':
                    tv==fcolor ? '@':
                    tv==scolor ? '#': 'X';
            }
            bf[j] = 0;
            puts(bf);
        }
}
```

11.4.2 Integrating Connectivity Filling in the Pixel Editor

Adding connectivity filling to the pixel editor requires modifications similar to those described in Section 10.7. A panel/menu selection should be provided that sets the event handler to `get_points()` and calls the `set_xyc_use()` function with a pointer to an intermediate function that eventually will call `fill()` of Listing 11.2.2 with `n` equal to 1. Listing 11.7 shows one possible implementation of the intermediate function. Because the drawing was saved in an integer array, defining `pPixel` as an integer is necessary.

Listing 11.7: Enhancement of Pixel Painting

```
typedef int pPixel;

interm_fill(int *xp, int *yp, int color)
{
        int *sp = &(pix[*xp/d0][*yp/d0]);
        fill(sp, color, color, MAX_WIDTH);
}
```

11.5 CONCLUSIONS

Connectivity filling is a useful tool for any pixel painting program, including programs that design icons such as `bitmap`. It also illustrates the fact that programs that appear to be simple (Listing 11.1) may be quite wasteful in terms of computing resources. An efficient program usually requires far more care to write and often is more complex than an inefficient program. Of course the converse is not true. A program can be both complicated and wasteful, and some efficient programs can be quite simple.

11.6 ASSIGNMENTS

1. Implement the algorithm of Listings 11.2 and 11.3 and incorporate it into the pixel painting program as suggested in Section 11.4.
2. Implementation of the algorithm described in this chapter is highly modular but inefficient because of the large number of function calls and the passing of a large number of arguments. Write a more efficient implementation by (a) incorporating `init_stack` and, in particular, `fill_line()` inside `fill()`; (b) storing the last three arguments of `fill()` in static variables where they can be accessed by `check_line()`.
3. The filling algorithm described in this chapter ignores the existing color of a pixel as long as it is different from the color used for filling or the border. Modify the algorithm so that pixels are filled as long as they have a particular target color. This modification would allow filling with different colors.
4. Expand the program of Assignment 3 to change the color used for filling each time a new seed is popped from the stack.
5. Expand the program of Assignment 3 to copy part of an image into the interior of a contour. In particular, the filling function should have the following argument structure.

```
fill(pPixel *seed, pPixel target_color,
   pPixel *color_source, int width)
```

6. Design a program that animates filling of a vase with liquid (see Figure 11.5). Users should be able to draw any shape, select a seed, and then fill the vase gradually to the top without overflowing and spilling any liquid.

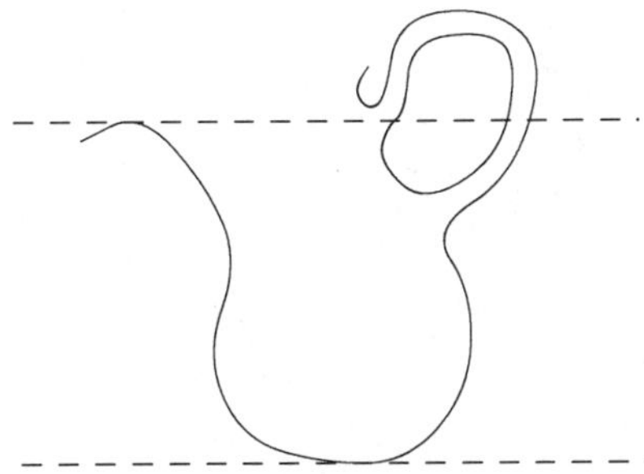

Figure 11.5 Upper and lower bounds for the shape of a vase that is to be filled with liquid.

Suggestions: Your progam should find the highest and lowest points of the contour that correspond to a closed shape, perform connectivity filling in a buffer, and then copy the buffer from the lowest point up. The `idle()` function might be called between displays so that the filling occurs gradually.

7. Modify Assignment 6 so that the liquid has an ice cube floating in it. The challenge is to allow for lateral motion when the ice cube hits an obstacle.

12

Filling Polygons

Scope of the Chapter

Filling polygons using a parity rule • Singular cases • Facilities of the Starter Toolkit for polygon filling

12.1 INTRODUCTION

In this chapter we discuss a technique of filling polygons called *parity filling*. In contrast to the method of Chapter 11, this method requires no seed, and it can find the interior pixels from the description of the outline. It is based on the *parity rule*, which can be expressed as follows.

Suppose that the outline of a region has been drawn with chalk on a sidewalk. A person walking along the sidewalk will be inside the region after crossing the outline *once*. Crossing the outline a second time means that the person is outside the region. If the region has a complex outline (such as the figures in the bottom row of Figure 11.1), the person may cross the outline more times. Crossing it for the third time will again put the person inside the region; for the fourth time, outside, and so on. Hence the following rule.

Parity Rule: *When we have crossed the outline of a region an odd number of times, we are inside the region; otherwise we are outside the region.*

Some complications result from the need to define crossing more precisely, as Figure 12.1 illustrates. Obviously, the footsteps on the left go first inside and then outside the triangle, but what about the footsteps on the right? We deal with such issues later when we try to translate the parity rule into useful programs.

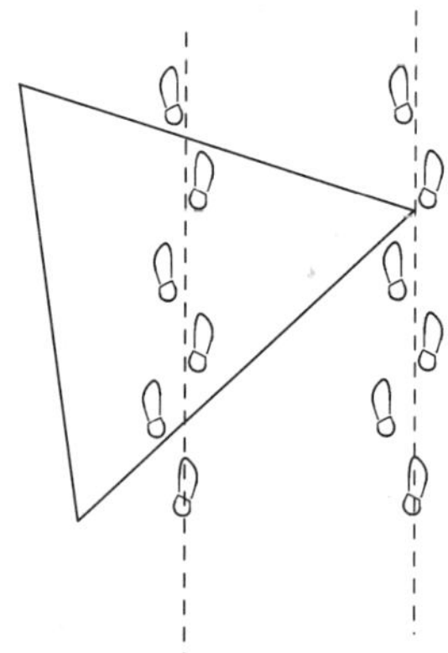

Figure 12.1 The footsteps on the left first go inside and then outside the triangle. But what about the footsteps on the right?

Both *Xlib* and the Starter Toolkit offer primitive functions that fill polygons (see Section 12.4). However, the algorithm used to fill polygons has other applications besides creating images, so we discuss it in some detail.

12.2 PARITY FILLING

12.2.1 The Basic Method

The parity rule can be used to fill the interior of a polygon with a solid color or texture by drawing a set of parallel lines and then displaying only the parts of the lines that are inside the polygon according to the parity rule.

Let `P[0]`, `P[1]`, ··· `P[n-1]` be the vertices of the polygon. (See Figure 12.2 for an illustration of the discussion. In that case `n` equals 19.) Let `L` denote a line of infinite length, given by an equation of the form $ax + by + c = 0$. Then, we must do the following.

1. Find the sides (`P[i]`,`P[i+1]`) that intersect line `L`. (We interpret the index `n` as `0` because the polygon must be closed.)
2. For each such side find the point of intersection with `L`. Let the points

be Q[0], Q[1], ···, Q[m-1]. Usually, m is a much smaller number than n. In Figure 12.2, m equals 8, and the points Q[] are indexed in the same order as the sides.

3. Sort the points Q along a direction parallel to line L.
4. Let R denote the sorted array. The parts of the line inside the polygon are the segments R[i],R[i+1], for i even. (Zero is considered to be an even number.)

Figure 12.2 Intersection of a line with a polygon where no simple rule (besides sorting) can specify which segments of the line are inside the polygon.

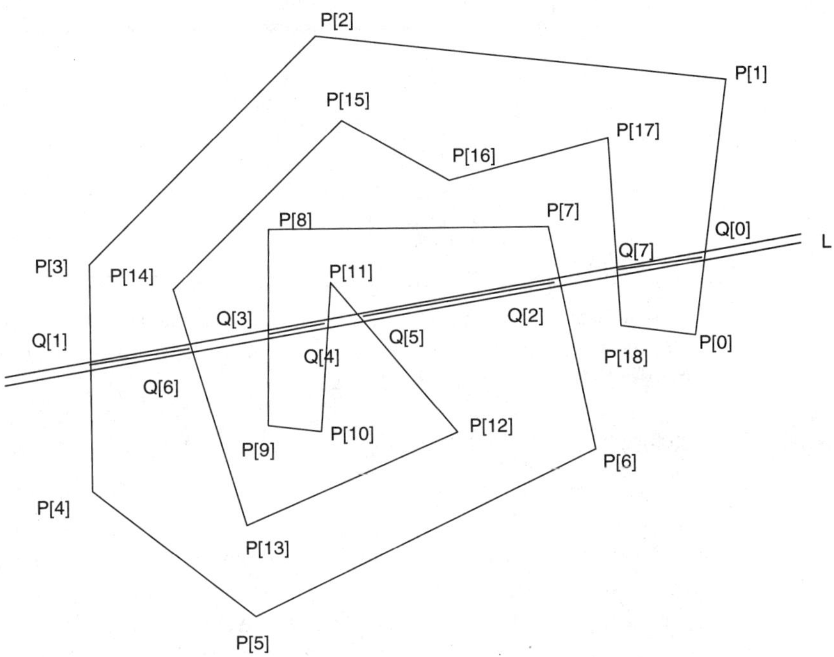

Figure 12.2 shows why the sorting is necessary. For complex polygons, if we find the intersection points by moving along the polygon boundary, they will be rather scrambled. Of course, if the sides are *presorted*, we may be able to avoid sorting the intersection points.

This procedure may fail if the line passes through a polygon vertex, as illustrated in Figure 12.3. When a line passes through a vertex we have the option of counting the vertex as a single intersection or as two, because it is a point that belongs to two sides. If we count such vertices as single, we have the correct answer for vertex *B* but the wrong answer for vertex *A*; the

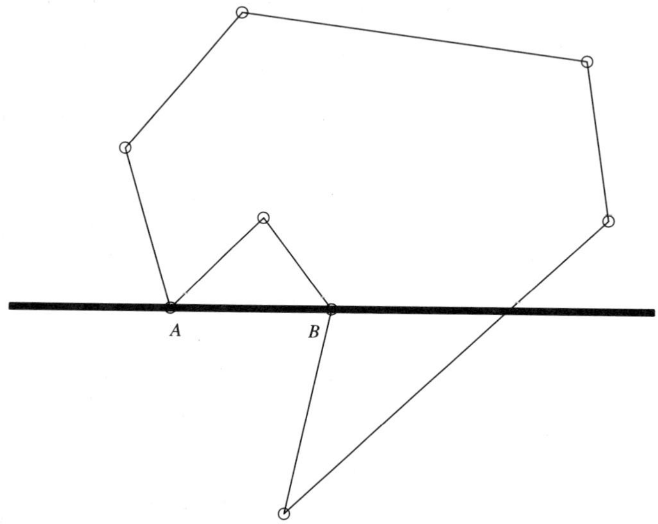

Figure 12.3 Demonstration of singular cases for finding the segments of a line that are inside a polygon.

opposite is true if we count such vertices as double. To find the correct answer we must count vertices such as A as double (or not count them at all) and vertices such as B as single.

12.2.2 Singularities

The cases where vertices of the polygon lie along the scanline `L` are called *singular* because they must be handled differently from the general case. Figure 12.3 shows that such singular cases must be handled differently when the line *pierces* the polygon and when it does not.

If the line pierces the polygon at a vertex (point B in Figure 12.3), clearly there is a crossing and it must be counted as such. If the polygon is not pierced (point A in Figure 12.3), there is no crossing and there should be no change in the parity count. We can see that better by shifting the line by a small amount. In the case of point B, nearby lines — either above or below — cross the outline, so the counting must proceed. In the case of point A, a line just below does not touch the polygon near A. A line just above A crosses the polygon twice. But crossing twice has the same effect on the parity of the count (being even or odd) as not crossing at all.

For simplicity we limit our discussion to the case when line `L` is horizontal, so it is defined by its vertical coordinate `yl`.

We can *finess* singular cases by carefully defining the intersection of a scanline with the sides of the polygon. If a scan line passes through the upper vertex of a side, that intersection is counted. But if a scanline passes through the lower vertex of a side, that intersection is ignored.

Thus when the scanline pierces the polygon at a vertex (point *B* in Figure 12.3), that vertex is counted only once. If the scanline passes through a vertex while the polygon is on one side (point *A* in Figure 12.3), that vertex is either not counted at all (if the polygon is above the scanline) or counted twice (if the polygon is below the scanline). In either case parity is not affected.

Horizontal lines can be ignored entirely. Indeed both vertices are either ignored (if they are thought of as "lower") or both counted (if they are thought of as "upper"). In either case the parity count remains the same.

Figure 12.4 Treatment of horizontal sides during parity fill. Filled triangles mark upper vertices (counted), and empty triangles mark lower vertices (not counted). Horizontal sides between the former are drawn; between the others are not.

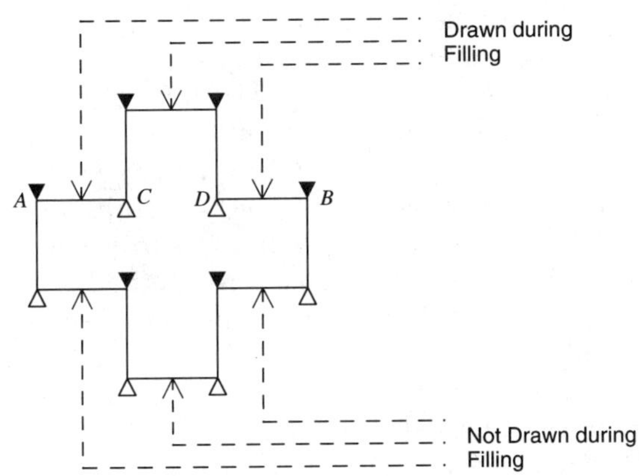

This approach has only one weakness: Certain parts of the boundary are not drawn. Figure 12.4 illustrates the situation. Filled triangles mark upper vertices that are counted during parity fill, and empty triangles mark lower vertices that are not counted. As a result, horizontal sides between vertices marked with a filled triangle are drawn. (Note that sides *AC* and *BD* are drawn as part of *AB*.)

If the resolution is high compared to the size of the polygon, the defect is difficult to spot. But for lower resolutions the defect is quite visible. The remedy is to make a list of all horizontal sides that have the polygon above them and draw them individually (see Assignment 1).

12.3 THE LINE SWEEP METHOD

12.3.1 Finding the Intersection of Many Parallel Lines with a Polygon

To find the intersections of a set of parallel lines with a polygon by testing the intersection of each line with all the sides is wasteful. A pair of parallel lines close to each other are likely to intersect the same sides of the polygon. We can solve the problem more efficiently by *sorting* the polygon sides along a direction perpendicular to that of the scanline `L`.

For simplicity, we assume in the rest of this chapter that `L` is horizontal. Then the sorting is done according to `y`.

If the number of sides is N and the sides are not sorted, we must consider all N sides for each scanline. If the number of possible scanlines is M, we must look for NM intersection points.

By presorting the sides, we can keep track of those whose lowest point is above the scanline or whose highest point is below the scanline. Then we need not check for the intersection of the scanline with those sides. If N_s is the average number of sides that do not belong to either group, we must look for $N_s M$ intersection points. Sorting has a cost of about $N \log_2 N$.

In practice, M is a much larger number than N because M is determined by the resolution of the display. Thus the dominant terms of the computational costs are those that depend on M.

In the example of Figure 12.2, N equals 19 while N_s is about 6. The number of possible scanlines, M, for the resolution used to print the image is about 400. Thus the method without sorting would require checking for $19 \times 400 = 7600$ line intersections. The method with sorting would require about $19 \log_2 19 = 95$ data-moving operations and about $6 \times 400 = 2400$ line intersections. Because finding the intersection of a line with the horizontal is probably more expensive than a data comparison and move operation, the cost of the method with sorting is about one-third the cost of the method that looks at all lines.

The method with sorting is a special case of the *line sweep* method for solving geometric problems. In all such methods the objects are sorted along a particular direction, and then a line perpendicular to that direction *sweeps* through the region.

After the sides have been sorted, they can be divided into three lists. An *active list* contains all sides that are intersected by the current scanline (or sweep line in general). A *waiting list* comprises sides that are below the current scanline and need not be examined now but may be examined in the future. A *discarded list* of the sides above the current scanline that have been examined in the past and will not be visited again. Initially all sides are in the waiting list, and at the end all should be in the discarded list.

12.3.2 Preparing the Segment List

To prepare the segment list we create a new structure, `Segment`, with four floating point type members so that we can perform arithmetic on them. Listing 12.1 contains this structure.

Listing 12.1: Definition of Segment Type — `File segment.h`

```
typedef struct {
    double x, y, X, Y;
    int status;
} Segment;
```

The `status` member is for future use. The code will also make use of the type `pPoint` defined in Section 10.6.

Next we fill an array, `sides[]`, of such structures by mapping each pair of adjacent polygon vertices, `P[i]`, `P[i+1]`, to one of them. The routine that does so while omitting horizontal sides is shown in Listing 12.2.1.

Listing 12.2.1: Construction of Sides from Vertices — `File fill.c`

```
#include <Starter.h>    /* for declaration of pPoint */
#include <segment.h>

int make_sides( pPoint *P, int n, Segment *sides)
{
    register i;
    register pPoint *pp;
    register Segment  *sp;
    double x, y, X, Y;

    sp = sides;
    x = (P+n-1)->x;    y = (P+n-1)->y;    /* last point */
    for(i=0, pp=P; i<n; i++, pp++) {
        X = pp->x;     Y = pp->y;
        if(Y != y) {  /* not a horizontal side */
            sp->x = x;    sp->y = y;
            sp->X = X;    sp->Y = Y;
            sp->status = 1;
            sp++;
        }
        x = X;         y= Y;
    }
    return(sp-sides);
}
```

Next we must sort the sides in the vertical direction. A convenient way to do so is to have a fixed relative position of the two points of a side. We choose to have the first point x,y higher than the second X,Y. The code in Listing 12.2.2 ensures this result.

Listing 12.2.2: Rearrangement of Side Endpoints — `File fill.c`

```
void flip_sides(Segment *sides, int ns)
{
    register i;
    register Segment  *sp;
    double tmpxy;

    for(i=0, sp=sides; i<ns; i++, sp++) {
        if(sp->Y < sp->y) {
            tmpxy = sp->y; sp->y = sp->Y; sp->Y = tmpxy;
            tmpxy = sp->x; sp->x = sp->X; sp->X = tmpxy;
        }
    }
}
```

12.3.3 Sorting the Segment List

The sorting of the sides along the vertical direction can be done using the C library routine

```
qsort( void *base, int number, int width,
    int (*comparator)(void *, void*) )
```

The argument `base` is a pointer to a byte array. Any structure is acceptable as long as `qsort()` is told its width, `width`, and the number of elements present, `numb`. Here, the first argument is the segment array start `sides`, the second argument is the number returned by `make_sides`, and the third argument `sizeof(Segment)`.

The element comparison routine, `comparator()` must be written by the applications programmer, and it takes as arguments two pointers to items in the array. It must return an integer that is greater than, equal to, or less than zero when the item pointed to by the first argument is greater than, equal to, or less than the item pointed to by the second argument. Listing 12.2.3 shows an implementation of the comparison function. It has been named `side_compar()`.

The segments are sorted primarily according to their `y` members. If the `y` members are equal, then the segments are sorted according to `x`. If both `x` and `y` are equal, the two sides are sharing a polygon vertex that is higher than either of its two neighbors. In that case the side to the left (the one with the smaller `X`) is placed ahead of the side to the right.

Listing 12.2.3: Comparison Function — `File fill.c`

```
#define COMP(A)    if(p1->A>p2->A) return(1);  \
        else if(p1->A<p2->A) return(-1);

int side_compar(Segment *p1, Segment *p2)
{
    COMP(y) else {
        COMP(x) else {
            COMP(X) else {
                COMP(Y) else return(0);
            }
        }
    }
}
```

Figure 12.5 shows the order in which the sides of a polygon are sorted according to the rules of the routine `side_compar()`. The horizontal dashed lines point to the vertices and are marked by pairs of numbers corresponding to the two sides meeting at a vertex.

Figure 12.5 A polygon with its sides numbered according to the rules of the routine `side_compar()`. The horizontal dashed lines point to the vertices and are marked by pairs of numbers corresponding to the two sides meeting at a vertex.

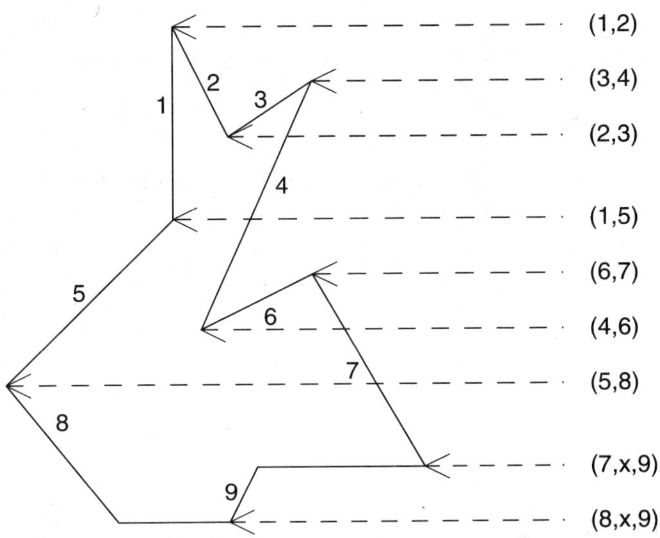

12.3.4 Traversal of the Segment List

We use Figure 12.5 to outline the segment list traversal. The markers < and > denote the bounds of the active list. Any side in the discarded list is enclosed in parentheses. Initially, all sides are in the waiting list, so our list of sides can be written as

```
<>1 2 3 4 5 6 7 8 9
```

First, the two top sides, 1 and 2, are brought into the active list so that the list of sides can be expressed as

```
<1 2> 3 4 5 6 7 8 9
```

When the scanline moves at the level of the second dashed line, sides 3 and 4 are added to the active list:

```
<1 2 3 4> 5 6 7 8 9
```

When the scanline moves past the third dashed line, sides 2 and 3 are moved into the discarded list:

```
<1 (2) (3) 4> 5 6 7 8 9
```

Crossing the fourth dashed line causes side 1 to be replaced by side 5 in the active list:

```
<(1) (2) (3) 4 5 > 6 7 8 9
```

Because all the discarded sides are contiguous, we may now move the first marker past side 3:

```
(1) (2) (3) <4 5 > 6 7 8 9
```

The subsequent changes in the list as the scanline moves lower are given without comment:

```
(1) (2) (3) <4 5 6 7 > 8 9
(1) (2) (3) <(4) 5 (6) 7 > 8 9
(1) (2) (3) <(4) (5) (6) 7 8> 9
(1) (2) (3) (4) (5) (6) <7 8> 9
(1) (2) (3) (4) (5) (6) <(7) 8 9>
(1) (2) (3) (4) (5) (6) (7) <8 9>
(1) (2) (3) (4) (5) (6) (7) <(8) (9)>
(1) (2) (3) (4) (5) (6) (7) (8) (9) <>
```

12.3.5 Implementation of the Traversal of the Segment List

In Listing 12.2.4 we provide the C code for performing the traversal described in Section 12.3.4. We need two pointers corresponding to the two markers (< and >) used in that discussion. We also need a way to mark segments that are in the discarded list and use the `status` variable for that purpose. Initially, `status` is set to 1 for all segments. Let `pstart` be the pointer corresponding to the start of the active list (the < marker) and `pend` be the marker corresponding to the end of the active list (the > marker). Here, `yc` is the current `y` coordinate of the scanline.

Listing 12.2.4: Polygon Scan Conversion — `File fill.c`

```
void draw();

void scan_convert(Segment sides[], int n) /* sides is sorted array */
{
    Segment *pstart, *pend, *sides_end;
    register Segment *sp;
    int yc, bottom;

    sides_end = sides + n;
    for(sp=sides; sp<sides_end; sp++) sp->status = 1;

    bottom = sides[0].Y;
    for(sp=sides+1; sp<sides_end; sp++)
        if(sp->Y > bottom) bottom = sp->Y;
    pstart = pend = sides;

    for(yc = sides[0].y; yc <= bottom; yc++) {
        /* bring into the active list*/
        while(pend->y <= yc && pend<sides_end) pend++;
        /* discard */
        for(sp=pstart; sp<pend; sp++) {
            if(sp->status) if (sp->Y <= yc) sp->status = 0;
        }
        /* move pstart for efficiency */
        while( pstart<sides_end && !(pstart->status) ) pstart++;

        /* find intersections */
        draw(pstart, pend, yc);
    }
}
```

The main loop contains four steps:

(1) All segments that have $y \leq$ `yc` are brought into the active list.

(2) All segments that have $y \geq$ `yc` are discarded by setting `status` = 0.

(3) The start of the active list is moved past all contiguous discarded segments (for purposes of efficiency only).

(4) Do the actual filling by calling the procedure `draw()`.

In the simplest case `draw()` finds the intersections of all the lines in the active list with the horizontal line at the height of its third argument.

New sides are brought into the active list when the top point equals `yc` and old sides are discarded when their bottom point equals `yc`. This procedure avoids the occurrence of singularities described in Section 12.2.2.

12.3.6 The Drawing Function

The code in Listing 12.2.5 is one possible implementation of `draw()`.

Listing 12.2.5: Drawing Scan Lines — `File fill.c`

```
#define NC     128  /* maximum number of sides intersecting a scanline */

void draw(Segment *p1, Segment *p2, int y)
{
     register Segment *sp;
     double dx, dy, xy;
     double xcut[NC];
     int n = 0;
     register i;
     int k;
     double xtmp;

     for(sp=p1; sp<p2; sp++) {
          if(!sp->status || sp->y==sp->Y) continue;
          dx = sp->X - sp->x;
          dy = sp->y - sp->Y;
          xy = sp->x * sp->Y - sp->X * sp->y;
          xcut[n++] = - (xy + y*dx)/dy;
     }
     do {
          k = 0;
          for(i=1; i<n; i++){
               if(xcut[i-1]>xcut[i]) {
                    xtmp = xcut[i-1];
                    xcut[i-1] = xcut[i];
                    xcut[i] = xtmp;
                    k = 1;
               }
          }
     } while(k);
     for(i=1; i<n; i += 2)
          put_line((int)xcut[i-1], y, (int)xcut[i], y);
}
```

The code of Listing 12.2.5 relies on the equation of a straight line joining two points. Equation (10.6) provides that result expressing y as a function of x. Because y is given this time and we need to find x, that equation is rewritten with the current notation as:

$$x = sp \rightarrow x + \frac{(sp \rightarrow X - sp \rightarrow x)}{(sp \rightarrow Y - sp \rightarrow y)}(y - sp \rightarrow y) \qquad (12.1)$$

Straightforward algebra yields the expression used in the code of `draw()` in Listing 12.2.5. If the segment is horizontal, dividing by $sp \rightarrow y - sp \rightarrow Y$ corresponds to division by 0 and should be avoided. The preceding implementation checks on whether the segment is horizontal, and if it is, ignores it. This is another example of defensive programming. Normally `draw()` should not encounter any such segments. Once written, however, the routine may be used for another application where horizontal segments have not been discarded.

Figure 12.6 The sides of the polygons are numbered according to their order in the sorted list. Connecting according to the order of the sides in the sorted list will give the correct answer for scanline `L1` but the wrong answer for scanline `L2`.

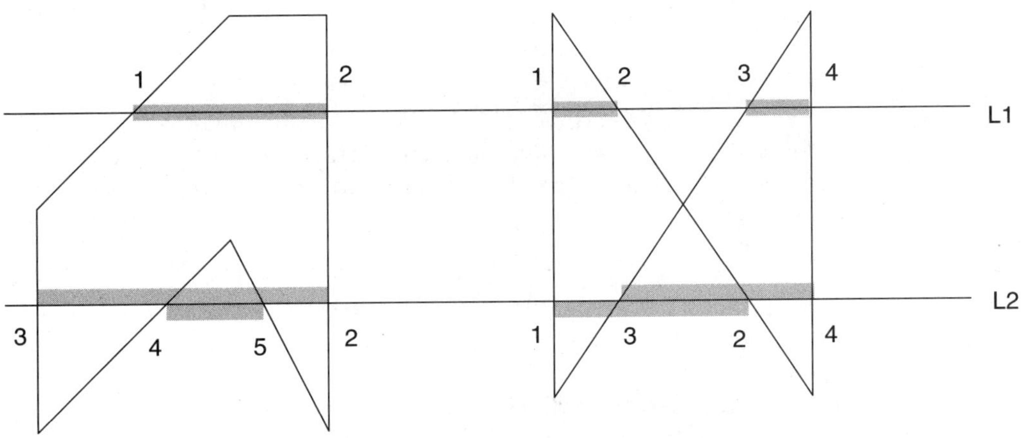

The order of the intersections found in the first part of `draw()` is not guaranteed to be correct, as the examples of Figure 12.6 show. Therefore a robust implementation must sort the intersection points (array `xcut[]`) along the horizontal direction. The next group of statements does the sorting using a *bubble* sort. This method is appropriate for this case (as opposed to the *quick* sort implemented by `qsort`) because (a) most of the time the points are already sorted; (b) n usually is small, most often 2, less frequently 4 or 6. The last statement in Listing 12.2.5 draws a line between alternating pairs of points.

12.3.7 Calling the Procedures

The routine in Listing 12.3 takes as argument a collection of points and attempts to fill the polygon defined by them. The routine can be called from any other program and it does not place any limits on the complexity of the polygon to be drawn.

Listing 12.3: Filling Function for Polygons

```
void fill_poly(pPoint *P, int n)
{
     Segment *pol_sides;
     int n_sides;

     pol_sides = (Segment *)malloc(sizeof(Segment)*n);
     n_sides = make_sides(P, n, pol_sides);
     flip_sides(pol_sides, n_sides);
     qsort(pol_sides, n_sides, sizeof(Segment), side_compar);
     scan_convert(pol_sides, n_sides);
}
```

We can easily modify `fill_poly()` to fill polygons with holes. We assume that the array containing the vertices of the polygon also contains some vertices that are used as markers to indicate that no side should be drawn between the previous and the next point. For example, the sequence

```
(89 67)(105 190)(185 100)(-1 -1)(111 94)(118 148)(153 108)
```

may describe two triangles using the pair `(-1 -1)` as separator. Then `fill_poly()` can be written as in Listing 12.4.

Listing 12.4: Filling Function for Polygons with Holes — `File call_fill.c`

```
#include <Starter.h>    /* for declaration of pPoint */
#include <segment.h>
#define marker(A) (A->x<0)

extern int side_compar();

void fill_poly(pPoint *P, int n)
{
     Segment *pol_sides, *cur_sides;
     int n_sides, i0, j, k;
     register i;
```

```
    register pPoint *pp;
    pPoint *pbase;

    pol_sides = (Segment *)malloc(sizeof(Segment)*n);
    cur_sides = pol_sides; n_sides = 0;  pbase = P;
    for(i=i0=0, pp=P; i<n; i++, pp++) {
        if(marker(pp)) {
            k = make_sides(pbase, i-i0, cur_sides);
            cur_sides += k;
            n_sides += k;
            pbase = pp + 1;
            i0=i+1;
        }
    }
    n_sides += make_sides(pbase, i-i0, cur_sides);
    flip_sides(pol_sides, n_sides);
    qsort(pol_sides, n_sides, sizeof(Segment), side_compar);
    scan_convert(pol_sides, n_sides);
}
```

The preceding code is based on the assumption that separator points have a negative `x`. Other conventions may be adapted by redefining the macro `marker()`. Figure 12.7 (on page 292) shows some examples of polygons filled with a program using the code described. Polygons are filled correctly regardless of horizontal sides, self-intersections, or holes.

Clearly, if a polygon is self-intersecting (as in the middle example in Figure 12.7), its interior is not well defined. The parity rule treats different regions like tiles and fills them alternatively.

12.3.8 Directional Parity Fill

Directional parity fill separates the intersections of a scanline with the sides of the polygon into two groups. Instead of counting the number of intersections, it keeps two counts: the DOWN count, which is the number of intersections by sides traversed from top to bottom during a clockwise traversal of the contour; and the UP count, which is the number of intersections by sides traversed from bottom to top during a similar traversal. A point is considered to be inside if the two counts are unequal.

If a polygon is not self-intersecting, the leftmost side contributes to the UP count, the next to the DOWN count, and so on. Therefore the two counts are unequal when the parity is odd, and the directional parity fill produces the same results as the ordinary parity fill. However the results differ for self-intersecting polygons, as illustrated in Figure 12.8 (page 292).

Figure 12.7 The polygon on the left has many horizontal sides, the polygon in the middle is self-intersecting, and the polygon on the right consists of two contours. All have been filled successfully.

Figure 12.8 According to directional fill, the dashed scanline segment between points 2 and 3 is not filled on the left polygon but it is filled on the right polygon.

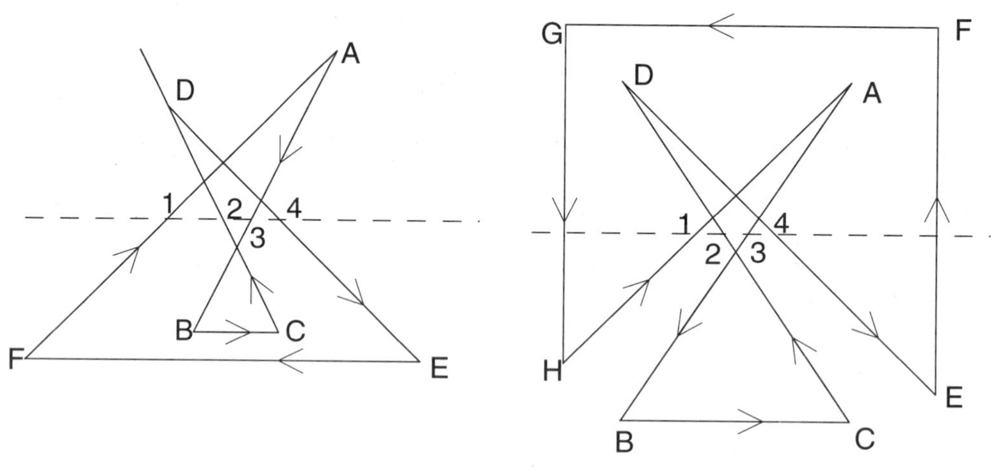

The parity of the intervals of the dashed scanline is given in the table below for the two polygons.

Interval	...,1	1,2	2,3	3,4	4,...
Left Polygon					
UP count	0	1	2	2	2
DOWN count	0	0	0	1	2
Parity count	0	1	0	1	0
Right Polygon					
UP count	0	1	2	2	2
DOWN count	1	1	1	2	3
Parity count	1	0	1	0	1

For the left polygon all the intervals (1,2), (2,3), and (3,4) have unequal count and are all filled. For the right polygon intervals (1,2) and (3,4) have equal counts and are not filled, whereas (2,3) has unequal counts and it is filled. If we used the parity count, (2,3) has a different color from (1,2) and (3,4) in both polygons.

To implement directional fill we need to add a member, `direction`, to the `segment` structure of Section 12.3.2. It should be set to 1 but changed to 2 in the `flip_sides()` function (Listing 12.2.2) when the segments are reversed. The main change will be in the function `draw()` (Listing 12.2.5).

12.4 CONCLUSIONS

Parity fill algorithms have been known for many years, and most graphics libraries include an implementation. (That is much less frequently the case with connectivity filling of the type described in Chapter 11.)

The Starter Toolkit includes a function that does parity filling of the kind described in this chapter. As it requires that the polygon vertices have coordinates declared as `short`, we use the type `pPoint` defined in Section 10.6.

☛ **`void poly_fill(pPoint v[], int n, char rule)`**
Fill the interior of the polygon with `n` vertices stored in `v[]` with the color of the foreground. If the argument `rule` has any value other than `'w'` use the ordinary parity rule; otherwise use the directional parity or winding rule.

Bugs: This routine invokes an *Xlib* function which has two limitations: (a) it does not handle polygons with holes; (b) it does not draw properly the original sides of the polygon (see Section 12.2.2). ☜

The algorithm described in this chapter produces better results than those obtained with `poly_fill()` but at the expense of greater traffic between application and display. Implementing the algorithm on the application side (client) requires that we send each scanline to the display (server) while `poly_fill()` does the filling in the server (see Section 1.3.2).

The algorithms of this chapter can be used not only to fill polygons but other contours as well. The main constraint is that the contour consists of arcs that do not bend in the vertical direction. If they do, they must be subdivided into parts that satisfy the constraint. Figure 12.9 illustrates the situation.

Figure 12.9 The contour on the left can be filled with a parity algorithm. Whether the contour in the middle can be filled depends on how the arcs are subdivided. If they are subdivided as at the top right, it cannot be filled. It can be filled with a parity algorithm if the arcs are subdivided as at the bottom right.

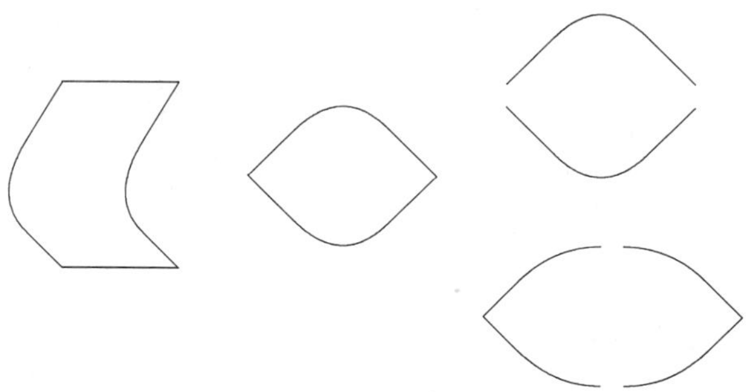

After the arcs are properly subdivided, the only part that needs modification is the `draw()` function. Incidentally, the implementation of this function as presented is rather inefficient if we are interested *only* in polygons. For polygons we can construct the intersection points by using a variation of the line plotting algorithm of Section 10.2 (see Assignment 3). However the code in Listing 12.2.5 is best suited for extensions. For arcs the segment structure must include additional members that can be used to compute the intersection of the arc with a horizontal line.

12.5 ASSIGNMENTS

1. Write a program to determine which of the horizontal sides of a polygon must be drawn after the filling operation.
2. Implement the parity fill of Listing 12.2 but, instead of filling all the area, draw only some of the segments (e.g., every 10 pixels vertically).

3. Modify the code of Listing 12.2.4 to avoid the arithmetic operations of `draw()` as follows. When a segment is added to the active list, start a line plotting process (using the method of Section 10.2). At each step collect all the *intervals* and sort them horizontally. Then use the parity rule to fill the gaps between them.
4. Modify the code of `draw()` (Listing 12.2.5) for the case of directional parity fill as suggested in Section 12.3.8.
5. Modify the filling algorithm to correctly fill contours composed of straight line segments and circular arcs. You must do three things: (a) check on whether each arc bends in the vertical direction, and if it does, subdivide it; (b) add the appropriate members to the `Segment` structure; (c) modify the first part of the `draw()` function to find intersections of horizontal lines with circular arcs. The proper choice of representation for a circular arc can simplify this problem significantly.
6. Investigate the difference in the speed of execution of the polygon filling algorithm described in this chapter for the following special cases of polygons: (a) polygons without holes; (b) polygons without self-intersections; (c) polygons where both (a) and (b) are true; and (d) convex polygons (i.e., polygons with the property that any straight line intersects them in at most two points).
7. Investigate possible simplifications of the polygon filling algorithm and corresponding savings in computation if you know *in advance* that the polygon has any of the four properties of Assignment 6. (In some of these cases you might be able to eliminate the sorting code in Listing 12.2.2 and replace it with a sorting of sides in the active list.)
8. Modify the `fill_poly()` function to construct a function that is called with an extra argument which is a pointer to a point and returns 1 if the point is inside the polygon and 0 otherwise.

   ```
   int point_in_poly(pPoint *P, int n, pPoint *q)
   ```

   As the question may be asked many times for a polygon, devise a *caching* scheme whereby some of the intermediate results are saved in static variables.
9. Use the results of Assignment 8 to add traps or hideaways in the video game of Chapter 3. In particular, modify Assignment 3 of Chapter 3 by replacing the rectangle with an arbitrary polygon drawn by the user.

13

Geometric Objects and Transformations

Scope of the Chapter

Representation of shapes as geometric objects rather than pixel arrays • Scaling • Translation • Rotation • Pointing to objects • Pointing to line segments

13.1 INTRODUCTION

13.1.1 The Limitations of Pixel Arrays

So far we have been working directly with pixels or with structures that are mapped directly into pixels. This work included the pixel painting program and the games with icons. Painting with pixels can be fun but it takes little advantage of the power of computers, and it does little more than can be done with pencil and paper. Pixel arrays have at least three serious inherent limitations.

Loss of identity: Once something has been drawn it loses its "identity." It is simply a set of pixels in the refresh memory of the display screen or, at best, in the `pix` array used in Chapter 2. For example, if we draw a polygon by repeated calls to the line routine, there is no way that we can copy it unless we copy a whole rectangle containing it. This approach eliminates one of the most attractive features of computer use: the ability to replicate data with little effort. It also makes editing difficult. We can modify the drawing by erasing and redrawing, but we cannot, for example, shift a line segment because there is nothing in the description of the picture to identify the line segment as such.

Lack of Scaling: Scaling a picture without significant loss in quality is impossible. Scaling is usually required in two cases: producing objects of different sizes after drawing one of them, and displaying the picture on devices of different resolutions. The first case means that even if we had fixed the identity problem, there are still limits on what we can do with the objects. The second case is probably the more important. If our screen has a resolution of 100 dots per inch and we want a hard copy on a laser printer that has 300 dots per inch, the result will be a picture that is one-third the size of the original. We may want to scale up the picture by a linear factor of 3, but a naive scaling also gives unsatisfactory results. Replacing a pixel by a 3×3 array of pixels produces unsightly "jaggies" (see Figure 13.1). And how about scaling by a factor of 1.5? Or reduction by a factor of 2? Discrete pictures *do not scale well.*

Figure 13.1 The shape in the middle is three times larger than the one on the left, but its shape has much more pronounced "jaggies" than the one on the left. More desirable as three times the shape on the left is the shape on the right, but it cannot be obtained from simple pixel operations.

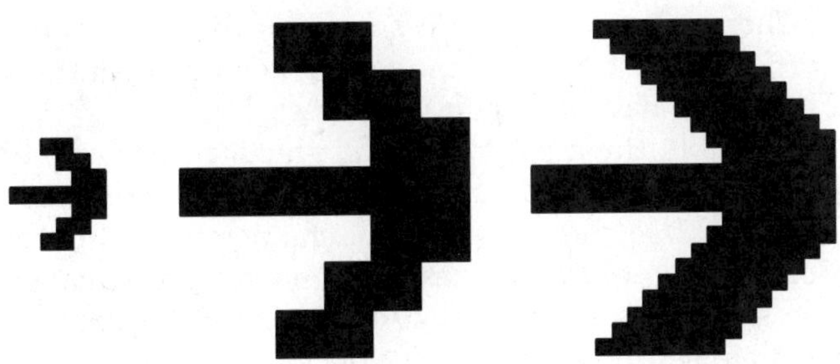

Difficulty of Geometric Transformations

Not only is it impossible to scale discrete pictures satisfactorily, but it also is very difficult to rotate them or apply other simple geometric transformations to them.

Although you may be convinced that simple scaling or rotation schemes fail, you may also think that "smart" scaling schemes that work for discrete pictures exist. There are complex theoretical reasons that such schemes cannot exist, related to the difficulties of digital plotting (Section 10.3). A complete discussion of this point is beyond the scope of this text but the following informal argument may convince you.

When we draw something using a pixel editor, we usually have in mind an analog picture that is approximated by the digital picture. When we apply scaling (or another transformation) we are looking for an approximation to a scaled (or transformed) version of the analog picture. What happens is the following. Let B be a digital picture that is a good approximation to an analog picture A. Usually, the scaled version of B is not a good approximation to the scaled version of A.

There is an additional complication. If the left shape of Figure 13.1 is the arrow at the end of a line in, say, an Engineering drawing, the right shape would not be an appropriate enlargement. The drafter might want to increase the size of the arrow *without* increasing its thickness. To scale properly such images we must distinguish between the linear dimension and the thickness and handle them independently.

13.1.2 Why Do We Care About the Limitations?

Object identity, scaling, rotations, and other transformation, are essential for many applications. Let's revisit the animation program of Chapter 3. Suppose that we want to have the graphins become larger or smaller as they move. We cannot do so unless the change in scale is an integer, and then we cannot avoid introducing major distortions. Having them rotate so that, for example, they face the direction of their motion also is impossible.

There is no way to access parts of the images. For example, if we want parts of their bodies to move, we need a separate bitmap for each frame. Their parts have lost their identities!

Probably the most important practical case of bitmap limitations is that of *font* libraries. Programs that display text (especially formatters such as *latex* and *troff*) need to display characters of different styles (roman, *italic*, **Bold**, and so on) and sizes. If bitmaps were scalable, we would need only one set of characters per style. Because they are not, we need to keep a separate set for each size. If you look at the font library of your system (a likely place is `/usr/lib/fonts`) you see files with names such as:

```
cour.b.10 cour.b.12 cour.b.14 ....
cour.r.10 cour.r.12 cour.r.14 ....
```

(See also Section 1.4.4.) Each file has the bitmaps for a font whose style is given by the single character after the first period (roman, bold, and so on) and whose size is given by the number after the second period (measured in typographers' points). *Scalable fonts* require representations other than bitmaps.

In this chapter we discuss techniques to overcome the three weaknesses described and we use these results in Chapter 14 to create a drawing editor.

To tackle the *object identity* problem we must develop appropriate data structures and procedures that let us pick the object or its parts after it has been drawn.

We study the three basic transformations: scaling, translations, and rotation, as well as some basic geometric operations, such as finding the distance of a point from a line.

13.2 OBJECT TYPES

So far we have dealt only with simple geometric objects such as points and straight lines. Before we start dealing with more complex objects we need to set up a framework that allows us to write programs efficiently. In particular, we should define *types* of objects so that we can write code with some generality and without extensive dependence on a particular platform.

13.2.1 Pixels and Points

The simplest object, of course, is a pixel and we defined an appropriate type, `pPixel`, in Section 11.1. The Starter Toolkit defines this type as

```
typedef unsigned char pPixel
```

Our code does not depend on this definition. It remains valid with other definitions, such as

```
typedef unsigned long pPixel
```

The position of a pixel can be defined either as `pPoint` (defined in Section 10.6) or as `fPoint`, defined in Listing 13.1.

Listing 13.1: Graphics Types, 1 — `File gtypes.h`

```
typedef struct {
    double x, y;
} fPoint;
```

For many programs we may need both definitions: `pPoint` is appropriate for plotting (and is part of the Starter Toolkit definitions), whereas `fPoint` is appropriate when performing certain transformations requiring high numerical precision.

Adding a `pPixel` member to the point structures so that we store color information is tempting. However, this addition is likely to be wasteful for most applications. Lines and curves that can be expressed as arrays of points usually have a fixed color. Full pictures in which color may vary a lot from point to point are best stored as arrays of pixels.

13.2.2 Lines, Polylines, and Circles

Even though adding a color member to individual points is not a good idea, such an addition makes sense for groups of points. We define a straight line segment type `fLine` in Listing 13.2.

Listing 13.2: Graphics Types, 2 — `File gtypes.h`

```
typedef struct Line {
     fPoint p, q;
     pPixel color;
     void (*plot)(struct Line * Line);
} fLine;
```

Listing 13.3 contains an implementation of a plotting function that can be used in conjunction with the `fLine` type. The function uses the `color` element directly as foreground color, which (as pointed out in Section 7.5.5) limits portability. (For example, the bit pattern corresponding to "orange" is not always the same.) The question of color is peripheral to the subject of this chapter, so we stay with the simpler implementation. However, you should be aware that the solution described at the end of Section 7.5.5 is preferable.

Listing 13.3: Function to Plot a Line Object

```
Show_Line(fLine *lp)
{
     set_foregr( (int)lp->color );
     put_line((int)(lp->p).x, (int)(lp->p).y,
          (int)(lp->q).x, (int)(lp->q).y)
}
```

A *polyline* or *open polygon* is a sequence of line segments, as shown in Figure 13.2. We define an `fPolyline` type as shown in Listing 13.4. Here, `pnts` is an array of points (with memory to be allocated) and `npnts` is the number of such points.

Listing 13.4: Graphics Types, 3 — `File gtypes.h`

```
typedef struct Polyline {
     fPoint *pnts;
     int npnts;
     pPixel color;
     void (*plot)(struct Polyline *);
} fPolyline;
```

Figure 13.2 Polyline (left) and polygon (right).

For a circle we define the graphics type as shown in Listing 13.5.

Listing 13.5: Graphics Types, 4 — `File gtypes.h`

```
typedef struct Circle {
    fPoint center;
    double radius;
    pPixel color;
    void (*plot)(struct Circle *);
} fCircle;
```

13.3 SCALING

13.3.1 Changing the Size of a Circle or a Polyline

We start with a simple example of a transformation, that of *scaling*: making an object larger or smaller without changing its position. For a circle this task is simple enough; we need only change the size of its radius. The routine for doing so is trivial, as shown in Listing 13.6.1. Note that we pass as argument a pointer to an object rather than the object itself. This approach makes the code far more efficient.

Listing 13.6.1: Scaling a Circle — `File scale.c`

```
#include <Starter.h>    /* for pPixel definition */
#include <gtypes.h>

void scale_circle(fCircle *cp, double scale_factor)
{
    cp->radius *= scale_factor;
}
```

For a polyline things are more complicated. We want to scale around a fixed position, so we must state what this position will be. The procedure in Listing 13.6.2 accepts three arguments: the polyline, the scale factor, and the fixed position expressed as a point.

Listing 13.6.2: Scaling a Polyline, A

```
void scale_polyline(fPolyline *lp, double scale_factor, fPoint *fixed)
{
     register i;    register fPoint *pp;
     for(i=0, pp=lp->pnts; i<lp->npnts; i++, pp++) {
          pp->x = (pp->x - fixed->x)*scale_factor + fixed->x;
          pp->y = (pp->y - fixed->y)*scale_factor + fixed->y;
     }
}
```

We can easily check to determine whether the coordinates of the points pointed to by `pp` and `fixed` are the same. If they are, the new position will be the same as the old one.

13.3.2 Center of an Object

Quite often we have no special preference about a fixed point. We simply want to scale an object as long as "it stays in the same position." This statement usually means that we want the center of the object to remain fixed. A circle has an obvious center, but a polyline does not. Listing 13.7.1 is a simple routine that finds the center of a polyline based on the formulas

$$x_c = \frac{1}{n}\sum_{i=0}^{n-1} x_i \quad \text{and} \quad y_c = \frac{1}{n}\sum_{i=0}^{n-1} y_i \tag{13.1}$$

where (x_i, y_i) are the coordinates of the vertices and (x_c, y_c) are the coordinates of the center.

Listing 13.7.1: Finding the Center of a Polyline — `File scale.c`

```
void polyline_center (fPolyline *lp, fPoint *pc)
{
     register i;    register fPoint *pp;
     pc->x = pc-> y = 0;
     for(i=0, pp=lp->pnts; i<lp->npnts; i++, pp++) {
          pc->x += pp->x;          pc->y += pp->y;
     }
     pc->x /= lp->npnts;           pc->y /= lp->npnts;
}
```

We can modify the `scale_polyline` procedure by checking on whether the pointer to `fixed` point is `NULL`. If it is, we compute the center, which is then used as `fixed` point. Listing 13.7.2 contains the modified procedure.

Listing 13.7.2: Scaling a Polyline, B — `File scale.c`

```
void scale_polyline(fPolyline *lp, double scale_factor, fPoint *fixed)
{
    register i;
    register fPoint *pp;
    fPoint tmp;

    if(fixed==NULL) polyline_center( lp, &tmp );
    else {
        tmp.x = fixed->x;
        tmp.y = fixed->y;
    }
    for(i=0, pp=lp->pnts; i<lp->npnts; i++, pp++) {
        pp->x = (pp->x - tmp.x)*scale_factor + tmp.x;
        pp->y = (pp->y - tmp.y)*scale_factor + tmp.y;
    }
}
```

13.3.3 A Simple Generalization

For each type we need a scaling routine, which can lead to a severe management problem as we create more and more object types. One solution is to create a *generic object* type and then give it parameters to represent specific types. Listing 13.8 is one attempt to do so.

Listing 13.8: Graphics Types, 5 — `File gtypes.h`

```
typedef struct _GGO {
    fPoint *pnts;
    int npnts;
    double param;
    void (*scale)(struct _GGO *, double, fPoint *);
} GGO;
```

The abbreviation `GGO` stands for generic geometric object. The definition includes a function pointer to bind the object to a particular scaling function. When the object is created, that pointer is set to a particular function. When we want to scale the object later, we need not worry about deciding which function to use. We may simply execute

```
p->scale (p, scale_factor, ...);
```

where p is a pointer to the object.

Although we have already used function pointers as members of structures, the example of Listing 13.8 is remarkable because the scaling functions for different types of objects vary systematically. There is a price to be paid for the convenience. All scaling functions must take the same type of arguments because, until execution time, which particular type will be called is not known. We encountered this situation before. In Chapter 2 we required that all event handlers take as their only argument a pointer to a pEvent structure. In Chapter 3 we required the graphin draw_me and move_me functions to take a pointer to a graphin structure as their only argument. Finally, the plot functions of Section 13.3.2 took as their only argument a pointer to the structure.

Because the structures contain any information that is needed, the uniformity is not a serious challenge. But scaling of different objects requires different types of information, so some care must be taken in planning for the arguments of the scaling functions.

Listing 13.9 is a reimplementation of the scale functions defined earlier.

Listing 13.9: Generic Scale Functions — File generic_scale.c

```
#include <Starter.h>    /* for pPixel definition */
#include <gtypes.h>

void scale_circle(GGO * op, double scale_factor, fPoint *fixed)
{
    op->param = scale_factor*op->param;
    /* Third argument is not used */
}

void scale_polyline(GGO * op, double scale_factor, fPoint *fixed)
{
    register i;
    register fPoint *pp;

    for(i=0, pp=op->pnts; i<op->npnts; i++, pp++) {
        pp->x = (pp->x - fixed->x)*scale_factor + fixed->x;
        pp->y = (pp->y - fixed->y)*scale_factor + fixed->y;
    }
}
```

Suppose now that in one application we have an array of objects. We may go ahead and scale them all by a simple statement such as

```
for(i=0, gp=g; i<64; i++, gp++) gp->scale(gp, scale, &fxp);
```

There is no need to perform any checks about the type of object that is to be scaled. (Declarations of `g` as an array of 64 elements of type `GGO`, etc., are assumed.)

13.4 GENERIC GEOMETRIC OBJECTS

The generic object that we defined in Section 13.3 is not general enough to take care of types other than the circle and the polyline. Listing 13.10 contains a definition that is more general than the one in Section 13.3. (It also repeats the definitions of `pPixel` and `fPoint` for completeness.) We provide additional definitions later.

Listing 13.10: Generic Geometric Object — `File geom_obj.h`

```
#ifndef GGO_DEFINED
#include <Starter.h>    /* for pPixel */

typedef struct fPoint {
    double x, y;
} fPoint;

typedef char Flag;
typedef int Number;
typedef char Text;
typedef double Param;

typedef struct _GGO {
    Flag type;      /* what type */
    fPoint *pnts;   /* point array */
    Number npnts;   /* how many points */
    Text *txt;      /* string */
    pPixel *px;     /* pixel pointer - can be used for colors */
    Param *param;   /* parameter array */
    Number nparam;    /* number of parameters */
    int (*plot)();    /* plotting routine */
    int (*scale)();   /* change size */
    int (*rotate)();  /* rotate around a point */
    int (*find)();    /* Check if a point is near it */
} GGO;
#define GGO_DEFINED
#endif
```

There are two reasons for introducing new data types such as `Number`. One is to make the declarations inside the program more intuitive; the other is to make porting from system to system easier.

The flag `type` is provided for convenience — a simple way to check the type of the object for whatever reason. Even though the member functions are made to reflect the type, we cannot be sure that there will never be any need to check the type.

The members `pnts` and `npnts` are as before, whereas `txt` and `px` provide the ability to associate a text string and or a pixel array with an object. Thus objects can be as diverse as text or full images. We could have used a `union` for some of these pointers, but doing so would have limited the type of objects that can be defined.

Pointers are provided for four functions: plotting the object, scaling, rotating, and determining whether an object is near a specified point. The last is useful for picking up objects with a mouse, and we discuss it at length in Section 13.7.

In one sense all GGOs are point pictures because the only spatial entities they have are sets of points on the plane. The plotting function actually specifies the category (as defined in Section 1.1.2) because it interprets the elements of the data structure in any of several ways.

13.5 TRANSLATION AND ROTATION

13.5.1 Translation

One simple transformation is to move an object by a certain distance in the `x` and `y` directions. No member function does that because the operation is the same for all types of objects. We can store the amount of translation in an `fPoint` and then use the general routine of Listing 13.11.

Listing 13.11: Object Translation — `File translate.c`

```
#include <geom_obj.h>

void translate(GGO * op, fPoint *shift)
{
     register i;
     register fPoint *pp;

     for(i=0, pp=op->pnts; i<op->npnts; i++, pp++) {
          pp->x += shift->x;
          pp->y += shift->y;
     }
}
```

13.5.2 The Rotation Equations

Rotation is the most complex of the transformations because it requires both a center of rotation and an angle for the amount of rotation. In addition we must deal with certain types of objects that present a special challenge to rotation, such as text and full images (presented as pixel arrays). We postpone such considerations for later and focus here on the formula that gives the location (X, Y) of a point (x, y) after it has been rotated by an angle θ around a point (x_0, y_0). (We may also think of an axis of rotation perpendicular to the plane and passing through (x_0, y_0).) See Figure 13.3.

Figure 13.3 Definition of the quantities used for the derivation of the equations for rotation: (x_0, y_0) is the point around which the rotation takes place; (x, y) is the initial position and (X, Y) is the final position; θ is the angle of rotation, and R is the distance between (x_0, y_0) and (x, y).

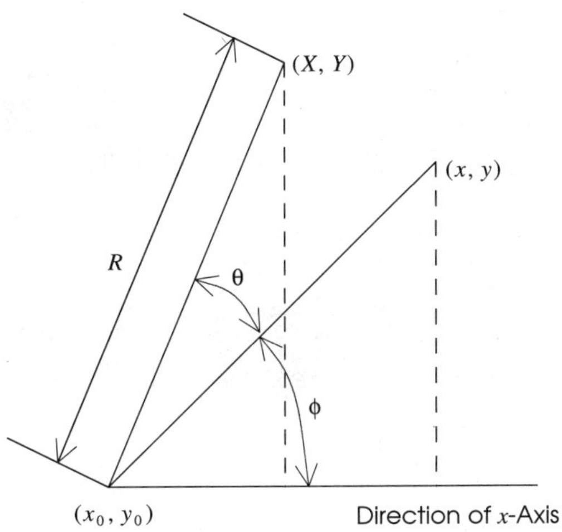

Let R be the length of the vector joining (x, y) to (x_0, y_0) and ϕ be the angle that this vector forms with the horizontal. After rotation by an angle θ, the length of the vector is still R but the angle is $\phi + \theta$. Therefore we have

$$x - x_0 = R\cos\phi \quad \text{and} \quad y - y_0 = R\sin\phi \tag{13.2a}$$

$$X - x_0 = R\cos(\phi + \theta) \quad \text{and} \quad Y - y_0 = R\sin(\phi + \theta) \tag{13.2b}$$

Expanding the cosine and sine functions in Equation (13.2b) we get

$$X - x_0 = R\cos\phi\cos\theta - R\sin\phi\sin\theta$$

and

$$Y - y_0 = R\sin\phi\cos\theta + R\cos\phi\sin\theta$$

Substituting the terms $R\sin\phi$ and $R\cos\phi$ from Equation (13.2a), we find that the new coordinates (X, Y) are given in terms of the old ones by the following equations:

$$X = x_0 + (x - x_0)\cos\theta - (y - y_0)\sin\theta \tag{13.3a}$$

$$Y = y_0 + (x - x_0)\sin\theta + (y - y_0)\cos\theta \tag{13.3b}$$

Rearranging the terms so that terms depending on x and y are separate from the others yields

$$X = x_0(1 - \cos\theta) + y_0\sin\theta + x\cos\theta - y\sin\theta \tag{13.4a}$$

$$Y = y_0(1 - \cos\theta) - x_0\sin\theta + x\sin\theta + y\cos\theta \tag{13.4b}$$

Such a separation is desirable because the same rotation may have to be performed for many points (different x and y) while the other terms remain the same.

13.5.3 The Rotation Program

The program of Listing 13.12 implements Equations (13.4a) and (13.4b) and performs the rotation of the points of an object.

Listing 13.12: Object Rotation — `File rotate.c`

```
#include <math.h>
#include <geom_obj.h>

void point_rotate(GGO *op , double angle, fPoint *axis)
{
	register i;
	register fPoint *pp;
	double c, s, u, v;

	c = cos(angle);
	s = sin(angle);
	u = (1-c)*axis->x + s*axis->y;
	v = (1-c)*axis->y - s*axis->x;

	for(i=0, pp=op->pnts; i<op->npnts; i++, pp++) {
		pp->x = u + c*pp->x - s*pp->y;
		pp->y = v + s*pp->x + c*pp->y;
	}
}
```

When you write a program of any mathematical complexity, you should check its results for at least a few simple cases in order to catch possible errors. The following are two useful checks for the rotation program.

Check No.1 Rotation by 90 degrees. Then c equals 0 and s equals 1 so that, after substitution of u and v, the replacement statements of the program are

```
pp->x = axis->x + axis->y - pp->y;
pp->y = axis->y - axis->y + pp->x;
```

If the axis of rotation is the origin, the first two terms are 0 and we obtain

```
pp->x = - pp->y;
pp->y =   pp->x;
```

with the expected result that y goes into negative x and x goes into y.

Check No.2 Rotation around one of the points: In this case there is some point whose coordinates, pp->x and pp->y, are equal to the coordinates of the axis, axis->x and axis->y, respectively. Again, after substitution of u and v, the replacement statements of the program are

```
pp->x = (1-c)*pp->x + s*pp->y + c*pp->x - s*pp->y;
pp->y = (1-c)*pp->y - s*pp->x + s*pp->x + c*pp->y;
```

In both statements all terms but one on the right-hand side cancel and yield

```
pp->x = pp->x;
pp->y = pp->y;
```

which is as expected: The axis does not move during rotation.

13.6 FINDING OBJECTS

13.6.1 The Easy (but User-Unfriendly) Way

Pointing to an object with a mouse or another pointing device actually points to a pixel on the screen. We need to search the list of objects to find which one is at or near the cursor. There are many possibilities for how to grab objects. One is to do so only by their visible points: polyline vertices, centers of circle, and so on. The other is by any pixel that their plot occupies.

Clearly, the first approach is the simpler to implement. We have to compute only the distance between the pointer location and the points of the object; if the distance is small enough we grab an object. (If more than one object have points near the pointer, we may look for the one with the smallest distance.) The following is a macro based on a simple expression for the distance between two points.

```
#define dist(A,B)  ( fabs(A->x-B->x) + fabs(A->y-B->y) )
```

It is called the *Manhattan* distance. As the calculation of the *Euclidean* distance requires taking a square root, we may use instead (for the sake of efficiency) its square, defining

```
#define dist(A,B)  ( (A->x-B->x)*(A->x-B->x) + \
                     (A->y-B->y)*(A->y-B->y) )
```

Finding the distance to a point from an object can be achieved with the code in Listing 13.13.

Listing 13.13: Distance Between Point and Object — File `obj_distance.c`

```
/* Find distance of point *q from object *op */
#include <math.h>
#include <geom_obj.h>
#define dist(A,B)  ( fabs(A->x-B->x) + fabs(A->y-B->y) )

double point_distance(GGO *op ,  fPoint *q) /* user unfriendly */
{
     register i;
     register fPoint *pp;
     double d, d0;

     pp=op->pnts;
     d0 = fabs( dist(pp, q) );
     pp++;
     for(i=1; i<op->npnts; i++, pp++) {
          d = fabs( dist(pp, q) );
          if(d < d0 ) d0 = d;
     }
     return( d0 );
}
```

13.6.2 The Hard (but User-Friendly) Way

The preceding code is easy to write, and it can be executed quickly, but it is not particularly user-friendly. The user has to know that only certain points of a display are accessible to the pointer. But now we have to worry about the shape of the objects.

The distance to a point from the circumference of a circle is computed easily from the property that all points of the circumference are at a fixed distance from the center. The function is shown in Listing 13.14.

Listing 13.14: Distance Between Point and Circle — `File circle_dist.c`

```
#include <math.h>
#include <geom_obj.h>

double point_circle_distance(GGO *op ,  fPoint *q)
{
    double dx, dy, d;

    dx = op->pnts->x - q->x;
    dy = op->pnts->y - q->y;
    d = sqrt(dx*dx + dy*dy);
    return( fabs(d - *(op->param)) );     /* op->param is the radius */
}
```

Things are far more complicated for a polyline. There we have to determine whether the pointer is near each side. For this task we need a way to find the equation of a line joining two points and a way to compute the distance to a point from a line segment. We try to solve this problem in Section 13.7 and then use the result for a "user-friendly" routine that computes the distance to a point from a polyline.

13.7 LINES AND POINTS

13.7.1 Equation of a Line Joining Two Points

A conceptually simple formula describes the equation of a line joining two points with coordinates (x_1, y_1) and (x_2, y_2)

$$\det \begin{bmatrix} x & x_1 & x_2 \\ y & y_1 & y_2 \\ 1 & 1 & 1 \end{bmatrix} = 0 \tag{13.5}$$

which can be expanded to

$$x(y_1 - y_2) + y(x_2 - x_1) + (x_1 y_2 - y_1 x_2) = 0 \tag{13.6}$$

probably the form more familiar to you. (We can also derive this equation from Equation (10.6).) We easily confirm the claim that this equation is that of the line joining two points by substituting for x and y, first with x_1 and y_1 and then with x_2 and y_2, and finding that the left-hand side is 0 in either case.

13.7.2 Distance to a Point from a Line Joining Two Other Points

If we take three points that do not lie on the same line, the determinant of the left-hand side of Equation (13.5) has a remarkable property: *It is twice the area of the triangle formed by the three points.*

We can provide a simple proof of this property by observing that the result should not depend on the coordinate system used. We select a convenient system by moving the origin to one of the points. The determinant then becomes

$$\det \begin{bmatrix} 0 & x_1 & x_2 \\ 0 & y_1 & y_2 \\ 1 & 1 & 1 \end{bmatrix} = \det \begin{bmatrix} x_1 & x_2 \\ y_1 & y_2 \end{bmatrix} \tag{13.7}$$

We can rotate the system of coordinates around the origin so that the x-axis coincides with one of the sides. Then, one of the y-coordinates becomes 0 and the determinant becomes

$$\det \begin{bmatrix} x_1 & x_2 \\ 0 & y_2 \end{bmatrix} = x_1 y_2 \tag{13.8}$$

But now x_1 is the length of the base of the triangle, and y_2 is the height (see Figure 13.4), which proves our statement.

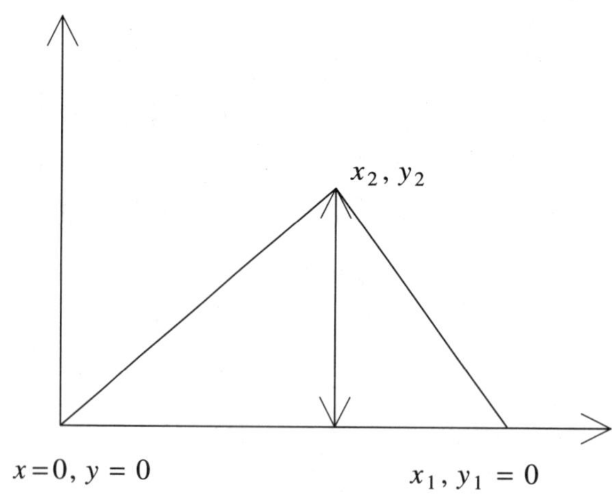

Figure 13.4 The area of the triangle of the three points (x, y), (x_1, y_1), and (x_2, y_2) is given by one-half the product $x_1 y_2$, provided the first point is at the origin and the line joining the first and the second is the x-axis.

The usual formula for the distance between two points gives the expression for the distance to a point (x, y) from the line joining the points with coordinates (x_1, y_1) and (x_2, y_2)

$$\frac{x(y_1 - y_2) + y(x_2 - x_1) + (x_1 y_2 - y_1 x_2)}{\sqrt{(x_1 - x_2)^2 + (y_1 - y_2)^2}} \tag{13.9}$$

Expression (13.9) may be positive or negative, depending on which side of the line the point lies. The sign is of no interest when we only want to check on whether a point is near a line or not, but it is useful for other problems that we deal with soon.

13.7.3 Distance to a Point from a Line

The last result can be generalized for other definitions of a straight line besides that of joining two points. Recall that the general equation of a straight line has the form

$$ax + by + c = 0 \tag{13.10}$$

When the line is defined by two points, a comparison of Equations (13.6) and (13.10) suggests that

$$a = y_1 - y_2, \quad b = x_2 - x_1, \quad \text{and} \quad c = x_1 y_2 - y_1 x_2 \tag{13.11}$$

Then, Expression (13.9) may be written as

$$\frac{ax + by + c}{\sqrt{b^2 + a^2}} \tag{13.12}$$

Suppose now that we multiply all coefficients of a line by a constant m. Doing so does not change the line or Equation (13.12) because m will be canceled from both the numerator and the denominator of the fraction. Therefore Equation (13.12) gives the distance to a point from a line expressed in the general form of Equation (13.10).

13.7.4 Distance of a Point from a Line Segment Joining Two Other Points

Expression (13.9) gives the distance to a point from an infinite line. For some applications, such as finding an object near a point, that is not enough. Figure 13.5(a) shows that a point can be near an infinite line but far from a segment of that line.

The distance to a point from the line equals its distance from the segment only if the point lies in the slab defined by the two lines perpendicular to the segment at its endpoints (see Figure 13.5(b)). When the point is outside this slab, its distance from the line equals the smaller of its two distances to the endpoints.

Our first task is to find the equations of the lines defining the slab. We know from analytic geometry that for a line described by Equation (13.10) the equation of a line perpendicular to it and passing from a point with coordinates (x_m, y_m) is

$$b(x - x_m) - a(y - y_m) = 0 \qquad (13.13)$$

Therefore the line passing through (x_1, y_1) satisfies the equation

$$(x_2 - x_1)(x - x_1) - (y_1 - y_2)(y - y_1) = 0 \qquad (13.14)$$

Similarly the perpendicular line passing through the other point is given by

$$(x_2 - x_1)(x - x_2) - (y_1 - y_2)(y - y_2) = 0 \qquad (13.15)$$

Figure 13.5 (a) Point C is near the line defined by A and B but quite far from the line segment defined by A and B. (b) Point C is distance CE from the line defined by points A and B, and its distances from these two points are CA and CB. The distance from the line segment is CE. For point D the distance from the segment is DA. DF is smaller than DA, but F does not belong to the *segment* defined by A and B.

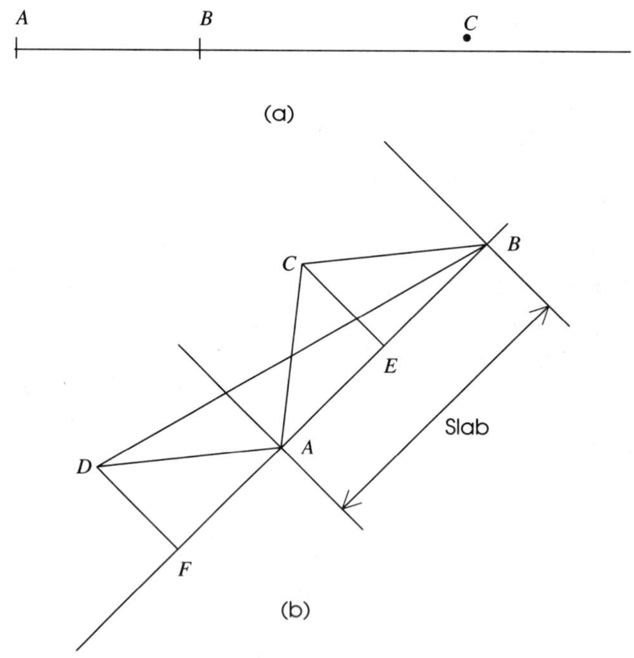

To find whether a point is inside the slab we must compute its signed distance from both lines and confirm that the two distances have opposite signs. Indeed, all points on one side of a line have the same sign for the distance. Let's compute these distances for the midpoint of the segment that obviously lies inside the slab and has as its coordinates $((x_1 + x_2)/2, (y_1 + y_2)/2)$. From Equation (13.14) we have

$$(x_2 - x_1)\left[\frac{x_1 + x_2}{2} - x_1\right] - (y_1 - y_2)\left[\frac{y_1 + y_2}{2} - y_1\right] = \frac{1}{2}(x_2 - x_1)^2 - \frac{1}{2}(y_1 - y_2)^2 \quad (13.16)$$

and from Equation (13.15) we have

$$(x_2 - x_1)\left[\frac{x_1 + x_2}{2} - x_2\right] - (y_1 - y_2)\left[\frac{y_1 + y_2}{2} - y_2\right] = -\frac{1}{2}(x_2 - x_1)^2 + \frac{1}{2}(y_1 - y_2)^2 \quad (13.17)$$

The two distances are indeed of opposite sign.

13.8 FINDING OBJECTS REVISITED

13.8.1 Implementation of the User-Friendly Distance Computation

We are now ready to write the code for computing the distance of a point from the vertices and sides of a polyline. First we need a routine to compute Expression (13.9), as in Listing 13.15.1.

Listing 13.15.1: Distance to a Point from a Line — `File distance.c`

```
/*
    Compute distance to point p0 from the
    straight line joining points p1 and p2
*/
#include <math.h>
#include <geom_obj.h>

double point_line_distance(fPoint *p1, fPoint *p2, fPoint *p0)
{
    double a, b, c, ll, d;

    a = p1->y - p2->y;
    b = p2->x - p1->x;

    if(!a && !b ) {
```

```
          /* Points p1 and p2 coincide, Compute p0,p1 distance */
          a = p1->y - p0->y;
          b = p1->x - p0->x;
          d = sqrt(a*a + b*b);
     }

     else {
          c = p1->x*p2->y - p1->y*p2->x;
          ll = sqrt(a*a + b*b);
          d = ( a*p0->x + b*p0->y + c ) / ll;
     }
     return(d);
}
```

Note that we have to do some error checking in case the line cannot be defined. If the two endpoints coincide, the routine returns the distance between the given point and the endpoint.

This function also contains all the quantities needed to compute the location of the given point with respect to the slab of Figure 13.5(b) so we may modify it to do that as well.

Listing 13.15.2: Distance to a Point from a Line Segment — `File distance.c`

```
/*
     Compute distance of point p0 from
     straight line segment joining points p1 and p2
*/
#include <math.h>
#include <geom_obj.h>

double point_segment_distance(fPoint *p1, fPoint *p2, fPoint *p0)
{
     double a, b, c, ll, d, d1, d2;

     a = p1->y - p2->y;
     b = p2->x - p1->x;

     if(!a && !b ) {
          /* Points p1 and p2 coincide, Compute p0,p1 distance */
          a = p1->y - p0->y;
          b = p1->x - p0->x;
          d = sqrt(a*a + b*b);
          return(d);
     }
```

```
    /*  Compute location with respect to slab*/
    d1 = b*(p0->x - p1->x) - a*(p0->y - p1->y);
    d2 = b*(p0->x - p2->x) - a*(p0->y - p2->y);

    if(d1*d2<0) { /* inside the slab; p1 and p2 have to be different */
         c = p1->x*p2->y - p1->y*p2->x;
         l1 = sqrt(a*a + b*b);
         d = ( a*p0->x + b*p0->y + c ) / l1;
         d = fabs(d);
    }
    else {
         a = p1->y - p0->y;
         b = p1->x - p0->x;
         d1 = sqrt(a*a + b*b);
         a = p2->y - p0->y;
         b = p2->x - p0->x;
         d2 = sqrt(a*a + b*b);
         d = d1 < d2 ? d1: d2;
    }
    return(d);
}
```

The distance from the polyline is then given by the computation in Listing 13.15.3.

Listing 13.15.3: Distance to a Point from a Polyline — `File distance.c`

```
#include <math.h>
#include <geom_obj.h>

double point_polyline_distance(GGO *op, fPoint *q) /* user friendly */
{
     register i;
     register fPoint *pp;
     double d, d0;

     pp=op->pnts;
     d0 = point_segment_distance(pp, pp+1, q);
     pp++;
     for(i=1; i<op->npnts-1; i++, pp++) {
          d = point_segment_distance(pp, pp+1, q);
          if(d < d0 ) d0 = d;
     }
     return(d0);
}
```

Of course, the last function is only the start. We need to develop similar functions for other kinds of objects, such as text. (We developed such a function for circles in Section 13.6.2.)

13.8.2 The Moral of the Story

User-friendliness comes at a price. A user-friendly program is far more difficult to write and requires more computational resources than a user-unfriendly program.

Sometimes the price is so high that the product is no longer friendly. For example, the additional computation may make the response of an interaction too sluggish. Or the additional development costs may make the product too expensive. Good engineering and marketing judgment require a balance between costs (both production and use) and the features of the product.

13.8.3 Issues of Efficiency

The implementation by `point_polyline_distance()` is correct, but it also is quite inefficient. The program already does much more computation than the simple version `point_distance()`. Thus we need to look for places where the computation could be reduced.

(1) Currently, we are computing the distance from each vertex of the polygon twice because a pointer to each vertex appears twice as an argument in the calls to `point_segment_distance()`. Precomputing the distances of the point from all the vertices and saving them in an array should save some time.

(2) The distance between an object and the cursor controlled by the mouse may have to be computed many times while the shape of the object does not change. We could speed things up by storing in an array the values of `a`, `b`, `c`, and `ll` for each side of the polygon.

(3) The cursor may be far from all the points of the polyline. For example, suppose that the polyline is a square with sides 50 pixels long and we find that the distance of the cursor from the first vertex is 500 pixels. There is no way that the cursor can be closer than 428 pixels from any other vertex, yet we go ahead and compute all the remaining distances! Remember that the reason we want to compute the distance is to identify the object pointed to by the mouse. Hence we do not care about the exact value of a distance unless it is small, at least compared to the dimensions of an object.

The first two cases are remedied by storing intermediate results. Such storage is a form of *caching*: keeping at hand some information that we know will be needed again soon. The third case can be handled by a different form of caching. We compute for each object a *bounding rectangle* by finding the extremes of the coordinates of its points:

```
xmin = min( ... p->x ... )   xmax = max( ... p->x ... )
ymin = min( ... p->y ... )   ymax = max( ... p->y ... )
```

We may enlarge the rectangle somewhat by decrementing `xmin` and `ymin` while incrementing `xmax` and `ymax`. These quantities can be made members of the GGO structure so that the following code can be inserted in the beginning of each distance computation routine.

```
#define INF 100000 /* or other huge number */
#define FAR_OUT(A,B) if(B->x < A->xmin || A->xmax < B->x \
    || B->y < A->ymin || A->ymax < B->y) return(INF);

double point_polyline_distance(GGO *op, Point *q)
{
    FAR_OUT(op, q)
    /* ... code from Listing 13.15.3, etc ... */
}
```

13.9 CONCLUSIONS

We introduced another example of object-oriented programming by treating shapes as geometric objects. We had presented an earlier example in the graphin structure. This new method offers considerable new opportunities. In particular, we can now replace the graphin icons with polygons that can be scaled continuously, creating the illusion of distance as graphins change in size.

A game using polygons rather than icons might be too slow on most hardware platforms unless we leave the polygons fixed. However, the approach is quite practical for stand alone systems and it is worth trying for its general educational value (Assignment 3).

We can also use the new structures to create a picture editor that is far more powerful than the pixel editor we have discussed so far. Its starting point can be the rubber banding routine described in Section 2.4, combined, for example, with the polygon filling routines of Chapter 12.

In addition to the geometric object structures, we discussed three basic transformations (scaling, translation, and rotation) and the computation of the distance of a point from a line and a line segment.

13.10 ASSIGNMENTS

Some General Comments: This chapter offers the basis for two programs that perform similar functions as the pixel / icon editor and the video game, but they have a different architecture. The architecture is drastically different in the case of the picture editor but less so in the case of the video game. This difference motivates the first two assignments. The remaining assignments refer to special cases or subsets of the first two.

1. Start the implementation of a graphics editor based on the GGO data structure by writing a polygon drawing program using the material of Section 2.4. (Assignment 3 of Chapter 2 can be used as the basis for the current assignment.) Include a feature for filling the last drawn polygon.
2. Recreate the graphin module for the video game of Chapter 3 by using images that have been drawn as sets of polylines (and polygons) rather than as icons.
3. Use Assignment 2 as a basis to create a "spinning" graphin. (As it moves, its image should rotate by a specified angle.)
4. In the original version of the video game (Chapter 3) many graphins could share the same icon. In the same way they can share the same group of polylines. Add a set of parameters that allow different graphins to share the same polylines but at different scales, colors, or orientations.
5. Modify Assignment 4 to allow sharing of parts of the image representing a graphin. You may have a basic "humanoid" figure that has different posture in each graphin (e.g., stretched arms or arms along the sides of the body).
6. Modify the video game of Chapter 3 so that when the player is on or near the line *segment* defined by any two graphins, the player loses the game. This modification can be made either in the original version or after the revision of Assignment 2.

   Hints: You need to use the material of Section 13.8, but you also need careful bookkeeping in considering possible pairs of graphins.

14

Programs for Drawing

Scope of the Chapter

Drawing various shapes • Usage functions • Grabbing and dragging • Selecting the object pointed by the user • Selection and operations on groups of objects • Callback structures for buttons that select editing operations

If I want to draw something on a piece of paper, I do not need a manual.
A teenage artist

14.1 INTRODUCTION

In Section 2.3 we discussed a simple pixel painting program, and in Section 2.4 we discussed a simple drawing program. In Chapter 7 we showed how to enhance such programs by adding color and features controlled by a selection panel. We discussed additional enhancements in Sections 10.7 and 10.8. Finally, in Chapter 13, we introduced structures and operations that are useful for drawing programs. In this chapter we approach the topic of computer drawing in a systematic way.

Before we go on we should clarify our terminology. We have used the term *painting* to describe actions whereby the program changes the color of pixels directly and the term *drawing* to describe actions whereby a geometric entity (e.g., a straight line segment) is created. The color of pixels changes when that entity is plotted. For practical reasons (see Section 10.7) all painting programs involve some drawing. That certainly is the case with the X Window System utility `bitmap` and other icon-creating programs. For this reason we use the term *drawing program* to include pixel painting programs.

The challenge of creating drawing programs is great because of the novelty of the field: Only in the late 1970s did the price of raster graphics displays come within the reach of people outside a few major industrial laboratories. Many software products have been introduced since then, but compared to, say, word-processing programs, have had limited use.

The purpose of this chapter is not to build one more such program. That is a major task and well beyond the scope of an introductory text. Instead, we focus on the issues involved in writing such programs.

14.1.1 Why Use a Computer to Create Pictures?

Why would anyone want to use a computer to paint or draw? After all pencil and paper (or even oil and canvas) are much simpler media. Of course, many of us have been using word processors for a long time and, maybe, we should try first to answer another question: Why would anyone want to use a computer to write? Here are some reasons.

- Correcting typing and spelling errors is easy.
- Revising text by inserting sentences here and there or by moving blocks of text around is easy.
- With a bit of practice, generating new documents from old ones is easy, *form letters* being the most obvious (and obnoxious) example of this practice.
- Full advantage can be taken of the many devices that can be connected to a computer; for example, using a cheap printer for drafts or a high-quality laser printer for the final copy.
- Computer programs can be used to "beautify" (format) the text by aligning margins, setting up tables, and the like.
- With text stored as strings of characters in a computer file, *information retrieval* is much easier. For example, finding all letters addressed to "George Smith" is much easier on a machine than searching through a cabinet of paper files.

The first four reasons also are valid for drawing. Corrections (big or small) are easy on a machine, and generating new pictures from old ones also is easy, and useful for applications such an animation. Having multiple output devices is attractive. Picture "beautification" is not as advanced as text formatting, but it is available, at least for simple drawings.

Only the last reason does not hold for pictures today. A machine has trouble finding all pictures in which a particular individual appears. Or even all pictures in which a human face appears. But progress is being made in this field, and, with all its other benefits, creating pictures by computer seems an attractive idea.

14.1.2 Drawing Editors

We use the term *drawing editor* for any program that creates pictures. So far word processor or text editing programs have been used far more widely than drawing editing programs for two reasons: (a) People write far more often than they draw; and (b) drawing editors programs require more computing resources than writing programs.

Today's computer hardware has become sufficiently cheap that a platform for a drawing editor is within most people's reach. Also, a good drawing editor lets people produce decent pictures regardless of artistic ability. So the time seems to be right to learn more about how to create such programs.

Because pictures have much greater variety than text, we expect to find also a greater variety of drawing editors. We can create full or flat pictures by assigning a specific color to each pixel. We call such programs *pixel editors*. They can also be used to draw curves or lines. Their main characteristic is that the only object they produce is a pixel array which is a copy of the display screen.

Some pixel editors are called *icon editors* because they are used to draw the icons used in many programs (see Chapter 3). As such icons usually are small (down to a size of 16×16 pixels), the pixel array is displayed magnified while it is being drawn. Most window systems include an icon editor.

Object editors are programs that do not manipulate pixels directly but create objects that can be translated into pixels in various ways. We can create an object drawing editor using the types of objects and operations introduced in Chapter 13.

Also, in Chapter 13 we pointed out the advantages of object representations for applying scaling and other transformations. Another major advantage is that such descriptions are portable and can be used on different types of devices and with different resolutions. This portability makes them particularly useful for *computer aided design* (CAD). For example, after an item has been drawn on the screen, the generated file can be fed into a program that may analyze various properties of the corresponding physical object, such as volume, weight, and strength.

Another application is the design of graphical user interfaces. Instead of writing a C program, the designer can draw the panels and buttons on screen and the C code can be generated automatically.

Today there are many commercial products that are object editors and offer many more features than what we describe here. Here we present some of the principles used in the design of such products. The main topic is the *interactive drawing of complex objects*, which we have mentioned only in passing so far.

14.1.3 A Potential Danger

Before going ahead we should also consider the disadvantages of word processing programs because drawing programs may inherit them along with the advantages. One disadvantage that most people mention is *user manuals* that sometimes are hefty volumes. Drawing involves many more operations than writing, so there is a justifiable fear that user manuals for drawing programs may look like encyclopedias.

Our goal should be to keep user manuals as small as possible, if not to make them disappear altogether — not only for drawing and writing but also for any other computer program. Ideally, the user should not have to look to a manual unless there is a malfunction or the user wants to do something unusual with the program.

The main challenge in designing programs with many options is to make their meaning as obvious as possible so that as little documentation as possible will be needed. (For example, having the cursor change to the color of the selected palette button provides a hint of functionality to the user so there is no need for a document describing the role of the palette.) We try to adhere to this practice in this text.

14.2 POLYGON DRAWING

14.2.1 Drawing Arbitrary Polylines

In Section 2.4 we described the *rubber banding* technique for drawing polylines; and in Section 7.3.3 how to have a panel menu that selects this operation. We now describe here how to use the drawn polyline, either to construct objects or for other purposes — for example, delineating objects.

For this purpose we will rely on the concept of *usage functions*, discussed in Sections 2.5.3, 7.6, and, particularly, 10.7. There they were called after the drawing was finished with two arguments: a pointer to the array of drawn points and the number of such points. The particular functions were selected by the messenger function `set_xyc_use()`. We start by modifying the code of Listing 2.7 to save points and then pass them to a usage function. The result is shown in Listing 14.1.

Listing 14.1: Draw and Save a Polyline — File polydraw.c

```
#include <Starter.h>
#include <geom_obj.h>

#define MAX_PTS    256

static fPoint buff[MAX_PTS];
static int bn = 0;
static fPoint *bp;
static void (*use)(fPoint *, int);    /* usage function */

void set_poly_use(void (*f)(fPoint *, int))
{
     use = f;
}

poly_draw(pEvent *p)
{
     static int initialized = 0;
     static int x0, y0, x1, y1;

     switch (p->kind+p->key) {
     case MOVE:                          /* rubber band */
          if(initialized){
               put_line(x0, y0, x1, y1);   /*erase*/
               x1 = p->x;
               y1 = p->y;
               put_line(x0, y0, x1, y1);   /*draw*/
          }
          return;
     case LEFT_PRESS:          /* add points to polyline */
          x0 = x1 = p->x;
          y0 = y1 = p->y;
          if(!initialized) {
               initialized = 1;
               bp = buff;    bn = 0;
          }
          bp->x = p->x; bp->y = p->y;
          if(bn >= MAX_PTS) {
               use(buff, bn);
               initialized = 0;
          }
          else {
               bp++;
               bn++;
          }
          return;
     case MIDDLE_PRESS:
     case RIGHT_PRESS:
          if(initialized){
               put_line(x0, y0, x1, y1);   /*erase*/
               initialized = 0;
```

```
                use(buff, bn);
            }
            return;
        }
}
```

The program just described draws open polylines. To draw a polygon (a closed polyline), you must explicitly select the first point again. In practice, this can be a rather delicate operation. The solution is to have two types of polylines, open and closed, with the relevant information stored in the `type` member of the `GGO` structure. This information is used by the plotting routine, but the last point is not stored explicitly.

We may omit any explicit action by having the `usage` functions check on whether the last point is close to the first one, and if so, discard the last point and set the type to be that of a closed polyline.

If we want to have a menu selection for creating objects that are polylines, we need a callback for the menu selection and a usage function. We may also use the same handler to draw polylines around objects and place all encircled objects in a group. Listing 14.2 lists the usage functions (without providing their implementation) and the respective callbacks for these two operations.

Listing 14.2: Callbacks for a Drawing Program — `File polydraw.c`

```
extern int poly_draw();

void create_polyline_object(fPoint bf[], int n)    /* usage function */
{
     /* code for object creation */
}

void objects_in_poly(fPoint bf[], int n)  /* usage function */
{
     /* code for finding the objects inside the polygon */
}

void draw_polyline()    /* callback for button labeled "Polyline" */
{
     set_poly_use(create_polyline_object);
     set_handler(poly_draw);
}

void form_group() /* callback for button labeled "Group" */
{
     set_poly_use(objects_in_poly);
     set_handler(poly_draw);
}
```

14.2.2 Drawing Right Rectangles (Boxes)

A right rectangle is a rectangle with one pair of sides vertical and the other horizontal. Such rectangles appear frequently in drawings as *boxes* in flow charts. We could use the general polyline drawing routine to create such a rectangle. However, providing a special procedure so that users will not have to be extra careful in keeping the lines exactly vertical or exactly horizontal is better.

Because of the frequent use of such objects, we define a special structure and inialization procedure for them in Listings 14.3.1 and 14.3.2.

Listing 14.3.1: Rectangle Structure Definition — `File rectangle.h`

```
typedef struct _Rectangle {
     double x, y, width, height;
     void (*plot)(struct _Rectangle *);
} Rectangle;
```

Listing 14.3.2: Rectangle Structure Initialization — `File rect.c`

```
#include <rectangle.h>

void plot_rect(Rectangle *r)
{
     put_rectangle( (int)(r->x), (int)(r->y),
          (int)(r->width), (int)(r->height) );
}

init_rectangle(Rectangle *r)
{
     r->plot = plot_rect;
}
```

Listing 14.4 shows a simple rubber band routine that draws such a box.

Listing 14.4: Rubber Band Rectangle — `File rectdraw.c`

```
#include <Starter.h>
#include <rectangle.h>

extern void plot_rect();
static int (*use)(Rectangle *);

void set_rect_use(int (*f)(Rectangle *))
{
```

```
	use = f;
}

void rect_draw(pEvent *p)
{
	static int initialized = 0;
	static Rectangle R;

	init_rectangle(&R);
	switch (p->kind+p->key) {
	case MOVE:	/* rubber rectangle */
		if(initialized) {
			R.plot(&R);	/*erase*/
			R.width  = p->x - R.x + 1;
			R.height = p->y - R.y + 1;
			R.plot(&R);	/*plot*/
		}
		return;
	case  LEFT_PRESS:
		if(!initialized) { /* first point */
			R.plot   = plot_rect;
			R.x = p->x;
			R.y = p->y;
			R.width  = 0;
			R.height = 0;
			initialized = 1;
		}
		else {		/* second point */
			R.plot(&R);	/*erase*/
			R.width  = p->x - R.x + 1;
			R.height = p->y - R.y + 1;
			R.plot(&R);	/*plot*/
			initialized = 0;
			use(&R);
		}
		return;
	default:
		return;
	}
}
```

When the left button is pressed for the first time, the rectangle structure is initialized with the upper left corner placed at the location of the cursor. When the mouse moves, the top left corner remains the same while the lower right corner follows the cursor. The rectangle is redrawn in the new position. When the left button is pressed a second time, the `use` function is called with a pointer to the drawn rectangle as argument. Then, the program is ready to draw another rectangle.

14.3 GRABBING AND DRAGGING

14.3.1 Grabbing and Dragging a Single Object

We now discuss a program for moving objects such as polylines to a different location from the one initially drawn. This operation requires two handlers: One for grabbing the object we want to move and the second for dragging it to the new location. The function `grab_object()` given in Listing 14.5.1 does the first task.

Listing 14.5.1: Grabbing an Object — `File grab_drag.c`

```
#include <Starter.h>
#include <geom_obj.h>

extern GGO *global_find();
extern void drag_object();
static GGO *current;

void grab_object(pEvent *p)
{
     if(p->kind+p->key==LEFT_PRESS) {
          current = global_find(p->x, p->y);
          if(current) set_handler(drag_object);
     }
}
```

When the left button of the mouse is pressed, a function `global_find()` is called. It looks at the list of drawn objects and finds one that has a point near the one with coordinates `p->x` and `p->y`. This routine uses the distance calculations described in Chapter 13 to decide when an object is near a point. However, the detailed distance calculations are hidden from this module because they are *encapsulated* within the function `find()`, which is a member of the structure `GGO` defined in Section 13.4 (see also Appendix A). Listing 14.5.2 provides one possible implementation of the function `global_find()`:

Listing 14.5.2: Finding an Object Near a Point — `File grab_drag.c`

```
/*   These declarations should be in the main part of the program */
static GGO g[128]; /* 128 is used only as an example */
static int gn;

GGO *global_find(int x, int y)
{
     register GGO *gp;
     register i;

     for(i=0, gp=g; i<gn; i++, gp++)
          if( gp->find(gp, x, y) ) return(gp);
     return( (GGO *)0 );
}
```

If no object is found, a null pointer is returned; otherwise a pointer to the object is given. If an object is found, the event handler is set to `drag_object`. This routine is presented in Listing 14.5.3 and is similar in structure to the polyline drawing routine.

Listing 14.5.3: Dragging an Object — `File grab_drag.c`

```
void drag_object(pEvent *p)
{
     switch(p->kind+p->key) {
     case MOVE:                /* drag object */
          if(!current) return;
          current->plot(current);/* erase */
          translate(current, p->x, p->y);
          current->plot(current);/* draw in new position */
          return;
     case LEFT_PRESS:          /* stop dragging */
          current = (GGO *)0;
          set_handler(grab_object);
          return;
     default:
          return;
     }
}
```

The function `drag_object()` is effective as event handler only if the variable `current` is nonzero. Checking whether `current` is 0 inside the procedure `drag_object()` may seem superfluous, but this is defensive programming. Once a procedure is available, we cannot anticipate all possible calling sequences; therefore we cannot rely on them to give meaningful values to all the variables.

The function `translate()` computes a new position for the object (see Assignment 6). When the left button is pressed, the program leaves the object in its last position, sets the object pointer `current` to null, and resets the event handler to `search`. The state diagram is shown in Figure 14.1.

Figure 14.1 A state diagram of a geometric object moving program.

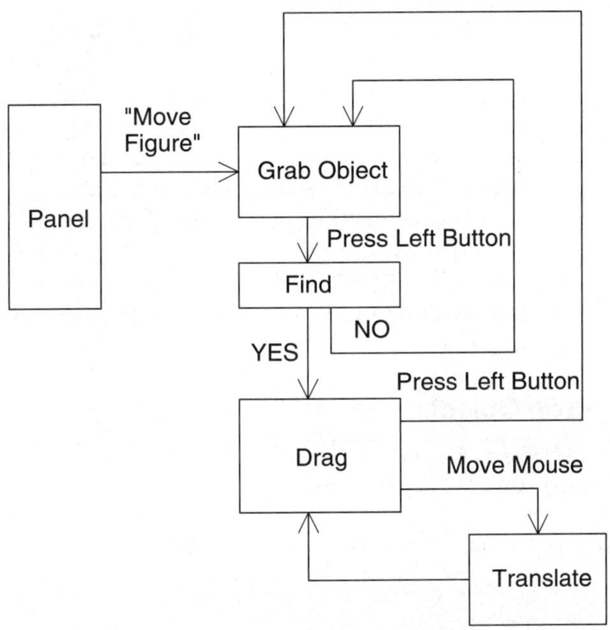

14.3.2 Grabbing and Dragging Many Objects: First Approach

Sometimes we want to move a group of objects. One possible way to do so is to enclose a group of them within a polygon and then grab and drag the polygon. This process involves:

1. Drawing a polyline using the handler `poly_draw()`. The program closes the polygon automatically.
2. Finding the objects inside the polygon and place pointers to them in the list `found_objects`.

3. Grabbing the polygon and dragging it by using the single object operations.
4. Computing the total amount of motion and applying it to the members of `found_objects`.
5. (Possibly) eliminating the original polygon.

The first two operations perform a *selection*, and the next two perform an operation on the selected object. Finally, the selection is canceled. There are two ways to implement such a combination of operations. One is to use two menu choices: first to select and then to move. The other is to combine them into one operation.

The details of the selection operation are described in Section 14.3.3. A procedure, say, `objects_in_poly()`, locates all objects inside the polygon, possibly highlights them, and places pointers to them in a special array. It may also add the drawn polygon to the list of objects with a special flag before relinquishing control of the program. When a grab and move operation is initiated later and the polygon with the special flag is grabbed, everything is done as for a single object with one exception. When we finish dragging, the program looks at the special array, translates all the objects in it, and then (possibly) destroys the polygon. To accomplish this task we need to modify slightly the procedure of Listing 14.5.3, giving Listing 14.6.

Listing 14.6: Drag an Object

```
/* Repeating definitions from Listing 14.5.1 */
static int (*use)(GGO *, int, int);

void set_drag_use( int (*f)(GGO *, int, int) )
{
     use = f;
}

void drag_object(pEvent *p)
{
     static int x0, y0;
     static int initialized = 0;

     if(!initialized) {
          initialized = 1;
          x0 = p->x;     y0 = p->y;
     }

     switch(p->kind+p->key) {
     case MOVE:                /* drag figure */
```

```
            if(!current) return;
            current->plot(current); /* erase */
            translate(current, p->x, p->y);
            current->plot(current); /* draw in new position */
            return;
        case LEFT_PRESS:        /* stop dragging */
            initialized = 0;
            if(use) use(current, p->x-x0, p->y-y0);
            current = (GGO *)0;
            set_handler(grab_object);
            return;
        default:
            return;
        }
}
```

The `use()` procedure will check on whether the object, which is its first argument, has a special flag indicating that it is a containing polygon. If so, it will use the other two arguments as a vector for translating the objects set aside in the special array.

Important Point *Whether to destroy the circumscribing polygon after we have finished is an engineering decision. We may want to keep the association of the objects in case we have to perform additional operations on them.*

14.3.3 Object Selection

So far we have not discussed how the procedure `objects_in_poly()` determines which objects are inside a polygon. It is a *static* operation in the sense that it does not involve user interaction but it can be rather complex for an arbitrary polygon. The most general solution is offered by Assignment 8 in Chapter 12, which suggests adapting the polygon filling algorithm for deciding whether a given point is inside an arbitrary polygon. However, the operation is relatively simple for a rectangle, and we may want to provide the user with a rectangle rather than an arbitrary polygon for selecting the objects. Of course, this costs the users some flexibility.

This situation is another example of the trade-off between program simplicity and user-friendliness besides the one discussed in Chapter 13. Here, we provide the procedure `objects_in_rect()` for the case of selection through a rectangle.

Listing 14.7: Find Objects Enclosed in Rectangle — File `rect_select.c`

```
#include <Starter.h>
#include <geom_obj.h>
#include <rectangle.h>
#define ENCLOSURE 11    /* example value */

int point_in_rectangle(fPoint *pp, Rectangle *pr)
{
     if(pp->x < pr->x || pp->x > pr->x+pr->width)  return(0);
     if(pp->y < pr->y || pp->y > pr->y+pr->height) return(0);
}

extern GGO * rect_to_object_list();

static GGO g[128]; /* 128 is used only as an example */
static int gn;
static GGO *gs[128];
static GGO **selected;

void objects_in_rect(Rectangle *r)
{
     register GGO *gp;
     register i, j;
     GGO *new_obj;

     selected = gs;

     for(i=0, gp=g; i<gn; i++, gp++) {
          for(j=0; j<gp->npnts; j++) {
               if(point_in_rectangle(gp->pnts+j, r)) {
                    *selected++ = gp;
                    break;
               }
          }
     }

     if(selected <= gs) return;  /* no selections made */
     /* We assume that a function for constructing objects from
     rectangles exists and it is used next */
     new_obj = rect_to_object_list(r);
     new_obj->type = ENCLOSURE;
}
```

The program of Listing 14.7 looks for objects that have at least one point inside the given rectangle. When such an object is found, it is added to the list of objects `gs[]`. If any such objects have been found, the rectangle itself is added to the global list of objects but with a special type. When an object is selected later and its type is `ENCLOSURE`, the relevant operation is applied not only to the object itself, but also to the objects in the array `gs[]`.

Having the array of pointers to selected object be static places certain limitations in the program: We cannot have more than one object with type `ENCLOSURE` at any given time. A better solution is to include such an array in the declaration of `GGO` (Listing 13.10), allowing for an object hierarchy. However, this solution will complicate the strategy for grabbing objects. What happens if the user points to an object that is a child of another? Does the program pick the individual object or its parent? Either solution has advantages and disadvantages.

The topic of hierarchies of geometric objects is beyond the scope of an introductory text because many considerations (both technical and human) require extended discussion. However, the mechanics of implementation of some strategies are rather simple (see Assignment 1).

14.3.4 Grabbing and Dragging Many Objects: Second Approach

If we do not want to make two selections for a single operation, we must somehow inform the system that we want a particular event handler after the selection procedure. We presented an example of such a strategy in Section 2.4.2 where we used two event handlers for the rubber band program.

The code of the following event handler could go into the `objects_in_poly()` procedure. But that code is unrelated to the procedure's main purpose (finding the objects inside a polygon), so creating a new procedure, `select_and_drag()`, which has the following form, is best.

```
void select_and_drag(GGO *pp)
{
	objects_in_poly(pp);
	current = /* address of last object */
	set_handler(drag_object);
}
```

The callback will be the same as before except instead of

```
	set_poly_use(objects_in_poly);
```

it will have now

```
	set_poly_use(select_and_drag);
```

The choice between the two approaches depends on which one is more convenient for the user: having to make two menu selections or one. One advantage of two separate menu selections is that the user may decide not to proceed with a particular operation. Also, the selection may be kept intact for subsequent operations.

14.3.5 The Many Meanings of the Word *Selection*

Selection is a word that has a specific technical meaning in the X Window System. It is an operation that lets one application communicate with another. In most cases the user selects a block of text in one window that then can be transferred into another window. We have used the word *selection* informally to mean selecting one or more objects in a window that then can be transferred into another part of the *same* window. However, the code of Listings 14.5 to 14.7 can be used as the basis for selecting and transferring objects *across* applications. The topic of communication between different applications is beyond the scope of this text, so we do not discuss how this is done. You should only be aware of the differences (and similarities) in meaning between the two uses of the word *selection*.

14.4 STRUCTURE OF THE CALLBACKS

In the preceding sections we described the code for drawing polylines and rectangles, picking up single objects, picking up groups of objects, dragging objects, and the like. Writing the code for scaling and rotation operations, as well as creating text (most of the code has been given in Section 2.5), is easy. Challenges in assembling such code into an object drawing program include constructing the callbacks of the panel buttons that specify editing operations and keeping track of the state of the program.

Each callback function must set the event handler and the usage function, and also provide a visual hint that reminds the users of the state of the program. We have already seen the use of different cursor icons for that purpose in Section 7.5.3 where we used a cursor like a pencil while drawing and a cursor with the word "Type" when keyboard input was expected. A message printed at the frame of the window or a text dialog area may convey more explicit information than the cursor.

Listing 14.8 provides some examples of callbacks for editing functions. It is based on the assumption that certain cursor icons have been created in the way described in Section 3.2. The icons are accessed through the variables `pencil_icon`, `box_icon`, and others. For the time being we are not concerned with the implementation of the function `user_hint()`.

Note that the same panel (menu) selections may be used both for groups of objects and individual objects if we grab the enclosing polygon or enclosing rectangle. There is no need to introduce different callbacks.

Listing 14.8: Callbacks for a Drawing Editor

```
extern void poly_draw();     /* In Listing 14.1 */
extern void rect_draw();     /* In Listing 14.3 */
extern GGO * poly_to_object_list();
extern GGO * rect_to_object_list();
extern void grab_object();   /* In Listing 14.5.1 */
extern void select();        /* In Listing 14.7 for rectangle */
extern void drag_object();   /* In Listing 14.5.2 */

/*   Callback for drawing polylines */
void draw_polyline()
{
     set_handler(poly_draw);
     set_poly_use(poly_to_object_list);
     active_cursor(pencil_icon);
     user_hint("Create polyline");
}

/*   Callback for drawing rectangles */
void draw_rectangle()
{
     set_handler(rect_draw);
     set_rect_use(rect_to_object_list);
     active_cursor(box_icon);
     user_hint("Create rectangle");
}

/*   Callback for moving objects */
void move_object()
{
     set_handler(grab_object);
     set_drag_use(drag_object);
     active_cursor(hook_icon);
     user_hint("Grab and move an object");
}

void select_objects()
{
#ifdef FRIENDLY
     set_handler(poly_draw);
     set_poly_use(select);
     active_cursor(rope_icon);
     user_hint("Enclose objects with a polyline");
#else
     set_handler(rect_draw);
     set_rect_use(select);
     active_cursor(box_icon);
     user_hint("Enclose objects with a rectangle");
#endif
}
```

14.5 CONCLUSIONS

We discussed the construction of some key parts of an object drawing program. Such a program is far more complex than a pixel painting program, and what we have described so far is only a small fraction of what must go into it. The following items are a few of the potential additions.

Object editing operations include adjusting the position of points, inserting points in a polygon or characters in a string of text, replacing part of a string of text, and the like. The challenge is to provide appropriate visual hints so that the user can select and perform such operations easily without having to consult a manual.

Geometric objects can be scaled easily (whereas bitmaps cannot), so adding zoom features to such programs is natural. For example, after selection of a set of objects (say, by the method of Section 14.3.3), selecting the "zoom" button from a panel and then pointing to the enclosing object will create a new drawing window in which the selected objects will be displayed at a larger scale. Creating such an editor stretches the abilities of the Starter Toolkit making necessary the direct use of the X Toolkit and *Xlib*. At the very least we must access some of the inner parts of the Starter Toolkit as described in Section 9.2.

Such editors also require extensive processing of the drawn objects by nongraphic means. After making a menu selection, we need only touch an object to have the selected operation performed on it. For example, we may draw a simple box (right rectangle) and have it replaced by a curve (spline) inscribed in it (see Section 17.2.1).

The discussion on grabbing and dragging objects has other applications besides editors. We pointed out in Section 14.3.5 that similar code underlies the mechanism that window systems use for communication between different application programs.

14.6 ASSIGNMENTS

1. Implement the `global_find()` function of Listing 14.5.2 for the case where the objects are stored in a tree (i.e., each object may have other objects as children) rather than in an array. Have the function return a pointer to the object actually picked by the user (see Figure 14.2).
2. Repeat Assignment 1 but make `global_find()` return a pointer to the highest ancestor of the object picked by the user. (See Figure 14.2.)
3. Write a program that takes as input a rectangle and then creates a shadow for it, as shown in Figure 14.3.

Figure 14.2 Hierarchy of Objects. When the user points to the object denoted 1, the function of Assignment 1 should return a pointer to 1. However, the function of Assignment 2 should return a pointer to the object denoted 2.

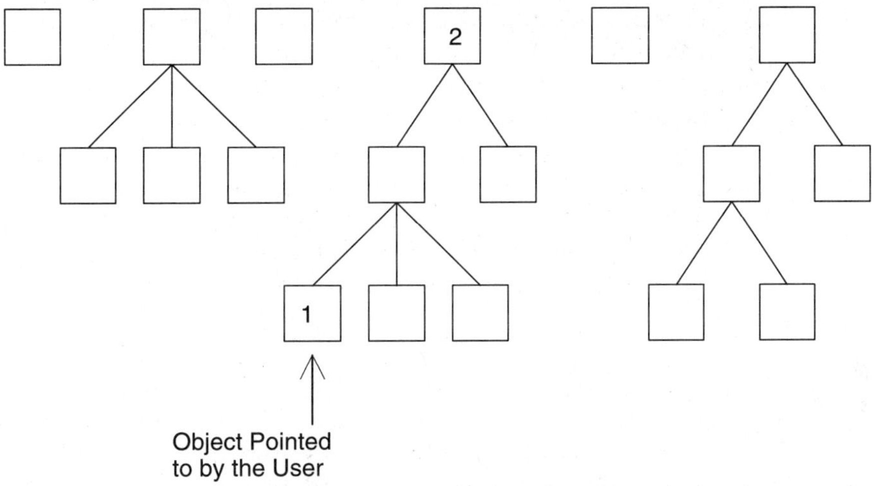

Figure 14.3 Rectangle with shadow.

4. Repeat Assignment 3 for an arbitrary polygon. (The task is much more difficult now.)
5. Implement the operations necessary to support scaling and rotating of polygons.
6. Implement the `translate()` function used in Listings 14.5.3 and 14.6. As the function takes as arguments only a pointer to an object and the current coordinates of the cursor, it is necessary to keep track of the coordinates of the cursor when the object was originally selected. Hence, the `find()` function and, possibly, the GGO structure must be modified.

7. Implement grid drawing for polygons. Establish a grid and make the necessary changes in the code of Listing 14.1 so that the vertices of the polygon are placed on the grid point nearest to the one selected by the user.
8. Implement confined slope drawing for polygons. Select a few slope values (e.g., 0°, ±45°, ±90°, and ±135°) and allow the sides of the polygon to have only those slopes. (Computing the slope and issuing warnings to the user is *not* an acceptable solution.)
9. Write an object drawing program that generates C code (using the Starter Toolkit functions) that when compiled and executed will reproduce the drawn image. You may want to limit the objects to boxes and text only. For example, if the user draws a rectangle with corners at (10, 24) and (64, 80), the program should output the statement

```
put_rectangle(10, 24, 54, 56);
```

10. Repeat Assignment 7, but have the program "beautify" the drawing. A simple beautification is to use a grid but you should do better than that here. For example, the width and height of rectangles may be made integer multiples of a number different from that of the grid spacing; or if text is drawn inside the rectangle it should be centered and the width of the rectangle adjusted to leave a certain (predefined) amount of space around the text.
11. Write an essay discussing how the program of Assignment 9 can be extended so that it will be useful for building graphical user interfaces. (The functions for supporting such an extension are not provided by the Starter Toolkit, but they are part of the X Window System and *Xlib*.)
12. Write a "table writing" program. The user should be able to place text over the screen and also draw lines (if desired) between rows and columns. The program should then perform some beautification by lining up the text in columns and rows.

15

Operations on Lines

Scope of the Chapter

Intersection of line segments • Mathematics of homogeneous coordinates • Relative position of points and/or line segments • Ideas for enhancing the video game of Chapter 3

15.1 INTRODUCTION

In Chapter 13 we examined relationships between points and straight line segments and gave a method for computing the distance to a point from such a segment. In this chapter we examine a group of related problems: finding the intersection of two line segments and finding the relative position of points with respect to line segments and of line segments with respect to each other. We approach such problems by using a new mathematical tool: *homogeneous coordinates*.

Finding the intersection of two lines is a straightforward application of elementary algebra. As the general equation for a straight line is

$$ax + by + c = 0 \tag{15.1}$$

the intersection of two lines can be found by solving the system of equations:

$$a_1x + b_1y + c_1 = 0 \tag{15.2a}$$

$$a_2x + b_2y + c_2 = 0 \tag{15.2b}$$

The solution is

$$x = -\frac{c_1b_2 - c_2b_1}{a_1b_2 - a_2b_1} \tag{15.3a}$$

and

$$y = \frac{c_1a_2 - c_2a_1}{a_1b_2 - a_2b_1} \tag{15.3b}$$

(See the Note at the end of the chapter showing how to find these answers.)

Clearly, these equations are valid only if $a_1b_2 - a_2b_1$ is nonzero. As this quantity is 0 when the two lines are parallel, we must add a check for parallelism to the routine that finds the intersection of two lines. A closer look at the results suggests that a check for parallelism may not be enough. The lines may intersect but at a distant point. We could eliminate such cases by adding a a criterion for "near parallelism," but still that is not enough.

Consider the example of Figure 15.1. There we define a point T as the intersection of the lines joining the pairs of points P, R and Q, S. These points in turn are defined by the intersections of the pairs of line segments AB, EF, and CD, GH, respectively. The four segments and T are within the display area, but points P, Q, R, and S are outside it. Although the coordinates of the final result are near those of the original data, some of the intermediate results are outside and can achieve very large values. In particular, we may place points S and Q quite far away, making the pair of angles RSP and PQR quite small and the pair of angles SPQ and SRQ near 180°. We need a way to handle very large values of coordinates (or large intermediate results while computing coordinates) without compromising the accuracy of the final result.

Let's introduce a scale factor w and replace x and y with u/w and v/w. Then Equation (15.1) becomes

$$au + bv + cw = 0 \tag{15.4}$$

It is still the equation of a straight line; to find the coordinates of its points we have to take the ratios u/w and v/w. If x or y is very large, u and v can be kept small by making w very small. We rewrite Equations (15.2a) and (15.2b) using this notation:

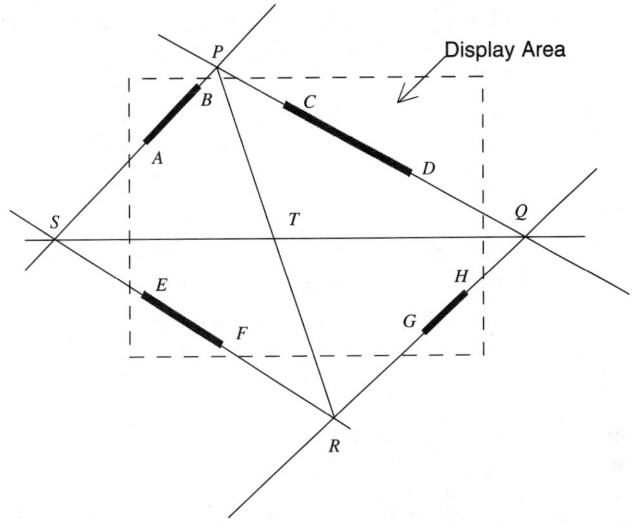

Figure 15.1 Problems with remote line intersections.

$$a_1 u + b_1 v + c_1 w = 0 \tag{15.5a}$$

$$a_2 u + b_2 v + c_2 w = 0 \tag{15.5b}$$

Let's now select u, v, and w to be

$$u = c_2 b_1 - c_1 b_2 \tag{15.6a}$$

$$v = c_1 a_2 - c_2 a_1 \tag{15.6b}$$

and

$$w = a_1 b_2 - a_2 b_1 \tag{15.6c}$$

Substituting these values into Equations (15.5a) and (15.5b) shows that they are indeed a solution. They are only one of many solution sets because the two equations now have three unknowns. But we can obtain any solution from another by multiplying the three values u, v, and w by a constant. Ultimately, we care only for the ratios u/w and v/w, so there is no problem in picking one solution over another.

The advantage of this approach is that we do not have to carry the division until we are ready for the display. The three values u, v, w are called the *homogeneous coordinates* of a point.

15.2 HOMOGENEOUS COORDINATES

We can change the expression of the equation for a line joining two points given by Equation (13.5) so that it is in terms of the homogeneous coordinates. The original expression is

$$\det \begin{bmatrix} x & x_1 & x_2 \\ y & y_1 & y_2 \\ 1 & 1 & 1 \end{bmatrix} = 0 \tag{15.7}$$

We replace x with u/w, x_1 with u_1/w_1, and so on and then multiply the first column by w, the second by w_1, and the third by w_2. These operations do not affect the value of the determinant so that we obtain

$$\det \begin{bmatrix} u & u_1 & u_2 \\ v & v_1 & v_2 \\ w & w_1 & w_2 \end{bmatrix} = 0 \tag{15.8}$$

Let's return to the problem in Section 15.1. Rather than ask for the coordinates of the intersection of two lines, we ask for the coefficients of all lines passing through the intersection. If these coefficients are a, b, and c, then (since the intersection must lie on that line) we have

$$a(c_2 b_1 - c_1 b_2) + b(c_1 a_2 - c_2 a_1) + c(a_1 b_2 - a_2 b_1) = 0$$

But the left-hand side is the expansion of a determinant; therefore we can write

$$\det \begin{bmatrix} a & a_1 & a_2 \\ b & b_1 & b_2 \\ c & c_1 & c_2 \end{bmatrix} = 0 \tag{15.9}$$

We observe now a remarkable property: The coefficients of a line passing through the intersection of two other lines satisfy the same equation as the coordinates of the points on a line joining two other points. Actually, there is no difference between points and straight lines; both are represented by a triplet of numbers.

15.2.1 Duality

The last two observations express the *duality* between points and lines on the plane when homogeneous coordinates are used. A set of three numbers may represent either a line or a point, so equations of a line defined by two points or that of a point defined by two lines are identical. The principle of duality is used extensively in *projective geometry*, a discipline that deals with geometric properties that are preserved under projection, a topic of great importance in three-dimensional graphics. For each property of points and lines, we can derive another result by interchanging point and line. Duality also may be used in graphics to economize on software. Thus the same procedure can be used to find either the intersection of two lines or the line joining two points. (In both cases it evaluates the minors of a 3×3 determinant.)

However, the applicability of duality is limited. In particular, duality does not hold over relationships that include distance. This limitation can be understood best with a simple experiment:

> Draw a rectangle with crossing diagonals on a transparency and use an overhead projector to display it on a tilted screen. All position and intersection relationships are preserved, but length relationships are not.

Figure 15.2 shows the shape of the original rectangle and its projection. Lengths *AE* and *EC* are equal, but the corresponding lengths, *ApEp* and *EpCp*, in the projection are not.

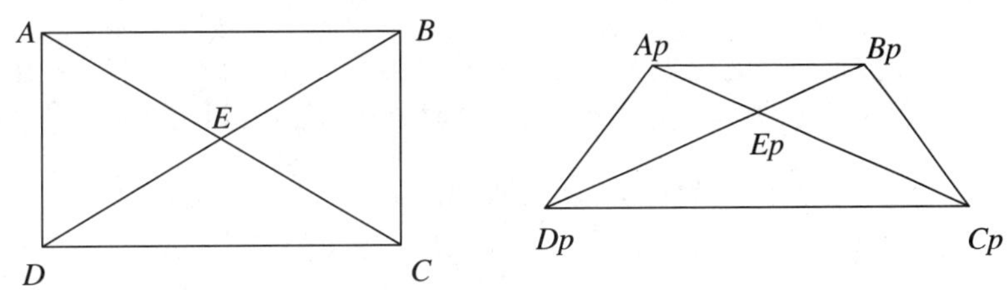

Figure 15.2 A rectangle (left) and its projection on a tilted screen (right).

15.2.2 Implementation

Listing 15.1 shows the definition of the basic type used in programs taking advantage of duality. We call the type a `triplet` rather than point or line because it may represent either.

Listing 15.1: Definition of the Triplet Type — `File triplet.h`

```
typedef struct {
    double u, v, w;
    } triplet;
```

Listing 15.2.1 shows the fundamental procedures for solving geometric problems with homogeneous coordinates.

Listing 15.2.1: Outer and Inner Products — `File lines.c`

```
#include <triplet.h>

void o_product(triplet *t1, triplet *t2, triplet *z)
{
     z->u = t1->v*t2 >w - t1->w*t2->v;
     z->v = t1->w*t2->u - t1->u*t2->w;
     z->w = t1->u*t2->v - t1->v*t2->u;
}

double s_product(triplet *t1, triplet *t2)
{
     return(t1->u*t2->u + t1->v*t2->v + t1->w*t2->w);
}
```

Procedure `o_product()` computes the minors of the determinants such as those shown in Equations (15.7) to (15.9). The minors form a vector known in analytic geometry as *outer product*; hence the prefix `o_`. Procedure `s_product()` computes the scalar product of two vectors known as the *inner product*. Let `P1`, `P2`, and `P3` be triplets representing the three columns of a matrix. Then to compute the determinant we allocate memory for another triplet, `Q`, and execute the code of Listing 15.2.2.

Listing 15.2.2: Computation of Determinant — `File lines.c`

```
double determinant(triplet *p1, triplet *p2, triplet *p3)
{
     triplet Q;

     o_product(p2, p3, &Q);
     return( s_product(p1, &Q) );
}
```

We split the computation of the determinant into two steps because the intermediate result is useful in solving geometric problems such as the one shown in Figure 15.1. If we use a triplet array `L[]` to store the coefficients of the lines, then the code fragment of Listing 15.3 computes the coefficients of the fifth line.

Listing 15.3: Computing the Arrangement of Figure 15.1 (Part)

```
/*   Program Solving the Problem of Figure 15.1       */
/*   Note: L+i is the address of L[i]                 */
triplet A, B, C, D, E, F, G, H, P, Q, R, S, T;
triplet L[8];
o_product(&A, &B, L);  /* compute coefficients of line joining A and B */
o_product(&C, &D, L+1);
o_product(&E, &F, L+2);
o_product(&G, &H, L+3);
o_product(L, L+1, &P); /* compute intersection of lines L and L+1     */
o_product(L+1, L+3, &Q);
o_product(L+2, L+3, &R);
o_product(L, L+2, &S);
o_product(&S, &Q, L+4);/* compute coefficients of line joining S and Q */
o_product(&P, &R, L+5);
o_product(L+4, L+5, &T);    /* the final answer */
```

The important feature of this code is that the *same* procedure is used to find the homogeneous coordinates of the intersection of two lines and to find the coefficients of a line joining two points.

15.2.3 Metrics: Finding the Midpoint of a Line Segment

Because homogeneous coordinates are scale independent, they must be used with care when metric relations are involved. For example, let's compute the coordinates of the midpoint P_0 of a line segment whose endpoints are P_1 and P_2. The definition of the new point relies on a metric relation, equality of lengths, so we must proceed cautiously. If we use conventional coordinates, we have a simple relationship:

$$x_0 = \frac{1}{2}(x_1 + x_2) \tag{15.10a}$$

$$y_0 = \frac{1}{2}(y_1 + y_2) \tag{15.10b}$$

To find the relationship for homogeneous coordinates we must replace all x's by u/w and all y's by v/w and simplify. The result is

$$u_0 = \frac{1}{2}(u_1 w_2 + u_2 w_1) \tag{15.11a}$$

$$v_0 = \frac{1}{2}(v_1 w_2 + v_2 w_1) \tag{15.11b}$$

$$w_0 = w_1 w_2 \tag{15.11c}$$

The procedure for computing the midpoint is given in Listing 15.4.1.

Listing 15.4.1: Midpoint Computation — `File midpoint.c`

```
#include <triplet.h>

void midpoint(triplet *p1, triplet *p2, triplet *p0)
{
     p0->u = (p1->u * p2->w + p2->u * p1->w)/2;
     p0->v = (p1->v * p2->w + p2->v * p1->w)/2;
     p0->w = p1->w * p2->w;
}
```

We can use this routine together with earlier ones for geometric constructions. For example, we can use it to find the point where the lines joining the vertices of a triangle with the midpoints of the opposite sides intersect. Figure 15.3 shows the notation used in Listing 15.4.2.

Figure 15.3
A triangle with the lines joining the midpoints of its sides.

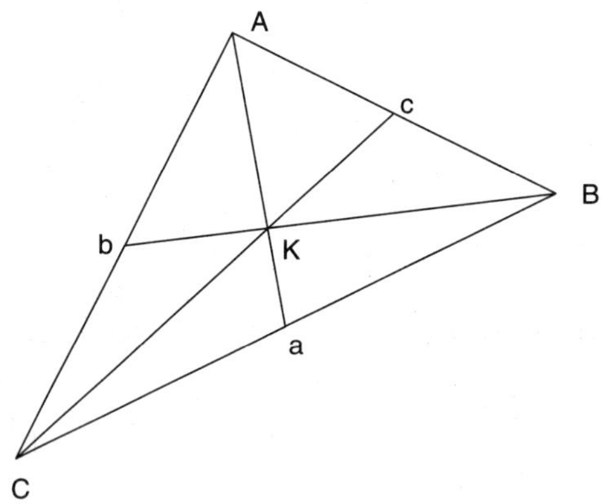

The last line checks the result of Euclidean geometry; that is, `K` indeed lies on line `Cc`. This check is simple but deficient because it does not allow for any numerical approximation errors. We need an expression to compute the distance to a point from a line.

Listing 15.4.2: Intersection of Three Lines — `File midpoint.c`

```
/*  Testing a theorem of geometry */

test_midpoint(triplet *A, triplet *B, triplet *C)
{
    triplet a, b, c;   /* midpoints */
    triplet  Aa, Bb, Cc;    /* lines */
    triplet K;    /* intersection */

    midpoint(A, B, &c);
    midpoint(B, C, &a);
    midpoint(C, A, &b);

    o_product(A, &a, &Aa);
    o_product(B, &b, &Bb);
    o_product(C, &c, &Cc);
    o_product(&Aa, &Bb, &K);
    if( ! s_product(&Cc, &K) ) error();
}
```

15.2.4 Metrics: Finding the Distance of a Point from a Line

The distance of a point from a line can be derived from Equation 13.12 in the same way that Equations (15.11) were derived from Equations (15.10). The distance is given by

$$\frac{au + bv + cw}{w\sqrt{a^2 + b^2}} \tag{15.12}$$

Expression (15.12) can be evaluated by the procedure in Listing 15.5.1 where the variables `lp->u`, `lp->v`, and `lp->w` correspond to the coefficients a, b, and c and the variables `pp->u`, `pp->v`, and `pp->w` correspond to the u, v, and w.

Listing 15.5.1: Distance of Point from Line — `File hdistance.c`

```
#include <math.h>
#include <triplet.h>

double line_dist(triplet *lp, triplet *pp)
{
    double d = s_product(lp, pp);
    if(lp->u || lp->v) {
        d /= pp->w * sqrt(lp->u*lp->u + lp->v*lp->v);
        return(d);
    }
    else error(); /* error condition */
}
```

Then, the statement for checking whether a line passes through a particular point can be written as

```
if( fabs( line_dist(&Cc, &K) ) > EPSILON) error();
```

If the line is defined by two points, the result for the determinant is

$$\frac{1}{ww_1w_2}\det\begin{bmatrix} u & u_1 & u_2 \\ v & v_1 & v_2 \\ w & w_1 & w_2 \end{bmatrix} \tag{15.13}$$

The result for the segment length is

$$\frac{1}{w_1w_2}\sqrt{(u_1w_2 - u_2w_1)^2 + (v_1w_2 - v_2w_1)^2} \tag{15.14}$$

We combine these two equations to obtain the expression of the distance to a point from the line joining two others:

$$\frac{\det\begin{bmatrix} u & u_1 & u_2 \\ v & v_1 & v_2 \\ w & w_1 & w_2 \end{bmatrix}}{w\sqrt{(u_1w_2 - u_2w_1)^2 + (v_1w_2 - v_2w_1)^2}} \tag{15.15}$$

These expressions can be evaluated by the procedure in Listing 15.5.2.

Listing 15.5.2: Distance of Point from the Line Joining Two Others — `File hdistance.c`

```
double p_line_dist(triplet *p1, triplet *p2, triplet *pp)
{
      double d, D;
      triplet z;

      o_product(p1, p2, &z);
      d = s_product(pp, &z);
      D = sqrt(z.u*z.u - z.v*z.v);
      if(D && pp->w) {
            d /= D*pp->w;
            return(d);
      }
      else error(); /* error condition */
}
```

15.3 APPLICATIONS

15.3.1 Composing Triplets

Let's create a new triplet from two others by taking a weighted sum of their terms using the code of Listing 15.6.1.

Listing 15.6.1: Composition of Triplets — `File compose.c`

```
#include <triplet.h>

void compose(triplet *p, double a, triplet *q, double b, triplet *t)
{
     t->u = a*p->u + b*q->u;
     t->v = a*p->v + b*q->v;
     t->w = a*p->w + b*q->w;
}
```

What does this code represent? We can prove with simple analytic geometry that, if the triplets are lines, the new triplet is a line passing through the intersection of the first two. If the triplets are points, the new triplet is a point on the line joining the two points (see Assignments 3 and 4). Figure 15.4 shows the arrangements.

Figure 15.4 A line (left) and a point (right) formed as the weighted sum of two other elements of the same kind. In the right-hand drawing the distance of t from the given points is proportional to the weights a and b; C is a constant.

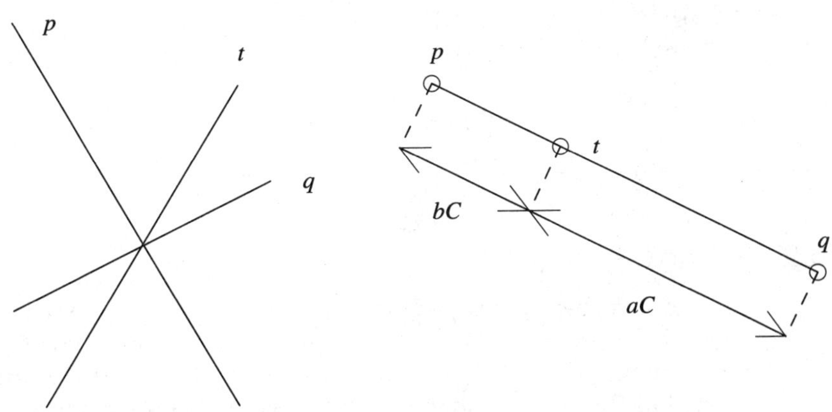

We use that routine to create a sweeping beam that takes successive positions as shown in Figure 15.5.

Figure 15.5
The dashed lines sweep the area between lines L_1 and L_2.

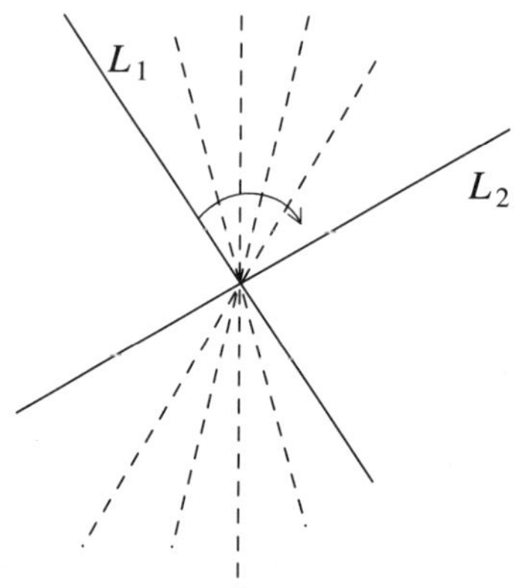

The code presented in Listing 15.6.2 produces a sequence of 11 such lines starting from the one pointed to by `p` and ending at the one pointed to by `q`.

Listing 15.6.2: Display of a group of Lines — `File compose.c`

```
display_line_bunch(triplet *p, triplet *q)
{
    double a;
    triplet T;

    for(a=0; a<=1; a += 0.1) {
        compose(p, a, q, 1-a, &T);
        /* display the line specified by the triplet T */
    }
}
```

15.3.2 Fun and Games

The procedures developed so far can be used to enhance the game described in Sections 3.4-3.7. For examples, we may create a "zap ray" effect by modifying the procedure of Listing 15.6.2: Any graphins near the sweeping line are eliminated. Before we revise the game we must decide how to resolve the incompatibility between the old code (integer point coordinates) and the new code (points expressed as triplets).

One solution is to change the graphin structure. The other is to change the procedures of the previous sections. The latter is preferable from an engineering viewpoint. The game takes place in a limited domain, and it requires the frequent computation of metric relations. The code conversion in the routines of this section is quite simple. Listing 15.7 shows an example of such integration.

Listing 15.7: Zap Ray

```
#include <graphin.h>
#include <triplet.h>
/*  Declarations from Listing  3.10.3, including graphin F[N] */
    and constant definitions from Listing 3.12.1             */

double m_line_dist(triplet *lp, graphin *mp)
{
    double d;
    triplet s;

    s.u = mp->x;  s.v = mp->y;  s.w = 1;
    d = s_product(lp, &s);

    if(lp->u || lp->v) {
        d /= sqrt(lp->u*lp->u + lp->v*lp->v);
        return(d);
    }
    else error(); /* error condition */
}

void zap_ray(triplet *p, triplet *q)
{
    double a;
    triplet *t;
    graphin *gp;

    for(a=0; a<=1; a += 0.1) {
        compose(p, a, q, 1-a, t);
        for(j=0, gp=F; j<how_many; j++, gp++) {
            if( gp->status == NUMB) continue;
            if( fabs( m_line_dist( t, gp) ) < EPSILON)
                gp->status = NUMB;
    }
}
```

This procedure becomes more interesting if we allow the graphins to be moving during the ray sweep. This can be achieved by breaking the loop (see Assignment 1).

A simplification is possible if we assume that the ray sweeps very fast so that anything in the sector defined by the two extreme lines is touched. Then, rather than compute proximity of graphins to lines, we need compute only their presence in the sector. We observe that when we compute the scalar product between a line and a point triplet, its sign will be positive on one side of the line and negative on the other. Thus, if we construct a triplet `s` from `gp` as done inside `m_line_dist()`, we need compute only two scalar products: `s_product(p, &s)` and `s_product(q, &s)`. As Figure 15.6 shows, there exist four possible configurations and the signs do not provide explicit information about the sector where a point lies (such a point is marked by a small box).

We need to find out which of the four configurations of Figure 15.6 exists in a particular situation. In particular, we have to specify which one of the four sectors is of interest. We do so by testing the signs for a known point. To simplify the program, we modify the sign of the coefficients of the line so that both are positive (i.e., we have the first configuration of Figure 15.6). To check on which graphins are contained in the specified sector we execute the code of Listing 15.8.

Figure 15.6 Four configurations for the signs of the quantity that `s_product()` returns for the point marked by a small box.

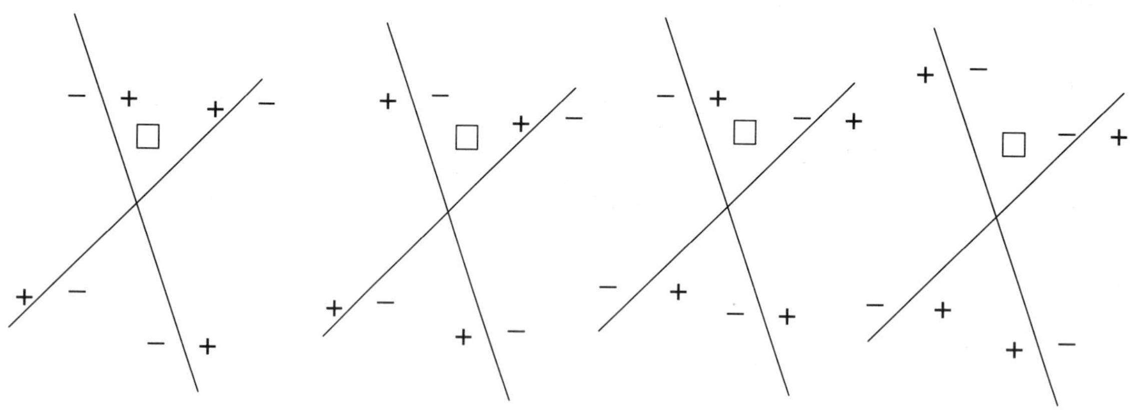

Listing 15.8: Zap Sector

```
#include <graphin.h>
#include <triplet.h>
/*   Declarations from Listing  3.10.3, including graphin F[N] */
/*   and constant definitions from Listing 3.12.1              */

double m_s_product(triplet *lp, graphin gp)
{
     triplet s;

     s.u = mp->x;  s.v = mp->y;  s.w = 1;
     return( s_product(lp, &s) );
}

zap_sector(triplet *p, triplet *q)
{
     graphin gp;

     for(j=0, gp=F; j<how_many; j++, gp++) {
          if( gp->status == NUMB) continue;
          if( m_s_product(p, gp) > 0 && m_s_product(q, gp) > 0 )
                    gp->status = NUMB;
     }
}
```

The preceding example is a relative position problem. Such problems occur in many applications in graphics, and we need a more systematic treatment than what we have done here.

15.4 RELATIVE POSITION OF POINTS AND/OR LINE SEGMENTS

15.4.1 Some Rules

When line segments are defined by their endpoints, the relative position of another point can be determined from the sign of `s_product()` provided we impose some rules in our representations.

- *Rule 1:* The scale factor `w` is never negative for points. If it turns out to be negative, the sign of all members of the triplet `(u, v, w)` should be changed. That leaves `x` and `y` unchanged. However, this rule should not be applied to triplets that represent lines.

- *Rule 2:* The vertical coordinate v increases upwards. This convention is the standard in analytic geometry, but not in many window systems where the higher a point is on the screen, the smaller is its vertical coordinate. Therefore all results should be conditioned in the implementation by the direction of increasing vertical coordinate.
- *Rule 3:* A point *lies to the right* of a line segment if it lies to the right of an observer walking along the line and going from the first endpoint to the second endpoint.

This condition is illustrated in Figure 15.7(a) where P lies to the right of both line segments L_1 and L_2.

Figure 15.7 Illustration of rules 3 and 4. (a) Point P lies to the right of both line segments L_1 and L_2. (b) Point 2 is the common point.

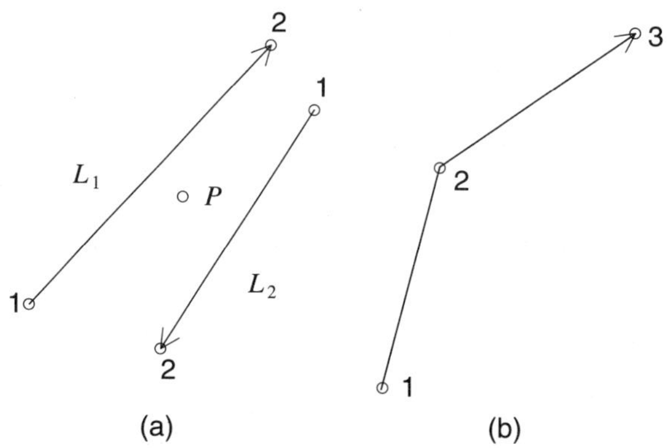

- *Rule 4:* If two line segments are joined, their endpoints are ordered in a consistent way. In particular, if M is the common point, it should be the second point of one segment and the first of the other.

In Figure 15.7(b) the middle point, 2, is the second point of the first segment and the first point of the second segment.

15.4.2 Position of a Point with Respect to a Line

We can use the determinant of Equation (15.8) to find the position of a point with respect to a line. This determinant is the equation of a line and is 0 when p points to a point on the line containing the line defined by p1 and p2. It also has a fixed sign for points on either side of the line. We claim that the following proposition is true.

Proposition: *If the point pointed to by* `p` *lies to the right of the line defined by* `p1` *and* `p2`, *then the determinant of Equation (15.8) is negative.*

Proof: Because the sign of the determinant is fixed on each side of the line we can show that the proposition is true by confirming that it returns the correct sign for a particular point. If the line is not horizontal and the first point is the lower of the two, points that have `x` greater than the points on the line will be to the right of the person walking from the first to the second point. If the first point is the higher of the two, points to the right will have `x` less than the points on the line.

We will compute the determinant for the point defined by:

$$\begin{aligned} P \rightarrow u &= p_1 \rightarrow u + p_1 \rightarrow w \\ P \rightarrow v &= p_1 \rightarrow v \\ P \rightarrow w &= p_1 \rightarrow w \end{aligned}$$

Here, the x coordinate of P is greater than the x coordinate of the first point of the line, so we should obtain a positive sign if the first endpoint is above the second and a negative sign if it is below. The result should be 0 if the line is horizontal. This is illustrated in Figure 15.8.

Figure 15.8 Selecting a point that lies to the right of a line.

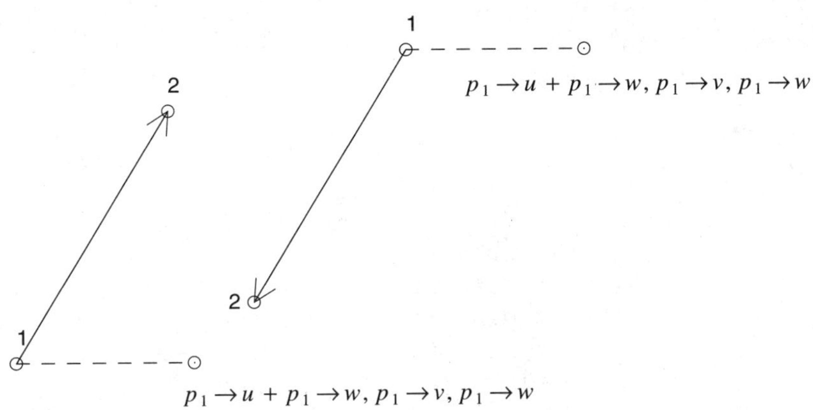

To verify that the signs are as we expect them to be, we compute the following determinant, which is what the sequence of `o_product()` and `s_product()` does:

$$D = \det \begin{bmatrix} p_1 \to u + p_1 \to w & p_1 \to u & p_2 \to u \\ p_1 \to v & p_1 \to v & p_2 \to v \\ p_1 \to w & p_1 \to w & p_2 \to w \end{bmatrix} \tag{15.16}$$

If we subtract the second column from the first, the determinant becomes

$$\det \begin{bmatrix} p_1 \to w & p_1 \to u & p_2 \to u \\ 0 & p_1 \to v & p_2 \to v \\ 0 & p_1 \to w & p_2 \to w \end{bmatrix} = p_1 \to w \det \begin{bmatrix} p_1 \to v & p_2 \to v \\ p_1 \to w & p_2 \to w \end{bmatrix} \tag{15.17}$$

The expansion of the last determinant yields

$$D = (p_1 \to w) \left[(p_1 \to v)(p_2 \to w) - (p_2 \to v)(p_1 \to w) \right] \tag{15.18}$$

which after division by the positive quantity $(p_1 \to w)^2 (p_2 \to w)$ becomes

$$\frac{p_1 \to v}{p_1 \to w} - \frac{p_2 \to v}{p_2 \to w} = y_1 - y_2 \tag{15.19}$$

This quantity is negative if the first endpoint is below the second and positive if the relative position is reversed which is what we expected.

If the line is horizontal we make a similar calculation by selecting a point:

$$P \to u = p_1 \to u$$
$$P \to v = p_1 \to v + p_1 \to w$$
$$P \to w = p_1 \to w$$

These calculations and the interpretation of Figure 15.8 are based on the four rules of Section 15.4.1. The second rule may not be valid in a particular window system, so we have to consider the effect that such a change will have on the results. Changing the direction that v increases will simply turn the diagrams of Figure 15.7 upside down and therefore interchange left and right. Hence in such a system the sign of the determinant will be positive.

The code in Listing 15.9 implements this analysis.

Listing 15.9: Point and Line Position — `File position.c`

```
/*   Return 1 if a point is to the right of an oriented line segment, */
/*   -1 if it is to the left, and 0 if it is on the segment.         */
#include <triplet.h>

int position(triplet *p1, triplet *p2, triplet *P)
    /* p1 and p2 point to the endpoints of the line segment */
{
    int k = determinant(p1, p2, P);

#   ifdef Y_INCREASES_UP
    return(k>0? 1: k<0? -1: 0);
#   else
    return(k>0? -1: k<0? 1: 0);
#   endif
 }
```

15.4.3 Intersection of Line Segments

We can use the result of Section 15.4.2 to check on whether two linear segments intersect and, if they do, to find the intersection. If the two segments are defined by pairs of points (`P[0]`,`P[1]`) and (`P[2]`,`P[3]`), the two segments will intersect if and only if the following two conditions are true.

1. The coordinates of `P[0]` yield a different sign from the coordinates of `P[1]` when they are substituted into the equation of the line joining `P[2]` and `P[3]`.
2. The coordinates of `P[2]` yield a different sign from the coordinates of `P[3]` when they are substituted into the equation of the line joining `P[0]` and `P[1]`.

Therefore we must call procedure `position()` four times.

```
S[0] = position(P+2, P+3, P);
S[1] = position(P+2, P+3, P+1);
S[2] = position(P, P+1, P+2);
S[3] = position(P, P+1, P+3);
```

The condition for intersection is that `S[0]` and `S[1]` differ in sign, and the same must also be true for `S[2]` and `S[3]`. Note that this condition is somewhat less stringent than the one used in the Proposition in Section 15.4.2 because we do not care what the signs are as long as they are different. Figure 15.9 shows the possible arrangements.

Figure 15.9 Possible configurations of two line segments.

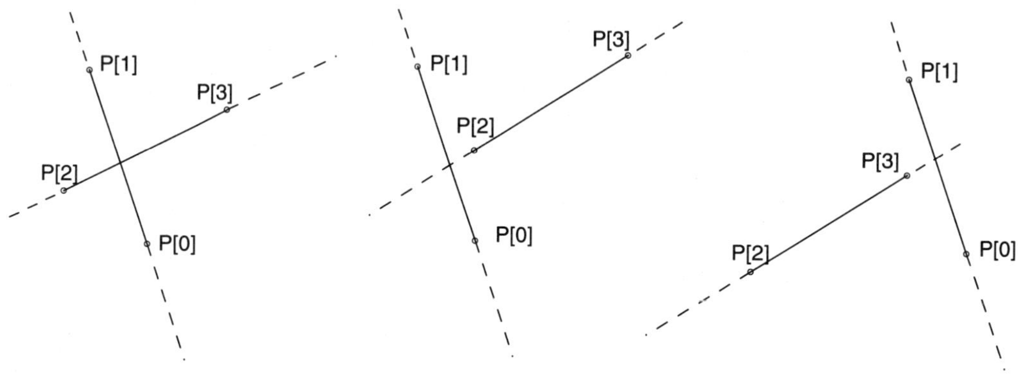

The code for checking is

```
if(S[0]*S[1]<0 && S[2]*S[3]<0) printf("Segments intersect");
```

If the conditions for intersection are satisfied, the coordinates of the common point `T` can be found by the following code.

```
o_product(P, P+1, &L12);
o_product(P+2, P+3, &L34);
o_product(&L12, &L34, &T);
```

If one or more of the returns of `position()` are 0, we have a singular case: One of the points lies in the line defined by the other two. Then we have to check on whether that point lies between the other two (see Assignment 5).

15.4.4 Murphy's Law in Computer Graphics

If anything can go wrong, it will.
(Murphy's Law)

We ended Section 15.4.3 by pointing out the need to examine the case of when one of the four points lies on the line joining the other two. Such an arrangement seems unlikely, so a natural question is: Why bother about it? But is it really unlikely?

If we select four points at random on the Euclidean plane, that any three of them will be collinear is, indeed, highly unlikely. But the situation is quite different in the discrete plane where coordinates are small integers (e.g., between 0 and 511). Figure 15.10 illustrates the situation. It shows an 8×8 grid with a line segment defined by two points (on the left) and three lines defined by three points on the right.

Figure 15.10 Black squares correspond to the defining points; gray squares correspond to the lines defined by each pair of them.

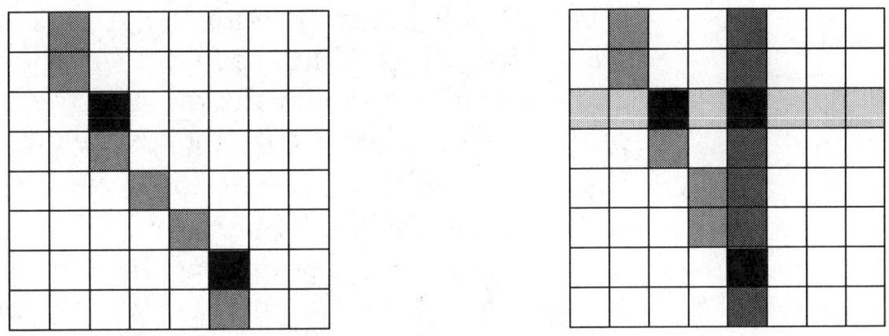

As 8 out of 64 squares are occupied by a line, the chances of picking up the third point on that line are 8 in 64, or 1 in 8. If the third point is not on that line, the chances of selecting the fourth on one of the three lines are even higher. The diagram on the right contains 20 marked squares, so the chances are 20 in 64 or 5 in 16, or almost 1 in 3.

These results are too pessimistic because in practice we use much larger grids than 8×8. If we use k bits per screen coordinate, the chances of three of four randomly selected points being collinear are approximately 1 in 2^{k-2}. For $k = 10$ (the range needed for a 1000×1000 screen), the odds are 1 in 256 — not very high, but not too low either. They are about the same as those for rolling a die for a 6 three times in a row.

15.5 CONCLUSIONS

We discussed issues concerning the relative position of points and line segments, extending the analysis of Section 13.7. Because of problems associated with scale (e.g., two line segments may intersect well beyond the limits of the screen) we introduced a new system of coordinates: homogeneous coordinates. Such coordinates not only solve certain numerical problems but also, because of the duality property, make the writing of programs for point/line position problems a little easier.

We also discussed the use of the analytical results to enhance the video games discussed in Chapter 3.

The following is a reference for additional reading on the subject of homogeneous coordinates.

- W. T. Fishback. *Projective and Euclidean Geometry.* New York: John Wiley & Sons, 1969.

15.6 ASSIGNMENTS

1. Modify the game program of Listing 15.7 so that the sweep loop (where `a` varies) is interleaved with the graphin motion loop in the following way. After all graphins have moved, the ray moves (new value of `a`) and proximity between the ray and the graphins is checked. Then the program checks for events, moves the graphins, and so on.
2. Design and implement a set of functions for an object drawing program so that a line can be defined from the intersection of two pairs of other line segments. For example, if the user has drawn segments `AB`, `CD`, `EF`, and `GH`, there should be a way to define a new segment joining the intersection of `AB` and `CD` with the intersection of `EF` and `GH`.
3. Prove that, if the triplets in Listing 15.6.1 represent straight lines, then the line corresponding to `t` passes through the intersection of the lines corresponding to triplets `a` and `b`.
4. Prove that if the triplets in Listing 15.6.1 represent points, then the point corresponding to `t` lies on the line joining the points corresponding to triplets `a` and `b`.
5. Complete the analysis begun in Section 15.4.3 (intersection of line segments) for the case where the endpoint of one segment lies on the line defined by the other segment.

15.7 NOTE

The system of Equations (15.2a) and (15.2b) can be solved by eliminating one of the variables between the two equations. To eliminate y, we multiply the first equation by b_2 and the second by b_1 and then we subtract the second from the first. The result is

$$(a_1 b_2 - a_2 b_1)x + (b_1 b_2 - b_2 b_1)y + c_1 b_2 - c_2 b_1 = 0$$

or

$$(a_1 b_2 - a_2 b_1)x + c_1 b_2 - c_2 b_1 = 0$$

If $(a_1 b_2 - a_2 b_1)$ is not 0, we can solve with respect to x:

$$x = -\frac{c_1 b_2 - c_2 b_1}{a_1 b_2 - a_2 b_1}$$

In this case we can substitute back into Equation (15.2a) and after a similar sequence of operations find

$$y = \frac{c_1 a_2 - c_2 a_1}{a_1 b_2 - a_2 b_1}$$

16

Operations on Polygons

Scope of the Chapter

Window clipping • Position of a point with respect to a convex or nonconvex polygon • Clipping a line segment by a convex polygon • Clipping of Polygons

16.1 INTRODUCTION

Polygons are used a lot in graphics because performing most operations on them is easier than on other shapes. They are point pictures and also the easiest to draw with a pointing device, such as the mouse. Using various mathematical techniques we can transform such point pictures to more complex forms, including full pictures.

We can see the computational advantages by comparing the computation required for filling an area (Chapter 11) to that for filling a polygon (Chapter 12). The program for filling an area seems simpler, but it requires far more time for its execution.

We can be convinced of the widespread utility of polygons by observing that any other shape can be approximated by a polygon with small enough sides (although there may be many such sides). Figure 16.1 shows the outlines of two swans drawn as polygons with 37 sides each. The polygonal nature of the outline is clearly visible in the larger swan but not in the smaller one. The larger the object, the more sides are needed to produce a smooth appearance.

Figure 16.1 Approximation of shapes with polygons. The outline of each of the two swans is a polygon with 37 sides.

The term *clipping* is used to describe many operations involving polygons. Clipping a straight line with respect to a polygon means finding the part of the line that is inside the polygon. Similarly, clipping polygon P with respect to polygon W means finding the part of P that lies inside W. Figure 16.2 shows some examples, with the clipped parts shown with heavier lines.

Figure 16.2 Left: Clipping a Line with a Polygon. Right: Clipping one Polygon (P) with another (W)

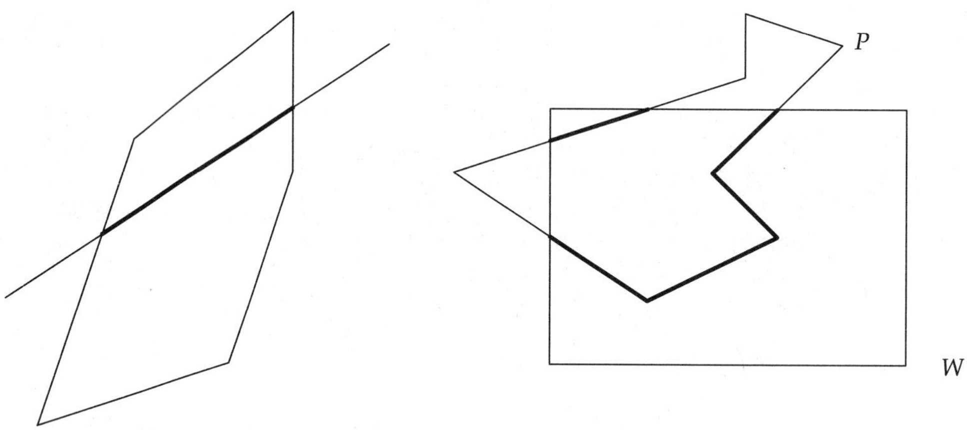

A special case of practical importance is clipping with respect to a polygon that is a right rectangle. Such a rectangle may represent the display area of a window, and the window system must determine which parts of a geometric figure can be drawn. Because of the simple shape of a right rectangle, many calculations are simplified. However, there also is a special need for speed because the computation is made so often.

In this chapter we start with window clipping and then discuss the problem of finding whether a point is inside or outside a polygon. Next, we discuss the position of a straight line with respect to a polygon, and, finally, the relation of two polygons with each other.

16.2 WINDOW CLIPPING

We use the expression *window clipping* to mean clipping a figure with respect to a right rectangle. The coordinates of the upper left corner of the rectangle are denoted `XMIN` and `YMIN`, and the coordinates of the lower right corner are denoted `XMAX` and `YMAX`. In a window system these values are in absolute screen coordinates. After clipping, the coordinates of the figure could be expressed relative to the upper left corner of the window by subtracting `XMIN` and `YMIN` from them. Normally, window clipping is performed by the system. Because window clipping is performed just before the final display, our discussion is in terms of ordinary rather than homogeneous coordinates.

16.2.1 Point Clipping

For a right rectangle point clipping is a trivial operation. A point with coordinates `x` and `y` is inside the window if

```
(XMIN <= x && x <= XMAX) && (YMIN <= y && y <= YMAX)
```

16.2.2 Line Clipping — Preliminaries

The calculation for a line segment is slightly more complex because parts of the segment may be inside a window even if neither of its endpoints is. Figure 16.3 shows four possibilities.

Line segment `L1` clearly is outside the window because both of its endpoints have a coordinate `x` that is less than `XMIN`. Line segment `L4` clearly is partly inside the window because one of its endpoints is inside the window. The answer for line segments `L2` and `L3` is not obvious. The relative positions of their endpoints with respect to the window sides is the same, yet part of `L3` is within the window while `L2` is entirely outside the window. Nevertheless the relative position of the endpoints provides *some* information, and we can use it to decide quickly the easy cases. Procedure `point_loc()` of Listing 16.1 computes a bit pattern that depends on the location of a point with respect to the boundaries of the window.

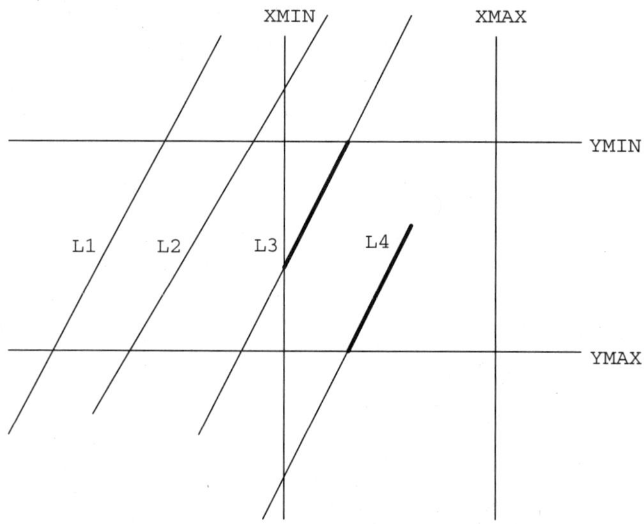

Figure 16.3 Relative position of four line segments with respect to a window. The part inside the window is shown with a heavier line.

Listing 16.1: Window Clipping (Part 1) — `File window_clip.c`

```
/*   SIDEs defined by octal patterns - bit pattern in comments */
#define LEFT_SIDE      01    /* 0001 */
#define RIGHT_SIDE     02    /* 0010 */
#define TOP_SIDE      010    /* 1000 */
#define BOTTOM_SIDE    04    /* 0100 */

static int XMIN, XMAX, YMIN, YMAX;

int point_loc(int x, int y)
{
     int c = 0;
     c = x<XMIN? LEFT_SIDE: x>XMAX? RIGHT_SIDE: 0;
     if(y<YMIN) c |= BOTTOM_SIDE;
     else if(y>YMAX) c |= TOP_SIDE;
     return(c);
}
```

Figure 16.4 shows the bit patterns calculated for each of the nine areas into which the sides of the window divide the plane.

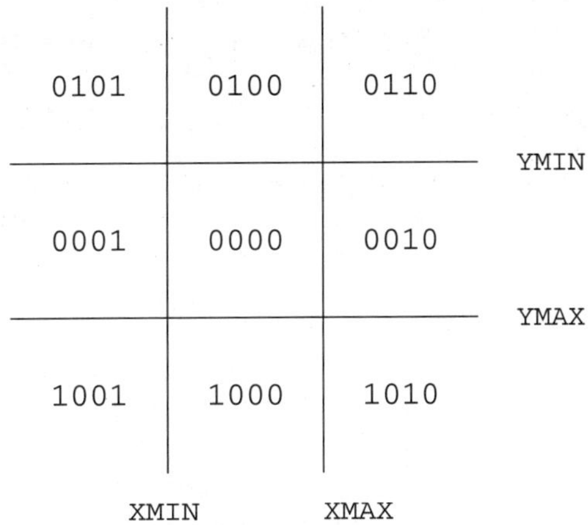

Figure 16.4 Relationship between the bit patterns computed by procedure `point_loc()` and the nine areas of the plane defined by the sides of a window.

If the value returned by `point_loc()` is 0 for both endpoints of a segment, both endpoints are inside the window and therefore so is the whole segment. The segment definitely will be invisible if both endpoints are on the same side of a boundary. In that case the returns from `point_loc()` will contain the bit pattern of that side. For example, if both endpoints are to the left of `XMIN`, both will contain the bit pattern `01`. If we perform a bitwise AND operation on these values, the result will be nonzero because both values contain the same pattern. Procedure `simple_clip()` of Listing 16.2 performs these checks and returns 1 if the segment is entirely within the window, – 1 if it is entirely outside, and 0 if it is ambiguous.

Listing 16.2: Window Clipping (Part 2, Temporary)

```
simple_clip(int x1, int y1, int x2, int y2)
{
     int c1, c2;
     c1 = point_loc(x1,y1);
     c2 = point_loc(x2,y2);
     if(!c1 && !c2) return(1);   /* && stands for logical AND */
     if(c1&c2) return(-1);       /* & stands for bitwise AND */
     return(0);
}
```

If `simple_clip()` returns 0, we must examine the exact position of the endpoints with respect to the sides. If a point is beyond a side of the window, we must replace it with the intersection of the line and that side. However, this step will not guarantee that the resulting line is ready to be displayed as line segments L2 and L3 of Figure 16.3 show. Therefore we have to check the endpoint location again.

16.2.3 Line Clipping — The Complete Solution

To find the part of a line segment contained inside a window we could either add a procedure to perform additional calculations when simple_clip() returns 0, or we could incorporate the calculations into simple_clip(). We do the latter because the bit pattern provides helpful information for these calculations. The new procedure is called complete_clip() and is shown in Listing 16.3. An assumption for the program is that y1 is less than or equal to y2, and, in case of equality, that x1 is less than x2. The procedure swap3() interchanges the values of the first three arguments with the values of the last three, and it is used to ensure that this assumption holds.

We apply the location test again after we replace one point because we may be able to decide immediately that the line is outside the window. In Figure 16.3, after the left endpoint of line L2 is moved to the left boundary of the window (the x of that endpoint is replaced by XMIN), it also moves above the top boundary so that c1 equals TOP. As c2 also equals TOP the procedure returns without any more tests.

Listing 16.3: Window Clipping (Part 2, Final) — File window_clip.c

```
int complete_clip(int *x1p, int *y1p, int *x2p, int *y2p)
{
     int x1, y1, x2, y2, c1, c2, visible;

     x1 = *x1p;     y1 = *y1p;
     x2 = *x2p;     y2 = *y2p;
     c1 = point_loc(x1,y1);
     c2 = point_loc(x2,y2);
     if(c1 & c2) return(-1);/* invisible segment */
     if(c1 || c2) /* not (!c1 && !c2) */
          visible = find_new_endpoints(x1p, y1p, x2p, y2p, c1, c2);
     else visible = 1;
     return(visible);
}

int find_new_endpoints(int *x1p, int *y1p, int *x2p, int *y2p, int c1, int c2)
{
     int visible = 1;

     while(c1 || c2){
          if(c1&c2) return(-1);   /* invisible segment */
```

```
        if(!c1) swap3(x1p, y1p, &c1, x2p, y2p, &c2);
        visible++;

        if(c1&LEFT_SIDE) { /* *x1p<XMIN */
            *y1p += (XMIN - *x1p)*(*y1p-*y2p)/(*x1p-*x2p);
            *x1p = XMIN;
            c1 = point_loc(*x1p,*y1p); continue;
        }
        if(c1&BOTTOM_SIDE) {    /* *y1p<YMIN */
            *x1p += (YMIN - *y1p)*(*x2p-*x1p)/(*y2p-*y1p);
            *y1p = YMIN;
            c1 = point_loc(*x1p,*y1p); continue;
        }
        if(c1&RIGHT_SIDE) {     /* *x1p>XMAX */
            *y1p += (XMAX - *x1p)*(*y1p-*y2p)/(*x1p-*x2p);
            *x1p = XMAX;
            c1 = point_loc(*x1p,*y1p); continue;
        }
        if(c1&TOP_SIDE) {  /* *y1p>YMAX */
            *x1p += (YMAX - *y1p)*(*x2p-*x1p)/(*y2p-*y1p);
            *y1p = YMAX;
            c1 = point_loc(*x1p,*y1p); continue;
        }
    }
    return(visible);    /* visible segment */
}

swap3(int *p1, int *p2, int *p3, int *q1, int *q2, int *q3)
{
    int t;
    t = *p1;  *p1 = *q1;    *q1 = t;
    t = *p2;  *p2 = *q2;    *q2 = t;
    t = *p3;  *p3 = *q3;    *q3 = t;
}
```

The expressions used for the new coordinates are based on the following computation. If the x coordinate of a point is X_{MIN}, then the corresponding y value can be found from the following equation, which is based on Equation 13.5.

$$\det \begin{bmatrix} X_{MIN} & x_1 & x_2 \\ y & y_1 & y_2 \\ 1 & 1 & 1 \end{bmatrix} = 0 \tag{16.1}$$

If we subtract the second column from the first, the value of the determinant does not change and the matrix has the form

$$\det \begin{bmatrix} X_{MIN} - x_1 & x_1 & x_2 \\ y - y_1 & y_1 & y_2 \\ 0 & 1 & 1 \end{bmatrix} = 0 \tag{16.2}$$

After expansion,

$$(X_{MIN} - x_1)(y_1 - y_2) - (y - y_1)(x_1 - x_2) = 0 \tag{16.3}$$

or

$$y = y_1 + (X_{MIN} - x_1)\frac{y_1 - y_2}{x_1 - x_2} \tag{16.4}$$

Similar analysis yields the expressions used for the other three window boundaries.

Listing 16.4 shows a program for testing the code given in Listings 16.1 and 16.3. The program displays a rectangle in foreground color inside the main window with the same subdivisions of the space as in Figure 16.3. By clicking a mouse button the user selects pairs of points that are marked with a small filled square. For each pair of points a line clipped by the rectangle is shown.

Listing 16.4: Test of Window Clip — `File test_clip_window.c`

```
/*   Program to test window clipping */

#include "window_clip.c"    /* Code of Listings 16.1 and 16.3 */

#include <Starter.h>
static int Width = 400, Height = 400, Margin = 100;

scene()
{
     fill_rectangle(Margin, Margin, Width-2*Margin, Height-2*Margin);
     put_line(0, Margin, Width, Margin);
     put_line(0, Height-Margin, Width, Height-Margin);
     put_line(Margin, 0, Margin, Height);
     put_line(Width-Margin, 0, Width-Margin, Height);
}

static int kount = 0, x[2],  y[2];

draw(pEvent *p)
{
```

```
    if(p->kind != BTN_PRESS) return;
    if(kount<2) {
        x[kount] = p->x;
        y[kount] = p->y;    kount++;
        fill_rectangle(p->x-2, p->y-2, 5, 5);
    }
    if(kount==2) {
        if(complete_clip(x, y, x+1, y+1) >0)
            put_line(x[0], y[0], x[1], y[1]);
        kount = 0;
    }
}

main()
{
    XMIN = Margin; XMAX = Width-Margin;
    YMIN = Margin; YMAX = Height-Margin;
    draw_window(scene, draw, Width, Height, "Clip Test");
}
```

This program can be easily modified to draw a line for each pair of points and then draw the clipped part thicker or in a different style or color.

16.2.4 Polyline Clipping by a Window

Finding the parts of the sides of a polyline that are visible through a window can be reduced to applying the procedure `complete_clip()` for each of its sides. That is wasteful, though, as each vertex is examined twice. A better way is to call `point_loc()` for each vertex and store the results in an array. Then the array can be traversed and the extra computation done only for the sides that would fail the test of `simple_clip()`. A function implementing this method is shown in Listing 16.5. It uses the structures `fPoint` (defined in Listing 13.1) and `fPolyline` (defined in Listing 13.4).

Listing 16.5: Polyline Clipping by Window — `File polyclip.c`

```
#include <Starter.h> /* for pPixel in gtypes.h */
#include <gtypes.h>      /* Definition of fPoint and fPolyline */

void poly_window_clip(fPolyline *Pp)
{
    register i;
    register fPoint * pp;
    int *cb;
```

```
    register int *cp;
    int x1, y1, x2, y2, visible;

    cb = (int *)malloc(Pp->npnts*sizeof(int));
    for(i=0, cp=cb, pp=Pp->pnts; i<Pp->npnts; i++, pp++, cp++)
            *cp = point_loc((int)pp->x, (int)pp->y);

    for(i=1, cp=cb+1, pp=Pp->pnts+1; i<Pp->npnts; i++, pp++, cp++){
        if(*cp & *(cp-1) ) continue;     /* invisible side */
        x1 = pp->x+0.5;          y1 = pp->y+0.5;
        x2 = (pp-1)->x+0.5;      y2 = (pp-1)->y+0.5;
        if( *cp || *(cp-1) )
        visible = find_new_endpoints(&x1, &y1, &x2, &y2, *cp, *(cp-1));
        else visible = 1;
        if(visible >= 1) put_line( x1, y1, x2, y2 );
    }
    free(cb);
}
```

The function of Listing 16.5 must be compiled with the functions of Listings 16.1 and 16.3. It can be tested with the program of Listing 16.4 if we replace the event handler of the latter with a rubber band drawing routine from Chapter 2. We need to modify the declaration of the buffer and also add the following code:

```
#include "window_clip.c"
#include "polyclip.c"
 ...
static fPoint buff[MAX_PTS];
static int bn = 0;
static fPoint *bp;
static fPolyline P;
 ...
/* when the right button is pressed terminating the drawing */
    P.pnts = buff;
    P.npnts = bn;
    set_line_width(4);
    poly_window_clip(&P);
    set_line_width(1);
```

This code will cause the new lines to be drawn thicker.

16.3 POSITION OF A POINT WITH RESPECT TO A POLYGON

16.3.1 The General Problem

In many applications we would like to know whether a point is inside a polygon. Assignment 8 in Chapter 12 asked for a modification of the polygon filling algorithm to solve this problem. Listing 16.6 offers a complete implementation. It differs from the method expected in Assignment 8 in Chapter 12 because the polygon sides are not presorted. If the point is on a horizontal side the answer varies according to the conditions described in Section 12.2.2 (particularly, Figure 12.4). The functions `cut_line()` and `xsort()` have code similar to that of function `draw()` in Listing 12.2.5. The main part of the algorithm is in the function `point_in_polygon()`.

Listing 16.6: Point in Polygon (Version 1) — `File point_in_poly.c`

```
#include <Starter.h>
#include <gtypes.h>

double cut_line(int x1, int y1, int x2, int y2, int y)
{
     double dx, dy, xy;

     dx = x2 - x1;
     dy = y1 - y2;
     if(!dy) return((x1+x2)*0.5);
     xy = x1 * y2 - x2 * y1;
     return( - (xy + y*dx)/dy );
}

void xsort(double xx[], int n)
{
     register i, k;
     int xtmp;

     do {
          k = 0;
          for(i=1; i<n; i++){
               if(xx[i-1]>xx[i]) {
                    xtmp = xx[i-1];
                    xx[i-1] = xx[i];
                    xx[i] = xtmp;
                    k = 1;
               }
          }
     } while(k);
}
```

```
int point_in_polygon(fPolyline *pol, fPoint *q)
{
	register i, j;
	static double xcut[64];
	int cut = 0;
	int n = pol->npnts;
	fPoint *pp, *pq;

	for(i=0, pp = pol->pnts; i<n; i++, pp++) {
		pq = i>0? pp-1: pol->pnts+n-1;
		if( (pp->y < q->y && q->y <= pq->y) ||
		    (pp->y >= q->y && q->y > pq->y) )
		    xcut[cut++] = cut_line(pp->x, pp->y, pq->x, pq->y, q->y);
	}
	if(!cut) return(0);
	xsort(xcut, cut);
	for(i=0; i<cut; i++) if(q->x < xcut[i]) break;
	return(i%2);
}
```

If the point pointed at by `q` has a `y` coordinate between those of the endpoints of a side, the intersection of that side with a horizontal line through the point is found. The result is stored in the array `xcut[]`. The functions of the preceding listing can be tested easily by using a rubber band drawing event handler, as described in Chapter 2. After drawing a polygon we may store it in an `fPolyline` structure, as described in Section 16.2.2 and then use the middle button of the mouse to check on whether a point is inside or not. The following code fragment could be used.

```
fPoint a;
	...
case MIDDLE_PRESS:
	a.x = p->x;	a.y = p->y;
	if(point_in_polygon(&P, &a))
			fill_rectangle(p->x-2, p->y-2, 5, 5);
	else put_rectangle(p->x-2, p->y-2, 5, 5);
```

16.3.2 A Method for Convex Polygons

The discussion of Section 15.4 suggests another method for checking whether a point is inside a polygon. If the vertices of a polygon are ordered clockwise, a point will be in the interior if it always is to the right of an observer traversing the sides in order. The routine of Listing 16.7 checks that and returns 1 if the point is always to the right.

Listing 16.7: Point in Polygon (Version 2) — `File psides.c`

```
/*   Position of a point with respect to the sides of a convex */
/*   polygon using the function  position() in Listing 15.9.    */
#include <triplet.h>

int point_in_polygon(triplet *p, int n, triplet *q)
{
     register i;

     if( position(p+n-1, p, q) >=0 ) return(0);
     for(i=1; i<n; i++) if( position(p+i-1, p+i, q) >= 0 ) return(0);
     return(1);
}
```

This method avoids finding the intersections of a line with all the sides and the sorting involved in the method of Listing 16.6, but it is applicable only to a special class of polygons. Figure 16.5 shows two situations where a point is inside a polygon, but the procedure `point_in_polygon()` returns 1 only for the situation on the left.

Figure 16.5 Two polygons which both contain a point marked with X but the procedure `point_in_polygon()` returns 1 only in the first case.

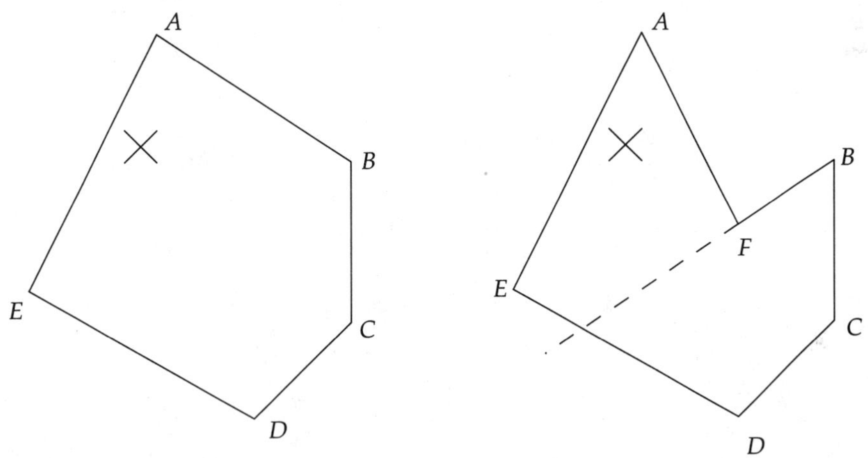

In the situation on the right the point in question lies to the left of side *FB*, even though it is inside the polygon. That happens because, when *FB* is extended (dashed part), it intersects side *DE*; therefore, points inside the polygon lie on both sides of *FB*. Polygons in which this does *not* happen are said to be *convex*.

Definition A polygon is convex if the angles of all its vertices are convex (i.e., less than 180°).

This definition is equivalent to that given in Assignment 6, Chapter 12. That is, a convex polygon is intersected by a straight line at no more than two points. With no concave angles (greater than 180°), none of the sides, when extended, have points inside the polygon.

Because the left polygon in Figure 16.5 is convex, the procedure `point_in_polygon()` can be used to determine whether a point is inside a polygon. In contrast, the right polygon of Figure 16.5 contains a concave angle (at vertex *F*), so it is not convex.

The efficiency of the function of Listing 16.7 can be improved by observing that procedure `position()` in Listing 15.9 calculates a determinant which in turns involves a call to `o_product()` followed by a call to `s_product()`. (See Listing 15.2.2.) We can save some time by precomputing an intermediate triplet and saving the results, as shown in Listing 16.8.

Listing 16.8: Point in Polygon (Version 3) — `File pconvex.c`

```
#include <triplet.h>

void sides(triplet p[], int n, triplet s[])
{
     register i;

     for(i=1; i<n; i++) o_product(p+i-1, p+i, s+i);
     o_product(p+n-1, p, s);
}

int point_in_polygon(triplet *s, int n, triplet *q)
{
     register i;

#    ifdef Y_INCREASES_UP
     for(i=0; i<n; i++) if(s_product(s+i, q) >0) return(0);
#    else
     for(i=0; i<n; i++) if(s_product(s+i, q) <0) return(0);
#    endif
     return(1);
}
```

The main procedure calls `sides()`, and then `point_in_polygon()`, for each point whose position with respect to the polygon must be found. We illustrate the application of this procedure using the convex polygon of Figure 16.6 whose vertices have the following coordinates. (Note that in this example y increases upward.)

$$(2, 7) \quad (11, 15) \quad (22, 9) \quad (22, -6) \quad (9, -6)$$

All of the points are on the display field, so we take w to be equal to 1 and u and v equal to x and y, respectively. A simple calculation gives the following triplets for the sides.

$$(-8, 9, -47)\ (6, 11, -231)\ (15, 0, -330)\ (0, -13, -78)\ (-13, -7, 75)$$

For the point with coordinates $(10, 10)$ the function `s_product()` returns the following values for each of the five triplets

$$-37,\ -61,\ -180,\ -208,\ -125$$

As all of these values are negative, `point_in_polygon` will return 1, indicating that the point lies inside the polygon, as it indeed does. On the other hand, for the origin $(0, 0)$ `s_product()` returns the values

$$-47,\ -231,\ -330,\ -78,\ 75$$

Because one of them is positive, `point_in_polygon` will return 0, indicating that the origin lies outside the polygon, as it indeed does.

Figure 16.6 Position of a point with respect to a convex polygon.

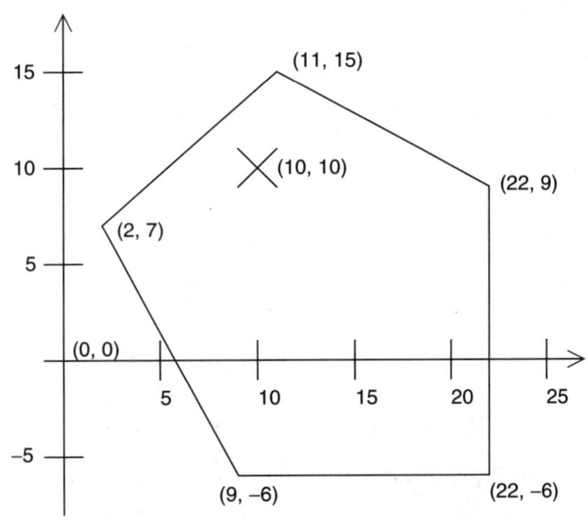

16.3.3 An Application of the Point in Polygon Routine

We can use the procedure `point_in_polygon()` of either Listing 16.6 or Listing 16.7 to add some features to the game we started in Chapter 3. One possibility is to have some traps in the form of convex polygons. When a graphin is inside such a polygon, it suffers whatever fate the programmer has decreed. Having the human player draw the trap polygons to encircle the graphins is also possible.

We need an array of polygons with each polygon being an array of triplets representing the equations of its sides. *If we assume* that the polygon is (a) convex and (b) its sides are ordered clockwise so that its interior is to the right of a person walking along them, the procedure `point_in_polygon()` in Listing 16.7 can be used to find when a "graphin gets trapped." We set aside for the moment the construction of the polygons and list the procedure for checking containment.

Listing 16.9: Traps for a Game — `File traps.c`

```
#include <triplet.h>

typedef struct {
     triplet *sides;
     int n;
} side_Polygon;

#define NT    12   /* number of traps, we assume 12 */
side_Polygon trap[NT];

int inside_trap(int x, int y)
{
     register i;
     triplet q;
     side_Polygon *tp;

     q.u = x; q.v = y; q.w = 1;
     for(i=0, tp=trap; i<NT; i++, tp++)
          if( point_in_polygon(tp->sides, tp->n, &q) ) return(1);
}
```

16.4 CLIPPING A LINE SEGMENT WITH A CONVEX POLYGON

When we dealt with the problem of clipping a line segment with a window (a right rectangle), we subdivided it into three cases: (1) Both endpoints were on the same side of one of the sides of the window, so the segment was definitely outside the window; (2) both endpoints were within the window, so the segment was contained within the window; and (3) neither (1) nor (2), which required quite a bit more computation.

The same is true when a line segment is clipped with a convex polygon. We can find which side of a polygon side a point is on by modifying the procedure `point_in_polygon()` of Listing 16.8. That procedure terminated and returned 0 if a point was found on the wrong side of a side. Now we want to determine whether both endpoints are on the wrong side of a side, so the pair must be examined simultaneously. Listing 16.10 contains the modified procedure. For simplicity we have removed the condition about the direction that `y` increases. We assume that it is downward.

Listing 16.10: Position of Segment with Respect to Polygon, A

```
/*   Position of segment with respect to sides of polygon. Returns: */
/*   1 if both endpoints inside, -1 if both outside, 0 otherwise.   */
/*   FUNCTIONS ASSUMES THAT Y INCREASES DOWNWARD                     */
#include <triplet.h>

int segment_in_polygon(triplet *s, int n, triplet *p, triplet *q)
{
     register i, k;
     int ps, qs;

     for(i=0, k=0; i<n; i++) {
          ps = s_product(s+i, p);
          qs = s_product(s+i, q);
          if(ps<0 && qs<0) return(-1);
          if(ps>=0 && qs>=0) k++;
     }
     if(k==n) return(1);
     else return(0);
}
```

In the same way as in clipping with a window, the challenging case is when `segment_in_polygon()` returns 0. Figure 16.7 (on page 380) shows a case where the segment *PQ* intersects all the *lines* defined by the sides of a polygon. Clearly, only the intersections with sides *AB* and *BC* are relevant. What distinguishes these sides from the others? Their endpoints are on either side of the given segment. Therefore we must make a list of the lines that are crossed by the segment so that later we can reverse the roles and check on whether the respective segments (as opposed to the lines) intersect. The modification of `segment_in_polygon()` shown in Listing 16.11 accomplishes that task.

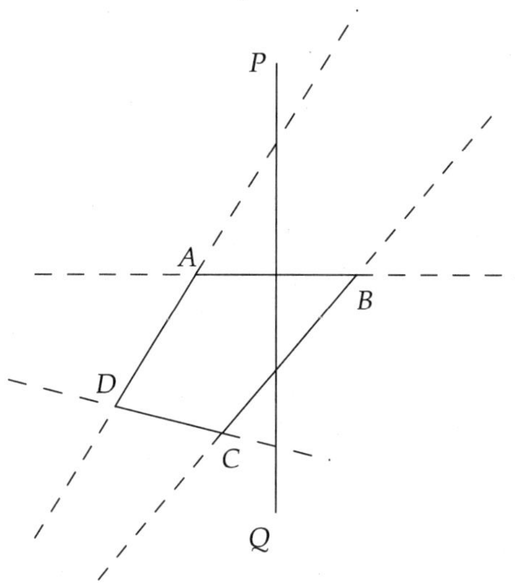

Figure 16.7 A convex polygon and a line segment that cause the function of Listing 16.10 to return 0.

Listing 16.11: Position of Segment with Respect to Polygon, B — `File line_cpoly.c`

```
/*   Position of segment with respect to sides of polygon. Returns: */
/*   1 if both endpoints inside, -1 if both outside, 0 otherwise.   */
/*   FUNCTIONS ASSUMES THAT Y INCREASES DOWNWARD                    */
#include <triplet.h>

int segment_in_polygon(triplet *s, int n, triplet *p, triplet *q,
     triplet *sbf[])
{
     register i, k;
     int ps, qs;
     triplet **sp;

     sp = sbf;
     for(i=0, k=0; i<n; i++) {
          ps = s_product(s+i, p);
          qs = s_product(s+i, q);
          if(ps<0 && qs<0) return(-1);
          if(ps>=0 && qs>=0) k++;
          else *sp++ = s+i;
     }
     if(k==n) return(1);
     else return(0);
}
```

16.5 CLIPPING OF POLYGONS

We can determine what part of an arbitrary polygon is inside a given convex polygon by calling the procedure `segment_in_polygon()` for each of its sides. We can also construct more efficient procedures in a manner similar to that presented in Listing 16.5. However, such a procedure would attempt the same checks for two polygons that are near each other as for polygons that are far apart. The total amount of computation can be reduced by associating with each polygon a bounding box, as shown in Figure 16.8.

Figure 16.8 Two polygons and their bounding boxes.

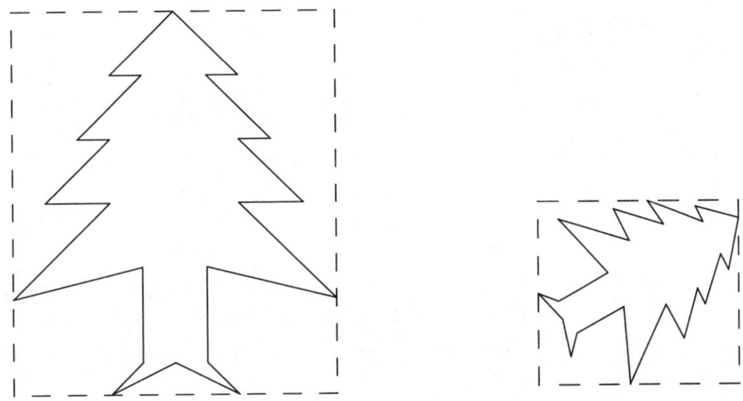

When an operation on a polygon needs to be performed, we may try it first on its bounding box. Because that is a right rectangle, most operations are simplified. We may also use bounding boxes for both polygons. Additional computation is performed only when the two boxes intersect each other.

16.6 CONCLUSIONS

Deciding whether a point is inside a polygon or finding the segment of a line that is inside a polygon are problems that are rather simple when the polygon is a right rectangle. They are more difficult when the polygon is convex (but not a right rectangle). When the polygon is not convex, the solution of both problems can be quite time consuming. Fortunately, the most common applications involve right rectangles. That is the shape of windows and, when something is drawn on a window, it is automatically clipped to its shape.

Various *Xlib* functions solve most of the polygon clipping and related problems in the most general case (see Chapter 18) — but only for drawing. Thus we can plot the intersection of two polygons using an *Xlib* function, but we cannot find a list of the vertices of the intersection using an *Xlib* function. Therefore, for many applications, using our own code is necessary.

We can enhance our video game by constructing a terrain where all the graphins are confined. However, the required computation can be quite extensive and slow down the game.

16.7 ASSIGNMENTS

1. Modify Listings 16.1 and 16.3 to use floating point arithmetic for the computation of the coordinates. Do the same for Listing 16.5.
2. Implement the testing of the polygon clipping algorithm suggested at the end of Section 16.2.4.
3. The method of Listing 16.5 draws only the sides of the polygon inside the window (shown on the left in Figure 16.9). Modify it to draw the window sides inside the polygon (shown on the right in Figure 16.9). (This problem is somewhat simpler for polygons, than for polylines. Handling the polyline case should be a separate assignment.)

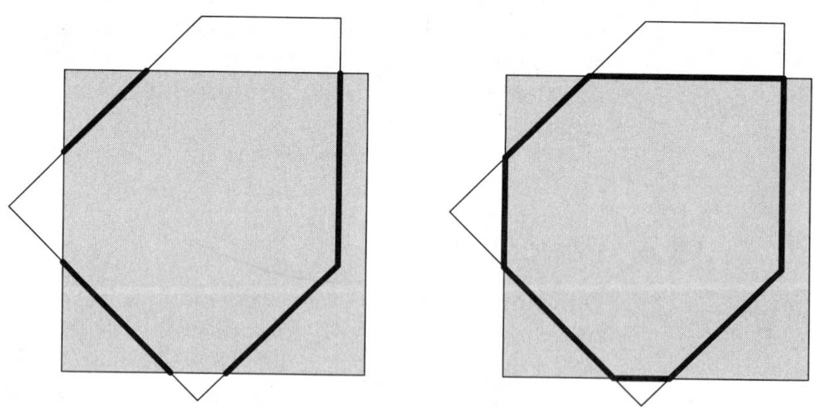

Figure 16.9 Two ways of clipping a polygon with a window.

4. Create a maze in a video game with sides that are either vertical or horizontal and confine the graphins to stay inside it. Figure 16.10 shows one possibility. You can arrange so that some graphins may enter a region while others cannot. (Suggestions for such regions are marked by different shading in the figure. For example, graphins that are strong could enter the regions marked by light gray. No graphin could enter the black regions.)

Figure 16.10 A maze that may be used to confine the movement of graphins in a video game.

5. Repeat Assignment 4 for a maze having sides with arbitrary directions.
6. Without implementing the code for either Assignment 4 or 5, identify the algorithms that must be used for each.
7. Modify the method of Listing 16.6 to handle the case when the y coordinate of the given point equals the y coordinate of one of the polygon vertices.

17

Splines

Scope of the Chapter

Need for curves whose shape can be determined through simple user interaction • Examples of interactive curve drawing and editing • Parabolic splines • Cubic splines

17.1 INTRODUCTION

17.1.1 The Need

Polygons can provide good approximations for any shape, but they are limited because their representations are not the most economical. To produce the appearance of a smooth curve may require a polygon with hundreds of sides. Clearly, using a curve rather than a collection of straight line segments to represent smooth shapes would be better.

The question is: What kind of a curve? *Curve* is not a precise mathematical term and many mathematical equations have smooth curve graphs. We cannot consider displays of curves without worrying about equations. But most of the time users are interested only in the shape of the curve and would prefer not to have to worry about the mathematical form used to generate the curve. Therefore, for a designer of graphics systems the natural question is: *''Which mathematical form is best for satisfying user requirements?''*

We should select a family of mathematical curves broad enough to produce any shape that a user might want to create in a display. But that is not enough: We also must be concerned about the ease of specification of a particular member of the family. Suppose that we decide to use circular arcs for curves. To specify an arc we need quite a few parameters. One possible choice is the following set: the coordinates of the center, x_c and y_c, the coordinates of the first point, x_1 and y_1, the angle of the arc ϕ, and the direction, *clockwise* or *counterclockwise*. This set of parameters specifies a circular arc completely, but it does not include the radius explicitly. Many users probably would like to specify an arc by its endpoints and the radius, but that is not a well-defined problem and it may have no, two, or four solutions.

Ideally, we want to provide an intuitive way for specifying a curve so that the *user* does not have to worry about the mathematics. A possible solution is to ask the user to specify some points at or near the curve and then have the program select a curve that matches the requirements. Note that finding such a curve is usually a more difficult mathematical problem than producing a curve from user-defined parameters. This situation is another instance of a well-known programming maxim:

Important Point: *The easier it is for the user, the more difficult it is for the programmer.*

17.1.2 Some Solutions

As the goal is to develop user-friendly facilities, designers of routines for drawing curves must be ready to tackle a fair amount of mathematics. Hence this chapter is not for the mathematically fainthearted.

In the rest of this chapter we assume that the user can enter points with a pointing device (e.g., a mouse) using a program similar to those of Listings 2.7, 10.4, or 14.1. Then we must decide how to interpret the points. We have the following choices.

(1) Have the curve pass exactly through the points specified. Finding such a curve is called *interpolation.* Usually, it is not a good solution unless we have great confidence in the points selected. We rarely do for points entered in an interactive graphics system, but we may if the points are produced by another program. For example, in computer aided design (CAD) we may want to produce a particular profile, and certain points on it have precise specifications. Figure 17.1 (top) shows an example of interpolation.

(2) Instead of insisting that the curve pass through the points, we may look for a curve that only passes near all of them. This approach is called

Figure 17.1 Comparison of interpolation, approximation, and smoothing for a given set of points. The "curve" used is a polyline (open polygon), and smoothness in this case means as few corners as possible.

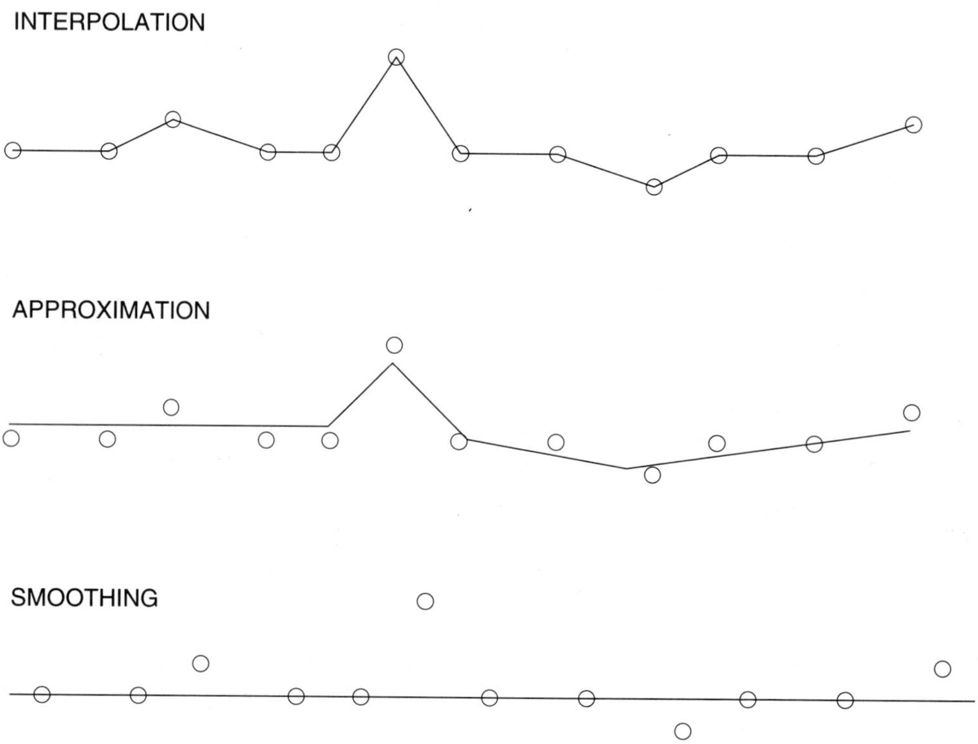

approximation and is illustrated in Figure 17.1 (middle). If the specified points are considered to be particularly unreliable, we may want to ignore some of them if they distort the shape of the curve significantly. This method is a special form of approximation called *smoothing* and is illustrated in Figure 17.1 (bottom).

(3) A third method for producing a curve from user-defined points is to interpret them as *control points* that "guide" the curve. The curve may be quite far from some of the points, but its shape is determined by them. At first sight this seems to be an unnatural method, but actually is the most user-friendly for computer graphics. The method was invented by French mathematician Pierre Bézier and it was first used for computer aided design (CAD) by the French car manufacturer Peugeot in the late 1940s.

Because of the many advantages of the third method, we limit our discussion to such curves. This way of specifying a curve requires some user training, but new families of curves developed over the last 40 years have reduced considerably the amount of training needed. Most people become quickly adept at manipulating the location of the control points to achieve the desired shape of the curve.

We start with a program illustrating the use of control points to draw and edit a curve and later provide the necessary mathematical descriptions.

17.2 DRAWING WITH SPLINES

17.2.1 Splines and Bézier Splines

Splines are curves that consist of pieces of smooth curves that are joined at points (called *knots*) with less smoothness than inside the individual pieces. A polyline is a trivial example of a spline. Straight line segments are smooth between their endpoints but not at the corners where they are joined.

We can construct a more interesting spline by joining segments of circular arcs. Figure 17.2 shows an example. The two arcs join at a point where they have a common tangent so the transition from one arc to another appears smooth but not entirely so.

Figure 17.2 Two circular arcs joining at a point with a common tangent.

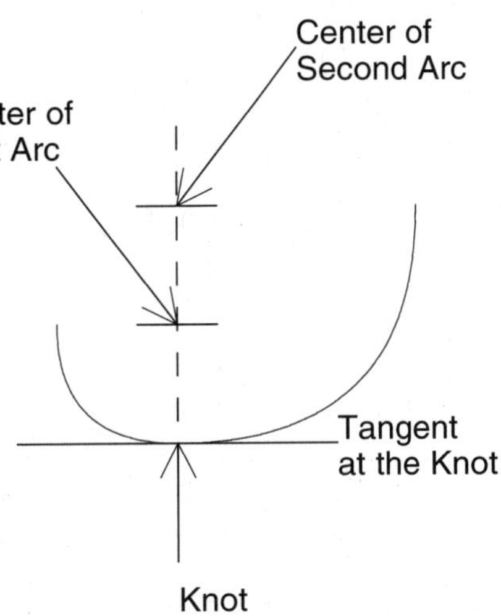

The driver of a car on a road with a center line of the shape shown in Figure 17.2 will sense a change in the centrifugal force when going from the large arc to the small arc. There is an abrupt change in curvature at the knot.

Definition A Bézier spline is a curve whose shape is determined by the position of certain control points.

In the rest of the chapter we describe how to write a program to plot such a curve; we show here how such a program can be used.

Figure 17.3 Three stages in drawing an oval outline. Left: A polygon is drawn. Middle: The drawn polygon is converted into a spline. Right: The shape of the spline is changed by moving one of the vertices of the polygon. In each stage the button selected from the control panel is shown in reverse video.

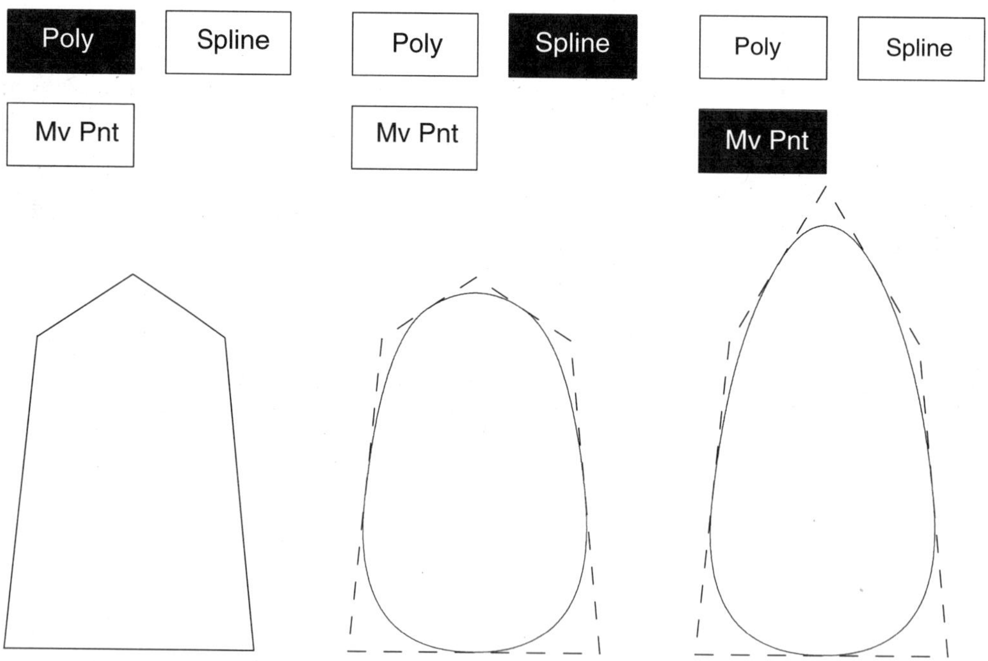

`void put_spline(fPoint P[], int n, double scale)`
Plot a smooth curve whose shape is controlled by n points with co-

ordinates stored in the array `P[]`. The argument `scale` is the distance between points that are plotted. The smaller it is, the more time is needed to create the plot. For a high-quality appearance it should be 1; for coarser plots 2 or 3 may be acceptable values. (*Not a part of Starter Toolkit.*) ☜

A spline plotting function has been deliberately left out of the Starter Toolkit because the X Window System does not provide for splines or any curves other than circular arcs. Readers may add the code (given in Listing 17.5) to their own library. Figure 17.3 shows three stages in a drawing session. The button corresponding to the selected action is shown in reverse video in each case.

First the user draws a polygon (left) using a program such as that of Listing 14.1. Then the user selects "Spline" from the control panel and touches the polygon. The program draws the spline controlled by the polygon and redraws the control polygon with dashed lines. Then the user selects "Mv Pnt" (move point) and moves one of the vertices of the polygon, adjusting the shape of the spline.

17.2.2 Functions for Drawing and Editing Splines

One possible implementation for the event handler used to convert a polygon into a spline is shown in Listing 17.1. It is designed to fit in the object editor of Chapter 14 (see Listings 14.5 and 14.6).

Listing 17.1: Callback for Making a Polygon a Spline

```
<include geom_obj.h>     /* See Listing 13.10 */

static GGO *current;
extern plot_spline();

poly_to_spline(pEven *p)
{
     if(p->kind+p->key==LEFT_PRESS){
          current = global_find(p->x, p->y);
          if(current){
               current->plot(current);/* erase */
               current->type = SPLINE;
               current->plot = plot_spline;
               current->plot(current);/* redraw */
          }
     }
}
```

The function plot_spline() takes as its argument a pointer to an object. It calls put_spline(), passing to it as arguments the array of control points pnts and their number npnts. The value for scale should be stored in a static variable by the application program because it has to do only with the quality of the plot rather than the object structure. The function plot_spline() might also draw the control polygon using the put_poly() functions described in Section 10.6 after setting the line style to dash. SPLINE is a predefined constant used to identify the object as a spline (see Section 13.4).

The "move point" event handler requires the use of a rubber band routine. One (not particularly efficient) implementation of it is shown in Listing 17.2.

Listing 17.2: Editing of Points

```
<include geom_obj.h>     /* See Listing 13.10 */

static GGO *current, fPoint *cp;
extern local_rubber_band();

move_point(pEvent *p)
{
      if(p->kind+p->key==LEFT_PRESS){
            current = global_find(p->x, p->y);
            if(current){
                  /* Find the point of current near p->x,p->y
                  and replace its coordinates by p->x,p->y.
                  Save a pointer to it in cp  */
                  set_handler(local_rubber_band);
            }
      }
}

local_rubber_band(pEvent *p)
{
      switch(p->kind+p->key) {
      case MOVE:
            current->plot(current);/* erase */
            cp->x = p->x; cp->y = p->y;
            current->plot(current);/* redraw */
            break;
      case LEFT_PRESS:    /* fix position */
            set_handler(move_point);
            break;
      }
}
```

The selected point follows the mouse until the left button is pressed. That event finalizes the change in shape. Note that the code of Listing 17.2 is applicable to any object, not just to splines. This advantage is a result of having the `plot()` function be a member of the object structure `GGO`.

17.3 CONTROLLED CURVES

17.3.1 Parabolic Arcs

We start the discussion of the mathematics underlying splines with a simple special case. Because two points define a straight line, we need at least three points for the simplest possible curve. Figure 17.4 shows a triplet of points and a curve guided by them.

Figure 17.4
Curve defined by three points.

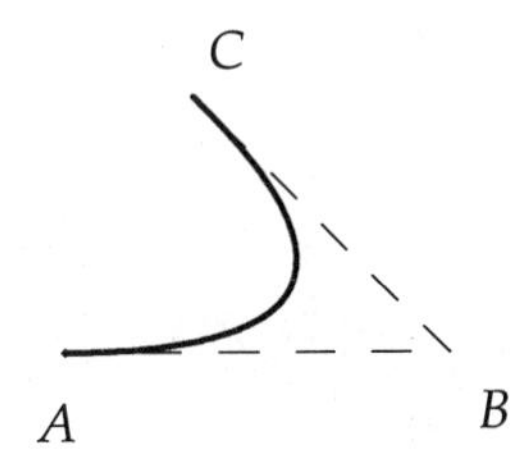

We now provide the mathematical expressions that generate a curve from points A, B, and C. Let x_a and y_a denote the coordinates of point A, with similar notations for the other two points. If t is a parameter that varies from 0 to 1, then the following pair of equations specify a curve:

$$x(t) = (1 - t)^2 x_a + 2t(1 - t)x_b + t^2 x_c \tag{17.1a}$$

$$y(t) = (1 - t)^2 y_a + 2t(1 - t)y_b + t^2 y_c \tag{17.1b}$$

The curve defined by Equations 17.1 is a *parabola* and the segment shown in Figure 17.4 is a *parabolic arc*. We can confirm that

$$x(0) = x_a \qquad y(0) = y_a$$

and

$$x(1) = x_c \qquad y(1) = y_c$$

In other words, for t equal to 0 the curve passes through A, and for t equal to 1 it passes through C. The curve stays away from B but is tangent to lines AB and BC. We prove that property in the next section. Here, we compute the coordinates of the point in the middle of the curve, which happens to be the one closest to B. We can confirm that

$$x(\tfrac{1}{2}) = \tfrac{1}{4}x_a + \tfrac{1}{2}x_b + \tfrac{1}{4}x_c$$
$$y(\tfrac{1}{2}) = \tfrac{1}{4}y_a + \tfrac{1}{2}y_b + \tfrac{1}{4}y_c$$

These expressions suggest a simple geometric construction for finding that point, as shown in Figure 17.5. Point M is the midpoint of line AB and N is the midpoint of line MB.

Figure 17.5
Construction of point N, which is nearest to B. Point M is the midpoint of line AB and N is the midpoint of line MB.

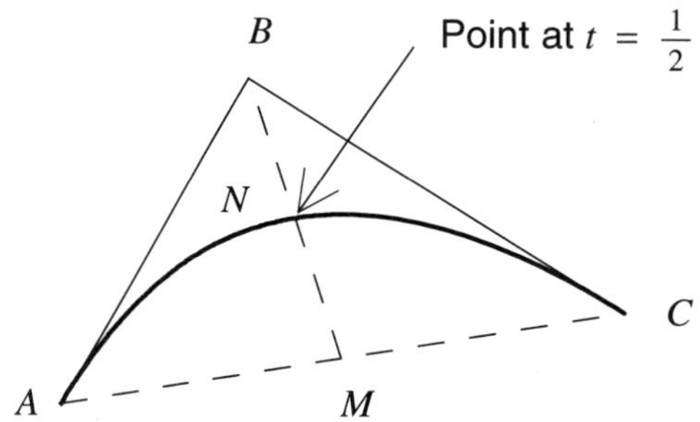

An interesting property of parabolic arcs is derived by observing that

$$(1 - t)^2 + 2t(1 - t) + t^2 = 1 \tag{17.2}$$

According to a theorem of analytic geometry, this equation means that the point with coordinates $x(t)$, $y(t)$ for t between 0 and 1 lies inside the triangle whose vertices are A, B, and C.

Although the mathematics may appear complicated, the program to generate a parabolic arc is rather simple. It is shown in Listing 17.3. The program uses the type `fPoint` defined in Listing 13.1 for its input and internal calculations, and the type `pPoint` (defined in Section 10.6) for its output.

Listing 17.3: Plotting a Parabolic Arc

```
/*   Not an efficient Program     */
#include <Starter.h>     /* for definition of pPoint */
#include <gtypes.h>      /* for definition of fPoint */

prep_arc(fPoint *ap, fPoint *bp, fPoint *cp, double dt, pPoint *v)
{
     double t, s;
     double tx, ty;
     register j = 0;

     for(t=0; t<=1; t+=dt, v++) {
          s = 1 - t;
          tx = s*s*ap->x + 2*s*t*bp->x + t*t*cp->x;
          ty = s*s*ap->y + 2*s*t*bp->y + t*t*cp->y;
          v->x = tx + 0.5;
          v->y = ty + 0.5;
     }
     return(j);
}
```

The array `v[]` can be used to plot the points by the Starter Toolkit function `put_poly()` (described in Section 10.6) by the code

```
fPoint A, B, C;
pPoint v[ ... ], n;
/* ... */
n = prep_arc(&A, &B, &C, v);
put_poly(v, n)
```

If the points computed by `prep_arc()` are near each other, the polygon appears as a smooth curve. Using a polygon to plot a curve may appear to contradict our stated purpose for studying curves — and in a way it is. As X servers do not know of any other curves besides circular arcs and ellipses, we have no choice but to draw a spline arc as a polygon. However, the amount of points is reduced for the *application*, which usually is not concerned with the details of the plotting routine.

This program of Listing 17.3 is inefficient because there are too many multiplications in the inner loop. A more efficient program is given in Section 17.4.3.

17.3.2 More Properties of Parabolic Arcs

Note: You may skip this section if you are not interested in the mathematical proof of the properties of parabolic arcs.

We prove here that the arc defined by Equation (17.1) is indeed tangent to lines AB and BC. We do so by computing the slope of a line segment joining two points of the curve. Let t_1 and t_2 be the values of the parameter t. Then, after some simple algebra, we obtain for the xs

$$x(t_1) - x(t_2) =$$

$$(t_1 - t_2)\left[-(2 - t_1 - t_2)x_a + 2(1 - t_1 - t_2)x_b + (t_1 + t_2)x_c\right] \tag{17.3a}$$

and similarly for the ys

$$y(t_1) - y(t_2) =$$

$$(t_1 - t_2)\left[-(2 - t_1 - t_2)y_a + 2(1 - t_1 - t_2)y_b + (t_1 + t_2)y_c\right] \tag{17.3b}$$

The slope of the line is expressed as

$$\frac{y(t_1) - y(t_2)}{x(t_1) - x(t_2)} =$$

$$\frac{-(2 - t_1 - t_2)y_a + 2(1 - t_1 - t_2)y_b + (t_1 + t_2)y_c}{-(2 - t_1 - t_2)x_a + 2(1 - t_1 - t_2)x_b + (t_1 + t_2)x_c} \tag{17.4}$$

When the line segment is near the start of the curve, both t_1 and t_2 are very small (nearly 0) and can be ignored so that (after dividing both terms of the fraction by -2) Equation (17.4) becomes

$$\frac{y(t_1) - y(t_2)}{x(t_1) - x(t_2)} \approx \frac{y_b - y_a}{x_b - x_a} \tag{17.5}$$

Thus near A the curve lies along line AB. At the other end we can replace both t_1 and t_2 with 1 (and also divide both terms of the fraction by -2) so that

$$\frac{y(t_1) - y(t_2)}{x(t_1) - x(t_2)} \approx \frac{y_c - y_b}{x_c - x_b} \tag{17.6}$$

In other words, near C the curve lies along line BC.

A rigorous proof that the curve is tangent to lines AB and BC can be given by using calculus to justify replacing t_1 and t_2 by 0 in one case and by 1 in the other.

17.3.3 Reintroducing Splines

A single arc is not very useful for describing complex shapes. We need to put many of these arcs together while making sure that the curve stays smooth. Let's take two triplets of points $\{A, B, C\}$ and $\{D, E, F\}$. The two arcs will touch if C coincides with D. However, the junction may not be smooth, as shown on the left in Figure 17.6. To make it smooth we need lines *BC* and *DE* to be extensions of each other with the result as shown on the right in Figure 17.6.

Figure 17.6 Because line segments *BC* and *DE* are not collinear, the two arcs on the left do not join smoothly. A smooth joint is achieved on the right because line segments *BC* and *DE* are collinear.

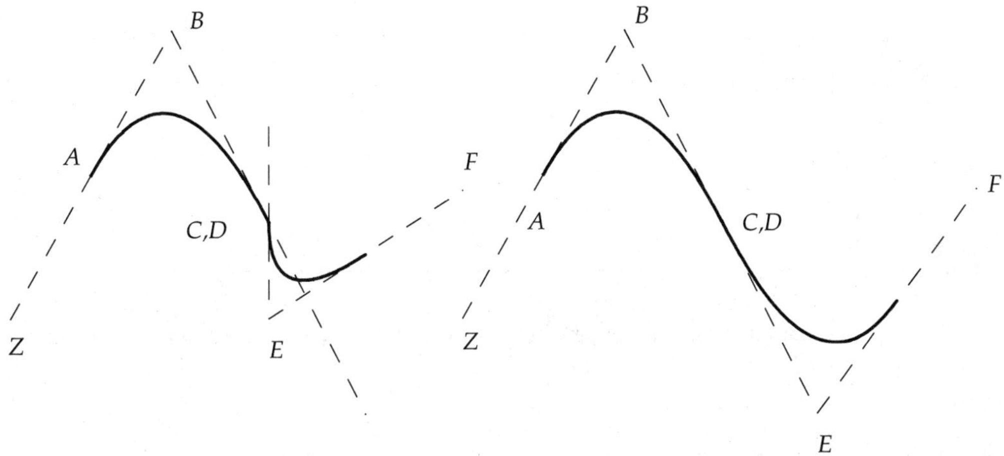

Clearly, points *C* and *D* are not independent of the others. What we need in order to define the pair of arcs are points *A*, *B*, *E*, and *F* and a number expressing a distance along segment *BE*. The number can be used to define the junction of the two arcs.

Anyone wanting to produce a smooth curve must first draw a polygon and then select points on the sides of the polygon. Each pair of such points with the vertex between them becomes a triplet that defines a parabolic arc. The arcs have the same tangent in their junctions so that the resulting curve appears smooth. An example of such a curve is shown in Figure 17.7. It is a special case of a Bézier spline: a *parabolic Bézier spline*. It consists of parabolic arcs that have common endpoints and the same tangent at these endpoints.

Adding the extra point on the sides requires additional work in an interactive system. For some applications it may be acceptable to give up

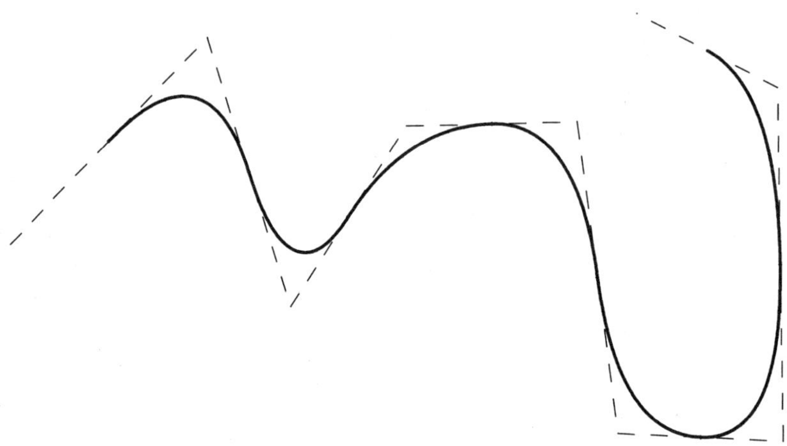

Figure 17.7 A smooth curve consisting of parabolic arcs defined by the polygon shown in dashed lines.

this extra degree of control for the sake of simplicity. Rather than select explicitly a point on the line segment *BE*, we opt always to use the midpoint of *BE*. Then, we should replace x_c and y_c in Equation (17.1) with

$$\frac{x_b + x_e}{2} \quad \text{and} \quad \frac{y_b + y_e}{2}$$

The same substitution should be made for the other endpoint. If we let *Z* be the point before *A*, instead of x_a and y_a we should use

$$\frac{x_z + x_b}{2} \quad \text{and} \quad \frac{y_z + y_b}{2}$$

Substituting these expressions into Equation (17.1a) yields

$$x(t) = \frac{1}{2}(1 - t)^2 x_z + \frac{1}{2}(1 - t)^2 x_b + 2t(1 - t)x_b + \frac{1}{2}t^2 x_b + \frac{1}{2}t^2 x_e \quad (17.7)$$

We group the terms that contain x_b and factor out the terms with t to obtain

$$\left[\frac{1}{2}(1 - t)^2 + 2t(1 - t) + \frac{1}{2}t^2\right]x_b$$

Carrying out some algebra simplifies this expression to

$$\frac{1}{2}\left[1 + 2t(1 - t)\right]x_b$$

We now rewrite Equation (17.1) as

$$x(t) = \frac{1}{2}(1-t)^2 x_z + \frac{1}{2}\left[1 + 2t(1-t)\right] x_b + \frac{1}{2}t^2 x_e \tag{17.8a}$$

$$y(t) = \frac{1}{2}(1-t)^2 y_z + \frac{1}{2}\left[1 + 2t(1-t)\right] y_b + \frac{1}{2}t^2 y_e \tag{17.8b}$$

The splines where the endpoints are the midpoints of the tangents are called *uniform parabolic Bézier splines*. However, there is a bit more work to do. In contrast to Equation (17.1), the variables in Equation (17.8) have no obvious meaning. Next, we introduce a more systematic and concise notation for the splines and an efficient program for plotting them.

17.4 PARABOLIC SPLINES

17.4.1 The Basics

Many of the Equations of Section 17.3 involve duplication because the forms for x and y are nearly identical. As a first step we introduce a more concise notation. We use a bold letter to denote a pair of coordinates, for example $\boldsymbol{A}$ stands for the pair x_a and y_a. If $\boldsymbol{P}(t)$ stands for the pair $x(t)$ and $y(t)$, we can rewrite Equation (17.8) as

$$\boldsymbol{P}(t) = \frac{1}{2}(1-t)^2 \boldsymbol{Z} + \frac{1}{2}\left[1 + 2t(1-t)\right] \boldsymbol{B} + \frac{1}{2}t^2 \boldsymbol{E} \tag{17.9}$$

The specific letters $\boldsymbol{Z}$, $\boldsymbol{B}$, and $\boldsymbol{E}$ correspond to the notation used in Figure 17.6.

Next we introduce an array $\boldsymbol{P}[\,]$ which holds the vertices of the polyline of the tangents. Then, the arc near the vertex $\boldsymbol{P}[i]$ is given by

$$\boldsymbol{P}_i(t) = \frac{1}{2}(1-t)^2 \boldsymbol{P}[i-1] + \frac{1}{2}\left[1 + 2t(1-t)\right] \boldsymbol{P}[i] + \frac{1}{2}t^2 \boldsymbol{P}[i+1] \tag{17.10}$$

Listing 17.4 shows a program for plotting a parabolic spline using the procedure of Listing 17.3.

Listing 17.4: Plotting a Spline

```
#include <gtypes.h>

void p_spline( fPoint *P, int n, double dt)
{
     register j;
     int k;
     pPoint v[1024];     /* Safe estimate */
```

```
    for(j=1; j< n-1; j++) {
        k = prep_arc(P+j-1, P+j, P+j+1, dt, v);
        put_poly(v, k);
    }
}
```

Both the program of Listing 17.4 and Equation (17.9) demonstrate a very useful property of the splines. If we change the position of a vertex of the polygon, we need to recompute only three arcs of the spline. This property gives the user local control of the shape of the curve. We use the term *control points* for the vertices of the polygon and the polygon itself is called the *control* or *guiding polygon*.

17.4.2 Efficient Computation of the Points of a Spline

The program of Listing 17.3 suggests that we need 14 multiplications for each spline point and there are approximately `1/dt` such points for each arc. We can reduce the amount of computation in two ways. First, we can rearrange the computation for each point to reduce the number of multiplications. Second, we can make `dt` vary with `t`. From a practical standpoint we want to obtain spline points that are close to each other within a particular distance. However, the points produced by the program of Listing 17.3 are not uniformly spaced. This lack of uniformity can be wasteful because, at the dense parts of the curve, we compute many more points than we need.

Another way of looking at the second problem is to realize that uniformly spaced points according to the parameter t do not correspond to uniformly spaced points in the plane.

We start with the first problem, cutting down the number of multiplications. Expanding the terms with t and then grouping all terms according to the powers of t transforms Equation (17.10) into

$$\boldsymbol{P}_i(t) = \frac{1}{2}\big[(\boldsymbol{P}[i-1] - 2\boldsymbol{P}[i] + \boldsymbol{P}[i+1])t^2 + 2(\boldsymbol{P}[i] - \boldsymbol{P}[i-1])t + (\boldsymbol{P}[i] + \boldsymbol{P}[i-1])\big] \tag{17.11}$$

We can reduce the operations even more by rewriting Equation (17.11) as

$$\boldsymbol{P}_i(t) = \frac{1}{2}\big[\big[(\boldsymbol{P}[i-1] - 2\boldsymbol{P}[i] + \boldsymbol{P}[i+1])t + 2(\boldsymbol{P}[i] - \boldsymbol{P}[i-1])\big]t + (\boldsymbol{P}[i] + \boldsymbol{P}[i-1])\big] \tag{17.12}$$

Now, we have only two multiplications per coordinate, or four per spline point. The computations can be clarified by introducing the following notation:

$$P_x^1 = \frac{1}{2}\Big[\boldsymbol{P}[i-1].x - 2\boldsymbol{P}[i].x + \boldsymbol{P}[i+1].x\Big] \quad (17.13a)$$

$$P_x^2 = \boldsymbol{P}[i].x - \boldsymbol{P}[i-1].x \quad (17.13b)$$

$$P_x^3 = \frac{1}{2}\Big[\boldsymbol{P}[i].x + \boldsymbol{P}[i-1].x\Big] \quad (17.13c)$$

$$P_y^1 = \frac{1}{2}\Big[\boldsymbol{P}[i-1].y - 2\boldsymbol{P}[i].y + \boldsymbol{P}[i+1].y\Big] \quad (17.13d)$$

$$P_y^2 = \boldsymbol{P}[i].y - \boldsymbol{P}[i-1].y \quad (17.13e)$$

$$P_y^3 = \frac{1}{2}\Big[\boldsymbol{P}[i].y + \boldsymbol{P}[i-1].y\Big] \quad (17.13f)$$

Then, Equation (17.12) reduces to

$$x_i(t) = (P_x^1 t + P_x^2)t + P_x^3 \quad (17.12x)$$

$$y_i(t) = (P_y^1 t + P_y^2)t + P_y^3 \quad (17.12y)$$

The second part (making dt vary with t) requires more work. We compute the coordinates of the spline at point $t+dt$ by using Equation (17.11) while ignoring terms with dt^2. As dt will be small, dt^2 will be even smaller. (A rigorous proof can be given using calculus.) We find

$$\boldsymbol{P}_i(t+dt) = \frac{1}{2}\big[(\boldsymbol{P}[i-1] - 2\boldsymbol{P}[i] + \boldsymbol{P}[i+1])(t^2 + 2t\,dt)$$
$$+ 2(\boldsymbol{P}[i] - \boldsymbol{P}[i-1])(t+dt) + \boldsymbol{P}[i] + \boldsymbol{P}[i-1]\big] \quad (17.14)$$

Subtracting Equation (17.11) from Equation (17.14) yields

$$\boldsymbol{P}_i(t+dt) - \boldsymbol{P}_i(t) =$$
$$dt\Big[(\boldsymbol{P}[i-1] - 2\boldsymbol{P}[i] + \boldsymbol{P}[i+1])t + \boldsymbol{P}[i] - \boldsymbol{P}[i-1]\Big] \quad (17.15)$$

The term in brackets represents a velocity by which the point moves along the spline arc as a function of t. We can convert this vector equation into two scalar equations by using Equations (17.13), as we did with Equation (17.12).

$$x_i(t+dt) - x_i(t) = dt2[2P_x^1 t + P_x^2] \quad (17.15x)$$

$$y_i(t+dt) - y_i(t) = dt2[2P_y^1 t + P_y^2] \quad (17.15y)$$

Because we want to keep the distance

$$[x_i(t+dt) - x_i(t)]^2 + [y_i(t+dt) - y_i(t)]^2$$

constant, dt should be inversely proportional to the velocity. Then, for some constant c, dt can be computed from

$$dt = \frac{c}{\sqrt{[(P_x^1)t + P_x^2]^2 + [(P_y^1)t + P_y^2]^2}} \tag{17.16}$$

Equation (17.16) has the disadvantage of taking a square root at each step. If we are interested in computational efficiency only, we may use the rather coarse approximation

$$dt = \frac{c}{|(P_x^1)t + P_x^2| + |(P_y^1)t + P_y^2|} \tag{17.17}$$

17.4.3 A Program for Computing Parabolic Splines

The derivations of the previous section let us write an efficient spline plotting program. The basic routine is given in Listing 17.5. The variable `scale` determines the density of points. The function `p_arc()` is a more efficient version of `prep_arc()` discussed in Section 17.3.1. (Note that the notation no longer corresponds to that used in Figures 17.5 and 17.6. Argument `*bp` still points to ***B***, but `*ap` and `*cp` point to ***Z*** and ***E***, respectively.)

Listing 17.5: Parabolic Arc Plotting (Revised) — File `p_spline.c`

```
/*   Plotting a spline arc defined by control points *ap, *bp, *cp    */
#include <Starter.h>
#include <gtypes.h>
#include <math.h>

int p_arc(fPoint *ap, fPoint *bp, fPoint *cp, double scale, pPoint *v)
{
     double P1x, P2x, P3x, P1y, P2y, P3y;
     double t, dt, ux, uy, gx, gy;
     fPoint *sp;
     int n;

     /*   Computation of Eqs. (17.13a-f)   */
     P1x = (ap->x + cp->x)/2 - bp->x;
     P2x = bp->x - ap->x;
     P3x = (ap->x + bp->x)/2;
     P1y = (ap->y + cp->y)/2 - bp->y;
     P2y = bp->y - ap->y;
     P3y = (ap->y + bp->y)/2;
```

```
    for(t=0, n=0; t<=1; n++, v++) {
        ux = P1x*t + P2x;
        uy = P1y*t + P2y;
        v->x = ux*t + P3x;
        v->y = uy*t + P3y;
        gx = ux + P1x*t;
        gy = uy + P1y*t;
        if(!gx && !gy) dt = 1;
        else {
#ifdef HIGH_QUAL
            dt = scale/sqrt(gx*gx + gy*gy);
#else
            dt = scale/(fabs(gx) + fabs(gy));
#endif
        }
        t += dt;
    }
    return(n);
}

void put_spline( fPoint *P, int n, double scale)
{
    register j;
    int k;
    pPoint  v[1024];    /* Safe estimate */

    for(j=1; j< n-1; j++) {
        k = p_arc(P+j-1, P+j, P+j+1, scale, v);
        put_poly(v, k);
    }
}
```

These programs are straightforward implementations of the analysis in Section 17.4.2. The only point we need discuss is the treatment of the case when *both* `gx` and `gy` are 0. In that case we skip to the last point. Later the polygon plotting function will draw a line from the point where `gx` and `gy` were 0 to the last point. We show in Section 17.4.5 that this is indeed the correct action.

17.4.4 A Geometric Method for Computing Parabolic Splines

Another method for plotting splines is based on reducing the computation of spline points to the computation of points of lines. We start with Equation (17.10), multiply both sides by 2, and subtract $\boldsymbol{P}[i]$ from each side:

$$2\boldsymbol{P}_i(t) - \boldsymbol{P}[i] = (1-t)^2\boldsymbol{P}[i-1] + 2t(1-t)\boldsymbol{P}[i] + t^2\boldsymbol{P}[i+1] \qquad (17.18)$$

After a bit of algebra the right-hand side of Equation (17.18) becomes

$$\boldsymbol{M} = (1-t)\Big[(1-t)\boldsymbol{P}[i-1] + t\boldsymbol{P}[i]\Big] + t\Big[(1-t)\boldsymbol{P}[i] + t\boldsymbol{P}[i+1]\Big] \qquad (17.19)$$

Each of the terms in brackets represents a point on a straight line. Thus point $\boldsymbol{M}$ is constructed by taking points on the line segments $\boldsymbol{P}[i-1]\boldsymbol{P}[i]$ and $\boldsymbol{P}[i]\boldsymbol{P}[i+1]$ at fractional distance t from the first point, joining these points with a line, and repeating the construction. (The fractional distance of point P on line segment AB is the ratio PA/AB.) Finally, the spline point is found as the midpoint of the line joining $\boldsymbol{M}$ and $\boldsymbol{P}[i]$, or

$$\boldsymbol{P}_i(t) = \frac{1}{2}\Big[\boldsymbol{P}[i] + \boldsymbol{M}\Big] \qquad (17.20)$$

This construction is illustrated in Figure 17.8.

Figure 17.8 Geometric construction of a parabolic spline.

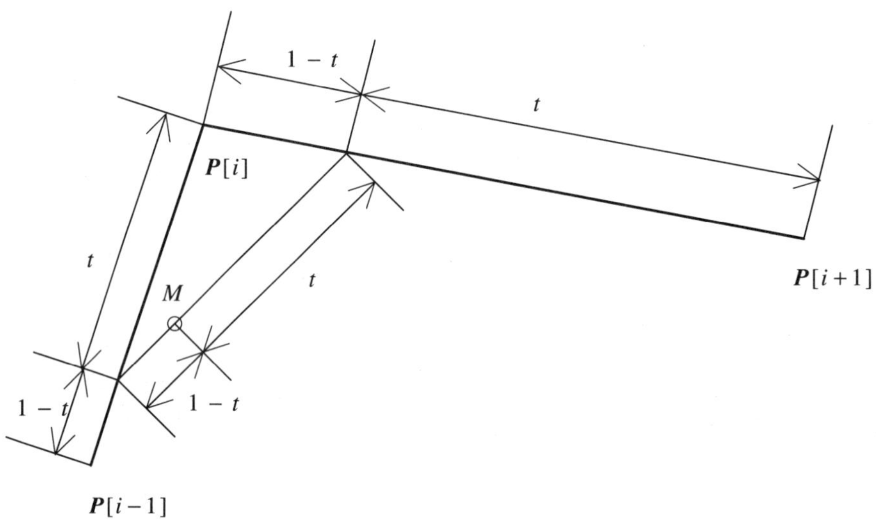

The velocity terms can also be expressed with a similar relationship. Indeed, the term in brackets on the right-hand side of Equation (17.15) can be written as

$$(\boldsymbol{P}[i-1] - \boldsymbol{P}[i])t + (1-t)(\boldsymbol{P}[i]-\boldsymbol{P}[i+1]) \qquad (17.21)$$

so that it can be computed also as a point on a line segment.

A procedure based on this observation is shown in Listing 17.6.

Listing 17.6: Geometric Spline Plotting

```
#include <gtypes.h>
#include <math.h>

int linepoint( fPoint *ap, fPoint *bp, double t, fPoint *rp)
{
    rp->x = (1^-^t)*ap->x + t*bp->x;
    rp->y = (1^-^t)*ap->y + t*bp->y;
}

int rec_p_arc(fPoint *ap, fPoint *bp, fPoint *cp, double scale, int x[], int y[])
{
    fPoint m1, m2, m3;
    int n;

    for(t=0, n=0; t<1; n++) {
        /* Compute Position */
        linepoint(ap, bp, t, &m1);
        linepoint(bp, cp, t, &m2);
        linepoint(&m1, &m2, t, &m3);
        x[n] = ( m3.x + bp->x )/2;
        y[n] = ( m3.y + bp->y )/2;

        /* Compute Velocity */
        m1.x = ap.x - bp.x;
        m1.y = ap.y - bp.y;
        m2.x = bp.x - cp.x;
        m2.y = bp.y - cp.y;
        linepoint(&m1, &m2, t, &m3);
#ifdef HIGH_QUAL
        dt = scale/sqrt(m3.x*m3.x + m3.y*m3.y);
#else
        dt = scale /( fabs(m3.x) + fabs(m3.y) );
#endif
        t += dt;
    }
    return(n);
}
```

Each call to `linepoint()` involves two multiplications, so even if we exclude the overhead of a procedure call (by making `linepoint()` a macro, for example), six multiplications are required for each spline point compared to four for the procedure of Listing 17.5. Two more multiplications are needed for the velocity, in contrast to the program of Listing 17.5

that does that computation as part of computing the point position. Thus the program of Listing 17.6 requires twice the amount of computation as the program of Listing 17.5. However, it seems to be easier to understand.

17.4.5 Corners in Splines

Many times we want to produce an outline that is smooth overall but also has some corners. This condition certainly is the case with the swan outline shown in Figure 17.9. Sharp corners are needed at three points. We could have divided the contour into three parts, but that would have required special caution because splines, in general, do not pass through the endpoints.

Figure 17.9 Control polygon (left) and resulting spline (right).

A better way is to make two vertices of the control polygon coincide. Suppose that $\boldsymbol{P}[i]$ equals $\boldsymbol{P}[i-1]$. Then Equation (17.11) becomes

$$\boldsymbol{P}_i(t) = \frac{1}{2}\left[(\boldsymbol{P}[i+1] - \boldsymbol{P}[i])t^2 + 2\boldsymbol{P}[i]\right] \tag{17.22}$$

or

$$\boldsymbol{P}_i(t) - \boldsymbol{P}[i] = \frac{1}{2}(\boldsymbol{P}[i+1] - \boldsymbol{P}[i])t^2 \tag{17.23}$$

Recall that this notation is shorthand for the coordinates of the points. If we write the pair of the coordinate equations and divide them by sides, we obtain

$$\frac{y_i(t) - y_i}{x_i(t) - x_i} = \frac{y_{i+1} - y_i}{x_{i+1} - x_i} \qquad (17.24)$$

In other words, the spline has been reduced to a straight line. Furthermore,

$$\boldsymbol{P}_i(0) = \boldsymbol{P}[i] \quad \text{and} \quad \boldsymbol{P}_i(1) = \frac{1}{2}(\boldsymbol{P}[i+1] + \boldsymbol{P}[i]) \qquad (17.25)$$

When a vertex of the control polygon is counted twice, the spline passes through the vertex and continues along the side of the polygon toward the next vertex until it reaches the midpoint.

The advantage of making a vertex double is that we do not have to modify the plotting routine at all. But we may want to detect such double vertices for the sake of computational efficiency. We can do so by adding some code to Listing 17.5 after the computation of `P1x`, ⋯ , `P3y`. If both `P2x` and `P2y` are 0, we know that the first two points coincide and in that case execute the code

```
v->x = ap->x;       v->y = ap->y;       v++;
v->x = (ap->x+cp->x)/2;v->y = (ap->y+cp->y)/2;v++;
return(2);
```

While we are discussing special cases, let's consider the case when the three control points are collinear. This condition is highly unlikely for control points drawn interactively but it may happen after such points are scaled or for control points produced by a program (recall Section 15.4.4). The following statement checks on whether the three control points are collinear.

```
if( P2x*(cp->y - bp->y) == P2y*(cp->x - bp->x) ) {}
```

We can prove that the preceding condition checks collinearity by using triangle similarity and observing that `P2x` and `P2y` equal `bp->x - ap->x` and `bp->y - ap->y`, respectively. In this case the spline arc reduces to a straight line, and the appropriate code is

```
v->x = P3x;         v->y = P3y;         v++;
v->x = (bp->x+cp->x)/2;v->y = (bp->y+cp->y)/2;v++;
return(2);
```

Straightforward algebra can also show that these two cases are the only ones where both `gx` and `gy` can be 0, so that if we add these checks to Listing 17.5 we can remove the code dealing with that situation. These modifications are another example of improving execution speed by making the code slightly more complex.

17.4.6 Estimating the Placement of Spline Arcs

Some applications require checking on whether two curves intersect or finding the intersection of a pair of curves. These tasks are rather difficult, and we would like to treat them as we did polygon clipping (discussed in Section 16.5). If each curve is confined in a region of simple shape, we have to deal with curve intersection only when the confining regions intersect. (If the confining areas of two curves do not intersect, we know that we need not check the curves themselves.) Hence we should make the confining area as tight as possible (without making it too complex).

In Section 17.3.1 we stated that, as a result of Equation (17.3), we know that a spline arc is confined within a triangle whose vertices are part of the control polygon. We can do better than that by showing that the spline is confined within a trapezoid, as depicted in Figure 17.10.

Figure 17.10 Confinement of spline arcs.

To do so we rewrite Equation (17.10) as

$$P_i(t) = \frac{P[i-1]+P[i]}{2}[(t-1)^2 + t(t-1)] + \frac{P_{[i-1]}+3P[i]}{4}2t(1-t)$$

$$+ \frac{3P[i]+P[i+1]}{4}2t(1-t) + \frac{P[i]+P[i+1]}{2}[t^2 + t(t-1)] \qquad (17.26)$$

We can verify that the four points are indeed the vertices of the trapezoid and that the sum

$$(t-1)^2 + t(t-1) + 4t(1-t) + t^2 + t(t-1)$$

equals 1.

17.5 CUBIC SPLINES

Parabolic Bézier splines are only one member of a large family of curves. A discussion of the general theory of splines is beyond the scope of this text, so we limit it to a few of the most common types. In this section we discuss *cubic Bézier splines*, which have arcs defined by four points. The term *cubic* reflects the fact that their defining equations include third powers of t. The counterpart of Equation (17.10) is

$$\begin{aligned} \boldsymbol{P}_i(t) &= \frac{1}{6}\Big[(1-t)^3\boldsymbol{P}[i-2] + (4 + 3t^3 - 6t^2)\boldsymbol{P}[i-1] \\ &\quad + [4 + 3(1-t)^3 - 6(1-t)^2]\boldsymbol{P}[i] + t^3\boldsymbol{P}[i+1]\Big] \end{aligned} \tag{17.27}$$

The coefficient of $\boldsymbol{P}[i]$ in Equation (17.27) can be simplified to

$$1 + 3t + 3t^2 - 3t^3$$

Cubic splines offer a greater degree of smoothness than parabolic splines do. However, they are not as tightly controlled by the polygon as parabolic splines are. First, we can confirm by substitution into Equation (17.27) the values for the endpoints of the arc:

$$\boldsymbol{P}_i(0) = \frac{1}{2}\left[\frac{1}{3}\boldsymbol{P}[i-2] + \frac{4}{3}\boldsymbol{P}[i-1] + \frac{1}{3}\boldsymbol{P}[i]\right]$$

$$\boldsymbol{P}_i(1) = \frac{1}{2}\left[\frac{1}{3}\boldsymbol{P}[i-1] + \frac{4}{3}\boldsymbol{P}[i] + \frac{1}{3}\boldsymbol{P}[i+1]\right]$$

These values suggest the following geometric construction. On the line joining the first ($\boldsymbol{P}[i-2]$) and second ($\boldsymbol{P}[i-1]$) points, pick a point, $\boldsymbol{A}$, at one-third the distance toward the second. On the line joining the second ($\boldsymbol{P}[i-1]$) and third ($\boldsymbol{P}[i]$) points, pick a point, $\boldsymbol{B}$, at one-third the distance toward the second. Then $\boldsymbol{P}_i(0)$ is the midpoint of the line joining points $\boldsymbol{A}$ and $\boldsymbol{B}$. A similar construction is possible for $\boldsymbol{P}_i(1)$. We can also show that the curve is tangent to line $\boldsymbol{AB}$ and to the similar line at the other end. Figure 17.11 shows the arrangement.

The following expression computes the midpoint of the arc.

$$\boldsymbol{P}_i(0.5) = \frac{1}{48}\left[\boldsymbol{P}[i-2] + 23(\boldsymbol{P}[i-1] + \boldsymbol{P}[i]) + \boldsymbol{P}[i+1]\right]$$

As 23/48 is nearly 1/2, for $t = 1/2$ the spline passes very near the midpoint of the line joining $\boldsymbol{P}[i-1]$ and $\boldsymbol{P}[i]$. We note that *a cubic spline does not touch the control polygon.*

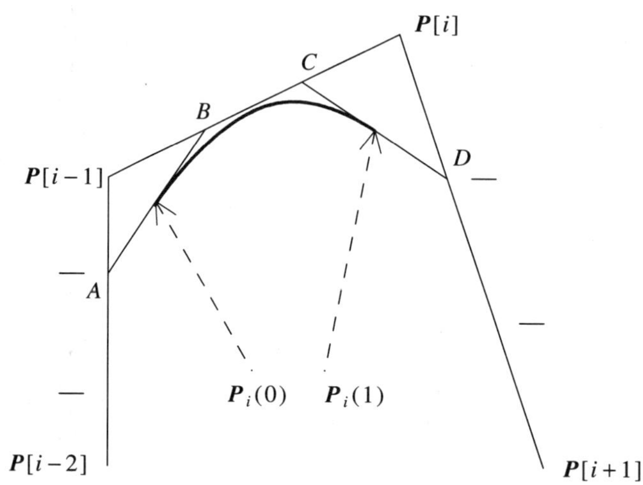

Figure 17.11 Cubic spline arc defined by four points: $\boldsymbol{P}[i-2]$, $\boldsymbol{P}[i-1]$, $\boldsymbol{P}[i]$, and $\boldsymbol{P}[i-2]$. The hash marks divide the first and third side into three parts.

The key to efficient plotting of cubic splines is the proper factorization of Equation (17.27) to reduce the number of multiplications required at each point. If we make C_i the coefficient of t^i, we have:

$$C_3 = \frac{\boldsymbol{P}[i+1] - 3\boldsymbol{P}[i] + \boldsymbol{P}[i-1] - \boldsymbol{P}[i-2]}{6} \tag{17.28a}$$

$$C_2 = \frac{\boldsymbol{P}[i] - 2\boldsymbol{P}[i-1] + \boldsymbol{P}[i-2]}{2} \tag{17.28b}$$

$$C_1 = \frac{\boldsymbol{P}[i] - \boldsymbol{P}[i-2]}{2} \tag{17.28c}$$

$$C_0 = \frac{\boldsymbol{P}[i] + 4\boldsymbol{P}[i-1] + \boldsymbol{P}[i-2]}{6} \tag{17.28d}$$

Then we can find the points of the cubic spline by evaluating the expression

$$C_0 + t[C_1 + t(C_2 + C_3 t)]$$

The description of a complete cubic spline plotting function is beyond the scope of this text.

Cubic splines are the most common type used, primarily for historical reasons. Originally splines in the form $y = f(x)$ were used instead of the form $x = x(t)$ and $y = y(t)$. The corresponding form for a parabolic spline is

$$y = ax^2 + bx + c$$

and the form for a cubic spline is

$$y = ax^3 + bx^2 + cx + d$$

If we define the endpoints and the tangents at them, we need four degrees of freedom, requiring use of the cubic form. However, the parametric form $x = x(t)$ and $y = y(t)$ has more degrees of freedom, allowing a parabolic arc to fit two endpoints and their tangents.

Because parabolic splines follow the shape of the control polygon more closely than cubic splines do, they are preferable for *simple* drawing programs. You should be aware that this preference may not be justified for advanced applications.

17.6 CONCLUSIONS

Numerous texts cover the topic of splines at various levels of sophistication and for different applications. The following is one of the earliest practical books containing many FORTRAN programs.

- C. de Boor. *A Practical Guide to Splines*. Heidelberg: Springer-Verlag, 1978.

The following three books emphasize graphics and are recommended for further reading. The third book contains an interesting introductory chapter by P. Bézier.

- I. D. Faux and M. J. Pratt. *Computational Geometry for Design and Manufacture*. Ellis Horwood Limited, 1979. Distributed by John Wiley & Sons, New York.
- B. Barsky. *Computer Graphics and Geometric Modeling using Beta-splines*. Heidelberg: Springer-Verlag, 1988.
- G. Farin. *Curves and Surfaces for Computer Aided Geometric Design*. San Diego: Academic Press, 1988.

Because the X Window System does not provide primitives for plotting curves, we have dwelled at some length on plotting parabolic splines. The issue of curve primitives is a tricky one: There are thousands of mathematical curves and, no matter how many we choose to add to the set of graphics primitives, most of them will be left out. The solution we use now is to represent each curve by a polygon and then plot the polygon. This approach has two disadvantages.

1. It generates a lot of traffic between the application (client) and the display (server).
2. It does not provide any guarantee of quality.

A better solution is to select a primitive curve that can easily and economically approximate any other curve. The author's favorite for this purpose is a *conic* spline. Such curves include as special cases not only the parabolic splines but also circular and elliptic arcs. A conic spline is a *rational* spline: Its points are given as the ratio of two polynomials. Because the nominator and denominator can vary at different rates, rational splines offer greater flexibility in determining the shape of curves than polynomial splines. (Rational splines are used extensively in computer-aided geometric design.)

Plotting conic arcs is relatively simple, so an extension to the X protocol can be created and plotting routines added to servers. The challenge is to map arbitrary curves into conic splines, a process that must be performed on the client side. For a further discussion of the problem of expressing arbitrary curves through conic splines see the following article.

- J. Hu and T. Pavlidis. "Function Plotting using Conic Splines." *IEEE Computer Graphics and Applications*, 1991, vol. 11, pp. 89-94.

17.7 ASSIGNMENTS

1. Modify the event handlers of Section 17.2 by constructing a single `pick_point()` handler and determine the rest of the operation through a `usage()` function.
2. Implement a function for plotting dashed parabolic splines. Two of the input parameters should be the lengths of the dash and the gap.
3. Investigate the question of plotting circles by approximating them with parabolic splines. Select a regular polygon (e.g., a hexagon) for a control polygon and compute the maximum difference between the points of the spline and a circle. Plot the maximum error as a function of the number of control points.
4. Extend Assignment 3 to deal not only with complete circles but also with circular arcs.
5. Incorporate the code suggested in Section 17.4.5 into the program of Listing 17.5 and use it to draw shapes with corners and flat sides.
6. Test the program of Assignment 5 with a simple rubber band program of the type used in Chapter 16 for testing polygon clipping (instead of using a full-fledged object drawing program).
7. You are given a spline that encloses an area A and the coordinates of a point. Devise a method for deciding whether the point is inside A. (This is an extension of the point in polygon problem discussed in Chapter 16.)

18

Advanced Plotting with Xlib*

Scope of the Chapter

Arc Plotting • Polygon plotting • Use of pixmaps for intermediate plotting • Polygon filling • Fill patterns • Regions • Region algebra

18.1 INTRODUCTION

In this chapter we discuss two kinds of *Xlib* functions: those used to implement the Starter Toolkit functions `put_arc()` (see Section 10.6), `put_poly()`, (see Section 10.6), and `poly_fill()` (see Section 12.4), as well as functions that have no Starter Toolkit counterpart. All *Xlib* drawing functions can be used in windows created by the Starter Toolkit functions by invoking a function that returns the needed arguments for *Xlib* functions: display pointer, window, and graphics context.

☛ **`int get_default_args(Display **dpp, Window *wp, GC *gcp)`**
Supply the values of the first three arguments of *Xlib* functions that are needed for drawing in the windows created by the Starter Toolkit. The function returns 1 on success and 0 on failure. ☜

---

* **This chapter may be skipped by those who want to use only the Starter Toolkit.**

Another function allows the use of the Starter Toolkit drawing functions in windows created by other means.

☛ **`void set_default_args(Display *dp, Window w, GC gc)`**
Set the default values of the first three arguments of *Xlib* functions that are used by the Starter Toolkit functions. ☜

The implementation of both functions was described in Section 5.2.1. If you use `set_default_args()`, do so cautiously because the Starter Toolkit performs other initialization operations besides setting the three parameters used in this function. In general, it may be used safely with such simple functions as `put_line()` and `fill_rectangle()`, but not with any function that does window manipulation.

The function `get_default_args()` is the most useful of the two because it allows the use of the full range of drawing functions of the X Window System within the Starter Toolkit environment. In turn, that makes possible keeping the Starter Toolkit small.

18.2 CIRCULAR AND ELLIPTICAL ARCS

18.2.1 Plain Arcs

Xlib has facilities for drawing circular or elliptical arcs, possibly filled. The function `XDrawArc()` accepts somewhat unusual arguments. It draws an arc within a rectangle of width `w` and height `h`, with upper left corner at `x`, `y`, and the extent specified by two angles, `start_angle` and `duration_angle`. The function call has the form

```
XDrawArc(Display *dp, Drawable dr, GC gc, int x, int y,
     unsigned int w, unsigned int h,
     int start_angle, int duration_angle);
```

If `w` equals `h` the drawn arc is circular; otherwise it is elliptical. Figure 18.1 shows the definition of the angles.

Angles are measured in sixty-fourths of a degree so that 90° should be passed as `90*64`, or `5760`. Listing 18.1 shows the implementation of the Starter Toolkit function `put_arc()` in terms of `XDrawArc()`. The coordinates of the top left corner are found by subtracting the radius (or axes) from the coordinates of the center. The dimensions of the bounding rectangle are found by doubling the radius (or axes).

One problem with these functions is that they have arguments that are not natural for many applications. A common practical statement of the

Figure 18.1
Definition of an arc in *Xlib* (see also Figure 10.6).

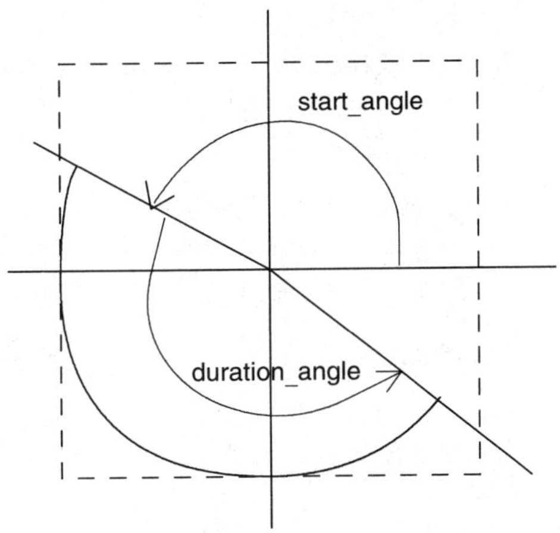

Listing 18.1: Function for Drawing Arcs — `File lib/paper_use.c (part of)`

```
put_arc(int cx, int cy, int rx, int ry, int start_a, int length_a)
{
    int x, y, w, h;

    x = cx - rx;
    y = cy - ry;
    w = 2*rx;
    h = 2*ry;
    start_a *= 64;
    length_a *= 64;

    XDrawArc(Dp, c_window, c_gc, x, y, w, h, start_a, length_a);
}
```

problem is: Plot a circular arc of a given radius r that joins two points, P_1 with coordinates (x_1, y_1) and P_2 with coordinates (x_2, y_2). To use the *Xlib* (or Starter Toolkit) functions we must find the center of the arc and the angles corresponding to the two endpoints.

In general, four different circular arcs satisfy the radius and endpoint conditions. Before doing any plotting we must specify which of the four arcs we want to plot. Therefore the solution to the problem "plot an arc of radius r joining P_1 and P_2" contains three parts:

1. Find the center(s) of the arcs.
2. Select the arc intended by the user.
3. Then plot that arc on a drawable (window or pixmap) by calling `put_arc()` or `XDrawArc()`.

The first part requires some computation, but it has a well-defined solution as long as the radius exceeds half of the distance between the two points. However, there is no clear-cut mathematical solution to the second part.

18.2.2 Filled Arcs

The function `XFillArc` takes exactly the same arguments as `XDrawArc` and the form of the filling is determined by the graphics context. The function

```
XSetArcMode(Display *dp, GC gc, int arc_mode)
```

can be invoked (before `XFillArc`) with either of the two possible values for `arc_mode`: `ArcChord`, which yields the shape on the left in Figure 18.2, or `ArcPieSlice`, which yields the shape on the right in Figure 18.2.

Figure 18.2 Definition of arc filling modes in *Xlib*.

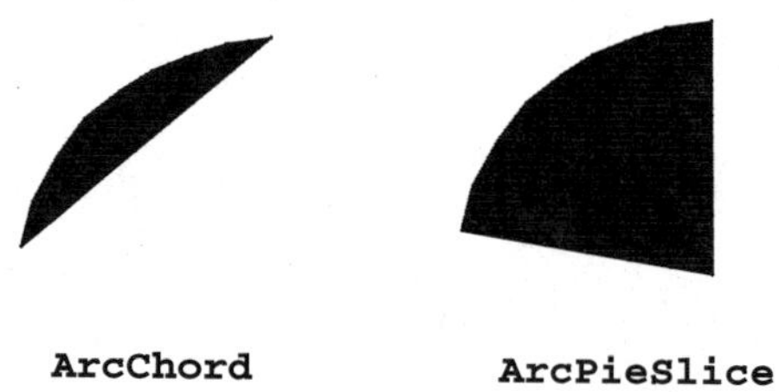

The program in Listing 18.2 generates a "rainbow pizza" in a visualization window of the Starter Toolkit as shown in Plate 4 (color insert). That code offers a concrete example of how to blend calls to *Xlib* functions with those of the Starter Toolkit. The program can be easily modified to allow colors from the standard input instead of being predefined (see Assignment 3 for specific suggestions).

Listing 18.2: Rainbow Pizza — `File pie.c`

```
#include <X11/Xlib.h>
#define ANGLE 3840 /* 60° times 64 */
static char *colors[] = { "red", "orange", "yellow", "green", "blue", "purple", 0};

rainbow_pizza(x, y, w, h)
{
     Display *d;
     Window   window;
     GC       gc;
     int i, a;

     get_default_args(&d, &window, &gc);
     XSetArcMode(d, gc, ArcPieSlice);
     for(i=0, a=0; i<5 && colors[i]; i++, a += ANGLE) {
          fore_color(colors[i]);
          XFillArc(d, window, gc, x, y, w, h, a, ANGLE);
     }
     if(colors[i]) fore_color(colors[i]);
     XFillArc(d, window, gc, x+10, y+5, w, h, a, ANGLE);
}

redraw()
{
     rainbow_pizza(50, 50, 200, 200);
}

main()
{
     vis_window(redraw, 300, 300);
}
```

18.3 POLYGON PLOTTING

18.3.1 The Basics

Xlib has a data type, `XPoint`, defined as in Listing 18.3.

Listing 18.3: X Window System Definition — `File X11/Xlib.h (part of)`

```
typedef struct {
     short x, y;
} XPoint;
```

This definition is equivalent to that of `pPoint` (Section 10.6) so that a Starter Toolkit function with an argument of type `pPoint` can pass it directly to an *Xlib* function with an `XPoint` argument.

The basic *Xlib* function for polygon plotting is `XDrawLines()`, which takes as arguments arrays of `XPoints`. It has the following argument structure.

```
XDrawLines(Display *dp, Drawable dr, GC gc,
        XPoint *v, int n, int mode);
```

Here, `n` is the number of points in the polyline. It must be no greater than 2046 to guarantee that the call will work on all X servers. The `mode` argument indicates how the coordinates will be interpreted. It can have one of two (predefined constant) values: `CoordModeOrigin`, or `CoordModePrevious`. The former specifies that all coordinates are absolute (i.e., with respect to the origin of the drawable). The latter specifies that all coordinates (except the first) are relative, (i.e., with respect to the previous point).

Some points may be drawn more than once, which implies that if we use the exclusive OR mode the plot will appear with gaps. Therefore a better way to do the plot is to use the copy (replacement) mode in a temporary pixmap and then copy the latter to the window with the exclusive OR mode. Listing 18.4 shows an implementation of `put_poly()` (omitting some of the error-checking statements).

Listing 18.4: Function for Drawing Polygons — `File lib/paper_use.c (part of)`

```
/* Dpy, c_window, and c_gc are defined in Section 5.2.1 */

void put_poly(pPoint P[], int n)
{
     Pixmap tmp_pix;
     static GC tmp_gc = 0;
     int xmin, ymin, xmax, ymax;
     int  width, height, depth;
     register i;

     xmin = xmax = P[0].x;  ymin = ymax = P[0].y;
     for(i=0; i<n; i++) {
          if(P[i].x < xmin) xmin = P[i].x;
          else if(P[i].x > xmax) xmax = P[i].x;
          if(P[i].y < ymin) ymin = P[i].y;
          else if(P[i].y > ymax) ymax = P[i].y;
     }
     for(i=0; i<n; i++) {
          P[i].x -= xmin;      P[i].y -= ymin;
     }
```

```
    width  = xmax-xmin+1;
    height = ymax-ymin+1;
    depth  = DefaultDepth(Dpy, DefaultScreen ( Dpy ) );
    if(!tmp_gc) tmp_gc = XCreateGC( Dpy, DefaultRootWindow( Dpy ),
                            NULL, NULL);
    XCopyGC(Dpy, c_gc, 0x1FFFF, gc_tmp);

    tmp_pix = XCreatePixmap(Dpy, c_window, width, height, depth);
    /* Clear Pixmap */
    XSetFunction(Dpy, tmp_gc, GXclear);
    XFillRectangle(Dpy, tmp_pix, tmp_gc, 0, 0, width, height);
    /* Draw on Pixmap */
    XSetFunction(Dpy, tmp_gc, GXcopy);
    XDrawLines(Dpy, tmp_pix, tmp_gc, P, n, CoordModeOrigin);
    XCopyArea(Dpy, tmp_pix, c_window, c_gc, 0, 0, width, height,
         xmin, ymin);
    XFreePixmap(Dpy, tmp_pix);

    /* restore values */
    for(i=0; i<n; i++) {
         P[i].x += xmin;      P[i].y += ymin;
    }
}
```

See Section 5.1.2 for a description of the functions `XCreatePixmap()` and `XCopyArea()`, as well as the reasons for clearing the pixmap.

The function `put_poly()` computes the extent of the plot by finding `xmin`, `xmax`, and so on, and then creates a temporary pixmap, just large enough to hold the plot. The origin is moved to `xmin`, `ymin`, and the polygon is plotted with replacement mode. After plotting, the values of `P[i]` are restored. The function uses its own graphics context but, except for the mode, all other parameters are copied from the graphics context of the Starter Toolkit drawing widget. Thus we are sure that the style, thickness, color, and so on of the lines will be correct.

18.3.2 More on Plots with Pixmaps

We can use pixmaps not only for temporary storage but also for static and thus speed-up programs, which contain displays with extensive computation. This method is a form of *caching* data needed for creating a display. Because we can always plot a curve by approximating it with a polyline, we modify the program of Listing 18.4 as follows:

Listing 18.5: Drawing Caching

```
typedef struct {
     Pixmap pxm;
     short width, height,
     short xoff, yoff;
} pix_plot_data;

void prepare_pix_plot(pPoint P[], int n, pix_plot_data *p)
{
     /* repeat code from Listing 18.4 until tmp_pix = ... */

     p->pxm = XCreatePixmap(Dpy, c_window, width, height, depth);
     /* Clear Pixmap */
     XSetFunction(Dp, tmp_gc, GXclear);
     XFillRectangle(Dp, p->pxm, c_gc, 0, 0, width, height);
     /* Draw on Pixmap */
     XSetFunction(Dp, tmp_gc, GXcopy);
     XDrawLines(Dp, p->pxm, c_gc, P, n, CoordModeOrigin);
     p->width  = width;
     p->height = height;
     p->xoff = xmin;
     p->yoff = ymin;
     /* restore values */
     for(i=0; i<n; i++) {
          P[i].x += xmin;      P[i].y += ymin;
     }
}

pix_plot(pix_plot_data *p, int dx, int dy)
{
     XCopyArea(Dp, p->pxm, c_window, c_gc, 0, 0, p->width, p->height,
          p->xoff + dx, p->off + dy);
}
```

We can speed the spiral plotting program of Section 1.5.2 by using the preceding approach. The following modifications are necessary. Because the function `prepare_pix_plot()` requires server resources, it must be called after the connection to the server has been established. If we insist on using `vis_window()`, we can achieve that by calling `create_spiral()` from within `show_spiral()` as shown in the following code fragment.

```
static pPoint Pol[MXP];
static pix_plot_data Pxp;
static int prepared = 0;
```

```
show_spiral()
{
     if(!prepared) {
          create_spiral();
          prepared = 1;
     }
     pix_plot(&Pxp, SIZE, SIZE);
}

main()
{
     vis_window(show_spiral, 2*SIZE, 2*SIZE);
}
```

In addition, the assignment statements

```
X[npts] = ... Y[npts++] = ...
```

within `create_spiral()` must be replaced with

```
Pol[npts].x   = x>=0? x + 0.5: x - 0.5;
Pol[npts++].y = y>=0? y + 0.5: y - 0.5;
```

and the following statement should be added after the loop

```
prepare_pix_plot(Pol, npts, &Pxp);
```

See Assignment 4 for more on this topic.

18.4 POLYGON FILLING

18.4.1 The Basics

The *Xlib* function for polygon filling is `XFillPolygon()`, which has the same arguments as `XDrawLines()` with one exception. The sixth argument of `XDrawLines()` (indicating relative or absolute coordinates) is the seventh argument of `XFillPolygon()`. The sixth argument of `XFillPolygon()` is used to indicate whether the polygon is convex or has holes. The predefined constant `Complex` is a safe choice.

The selection between parity fill (called in *Xlib* documentation `EvenOddRule`) and directional fill (called in *Xlib* documentation `WindingRule`) is done through the graphics context. Listing 18.6 shows the implementation of `poly_fill()`, whose use was documented in Section 12.4.

Listing 18.6: Polygon Filling — `File lib/paper_use.c (part of)`

```
/* Dpy, c_window, and c_gc are defined in Section 5.2.1 */

poly_fill(pPoint v[], int n, char rule)
{
     if(rule=='w') XSetFillRule(Dpy, c_gc, WindingRule);
     else XSetFillRule(Dpy, c_gc, EvenOddRule);

     XFillPolygon(Dpy, c_window, c_gc, v, n, Complex,
          CoordModeOrigin);
}
```

The function `XFillPolygon()` draws part but not all of the boundary. Therefore for better quality results we should use an intermediate pixmap and also call `XDrawLines()` for the boundary (see Section 18.3 and Assignment 5). An alternative is to use a robust algorithm such as the one described in Chapter 12.

18.4.2 Fill Patterns

Filling the inside of a region involves two steps. The first is to find the pixels inside the region, and the second to assign a color to those pixels. Although *Xlib* provides facilities only for *X regions* (i.e., unions of polygons and/or rectangles discussed in Section 18.5) the two-step approach is valid for any region, including an arbitrary plane region of the type discussed in Chapter 11. In principle, there are three ways to color the pixels of a region.

1. *Solid Fill* assigns the same color to all of them. It usually is implemented by setting the foreground to the selected color (using `XSetForeground()`) and then calling one of the `XDraw` or `XFill` functions. This style usually is the default in the graphics context and can be set explicitly by

```
XSetFillStyle(Dpy, gc, FillSolid);
```

2. *Pattern Fill* assigns a color to each pixel according to some predefined repetitive pattern. *Xlib* distinguishes between patterns that are pixmaps (`Tiles`) and patterns that are bitmaps (`Stipples`). In the first case we need the following calls:

```
XSetTile(Dpy, gc, some_pixmap);
XSetFillStyle(Dpy, gc, FillTiled);
```

In the second case we need

```
XSetStipple(Dpy, gc, some_pixmap);
XSetFillStyle(Dpy, gc, FillStippled);
```

3. *Image Fill* copies the color of a given image to each pixel. This task can be accomplished with tiling if the image is not too big; otherwise we should set the clip mask of the graphics context to the polygon and then draw the image. Only the parts inside the polygon will be shown. (Full image display with *Xlib* is discussed in Section 22.3.)

Listing 18.7 shows a program that fills two figures with repetitions of an icon pattern. (See Section 3.2.1 for a description of icon files.)

Listing 18.7: Filling with Stipple — `File txic.c`

```
#include <X11/Xlib.h>
#include <boat.icon>

static Display *Dpy;
static Window   wn;
static GC       gc;
static Pixmap   stipple_fill;
static int    init = 0;

/*  Create stipple from a boat icon  */
make_stipple()
{
    get_default_args(&Dpy, &wn, &gc);
    stipple_fill = XCreateBitmapFromData(Dpy, wn,
        boat_bits, boat_width, boat_height);
    XSetStipple(Dpy, gc, stipple_fill);
    use_replace_mode(); /* XSetFunction(Dpy, gc, GXcopy); */
}

static XPoint triangle[] = { 140, 20, 40, 193, 240, 193, 140, 20};

redraw()
{
    if(!init) {
        make_stipple();
        init = 1;
    }
    XSetFillStyle(Dpy, gc, FillStippled);

    /* Fill an Equilateral Triangle */
    XFillPolygon(Dpy, wn, gc, triangle, 3, Complex, CoordModeOrigin);
```

```
    /* Fill an Ellipse - Note: 64*360 equals 23040 */
    XFillArc(Dpy, wn, gc, 40, 220, 200, 100, 0, 23040);

    /* Draw Outlines */
    XSetFillStyle(Dpy, gc, FillSolid);
    XDrawLines(Dpy, wn, gc, triangle, 4, CoordModeOrigin);
    XDrawArc(Dpy, wn, gc, 40, 220, 200, 100, 0, 23040);
}

main()
{
    vis_window(redraw, 280, 400);
}
```

One of the figures is an equilateral triangle and the other an ellipse. We use the replacement drawing mode because part of the outline is drawn during filling. We also need to set the fill style to solid before drawing outlines. If we do not, the lines will be drawn using the stipple pattern. We will show why this might be desirable in Section 18.4.3. (What would happen if the statement

```
XSetFillStyle(Dpy, gc, FillStippled);
```

was inside the `make_stipple()` function rather than inside `redraw()`?)

Listing 18.7 offers another illustration of combining code from the Starter Toolkit and *Xlib* functions. Note that, after we copy the default arguments by the call to `get_default_args()`, we have to be careful about using Starter Toolkit calls. Because `GC` is a pointer, we can safely use the `use_replace_mode()` in this case (and in the example of Listing 18.2). A direct call to `XSetFunction(Dpy, gc, GXcopy)` would have been an alternative. Figure 18.3 shows the output of the program of Listing 18.7.

18.4.3 Drawing on Tiles and Stipples

The function `XSetFillStyle()` selects not only how pixels are colored during filling but also how they are colored during drawing. In particular, the pixels that normally are given the foreground color are now assigned a value from the stipple or tile pattern. As a result, drawing with an exclusive OR operation on the filled area will produce images with color corresponding to the 0 value, usually white. To draw with lines of another color we must create a pixmap (or bitmap) by using an exclusive OR of the fill pattern pixmap with the target color, as shown in Listing 18.8.

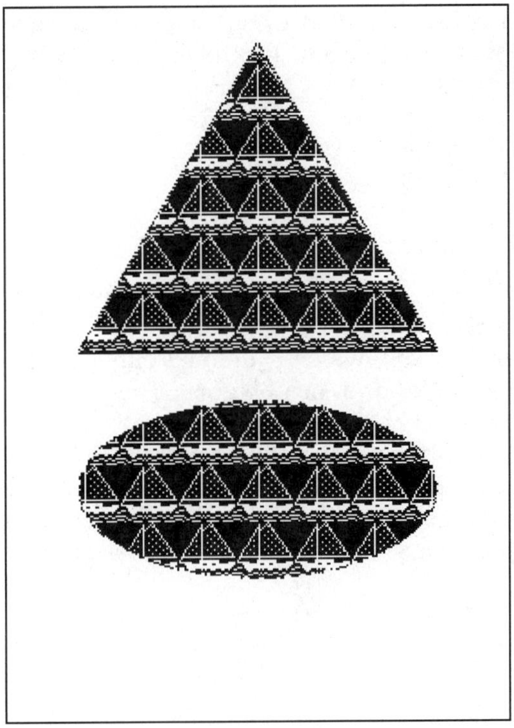

Figure 18.3 Examples of stipple fill.

Listing 18.8: Setup Tiles

```
static Pixmap fill_px, black_px;

fill_area( /* ... */ )
{
     /* create pixmaps fill_px and black_pix with
     black_pix = fill_px ^ black . See Chapter 22
     for details */

     XSetFillStyle(Dp, c_gc, FillTiled);
     XSetFunction(Dp, c_gc, GXxor);
     XSetTile(Dp, c_gc, fill_px);
     XFillPolygon(Dp, c_window, c_gc, /* ... */ );
     /* or XFillRectangle(Dp, c_window, c_gc,  ... ); */
     XSetTile(Dp, c_gc, black_px);
}
```

The last statement sets the tiling pixmap to `black_px`. Anything drawn (text or lines) on the tiled area will appear as black. If that statement had been omitted everything would have been drawn as white (if 0 was used for white and 1 for black, and the reverse for systems where 1 is white and 0 black).

18.5 REGIONS

18.5.1 The Basics

Xlib has several functions implementing polygon clipping and other operations involving polygons. Fundamental to such operations is the concept of an *X region,* which is defined either as the area enclosed within a union of rectangles and/or polygons. The type `Region` is used to refer to the area enclosed by these shapes.

Regions are used in connection with the graphics context to set up a *clip mask* for everything drawn by a function that includes the graphics context as argument. Listing 18.9 shows how a region is constructed from a polygon.

Listing 18.9: Region Creation

```
#include <X11/Xutil.h>
     /* ... */
     Region poly_region;
     /* ... */
     poly_region = XPolygonRegion(P, n, EvenOddRule);
```

Here, `P` is an array of `XPoints` and `n` is the number of points in the array. The `Region` type is not defined in `X11/Xlib.h` but in `X11/Xutil.h`, which must be included in any files using regions. Note the lack of a reference to the server or a drawable. A `Region` is a description of the interior of the polygon. The statement

```
XGetGCValues(Dpy, c_gc, GCClipMask, &gvalues);
```

saves the current clip mask in a structure `gvalues` of type `XGCValues`, and the statement

```
XSetRegion(Dpy, c_gc, poly_region);
```

sets a new clip mask equal to the interior of the polygon with vertices in the array `P`. If we draw a line by the statement

```
XDrawLine(Dpy, c_window, c_gc, x1, y1, x2, y2);
```

it will appear clipped by the polygon with vertices in `P`. We can restore the original clip mask with the statement

```
XSetClipMask(Dpy, c_gc, gvalues.clip_mask);
```

Listing 18.10 (in two parts) shows a complete program illustrating clipping by regions. For the most part it is similar to the program of Listing 16.4 that was used to test window clipping. The interesting new function is `create_clipping_region()`. Rather than restore the clip mask of the graphics context, we copy the current context into a new one (the argument mask `0xFFFFFF` selects all values). Then we set the clip mask of the new region to be the interior of the given polygon. The particular polygon of the listing is self-intersecting.

Listing 18.10.1: Clipping Lines through Regions (Part 1) — `File clip.c`

```
#include <X11/Xlib.h>
#include <X11/Xutil.h>
#include <Starter.h>

static Display  *Dpy;
static Window   window;
static GC       c_gc;
static GC       g_clip;
static int init = 0;
static XPoint P[5] = { 80, 80, 300, 140, 140, 300, 140, 20, 80, 80 };
static int Pn = 5;

create_clipping_region()
{
    Region poly_region;
    XGCValues v;

    poly_region = XPolygonRegion(P, Pn, EvenOddRule);

    /* create second graphics context */
    get_default_args(&Dpy, &window, &c_gc);
    g_clip = XCreateGC(Dpy, window, 0, 0);
    XCopyGC(Dpy, c_gc, 0xFFFFFF, g_clip);
    v.line_width = 4;
    XChangeGC(Dpy, g_clip, GCLineWidth, &v);

    /* define the clipping region of g_clip as poly_region */
    XSetRegion(Dpy, g_clip, poly_region);
}
```

The second part is similar to the program of Listing 16.4 that was used to test window clipping. Each line is drawn twice but with a different graphics context each time.

Listing 18.10.2: Clipping Lines through Regions (Part 2) — `File clip.c`

```
scene()
{
     if(!init){
          create_clipping_region();
          init = 1;
     }
     put_poly(P, Pn);    /* show the clipping polygon */
}

static int kount = 0;
static int x[2], y[2];

draw(pEvent *p)
{
     if(p->kind != BTN_PRESS) return;
     if(kount<2) {
          x[kount] = p->x;
          y[kount] = p->y;   kount++;
     }
     if(kount==2) {
          /* draw a full line */
          XDrawLine(Dpy, window, c_gc, x[0], y[0], x[1], y[1]);
          /* draw a (thick) clipped line */
          XDrawLine(Dpy, window, g_clip, x[0], y[0], x[1], y[1]);
          kount = 0;
     }
}

main()
{
     draw_window(scene, draw, 400, 400, "Clip Test");
}
```

Other operations using regions do not require the use of a graphics context. For example, to find whether a point is within a polygon we can simply call a function available for the purpose. Thus

```
if( XPointInRegion(poly_region, x, y) == True)
    printf("Point %d %d is inside0, x, y);
```

Many of the operations described in Chapters 15 and 16 can be performed directly with the region functions of *Xlib*. Why then bother with writing our own polygon operation routines? The reason is that an X `Region` is defined as a set of pixels on a drawable rather than a list of vertices with particular combination rules. Thus, for example, we cannot find the vertices of a polygon that is the intersection of two other polygons. We can find only the area of the intersection. Finding the area is sufficient for plotting operations but not when the intersection must be used for other geometric operations.

18.5.2 Region Algebra

In addition to the functions described in Section 18.5.1, *Xlib* provides more than a dozen other functions that can be used for region operations. Most are useful only for drawing operations, but one of them returns values that can be used for other operations. The function `XClipBox()` takes as arguments a region and a pointer to an `XRectangle`. It returns in its second argument the smallest rectangle that encloses the given region. Thus the sequence of statements in Listing 18.11 yields the bounding box of a polygon with `n` vertices in the array `P` of `XPoint` structures. The statement `XDestroyRegion()` frees the memory associated with the region.

Listing 18.11: Finding a Bounding Box through Regions

```
typedef struct {
     short x, y;
     unsigned short width, height;
} XRectangle;

bounding_box(XPoint P[], int n, int *xp, int *yp, int *wp, int *hp)
{
     Region poly_region;
     XRectangle BB;
     /* ... */
     poly_region = XPolygonRegion(P, n, EvenOddRule);
     XClipBox(poly_region, &BB);
     XDestroyRegion(poly_region);
     *xp = BB.x;          *yp = BB.y;
     *wp = BB.width;      *hp = BB.height;
}
```

Of course we can find the same information by looking for extremes in the values of the coordinates of the polygon vertices, as we did in Listing 18.4. The approach used in Listing 18.11 is useful for complex regions that are formed by union and intersection operations. Thus

```
XUnionRegion(A, B, C)
```

computes `C` as the union of regions `A` and `B`. Similarly

```
XIntersectRegion(A, B, C)
```

computes `C` as the intersection of regions `A` and `B`.

Note that a region cannot be plotted directly. One way to visualize it is to perform the sequence

```
XSetRegion(Dp, c_gc, R);
XFillRectangle(Dp, c_window, c_gc, 0, 0, 2000, 2000 );
```

This sets the clip mask of the graphics context to the region of interest and then draws a large rectangle. Only the part of the rectangle within the region will be visible.

18.6 CONCLUSIONS

We showed how to combine the function of the Starter Toolkit with *Xlib* functions. The Starter Toolkit takes care of the window creation process, handling of events, and the like so that applications programmers need be concerned only with graphics issues. However, after the default arguments have been copied, you should be careful about which functions of the Starter Toolkit you use. You should never call functions that create windows or the `draw_area()` function because they define the default arguments. Calling any of the plotting functions or those that manipulate the graphics context is safe.

In programs that deal with many windows, the safest approach is to call the `get_default_args()` from inside each procedure that needs the default arguments.

18.7 ASSIGNMENTS

1. Derive the analytic expressions needed for finding the center of a circular arc with a given radius and endpoints.
2. Write an interactive program for drawing arcs. Start with a rectangle drawing function, such as the one shown in Listing 14.4, and then add facilities to specify the rays bounding the arc.
3. The X utility `showrgb` displays the color name database. The following Unix shell script strips the RGB values, packs spaces, and eliminates duplicate entries.

```
showrgb  | awk '{print substr($0,14) }' |
sed "s/ //g" | sort -u
```

(The code assumes that the color names start after the fourteenth location.) Modify the `pie.c` program of Listing 18.2 to read its standard input for color and place it at the end of a Unix pipe containing the preceding script and a `grep` statement. Use that script to display variations of colors. (This is similar to Assignment 13 of Chapter 2.)

4. (a) Modify the program of Listing 3 of Chapter 1 (display of spiral) by using the suggestions of Section 18.3.2. Eliminate the `SIZE` constant during the computation of the points and use it only during the display. In particular, provide an option to fit the window size to the size of the spiral.

   (b) Modify the `prepare_pix_plot()` function to get around the server limit on the maximum number of points.

5. Modify the code of Listing 18.6 to use an intermediate pixmap as in Listing 18.4 in the way suggested at the end of Section 18.3.2.

6. Incorporate the stipple filling functions of Listing 18.7 into a pixel painting program. In particular, have a menu button marked with an icon so that when that button is selected all subsequent painting is done with a stipple produced by that icon.
   Note: The problem is rather simple when the rectangle used to paint pixels is of the same size as the icon. The more challenging version is when the size of the painting rectangle is arbitrary — not even an integer multiple or submultiple of the icon size.

7. Modify the program of Listing 18.7 by defining a `Region` from the triangle, setting the clip mask to that region and then filling a large rectangle. The appearance should not change. (However, the ellipse will have to be dropped because `Regions` can have only rectilinear boundaries.)

19

Projections and Visibility

Scope of the Chapter

Introduction to three-dimensional graphics • Homogeneous coordinates in three dimensions • Projections (finding plane descriptions for objects defined in space) • Visibility (finding which objects may obscure others) • Ray tracing (finding what is seen from a point on the display screen)

19.1 INTRODUCTION

19.1.1 What Is a Projection?

So far we have dealt only with flat objects, such as polygons. Of course, most real objects are solids, and we need to look into *three-dimensional* graphics in order to display them. As most graphics displays are flat (two-dimensional) we must find a way to compute the two-dimensional appearance of a three-dimensional object. Such an operation is called a *projection*.

You can understand projections better by doing some simple experiments. In a dark room, use only one light and observe the shadow of various solid objects. The shadows are flat (two-dimensional) and show the result of the projection. If an object is held at a distance from the light source its shadow provides a rather accurate representation of its shape. But, if the object is held close to the source, the shape of its shadow is quite distorted, especially if the light is small (such as a flashlight) and the object is large (for example, a basketball).

Figure 19.1 shows two arrangements. When the light comes from a living room lamp, the shadow of a small sphere, such as a baseball, is a circle. When the light source is a flashlight and the object is a basketball, the shape of its shadow is distorted. For some relative positions it is a circle, but for others it is an ellipse. The first type of projection is called *parallel* because all the light rays around the object are parallel. The second type of projection is called *central* because the light rays all start from a central point. A more common name for the same type of projection is *perspective* because this term is used by artists to describe the same process.

Figure 19.1 Projection Experiment.

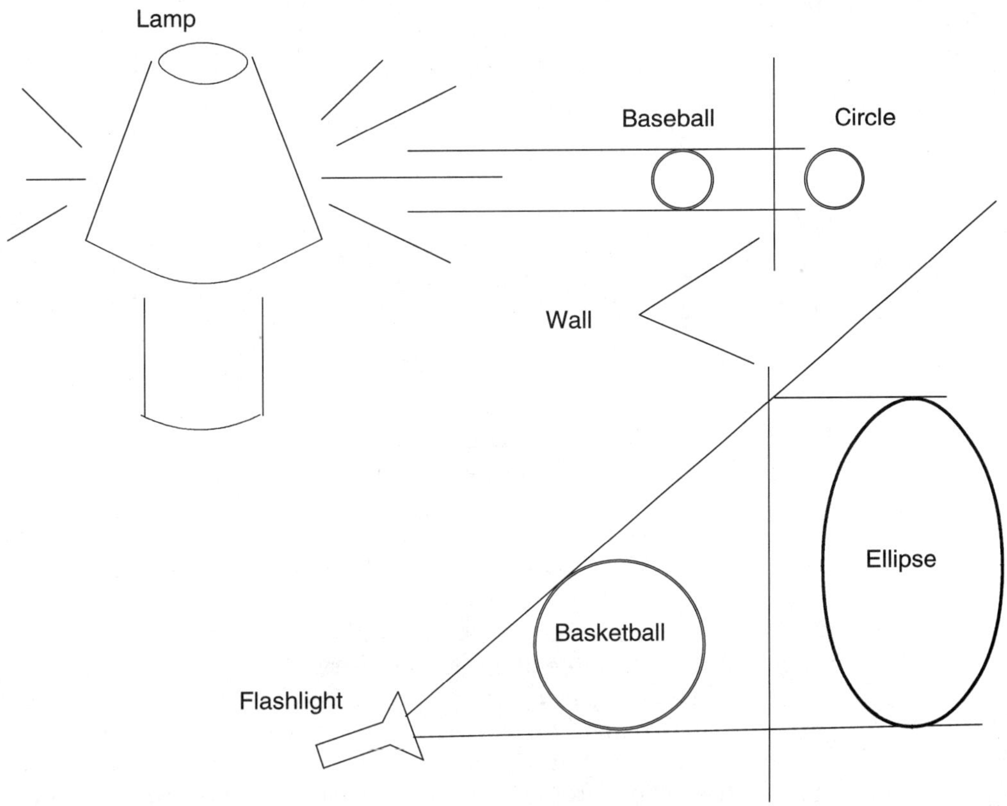

When we take a photograph, we capture projections of objects on the film. Shadows are the result of blocking light, but the lens of a camera collects the light reflected from a object and directs it onto the film. Figure 19.2 outlines how an image is formed on the film.

Figure 19.2 Image formation on film.

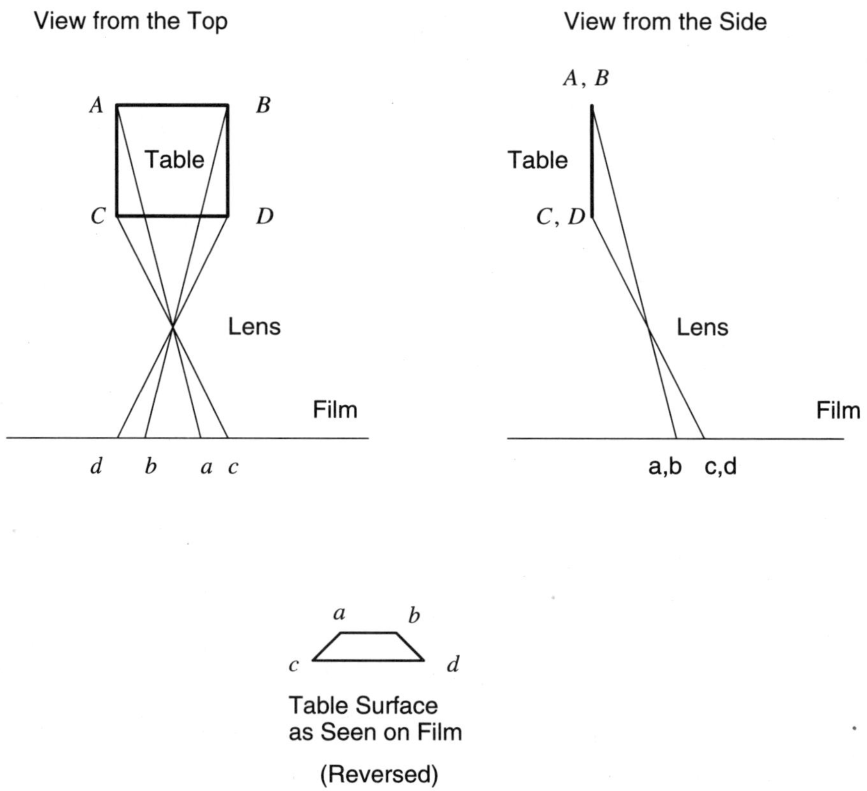

The object is a table whose top is shown as a rectangle. The camera is slightly above the table (diagram on the right). The lens plays the same role as the light source in a central projection. The far side of the table, *AB*, appears shorter than the front side, *CD*, so the image formed is a trapezoid as shown in the bottom diagram. In this case the projection is central. The farther the table is from the camera, the smaller is the discrepancy between lengths *ab* and *cd* so that the projection becomes parallel.

When we create a screen display from a group of three-dimensional objects, we must carry out the photographic process. The eye of the viewer takes the place of the camera lens. Also customary is to place the display screen in front rather than behind the viewer, as in the case of the film. Figure 19.3 shows that this position does not affect the geometry.

We provide analytical expressions for computing projections in Section 19.3.

Figure 19.3 Equivalence between projection on film and projection on a display screen.

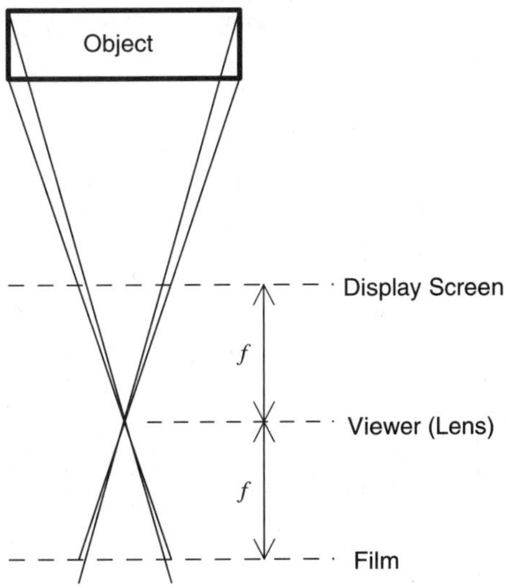

19.1.2 What Is Visibility?

When we project more than one object on a screen, some may obscure others, making their projections invisible. Deciding which parts of an object are visible requires the solution of two problems: (1) finding which projections overlap; and (2) deciding which object is nearer the viewer. We use the word *visibility* to describe the class of such problems. We prefer it to the older term, "hidden surface elimination," because it is shorter and more general.

There are two fundamental ways to solve this pair of problems: in *object space* or in *display space*. The first way works around the list of objects in the scene by using a modification of the techniques discussed in Chapter 16 to find which projections overlap. If the projections of two objects are both polygons, we determine which parts of one polygon are inside the other. In Figure 19.4, when polygon P_1 is clipped with respect to polygon P_2, we find that polyline ADC is inside P_2. When polygon P_2 is clipped with respect to polygon P_1, we find that polyline ABC is inside P_1. Region $ABCD$ is given the color of whichever polygon is nearer the viewer. This assignment is made by comparing the distance from the screen to the points from the original objects that are projected on A, B, C, and D. Two points from the objects are projected onto each polygon. Let's denote them A_1, A_2, B_1, B_2, and so on. If A_1 is nearer the screen than A_2, then P_1 is in front of P_2. The reason we examine more than one set of pairs is the possibility that one object may pierce another.

Figure 19.4 The heavy lines outline the intersection of the two polygons.

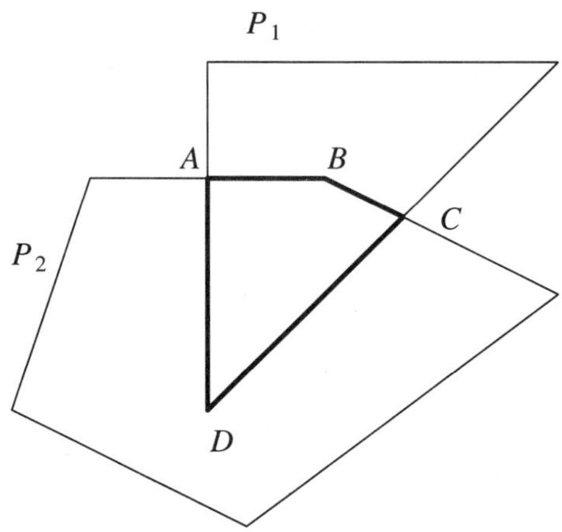

Figure 19.5 shows two possible appearances of the polygons, depending on the relative position of the original objects.

This approach can be quite efficient for dealing with only a few objects, but it can become cumbersome in a scene with many objects, especially if they have complex shapes. It can be accelerated by using bounding boxes for all objects and finding bounding rectangles on the display plane. Only when the bounding rectangles for two objects intersect do we need to consider the relationship between the objects themselves. Still, the method can be overwhelmed easily, especially when objects have complex shapes so that one part can obscure another (for example, the handle of a cup may obscure part of the cup itself).

Figure 19.5 Left: The object projected on P_2 is in front of the object projected on P_1. Right: The object projected on P_1 is in front of the object projected on P_2.

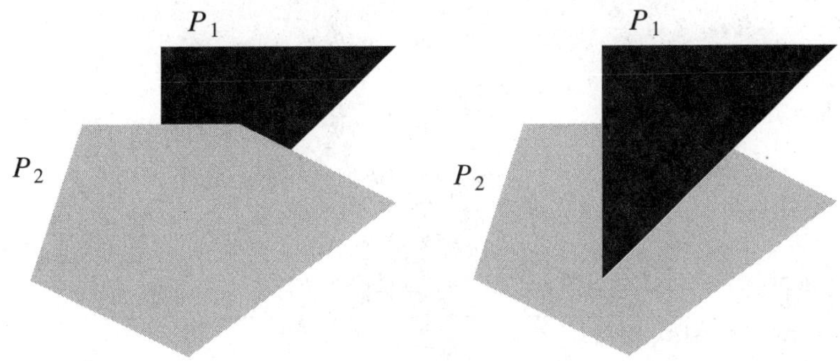

Visibility in display space is a general method, but it requires a large memory buffer, which essentially is a copy of the frame buffer. Rather than go through the list of objects repeatedly, we maintain a copy of the screen called the z buffer where we store the z values (distances from the screen) of the points projected on the screen. For example, when we compute the projection of polygon P_1 not only do we assign the screen pixels the color of P_1, we also place the z values of the corresponding points in the z buffer. Note that this operation must be done not only for the vertices of P_1 but also for all the points in its periphery and interior (using, for example, the methods of Chapter 12). Later, when we compute the projection of P_2, we compare the z values of its points to those in the z buffer. If the new value is greater than the existing one, we ignore the point because it is farther from the screen.

A discussion of the various visibility algorithms is beyond the scope of this text because most of them involve operations away from the display.

19.2 HOMOGENEOUS COORDINATES IN SPACE

19.2.1 Points and Planes

Before deriving any analytical expressions for projections or doing any other computations in three dimensions we introduce homogeneous coordinates. Homogeneous coordinates are even more useful in three dimensions than in two. If the coordinates of a point in space are (x, y, z), its homogeneous coordinates will be u, v, t, and w, and the following relationships hold:

$$x = \frac{u}{w}, \quad y = \frac{v}{w}, \quad \text{and} \quad z = \frac{t}{w} \tag{19.1}$$

The equation for a plane, which in analytic geometry is expressed as

$$ax + by + cz + d = 0 \tag{19.2}$$

now becomes

$$au + bv + ct + dw = 0 \tag{19.3}$$

Note that we can represent both points and planes as `quadruplets`, as defined in Listing 19.1.

Listing 19.1: Definition of quadruplet — `File quadruplet.h`

```
typedef struct  quadruplet {
     double u, v, t, w;
     } quadruplet;
```

The three-dimensional scalar product can be computed by the simple procedure in Listing 19.2.1.

Listing 19.2.1: 3D Scalar Product — `File plane.c`

```
#include <quadruplet.h>

double s3_product(quadruplet *q1, quadruplet *q2)
{
     return(q1->u*q2->u + q1->v*q2->v + q1->t*q2->t + q1->w*q2->w);
}
```

Things are a bit more complicated for the outer product. First, we note that the equation of a plane defined by three points is given by

$$\det \begin{vmatrix} u & u_1 & u_2 & u_3 \\ v & v_1 & v_2 & v_3 \\ t & t_1 & t_2 & t_3 \\ w & w_1 & w_2 & w_3 \end{vmatrix} = 0 \tag{19.4}$$

The coefficients of the plane equation are the 3×3 minors of the 4×4 determinant. Rather than write a new routine for computing the determinants we may use the procedure of Listing 15.2.2 (Section 15.2.2). That procedure is expressed in terms of triplets, so we need a routine to construct triplets from quadruplets. Listing 19.2.2 provides such a function together with the function computing the coefficients of the plane.

Listing 19.2.2: 3D Outer Product — `File plane.c`

```
#include <triplet.h>

void qt(quadruplet *q, triplet *t, int n)
{
     t->u = n==0? q->v: q->u;
     t->v = (n==0 || n==1)? q->t: q->v;
     t->w = n==3? q->t : q->w;
}

void o3_product(quadruplet *q1, quadruplet *q2, quadruplet *q3, quadruplet *g)
{
     int n;
     triplet P, Q, R;
     double v[4];

     for(n=0; n<4; n++) {
          qt(q1, &P, n);
          qt(q2, &Q, n);
          qt(q3, &R, n);
          v[n] = determinant(&P, &Q, &R);
     }
     g->u = v[0];  g->v = -v[1];
     g->t = v[2];  g->w = -v[3];
}
```

The three quadruplet pointers, `q1`, `q2`, and `q3`, point to the second, third, and fourth columns, respectively, of the determinant of Equation (19.4). `v[n]` is the minor of that determinant with respect to the nth element of the first column. Before the final result is stored in the quadruple `*g`, the signs are adjusted according to the determinant expansion rule. The numerical value of a 4×4 determinant can be computed by using the `s3_product()` function of Listing 19.2.1 with arguments a quadruple pointing to the first column and the quadruple with the results of `o3_product()`.

19.2.2 Straight Lines

The definitions of Section 19.2.1 and the procedures of Listing 19.2 allow us to work with points and planes, but they do not deal with straight lines.

Planes are described by a single equation, but straight lines in three dimensions are defined by a *pair* of equations. A straight line is the intersection of two planes, so its general equation has the form

$$au + bv + ct + dw = 0 \tag{19.5a}$$

$$eu + fv + gt + hw = 0 \tag{19.5b}$$

To understand why, let's first set the scale factor w to 1 and then consider the two-dimensional case. In the plane, if we specify one coordinate of a point on a line, the other coordinate can be found by solving the equation of the line. In three dimensions we also need a similar property. If we specify one coordinate of a point and we know that the point is on the straight line, then the point must be defined completely. But two more coordinates are to be determined, so we need two equations.

An important case is when a straight line is defined by a pair of points. In this case the projections of the points onto the coordinate planes (x-y, y-z, and z-x) define the projections of the line. By choosing two of the planes we can write the equations for the line:

$$\det \begin{vmatrix} u & u_1 & u_2 \\ v & v_1 & v_2 \\ w & w_1 & w_2 \end{vmatrix} = 0 \tag{19.6a}$$

and

$$\det \begin{vmatrix} u & u_1 & u_2 \\ t & t_1 & t_2 \\ w & w_1 & w_2 \end{vmatrix} = 0 \tag{19.6b}$$

The first equation does not have a t term and the second does not have a v term so that c and f will be 0 if we want to write the equations in the form of Equations (19.5). We can use the expressions in Section 15.2 to compute the rest of the coefficients. In particular,

$$a = v_1 w_2 - v_2 w_1$$

$$e = t_1 w_2 - t_2 w_1$$

and so forth.

Listing 19.3: 3D Line Defined by a Pair of Points — `File line_3d.c`

```
/*  vector Lines[] holds the eight coefficients of the two equations */
#include <quadruplet.h>
#include <triplet.h>

line_3d(quadruplet *q1, quadruplet *q2, double Lines[])
{
    triplet A, B, C;
```

```
    qt(q1, &A, 2);      /* eliminate t coordinate */
    qt(q2, &B, 2);
    o_product(&A, &B, &C);
    Lines[0] = C.u;     Lines[1] = C.v;    Lines[2] = 0; Lines[3] = C.w;
    qt(q1, &A, 1);      /* eliminate v coordinate */
    qt(q2, &B, 1);
    o_product(&A, &B, &C);
    Lines[4] = C.u;     Lines[5] = 0; Lines[6] = C.v;     Lines[7] = C.w;
}
```

19.3 ANALYTIC EXPRESSIONS FOR PROJECTIONS

19.3.1 The Basic Expressions

The expressions for the coordinates of the projection can be derived from Figure 19.3. For convenience the basic diagram has been redrawn as Figure 19.6. Using triangle similarity, we conclude that

$$\frac{x^p}{x} = \frac{f}{z + f} \tag{19.7}$$

Solving with respect to the coordinate of the projection y^p and dividing by f yields

$$x^p = \frac{x}{1 + (z/f)} \tag{19.8a}$$

The same situation holds for the y coordinate so that

$$y^p = \frac{y}{1 + (z/f)} \tag{19.8b}$$

Of course,

$$z^p = 0 \tag{19.8c}$$

Equations (19.8a)-(19.8c) provide the general expression for a perspective projection along the z-axis on the plane $z = 0$. If the viewer is far from the display screen compared to the distance to the objects from the screen, f is much greater than all the z's. Therefore the ratio z/f is close to 0 and can be ignored. The same situation holds for all three coordinates, giving the projection equations

$$x^p = x \tag{19.9a}$$

$$y^p = y \tag{19.9b}$$

$$z^p = 0 \tag{19.9c}$$

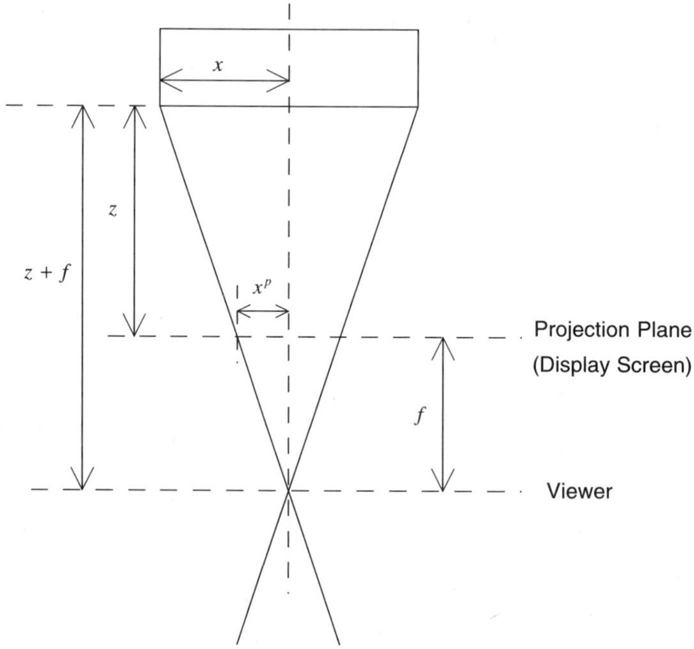

Figure 19.6 Derivation of the projection equation.

Such a projection is called *orthographic*.

From now on we use the word *projection* to mean an orthographic projection, and we refer to perspective projections explicitly.

19.3.2 The Perspective Projection Matrix

Homogeneous coordinates are particularly convenient for computing projections. Let's go back to Equations (19.8) and express them in terms of homogeneous coordinates by replacing x with u/w, x^p with u^p/w^p, and so on, and noting that wz equals t. We find that

$$\frac{u^p}{w^p} = \frac{u}{w + (t/f)} \tag{19.10a}$$

$$\frac{v^p}{w^p} = \frac{y}{w + (t/f)} \tag{19.10b}$$

$$t^p = 0 \tag{19.10c}$$

We have not yet defined w^p, so we may select it to be

$$w^p = w + \frac{t}{f} \tag{19.11}$$

which gives $u^p = u$ and $v^p = v$. In other words, the perspective projection affects only the fourth coordinate! Well, almost, because t^p is set to 0.

You will soon see reasons for also applying the projection transformation on t so that t^p equals t rather than 0. Clearly, keeping track of an additional coordinate is not going to hurt. When we create the display we set t^p equal to 0 again. However, the other value is available for any intermediate calculations that we may want to carry out. If we allow t to behave like the other coordinates, we can define the following *projection matrix*

$$P = \begin{bmatrix} 1 & 0 & 0 & 0 \\ 0 & 1 & 0 & 0 \\ 0 & 0 & 1 & 0 \\ 0 & 0 & \frac{1}{f} & 1 \end{bmatrix} \tag{19.12}$$

If $\boldsymbol{V}$ denotes the vector (u, v, t, w) and $\boldsymbol{V}^p$ denotes the vector (u^p, v^p, t^p, w^p), the projection is

$$\boldsymbol{V}^p = P\boldsymbol{V} \tag{19.13}$$

The program of Listing 19.4 implements Equation (19.4).

Listing 19.4: Projection Equation — `File project.c`

```
#include <quadruplet.h>

projection( quadruplet *q1, quadruplet *q2, double f )
{
     q2->u = q1->u;     q2->v = q1->v;     q2->t = q1->t;
     q2->w = q1->w + q1->t/f;
}
```

A simple observation from Equations (19.10) and (19.11) and from Listing 19.4 is that the farther an object is from the screen (i.e., the larger is t/w), the larger is the scale factor of the projection (w^p or `q2->w`). As the final display is achieved by dividing all other coordinates by the scale factor, a large t/w will result in a small object, which is what we would expect. The objects farthest from the screen should appear smallest.

To work with the ordinary coordinates, we can use the program of Listing 19.5.

Listing 19.5: Perspective Equation — `File perspective.c`

```
perspective(double x, double y, double z, double f,
    double *xp, double *yp, double *zp)
{
    double u;

    u = 1 + z/f;
    *xp = x/u;    *yp = y/u;    *zp = z/u;
}
```

19.3.3 Why Project in Three Dimensions? Visibility Issues

In this section and the rest of the chapter we discuss in detail the construction of projections and related problems. Representing two dimensions on paper is easy, but three-dimensional drawings are harder to make. In particular, we have to project each arrangement on paper, and right away we run into a problem. We cannot depict in a text (printed on two-dimensional paper) the construction of projections except through other projections!

We have opted for the following solution. Rather than show the projection of three-dimensional objects onto two dimensions we will show projections of two-dimensional objects onto one dimension. We can interpret such drawings as views of the three-dimensional world from the top. Assume that you look at the x-z plane with the y-axis going away from you.

Figure 19.7 shows the meaning of assigning a value to the t or z coordinate. We use a simple geometric construction to compute the projections. The projection P' of point P is found as the intersection of line PV and the x-axis. Point P'' lies at the intersection of line OP joining the origin and P and a vertical line through P' (shown as a dashed line in Figure 19.7).

The proof of the construction shown in Figure 19.7 is simple:

$$\frac{z^p}{f} = \frac{z}{f + z} \tag{19.14}$$

because of triangle similarity. If we consider two points, we can use simple algebra to show that the z values of the projection have the same relationship as the original values. In particular,

$$z_1^p > z_2^p \quad \text{if and only if} \quad z_1 > z_2 \tag{19.15}$$

This relationship is not valid for x^p, as Figure 19.8 shows.

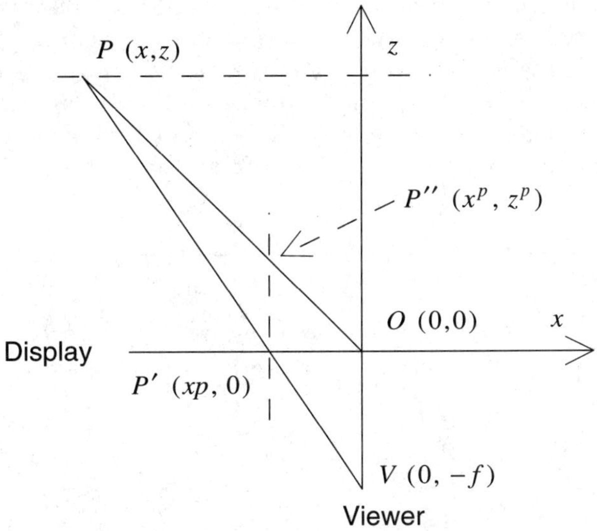

Figure 19.7 Construction of the three-dimensional perspective projection. The y-axis is away from the viewer.

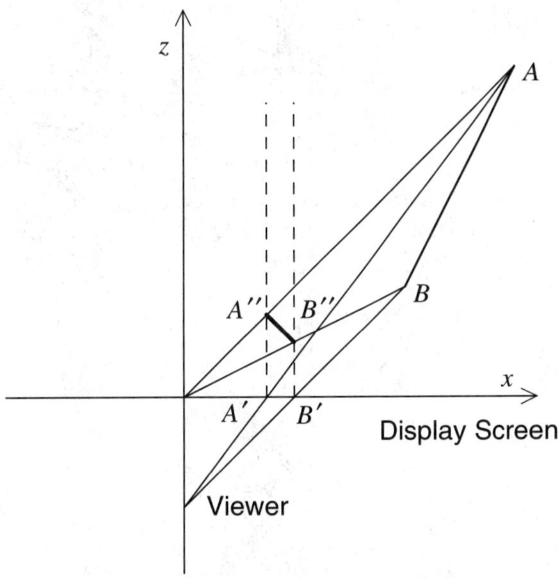

Figure 19.8 Construction of the three-dimensional perspective projection of a line segment. The y-axis is away from the viewer.

The reason we use the third dimension has to do with deciding what parts of a scene are visible. Figure 19.9 shows two line segments, *AC* and *BD*, which are projected onto $A'C'$ and $B'D'$. Because the projections overlap, we have to decide which color the segment $B'A'$ will be: that of *AC* or of *BD*. As *BD* is in front of *AC*, we should choose the color of *BD*. If we projected only on the plane (shown as a line in Figures 19.6-19.8), we would have to go back to the original data. But we have the values of *z*, so we can make the decision on the basis of line segments $A''C''$ and $B''D''$.

Figure 19.9 Construction of the three-dimensional perspective projections of two line segments. The *y*-axis is away from the viewer.

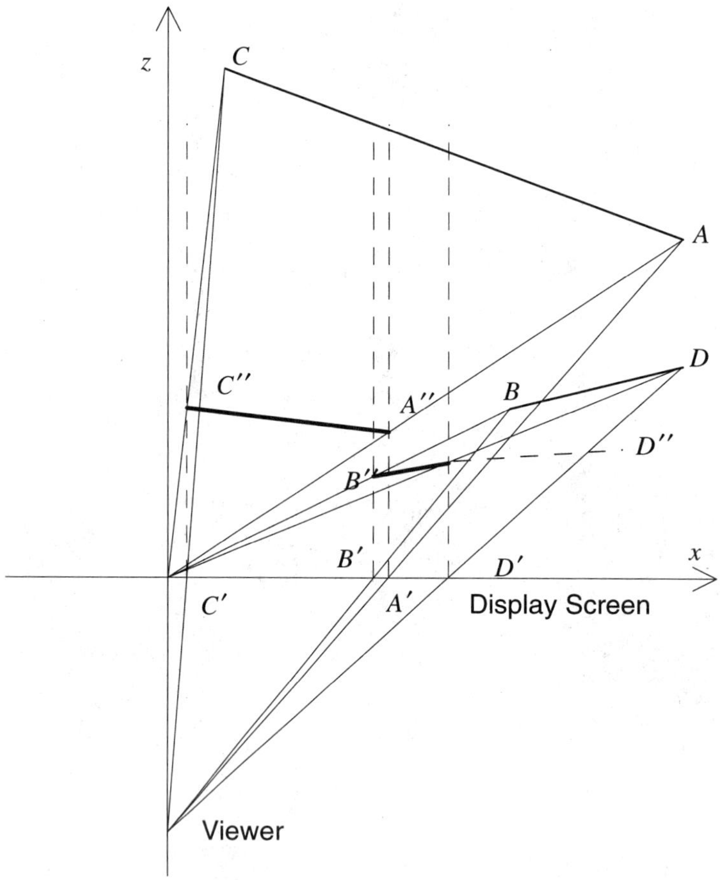

The advantage of this approach is that we *separate* the construction of the perspective projection from the problem of *visibility*. First, we apply the perspective projection transformation by using the procedures of either Listing 19.4 or Listing 19.5. Then, we construct the final projection by applying an *orthographic projection* (i.e., setting z to 0) on the result while deciding the visibility issue.

19.3.4 Some Examples

Figures 19.10 and 19.11 show constructions similar to Figures 19.6-19.8 for a square and a circle. The square is transformed into a trapezoid and the circle into an ellipse.

Figure 19.10 Projection of a Square.

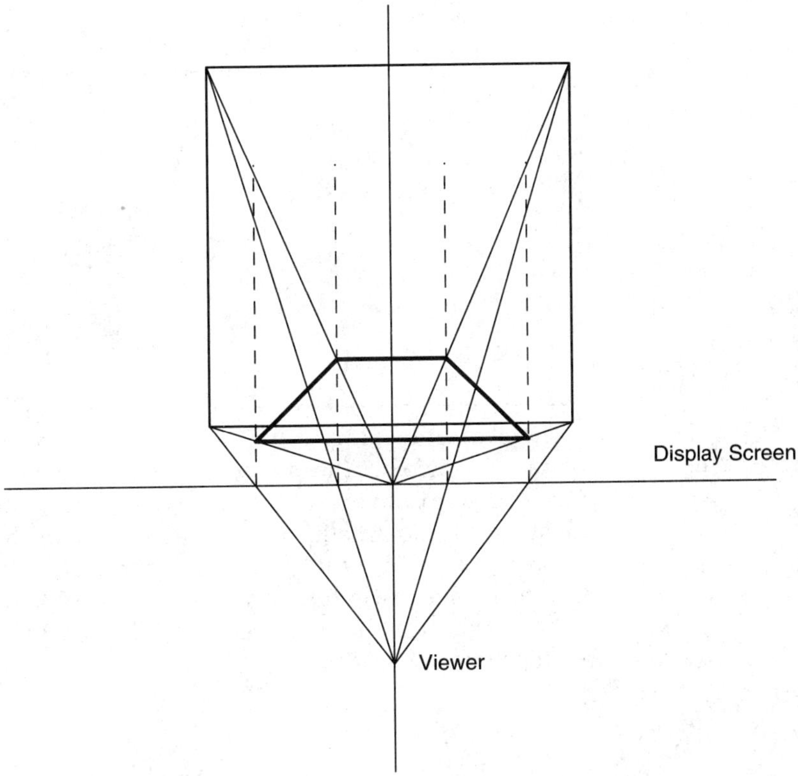

Figure 19.11
Projection of a Circle.

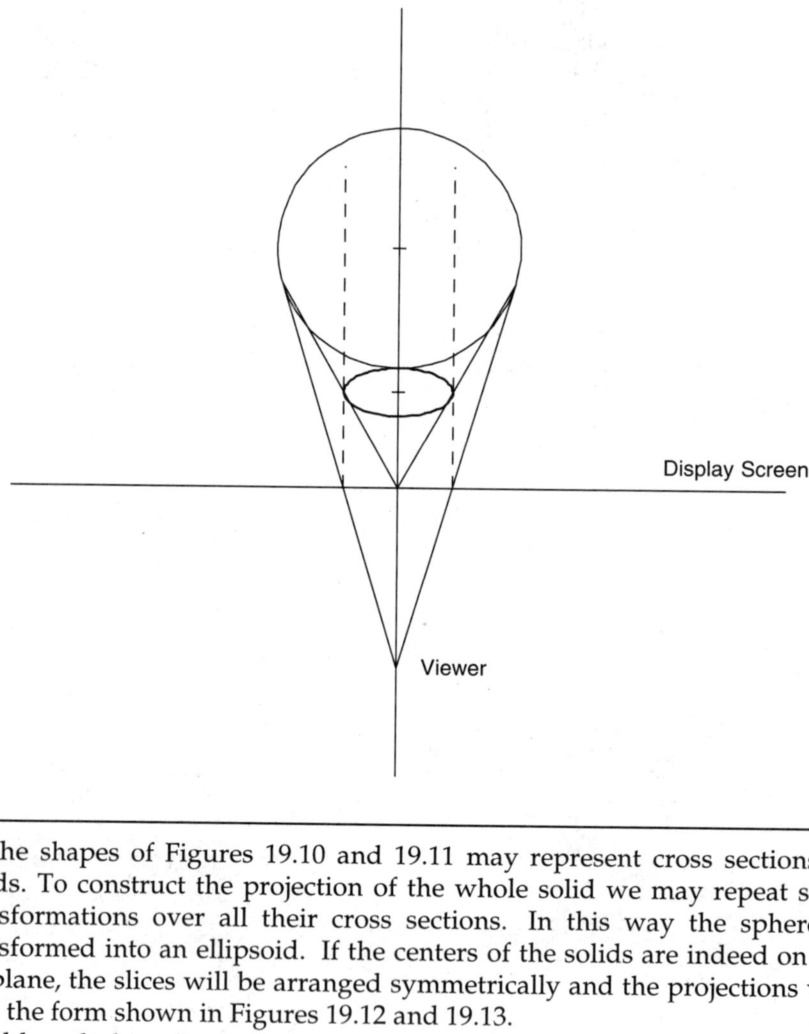

The shapes of Figures 19.10 and 19.11 may represent cross sections of solids. To construct the projection of the whole solid we may repeat such transformations over all their cross sections. In this way the sphere is transformed into an ellipsoid. If the centers of the solids are indeed on the *x-z* plane, the slices will be arranged symmetrically and the projections will take the form shown in Figures 19.12 and 19.13.

Although the sphere projection of Figure 19.13 is a circle, the solid in the *x-y-z* space is lens-shaped.

Figure 19.12 Projection of a Cube on the x-y plane.

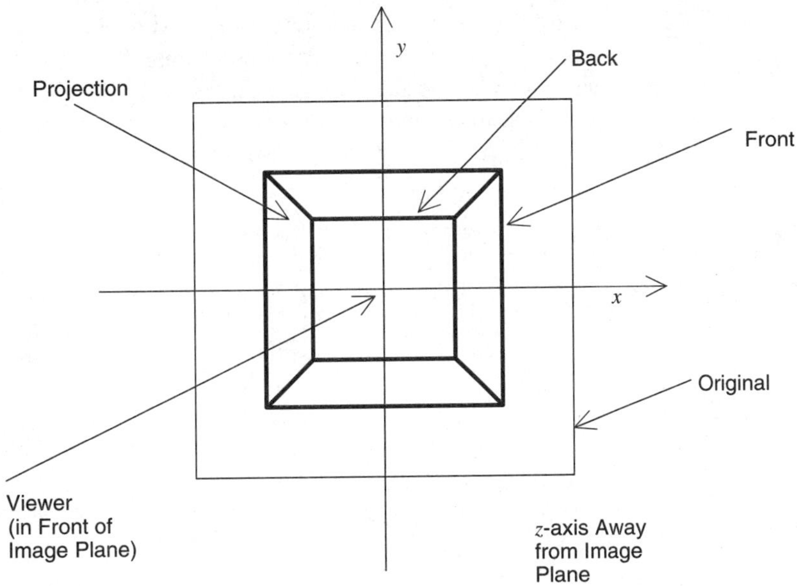

Figure 19.13 Projection of a Sphere on the x-y plane.

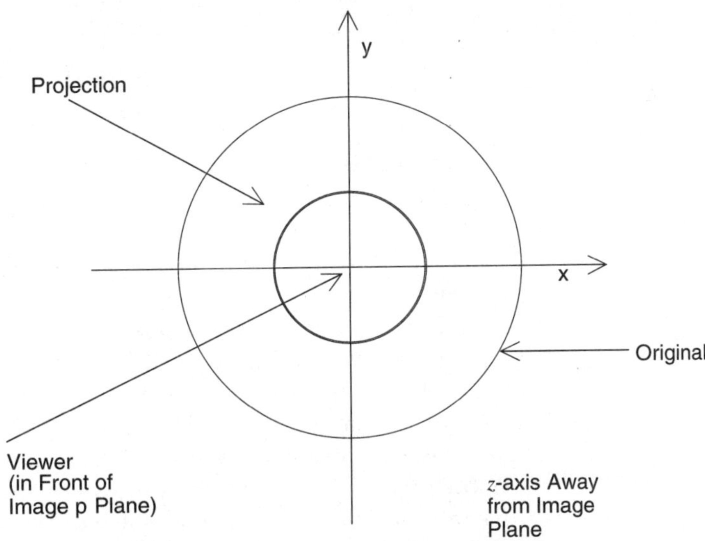

19.4 RAY TRACING

In general, the appearance of an object depends on those around it. Certainly, a shiny surface will mirror the objects around it, but dull surfaces also may show some dim reflections. Therefore, when we construct a projection, we should look not only at a particular point on the screen but also go back and examine other points in the scene that might be reflected on the first point. Figure 19.14 illustrates this type of construction.

Figure 19.14 Basic Ray Tracing projected on the x-z plane.

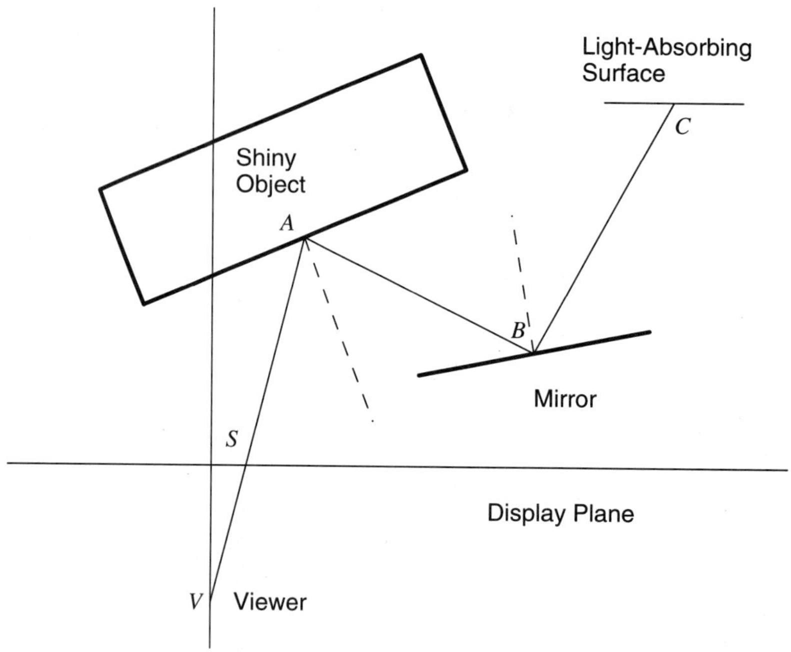

To find what should be at point S of the display screen a line (VS) between the viewer and that point is defined. The line is extended until it meets an object, in this case at point A. If that object did not reflect any light, we could have assigned its color to pixel S. Because it happens to be reflective, we construct a new line, which is the reflection of VA on the surface of the object. The dashed line shows the normal on that surface, and AB is the continuation of the *ray* that started from V. This ray is traced until it hits a second object, a mirror, and then is reflected again.

The viewer sees a reflection of C on the first object through the mirror at B. Because light is attenuated as it is reflected, the final color assigned to pixel S is a blend of the colors of the objects encountered by the ray as it travels through the scene.

Ray tracing does not deal directly with projections or visibility. In a sense it is a brute force approach and as such it is quite expensive computationally. Describing specific algorithms for this method is beyond the scope of this text.

19.5 CONCLUSIONS

Numerous texts cover the topics of visibility, ray tracing, and other three-dimensional graphics problems. We presented only a framework for computing projections because that is a direct extension of the material covered in Chapter 15. Such material is sufficient for writing simple programs that provide the illusion of motion toward or away from the viewer.

The material in this chapter sets the stage for writing programs under the X Window System that simulate three-dimensional motion. Listings 19.6.1 and 19.6.2 provide a simple program that shows a rectangle moving back and forth.

The first part of the program contains the declarations of two data types (a three-dimensional point with floating point coordinates and a point on the plain with integer coordinates), the definition of a rectangle tilted with respect to the viewing plane, and a function to compute the projection and display it.

Listing 19.6.1: Simple 3D Motion (Part 1) — `File fzoom.c`

```
#include <Starter.h>

typedef struct {
     double x, y, z;
     } f3Point;

static f3Point P[4] = {
          50., 150., 20.,
          50., 200., 20.,
          150., 200., 60.,
          150., 150., 60.
     };

static double f = 200.;

static pPoint p[4];
```

```
void project()
{
     register i;
     double u;

     for(i=0; i<4; i++) {
          u = 1 + P[i].z/f;
          p[i].x = P[i].x/u;
          p[i].y = P[i].y/u;
     }

     for(i=1; i<4; i++) put_line(p[i-1].x, p[i-1].y, p[i].x, p[i].y);
     put_line(p[3].x, p[3].y, p[0].x, p[0].y);
}
```

The second part contains a function (`zoom()`) that erases the old projection, computes a new position, displays the new projection, and then sleeps for about ten milliseconds. This function is a background procedure registered with the `add_work()` call (highlighted statement in the listing). A simple event handler causes a reversal of motion when the left mouse button is pressed.

Although this program is trivial, it contains the basic ingredients for building more interesting programs.

Listing 19.6.2: Simple 3D Motion (Part 2) — `File fzoom.c`

```
static int dz = -1;

int move_around()
{
     register i;

     project();
     for(i=0; i<4; i++) P[i].z += dz;
     project();
     idle(10000);
     return(0);
}

void motion_direction(pEvent *p)
{
     switch(p->kind+p->key){
     case LEFT_PRESS: dz = -dz; break;
     case RIGHT_PRESS: exit();
     }
}
```

```
main()
{
     begin_display(400, 400, "Move Around");
     complete_display();
     set_redraw(project);
     set_handler(motion_direction);
     use_xor_mode();
     add_work(move_around);
     wait_for_event();
}
```

19.6 ASSIGNMENTS

1. Write a program to display an object moving vertically to the screen. You may use the program of Listing 19.6 as basis, but select a more interesting shape than a rectangle.
2. Modify the program of Assignment 1 so that the object has a more complicated trajectory — for example, moving along a circle whose plane is tilted with respect to the screen. In this case the `move_around()` function should recompute all three coordinates. You may want to have explicit functions of a time parameter *t*.
   Note: We have not discussed three-dimensional rotation, so the motion of the object always should be parallel to itself.
3. Repeat either Assignment 1 or 2 for more complex plane shapes. In particular, select a rectangle with some text in it. Because bitmaps do not scale well, you may construct polygonal outlines for the letters. That should be easy for such characters as T, E, and the like, so displaying a word such as TILE also should be easy.
4. Instead of plane objects, use simple solids (e.g., a cube). In this case you must solve the visibility problem at each iteration. (The simple method of Section 19.1.2 should be adequate.)
5. Modify the game program of Chapter 3 to have three-dimensional graphins. Each graphin can be formed by a few planes and have motion of the type described in Listing 19.6. Note that you need change only the graphin structures. The rest of the program stays the same.

20

Full Pictures

Scope of the Chapter

Definition of the term *full pictures* • Real and synthetic full pictures • Scanning and displaying • Dealing with jaggies (''anti-aliasing'') • Colormaps for full pictures • Display tools

20.1 INTRODUCTION

20.1.1 Requirements for Displaying Full Pictures

In Chapter 1 we defined as *full pictures* those that have graduations in shade and color so as to give the impression of a photograph or television display. Such pictures require a large refresh memory because of the need to display many intensity and color levels per pixel.

Anyone who has worked with full pictures knows that the proverb ''A picture is worth a thousand words'' is an understatement. We need close to half a million computer words (16 bits each!) to store the information contained in a color television frame. Indeed, for high-quality pictures we need at least 6 bits per color, although 8 are preferable. This requirement translates into 8 bits per pixel for grayscale full pictures and 24 bits per pixel for color full pictures. Thus a 512-square full color picture requires more than 6 million bits.

Such large memories are not always available, and full pictures are often displayed by a process called halftoning. This process uses fewer bits per pixel, but it creates the illusion of more gray scale or color levels. This is the process used to print, for example, photographs in newspapers. The ordinary printing process is equivalent to a 1 bit display (all black areas have the same reflectivity), but the use of small dots in various arrangements can create the impression of gray scale. Halftoning is discussed in detail in Chapter 21.

Under the X Window System programs can be written to check the available number of bits per pixel and use either a straight display if there are enough bits or a halftoning process if there are not enough. The Starter Toolkit function `setup_image()` does this task automatically. We describe its use in Section 20.4.2 and its implementation in Chapter 22.

Another challenge presented by full pictures is that they usually require all the locations of the video lookup table for their own colormap. We can arrange for the window manager to load such a colormap any time the cursor is on the window where the picture is displayed so that all colors are shown properly. However, having a special colormap for one window causes the other windows to appear with the wrong colors. This issue is discussed in Section 20.3.

Full pictures can be obtained either by *scanning* a real scene or by *synthesizing* one from a mathematical description. An issue common to both processes is that of selecting the right *resolution* for both space and intensity. Spatial resolution is the number of pixels that correspond to a unit of length. Intensity resolution is related to the number of bits per pixel: k bits can display 2^k levels.

20.1.2 Pictures and Their Descriptions

The large memory requirements for full pictures surprise many people. Six millions bits of information in a television frame? The reason for the surprise is that we talking about the memory needed to re-create the original picture on a computer display. It is a different story if we try to count the words needed to describe the content of a picture. The phrase "cloudy sky" could be stored in five 16-bit words, but we may need 20 or more times that many to describe a frame from a sports event. There is a big difference between the *description* of a picture and the *picture* itself. This distinction is at the core of a classification of the technical disciplines that deal with pictures.

Image Synthesis is the creation of images from (usually) mathematical descriptions. Much of the computer graphics literature deals with this problem.

Image Analysis is the inverse process: attempting to extract descriptions of objects from a scanned picture. Names given to the study of such problems include *Computer Vision*, *Robot Vision*, and *Image Understanding*. We prefer the term *Image Analysis* because it avoids any suggestion that computers replicate human behavior that words such as "vision" or "understanding" convey.

Image Processing refers to transformations of one picture onto another. Contrast sharpening is an example of such a transformation. Figure 20.1 illustrates the connection among these terms.

Figure 20.1 Relationships among Image Synthesis (Graphics), Image Analysis, and Image Processing.

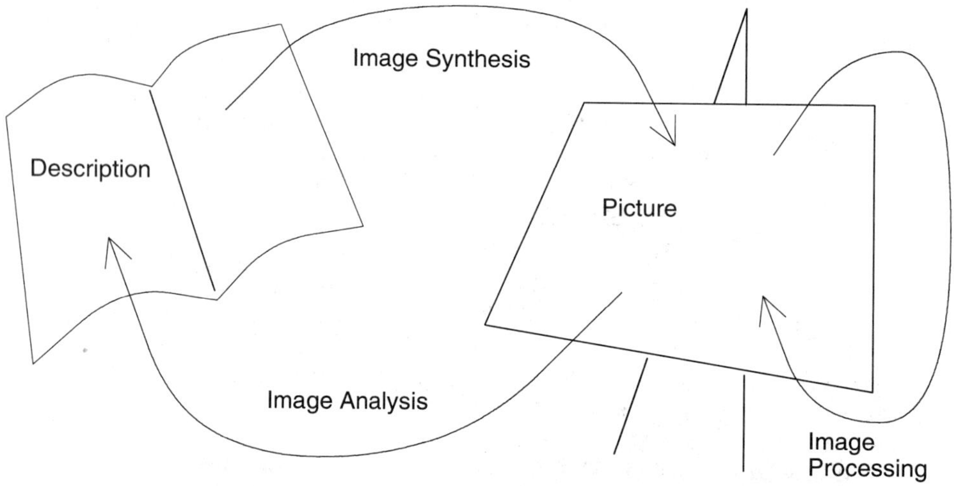

In this text we focus only on display and interactive synthesis of simple images. However, the tools we develop are necessary for most development or production work in any of the three areas.

20.2 CREATING FULL PICTURES

20.2.1 Scanning

A television camera offers a convenient way to capture a natural scene and store it in a computer. Flatbed scanners are based on photodiode arrays or charged coupled devices (CCD arrays) and usually have more accuracy than television camera devices. They are appropriate for pictures that are already printed on paper. Both types of devices convert the optical signal into an electrical signal.

Computers can deal only with numbers, so the electrical signal must be converted into an array of numbers. This conversion involves two steps: sampling and quantization.

Definition *Sampling* is the selection of particular instances in time or space when the value of the signal is measured and then input to the computer. The *sampling rate* or *resolution* measures the number of points per unit of time or length. The distance between adjacent sampling points is called the *sampling interval.*

For example, a speech signal may be measured every 0.1 millisecond, or a picture may be measured every 0.01 inch. Obviously, the sampling rate must exceed the rate of signal changes; otherwise, information is lost.

Definition *Quantization* is the conversion of a signal value into a number having a fixed number of bits so that each sample can be stored in some location of computer memory.

For example, the values from a full image may be described by 8 bit numbers, whereas the values from a flat image may be described by 1 bit.

Both sampling and quantization are performed by an *analog-to-digital* (A/D) converter, a device that measures the intensity of a signal at frequent intervals and stores it as fixed length number. For color images, filters must be used to separate the signal into three basic colors, each of which is sampled and quantized separately.

When we perform such an input operation, what is stored in the computer memory differs from the original in three principal ways: spatial resolution, blurring, and quantization.

Spatial Resolution: Because intensity (and possibly color) are measured only at certain points of the image, some information is lost inevitably. A sampling interval should be as small as possible in order to capture all the detail in a picture. For example, a printed page must be sampled at a rate of at least 200 samples per inch and often is sampled at rates as high as 400 samples per inch.

Blurring: Each sensor measures intensity not only from a single point in the picture but also from a small area around it. Therefore the values of the samples depend on an aggregate of values, which tends to reduce contrast and blurs the image. Note that sampling at a high rate is not enough to preserve detail. We must also ensure that each sensor looks as little as possible at the areas of its neighboring sensors.

Quantization: The values of the original signal are not reproduced exactly. The situation is worse than it might seem because of the interaction between quantization and the other two processes. For example, consider a page of text scanned at a low resolution. You may get the same value for a sample on a thin black line (because it is averaged with the white areas around it) and for a sample on a white narrow gap between two black areas. Regardless of the quantization rule used, one of the two values is going to be wrong.

20.2.2 Synthesis

Full pictures can be synthesized from mathematical descriptions of objects that, in principle, have infinite resolution. So once again, we face the problems of sampling and quantization. Let's look at a simple problem, displaying the projection of a sphere with center at x_c, y_c, z_c, and radius R. The surface of the sphere does not have uniform brightness or color, but the colors at each point of each surface are given by three functions:

$$red(x,y,z) = f_r(x,y,z) \tag{20.1a}$$

$$green(x,y,z) = f_g(x,y,z) \tag{20.1b}$$

$$blue(x,y,z) = f_b(x,y,z) \tag{20.1c}$$

where

$$(x - x_c)^2 + (y - y_c)^2 + (z - z_c)^2 = R^2 \tag{20.1d}$$

The details of these functions are not pertinent right now. Their only important property is that they provide a value for any combination of x, y, and z that satisfies Equation (20.1d). In order to display the sphere we must first find its projection, which (for orthographic projection) will be a circle. Some of the points on the surface of the sphere will be mapped into points inside or on the circle. We also must decide how big the display will be.

If R is mapped into only a few pixels, the projection of the sphere will be too small to show any color variation details on its surface. We want to convert the abstract units of length in the definition of the sphere into pixel distances large enough to provide an accurate display. For example, if R is 0.3, we may desire to map the distance between two pixels into 0.01 so that the projection of the sphere will be a circle with radius of 30 pixels. This procedure is equivalent to establishing a sampling rate: how frequently we perform the computations of Equations (20.1a)-(20.1d).

A similar issue arises with the mapping of the *red*, *green*, and *blue* values into pixels. The equations may have a large range — for example, from 0 to 15,000 — but we may have, say, only 4 bits per color. Thus we face a quantization problem.

The only difference with scanned images is that no blurring occurs. However, we show in Section 20.2.6 that introducing some blurring deliberately is a good idea.

20.2.3 The Theory of Displaying

Both the scanning and the synthesis processes create an array of numbers that approximate the color and brightness of various points on the original picture. These numbers are stored in the refresh memory and then are used to create an image on the face of a CRT display, which is the picture that we actually see. However, we must keep one fact in mind: We are dealing with three pictures: the *original* (either a physical image or a mathematical description), the *discrete* version (the numbers in the refresh memory), and the *reconstructed* (what is shown on the screen).

Figure 20.2 shows the relationship among the three pictures by displaying a segment of a scanline. The horizontal axis represents distance along a scanline and the vertical axis intensity at each point. The dashed lines

Figure 20.2 Three representations of a full picture: original scanline profile (top); pixel values stored in refresh memory (middle); and reconstructed scanline profile (bottom).

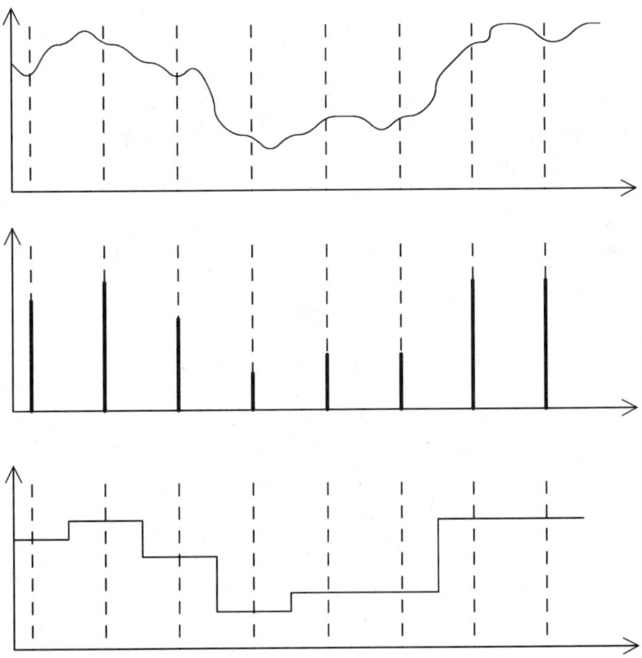

represent the sampling points. The top plot is the original intensity profile. The middle plot shows the values of the samples and corresponds to what is stored in the refresh memory. The bottom plot is the reconstruction of the intensity profile as seen on the display screen. It has a "staircase" appearance because the intensity values between samples have been lost; each area of the screen is painted with a constant intensity and color.

The jagged appearance becomes quite pronounced when we look at the whole picture. Such staircases are obvious along both the x- and along the y-axes so that each pixel corresponds to a square area of constant intensity and color. The higher the sampling rate (resolution) is, the smaller is the size of such squares, and the less likely they are noticeable. Figure 20.3 shows a shape at two different resolutions.

Figure 20.3 Increase in jagged appearance caused by low resolution (right) compared to high resolution (left).

Although the jagged appearance becomes less noticeable at high sampling rates, it always is there. One way to eliminate it completely is by changing the rule for reconstructing a picture from the pixel values. This approach is illustrated in Figure 20.4. It is similar to Figure 20.2, except that the intensity and color of the image on the screen is formed not by coloring with a constant value around each pixel, but by using a weighted sum of the colors and intensities of all the neighboring pixels.

20.2.4 Reconstruction Filters

The term *reconstruction filter* is used to describe the rule used to produce an analog image from pixel values. Normally such filters are not implemented in software but by the hardware of the display device.

Let f_{ij} be the value of a pixel with coordinates x_i and y_j, and $g(x,y)$ be the value of the reconstructed image intensity function. Then the reconstruction rule used in Figure 20.2 can be expressed as

$$g(x,y) = f_{ij} \tag{20.2}$$

for $x_i < x < x_{i+1}$ and $y_j < y < y_{j+1}$.

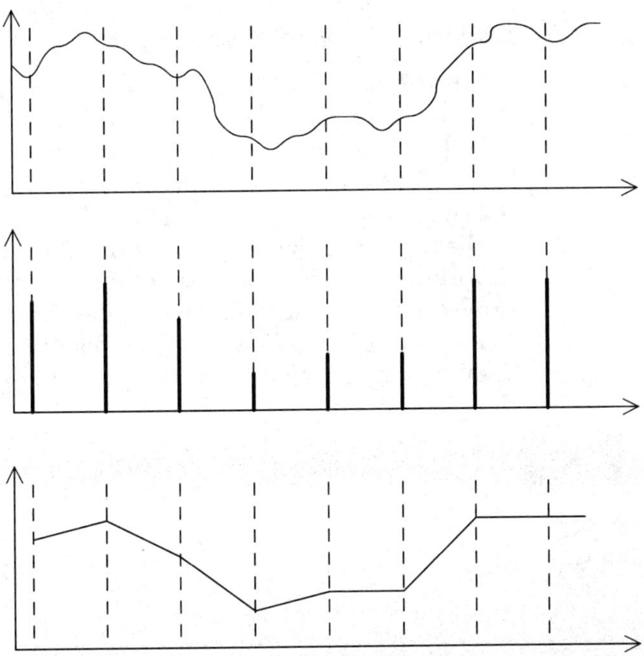

Figure 20.4 Three representations of a full picture: original scanline profile (top); pixel values stored in refresh memory (middle); and reconstructed scanline profile using intermediate values between pixels (bottom).

Color pictures require three copies of such an equation, one for each basic color. The hardware for implementing such a filter is simple: When the refresh memory is scanned, a beam spot of size $s \times s$ is used to paint the screen.

The reconstruction rule used in Figure 20.4 can be expressed as

$$g(x,y) = \frac{x_{i+1} - x}{x_{i+1} - x_i}\left[\frac{y_{j+1} - y}{y_{j+1} - y_j} f_{ij} + \frac{y - y_j}{y_{j+1} - y_j} f_{i,j+1}\right] + \frac{x - x_i}{x_{i+1} - x_i}\left[\frac{y_{j+1} - y}{y_{j+1} - y_j} f_{i+1,j} + \frac{y - y_j}{y_{j+1} - y_j} f_{i+1,j+1}\right] \quad (20.3)$$

for $x_i < x < x_{i+1}$ and $y_j < y < y_{j+1}$. We can confirm that

$$g(x_i, y_j) = f_{ij}$$

Obviously the filter of Equation (20.3) is much more complex than the filter of Equation (20.2). A hardware implementation is likely to be far more expensive for the second filter than for the first. So, even though such filters give much smoother appearance to images, they are not implemented in any of the display systems available today.

20.2.5 Choosing the Right Sampling Rate

The first factor that influences the choice of the sampling rate is how frequently colors and intensities change in the original. Suppose, for example, that the sphere described in Section 20.2.2 has color bands with widths of 0.005. Choosing the distance between pixels to be 0.01 will cause some of the color bands to be lost. Therefore we must sample at least as frequently as the narrowest width of color or intensity. Figure 20.5 shows the kind of distortion that results when we do not follow this rule. The top drawing shows a scanline profile that varies from high to low values more than twice between two samples. The bottom drawing shows the reconstructed scanline profile that varies from high to low values once every two samples.

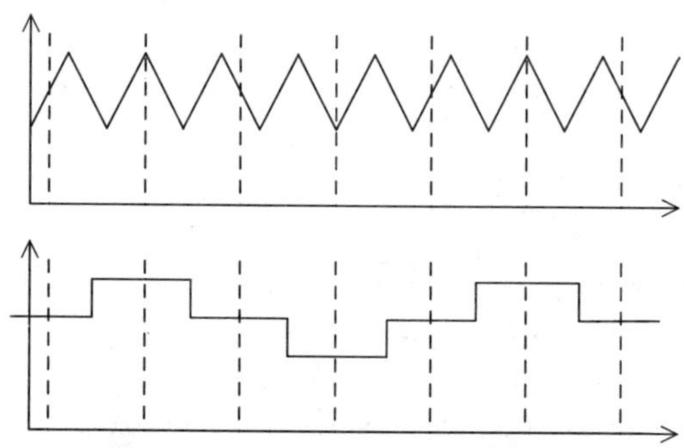

Figure 20.5 The rapid changes in intensity (top) are reduced to much slower changes because of undersampling (bottom).

Because of inadequate sampling, a high-frequency variation has been *aliased* into a low-frequency variation. Not only did we lose information, we also ended up with misinformation. Caution: The term *aliasing* has been used with a different meaning in computer graphics, which we discuss later. The term originated in signal processing, and its original meaning is the one just given.

A theorem in signal processing (attributed to Nyquist or Shanon) states (roughly) that "A signal can be reconstructed perfectly if it is sampled once per intensity zone." This result is quoted often in the computer graphics literature but *actually is irrelevant*. The reason is that the reconstruction assumed by the theorem uses quite a complex filter (much more complex than the second filter of Section 20.2.4). In graphics displays we use much simpler reconstruction filters, so we must sample at much higher rates than the theoretical minimum.

20.2.6 Creating Smooth Displays

The jagged appearance of the contours of Figure 20.3 is undesirable for high-quality graphics, and we review here briefly ways for removing such jaggies. Reducing jaggies often is referred to as *anti-aliasing*, but this term is a misnomer: the *jaggies* are the result of introducing abrupt changes in the display, whereas *aliasing* is the term used in signal processing for converting rapid changes into slow changes. The origin of this confusion lies probably in the fact that both aliasing and the jaggies can be reduced by higher sampling rates or by smoothing the picture before sampling.

The real reason for jaggies is the use of too simple a reconstruction filter. Hence the best way to reduce them is to preprocess the image so that the behavior of a simple reconstruction filter can be closer to the behavior of the one described by Equation (20.3). In other words, we should reduce in advance the difference between adjacent pixels. Such a reduction is achieved by deliberate blurring of the image before digitization.

A complete discussion of this topic is beyond the scope of this text but you can have an idea of what is involved by considering the problem of drawing straight lines without jaggies. We can do so by using a method where each pixel is given an intensity that differs from the ideal color in proportion to its distance from the ideal line segment. Such a method would assign colors to a band of pixels along the line. If the ideal color is black, a few of them might actually be black, but most will be various hues of gray. In contrast, the method of Section 10.2.2 assigns the ideal color to the nearest pixel to the ideal line at each x (or y) and leaves the others unmarked.

20.3 COLOR AND COLORMAPS

20.3.1 The Basics of Colormaps

In computer graphics color is virtually synonymous with colormaps. As we explained in Section 1.2.3, information in the refresh memory is stored only through bit patterns, which are translated into color through the video lookup table. A *colormap* is a data structure that when loaded in the video lookup table determines how the contents of the refresh memory are translated into voltage that controls the red, green, and blue beams of the display device.

In almost all modern devices the colormap can be controlled by the applications program. Such control is very useful because most devices offer the potential of a much larger number of colors than can be stored in a pixel. The applications programmer decides which colors to use.

Sometimes the term *hardware colormap* is used to describe the video lookup table, and the term *virtual colormap* is used to refer to what we simply call colormap in this text.

We can implement a colormap by using three pixel arrays: `red`, `green`, and `blue`. For a pixel with value `n` we can define the amount of each color to be displayed with statements such as the following.

```
red[n]   = n1;
green[n] = n2;
blue[n]  = n3;
```

After constructing these arrays we must load them into the proper hardware location. Software tools are available for doing so.

Although the basic idea behind colormaps is simple, things become much more complex in window systems. The reason is that there usually is only one piece of hardware that translates the pixel values of the refresh memory into colors. If each window has a different colormap, a contention problem arises. The usual solution is to load into the hardware the colormap of the currently active window (usually the one where the cursor is). Unfortunately, this is likely to cause distortions in the appearance of windows that have other colormaps.

Therefore loading a new colormap is too drastic an action. The X Window System encourages applications programmers to leave colormaps alone in order to maintain a consistent appearance of the display screen as users go from one window to another. A *default colormap* is maintained by the system and usually has room for a few new colors without disturbing other windows. So far, we have stayed away from colormaps, using instead the Starter Toolkit function `add_named_color()` to add new colors to the default map, provided such colors exist in the color database of the X Window System.

This strategy is inadequate for full pictures for three reasons.

1. There may be no names for all the colors appearing in the picture. This is not a serious problem because the X Window System provides functions for adding a color by its red, green, and blue values.
2. There may not be enough space in the existing colormap to add all the needed colors.
3. Even if there is space, the values returned by `add_named_color()` (or its equivalents) are not necessarily contiguous. For example, let

pixel value `i` have colors `red[i]`, `green[i]`, and `blue[i]`. When the color triplet is added to the default colormap, it probably will not occupy the `i`th cell. If we let `j[i]` denote its actual location, to display a picture we must transform all the pixel values according to a table mapping the original pixel values `i` to new values `j[i]`. If the values are *contiguous*, that is, `j[i+1] = j[i]+1`, the transformation is simple: We add to each pixel a constant value; `j[i]-i`. Otherwise we must do more work.

The second reason is the most serious obstacle. To overcome it we must use a different approach for full images and create new colormaps for them.

20.3.2 Colormaps for Real Color

Most true color images have 24 bits per pixel, 8 each for red, green, and blue. If our display has 24 bits per pixel, then life is easy; we simply copy the pixels from the file into the refresh memory. Things become complicated when the display does not have enough bits to accommodate all colors. Let's consider in some detail the common case of an 8-bit-per-pixel refresh memory. In such displays each of three (red, green, and blue) D/A converters accepts an input of 8 bits. We have 2^{24} (16,777,216) possible color hues but only 1 byte per pixel in the refresh memory. Thus we can use at any one time only 2^8 (256) of the 16,777,216 colors. Doing so means allocating only a few bits per color and then relying on the colormap to create the proper image.

We need to do two things: construct the colormap and combine the images of different colors. Suppose that we allocate three bits for red, three for green, and two for blue; starting with the most significant bit, as shown in Figure 20.6.

Figure 20.6 Bit allocations for color.

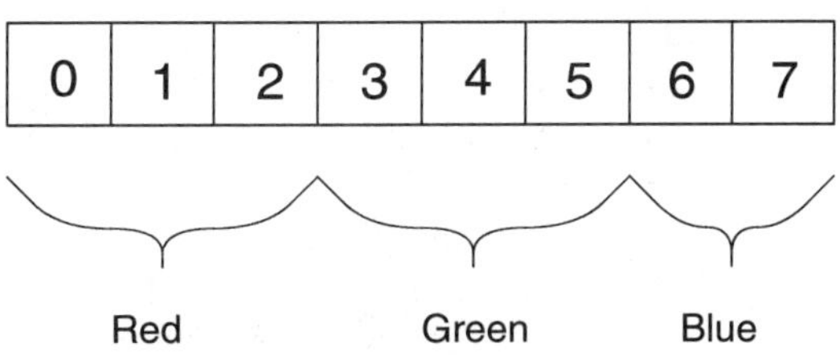

The function shown in Listing 20.1 constructs the three arrays that must be loaded into the colormap. For example, if `n` equals octal `034`, the green value should be the maximum for 3 bits, i.e., octal `0340`.

Listing 20.1: Construct RGB Arrays

```
void make_332_RGB(int red[], int green[], int blue[])
{
    register n;

    for(n=0; n<256; n++){
        red[n]   =      n&0340;  /* copy the 3 most significant bits */
        green[n] = (n<<3)&0340;  /* shift the next 3 bits and copy */
        blue[n]  = (n<<5)&0300;  /* shift the next 2 bits and copy */
    }
}
```

Next, we must place the most significant bits of each color in the appropriate places in each byte. We do so with the following code fragment.

```
green[y][x] >>= 3; /* shift by three bits */
blue[y][x]  >>= 6; /* shift by six bits   */
comp[y][x]    = (red[y][x]&0340) | (green[y][x]&034) |
                                        (blue[y][x]&03);
```

We can view the processes as an effort to deal with a bottleneck in the display system: The refresh memory has only one byte per pixel. Therefore we pack the color information into one byte (the preceding code fragment) and then use the colormap to unpack it.

Depending on the picture, we may use different color distributions. For example, for a fall foliage picture we want to emphasize the red and yellow (a combination of green and red), so we may assign four bits to red, three to green, and only one to blue. For a picture of a beach we may want to use far more blue and green, so we may use three bits each for green and blue and two for red. That is why associating a colormap with each picture is important.

Pictorial databases that store combined images normally also store a colormap with each image. Quite often a halftoning technique (see Chapter 21) also is used.

The colormap of Listing 20.1 uses all 256 locations of the video lookup table, so the appearance of the rest of the windows will change significantly. Many systems use 0 for white and 1 for black. In the colormap of Listing 20.1, 0 is black and 1 is dark blue, so that the rest of the display will appear black. We can construct colormaps that do not have such drastic effects on the rest of the display by not assigning values to all 256 locations. For example, we preserve the first two locations by assigning

```
red[0] = green[0] = blue[0] = 255;
red[1] = green[1] = blue[1] = 0;
```

But then we must ensure that the values 0 and 1 do not appear in the image. The following code fragment does that.

```
if(comp[y][x]==1) comp[y][x] = 2;     /* slightly brighter blue */
else
   if(comp[y][x]==0) comp[y][x] = 1; /* new location of black */
```

20.3.3 Facilities for Colormaps of the Starter Toolkit

If we associate a colormap with a window, when the window becomes active, the window manager automatically loads its colormap into the video lookup table. However, this process may not work for subwindows (it depends on the implementation of the server). This poses a challenge because the colormap of the top window of an application may not be entirely under the control of the applications programmer.

For example, when `begin_display()` is called, it creates a window from a widget set such as *Motif* or *OLIT*; such systems require certain entries of the colormap. The solution adopted by the Starter Toolkit is to create pop-up windows for displaying pictures that require their own colormap and to hide all the details of colormap installation from the applications programmer. The red, green, and blue arrays are part of the image structure discussed in Section 20.4. The Starter Toolkit looks at the image structure and issues the appropriate *Xlib* calls. For now, we merely point out the simplicity of the scheme. For example, if `img` is a pointer to the image structure and we want to associate with it the three arrays created in Section 20.3.2 we must execute the following code.

```
img->red   = red;
img->green = green;
img->blue  = blue;
```

Similarly, the data are assigned by the statement

```
img->pstart = comp;
```

Of course, the four arrays `comp`, `red`, `green`, and `blue` must remain allocated while the program is running. In Chapter 22 we discuss methods for dealing with colormaps directly.

After a colormap has been installed, checking the correspondence between colors and pixel values is easy. The following code displays a series of 256 vertical lines, each with the color corresponding to the pixel value of its position. (For example, the twentieth line has the color of pixels with value 20.)

```
display_colormap()
{
     register i;

     for(i=0; i<256; i++) {
              set_foregr(i);
              put_line(i, 0, i, 100);
     }
}
```

20.4 DISPLAY OF FULL PICTURES

20.4.1 Image Structure and Image Files

Whether scanned or synthetic, full pictures usually are stored in a file that contains not only the pixel values but also their dimensions and information about the appropriate colormaps. (We first explained the need to store the colormap with the pixel values in Section 7.5.5, and it also should be obvious from the discussion in Section 20.3.2.) After we read such a file, it is advisable to keep all this information together. The Starter Toolkit uses the data structure shown in Listing 20.2 for storing both the information about the original image and the related colormap.

Listing 20.2: Definition of Image structure — `File include/Starter.h (part of)`

```
typedef unsigned char pPixel;

typedef struct {
     pPixel *pstart;
     int width;
     int height;
     int depth;
     int ID;
     int pix_w;         /* used by halftoning process */
     int pixel_offset; /* to accommodate other colors */
     int cmap_type;     /* used to avoid colormap duplication */
     int cmap_len;
     pPixel *red, *green, *blue;
} pImage;
```

The `pImage` structure is quite small and space is allocated as needed. The member `pstart` points to the pixel array. `width` and `height` refer to the dimensions of the image, and `depth` is the number of bits per pixel in the original image.

`ID` is a reference number that is discussed in the next section (see also Section 22.3.2). `pix_w` is used to store an adjusted width if the image is going to be displayed by halftoning.

The remaining members deal with colormaps. `pixel_offset` is a value that is added to all the pixels to accommodate colormaps that do not start at 0. When many full pictures are used by an application, `cmap_type` can be used to avoid the replication of colormaps. When a new picture is loaded, the Starter Toolkit checks on whether pictures with the same value of `cmap_type` have already been loaded; if so, it does not create a new colormap. *Caution:* Most types of image files do not contain the colormap type explicitly. It must be inferred from the RGB values. `cmap_len` is the length of the colormap, and the pointers to arrays (`red`, etc.) store the values to be loaded into the colormap.

Many standards exist for image formats with headers. In this text we assume that a routine is available for reading images and filling the `pImage` structure defined in Listing 20.2. The read routine has the form

```
int read_image( char *fname, pImage *result)
```

The argument `fname` is the name of the file where the image is stored, and `result` is the structure where the data are read. The function returns 0 on successful execution and a negative number on failure. After the `pImage` structure has been filled, we can forget about the original image format file.

20.4.2 Windows for Full Pictures

As we pointed out in Section 20.3.3, the Starter Toolkit creates special pop-up windows for full pictures and has various functions for accomplishing this task. The key function is

☛ **`void imgwin(char *label, int (*handler)(), pImage *img)`**
Create a pop-up window of sufficient size to display the image of the structure `img` and also create a colormap for the window from the information in the same structure. The argument `label` is the window label, and `handler` is the event handler for that window. ☜

The trivial function of Listing 20.3 illustrates the use of this function.

If no colormap is associated with the image, we should create one before calling `imgwin()`. In Section 20.4.2 we demonstrate how to do so for the common case of grayscale pictures.

The Starter Toolkit contains two functions that normally are called from inside `imgwin()` but they may also be called directly.

Listing 20.3: Create Image Window from File — `File lib/pixwin.c (part of)`

```
int pixwin(char *fname, int (*handler)() );
{
	pImage Imp;

	if( read_image( fname, &Imp ) ) {
		/* error message */
		return(-1);
	}
	imgwin(fname, handler, &Imp);
	return(0);
}
```

☛ **`int setup_image(pImage *img)`**
If the display is monochrome, this function creates a halftone of the image and copies it into a bitmap. If the display has enough bits, it creates a pixmap and copies the image there. The XID of the bitmap or the pixmap is copied onto `Ip->ID` and is used later for all displays of the picture. ☜

☛ **`void put_image(pImage *img, int x, int y)`**
Displays the image pointed to by `img` with its upper left corner at the point with coordinates `x` and `y`. It uses the `ID` member to find a pointer to the appropriate data. ☜

The implementation of these functions trades off server memory for faster execution. A third function is useful for interacting with the windows in which images are displayed (see Assignment 6).

☛ **`pImage *get_image(pEvent *p)`**
Return a pointer to the structure of the image displayed in the window in which the event occurred. ☜

These functions can be used to perform interactively certain image enhancement operations. Listing 20.4 shows an example of an appropriate event handler.

Listing 20.4: Interactive Image Operations — `File xpix.c`

```
#include <Starter.h>
extern pImage * get_image();

void image_handler(pEvent *p)
{
	pImage *Ip;
	pPixel *cp;
	register x, y;

	if(p->kind != BTN_PRESS) return;
	Ip = get_image(p);
```

```
    /* Invert in Place */
    for(y=0, cp=Ip->pstart; y<Ip->height; y++)
         for(x=0; x<Ip->width; x++, cp++)
         *cp = ~(*cp);
    setup_image(Ip);
    clear_screen(-1);
    put_image(Ip, 0, 0);
}
```

The code of Listing 20.4 simply inverts the image, something that could have been done more simply by changing the colormap. It is used here only because of its relative simplicity; you can think of more interesting operations. Calling `setup_image()` creates a new pixmap from the modified image that is then copied on the screen.

20.4.3 Colormaps for Grayscale Pictures

Colormaps are necessary even for displaying pictures without color if they have more than one bit per pixel. In such cases the three arrays, `red`, `green`, and `blue`, are the same. Because colormaps for grayscale pictures are trivial, they may be omitted from the image file. They may be added to the `pImage` structure after a picture has been read. The remaining pictures need have only the same `cmap_type`.

The key to creating a friendly (to other windows) colormap for such pictures is to realize that human observers have difficulty distinguishing more than 1% changes in intensities so that 7 bits usually are enough to describe a grayscale image. Therefore the least significant bit of their pixels may be sacrificed without being noticed by viewers.

Important *Although a person cannot see certain details in a picture, such details may become visible after appropriate image enhancement techniques have been applied to the data. Dropping the least significant bit is wrong in such cases.*

When we are looking for hidden details, we should apply an enhancement method before display and include the requirement that the output be only 7 bits. For example, if the image is underexposed, the only values may be in the range of 0-100. The correct solution is first to double each value (making the range 0-200) and *then* drop the last bit (always 0 in this case). Such situations arise often in medical and forensic applications.

Discussing image enhancement techniques is beyond the scope of this text, so we stay with the simple approach of dropping the last bit. The code of Listing 20.5 starts with that step and then creates the red, green, and blue arrays. Finally, it gives appropriate values to the rest of the `pImage` structure.

Listing 20.5: Friendly Color Maps for Gray Pictures — `File lib/p_fullpix.c (part of)`

```
void prepare_gray(pImage *img)
{
    register i, j;
    register pPixel *cp;
    register pPixel *red, *green, *blue;

    if(no_depth()) return; /* One bit per pixel server */
    /* Drop last bit */
    for(j=0, cp = img->pstart; j<img->height; j++) {
        for(i=0; i<img->width; i++, cp++) *cp = (*cp>>1)&0177;
    }

    img->cmap_len      = 128;
    img->cmap_type     = 1;
    img->pixel_offset  = 64;
    red   = img->red   = (pPixel *)malloc(128*sizeof(pPixel));
    green = img->green = (pPixel *)malloc(128*sizeof(pPixel));
    blue  = img->blue  = (pPixel *)malloc(128*sizeof(pPixel));

    for(i=0; i<128; i++) *red++ = *green++ = *blue++ = i<<1;
}
```

Note that the *i*th position of the colormap has value `2*i` in order to recover the original brightness of the image. When the colormap is created, the first `pixel_offset` positions (64, in this case) of the default colormap will be copied into the new one so that, even when the new map is loaded, the appearance of the other windows is likely to be preserved. The sum of `pixel_offset` and `cmap_len` must be no greater than 256.

The program of Listing 20.5 destroys the original image when it produces one with 7 bits. A more conservative approach is to allocate memory for a new array and create the 7 bit image there.

20.4.4 Creating an Application That Displays Full Pictures

Listing 20.6 shows a program for displaying a set of grayscale images stored in files whose names are passed as argument to the program. When a file is read successfully, the image is displayed. Figure 20.7 shows a display resulting from a grayscale image. The same program can display color images since all information about the color map is in the `pImage` structure.

Listing 20.6: Picture Browser — `File xpix.c`

```
/*   Interpret command line arguments as image file names     */
/*   Uses function of Listing 20.5                          */

main(int arc, char **arv)
{
     pImage I[256], *Ip;

     begin_display(100, 20, "Picture Browser");
     complete_display();
     Ip = I;
     while(arc>1) {
          if( !read_image(arv[1], Ip) ) {
               imgwin(arv[1], image_handler, Ip);
               Ip++;
          }
          arc--; arv++;
     }
     wait_for_event();
}
```

Figure 20.7 Display generated by the program of Listing 20.6 after it was run with a file containing the picture of the swan as argument.

20.5 CONCLUSIONS

Full pictures are of great importance in *multimedia* applications, and, as far as the actual display goes, there is little difference between synthetic and scanned images. It matters only as so far as the creation of the `pImage` structure. In this chapter we provided a set of simple functions for displaying such images in pop-up windows. Chapter 22 describes facilities of the X Window System beyond those of the Starter Toolkit that allow greater flexibility in the creation of displays.

In general, manipulation of colormaps under the X Window System is rather limited because of the concern of maintaining the correct appearance for all windows on a screen.

20.6 ASSIGNMENTS

1. Write a program that displays "anti-aliased" lines as suggested in Section 20.2.6. Compare the appearance of such lines with those produced by `put_line()`.
2. If you have a scanned picture available, write a program that first reads in and displays the image with the correct colormap. Then it lets the user select a *subsampling* rate, which displays only some of the pixels (e.g., one of four) but using a rectangle rather than a single point (in the same way as in the pixel painting program) so that the total size of the picture remains the same. Have the second picture appear in another pop-up window.
3. Write a program to display the negatives of grayscale images.
4. Modify the program of Listing 20.6 so that it forms a panel with buttons labeled by the image file names. Then selecting a button would result in the actual display. (This procedure is similar to the program that created the display of Figure 1.2.)
5. Add a facility to the program of Assignment 4 for displaying both positive and negative images.
6. Write a program that lets the user create subimages of the displayed images. You will need the following components: (1) an event handler for the image windows that lets the user create a rectangle over the image window; (2) a procedure that translates the window coordinates into positions in the image array `pstart` and uses that information to create a new image structure. You will first need to use the Starter Toolkit function `get_image()` specified in Section 20.4.2; (3) copy the colormap information; and (4) create a new window for displaying the subimage.

7. Modify Assignment 6 to allow for various types of processing of the selected subimages — for example, modifying them as suggested in Assignment 2.
8. Graphins with many colors may be created by using images drawn with a pixel painting program, such as those described in Chapters 2 and 7, instead of icons. This approach makes a video game more interesting. Write a function that reads the output of a pixel painting program (including the table of colors) and use the Starter Toolkit function `make_image()` to create a graphin member that is a `pImage`. (See Appendix B for the documentation of `make_image()`.) Note that the only changes in the code for the game will be replacing the part that creates icons with the part that creates images and in the function that draws graphins. (The function `put_image()` should replace `draw_icon()`.) Plate 5 shows a snapshot of the screen of such a game.

21

Halftoning

Scope of the Chapter

Techniques for displaying full pictures so that they appear to have a larger variety of colors and intensity than the display device is capable of providing • Dither halftoning • Error diffusion halftoning • Color halftoning

21.1 INTRODUCTION

21.1.1 Statement of the Problem

Many times we want to display a picture with more color hues than the display device can support, as when we print a grayscale or full color image. Printing on paper allows only one hue per color. Another example is when we allocate only 2 or 3 bits per basic color as we did in Section 20.3.2. We can create the illusion of more hues by using the *halftoning* process.

In a newspaper pictures usually are printed on paper with black ink only. The impression of gray is created by using different densities of black dots, depending on the gray values of the nearby input pixels. The basis of halftoning is to trade spatial resolution for color resolution. We may be using only one intensity of color, but we vary the area over which it is applied so that *average* value of pixel intensity is close to the original pixel values.

If the display device has very high resolution we can map an input pixel into a *group* of pixels so that *their* average value is close to the value of the original pixel. Such a method is applicable to high-quality printers where resolutions of 1000 pixels per inch are possible.

Electronic displays have much lower resolutions (about 100 pixels per inch), and ordinary laser printers usually do not go higher than 300 pixels per inch. In such cases we must work with the assumption that the output (the halftone picture) has the same resolution as the input (the original full picture).

In this chapter we discuss halftoning processes for digital displays, first for grayscale and then for color images.

21.1.2 Outline of Solutions

In order to display a full picture on a 1-bit-per-pixel screen, we must find a rule by which a value is mapped to 1 or 0. Most such rules involve some form of *thresholding*. Pixels with values above the threshold are mapped into 1's and pixels with values below the threshold are mapped into 0's. If we use a fixed threshold for the whole image, the results are rather unsatisfactory. Figure 21.1 shows the result of simple thresholding on an image that looks much better when printed in halftone (by a method to be explained later) in Figure 21.2. Both figures appear on page 476.

We can achieve better results by using *different* thresholds at each pixel. For example, we may select four thresholds `t[0]`, `t[1]`, `t[2]`, `t[3]`, and have a rule for choosing one of them for each pixel. One possible rule is to select `t[j]` for the pixel at `(X,Y)` where

```
j = X%2 + 2 * (Y%2)
```

(The expression **%2** means *modulo 2*.) Thus pixels with both coordinates even are compared to `t[0]`, those with `X` even and `Y` odd to `t[2]`, etc. If the intensity value `f[Y][X]` exceeds `t[j]`, the pixel is given the background color (white); otherwise it is given the foreground color (black). Areas that are very dark or very light will appear as solid dark or solid white because the brightness of each pixel will be on the same side of all the thresholds. Areas with intermediate values will have a "salt and pepper" appearance (creating the illusion of gray) because the values may be greater from some of the thresholds and less from some of the others. This process is called *dithering* and is discussed in Section 21.2.

A second way of halftoning is by *error diffusion*. Rather than vary the threshold value, we change the pixel values. After assigning a pixel to be white or black, we are left with an error: the difference between the picture value and the display value. Then we distribute that error to neighboring

Figure 21.1 Display of thresholded version of the image.

Figure 21.2 A halftone display of the image whose thresholded version is shown in Figure 21.1.

pixels so that their values decrease if we map a light pixel into white and increase if we map a dark pixel into black. This procedure will not affect the color of pixels in very light or very dark areas: The pixels will be on the same side of the threshold anyway. But it will move pixels to opposite sides in areas with intermediate values, creating again a salt and pepper appearance. The method is discussed in Section 21.3. Both techniques can be applied to multibit output as we explain in Section 21.4.

21.2 DITHER HALFTONING

21.2.1 Analysis of Dither Halftoning

The dither method uses a set of thresholds. Thresholds can be selected either systematically (*ordered* dither) or randomly (*random* dither). We show later that random dither gives rather poor results, and for this reason it is rarely, if ever, used. As long as there is no danger of confusion, we use the term *dither* to mean ordered dither. The justification for the technique is as follows.

Let R be a region of uniform intensity with all pixels having intensity `g` and which also is large enough so that it has more pixels than number of thresholds n. If the value `g` is greater than `t[i]` and less or equal to `t[i+1]`, then `i` out of `n` times a pixel will be white, and the relative intensity of the region will be `i/n`. Dithering is actually a quantization technique that works well for large regions with uniform intensity. For regions with fewer pixels than `n`, the result is unpredictable, so some detail is bound to get lost.

Various techniques may be used to select thresholds. An important consideration is the need to avoid visible patterns in the output. Therefore the high and low values of the thresholds should be mixed in space. A commonly used strategy for achieving that goal involves arranging the thresholds in a square matrix with which we tile the picture. Therefore `n` must be an even power of 2: 4 (2×2 matrix), 16 (4×4 matrix), or, in general, 2^{2k} for some k. Furthermore, for simplicity of notation, we assume that the `n` thresholds are successive numbers from 0 to 2^{2k-1}. This assumption is not a restriction because we can always scale the values we find. If n equals 4, we start with the dither matrix

$$D_2 = \begin{bmatrix} 0 & 2 \\ 3 & 1 \end{bmatrix} \tag{21.1}$$

We define an auxiliary matrix U_n, which has ones for all its entries and an operation $\times$ between two matrices A and B as follows: the matrix $A \times B$ is obtained by replacing each element of A with matrix B multiplied by that element. Thus, if A is an $n \times n$ and B an $m \times m$ matrix, $A \times B$ will be $nm \times nm$. (This result is called the tensor product of two matrices.) Using this rule, we find that

$$U_2 \times D_2 = \begin{bmatrix} 0 & 2 & 0 & 2 \\ 3 & 1 & 3 & 1 \\ 0 & 2 & 0 & 2 \\ 3 & 1 & 3 & 1 \end{bmatrix} \tag{21.2a}$$

and

$$D_2 \times U_2 = \begin{bmatrix} 0 & 0 & 2 & 2 \\ 0 & 0 & 2 & 2 \\ 3 & 3 & 1 & 1 \\ 3 & 3 & 1 & 1 \end{bmatrix} \tag{21.2b}$$

If we multiply the matrix of Equation (21.2a) by 4 and add it to the matrix of Equation (21.2b), we obtain

$$D_4 = \begin{bmatrix} 0 & 8 & 2 & 10 \\ 12 & 4 & 14 & 6 \\ 3 & 11 & 1 & 9 \\ 15 & 7 & 13 & 5 \end{bmatrix} \tag{21.3}$$

This is a 4×4 matrix whose elements are the 16 numbers from 0 to 15.

We generalize this process by using the relation

$$D_{2n} = 4U_2 \times D_n + D_2 \times U_2 \tag{21.4}$$

21.2.2 A Program to Generate Dither Matrices

Listing 21.1 shows a program implementing Equation (21.4). We cannot use subscripts in a C program, so we use the notation `D_n` to denote the matrix D_n. The function `newd(D_n, D_2, D_2n, n)` takes as arguments pointers to the matrices D_n, D_2, and D_{2n} and the value of n. The matrices are stored as linear arrays because the C language does not handle two-dimensional arrays well.

Listing 21.1: Creation of Dither Matrices — `File lib/p_util.c (part of)`

```
/*   Implementation of D_2n = 4U_2 x D_n + D_2 x U_2 */

typedef unsigned char pPixel;
#define D_2_SIZE 2
#define D_n_SIZE n

void newd(pPixel *D_n, pPixel *D_2, pPixel *D_2n, int n)
{
     register i, j;
     int im, id;
     pPixel c, d, *v;
     int n2;

     n2 = 2*n;
     v = D_2n;
     for(i=0; i<n2; i++) {
          im = i%n; id = i/n;
```

```
            for(j=0; j<n2; j++) {
                c = *(D_2 + id*D_2_SIZE+j/n); /* c = D_2[i/n][j/n] */
                d = *(D_n + im*D_n_SIZE+j%n); /* d = D_n[i%n][j%n] */
                *v++ = 4*d + c;
            }
        }
}
```

We start with matrix D_2 from Equation (21.1). A call to

```
newd(D_2, D_2, D_4, 2)
```

produces the matrix D_4 of Equation (21.3). Then a call to

```
newd(D_4, D_2, D_8, 4)
```

produces the matrix D_8:

$$D_8 = \begin{bmatrix} 0 & 32 & 8 & 40 & 2 & 34 & 10 & 42 \\ 48 & 16 & 56 & 24 & 50 & 18 & 58 & 26 \\ 12 & 44 & 4 & 36 & 14 & 46 & 6 & 38 \\ 60 & 28 & 52 & 20 & 62 & 30 & 54 & 22 \\ 3 & 35 & 11 & 43 & 1 & 33 & 9 & 41 \\ 51 & 19 & 59 & 27 & 49 & 17 & 57 & 25 \\ 15 & 47 & 7 & 39 & 13 & 45 & 5 & 37 \\ 63 & 31 & 55 & 23 & 61 & 29 & 53 & 21 \end{bmatrix} \tag{21.5}$$

The code to produce this matrix is given in Listing 21.2.

Listing 21.2: Creation of an 8x8 Dither Matrix — `File lib/p_util.c (part of)`

```
static pPixel dmatrix[8][8];

void makedither()
{
    register i, j;
    pPixel a[4], b[4], c[16], d[64];

    a[0] = a[1] = a[2] = a[3] = 1;
    b[0] = 0;b[1] = 2;b[2] = 3;b[3] = 1;
    newd(b, b, c, 2); newd(c, b, d, 4);
    for(i=0;i<8;i++) for(j=0;j<8;j++) dmatrix[i][j] = 4*d[i*8+j];
}
```

The preceding code multiplies the final values of the matrix by a constant so that the values are distributed uniformly in the 0 to 255 interval.

As the values of D_8 vary from 0 to 63, multiplication by 4 changes the range from 0 to 252.

Another approach is to create an array of 64 thresholds, `t[]`, and replace the element of the dither matrix with value `k` by `t[k]`. Such thresholds may vary from image to image, so we can utilize best the dynamic range of the device. However, such *adaptive* halftoning may change the appearance of the image — for example, make an underexposed (too dark) image lighter. Whether this result is desirable depends on the application. Leaving manipulations of the dynamic range to another process probably is best so that halftoning keeps the overall appearance of the image.

21.2.3 Implementation of Dither Halftoning

Implementation of the overall method also is simple. If the dither matrix is $m \times m$ (i.e., $n = m^2$), we compare the pixel at (X, Y) with the D_m entry that is the $X\%m$ row and $Y\%m$ column. The key statement is

```
if(picture[x][y] > dither[x%m][y%m]) picture[x][y] = WHITE;
else  picture[x][y] = BLACK;
```

for predefined values of `WHITE` and `BLACK`. However, the preceding formulation is not efficient. Because the halftone image has 1 bit per pixel, using a byte per pixel (as the expression implies), it uses eight times more space. A byte vector whose bits correspond to pixels must be used. We have already used such a vector to store icons (see Section 3.2.1). The code of Listing 21.3 shows a function that creates such an array using the matrix `dmatrix` created by the code of Listing 21.2.

Listing 21.3: Producing a Dither Halftone — `File lib/p_util.c (part of)`

```
/*   ---- Dither program for monochrome displays -----   */
static pPixel dmatrix[8][8];
static int d_m_done = 0;
static int LSBfirst_mask[] = { 01, 02, 04, 010, 020, 040, 0100, 0200 };
static int MSBfirst_mask[] = { 0200, 0100, 040, 020, 010, 04, 02, 01 };

void dither(pImage * img, pPixel bit_vector[], int bitorder)
{
     int y, xv, j, extra_w;
     register x, k;
```

```
    register pPixel *cp;
    int *hmask;

    if(!d_m_done) {                          /* --- 1 --- */
         makedither();
         d_m_done = 1;
    }
    if(bitorder) hmask = MSBfirst_mask;
    else hmask = LSBfirst_mask;

    extra_w = img->width%8;
    img->pix_w = img->width - extra_w;       /* --- 2 --- */

    x = y = 0;     j = 0;
    cp = img->pstart;                        /* --- 3 --- */
    do{
         xv = 0;
         for(k=0; k<8; k++, x++, cp++)       /* --- 4 --- */
              if(*cp < dmatrix[y%8][x%8]) xv |= hmask[k];
         bit_vector[j++] = xv;
         if(x >= img->pix_w) { x = 0;        cp+= extra_w; y++; }
    } while(y<img->height);
}
```

The following observations are pertinent. The function is called with three arguments: a pointer to an image structure (input image), a pointer to a bit array (output), and a flag indicating whether the display device uses the most significant or the least significant bit of a byte for the leftmost pixel. The Starter Toolkit uses this function to prepare full images for one-bit displays (see Section 22.3.4).

The static variable `d_m_done` indicates whether the dither matrix has been computed (Statement 1). Statement 2 forces the output image width to be a multiple of 8. This constraint is not only convenient for the construction of the bitmap but also for its later display.

The essential work starts with Statement 3. The variable `cp` points to the input data whose value is compared in Statement 4 with values of the dither matrix. If it is below the threshold, a pixel is set to 1 by the bitwise OR operation with the appropriate mask. Figure 21.3 was produced by this method.

Figure 21.3 Halftone display of an image produced by the dither matrix of Equation (21.5).

21.2.4 Properties of Dither Halftoning

The pattern of thresholds in the dither matrix achieves a maximum dispersion of black versus white pixels in the output. For example, if we have a picture with a constant intensity of 8 and compare it to the dither matrix of Equation (21.3), we find the pattern shown in Figure 21.4, where the black squares represent pixels with values greater than the threshold, and the white squares all other pixels.

Figure 21.4 Results of applying the dither matrix of Equation (21.3) to a picture of uniform density equal to 8.

The main disadvantage of dithering is that, because of the repetition of the dither matrix, the results have an artificial texture. For example, a uniform area of intensity 60 dithered with the matrix of Equation (21.5) will have 4 black pixels for each group of 64, and they will be repeated across the area (places where D_8 has values of 60, 61, 62, and 63). This problem is visible in Figure 21.3. One apparent (but not real) remedy is to use random dither. At each pixel we select at random one number from the interval [0,63] and use it as a threshold (or threshold pointer). This method will certainly remove any regularly repeating pattern, but the result is disappointing, as Figure 21.5 shows. In addition, the computational costs are much higher for random dither than they are for ordered dither because the (pseudo)random generator function is called at each pixel. In contrast the ordered dither matrix need be computed only once.

Figure 21.5 Halftone display of an image produced by random dither.

21.3 ERROR DIFFUSION HALFTONING

21.3.1 Analysis of Error Diffusion Halftoning

The error diffusion method uses a fixed threshold, T, for all pixels, but it modifies the value of the pixels themselves. Let's consider a region of constant intensity $g > T$. The first pixel is painted white with intensity W. If we spread the error over m other pixels in proportions $p_1, p_2, \cdots, p_m$, their values will be

$$g - p_i(W - g) = (1 + p_i)g - p_i W \quad i = 1, 2, \cdots, m \tag{21.6}$$

As $g < W$, the new value will be smaller and may even be less than T. If it is not, the error will be propagated to a new set of pixels whose values will become

$$g - p_j(W - [(1 + p_i)g - p_i W]) \tag{21.7}$$

or

$$(1 + p_j(1 + p_i))g - p_j(1 + p_i)W \tag{21.7a}$$

and so on. The complete analysis of the method is rather involved, so we present a simpler version here.

The typical implementation of the method uses $m = 3$, and the error is spread to the pixels directly to the right of the current one, the one directly below, and the one right diagonally below (see Figure 21.6). In this case if the value is still above T after n pixels along a scanline, the next value will be

$$(1 + p + p^2 + \cdots + p^n)g - (p + p^2 + \cdots + p^n)W \quad (21.8)$$

where we write p for p_1.

Figure 21.6
Distribution of error from pixel C.

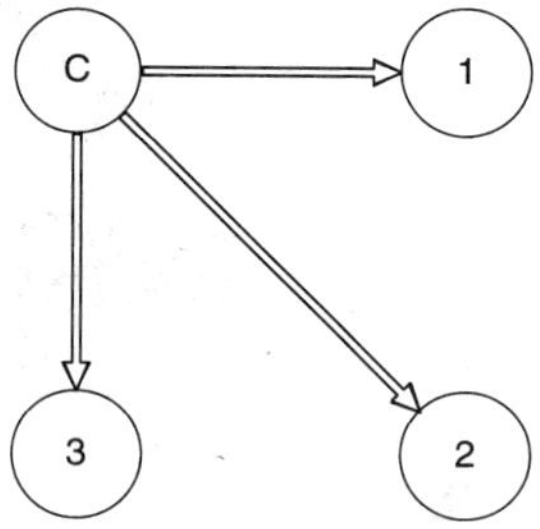

The expression multiplying g is the sum of geometric series which, according to elementary algebra, is

$$\frac{p^{n+1} - 1}{p - 1} = 1 + p\frac{p^n - 1}{p - 1} \quad (21.9)$$

Substitution then simplifies Equation (21.8) to

$$g + p\frac{p^n - 1}{p - 1}(g - W) \quad (21.10)$$

If we assume that the threshold T equals $W/2$, we can try to find the value of n when the pixel value will be less or equal to T, or

$$g + p\frac{p^n - 1}{p - 1}(g - W) \leq \frac{W}{2} \quad (21.11)$$

This inequality will hold if

$$\frac{g}{W} \leq \frac{p - 1 + 2p(p^n - 1)}{2(p^{n+1} - 1)} \quad (21.12)$$

For $p = 3/8$, the following table gives the values of the right-hand side of Equation (21.12) for various n.

n	1	2	3	∞
RHS of Equ.(21.12)	$\frac{7}{11} = 0.6364$	$\frac{65}{97} = 0.6701$	$\frac{2735}{4015} = 0.6812$	$\frac{11}{16} = 0.6875$

Note that the right-hand side of Equation (21.12) approaches an asymptote as a function of n. If g is close enough to W, no pixel will ever have a value of less than T. This outcome corresponds to the highest threshold in the dither method. The advantage of the method is the removal of the texture introduced by the dither.

21.3.2 Implementation of Error Diffusion Halftoning

Listing 21.4 shows a preliminary implementation of error diffusion halftoning based on the arrangement of Figure 21.2 with

$$p_1 = p_3 = \frac{3}{8} \quad \text{and} \quad p_2 = \frac{1}{4}$$

The particular algorithm used is due to Floyd and Steinberg. The routine reads an array `bf`, where the input is stored as a byte per pixel. If an input pixel has a value greater than the threshold value, the output pixel is set to 1.

Listing 21.4: Error Diffusion Halftoning (Preliminary Version)

```
/*   Floyd-Steinberg Algorithm: Halftone by Error Diffusion   */
typedef unsigned char pPixel;

static int mask[]; /* Initialized as in Listing 21.3 */

pPixel *error_dif(pImage *img)
{
        register x, y;
        register pPixel * cp;
        register j = 0, k = 0;
        int e;
        int g, white=255, black=0;
        int tout;
        pPixel *bit_vector;

        bit_vector = (pPixel *)malloc(img->height*img->width);
        img->pix_w = img->width - img->width%8;

        for(y=0, cp=bf; y<img->height; y++) {
                for(x=0; x<img->width; x++, cp++){
                        tout =    *cp>g?    0:   1;
                        e = tout?     *cp - black:  *cp - white;
                        /* output only if within multiple of 8 */
                        if(x < img->pix_w) {
```

```
                if(tout) xv |= mask[k];
                k++;
                if(k>7) {
                    bit_vector[j++] = xv;
                    k = 0;          xv = 0;
                }
            }
            /*  distribute error   */
            *(cp+1) += (3*e)/8;
            *(cp+img->width) += (3*e)/8;
            *(cp+img->width+1) += e/4;
        }
    }
}
```

The program of Listing 21.4 is not correct because: (a) it does not check for the possibility of overflow when the error is distributed; and (b) it also does not check for boundaries. The second problem is easy to fix. The first can be solved by copying the pixel value into an integer, adding the (positive or negative) error, and then copying a clipped value into a byte. (By *clipped* we mean replacing values above 255 by 255 and below 0 by 0.)

Such a program will still have an important weakness: It will be modifying the input data, which is not a good programming practice. We can avoid that by copying the image data into an array of `short` integers, which will solve the overflow problem as well. However, this solution requires a lot of extra memory.

21.3.3 Improved Implementation of Error Diffusion Halftoning

Listing 21.5 shows the final version of the error diffusion algorithm. It uses two integer buffer arrays where all the calculations are performed. The function `copy_line()` copies a pixel scanline into an integer array.

The program uses two integer arrays in a cyclic manner. One, pointed to by `s1`, contains the current scanline, and the other, pointed to by `s2`, contains the next scanline. At the start of each iteration, `s1` is made to point to the array that `s2` used to point to, thus advancing by one scanline. (What used to be the next scanline is made the current scanline.) Then a new scanline is copied to the space pointed at by `s2`. The program is initialized by copying the first scanline into the space pointed to by `s2`.

Listing 21.5: Error Diffusion Halftoning — `File htone.c`

```
/*   Improved Implementation of Floyd-Steinberg Algorithm    */
#include <Starter.h>

pPixel *copy_line(int int_buf[], int width, pPixel *pix_start)
{
    register int  x;
    register pPixel   *cp;
    register int  *sp;

    for(x=0, cp=pix_start, sp=int_buf; x<width; x++)  *sp++ = (*cp++)&0377;
    return(cp);
}

#define BN 4096    /* bigger than the widest expected image */

static int LSBfirst_mask[] = { 01, 02, 04, 010, 020, 040, 0100, 0200 };
static int MSBfirst_mask[] = { 0200, 0100, 040, 020, 010, 04, 02, 01 };

void error_dif(pImage *img, pPixel bit_vector[], int bitorder)
{
    int y;
    register x, k;
    pPixel * cp;
    int *s1, *s2, *st;
    static int sbf1[BN], sbf2[BN];
    register int *sq, *sp;
    int j, tout, e, *mask;
    int pmid = 127, white = 255, black = 0;

    /* select mask according to bit order of device */
    if(bitorder) mask = MSBfirst_mask;
    else mask = LSBfirst_mask;

    /* make the width multiple of eight to keep the code simple */
    img->pix_w = img->width - img->width%8;

    /* initialize and copy the first line of the image into s2 */
    cp = img->pstart;
    s1 = sbf1;    s2 = sbf2;
    cp = copy_line(s2, img->width, cp);

    j = 0;   k = 0;   bit_vector[j] = 0;
    for(y=0; y<img->height; y++) {
        /* switch s1 and s2 */
        st = s2; s2 = s1; s1 = st;
        if(y<img->height-1)  cp = copy_line(s2, img->pix_w, cp);

        for(x=0, sp=s1, sq=s2; x<img->pix_w; x++, sp++, sq++){
```

```
                    tout =    *sp > pmid?   0:   1;
                    e =  tout?     *sp - black:  *sp - white;

                    /* pack pixels into bytes */
                    if(tout) bit_vector[j] |= mask[k];
                    k++;
                    if(k>7) {
                         j++;
                         bit_vector[j] = 0;
                         k = 0;
                    }

                    /* diffuse the error */
                    if(x<img->pix_w-1) *(sp+1) += (3*e)/8;
                    if(y<img->height-1) {
                         *sq += (3*e)/8;
                         if(x<img->pix_w-1) *(sq+1) += e/4;
                    }
               }
          }
}
```

The program of Listing 21.5 can be improved in many ways. One improvement is to allocate memory for the arrays `sbf1[]` and `sbf2[]` dynamically on the basis of the `img->width` value.

21.4 MULTILEVEL AND COLOR HALFTONING

The techniques discussed so far deal with displaying a full image on a one-bit display. In certain situations the output display may have 2 or more bits. This condition is particularly true for color images when we try to squeeze 3 bytes of color information into 1 byte of refresh memory. We discuss first the modification of dithering and then of error diffusion methods for multilevel halftoning while showing how such techniques can be applied to color images.

21.4.1 Multilevel Dithering

In regular dithering we compare the value of each pixel with a threshold that varies from pixel to pixel. For multilevel thresholding we simply need a set of thresholds. For example, if we have 2 bits, then we need 3 thresholds for selecting one of the four 2-bit combinations as shown in Figure 21.7.

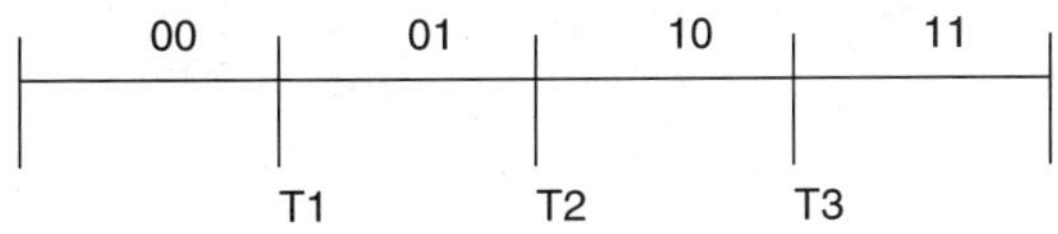

Figure 21.7 Distribution of thresholds for multibit halftoning with dither.

In general, if we have k bits, there will 2^k levels and we need $2^k - 1$ thresholds for separating them. A simple way to construct the thresholds is to normalize the dither matrix so that its values are between two intermediate levels rather than between 0 and 255. Let

```
q[0], q[1], ... , q[L-1]
```

be `L` levels with constant distance

```
dq = 256/(L-1);
```

between them. Then each element of the 8×8 matrix is multiplied by `dq/64` or `8/(L-1)` to yield a new matrix `D`. (`dq` should be declared a floating point variable.) For a pixel value at `x,y` we have to first find the interval where it belongs, say `q[i-1],q[i]`, and then compare the value with `q[i-1]+D[y%8][x%8]`. If it is less, we output `i-1`; otherwise, we output `i`.

Rather than output the bit pattern itself, we may define a value array with elements

```
v[0], v[1], ... , v[L-1]
```

where `v[i]` need not equal `i`. This method is particularly useful in dealing with color. Let `cp` be a pixel pointer of the red image and let's assume that the three most significant pixels of an 8-bit output image correspond to red. Then we have

```
static int v[8] = {0, 040, 0100, 0140, 0200, 0240, 0300, 0340};
```

If `jp` is the output pointer, the core of the C x-y loop (starting with Statement 4) in Listing 21.3 will be

```
k = *cp/dq;
if( *cp < q[k]+d[y%8][x%8] )  *jp |= v[k];
else *jp |= v[k+1];
```

21.4.2 Multilevel Error Diffusion

With dithering we have a variable threshold, but in error diffusion we change the pixel values by the difference from the threshold. That requires two steps: (1) find the proper range for the value; and (2) perform the error diffusion for the selected value. Listing 21.6 shows a code fragment that performs these operations while mapping the red values from 8 bits to 3 bits.

Listing 21.6: Error Diffusion for Color — `File lib/p_util.c (part of)`

```
/* output values */
static pPixel v3[8] = { 0, 060, 0120, 0160, 0220, 0260, 0320, 0377 };

/* error diffusion macro    */
#define spread(e, x, y, width, height, color)        \
     if(x<width-1) *(color+1) += (3*e)/8;       \
     if(y<height-1) {                     \
          *(color+width) += (3*e)/8;        \
          if(x<width-1) *(color+width+1) += e/4;     \
     }

/* Following code is part of color_htone(), called by compose_color() */
/* red_i points to integer array of red values, v index in v3[] */
/* vred is output value, e the error */
     /* select interval of input value */
     v = *red_i>>5; if(v>7) v = 7; if(v<0) v = 0;
     vred = v3[v];
     e = *red_i - vred;
     spread(e, x, y, Ip->width, Ip->height, red_i) /* no ";" */

     /* repeat for green and blue */
     /* compose color values into 8 bits */
     *cp = vred&0340 | (vgreen>>3)&034 | (vblue>>6)&03;
```

The last statement combines 3 bits from red, 3 from green, and 2 from blue into a single byte. The overall function has the same structure as the 1 bit error diffusion of Listing 21.5.

Halftoning improves significantly the appearance of a color picture displayed with few bits per color. Plates 6-9 illustrate the effects of color halftoning for two types of color images: a synthetic (Plates 6 and 7) and a scanned (Plates 8 and 9). Plates 6 and 8 show images constructed with the equivalent of the following composition operation.

```
*cp = (*red_i&0340) | (*green_i>>3)&034 | (*blue_i>>6)&03;
```

Unpleasant *contouring* artifacts are obvious. The few hues of each color used are quite far apart and are easily visible to the human eye. In Plates 7 and 9 halftoning has eliminated these artifacts. The Starter Toolkit has a function for packing 24-bit-per-pixel images into 8-bit-per-pixel images with or without halftoning.

☛ **`void compose_color(pImage *Ip, int use_htone)`**
This function converts images with 24 bits per pixel to images with 8 bits per pixel. If `Ip` does not point to a 24-bit-per-pixel image, the function returns immediately. The function assumes that the 8 most significant bits are for blue, the next 8 for green, and the last 8 for red. If `use_htone` is not 0, the conversion uses color halftoning which results in much better results but requires more time than when `use_htone` is 0. The original 24-bit data are discarded at the end of the conversion. ☜

21.5 CONCLUSIONS

Halftoning is much older than computing because it was required for printing full pictures on a medium (printed paper) that allowed no controlled variations in intensity. The following book provides additional background material.

- R. Ulichney. *Digital Halftoning.* Cambridge, Mass.: M. I. T. Press, 1987.

The Starter Toolkit provides facilities for testing image processing programs, and Listing 21.7 shows some of them. The key to all of them is the function `imgwin()`. The listing invokes the `dither()` function, which is part of the Starter Toolkit. This function can be replaced with any other halftoning technique.

Listing 21.7: Testing Halftoning Methods — `File pix_test.c`

```
#include <Starter.h>
static void img_handler();

static pImage Im[256]; /* no more than 256 images expected
                 at one time */


main(int arc, char **arv)
{
     pImage *Imp = Im;

     if(arc<2) exit(-1);
     begin_display(200, 200, "Halftone Test");
     complete_display();
     /* Read images from files whose names were
        passed as command line arguments */
     while(arc>1) {
```

```
        if(read_image( arv[1], Imp )) exit(-1); /* too drastic */
        /* Create a popup window to display that image */
        imgwin(arv[1], img_handler, Imp);
        arc--; arv++; Imp++;
    }
    wait_for_event();
}

/* Event Handler */
extern pImage * get_image();     /* Starter Toolkit function */

static void img_handler(p)
    pEvent *p;
{
    pImage *pointed_image;
    pPixel *ibits;
    pImage *new_img;

    if(p->kind == BTN_PRESS) {
        /* find image displayed in the window
           where the mouse button was pressed */
        pointed_image = get_image(p);
        /* Allocate a bit vector for the halftone */
        ibits = (pPixel *)malloc(
             pointed_image->height*
             pointed_image->width*sizeof(pPixel));
        if(!ibits) exit(-1);    /* No memory available */
        dither(pointed_image, ibits, 1);
        /* make a new pImage to display the results */
        new_img = (pImage *)malloc(sizeof(pImage));
        if(!new_img) exit(-1);
        new_img->width  = pointed_image->pix_w;
        new_img->height = pointed_image->height;
        new_img->depth  = 1;
        new_img->pstart = ibits;
        /* create a new window without handler */
        imgwin("Results", 0, new_img);
    }
}
```

The program of Listing 21.7 can be improved in at least two ways: by the addition of diagnostic messages before the exit statements and by having a panel that lets the user select the processing function.

21.6 ASSIGNMENTS

1. Implement the testing program of Section 21.5 and use it to test the error diffusion method for halftoning.
2. This assignment requires access to an image with red, green, and blue pixel values. Allocate bits to each color (for example, 3, 3, 2) and produce two composite images. For the first use the most significant bits. For the second use multibit halftoning to map the original bits to the reduced number. Display the two images and observe the difference in quality. (This assignment repeats the process that produced the pairs of Plates 6, 7 and 8, 9 so that you can see the difference in an electronic display without the interference of the printing process.)

22

Image Display in the X Window System*

Scope of the Chapter

Colormaps and visuals • Colormap types • The *Xlib* `XImage` function and its use in displaying full images and halftones • Creating images from bitmaps and icons • Image display widgets

22.1 COLORMAPS AND VISUALS

22.1.1 The Basics of Colormaps

Recall that the `Colormap` type is an XID that refers to a server structure that contains the colormap information. We can access a colormap XID in three ways: by using the `DefaultColormap()` macro, as described in Section 5.3.1; by getting the value of the colormap resource of a widget, as described in Section 22.2.2; or by creating a new colormap by a call

```
cmap = XCreateColormap( display, root_window, visual, AllocAll);
```

The first two arguments are self-explanatory. The argument `visual` is an

* **This chapter may be skipped by those who want to use only the Starter Toolkit.**

XID of type `Visual`, which is supposed to describe the hardware of the video lookup table. The argument `AllocAll` is a flag that, in essence, specifies that all colormap entries are to be under the complete control of the application. If the fourth argument has the value `AllocNone`, the server has more flexibility in the allocation of colormap entries so that they may be shared with other applications.

If an application relies on the X Toolkit and a widget set such as *Motif*, there usually is no need to create a new colormap because one already exists with no allocated color cells. We then add new colors to it by using the methods detailed in Section 5.3. The only time we need to invoke `XCreateColormap()` is when we deal with applications that display full pictures.

Application programs that deal with full pictures are usually simpler if we allocate *contiguous* colors. That is, if two pixels have values that differ by an amount `k`, the corresponding colormap indices differ by the same amount `k`. If we are using an existing colormap we may obtain a contiguous block of color cells by calling the function `XAllocColorCells()` but this will not work if not enough space is left in the map. A better solution is to create a new colormap with the fourth argument set to `AllocAll` so that we can allocate contiguous colors. To preserve the appearance of other windows on the screen we may copy some of the default colormap entries to the new map, if there is space. These procedures are followed in the Starter Toolkit (see Section 22.2). Their effect is to give priority to the correct appearance of the full picture display over that of the rest of the screen.

The call to `XCreateColormap()` initializes a data structure only and neither assigns values to the entries of the colormap nor loads it in the video lookup table. All such operations come later: Values are added by the `XAllocColors()` or `XStoreColors()` functions; the colormap is loaded onto the hardware by the window manager (usually) when the cursor enters a window.

22.1.2 Overview of Visuals

Xlib has a structure, `Visual`, that contains information about the color display abilities of the server. Because the macro `DefaultDepth()` provides information about the number of bits per pixel, `Visual` is useful mainly for information about the video lookup table. Application programs are not allowed to access the contents of the structure directly but only through the function `XGetVisualInfo()`. This function stores relevant data in a structure of type `XVisualInfo`.

You should be aware that the information provided by visuals reflects what the hardware *can do* rather than what it *actually does*. Replacing a color monitor with a monochrome monitor is easy: Simply combine the output of the red, green, and blue D/A converters. There is no way to ensure that the server is aware of such an external wiring change, so interrogating the visual structure will provide the answer that the display supports color, whereas in reality it does not.

Finding the type of the display device and adjusting the program accordingly is important for programs that are required to run on a variety of platforms. However, the information provided by the visual can tell the program with certainty only what the device *cannot do*.

For example, in the pixel painting program discussed in earlier chapters we may provide two palettes of colors: one with real color and the other with shades of gray. If the visual says that there is no support for color, the program selects the second palette. However, if the visual says that there is color support, the program may check a user-provided flag or environmental variable before selecting the real color palette.

The easiest way to deal with visuals is to select one associated with the X Toolkit widget we are using (see Section 22.2.2). If the widget has no associated visual, we can find the default visual and use it as an argument to the functions that create colormaps or image structures. We do so with the macro `DefaultVisual()`, which takes as arguments a pointer to a `Display` structure and a screen number. The latter can also be the default so that the return of

```
DefaultVisual( display, DefaultScreen(display) )
```

should suffice as an argument when a `Visual` type is required.

Because of the uncertainty about monitors, the Starter Toolkit relies on the depth information (how many bits per pixel) to decide whether to use a colormap or a halftone approximation of a full picture. When a visual is needed as argument to an *Xlib* function, it is supplied by one of the ways just described.

22.1.3 Checking Visuals

Although the Starter Toolkit does not check visuals, we describe here how it is done for those who want to write programs that take advantage of this feature of the X Window System. The key information about the video lookup table is contained in the `class` member of the information structure. There are six classes, and they are referred to by the symbolic names `DirectColor`, `PseudoColor`, `GrayScale`, `TrueColor`, `StaticColor`, and `StaticGray`.

The classes `DirectColor` and `TrueColor` imply that the refresh memory can accommodate three separate indices for the red, green, and blue colors and, of course, three D/A converters (see Figure 1.3) so that the full range of colors supported by the device can be displayed at the same time. (These classes are often found in color displays with 24 bits per pixel.) The classes PseudoColor and StaticColor imply that there is only one such index but three D/A converters. You can show color pictures on such a device but with a limited range of colors. (These classes are often found in color displays with 8 bits per pixel.) The classes GrayScale and StaticGray imply that there is only one D/A converter. Note that a device with a black and white monitor and three D/A converters will be capable of displaying only gray scale pictures even though it will have a PseudoColor class visual.

Also DirectColor, PseudoColor, and GrayScale imply that different colormaps can be stored in the video lookup table, but the other three imply that that is not possible. In other words, devices whose only visuals are TrueColor, StaticColor, or StaticGray have fixed colormaps.

Clearly, there is a hierarchy amongst the three types of devices: If a device can support PseudoColor it can also support GrayScale by setting the values of the three basic colors equal to each other. Similarly, if a device can support DirectColor it can also support PseudoColor by setting the three color indices equal to each other.

Listing 22.1 shows a function that checks on whether a particular visual is available.

Listing 22.1: Visual Checking

```
Visual *proper_visual(needed_depth)
{
     XVisualInfo  vtemp;
     XVisualInfo *vlist;
     Visual *found_visual;
     int nv;

     vtemp.screen = DefaultScreen ( display );
     vtemp.depth = needed_depth;
     vtemp.class = PseudoColor;
     vlist = XGetVisualInfo(display,
          VisualScreenMask | VisualDepthMask | VisualClassMask,
          &vtemp, &nv);
     if(nv<1) found_visual = (Visual *)0;
     else found_visual = vlist[0].visual;
     XFree(vlist);
     return( found_visual );
}
```

The function XGetVisualInfo() uses a visual information structure (vtemp in Listing 22.1) as its third argument in order to specify the desired properties for a visual. The function returns a pointer to an array of all such structures that have these properties. The second argument is a mask, indicating which properties are of interest, and the fourth points to an integer where the number of visuals with the desired properties is stored. In Listing 22.1 we specify the screen, the needed depth, and the class that is set to `PseudoColor`, which allows us to run all the examples we are discussing in this text. If no such visual is found, the function returns a null value; otherwise, it returns a pointer to the `Visual` structure of the first visual returned.

22.2 CREATING AND USING COLORMAPS

22.2.1 Color Cells and Their Allocation

The basic data structure for dealing with color is `XColor`, which we introduced in Section 5.3.1. Its definition is repeated here for convenience.

```
typedef struct {
     unsigned long pixel;
     unsigned short red, green, blue;
     char flags;
     char pad;
} XColor;
```

In Section 5.3.1 we also introduced two functions that deal with `XColor`: `XAllocColor()` and `XStoreColor()`. When the former is called, it checks on whether the colormap already contains an entry with the colors specified, and, if so, it returns the value of `pixel` for that entry. If no such entry exists, it creates a new one and returns the `pixel` value for it. In contrast, `XStoreColor()` expects a pixel value and places the color values in the entry of the colormap specified by `pixel`. Therefore `XStoreColor()` is appropriate for creating colormaps with contiguous pixel values (the type needed for full pictures). However, it can be used only if the colormap has been created with the `AllocAll` parameter or after a previous call to `XAllocColorCells` for other types of colormaps.

To fill a colormap structure with given red, green, and blue arrays of colors we must create an array of color cells and fill the individual red, green, and blue entries of each cell from the array. The code of Listing 22.2 does that.

Listing 22.2: Storing Colors — `File lib/p_fullpix.c (part of)`

```
#define MAX_CMAP_SIZE  256

int set_RGB_colors(Colormap kmap, int skip_cells,
```

```
    pPixel red[], pPixel green[], pPixel blue[], int n)
{
    register i;
    unsigned short j;
    XColor colors[MAX_CMAP_SIZE], color;

    if(no_depth()) return(-1);
    if( n+skip_cells > MAX_CMAP_SIZE) return(-1);

    /*  Create array of color cells */
    for(j=0, i=skip_cells; j<n; i++, j++) {
         colors[j].pixel  = i;
         /* shift the color values because the XColor
            structure has 16 bit members */
         colors[j].red = red[j]<<8;
         colors[j].green = green[j]<<8;
         colors[j].blue = blue[j]<<8;
         colors[j].flags = DoRed | DoGreen | DoBlue;
    }
    /*  Add new colors  */
    XStoreColors(Dpy, kmap, colors, n);
    return(0);
}
```

The argument `skip_cells` equals the number of colors that can be spared for preserving the appearance of the other windows on the screen (see Section 22.1.1). It is used as the starting value for `pixel`. The `XColor` structure has 16 bits per color — hence the need for the 8 bit shift. Once the array is filled, its contents are sent to the server by the instruction `XStoreColors()`, which is similar to `XStoreColor()` except that it transfers the contents of an array of color cells rather than a single color cell. The argument `Dpy` is a pointer to a display (server), and `no_depth()` is a function that returns 1 if there are not enough bits per pixel in the display.

22.2.2 Initializing Colormaps

Listing 22.3 shows the Starter Toolkit function that initializes colormaps. Calls to this function were described in Sections 9.2.2 and 9.3.1.

Listing 22.3: Initial Colormap — `File lib/p_fullpix.c (part of)`

```
#define FULL_DEPTH 8
static Display  *Dpy;
static Colormap cmap;
static Visual *visual; /* also needed for XImage */
static int    monochrome = 0;
```

```
int no_depth() {
     return(monochrome);
}

void init_color_map(Widget w)
{
     int screen_depth;

     Dpy = XtDisplay(w);     /* Find server used by the widget */

     /*  Find if the server screen has appropriate depth     */
     screen_depth  = DefaultDepth(Dpy, DefaultScreen ( Dpy ) );
     monochrome    = screen_depth <  FULL_DEPTH? 1: 0;
     if(monochrome) {
          /* print warning message */
     }
     else      /*  Obtain the Xt  colormap and visual    */
     XtVaGetValues(w, XtNcolormap, &cmap, XtNvisual, &visual, NULL);
}
```

The preceding code can be used as a template for any applications that deal with color. The key step is finding the depth of the display (server). If the number of bits is less than some desired value, the flag `monochrome` is set. The trivial function `no_depth()` allows the flag to be checked later by any procedure that deals with color (even if the procedure is in another module). The colormap obtained by the call to `XtVaGetValues` need not be the default colormap; it is whatever colormap the X Toolkit has assigned to the widget `w`. The colormap used by the function `add_named_color()` is obtained in this way.

Things are more complicated for widgets that are intended for the display of full pictures. The relevant code is given in Listing 22.4. The function `make_special_map()` is called after an image has been read and the color arrays of the `pImage` structure either have been read from a file or computed as shown in Listing 20.5 (Section 20.4.3). In the Starter Toolkit this function is called from inside the `imgwin()` function whose use was described in Section 20.4.2. (We discuss implementation of `imgwin()` in Section 22.4.)

Listing 22.4: Special Colormap — `File lib/p_fullpix.c (part of)`

```
void make_special_map(Widget w, pImage *img)
{
     register i;
```

```
	int cmap_offset;
	XColor colors[MAX_CMAP_SIZE];
	Colormap w_cmap;

	if(no_depth()) return;

	w_cmap = XCreateColormap( Dpy, DefaultRootWindow(Dpy),
			DefaultVisual(Dpy, DefaultScreen(Dpy)), AllocAll);

	cmap_offset = img->pixel_offset;
	/*   save some colors from the Xt   colormap    */
	if(cmap_offset) {
		for(i=0; i< cmap_offset; i++) {
			colors[i].pixel = i;
			colors[i].flags = DoRed | DoGreen | DoBlue;
		}
		XQueryColors(Dpy,  cmap, colors, cmap_offset);
		XStoreColors(Dpy, w_cmap, colors, cmap_offset);
	}
	set_RGB_colors(w_cmap, cmap_offset,
			img->red, img->green, img->blue, img->cmap_len);

	XtVaSetValues(XtParent(w), XtNcolormap, w_cmap, NULL);
}
```

If the display does not have enough depth, the function returns immediately. If there is enough depth, it creates a new colormap, which involves the following steps. If space is available, `cmap_offset` color cells are copied from the colormap identified by the call to `init_color_map()` `(cmap)` to the new map `(w_cmap)`. Normally the widget passed as an argument to `init_color_map()` is the top widget of an application and the widget passed to `make_special_map()` is that of a pop-up window for full picture display.

Copying colormaps is not done directly but it requires the following steps. First, we assign values to the `pixel` members of the `Xcolor` structure `colors`, then call `XQueryColors()`, which copies the color cells of the default colormap into `colors[]`, and then copy `colors[]` into the structure of the new colormap.

The new colormap is attached to the *parent* of the widget by the last statement. This step is a special feature of the Starter Toolkit whereby widgets for the display of full pictures are created as children of pop-up shell widgets. Having the colormap attached to a top widget is a better solution than attaching it farther down the widget tree because of potential problems with window manager implementations.

Associating the red, green, and blue arrays with each picture may appear wasteful, but it is not. If many pictures share the same colormap, we can create three static arrays with the color intensities and simply store pointers to them in the image structure, as was done in Section 20.4.3. Even if we store the full array with the image, the amount of space required (3×256 or 768 bytes) is minute compared to the space needed for the whole picture. A rather small 256×256 picture requires 65,536 bytes, or more than 80 times the space for the colormap.

22.3 IMAGE STRUCTURES

22.3.1 The XImage Structure

In Section 5.1 we introduced pixmaps as regions of the refresh memory or regions that can be copied intact into the refresh memory. Together with windows they are the X `drawable` type where pictures or graphic data can be stored. Note that a `drawable` is a server structure.

Clearly, we need a structure on the application (client) side to store data that can be copied onto a drawable (window or pixmap). This capability is essential for full pictures for which we must specify the bit pattern of each pixel in the refresh memory. (For flat and line pictures we can keep on the client only a concise description, which the plotting functions expand.) The structure provided by *Xlib* for that purpose is `XImage`. It has more than 20 members, and `pImage`, in effect, is a simplified version of it. Various *Xlib* functions manipulate the members of `XImage`, so we never have to deal with them directly.

Of the functions that manipulate this structure, the following are the most important.

The `XCreateImage()` function creates an `XImage` structure and returns a pointer to it. The data must be given in byte array form and must be preserved because the function does not copy them; it only stores a pointer to them in one of the `XImage` structure members. The number of bits per pixel is under program control.

The `XPutImage()` function copies the image data onto a drawable. If the drawable is a visible window, the image is displayed.

The `XAddPixel()` function adds a constant value to all pixels. It is useful when the colormap does not start from 0. If we use the code of Listing 22.4 to create the colormap, `img->pixel_offset` should be added to all pixels.

The `XGetImage()` function is the equivalent of a screen dump. It will copy the contents of a drawable into an `XImage` structure.

22.3.2 Where to Store Image Data

When creating an image display application, we have two choices in the implementation. Because windows may have to be redrawn repeatedly in response to exposure events, we must decide where we want to keep the pixel data. If we keep them in the client using an `XImage` structure, we must copy them to the server each time an image has to be redrawn. This copying generates substantial traffic between client and server. If we keep them in the server by storing them in a `Pixmap`, we avoid the traffic but double the server memory requirements by keeping, in effect, a backup copy of all windows that display images.

In both cases we need to create an `XImage` structure from the `pImage` structure. If we keep the pixels in the client, any time we need to redisplay the picture we need to call the function `XPutImage()` with a window argument. If we keep the pixels on the server, we must create a `Pixmap`, and call `XPutImage()` only once with the pixmap as an argument. The image can then be displayed by a call to `XCopyArea` or `XCopyPlane`, depending on the number of bits per pixel. In the following sections we present both methods as alternative implementations of the related Starter Toolkit functions `setup_z_image()` and `setup_b_image()`. These functions are called from `setup_image()`, whose use was described in Section 20.4.2 and whose code is shown in Listing 22.5.

Listing 22.5: Image Display Initialization — `File lib/p_fullpix.c (part of)`

```
void setup_image(pImage *img)
{
     if(img->depth<2) { /* 1 bit image */
          setup_j_image(img);
     }
     else {
          if(no_depth()) setup_b_image(img);
          else setup_z_image(img);
     }
}
```

The function `setup_image()` also has provisions for handling 1-bit images that are packed 8 pixels per byte. Because these images have more modest requirements than byte-per-pixel images, the Starter Toolkit always stores them in the server using the function `setup_j_image()`.

22.3.3 Creating XImages with Full Depth

When image data are kept in the client, the implementation of `setup_z_image()` is very simple, as shown in Listing 22.6.

Listing 22.6: Creating an XImage — `File lib/p_fullpix.c (part of)`

```
void setup_z_image(pImage *img)
{
     XImage *xi;

     xi = XCreateImage(Dpy, get_visual()
          8, ZPixmap, 0,      /* bit/byte arrangement */
          img->pstart, img->width, img->height, 8, 0);

     XAddPixel(xi, (long)img->pixel_offset);
     img->ID = (int)xi;
}
```

(Note: Actual implementation of the function in the Starter Toolkit is slightly different from those in Listings 22.6 and 22.7.)

The function `XCreateImage` takes 10 arguments, of which the first two are self-explanatory. (They have the values determined by the code of Listing 22.3.) The next three arguments describe the arrangement of the input data.

The third argument is the number of bits per pixel (8 in this case). The fourth argument (`ZPixmap` in Listing 22.6) is a flag that indicates the relationship between bytes and pixels. The predefined constant `ZPixmap` states that the values of pixels are stored in scanline order in the byte array, with the number of bits per pixel given by the third argument. The fifth argument is an offset value that indicates how many pixels to ignore in the beginning of the data array.

The sixth argument always must be an array of bytes containing the data (the `pstart` member of the `image` structure in the example of the table). The seventh (`img->width`) and eighth (`img->height`) arguments are self-explanatory.

The ninth argument is an integer that must be an integer submultiple of the scanline length: Only the values 8, 16, and 32 are acceptable. If the actual length of a scanline is not a multiple of these numbers, the data must be padded. The last argument has the value 0, indicating that the scanlines are contiguous.

The next statement in the listing adds to all the pixels the pixel offset that was used in creating the color map. Finally, the pointer to the `XImage` structure returned by `XCreateImage()` is stored in the `ID` member of the `pImage` structure. Casting into integer avoids compiler complaints and has no detrimental effects.

When the data are kept in the server, we need to do more work in the beginning. The implementation is shown in Listing 22.7.

Listing 22.7: Creating a Pixmap — `File lib/p_fullpix.c (part of)`

```
void setup_z_image(pImage *img)
{
    XImage *xi;
    Pixmap  px;
    static  GC gc = 0;

    xi = XCreateImage(Dpy, get_visual()
        8, ZPixmap, 0,      /* bit/byte arrangement */
        img->pstart, img->width, img->height, 8, 0);

    XAddPixel(xi, (long)img->pixel_offset);

    px = XCreatePixmap(Dpy, DefaultRootWindow(Dpy),
            img->width, img->height,
            DefaultDepth(Dpy, DefaultScreen(Dpy)) );
    img->ID = (int)px;

    if(!gc) {
        gc = XCreateGC( Dpy, DefaultRootWindow( Dpy ), NULL, NULL);
        XSetFunction(Dpy, gc, GXcopy);
    }
    XPutImage(Dpy, px, gc, xi, 0, 0, 0, 0, img->width, img->height);

    XFree((caddr_t)xi);
```

The second and third statements are the same as in Listing 22.6. Then a pixmap is created (see Section 5.1.2), and its XID is stored in `ID` member of the `pImage` structure. A trivial graphics context is created and is used to copy the `XImage` onto the pixmap. We discuss the `XPutImage()` call in Section 22.3.6. Finally, the space for the `XImage` structure is freed because we do not need it anymore.

22.3.4 Creating XImages with Halftoning

If the picture is going to be displayed by means of halftoning, the code shown in Listing 22.8 must be used. Rather than list two versions, we present one listing with conditional statements.

Listing 22.8: Creating a Halftone Image — `File lib/p_fullpix.c (part of)`

```
void setup_b_image(pImage *img)
{
    pPixel *ibits;
```

```
    int bitorder;
    XImage *xi;
#ifdef SERVER_STORE
    Pixmap  px;
    static  GC gc = 0;
#endif

    bitorder = BitmapBitOrder(display)==MSBFirst? 1: 0;     /* -- 1 -- */
    ibits = (pPixel *)malloc(img->height*img->width);
    /* error checking needed if ibits is null */

    dither( img, ibits, bitorder ); /* Function of Listing 21.3 */

    xi = XCreateImage(Dpy, get_visual(),                   /* -- 2 -- */
        1, XYBitmap, 0,    /* bit/byte arrangement */
        ibits, img->pix_w, img->height, 8, 0) );

#ifdef SERVER_STORE
    px = XCreatePixmap(Dpy, DefaultRootWindow(Dpy),
            img->width, img->height,
            DefaultDepth(Dpy, DefaultScreen(Dpy)) );
    img->ID = (int)px;

    if(!gc) {
        gc = XCreateGC( Dpy, DefaultRootWindow( Dpy ), NULL, NULL);
        XSetFunction(Dpy, gc, GXcopyInverted);
    }
    XPutImage(Dpy, px, gc, xi, 0, 0, 0, 0, img->width, img->height);

    XFree((caddr_t)xi);
#else
    img->ID = (int)xi;
#endif
}
```

In bitmaps each byte contains 8 pixels and, depending on the server hardware, the leftmost pixel may be either the most significant or the least significant bit. The macro `BitmapBitOrder()` returns one of the predefined constants `MSBFirst` or `LSBFirst`. To have halftoning functions that are independent of the X Window System, these predefined values are translated to 0 or 1 by Statement 1 and that result is used as the third argument to the halftoning function. The byte array `ibits` is where the halftoning function will store the data, pixel per bit. The call to the function `XCreateImage()` differs from that of Listing 22.6 only in the middle arguments. Now, there is 1 bit per pixel, the format is a bitmap indicated by the flag `XYBitmap`, there is no initial offset, and the data will be taken from the array `ibits`. As `XCreateImage()` does not copy the data but only stores a pointer to them, the data pointed to by `ibits` should not be freed.

In Listing 22.8 the function `dither()` is used for halftoning but any of the other functions of Chapter 21 could be used instead. To keep an integer number of bytes per scanline, the halftoning functions may truncate the width of the image and return the new value in `pix_w`. Better solutions are possible, but we opted for simplicity here.

The code for server storage is identical to the code of Listing 22.7.

22.3.5 Images from Bitmaps and Icons

Sometimes we need to display a bitmap as an image. We can create a pixmap directly from such data (without creating an `XImage`) by using the *Xlib* function `XCreatePixmapFromBitmapData()`. Listing 22.9 shows the relevant Starter Toolkit implementation.

Listing 22.9: Creating a 1-Bit Image (Version A) — `File lib/p_fullpix.c (part of)`

```
void setup_j_image(pImage *img)
{
     int  Scr = DefaultScreen(Dpy);
     Pixmap   px;
     unsigned long fg, bg;

     /* Find the proper values for black and white pixels */
     fg = BlackPixel(Dpy, Scr);
     bg = WhitePixel(Dpy, Scr);
     flip_bytes(img);

     px = XCreatePixmapFromBitmapData(Dpy, DefaultRootWindow(Dpy),
          img->pstart, img->width, img->height,
          fg, bg, DefaultDepth(Dpy, DefaultScreen(Dpy)) );

     img->ID = (int)px;
}
```

If we do not use server storage, we can create an `XImage` by the following code. (The implementation of the Starter Toolkit always uses server storage because such images are usually small.)

Listing 22.10: Creating a 1-Bit Image (Version B)

```
void setup_j_image(pImage *img)
{
     XImage *xi;

     xi = XCreateImage(Dpy, get_visual(),
          1, XYBitmap, 0,
          img->pstart, imp->width, img->height, 8, 0);
      img->ID = (int)xi;
}
```

A related topic is the creation of images used to label selection panel buttons. In this case we have two choices: Create a pixmap for the icon and store it in the server, or create an `XImage` and store it in the client. As we mentioned in Section 9.3.3, the first solution is used in *Motif* and the second in *OLIT*. The function `icon_image()` was used there, and Listing 22.11 shows its implementation.

Listing 22.11: Creating an XImage from an Icon — `File lib/p_fullpix.c (part of)`

```
XImage *icon_image(char *cv, int w, int h, int inconsistent)
{
     XImage *xi;

     xi = XCreateImage(Dpy, visual,
          1, XYBitmap, 0,     /* bit/byte arrangement */
          cv, w, h, 8, 0);

     if(inconsistent) {
          if(BitmapBitOrder(Dpy)==MSBFirst)
               xi->bitmap_bit_order = LSBFirst;
          else xi->bitmap_bit_order = MSBFirst;
          if(ImageByteOrder(Dpy)==MSBFirst) xi->byte_order = LSBFirst;
          else xi->byte_order = MSBFirst;
     }
     return(xi);
}
```

The call to `XCreateImage()` is similar to Statement 2 of Listing 22.8. The icon bit vector is used in place of the bit vector returned by the halftoning function. The block of statements executed when the `inconsistent` flag is set may be needed if the icon has been created by an editor that has a different view of the world.

Listing 22.12 shows a function for creating pixmaps for icons; it was used in Section 9.3.3 for creating the *Motif* icon buttons.

Listing 22.12: Create a Pixmap from an Icon — `File lib/p_fullpix.c (part of)`

```
Pixmap icon_pixmap(char *iconbits, int width, int height, depth )
{
    return
        XCreatePixmapFromBitmapData( Dpy, DefaultRootWindow(Dpy),
        iconbits, width, height, depth, 0,
        DefaultDepth(Dpy, DefaultScreen ( Dpy ) ) );
}
```

22.3.6 Image Display with the Starter Toolkit

The `put_image()` function is used for image display in the Starter Toolkit. It is shown in Listing 22.13 with a conditional definition that corresponds to the implementation of the image setup functions discussed in the preceding two sections.

Listing 22.13: Displaying an Image — `File lib/paper_use.c (part of)`

```
void put_image(pImage *img, int x, int y)
{
#ifdef SERVER_STORE
    Pixmap px = (Pixmap)img->ID;

    if(no_depth()) XCopyPlane(Dpy, px, c_window, c_gc, 0, 0,
        img->width, img->height, x, y, 1);
    else          XCopyArea(Dpy, px, c_window, c_gc, 0, 0,
        img->width, img->height, x, y);
#else
    if(img->depth>1) XPutImage(Dpy, c_window, c_gc,
        (XImage *)img->ID, 0, 0, x, y, ximg->width, ximg->height);
    else {
    /*  The Starter Toolkit always uses server store for
        images with depth 1. Repeat previous block of code*/
    }
#endif
}
```

The functions `XCopyArea()` and `XCopyPlane()` were discussed in Sections 5.1.2 and 5.4.1, so we focus here on `XPutImage()`. Most of the arguments are self-explanatory. The fifth and sixth indicate the `x` and `y` offsets from the upper left corner of the image; the ninth and tenth indicate the dimensions of the image to be copied. The values shown in Listing 22.13 apply to display of an entire image. When `XPutImage` was used in Listing 22.7, the fifth and sixth arguments were 0 because the upper left corner of the image was placed on the upper left corner of the pixmap.

If the image format is `ZPixmap`, the color is determined only by the colormap. If the format is `XYBitmap`, pixels with a value of 1 are shown in the foreground color and those with a value of 0 in the background color, *as determined by the graphics context.*

The code of the `setup_` functions may be combined with the display function code, but that is wasteful because the same image may be displayed repeatedly in response to exposure events. In Section 22.4 we show an example of an integration.

22.4 AN IMAGE DISPLAY PROTOTYPE WIDGET

Creating a window for displaying full pictures involves a certain core of operations, which justifies creating a prototype widget in the same way we created a slider prototype widget in Section 9.2.4. This is what the function `imgwin()` (introduced in Section 20.4.2) does. Implementation of this function is shown in the three parts of Listing 22.14. The first part contains the declarations, including a state structure.

Listing 22.14.1: Full Picture Widget (Part 1) — `File lib/pixwin.c (part of)`

```
/*   Image Processing Widget Prototype     */
#include <X11/StringDefs.h>
#include <X11/Intrinsic.h>
#include <X11/Shell.h>
#include <Paper.h>
#include <Starter.h>

typedef struct {
     pImage Im;
     pImage iIm;
     char *label;
     } pixwin_state;

extern Widget create_paper_widget();
extern Widget img_window();
extern pixwin_state  ** paper_hanger();   /* actually XtPointer */

void imgwin(), copy_image(), copy_cmap_info();
```

The first part of the code of `imgwin()` is straightforward. The image structure *and all the data* are copied in the state structure so that they can be accessible while the widget is in use, even if the original memory locations are freed. (The actual code in the Starter Toolkit is slightly different.)

Listing 22.14.2: Full Picture Widget (Part 2) — `File lib/pixwin.c (part of)`

```
void imgwin(char *label, int (*handler)(), pImage *img);
{
    Widget pix_widget = 0;
    pixwin_state *pwp = (pixwin_state *)malloc(sizeof(pixwin_state));
    struct image *Imp;

    mk_label(&(pwp->label), label);
    copy_image(img, &(pwp->Im));
    copy_image(img, &(pwp->iIm));
    Imp = &(pwp->Im);

    pix_widget =  create_paper_widget(0, handler,
            Imp->width, Imp->height, PopUpChild, label);
    XtAddCallback(pix_widget, XtNredrawCallback, pixdraw, Imp);

    /* Take care of color maps */
    if(Imp->depth>1) {
        if(!Imp->cmap_type) prepare_gray(Imp);
        make_special_map(pix_widget, Imp);
    }

    setup_image(Imp); /* last thing, after color maps */

    *paper_hanger(pix_widget) = pwp;
    popup(pix_widget, 1);

    if(!no_depth()) image_tile(pix_widget, Imp);
}
```

The last statement arranges that the image itself be used as tile for drawing operations. In this way we can use exclusive OR to draw on top of an image display window.

Two convenience functions allow accessing the widget state from other programs.

Listing 22.14.3: Full Picture Widget (Part 3) — `File lib/pixwin.c (part of)`

```
char * get_pix_name(pEvent *p)
{
     PaperWidget w;
     pixwin_state *pwp;

     w = (PaperWidget)p->origin;
     pwp = *paper_hanger( w );

     return pwp->label;
}

pImage * get_image(pEvent *p)
{
     PaperWidget w;
     pixwin_state *pwp;

     w = (PaperWidget)p->origin;
     pwp = *paper_hanger( w );

     return &(pwp->iIm);
}
```

22.5 CONCLUSIONS

We discussed the *Xlib* facilities for displaying full pictures, including colormaps and image structures. Full pictures are big consumers of memory and usually demand their own colormaps. Displaying full pictures with color (as opposed to grayscale) on 8-bit displays is a challenge but it can be done with color halftoning.

The handling of colormaps with the X Window System is more complicated than with many earlier graphics systems. The reason is that X tries to preserve the proper appearance for all windows in a display and therefore imposes various restrictions on the use of colormaps. This approach is reasonable for graphical user interfaces, but it creates complications for graphics and image processing applications where user attention may be focused only on one or two windows.

If a display with 24 or more bits per pixel is available, displaying full pictures in color at the same time as other applications presents no problem. The same is impossible for displays with, say, only 8 bits per pixel. For such displays the Starter Toolkit provides for the creation of pop-up windows (with the `imgwin()` function) that have their own colormaps. When the cursor is in one of those windows, the window manager loads the appropriate colormap to show properly the image in that window.

22.6 ASSIGNMENTS

1. Write a program to list *all* visuals supported by a display device. Use the code of Listing 22.1 as a starting point.
2. Create an image wherein the color varies smoothly along the horizontal axis from pure red to pure green.
3. Listing 22.4 copies as many colors from the X Toolkit colormap as there is space for accommodating them in the image colormap. Modify the latter to examine the number of colors actually used in the former and copy only those, if they are fewer than the available space.
4. The Starter Toolkit uses a compile time flag for deciding whether to store images in the server. Use the code of Listings 22.6-22.10 and 22.14 to create a prototype image widget that makes that decision at run time. Then compare the performance of the program under the two options.

A

Object-Oriented Programming

Scope of the Appendix
Overview of the main features of object-oriented programming

A.1 INTRODUCTION

Object-oriented programming is a technique that has been used to manage the complexity of large programs. Although it is not a panacea for all software development ills, it is a helpful technique and it has been used throughout this text. Its first visible use was in the definition of graphins in Section 3.4 (Listing 3.6). This Appendix provides an overview of the topic for those of you who may be unfamiliar with it.

Some confusion exists between object-oriented programming and languages that *support* object-oriented programming. Such languages (for example, C++) make object-oriented programming easier but object-oriented programs can be written in *any* language. Conversely, writing a program in, say, C++ does not guarantee that it is object-oriented, or that it takes full advantage of the technique.

The X Window System relies heavily on object-oriented programming even though the programs are written in C, which is not a language that supports the technique. This makes programs a bit more cumbersome than if they had been written in C++, but most of the advantages of object-oriented programming can be obtained with some careful planning. Listing A.1 (a copy of Listing 3.6) shows a typical object definition.

Listing A.1: Graphin Structure — `File graphin.h`

```
typedef struct graphin {
    int icon;                   /* its shape */
    int color;                  /* its color */
    int x, y;                   /* its location */
    int dx, dy;                 /* its motion */
    int status;                 /* for future expansion */
    int nature;                 /* for future expansion */
    void (*draw_me)(struct * graphin);    /* function to draw a graphin */
    void (*move_me)(struct * graphin);    /* function to move a graphin */
} graphin;
```

We can distinguish two kinds of elements: *members* such as `status`, which are distinct for each *instance* of an object; and *methods*, which are pointers to functions. When a graphin is to be drawn, its drawing function is called with a pointer to the object as argument; for example,

```
graphin G1;
/* ... */
G1.draw_me(&G1);
```

In a language that supports object-oriented programming (C++, for example) the corresponding call would have been simpler:

```
G1.draw_me();
```

However, at the expense of slightly longer expressions, we can have object-oriented programs in C.

Another example of an object is the basic window object defined in Listing 8.1. The object has members such as its dimension and label and methods such as the functions for redrawing the window and handling user input.

In general, members of an object are unique to the object, whereas methods are shared. This distinction does not mean that two graphins cannot have the same icon. They can, but each one has a separate memory location where the icon identifier is stored. However, the code for the methods is kept outside the object structure.

A.2 ENCAPSULATION

A major advantage of object-oriented programming is *encapsulation* or *information hiding*. Many of the members of an object may be hidden from applications programmers, thus simplifying the code they have to write and also reducing the possibility of errors. The Starter Toolkit used in the examples of this text relies heavily on such information hiding. For instance, the function `draw_window`, in effect, creates a basic object for which applications programmers supply only certain items: the redrawing and event handling functions, the label, and the dimensions of the window. All other properties of the window and the functions associated with it are hidden.

The game program in Chapter 3 provides a good illustration of the advantages of encapsulation. We can introduce new graphin types without changing the main routines. For example, instead of icons we may use polygons (Section 13.1.2), sets of planes (Assignment 5 of Chapter 19), or pixmaps (Assignment 8 of Chapter 20).

Object-oriented programming also is a software management tool. If a team of programmers undertakes a task, the more experienced members may write the code for the object library while the less experienced staff use the objects to create application programs. That is exactly the role of the X Window System Toolkit described in Chapter 8. Applications programmers do not have to create windows from scratch but, instead, they can use *widgets* which are windows with certain functionality associated with them. The Starter Toolkit creates additional objects from the objects of the X Toolkit, further simplifying the writing of simple application programs. For example, the function `vis_window()` relies on an object for which the application must provide only a method (the redrawing function) and two members (the dimensions of the window).

One of the best examples of the power of encapsulation is unrelated to graphics but comes from an application that is familiar to everyone: the calculation of dates. Calculations involving dates tend to be rather tricky because the rules used by calendars are the results of history and culture rather than concern for efficient computation. Finding the date 145 days after February 20, 1994, is not a trivial matter. If we add 145 to 20 we get 165, which clearly, is not a legitimate date. We have to start subtracting the number of days in the month while incrementing the month until we find a legitimate date. In this example we find that the date 145 days after February 20, 1994, is July 15, 1994.

Clearly, we need a function that will perform this computation. Even better would be a set of functions that perform all calculations that have to do with dates. For example, functions could be written to find the number of days between two particular dates, parsing a string such as "Feb. 20, 1994" to obtain the three numbers for day, month, and year, etc. The problem is how to keep track of all these functions. We can achieve that by creating an object that includes not only the elements of the date (day, month, and year) but also the functions that make computations involving dates. Listing A.2 provides a simple example.

Listing A.2: Date Object

```
/*   Definition that should be in a file date.h     */
typedef struct {
     int day, month, year;
     int    (*make)();    /* construct date from string */
     void   (*incr)();    /* add days to date */
     void   (*show)();    /* construct string from date */
} date;
```

The structure includes pointers that can be set to three functions that manipulate dates. (A more realistic example would have more functions than three.) After setting up this structure, a programmer will have to write only a statement of the form

```
a->incr(a, n, b);
```

where `a` and `b` are pointers to `date` structures and `n` is the number of days to be added to the date pointed to by `a` to find a new date that is stored in the structure pointed to by `b`. The program would need to declare the pointers with a statement

```
date *a, *b;
```

and then create the structures by calling an initialization function, such as the one shown in Listing A.3. This function allocates memory for the structure and also binds the pointers to functions with the real functions.

Listing A.3: Initialization of the Date Object

```
#include <date.h>
extern int  date_from_string();
extern void add_to_date(), show_date();

init_date(Dpp)
     date **Dpp;
{
     (*Dpp) = (date *)malloc(sizeof(date));
     (*Dpp)->make = date_from_string;
     (*Dpp)->incr = add_to_date;
     (*Dpp)->show = show_date;
}
```

What we have achieved by this mechanism is to *hide* the specific numbers of `day`, `month`, and `year` from programmers who use the library. These members can be accessed only through the functions `make()`, `incr()`, and `show()`. Information hiding protects against errors, such as changing one number without changing others that depend on it and against assigning illegal values. A language, such as C++, that supports object-oriented programming allows the overloading of operators so that instead of writing

```
a->incr(a, n, b);
```

we can write

```
b = a + n;
```

This example, shows that the proper design of objects and implementation of the necessary methods are essential to the successful use of object-oriented programming.

A.3 MESSENGER FUNCTIONS

A special case of information hiding is the use of *messenger* functions. Consider the function that must redraw a window in response to an `Expose` event. This function must be known to the event handler of the window, but it must be written by the applications programmer who knows what should be in the display.

We could declare a global variable that is a pointer to a function and have both the event handling code and the applications code share it. However, global variables are not good programming practice. Because they can be changed by any part of the program and because different parts may be written by different people at different times, they are one of the most likely places for errors to occur.

Instead, we can call the messenger function `set_redraw()` which assigns its argument to an underlying object. A relatively simple example of a messenger function was shown in Section 2.5 in connection with text entry. We may think of the module that collects typed text as a single object with members that are the static variables declared in Listing 2.9.2 and methods comprising the functions `init_text()` and `collect_text()`. The function `set_string_use()` is a messenger function telling the object what to do with the typed text. (See the Assignment at the end of this Appendix for more on this topic.)

If we use the material of Section 8.1 and let `drawing_window` denote a static structure in the file that has the declarations for the drawing area, the following will be a possible implementation of the messenger function

```
set_redraw().

set_redraw(f)
     int (*f)();
{
     drawing_window.draw = f;
}
```

The statement

```
set_redraw(show);
```

in the application module sends a message to the window module that the function `show()` should be called in response to an `Expose` event. Similarly, the messenger function `set_handler()` can be implemented as

```
set_handler(f)
     int (*f)();
{
     drawing_window.events = f;
}
```

With such functions, applications programmers do not have to worry about the internal structure of the window modules. If they decide to create applications with multiple drawing windows, the same approach will be valid if the messenger functions take a second argument to identify the window.

Caution: Actual implementation of these two functions in the Starter Toolkit is quite different. They call messenger functions of the X Toolkit in turn rather than access widget members directly (see Section 9.1.2).

A.4 INHERITANCE

New objects may be created from old ones by providing their structures with additional new members while retaining the members of the old structure. Languages that support object-oriented programming (e.g., C++) provide convenient mechanisms for inheritance. The process is somewhat awkward in C, but using it to keep some order among the various object types is a good idea. Of the various solutions to this problem, none is entirely satisfactory. We describe here the approach used in the X Toolkit and use the graphin example to illustrate it.

Suppose that we want graphins to have various possessions depending on their type. Some may have weapons, others may have magic spells, and so on. Listing A.4 shows the definition for a wizard graphin.

Listing A.4: Wizard Definition

```
/*   Definitions that could be in graphin.h */

typedef struct wiz_part {
     int n_Spells;
     int n_spells;
     void (*Spell)(struct *wiz_part);
     void (*spell)(struct *wiz_part);
} wiz_part

typedef struct {
     graphin  basis;
     wiz_part w;
} wizard
```

The new object contains a copy of the parent object (graphin, in this case) and a new structure. If we declare

```
wizard A;
```

then the drawing function will be called as

```
A.basis.draw_me(&(A.basis));
```

A somewhat simpler syntax could be achieved by declaring the following macro.

```
#define graphin_draw(G) G.basis.draw_me(&(G.basis))
```

Then we could just call

```
graphin_draw(A);
```

To cast a spell we need a call such as

```
A.wiz_part.spell(&(A.wiz_part));
```

which could be abbreviated through the macro

```
#define wizard_spell(W) W.wiz_part.spell(&(W.wiz_part))
```

to

```
wizard_spell(A);
```

A warrior graphin could be constructed similarly as

```
typedef struct war_part {
     /* ... */
} war_part;
```

```
typedef struct {
     graphin  basis;
     war_part w;
} wizard
```

We can create additional new classes by combining the existing structures with new ones. For example, a flying wizard would be

```
typedef struct flight_part {
     /* ... */
} flight_part;

typedef struct {
     graphin      basis;
     wiz_part w;
     flight_part  f;
} flying_wizard;
```

A.5 CONCLUSIONS

We outlined the main concepts of object-oriented programming: encapsulation, messenger functions, and inheritance. We also demonstrated that the technique can be implemented in any language, including C.

A.6 ASSIGNMENT

Modify the code of Section 2.5 so that the static variables and the functions belong to an object structure. Associating a distinct object with each window results in a program allowing users to type simultaneously in two windows, something that cannot be done now. In the current version, when a user starts typing in one window, `name_started` is set and subsequent calls to `init_text()` cause an immediate return. With the proposed organization, each object will have a different status member so that, if `o1.name_started` has been set to 1, we could still call the function `o2.init_text(&o2, ... )` and initialize another text entry process.

B

The Starter Toolkit

Scope of the Appendix
Organization of the Starter Toolkit • Structures used by the toolkit (the `Starter.h` file) • Documentation of the functions

B.1 ORGANIZATION

We have discussed the Starter Toolkit throughout the text. Most of its functions were documented in the chapters dealing with graphics, and some of its implementation code was used for case studies in the chapters dealing with X. Here we present an overview of its organization and the thinking behind its design.

A major motivation behind its development was the realization that the X Toolkit and widget sets such as *Motif* were oriented primarily toward supporting the development of Graphical User Interfaces (GUIs). Therefore widgets tended to have a predefined form that could be changed by varying certain parameters. This situation is very different from the normal graphics case, in which the goal of the application is to create a completely new display in a window.

Another motivation is the need to enable those with limited programming skills to write interesting programs quickly while introducing them to the concepts used in the X Window System in general and the X Toolkit in particular. The need for a gradual transition requires that the complexity of

X be hidden in a controlled way and that the simplified function calls can be mixed with calls to *Xt* and *Xlib* functions.

Integration of the Starter Toolkit with the rest of the X Window System is particularly important for programming assignments that go beyond those of an introductory course. You can take a program written with the Starter Toolkit and enhance it by calling directly functions of the X Toolkit or *Xlib*.

The core of the Starter Toolkit is `PaperWidgetClass`, a new widget class, which is a subclass of `Core` and supports not only the various graphics operations but also the selection mechanism of X. As a result, it can be used either as stand-alone or within another widget set, such as *Athena*, *OLIT*, or *Motif*.

The Starter Toolkit has the concept of an *active widget* which provides the display, window, and graphics context arguments needed by the *Xlib* functions. Therefore, applications can execute drawing operations with simple calls such as `put_line(x1, y1, x2, y2)`. The toolkit also provides facilities for prototype widgets, as described in Chapters 9 and 22.

Two aspects of the Starter Toolkit have been deliberately left out of the main text: Selections and Resources, even though the toolkit supports both. The following code fragment, for example, is part of an event handler (similar to `get_string` discussed in Section 2.5.3) that for text entry starts by copying the selection in the text area.

```
void typist(pEvent *p)
{
     switch(p->kind) {
     case BTN_PRESS:
          if(name_started) return(0);
          /* ... */
          get_selection(grab_text);
          return;
     /* ... */
}
/*   Selection Callback */
grab_text(char *s)
{
     int sel_w, sel_h;

     strcpy(str_buffer, s);
     x1 = x0 + put_NL_text(str_buffer, x0, y0, 1, &sel_w, &sel_h);
     y1 = y0 + sel_h;
     /* ... */
}
```

The selection mechanism is both too complex and of limited interest to elementary graphics to justify its inclusion in an introductory text. (However, we discussed the graphics needed to implement some operations related to selections in Section 14.3.5.)

Resources are described in the text only in conjuction with the X Toolkit in order to explain the nature of the arguments of its functions. The resource mechanism is useful for customizing frequently used programs, but that is not the case with programs written as class assignments or introductory student projects. Most such programs are never used again after they are graded.

The code of the Starter Toolkit is in the directory `Starter`, which includes three subdirectories: `pwidget`, `include`, and `lib`. The contents of each directory with brief comments on their files follow.

- **`pwdiget`**

  Implementation of the paper widget. Files:

  `Paper.h`: public definitions, linked to the `include` directory.

  `PaperP.h`: private definitions.

  `paper.c`: functions of the paper widget .

- **`include`**

  Definitions of the public Starter Toolkit structures.

  `Paper.h`: public definitions of the paper widget, linked to the `pwidget` directory.

  `Starter.h`: definitions of the structures and event types used in the application programs and listed in Section B.2.

- **`lib`**

  Functions of the Starter Toolkit.

  `dialog.c`: Prototype widget for dialogue.

  `p_fullpix.c`: Functions for dealing with colormaps and other needs of full pictures.

  `p_panel.c`: Selection panels and container widget functions. This file must be compiled with one of three flags indicating the widget set used — *Athena*, *Motif*, or *OLIT*.

  `p_util.c`: Various utility functions used for tasks such as text collection and halftoning.

  `paper_mate.c`: Creation of paper widget instances.

  `paper_use.c`: Graphics functions including those that manipulate the graphics context; includes the function `draw_area` that selects the active paper widget.

  `pixwin.c`: Prototype widget for the display of full images.

  `slider.c`: Prototype slider widget.

  `x_rfile.c`: I/O for image files; copy supplied deals only with SUN raster files and should be rewritten for other image formats; contains only one feature of the Starter Toolkit, the `pImage` structure.

`xdef.c`: Structure with event names; used for debugging only.

Warning *Not all facilities of the Starter Toolkit are used in the text. This appendix includes information about structures or functions that are not used elsewhere. They are intended only for those who want to use the toolkit for applications beyond those described in the text.*

B.2 STRUCTURES AND DEFINITIONS: THE Starter.h FILE.

Listing B.1 contains the definition file `Starter.h`.

Listing B.1: Structures and Definitions — `File include/Starter.h`

```
#ifndef STARTER

/*   Paper Widget Types used by paper_mate.c    */
#define NormalChild          0
#define PopupChild_P         1
#define PopupChild           2
#define IndependentChild     3
#define PopupChild_Q         4

/*   Image Related Types     */
typedef unsigned char pPixel;

typedef struct image {
     pPixel *pstart;
     int width;
     int height;
     int depth;
     int ID;
     int pix_w;              /* used by halftoning process */
     int pixel_offset;       /* to accommodate other colors */
     int cmap_type;          /* used to avoid colormap duplications */
     int cmap_len;
     pPixel *red, *green, *blue;
}  pImage;

/*   Definitions for Menus   */
struct action_pair {
     char *label;  /* item label */
     int (*fun)(); /* function called when selection is made */
};
```

```
struct value_pair {
     char *label;  /* item label */
     int value;    /* value returned when selection is made */
};

typedef struct action_pair pAction;
typedef struct value_pair  pValue;

/*   Definitions for Events */
#define LEFT              1 /* Left button pressed/released/dragged */
#define MIDDLE            2 /* Middle button pressed/released/dragged */
#define RIGHT             3 /* Right button pressed/released/dragged */
#define BTN_PRESS         4 /* Left button pressed */
#define BTN_RELEASE       8 /* Button (any) released */
#define MOVE             12 /* The pointing device moved */
#define DRAG             16 /*Motion with a button pressed */
#define KEY_RETURN       20 /* A return or new line key was pressed */
#define KEY_ERASE        24 /* A back-space or delete key was pressed */
#define ESCAPE           28 /* The ''escape'' key was pressed */
#define KEY_NORMAL       32 /* A printable key was pressed on the keyboard */
#define NULL              0 /* Default (action of no interest to the program) */
/*   Composite kind+key */
#define LEFT_PRESS        5 /* Left button pressed */
#define MIDDLE_PRESS      6 /* Middle button pressed */
#define RIGHT_PRESS       7 /* Right button pressed */
#define LEFT_RELEASE      9 /* Left button pressed */
#define MIDDLE_RELEASE   10 /* Middle button pressed */
#define RIGHT_RELEASE    11 /* Right button pressed */
#define LEFT_DRAG        17 /*Motion with Left button pressed */
#define MIDDLE_DRAG      18 /*Motion with Middle button pressed */
#define RIGHT_DRAG       19 /*Motion with Right button pressed */

struct pen {
     int x, y; /* location of the cursor */
     int kind; /* what kind of event occurred */
     char key; /* what key was struck on the keyboard, if any */
     long origin;  /* where it came from (widget) */
};

typedef struct pen pEvent;

/*   Other definitions  */
typedef struct {
     short x, y;
     } pPoint;

#define STARTER
#endif
```

B.3 FUNCTIONS

This section provides documentation for most (but not all) functions of the Starter Toolkit. The omissions are functions that are used to support other functions of the toolkit. The section number where a function is first used in the text is given at the end of each item.

Notation: Functions are marked according to the following system.

- ☛☛ Functions used frequently in the examples of the text. Most assignments can be carried out with them alone.
- ☛ Other functions discussed in the graphics chapters of the text.
- ❏ Functions requiring either knowledge of the X Toolkit and/or *Xlib* (starred chapters), or used in conjunction with functions that need such knowledge.
- ☞ Functions not discussed in the text.
- ❖ (Used in addition to one of the above symbols.) Functions that depend on another widget set: *Athena*, *Motif*, or *OLIT*. The widget set must be selected at compilation time. If none is selected, the library of the Starter Toolkit will be created but without these functions. Most simple programs (such as those described in Chapters 1 and 2) do not need them.

☛☛ **`void active_cursor(int n)`**
Make the visible cursor be the one with index `n` in the icon array. The number `n` returned by a previous call to either `make_cursor()` or `make_color_cursor()`. If `n` is negative, the default cursor becomes visible. The program will fail if it is called with a nonnegative value that is not one returned by a call to the cursor creation functions. (Section 3.2.3.)

☞ **`int add_RGB_color(pPixel red, pPixel green, pPixel blue)`**
Create an entry in the colormap with the color values passed as arguments and return the index of the colormap entry. If there is no space for the new color, the function returns `-1`. In general, using `add_named_color()` instead of this function is better. Use `add_RGB_color()` in such programs as a slider that uses gradual changes in color to indicate value. (Not discussed in the text.)

☛ **`void add_colors_by_name(pValue clist[])`**
Only the labels of the value pair list need be initialized and each name must be preceded by a "-" — for example, `-white`. Then, the function `add_named_color()` is called for each named color (after skipping the first character), and the returned value is stored in the corresponding value member of the structure. If the value returned by `add_named_color()` is negative, the value of the previous entry is copied except for the first element when the value is set to 0. The function returns when a 0 label is found in `clist[]`. (Section 7.5.1.)

☛ **`int add_named_color(char *cname)`**
Find the named color in the database of the X Window System and determine whether its red, green, and blue values are in the colormap used by the application. If not, make a new entry in the colormap as long as there is space. In either case return the index of the colormap entry. If the name is not in the database or if it is found but there is no space for the new color, the function returns `-1`. (Section 2.6.2.)

☛ **`int add_work( int (*f)() )`**
The function `f()` will be called when no events are waiting in the queue. The return of `f()` is important. If it is nonzero, the function is removed from the system. See also the functions `grab_draw_area()` and `release_draw_area()`. (Section 3.4.2.)

☛ **`int back_color(char *cname)`**
Set the background color to the given name, (e.g., "red," "orange," etc.). It returns 0 if the color has been set successfully; otherwise, it returns `-1`. (Section 1.4.3.)

❑ **`Widget base_widget()`**
Return the widget that is to be used as parent of a drawing widget. It is either a container widget or a pop-up shell. (Section 9.3.1.)

☛☛❖ **`void begin_display(int w_width, int w_height, char *window_label)`**
Start the program by connecting to the display (server) and initialize internal data structures to allow the creation of a drawing window with width `w_width` and height `w_height`. The string `window_label` is used as a label in the frame of the window. This function should be called before any other procedure of the Starter Toolkit. The only exceptions are the two functions `vis_window()` and `draw_window()` that contain equivalent code to `begin_display()`. (Section 3.3.1.)

☛ **`void clear_screen(int x, int y, int W, int H)`**
If any argument is negative, the entire drawing window is erased. Otherwise, only a rectangle with upper left corner coordinates `x`, `y` and dimensions `W` and `H` is erased. (Section 1.4.2.)

☛ **`void collect_text(pEvent *p)`**
Event handler for collecting strings of characters typed on the window. See also `init_text()`, `set_string_use()`, and `get_string()`. (Section 2.5.2.)

`void color_slider(void (*usage)(double), char *label, char *fore, char *back)`

Create a slider widget with background color `back` and foreground color `fore`. The slider displays a scale between 0 and 100 and the user may select any intermediate position. When a selection is made, the function `usage()` is called with the selected value as an argument. The argument must be declared as `double`. The value is also displayed near the upper left corner of the window. The argument `label` is displayed near the right side of the window and is truncated to 14 characters if it is longer than that. The dimensions of the slider cannot be changed. (Section 7.6.)

`void complete_display()`

Creates and displays a drawing window and any other windows that have been requested. (Section 3.3.1.)

`void compose_color(pImage *Ip, int use_htone)`

This function converts images with 24 bits per pixel to images with 8 bits per pixel. If `Ip` does not point to an image with 24 bits per pixel, the function returns immediately. The function assumes that the 8 most significant bits are for blue, the next 8 are for green, and the last 8 are for red. If `use_htone` is not 0, the conversion uses color halftoning which results in much better results but requires more time than when `use_htone` is 0. (Section 21.4.2.)

`Widget create_paper_widget( int (*redraw)(), int (*handler)(pEvent *), int width, int height, int relationship, char *window_name )`

Create a paper widget that provides a drawing window of dimensions `width` and `height` with frame label `window_name`. The function `redraw()` is called in response to exposure events and the function `handler()` is called in response to mouse and keyboard events. The argument `relationship` is a flag that can have one of the following predefined values: `NormalChild`, `PopupChild`, or `IndepedentChild`. When this function is used, files `<X11/StringDefs.h>` and `<X11/Intrinsic.h>` must be included. (Section 9.2.1.)

`void default_destination()`

Restore the widget of the main drawing window for destination of the output of the Starter Toolkit graphics functions. (Section 9.2.2.)

`void draw_area(PaperWidget w)`

Copy the display pointer, window, and graphics context associated with `w` to the static variables of the module that contains the drawing functions of the Starter Toolkit, such as `put_line()` and `fore_color()`. (Section 9.2.2.)

☛☛ **void draw_icon(int k, int x, int y)**
Display the icon pointed at by `k` at location `x, y`. The integer `k` must have been returned by a `make_icon()` call. (Section 3.2.3.)

☛☛ **void draw_window(void (*f)(), void (*g)(pEvent *), int w, int h, char *s)**
The argument `f` is a pointer to a drawing function, as in `vis_window()`; `g` is the event handler, `w` and `h` are the width and height of the window, and `s` the window label. (Section 2.2.3.)

☛ **void end_dialog()**
Erase the dialogue panel and wait for another panel selection. (Section 7.5.4.)

☞ **void erase()**
Set foreground color the same as the background color, so any future drawing using replacement mode will result in erasures. The original foreground color can be restored with `resume()`. (Not discussed in the text.)

☛☛ **void fill_rectangle(int x, int y, int W, int H)**
Display a filled rectangle with upper left corner coordinates `x, y` and dimensions `W` and `H`. (Section 1.4.2.)

☛ **int fontlength(char *text_string)**
If a font has been selected, it returns the length (in pixels) of the text string given as the argument. If there is no selected font, it returns the number of characters in the string multiplied by 12. (Section 1.4.4.)

☛☛ **int fore_color(char *cname)**
Set the foreground color to the given name (e.g., "red," "orange," etc.). It returns 0 if the color has been set successfully; otherwise, it returns `-1`. (Section 1.4.3.)

❑ **void get_default_args(Display **dpp, Window *wp, GC *gcp)**
Return the values of the first three arguments of *Xlib* functions that are needed for drawing on the windows created by the Starter Toolkit. (Section 18.1.)

☛ **int get_font_height()**
If a font has been selected, it returns the maximum vertical span of characters in the font used in the display. If there is no selected font, it returns 20. (Section 1.4.4.)

☛ **pImage *get_image(pEvent *p)**
Return a pointer to the structure of the image displayed in the window where the event occurred. (Section 20.4.2.)

☞ **`void get_selection(void (*f)(char *))`**
Ask the server for the primary *selection* of type text and call `f()` with the selection string as argument. (Not discussed in the text.)

☛ **`void get_string(pEvent *p)`**
Event handler that when the user presses a mouse button, places a prompt at the point where the cursor is and then displays typed text there. It calls `init_text()` and `collect_text()`. (Section 2.5.3.)

☛ **`void grab_draw_area()`**
Function that should be called before any graphics operations in a background procedure (one that is passed as argument to `add_work()`). Essential if the application chosen has more than one window. See also `release_draw_area()`. (Section 7.6.)

☛ **`void idle(int n)`**
Suspend execution (sleep) for (approximately) `n` microseconds. (Section 3.4.2.)

☛ **`void imgwin(char *label, int (*handler)(pEvent *), pImage *img)`**
Create a pop-up window of sufficient size to display the image of the structure `img` and also create a colormap for the window from the information in the same structure. Argument `label` is the window label, and `handler()` is the event handler for that window. (Section 20.4.2.)

☛ **`init_text(int x, int y, int k)`**
Initialize text collection *when the event handler is* `collect_text()`. Characters typed on the keyboard will appear on the application window starting at location with coordinates `x, y`. If `k` is nonzero, hitting the RETURN key terminates text entry. Otherwise, the user must hit the ESC key to terminate text entry. See also `set_string_use()`. (Section 2.5.1.)

☛ **`int make_color_cursor(unsigned char iconbits[], int hx, int hy, char *color, char *mask_color)`**
Create a 16 × 16 cursor icon using the array `iconbits`. Arguments `hx` and `hy` are the coordinates of the "hot spot" of the cursor, the point whose coordinates are returned by the event handler. The upper left corner of the icon is 0, 0. The last two arguments should be character strings specifying the color of the cursor and its mask. The function returns an integer used to reference the cursor from the applications program. The function returns a negative index when not enough memory is left to create the structure. There is no need to supply a mask; it is created automatically. (Section 3.2.3.)

☛☛ **int make_cursor(char iconbits[], int hx, int hy)**
Function calls `make_color_cursor()` (see above) with color arguments "black" and "white." (Section 3.2.3.)

☛ **void make_dash()**
All lines will be drawn dashed. (Section 1.4.3.)

☛☛ **int make_icon(char iconbits[], int w, int h, int cx, int cy)**
Argument `iconbits` is the array that contains the pixel description, `w` and `h` are the width and height of the icon, respectively, and `cx` and `cy` are the coordinates of the center with respect to the upper left corner. The center is used to display the icon in a particular location. The function returns an integer that is used to reference the icon from the applications program. The function returns a negative index when not enough memory is left to create the structure. (Section 3.2.3.)

☛ **void make_solid()**
All lines will be drawn solid. (Section 1.4.3.)

☛ **void mk_label(char **target, char *source)**
Copy the string pointed at by `source` to the memory location pointed at by `*target` after allocating sufficient memory to the latter location. Note the asymmetric use of the two arguments. If we have the declaration `char *a, *b;` we should call this function as `mk_label(&a, b)`. (Section 7.4.2.)

☞ **void own_error(int serious, char *msg)**
Print the message `msg` in the window that originated the application. If `serious` is nonzero, terminate execution; otherwise, continue. (Not discussed in the text.)

☞ **int own_selection(int x, int y, char *s)**
Tell the server to make `s` the text selection. Arguments `x` and `y` are the coordinates of the start of the baseline where the text is displayed. Return `TRUE` or `FALSE`, depending on whether the server granted the request. (Not discussed in the text.)

❑ **XtPointer * paper_hanger(PaperWidget w)**
Return a pointer to a pointer associated with the widget `w`. This function is used to associate a structure with the widget `w`. (Section 9.2.2.)

☛ **void poly_fill(pPoint v[], int n, char rule)**
Fill the interior of the polygon with `n` vertices stored in `v[]` with the color of the foreground. If the argument rule has any value other than `'w'`, use the ordinary parity rule; otherwise, use the directional parity or winding

rule. Bugs: This routine invokes an *Xlib* function that does not handle polygons with holes or the proper drawing of the original sides of the polygon. (Section 12.4.)

❑ **`void popdown(Widget w)`**
Cause the window of the widget `w` to disappear. The widget must have been created as the child of a pop-up shell. (See `popup()` for more on this point.) (Section 9.2.2.)

❑ **`void popup(Widget w, int easy)`**
Cause the window of the widget `w` to appear. The widget must have been created as the child of a pop-up shell — for example, by calling `create_paper_widget()` with `PopupChild` as its fifth argument. If the flag `easy` is 0, all keyboard and mouse input is ignored unless directed to that widget. This setting is appropriate for dialogue widgets. (Section 9.2.2.)

☞ **`int put_NL_text(char *s, int x, int y, int compdim, int *wp, int *hp)`**
Display a text string that contains new lines. The first three arguments are as in `put_text();` the rest have the following meaning. If `compdim` is nonzero, the function computes the dimensions of the displayed block of text and stores the width and height (in pixels) in the locations pointed at by `wp` and `hp`, respectively. The function returns the length of the last line in pixels. (Not discussed in the text.)

☛ **`void put_arc(int cx, int cy, int rx, int ry, int start_a, int length_a)`**
Plot a circular or elliptical arc with center coordinates `cx` and `cy`, starting at angle `start_a` (expressed in degrees) and spanning an angle of `length_a` degrees. If `rx` and `ry` are equal, the arc is circular with radius `rx`. Otherwise, it is elliptical with a horizontal axis of `rx` and a vertical axis of `ry`. To plot a complete circle with radius `r`, the appropriate call is `put_arc(cx, cy, r, r, 0, 360)`. The arc is drawn counterclockwise if `length_a` is positive and clockwise if it is negative. Starting angles are measured from the horizontal and can be either positive or negative. (Section 10.6.)

☛ **`void put_image(pImage *img, int x, int y)`**
Displays the image pointed to by `img` with its upper left corner at the point having coordinates `x`, `y`. It uses the ID member to find a pointer to the appropriate data. (Section 20.4.2.)

☛☛ **void put_line(int x1, int y1, int x2, int y2)**
Display a straight line segment joining a pair of points with coordinates `x1, y1`, and `x2, y2`, respectively. (Section 1.4.2.)

☛ **void put_poly(pPoint v[], int n)**
Plot a polygon with `n` vertices whose coordinates are stored in the array `v[]`. The value of `n` must be at least 1. (Section 10.6.)

☛☛ **void put_rectangle(int x, int y, int w, int h)**
Display an unfilled rectangle with upper left corner at `x, y`, width `w`, and height `h`. (Section 1.4.2.)

☛☛ **int put_text(char *text, int x, int y)**
Display the string text so that it starts at `x` and its baseline is at `y`. It returns the width of the displayed text in pixels. *Warning:* The function does not work correctly if the string contains new line characters. Use `put_NL_text()` for such strings. (Section 1.4.2.)

❑ **void restore_destination()**
Restore the previous widget for destination of the output of the Starter Toolkit graphics functions. (Section 9.2.2.)

☛ **int read_image(char *fname, pImage *result)**
Read a raster image from file `fname` and store the pixel values, dimensions, and colormap information in the `pImage` structure pointed at by `result`. Return 0 on success, nonzero on failure. Current implementation is for SUN raster files. (Section 20.4.1.)

☛ **void release_draw_area()**
This function should be called after all graphics operations in a background procedure and *before* calling `idle()`. See also `grab_draw_area()`. (Section 7.6.)

☞ **void resume()**
Restore the original foreground color after an `erase()` call. (Not discussed in the text.)

☛ **int select_font(char *font_name)**
Select the named font to be used for displaying text. The function returns 1 upon success and 0 otherwise. Note that a font corresponds to both a specific style and a specific size. (Section 1.4.4.)

☛ **void set_backgr(long c)**
Set the background color to the value `c`. (Section 1.4.3.)

❑ **`void set_default_args(Display *dp, Window w, GC gc)`**
Set the default values of the first three arguments of *Xlib* functions that are used by the Starter Toolkit drawing functions. Function should be used cautiously to avoid unwanted interference with the operation of the Starter Toolkit. (Section 18.1.)

☛ **`void set_foregr(long c)`**
Set the foreground color to the value `c`. (Section 1.4.3.)

☛☛ **`void set_handler(void (*f)(pEvent *))`**
Argument `f` is the name of a procedure that takes exactly one argument, a pointer to a pen structure. When an event occurs, the event handler of the Starter Toolkit calls `f` with a pointer to a `pEvent` structure as an argument. (Section 2.4.2.)

☛ **`void set_line_width(int n)`**
All lines (dashed or solid) will be drawn with thickness `n`. (Section 1.4.3.)

☛☛ **`void set_redraw( void (*f)() )`**
Argument `f` is the name of a function that normally takes no arguments which should be called whenever there is a need to redraw a window. ❑*Advanced Use:* In reality, the Intrinsics call `f` with the widget where an expose event occurred as its argument. Applications that deal with multiple windows may find this feature to be useful. (Section 3.3.1.)

☛ **`void set_string_use(void (*f)(char *))`**
To be used when the event handler is `collect_text()`. After the user terminates text entry, the function `f` is called with the entered text as its argument. (Section 2.5.1.)

☛☛❖ **`int setup_a_panel(char *name, pAction a[],`**
`void (*rfun)(), char *icdata[])`
Set up a panel with button labels and callbacks as specified by the array `a[]`. The last element of the array must be a structure with a null label. If `a[].fun()` returns a nonzero value for some entry, the panel button pops back up after that entry has been selected; otherwise, it remains depressed. The argument `name` is used to identify the class of actions of the panel. The function `rfun`, if provided, is called before each callback. Its purpose is to take care of any general operations that must be carried out before the callback — for example, cleaning up the results of an earlier selection. The array of character strings `icdata[]` is used for setting panels with icons rather than text labels. Each element of the array should be the name of an icon byte array. The argument `icdata` can be omitted for panels having text labels only. Only one selection can be made at one time, so the panel behaves like a "radio box." If a label starts with "–," the rest of the label is

interpreted as a color and the button is filled with the color. If a label starts with "@," the rest of the label is interpreted as the dimension of a square icon. An icon is then formed from the corresponding entry of `icdata[]` and is used to label the button. (Section 7.3.2.)

`int setup_v_panel(char *name, pValue v[],`
`int (*cfun)(int), char *icdata[])`
Set up a panel with button labels and values as specified by the array `v[]`. The last element of the array must be a structure with a null label. The function pointer `cfun` is the common callback function and always must be provided. It is called with the selected value as an argument. If it returns a nonzero value, the panel button pops back up after each selection; otherwise, it remains depressed. The argument `name` is a label for the panel. The array of character strings `icdata[]` is used for setting panels with icons rather than text labels. Each element of the array should be the name of an icon byte. The argument `icdata` can be omitted for panels with text labels only. Only one selection can be made at one time, so the panel behaves like a "radio box." See `setup_a_panel()` for the interpretation of labels. (Section 7.3.2.)

`void setup_canvas(int width, int height)`
Create a drawing window of the given dimensions. (Section 7.4.1.)

`int setup_image(pImage *img)`
If the display is monochrome, this function creates a halftone of the image and copies it into a bitmap. If the display has enough bits, then it creates another pixmap and copies the image there. The XID of the bitmap or the pixmap is copied onto the `img->ID` and is used later for all displays of the picture. (Section 20.4.2.)

`void slider(void (*usage)(double), char *label)`
Create a slider widget with a white background and black foreground. See the entry for `color_slider()` for the rest of the documentation. (Section 7.6.)

`void start_dialog(pAction messages[])`
Cause a dialogue panel to appear, displaying `messages[0].label` and an underscore. The user is expected to type a string ending with Return or Escape. (Errors are corrected by backspacing.) Then the function `messages[0].fun()` is called with the typed string as argument. If `messages[0].fun()` contains any `to_dialog()` calls, their strings are displayed before `messages[1].label` is displayed. The process continues in this manner until a 0 label is found. (Section 7.5.4.)

☛ **void take_from_file(int fid, int (*fun)(long, int *))**
Argument `fid` is a file descriptor, and `fun` is the function called to read data from the file descriptor when such data become available. (Section 7.7.1.)

☛ **void to_dialog(char *s)**
Display the string `s` in the dialogue panel. (Section 7.5.4.)

☛ **void two_way_pipe(char *cmd, int *to_child_p, int *from_child_p)**
Start execution of the Unix command `cmd` and return pointers to two file descriptors: `to_child_p` for providing input to the command and `from_child_p` for taking output from the command. (Section 7.7.2.)

☛ **void use_replace_mode()**
Set the drawing mode to replacement. (The old value is replaced by the new.) (Section 1.4.3.)

☛☛ **void use_xor_mode()**
Set the drawing mode to exclusive OR. (The value in the refresh memory is formed by the bitwise exclusive OR of the old and the new value.) (Section 1.4.3.)

☞ **void version()**
Print the version number of the Starter Toolkit. (Not discussed in the text.)

☛☛ **void vis_window(void (*f)(), int w, int h)**
Create a window with width `w` and height `h` or the default values if the arguments are unreasonable. When the window is ready, call `f()` to create the contents of the display. The function `f()` is also called anytime the window has to be redrawn in response to changes in the display — for example, if the window was obscured by another and then becomes visible again. (Section 1.5.1.)

☛☛ **void wait_for_event()**
Go into an infinite loop, but at each iteration check on whether an event has occurred (e.g., the mouse moved) and call the appropriate event handler. (Section 3.3.1.)

☛ **int write_image(char *fname, pImage *given)**
Create a raster image in file `fname` from the pixel values, dimensions, and colormap information in the `pImage` structure pointed at by `given`. Return 0 on success, nonzero on failure. Current implementation produces SUN raster files. (Not discussed in the text.)

☛ **`void xflush()`**
Flush the graphics instructions to the server. Normally, any drawing instructions are buffered until there are events in the server queue. Calling this function causes immediate execution. (Section 1.4.2.)

☛ **`void xor_fore()`**
Function is useful for drawing with exclusive OR on nonzero background. The applications programmer can select the desired colors for foreground and background and, by calling this function, can be sure that the correct colors will appear. Function should be called immediately after a change in foreground of background color. (Section 1.4.3.)

C

Installation of the Software

Scope of the Appendix
Requirements • Procedures for installing the Starter Toolkit • Testing • Documentation

C.1 REQUIREMENTS

You must have a machine that runs Unix, or any of its variants, such as Linux or FreeBSD, as well as the X Window System (X11R4 or later version). The Starter Toolkit occupies very little space compared to these systems, so disc space should not be a problem unless your system is filled to capacity.

You do not have to be a Unix or X guru to install the software that comes with this text, but you should have some programming experience *using* Unix. In particular, you should be familiar with the *make* command and know how to search directories.

The main part of the software is the Starter Toolkit, and it is the one part whose installation requires some care. Currently, the Starter Toolkit has been ported to the following systems: Sparcs and SUN3s (*OLIT*, *Motif*, and *Athena* widget sets), various Hewlett-Packard workstations (*Motif* and *Athena*), Sony NWS-3710 (*Motif*), SGI Iris (*Motif*), 486 running FreeBSD

(*Athena*), and 486 running Linux (*Motif*). During the first few ports, idiosyncrasies of the software were removed and from then on porting meant editing the `Makefile` and then executing a series of `make` commands. Undergraduate students did the porting in several instances.

C.2 PROCEDURES

C.2.1 Bringing the Files Onto Your System

The Starter Toolkit is part of a software package that comes with this text. The entire package is contained in the diskette attached to the back cover of the book and it can also be obtained by anonymous `ftp`. The package consists of a compressed archive, `IGX.tar.Z` and a `readme.txt` file. The latter contains a copyright notice and unpacking instructions.

- **From the Diskette:** The files can be extracted by a command such as
```
tar -xvf /dev/rfd0
```
- **Through `ftp`:** You can use either of the following two sites:
```
ftp.pws.com:/pws/compsci/pavlidis
ftp.cs.sunysb.edu:/pub/TechReports/pavlidis/Xstart
```
  Note that the `ftp` mode must be set to binary before taking the `IGX.tar.Z` file.

Whether you obtained the `IGX.tar.Z` file from the diskette or from an `ftp` site the rest of the installation is the same. Be sure that the file is in a directory for which you have write permission and then execute the following two Unix commands.

```
uncompress IGX.tar.Z
tar -xvf IGX.tar
```

These commands create four directories:

- `starter`, containing the Starter Toolkit.
- `examples`, containing the files that are referred by a single name in the listings throughout the text (e.g., `world.c` in Listing 1.2).
- `images`, containing two image files that can be used to test the code of the examples in Chapters 20-22.
- `demos`, containing programs outside the text that have been written mainly by students using the Starter Toolkit. *Caution:* The contents of this directory are more likely to contain bugs or present portability problems than the the contents of the other three directories.

If you use an `ftp` site you should be aware that in some sites there may be additional files related to the Starter Toolkit. Such files can be one of three kinds: (1) Files that correspond to the parts of `IGX` — for example, `Starter.tar.Z`. If you take the `IGX.tar.Z` file you may safely ignore such files; (2) Files related to other applications of the Starter Toolkit; (3) Files with names starting with `IGX.update`. You may wish to take those, although they are not essential for getting started.

C.2.2 Installing the Starter Toolkit

Directory `starter` contains four subdirectories, the three discussed in Section B.1 (`pwidget, include`, and `lib`) and a fourth, `docum`. To install the toolkit you must do the following.

1. `cd pwidget` and edit the `Makefile` shown in Listing C.1 to reflect correctly the path names in your system.

Listing C.1: Makefile for Paper Class Widget — `File pwidget/Makefile`

```
INCLUDE  =     -I${OPENWINHOME}/include
#INCLUDE =     -I/usr/include/X11R4
paper:
     $(CC) ${INCLUDE} -I.  -c paper.c
```

The listing corresponds to the correct setting for a SUN system. For most other systems removing the `#` character from the second line and placing it in the first is enough. Then type `make`, which will created the paper widget object file `paper.o`. (Note that the source file does not conform to ANSI C).

2. `cd ../lib` and edit the `Makefile` shown in Listing C.2 to reflect correctly the path names in your system.

Listing C.2: Makefile for Library of the Starter Toolkit — `File lib/Makefile`

```
#Sun OpenLook version
INCLUDE =-I${OPENWINHOME}/include
LIB  =    -L${OPENWINHOME}/lib
RANLIB   =    ranlib
WLIB =    -lXol
WSET =    -DOLIT

#System V Motif version
#INCLUDE  =   -I/usr/include/X11R4 -I/usr/include/Motif1.1
#LIB   =  -L/usr/lib/X11R4 -L/usr/lib/Motif1.1
#RANLIB      =  echo
#WLIB        =  -lXm
#WSET        =  -DMOTIF
```

```
CFLAGS    =    ${INCLUDE} -I. -I../include -g ${WSET}
#ANSI version
#CFLAGS   =    ${INCLUDE} -I. -I../include -g ${WSET} -DNEW_C

START_LIB  =  paper_mate.o paper_use.o p_fullpix.o \
        p_util.o x_rfile.o p_panel.o ../pwidget/paper.o \
        slider.o dialog.o pixwin.o

libStW.a: $(START_LIB)
        ar rv libStW.a $(START_LIB)
        ${RANLIB} libStW.a

START_LIB:    ../include/Starter.h
```

The `Makefile` of the listing is set for compilation on a SUN system with the *OLIT* widget set. There is a commented out version for *Motif* on a "System V" system (e.g., the Hewlett-Packard workstations). The actual file contains additional commented out options that serve as examples for the needed modifications. If you want to compile an ANSI version, add the C-compiler flag `-DNEW_C` and any other flags needed in your system.

After editing the `Makefile`, type `make`. Doing so creates the library `libStW.a` that contains all functions of the Starter Toolkit.

C.2.3 Testing the Starter Toolkit

After creating the file `libStW.a`, go to the `examples` directory and edit its `Makefile` as needed. The file is shown in Listing C.3 for the SUN/*OLIT* version.

Listing C.3: Makefile for Examples — `File examples/Makefile`

```
STARTER =../starter

INCLUDE =-I${OPENWINHOME}/include  -I${STARTER}/include -I.
LIB  =    -L${OPENWINHOME}/lib -L$(STARTER)/lib
WLIB =    -lXol

CFLAGS   =    ${INCLUDE}

$(PGM): $(PGM).o
     $(CC)  $(PGM).o $(LIB) -lStW  $(WLIB) -lXt  -lX11 -lm -o $(PGM)
```

To compile and link a program, (e.g., `spiral`) just type

```
make PGM=spiral
```

Before you run the program you must be sure that the library load path is correctly set. Most of the time there is no need for that, but, if you running a different widget set than normally used in the system, you may have to give priority to that library. The following statment is an *example* of a situation where the *Motif* widget set is used on a SUN workstation.

```
setenv LD_LIBRARY_PATH /home/motif/usr/lib:/usr/openwin/lib
```

Including such a statement in the user `.cshrc` (or equivalent) files is a good idea. After you have made sure that the path is set correctly, typing

```
    spiral
```

will create a window with a display similar to that in Figure 1.8.

The (edited) makefile of Listing C.3 must be copied by all users of the Starter Toolkit. *They do not need to copy anything else* in their own directories.

C.2.4 Documentation of the Starter Toolkit

Go to directory `docum` and edit the first line of the file `help` to reflect the correct path for file `doclib`. The file `help` is an awk/shell script and should be moved into a directory that should be in the `PATH` of all users — for example, `/usr/local/bin`. You should change the mode of `help` to executable with the statement

```
chmod 755 help
```

The file `doclib` contains documentation of the Starter Toolkit functions sorted alphabetically by function name. It is essentially the same as Appendix B. The entry for each function is preceded by a line with the string `.Ls` and is followed by a line with the string `.Le`. These strings can be used for formatting (after the user defines appropriate macros) or for online documentation search through `help`.

For example, typing `help put_line` yields

```
void put_line(int x1, int y1, int x2, int y2)

Display a straight line segment joining a pair of points with
coordinates x1, y1, and x2, y2, respectively. (Section 1.4.2.)
--
```

The Section reference is for the place where the function was used first in the text. (The Starter Toolkit also contains functions not discussed in the text.) Documentation for a group of commands may be obtained by providing a common substring to help — for example, `help void` or `help put_`. A partial substring also is enough `help xor` yields documentation for `use_xor_mode()`.

Index

A

active_cursor(), 72, 75, 127, 527
Active segment list, 282
Active window, 102
add_colors_by_name(), 169-70, 527
add_named_color(), 58, 123, 169, 462, 528
add_RGB_color(), 527
add_work(), 77, 209, 528
Aliasing, 460, 461
Analog-to-digital converter, 455
Animation
- generating erratic motion, 80-81
- of a graphin, 77-79
- interaction among graphins, 86-90
- of many graphins, 79-80
- Sea World example of simple, 81-86
- video game example, 90-92

Anti-aliasing, 461
Application (client), use of the term, 96
Application context, 229
Approximation, 386
Arcs
- *See also* Circular arcs
- parabolic, 391-97
- plotting filled, 414-15
- plotting parabolic, 259-60
- plotting plain, 412-14
- spline, 406

Area filling. *See* Connectivity filling; Polygon filling
Asente, P. J., 210
Asynchronous communication, 13, 108
Athena, widget set 195, 215-16
Atoms, 110-11
Attenuation factor, 254-55
Attributes, 109-10

B

back_color(), 16, 123, 528
Background color, 16
Background function, 77
Backing up windows, 103-4
Backup, creating a, 44-45
Barsky, B., 409
base_widget(), 227, 228, 528
begin_display(), 73, 74, 165, 231, 233, 528
Bézier, Pierre, 386
Bézier splines, 387-91
- cubic, 407-9
- parabolic, 395
- uniform parabolic, 397

Bitmap(s), 8-9
- icon creation and, 67
- images from, 507-9
- limitations, 298

problems of geometry on, 247-50
Blurring, 455
Boor, C. de, 409
Bounding rectangle, 319
Bresenham, J. E., 261
Bresenham's method for plotting line segments, 243
Bubble sorting, 289-90
Button(s)
functions of Starter Toolkit, 236-38
mouse, 134-35, 138
panel, 156

C

Caching, 318-19, 417-19
Callbacks/callback functions, 148-49, 159, 205-6, 336-37
Canvas
subwindow, 56
use of the term, 142
Cathode ray tubes (CRTs), 5
Central/perspective projections, 431
check_line(), 269-70
Circles
changing the size of, 301-2
defined, 301
Circular arcs
plotting, 250-52
plotting, with straight lines, 252-55
plotting functions for, 255-56
clear_screen(), 15, 118, 528
Client (application), 12, 95-96
client_data, 185, 236
Clip mask, 424-25
Clipping, 364
Clipping, window
line segment with a convex polygon, 378-80
line window, 365-71
point window, 365
polygons, 381
polylines, 371-72
collect_text(), 50, 56, 528
Color(s)
cells, 120-22, 498-99
of cursors, 72
of icons, 72
painting with, 56-61
palette of, 56, 58-61
pixels of a region, 420-22
using, by name, 122-24
Colormaps
basics of, 461-63, 494-95
creating and using, 498-502
default, 462
defined, 7, 461
for grayscale pictures, 469-70
hardware, 462
for real color, 463-65
Starter Toolkit facilities for, 465-66
use of, 120-22
virtual, 462
color_slider(), 180, 529
complete_display(), 74, 165, 228, 234, 529
compose_color(), 491, 529
Composite widget class, 199
Computation, visualization of, 22-24
Computational Geometry for Design and Manufacture (Faux and Pratt), 409
Computer aided design (CAD), 323, 385, 386
Computer Graphics and Geometric Modeling using Beta-splines (Barsky), 409
Conic/rational splines, 410
Connectivity filling, 264
basics of, 267-68
calling the filling module, 268-69
color leaking, 272
filling a line segment, 269-71
testing, 272-74
with line segments, 266-67
Constraint widget class, 199
Control points, 386, 398
See also Splines
Control polygon, 398
Convenience functions, 111-12
Core widget class, 198-201
create_canvas(), 142-43, 193
create_gc(), 143-44
create_paper_widget(), 216-17, 226-28, 529
create_spiral(), 22-23
Cubic splines, 407-9
Cursor(s)
changing the icon, 74-75
color of, 72

creating, from icons, 126-27
defined, 1, 66
varying the cursor to match a panel selection, 172-75
Cursor masks, creating, 68-71
Curves
See also Circular arcs
plotting, 259-60
shape versus mathematical form for, 384-87
Curves, drawing. *See* Splines
Curves and Surfaces for Computer Aided Geometric Design (Farin), 409
cuserid(), 26

D

Data, visualization of, 24-26
Default colormaps, 462
DefaultColormap(), 121, 494
default_destination(), 219, 225, 529
Defensive programming, 272
Depth, defined, 9
Dialogue panel, 175-76
Dialogue widget, 220-23
Digital Halftoning (Ulichney), 491
Digitizing tablets, 10
Directional parity filling, 291-93
Discarded segment list, 282
dispatch_event(), 194
Display
See also Server
list, 12
space, 433, 435
use of term, 96
Displaying full pictures, 457-58, 466-71
See also Halftoning
Distance, finding the
to a point from a line, 313, 315-16
to a point from a line joining two points, 312-13
to a point from a line segment joining two points, 313-15, 316-17
to a point from a polyline, 317-18
Dither halftoning
defined, 475
generating dither matrices, 478-80
implementation of, 480-81
multilevel, 488-89
ordered versus random, 476-78
properties of, 482-83
Dragging objects, 329-36
Drawables, 114-15
draw_area(), 218, 529
draw_icon(), 72, 73, 125, 530
Drawing
basics of, 114-18
callbacks and, 336-37
circular and elliptical arcs, 412-15
drawables and pixmaps, 114-16
editors, 323-24
function correspondence, 118-19
grabbing and dragging objects, 329-36
graphics context, 116-18, 119-20
mode, 17
polygons, 324-29
primitives, 118-19
reasons for using a computer in, 322-23
right rectangles/boxes, 327-29
scan lines, 288-90
on tiles and stipples, 422-24
use of the term, 322
a widget, 226-28
with splines, 387-91
Drawing curves.*See* Splines
Drawing window
Athena used to create a, 215-16
creating a single, 213
Motif used to create a, 214
OLIT used to create a, 214-15
draw_window(), 40-41, 73-74, 140-45, 149, 190, 213, 239, 530
Duality, 344-45

E

Encapsulation/information hiding, 516-18
end_dialog(), 176, 223, 530
erase(), 530
Error diffusion halftoning
analysis of, 483-85
defined, 475-76
implementation of, 485-88
multilevel, 489-91
Event(s)
checking for, 131-32

defined, 32-33
difference between interrupt handling and, 33-34
driven computing, 33
exposure, 103, 134
function pointers, 36-37
generated by server/window manager, 139-40
generated by user action, 138
graphics context selection of, 139
input selection, 135-36
interpretation by the Starter Toolkit, 38-40
mouse, 134-35
programming styles for handling, 34-36
queue, 33, 58, 131-32
selection of, 138-39
translation by Starter Toolkit, 145-48
types of, 37-38
window manager, 136-38
XEvent data structure, 133-34

Event handlers
for drawing polylines, 46-50
resetting, 260
Starter Toolkit, 40-41, 206-8
for text, 50-54
writing useful programs, 261

Event-window correspondence, 194
Exclusive OR, 17, 115
Exposure events, 103, 134

F

Farin, G., 409
Faux, I. D., 409
File
descriptor, 106
manager, 2
saving a, 176-79

fill(), 265, 268-74
Filled arcs, plotting, 414-15
Filled polygons. *See* Polygon filling
fill_poly(), 290-91
fill_rectangle(), 15, 118, 412, 530
find_font(), 128-29
Finding objects, 309-11, 315-18
find_neighbors(), 265
Fishback, W. T., 361
Flanagan, D., 210
Flat picture, defined, 4
Flood filling, 264
fontlength(), 19, 129-30, 530
Fonts, 18-20, 26-27, 128-30
scalable, 298

fore_color(), 16, 122, 123, 530
Foreground color, 16
Frame buffer, 6
Full pictures
See also Halftoning
creating, 454-61
creating smooth displays, 461
defined, 4, 452
description versus, 453-54
displaying, 457-58, 466-71
image structure and files, 466-67
reconstruction filters, 458-60
requirements for displaying, 452-53
scanning, 453, 454-56
selecting the right sampling rate, 460-61
synthesizing, 453, 456-57
windows for, 467-69

Function pointers, 21-22, 36-37

G

Games, homogeneous coordinates used in, 352-55
Games, icons in
animating a graphin, 77-79
animating many graphins, 79-80
creation of game objects/graphin, 76-77
erratic motion, generating, 80-81
interaction among graphins, 86-90
Sea World example of simple animation, 81-86
video game example, 90-92

Generic geometric objects (GGO), 303-6
Geometric objects
equation for a line joining two points, 311
finding the distance to a point from a line, 313, 315-16
finding the distance to a point from a line joining two points, 312-13
finding the distance to a point from a line segment joining two points, 313-15, 316-17
finding the distance to a point from a polyline, 317-18
generic, 303-6
limitations of pixel arrays, 296-99

lines, polylines, and circles, 300-301
pixels and points, 299
pointing/finding, 309-11, 315-18
rotation, 307-9
scaling, 301-5
translation, 306
Geometry, projective, 345
geometry_layout(), 192
Geometry on bitmaps, problems of, 247-50
get_color_cell(), 127
get_default_args(), 119, 411, 412, 530
get_font_height(), 19, 26-27, 129-30, 530
get_image(), 468, 530
get_palet(), 58, 60
get_points(), 257-58
get_selection(), 531
get_string(), 56, 531
Gettys, J., 112
global_find(), 329-30
Grabbing objects, 329-36
grab_draw_area(), 180, 531
Graphical computing
menus, 152-64
panels, 165-69
pipes, 181-86
pixel painting panels, 169-79
role of, 151-52
video game example, 179-81
Graphical user interfaces (GUIs), 181, 187
Graphics context, 16, 116-18, 119-20
selection of events by, 139
Graphics file, 11-12
Graphics hardware
bitmaps, pixmaps, and planes, 8-9
input devices, 10
for picture display, 5
raster, 5, 6-7
refresh memory, 6, 8
vector, 6
Graphics metafile, 12
Graphics primitives, 11
Graphin(s)
animating a, 77-79
animating many, 79-80
creation of game, 76-77
defined, 76
erratic motion, generating, 80-81
interaction among, 86-90
Sea World example of simple animation, 81-86
traps for, 378
video game example, 90-92
Grayscale pictures, 4
Guiding polygon, 398

H

Halftoning
creating XImages with, 505-7
dither, 475, 476-83
error diffusion, 475-76, 483-88
multilevel, 488-91
purpose of, 452-53, 464, 474
thresholding, 475
Handles, 108
Handwriting recognition by computers, 152
Hardware colormap, 462
Hints (for window manager) 106
Homogeneous coordinates, 341, 344-50
in games, 352-55
in space, 435-39
Hu, J., 410

I

Icon(s)
changing the cursor, 74-75
color of, 72
creating, 124-25
creating cursor masks, 68-71
creating cursors from, 126-27
defined, 1, 65-66
editors, 66-67, 323
file formatting with, 67-68
in games, 75-81
images from, 507-9
making icons useful, 71-73
panels with, 171-72
icon_image(), 508-9
Identity, loss of, 296-97
idle(), 78, 531
Image analysis, 453-54
Image display prototype widget, 510-12
Image fill, 421
Image processing, 454

Image structures and display
  creating XImages with full depth, 503-5
  creating XImages with halftoning, 505-7
  from bitmaps and icons, 507-9
  XImage, 502
  storage of image data, 503
  with Starter Toolkit, 509-10
Image synthesis, 453
imgwin(), 467-68, 491, 510-11, 531
Information hiding, 516-18
Information structure, 128
Inheritance, 519-21
init_color_map(), 230, 233
Initialization of an application, 228-30
init_stack(), 267
init_text(), 51, 531
Inner product, 346
Input devices, 10
Input selection, event, 135-36
Insanely Great (Levy), 28
Installation of software, 539-43
Intensity resolution, 453
Inter-Client Communication Conventions Manual (ICCCM), 149
Interpolation, 385
Interrupt driven computing
  defined, 32
  difference between event driven and, 33-34
Intersection of line segments, finding
  algebraic equations for, 341-43
  composing triplets, 351-52
  duality, 344-45
  finding the distance of a point from a line, 349-50
  finding the midpoint of a line segment, 347-49
  homogeneous coordinates, 341, 344-50
  relative position of points and/or line segments, 355-61
  used in games, 352-55
Intrinsics, 13, 196

J
Jaggies, 297, 461

K
Keyboard, 101, 102
Kimball, P. E., 210
Knots, 387

L
Levy, S., 28
Line drawings, defined, 4
Line joining two points, equation for, 311
  See also Distance, fiding the
Lines, plotting straight
  basics of, 242-43, 258-59
  Bresenham's method for, 243
  mathematical foundations, 243-45
  plotting arcs with straight lines, 252-55
  problems of geometry on bitmaps, 247-50
  program for, 245-47
Line segments
  See also Intersection of line segments, finding
  clipping, with a convex polygon, 378-80
  connectivity filling of, 264, 266-74
  relative position of points and/or, 355-61
  window clipping, 365-71
Line sweep method, 282-93
Line window clipping, 365-71
Liquid crystal displays, 5

M
McIlroy, M. Doug, 262
Mailtool, 2-3
make_button(), 236-38
make_color_cursor(), 73, 126-27, 531
make_cursor(), 72, 126, 532
make_cursor_mask(), 70, 71, 127
make_dash(), 18, 120, 532
make_icon(), 71, 73, 125, 532
make_label(), 168, 191, 532
make_solid(), 18, 120, 532
Manager, window, 101-3
  events generated by, 139-40
Manhattan distance, 310
Menus
  See also Panels
  advantages of, 154
  defined, 152-54
  panels, 156-57
  pointing to items, 154-55
  pop-up, 156
  programs behind graphical, 159-64

pull-down, 155-56
Messenger functions, 518-19
Modular programming, 41
Monochrome pictures, 4
Motif widget set, 195, 196, 199, 200, 201, 214
button functions, 236, 238
creating widgets, 231-34
Motion sensing devices, 10
Mouse, 1, 10, 47
buttons, 134-35, 138
events, 134-35
move_me(), 76
move_objects(), 86
Multilevel halftoning, 488-91
Multimedia screen, 3
Multiplexing, 259
Multitasking, windows and, 100-101

N

Nested event servers, 34-35
Nye, A., 112, 210

O

Object editors, 323
Object-oriented programming, 189
encapsulation/information hiding, 516-18
inheritance, 519-21
messenger functions, 518-19
overview of, 514-15
Object space, 433-34
OLIT (Open Look Intrinsics Toolkit) widget set, 195, 199, 200, 201, 214-15
button functions, 236, 238
creating widgets, 231-34
One-way pipes, 181-83
Ordered dither, 476-78
Orthographic projection, 440
Ousterhout, John K., 238, 239
Outer product, 346
own_error(), 267, 532
own_exit(), 141
own_handler(), 207, 208
own_selection(), 532
O'Reilly, T., 210

P

Painting
with color, 56-61
with pixel panels, 169-79
with pixels, 41-45
use of the term, 321-22
paint_line(), 258-59
paint_rectangle(), 259
Palette of colors, 56, 58-61
Palette subwindow, 56
Panels
creating and using, 165-69
defined, 156-57
dialogue, 175-76
functions of Starter Toolkit, 234-36
painting with pixel, 169-79
Starter Toolkit function for action, 159-161
Starter Toolkit function for value, 161-63
value, from an integer array, 167-68
value, from a string array, 168-69
varying the cursor to match a, 172-75
with icons, 171-72
paper_hanger(), 219-20, 532
PaperWidgetClass, 197
Parabolic arcs
drawing with, 391-97
plotting, 259-60
Parabolic Bézier splines, 395
uniform, 397
Parabolic splines
basics of, 397-98
computing points, 398-400
corners in, 404-5
estimating the placement of arcs, 406
geometric method for computing, 401-4
program for computing, 400-401
Parallel projections, 431
Parity filling, 277-81
directional, 291-93
singularities, 280-81
Parity rule, 277
Pattern fill, 420-21
Pavlidis, T., 410
Pel, use of term, 8
Perspective projections, 431
matrix for, 440-42

pEvent, 39, 145
Pew, J. A., 210
pImage, 466, 470-71, 502
Pipes
- one-way, 181-83
- two-way, 183-86

Pixel(s)
- accelerating painting of, 256-60
- changing the size of, 42-43
- defined, 8, 299
- editors, 45, 274, 323
- painting with, 41-45
- painting with pixel panels, 169-79

Pixel arrays, limitations of, 296-99
Pixmaps
- copying, 116
- creation of, 115-16
- defined, 9, 114-15
- plotting with, 417-19

Planes, 9
PLOT libraries, 11-12, 96, 97
Plotting with *Xlib*
- filled arcs, 414-15
- pixmaps and, 417-19
- plain arcs, 412-14
- polygons, 415-19

Pointers, function, 21-22, 36-37
Pointing
- to items in menus, 154-55
- to objects, 309-11, 315-18

point_in_polyline(), 373-78
point_polyline_distance(), 318
Points
- collecting an array of, 257-58
- defined, 299
- position of, with relation to a polygon, 373-78
- relative position of points and/or line segments, 355-61
- window clipping, 365

poly_fill(), 293-94, 411, 419-20, 532-33
Polygon(s)
- clipping, 381
- clipping line segment with a convex, 378-80
- control/guiding, 398
- convex, 376
- defined, 46
- drawing, 324-29
- open, 300
- plotting, 415-19
- position of a point with relation to a, 373-78
- utility of using, 363-65

Polygon filling
- basics of, 419-20
- drawing on tiles and stipples, 422-24
- drawing scan lines, 288-90
- filling function for, 290
- filling function for, with holes, 290-91
- fill patterns, 420-22
- finding the intersection of many parallel lines with a polygon, 282
- line sweep method, 282-93
- parity filling, 277-81, 291-93
- segment list, 283-88
- singular vertices, 280-81

Polylines
- changing the size of, 301-2
- defined, 46, 300
- finding the center of, 302-3
- plotting functions for, 255-56
- window clipping, 371-72

Polylines, drawing
- of arbitrary, 324-27
- event handler for, 46-48
- using two event handlers, 48-50

popdown(), 219, 533
popup(), 219, 533
Pop-up menus, 156
Popup widgets, 203, 219
pPixel, 266, 299
pPoint, 256, 299
Practical Guide to Splines, A (Boor), 409
Pratt, M. J., 409
process_event(), 144-45, 190
Projection matrix, perspective, 440-42
Projections
- basic expressions for, 439-40
- central/perspective, 431
- defined, 430-33
- examples, 445-47
- orthographic, 440
- parallel, 431
- reasons for three-dimensional, 442-45

Projective and Euclidean Geometry (Fishback), 361
Projective geometry, 345
Properties, 109, 110-11
Prototype widgets, 219
proximity(), 75, 89
Pull-down menus, 155-56
put_arc(), 255-56, 411, 412-14, 533
put_image(), 468, 509, 533
put_line(), 15, 23-24, 118, 241, 256, 412, 534
put_NL_text(), 533
put_pixel(), 242
put_poly(), 256, 411, 416-17, 534
put_rectangle(), 15, 26-27, 118, 259, 534
put_text(), 15, 21, 118, 534

Q

Quantization, 455, 456
quit(), 41

R

random(), 80
Random dither, 476-77
Raster graphics, 5, 6-7
Rational splines, 410
Ray tracing, 448-49
read_from_child(), 182, 185
read_histogram(), 25
read_image(), 467, 534
Reconstruction filters, 458-60
Rectangle(s)
  bounding, 319
  drawing right, 327-29
  plotting a, 259
redraw_pixels(), 45
Refresh memory, 6, 8, 104
region(), 56, 58
Region algebra, 427-28
Regions
  See also Connectivity filling; Polygon filling
  creating and clipping, 424-27
  defined, 264
release_draw_area(), 181, 534
Reparenting, 108-9
reset_handler(), 258, 260
Resolution, spatial and intensity, 453, 455
Resources, 203-4
restore_destination(), 218, 534
resume(), 534
Retraceability, 248
Rotation of objects, 307-9
Rubber banding, 47, 324, 327-28

S

Sampling, 456
Sampling rate, selection of, 460-61
save_file(), 178
Saving a file, 176-79
Scaling
  changing the size of circles of polylines, 301-2
  generic, 303-5
  lack of, 297-98
Scan conversion, 264
Scanners, 10
Scanning full pictures, 453, 454-56
Scheifler, R. W., 112
Screen
  description of Windows, 1-3
  difference between physical and logical, 7
Scrollbars, 157-58
Seed, 264
Seed filling, 264-66
segment_in_polygon(), 379-80, 381
Segment list
  preparing the, 283
  sorting the, 284-85
  traversal of, 286-88
select_font(), 19, 128, 129, 130, 534
select_input(), 139-40
Selection, use of the term, 336
Server
  See also Display
  connecting to, 105-6
  defined, 12, 95-96
  events generated by, 139-40
  resources, 104
set_backgr(), 16, 534
set_default_args(), 119, 412, 535
set_foregr(), 16, 120, 535
set_handler(), 48-49, 73, 207, 535
set_line_width(), 18, 120, 535
set_redraw(), 74, 205-6, 535
set_server(), 230, 233

set_string_use(), 52, 535
setup_a_panel(), 161, 163-64, 171, 234-36, 239, 535-36
setup_canvas(), 167, 536
setup_image(), 453, 468, 469, 503, 536
setup_v_panel(), 162-64, 170, 171, 234, 536
setup_z_image(), 503-5
Shell widgets, 199
Shell window, 101
side_compar(), 284-85
Singularities, 280-81
slider(), 179-80, 224-26, 536
Sliders, 157
Slider widget prototype, 220, 223-26
Smoothing approximation, 386
Software, installation of, 539-43
Solid fill, 420
Spatial resolution, 453, 455
Speech recognition by computers, 152
Splines
  conic/rational, 410
  cubic, 407-9
  drawing with, 387-91
  points, 387
Splines, parabolic
  basics of, 397-98
  computing points, 398-400
  corners in, 404-5
  estimating the placement of arcs, 406
  geometric method for computing, 401-4
  program for computing, 400-401
Sprite, 1
Stacking order, 101
Stack memory, 265
start_dialog(), 175-76, 220-22, 536
Starter Toolkit, 13-14
  button functions of, 236-38
  colormaps, 465-66
  documentation for, 543
  event handler by, 40-41
  event interpretation by, 38-40
  event translation by, 145-48
  examples, 20-27
  fonts, 18-20, 26-27
  function for action panels, 160-62
  function for value panels, 162-64
  functions, list of, 527-38
  graphics context, 16-18
  image display with, 509-10
  installation of, 539-43
  overview of, 14, 522-25
  panel functions of, 234-36
  primitive drawing functions, 15-16
  relationship between *Xlib*, X Toolkit, widget sets and, 196-98
  structures and definitions, 525-26
  testing the, 542
  using the X Toolkit with, 216-20
State variable, 35-36
Stipples, drawing on, 422-24
Straight line plotting. *See* Lines, plotting straight
Subclass of Core Widget class, 199
Swick, R. R. 210
Synthesizing full pictures, 453, 456-57

T

take_from_file(), 182, 537
Tcl, 238
Tcl and the Tk Toolkit (Ousterhout), 239
Text, event handlers for
  main part, 52-54
  preliminaries, 50-52
  using typed text, 54-56
Text editor, 2
Texture, 66
The X Toolkit Cookbook (Kimball), 210
The X Window System: Programming and Applications with Xt — Open Look Edition (Young and Pew), 210
The X Window System: Programming and Applications with Xt — OSF/Motif Edition (Young), 210
Thresholding, 475
Tiles, drawing on, 422-24
Tk toolkit, 238-39
to_dialog(), 176, 223, 537
Toolkits
  See also Starter Toolkit; X Toolkit
  defined, 13-14, 195
  relationship between *Xlib*, X Toolkit, widget sets, Starter Toolkit, 196-98
  Tk, 238-39
Touch sensitive screens, 10, 151, 152, 154

Trackball, 10
Translation of objects, 306
Traps
  in the form of convex polygons, 378
  for graphins, 378
two_way_pipe(), 184, 537
Two-way pipes, 183-86

U

Ulichney, R., 491
Unix PLOT libraries, 11-12, 96, 97
Usage functions, 324
use_replace_mode(), 17, 120, 537
use_xor_mode(), 17, 120, 537

V

Value mask, 109, 110
Vector graphics, 6
version(), 537
Video lookup table, 7, 101, 120-21
Virtual colormap, 462
Visibility, defined, 433-35
Visualization examples, 20-27
Visuals
  checking, 496-98
  overview of, 495-96
vis_window(), 20-22, 537

W

wait_for_event(), 74, 537
Waiting segment list, 282
Widgets, 13
  classes, 195, 198-201
  Core widget class, 198-201
  creating, 226-28
  creating drawing, 230-31
  creating *Motif* and *OLIT*, 231-34
  hierarchy, 198-201, 202
  instance of, 201-2
  popup, 203, 219
  prototype, 219
  tree, 201-3
Widget sets, relationship between *Xlib*, X Toolkit, Starter Toolkit and, 196-98
Window(s)
  active, 102
  backing up, 103-4
  creating, 99, 106-7, 191-93
  creating objects, 190-91
  defined, 99-100
  features of, 109-12
  for full pictures, 467-69
  grouping of, 189
  managers, 3, 101-3
  mapping of, 100, 106-7
  multitasking and, 100-101
  objects, 188-91
  overlapping of, 100
  screen of, 1-3
  shell, 101
  subdividing, 56-58
  tree, 189
  types of pictures displayed on, 3-4
Window clipping
  line, 365-71
  line segment with a convex polygon, 378-80
  point, 365
  polygons, 381
  polylines, 371-72
  use of the term, 365
window_object, 190-91
Window program, example of simple, 104-9
write_image(), 537

X

XAddPixel(), 502
XAllocColor(), 121-22, 495, 498-99
XCheckIfEvent(), 132
XCloseDisplay(), 106
XColor(), 121498
XCopyArea(), 116, 125, 509
XCopyPlane(), 125, 509
XCreateBitmapFromData(), 124, 126
XCreateColormap(), 494-495
XCreateGC(), 117-18
XCreateImage(), 502
XCreatePixmap(), 115
XCreatePixmapCursor(), 126
XCreateWindow(), 106
XDefineCursor(), 126
XDrawArc(), 412-14
XEvent(), 133-34

XFillArc(), 414
XFillPolygon(), 419, 420
XFlush(), 16, 136, 538
XGetImage(), 502
XGetVisualInfo(), 497
X identity numbers (XID), 107-8
XImage structure, 502
  with full depth, 503-5
  with halftoning, 505-7
Xlib, 13, 96-99, 103, 112
  advanced plotting with, 411-28
  image display using, 494-513
  relationship between X Toolkit, widget sets, Starter Toolkit and, 196-98
Xlib Protocol Reference Manual (Nye), 112
Xlib Reference Manual (Nye), 112
XLoadQueryFont(), 129
XMapWindow(), 106
XNextEvent(), 132, 133, 136
XOpenDisplay(), 105-6, 191
XOR, 17
xor_fore(), 18, 538
XParseColor(), 122, 124
XPoint, 415-16
X Protocol, 12-13, 96-99
XPutImage(), 502
XrmStringToQuark(), 124
XSelectInput(), 109, 136, 138
XSetFont(), 130
XStoreColor(), 121, 122, 495, 498-99
XtAddWorkProc(), 209
XtAppAddInput(), 209
XtAppInitialize(), 229, 230
XtCreateManagedWidget(), 231
XtDisplay(), 230
XTextWidth(), 118
X Toolkit, 13-14, 195, 212-16
  relationship between *Xlib,* widget sets, Starter Toolkit and, 196-98
  using Starter Toolkit with, 216-20
XtVaCreateManagedWidget(), 231
XtVaSetValues(), 230
X Toolkit Intrinsics Programming Manual (Nye and O'Reilly), 210
X Toolkit Intrinsics Reference Manual (Flanagan), 210
X Window System
  components of toolkit, 194-98
  defined, 12-13
  historical background, 11-12
  toolkits, 13-14, 195, 196-98
X Window System (Scheifler and Gettys), 112
X Window System Toolkit (Asente and Swick), 210

Y

Young, D. A., 210